SELECTED WORKS OF
JOSEPH CARDINAL BERNARDIN

Selected Works of Joseph Cardinal Bernardin

VOLUME 1

Homilies and Teaching Documents

Alphonse P. Spilly, C.PP.S.
Editor

Foreword by
Roger Cardinal Mahony

A Liturgical Press Book

THE LITURGICAL PRESS
Collegeville, Minnesota

Cover design by Ann Blattner

Excerpts are taken from the New American Bible, © 1970 by the Confraternity of Christian Doctrine, 3211 Fourth Street N.E., Washington, D.C. 20017-1194, and are used by permission of the copyright holder. All rights reserved.

Excerpts are also quoted from *Vatican Council II: The Conciliar and Post Conciliar Documents*, © 1975 and 1986 by Harry J. Costello and Reverend Austin Flannery, O.P., Costello Publishing Co., P.O. Box 9, Northport, NY 11768, U.S.A.

Volume 1: ISBN 0-8146-2583-5

1	2	3	4	5	6	7	8

Library of Congress Cataloging-in-Publication Data

Bernardin, Joseph Louis, 1928–
    [Selections. 2000]
    Selected works of Joseph Cardinal Bernardin / Alphonse P. Spilly, editor ; foreword by Roger Cardinal Mahony.
        p.   cm.
    Includes bibliographical references and index.
    Contents: v. 1. Homilies and teaching documents.
    ISBN 0-8146-2583-5 (alk. paper)
    1. Catholic Church—Doctrines.   I. Spilly, Alphonse P., 1939– .
II. Title.

BX4705.B38125 A25   2000
282'.77311—dc21   99-039499
                                                 CIP

Contents

First Days in Chicago

Advent–Christmas Season

Ordinary Time

Special Occasions

a. Personal

b. Archdiocese of Chicago

The Challenges of the Last Years

Foreword

When remembering the late and deeply cherished Joseph Cardinal Bernardin, several dimensions of his life and legacy come to mind. Recalling the years of our acquaintance, especially the time of his struggle with the cancer that would take his life on November 14, 1996, what I remember most vividly is how firmly anchored he was in the person of Jesus Christ, how deep his faith in him. Cardinal Bernardin's life of prayer and witness, his ecclesial vision, his strengths as a leader and reconciler of people, as well as his keen pastoral insight all found their source and sustenance in a faith, hope and love firmly rooted in the person of Jesus Christ.

Cardinal Bernardin will be remembered by many as one of the great Catholic churchmen of the twentieth century. Deeply revered by his brother bishops, by priests, deacons, religious, and laypeople, his contributions to the Church and to society are far too extensive to enumerate. But of all these, Cardinal Bernardin's name will always be linked with "the seamless garment," an image he drew upon to articulate a consistent ethic of life, one which safeguards human life from conception to natural death while attending to the many dimensions of life in all its complexity, not just one. His name will also be associated for many years to come with the Catholic Common Ground Initiative, begun at his initiative in the hope of recovering a spirit of civility, mutual respect, and sincere dialogue among Catholics who seem to line up all too easily around secondary issues, thereby losing sight of the centrality of our one faith in Christ and the charity which is to be the hallmark of all who profess faith in him. But, above all else, it is the legacy of personal witness to the power of the love of Christ amidst his own illness, suffering, diminishment and death, that was and is the greatest gift of our "Brother Joseph" to those of us still on the journey toward the glory which he now shares more fully.

This collection includes a wide variety of writings, carefully selected and edited by Father Alphonse P. Spilly, C.PP.S., Special Assistant to the Archbishop of Chicago, Cardinal Bernardin, for nearly thirteen years. While it is not a comprehensive collection, *Selected Works of Joseph Cardinal Bernardin* may be considered the essential Bernardin, including as it does his most important writings. What is quite striking about his writing, whether it is a pastoral letter, a synodal intervention, a reflection on the challenge facing catechists, or a homily, is the consistency of his message. There is indeed a common ground throughout his large literary corpus. First, Bernardin speaks and writes *from* and *to* the lived experience of faith in the Church of his day, attentive to the complexities and ambiguities of contemporary Christian life. Second, he examines human and Christian experience in all its beauty and its brokenness in the light of Christian history and tradition, then sounds a prophetic utterance directed to all of us in the Church and in the world who squander and betray God's gift. Third, he seeks always to rekindle the gift of hope and cultivate resources of creativity as the Church looks to the future, searching out ways to meet contemporary needs and future challenges with the confidence that can only spring from faith, hope, and love, indeed from a whole way of life, fixed on Christ.

What is most striking about these writings, however, is their profoundly personal tone. Cardinal Bernardin was a man of great modesty and reticence. Nonetheless, even as he addressed the large issues and pressing concerns in Church and society, he spoke and wrote in his own voice. Authenticity rings through every one of his words. At the same time, his words are never intrusive or embarrassingly familiar even, for example, when addressing the challenges facing Catholic health care in the United States while he himself was a cancer patient. This is because he was, in fact, not speaking of himself, but of the Christ living in him, the Shepherd with whom he united himself by laying down his life for his flock. True to his episcopal motto, while he was among us Cardinal Bernardin remained as one who serves.

Reading these pages provides occasion to drink of the same spiritual springs that gave life and light to Joseph Cardinal Bernardin, indeed to partake of the same Christian spirituality as his. This is a spirituality, a distinctive approach to living the Gospel, in which nothing is preferred to the love of Christ. It is a spirituality shaped by a deep love of the Church in all its grandeur and grit. This is a spiritual journey that is altogether apostolic, responsive to the mandate to spread the word and work of Jesus as the Good News for which the human heart longs. And it is a prophetic path of proclaiming God's Word in word and deed, in a whole way of life of witness against any compromise of the values of the Gospel. Finally, this is a spirituality shaped through and through by a life of prayer which is nurtured, cultivated and sustained in and through the Liturgy of the Church, especially the Eucharist, the source and summit of Catholic faith and life.

Receive and celebrate Joseph Cardinal Bernardin's great gift to us in and through these pages. May the gift of wisdom expressed in his words unite us more deeply as the one Body of Christ gathered and sent by Word and Sacrament. And help us discern in our midst, as Cardinal Bernardin did, the presence of the living Christ given for the life of the world.

✠ Roger Cardinal Mahony
Archbishop of Los Angeles

Preface

As bishop, archbishop, and cardinal, Joseph Louis Bernardin (1928–1996) served the Catholic Church in the United States and the universal Church with great distinction. He was truly a man of faith, a Church leader who had a significant impact on countless people. Although he was not naïve, he was humble. He would have been surprised at the great outpouring of respect and affection that his family and friends witnessed at the time of his death and funeral. Likewise he would have been amazed at the popularity of his best-selling, posthumous work, *The Gift of Peace* (Loyola Press, 1997), which has also been published in ten foreign versions, and the warm response to a one-hour documentary on his life, *Bernardin*, produced by Martin Doblmeier and Frank Frost and first viewed on PBS stations throughout the nation in 1998.

There were many dimensions to his personality, his ecclesial vision, and his pastoral ministry, but he devoted special care to his teaching role as a bishop. This collection of some of his talks and writings as archbishop of Chicago (1982–1996) is evidence of his commitment to this responsibility.

When I began to work full-time for Cardinal Bernardin in 1984, Fr. James Roache, the vicar general, told me that I was to follow two general criteria. First, the cardinal was fully committed to presenting the authentic teaching of the Church ("theologically impeccable" was the phrase used) and second, he wanted to be "pastorally sensitive." It is a constant challenge to be both "theologically impeccable" and "pastorally sensitive," but Cardinal Bernardin was determined to do both. Not surprisingly, one of his favorite biblical phrases was to "proclaim the truth in love" (Eph 4:15).

Cardinal Bernardin's teaching style was quite simple even though the content was often profound. He seemed to know instinctively that, while all of the three components of communication are essential—speaker, message, and audience—the key to effective communication is knowing, respecting, and effectively addressing the **audience.** He was always very concerned to deliver his message in a way that would be understandable to his listeners or readers.

This corresponds with a personal characteristic of his. As archbishop of Chicago and a cardinal, a widely recognized Church leader and media personality, he was almost always in the spotlight—whether he was presiding at a parish liturgy, delivering a major address, or simply strolling down a street. However, to the extent that it was possible, he tried to turn the focus of attention to the audience he was addressing or the person with whom he was speaking at the moment. In long receiving lines he looked each person in the eye, frequently holding a hand or touching a shoulder, always listening attentively and responding warmly and gently to whatever was said to him. It seems that nearly everyone who met him—if only briefly and on a single occasion—had the impression that he somehow cared about them. He truly did, and in this way he mediated God's love to people. And people usually responded in kind. As Bishop Raymond Goedert of Chicago said at Cardinal Bernardin's funeral, he was "the most beloved human being who has ever graced the Archbishop's throne in [that] historic Cathedral."

Although Cardinal Bernardin never seemed to be fully comfortable with being in the spotlight, he knew it gave him wonderful opportunities both to affirm the persons he was addressing and to challenge them to live in accord with God's word and their God-given potential. He could effectively proclaim some of the "hard sayings" of the gospel because he first reached out to people with compassion, understanding, and love. When there was a bond of mutual trust and respect between himself and his audience, he could gently but firmly lead them to face challenges. He did not shy away from speaking the truth, even when it went beyond a challenge of the moment to a thorough conversion of life.

He was an evangelizer after the model of the Good Shepherd. Indeed, at his installation as archbishop of Chicago he said that he modeled his episcopal ministry on that of the Good Shepherd, adding with characteristic simplicity: "I have come to Chicago with only one desire: to do all in my power to proclaim the Lord Jesus Christ and his Gospel in word and deed." Frankly, this sounded rather simplistic at the time. But after seeing and hearing him faithfully witness the Lord Jesus in word and deed during his fourteen years in metropolitan Chicago, it became clear how powerful and effective that simple focus can be.

Cardinal Bernardin usually spoke in public from a written text. At times that made for a less than lively delivery, especially if he was particularly tired at the moment. The first two times I heard him deliver a homily, when he was still archbishop of Cincinnati, I wondered why he used a written text at the risk of boring his audience. As his Special As-

sistant for nearly thirteen years, I had to learn how to give a credible answer when others asked the same question! My answer is threefold, and
it is based on conversations with him over the years.

First, Cardinal Bernardin wanted to ensure that he had something to
say and that he said it precisely in the way he wanted. He loved language,
and, because he could see elements of truth on both sides of an argument,
his position was often balanced and very nuanced. (A coworker used to
refer to those of us who worked with the cardinal on his talks and writings as the "Community of the Careful Nuance.") Moreover, the cardinal
often spoke on more than one occasion on a given day and several times
on a weekend. He wanted his message to be tailored to the specific circumstances of each group and occasion. Further, he was frequently exhausted and did not rely on his memory or capacity to improvise under
those circumstances. When he did speak "off the cuff," he was very effective. However, even when he was asked to give a fairly simple invocation or benediction, he usually preferred a written text.

Second, he wanted a written record of precisely what he had said. Especially if a talk was well received, it would be fairly easy to "recycle" it
on another occasion with appropriate editing and updating. Moreover,
people frequently asked for a text of his talk afterward. It was also helpful to have a copy at hand when someone criticized what he had said or
was reported to have said. When provided with a full text of his presentation, critics often retracted their objections, having based their original
critique on a media report that did not give the full quote or took his words
out of their context. Needless to say, a text did not resolve all controversies or objections. Indeed, at times his written words added fuel to the
fire of a controversy, even if that was not his intention.

Third, Cardinal Bernardin was firmly convinced that a record of a diocesan bishop's words and deeds should be preserved in the diocesan
archives for historical research. As chancellor of the Diocese of Charleston, he had been canonically responsible for the archives of that historic
see. When he discovered that some valuable diocesan records were gathering mold in the damp basement of the chancery building, he immediately began to rectify the matter and salvage what could be saved. His
interest in archives continued throughout his episcopal ministry.

When he came to the Archdiocese of Chicago, the archdiocesan archives
and records, for the most part, were stored in a large room in the nearly
vacant Philosophy Building at Mundelein Seminary, overseen by a small
staff without any computerization or modern methods. In 1985, he started
the process of combining records management and archives. The archives
and noncurrent administrative records were moved into a safer and more
accessible location, and in 1986 he hired a professional archivist and
records manager.

Shortly before Cardinal Bernardin died, he moved the archdiocesan archives and records to a first-rate facility on the western edge of the Loop in Chicago. After his death it was dedicated as the Archdiocese of Chicago's Joseph Cardinal Bernardin Archives and Records Center. Because of the meticulous way he kept his personal papers, correspondence, talks, and writings during his years in Chicago, it will one day be possible for serious researchers to reconstruct virtually every day of his life as archbishop of Chicago. The original copies of his talks and writings are stored at the center along with their corresponding diskettes, when they are available on diskette, and are currently available for research.

The archives of Cardinal Bernardin's works include over 450 major addresses, about 1,600 homilies, over 600 texts of briefer remarks, and a lesser number of invocations and welcomes. In addition, he wrote a weekly column for the archdiocesan newspaper for nearly fourteen years, usually taking two months off from this responsibility each summer.

Obviously, no one person could have drafted and edited this enormous volume of talks and writings, let alone the archbishop of the second largest archdiocese in the nation. A "resource group" helped Cardinal Bernardin draft his talks and writings on a regular basis. This anonymous group numbered from three to ten persons over the years. In addition, many others—within the archdiocese and across the country—helped with specific talks and writings. At times, the cardinal prepared an initial draft himself. Drafts prepared by others were usually routed through my office where they were entered into a computer and edited in accord with the cardinal's thought and style. Then he himself edited the drafts, sometimes several times. If he were not a bishop, he would have made an excellent editor or publisher. He was very concerned that, even though others often helped him prepare his talks and writings, he always made the texts his own. He did not say anything he did not want to say. It usually seemed clear to his listeners and readers that he spoke from his heart even if others had helped him find the right words to convey his message.

This two-volume collection of Cardinal Bernardin's addresses and writings is to be understood as the "essential" Bernardin. It is not a comprehensive work; many of his talks were relevant primarily to a specific occasion and audience, and including all of them in a single collection does not seem feasible or desirable. Some of the texts included in the two volumes were originally published in *Origins*. Others have been published by St. Anthony Messenger Press ("*Christ Lives in Me*," 1985), Sheed & Ward (*Consistent Ethic of Life*, 1988), Liturgy Training Publications (*A Blessing to Each Other*, 1996), Georgetown University Press (*A Moral Vision for America*, 1998), and the Catholic Health Association (*Celebrating the Ministry of Healing: Joseph Cardinal Bernardin's Reflections on Healthcare*, 1999).

The idea for this collection of Cardinal Bernardin's works arose on October 9, 1996, when Mr. Michael Glazier telephoned me about a desire to have some of Cardinal Bernardin's talks and writings published. I discussed this with the cardinal, and he quickly gave his approval for the project. However, the next weeks were filled with several other projects, including the preparation of his last two reports on the archdiocese for the Holy See and *The Gift of Peace*.

I met with Cardinal Bernardin for the last time on a gloomy, drizzly November 7, 1996. In effect, we were clearing the table of work before us. He was feverish and quite weak. His breathing was a bit labored. Toward the end of our conversation we talked about one last item, "the Glazier project." His eyes lit up, and he smiled gently, saying, "Al, you'll have to do that for me." I nodded my head in agreement. He died a week later.

Carrying out his wish has been a long endeavor but a work of love. The works included in these two volumes have value and interest well beyond their original audiences. They make available to others the faith, ecclesial vision, and pastoral insights of a great Churchman in his own words. Future generations will undoubtedly discover that the Church has changed from the time when Cardinal Bernardin served as archbishop of Chicago with such distinction, but they will also find here "pearls of great value" whose relevance and inspiration extend well beyond the twentieth century into the third millennium of Christianity.

Alphonse P. Spilly, C.PP.S.

Acknowledgments

My first debt of gratitude is to Mr. Michael Glazier, who contacted Cardinal Bernardin about this collection about five weeks before the latter's death. Mr. Glazier has been a constant source of encouragement, support, and guidance during the entire project.

I am grateful to Francis Cardinal George, O.M.I., who has enthusiastically backed this endeavor and accepted that I was less accessible to him at times as his special assistant because of the "Bernardin Project." I also thank Bishop Raymond Goedert, Diocesan Administrator after Cardinal Bernardin's death and vicar general to both archbishops, for his ongoing interest in this and other publications of Cardinal Bernardin's works.

I also acknowledge with gratitude the ongoing support of Mrs. Elaine Addision, Cardinal Bernardin's sister, and Ms. F. Octavie Mosimann, his executive secretary for over thirty years. Others who made this collection possible through the years are Mrs. Mary Duffy, my administrative assistant, and later Mrs. Marie Knoll, communications associate in the Archbishop's Office, as well as members of the Resource Group who helped Cardinal Bernardin prepare many of his talks and writings.

Throughout the project I consulted with several people who worked closely with Cardinal Bernardin during his ministry in the Archdiocese of Chicago and/or were familiar with his thinking. I am especially grateful to Msgr. Kenneth Velo, Sister Mary Brian Costello, R.S.M., and Fathers Michael Place, Francis Kane, Louis Cameli, and Robert Schreiter, C.PP.S.

Mr. John J. Trainor, vice chancellor and director of the Archdiocese of Chicago's Joseph Cardinal Bernardin Archives and Record Center, and his staff were very helpful in facilitating research on some of the content of these volumes.

All of us owe a great debt of gratitude to the staff of The Liturgical Press for undertaking this extensive work and making these works of Cardinal Bernardin accessible to a wider audience and future generations.

Finally, I thank my widowed mother, Helen, with whom I have lived the last fourteen years, for her patience, her understanding, and her sharp eye for "typos" in the proofs.

Father Al Spilly, C.PP.S.

Part One

TEACHING DOCUMENTS

Introduction to Part One:
Teaching Documents

Historians will undoubtedly identify Joseph Cardinal Bernardin (1928–1996) as one of the greatest figures in the Catholic Church in the United States during the twentieth century. He was a gentle, prayerful, pastoral leader who also enjoyed a reputation as an able administrator in various diocesan offices in Charleston, as auxiliary bishop in Atlanta, as archbishop in Cincinnati and Chicago, and as general secretary and president of the U.S. episcopal conference. Ordained a bishop in 1966 at the age of thirty-eight, he carried out his entire episcopal ministry within the vision and spirit of the Second Vatican Council, whose last session he attended as a guest of his diocesan bishop.

While the two volumes in this series reflect the faith, the mind, and the vision of the man, this first volume offers an introduction to the care and sensitivity with which he carried out his teaching ministry as a diocesan bishop. All of these works have been published earlier, primarily within the Archdiocese of Chicago; they are gathered here for readers in the broader Church and for future generations.

As archbishop of Chicago, Cardinal Bernardin issued four pastoral letters, three pastoral reflections, and five pastoral statements. While these documents were primarily addressed to the archdiocese and intended to guide its mission and ministry, they have relevance and interest beyond that local church. A pastoral letter was understood to have more importance than a pastoral reflection or statement, but the cardinal undertook each of these projects with great interest and diligence.

He always consulted widely within, and often beyond, the archdiocese with persons whose views he trusted along a rather broad spectrum of viewpoints. This took time. His pastoral letter on the Church, for example, was in preparation for well over two years, and there were more than a

3

dozen major consultants. Version after version was revised until Cardinal Bernardin was satisfied that it said precisely what he wanted to say. Most of these documents were translated into Spanish and some into Polish.

Pastoral Letters. Cardinal Bernardin issued his first pastoral letter as archbishop of Chicago to mark the twentieth anniversary of the Second Vatican Council's Constitution on the Sacred Liturgy. In *Our Communion, Our Peace, Our Promise* he evaluated what had occurred in liturgical renewal during the preceding two decades and offered challenges for the future.

In his second pastoral letter, *In Service of One Another,* Cardinal Bernardin addressed current questions and tensions regarding various forms of ministry, offered clarification about the concept, and affirmed new developments in ministry, encouraged their coordination, and offered some directions for the future.

In order to deepen Catholics' understanding of the mystery of the Church and to give sharper focus to the identity and mission of the archdiocese, Cardinal Bernardin devoted considerable time and other resources to the development of a pastoral letter on the Church, *The Family Gathered Here Before You.* In it he reflects on Catholics' experience of the Church, the mystery of the Church itself, and the future of the Church in metropolitan Chicago. This is the longest of his pastoral letters, and in order to help parishes reflect on it, discussion guides were made available in English, Spanish, and Polish.

Throughout his ministry as archbishop of Chicago, Cardinal Bernardin took a keen interest in issues related to Catholic health care. While he had decided to issue a pastoral letter on the topic before the discovery of his pancreatic cancer, the project took on a more personal tone and greater urgency after he became a cancer patient himself and unofficial chaplain to hundreds of other patients. *A Sign of Hope* appeared in October 1995, while he was still convalescing from postoperative treatments for cancer and about the time he began to experience serious problems with his legs and spine (as the result of spinal stenosis and the collapse of four vertebrae). In his letter he offered his reflections on Catholic health care, described a bishop's ministry in health care, and offered some proposals about health care ministry in the local church.

Pastoral Reflections. Work on the first of his pastoral reflections as archbishop of Chicago, *"Christ Lives in Me": A Pastoral Reflection on Jesus and His Meaning for Christian Life,* began while he was still archbishop of Cincinnati, but it was completed in 1985 when he had been archbishop of Chicago for nearly three years. While the letter reflects familiarity with contemporary developments in christology, it has a decidedly personal tone. After examining the pastoral relevance of christology, he reflects upon the Christian response in faith to Jesus and the following of Christ.

In 1983 Pope John Paul II established a Pontifical Commission of three U.S. bishops (Archbishops John Quinn and Thomas Kelly, and Bishop Raymond Lessard) to study religious life in the United States. In the Archdiocese of Chicago the first phase of the study consisted primarily of meetings in which Cardinal Bernardin and the auxiliary bishops listened to the experience of women and men religious and responded briefly to what they heard. In the second phase the participants were challenged to come to grips with six essential elements of authentic religious life. In the fall of 1986, in order to offer guidance to this second phase, Cardinal Bernardin issued *Reflections on Religious Life*, focusing on the six dimensions: identity and charism, community, obedience, structures of authority, consecration and mission, and public witness.

Cardinal Bernardin had a lifelong interest in religious education. His 1986 pastoral statement, *The Challenges We Face Together*, was directed primarily to archdiocesan religious educators and was intended both to affirm the importance of this ministry and to clarify some issues that many educators had raised with him. In particular he dealt with three questions: (1) Does the Church's faith change? (2) Where is the Church's faith expressed? (3) How do we deal with disagreement within the Church? A few years later he also published *Growing in Wisdom, Age, and Grace: A Guide for Parents in the Religious Education of Their Children* (Sadlier, 1988; revised edition 1997).

Pastoral Statements. When AIDS began to reach crisis proportions in the mid-1980s, Cardinal Bernardin appointed a task force to study how the Church might best minister to the growing number of people with AIDS in the archdiocese. In October 1986, upon the task force's recommendation, he issued a pastoral statement on AIDS, *A Challenge and a Responsibility*, a forerunner of the U.S. bishops' 1987 pastoral statement on the topic: *The Many Faces of AIDS: A Gospel Response*. In his own brief statement Cardinal Bernardin considered AIDS in the light of the gospel, the spread of AIDS in our society, and the Church's response to the crisis.

When the leaders of the archdiocesan Catholic charismatic renewal asked Cardinal Bernardin to give public support to their movement, he issued a pastoral statement, *"Come, Holy Spirit"* in 1988. His primary intent was to strengthen the Catholic charismatic renewal and help bring about a new Pentecost in the Church of metropolitan Chicago. He also clarified certain aspects of the movement (conversion, "baptism in the Spirit," and "charisms") and offered some challenges to its members (a *Catholic* reading of Scripture, the balance of personal spirituality and service, and integration in the local ecclesial community).

Since the Second Vatican Council, the Archdiocese of Chicago has had more permanent deacons than any other diocese in the world. Cardinal Bernardin's pastoral statement on the permanent diaconate, *The Call to Service*, marked the twenty-fifth anniversary of the restoration of the permanent diaconate in the Western Church. In it he reflected upon diaconal ministry and identity as well as the vocation, formation, and assignment of deacons. He also provided vision to guide the future of the permanent diaconate in the local church.

Cardinal Bernardin enjoyed talking with young people and wanted to reach out to them with a special pastoral statement on youth. He issued a videotape, *Here and Now*, featuring four teens and himself in a question-and-answer format. A written version, based on the videotape, was published as a teen newsletter, whose text is included in this volume.

In 1976, a Parish Sharing program was established in the Archdiocese of Chicago, matching up certain parishes with others for their mutual benefit. It was a way to build unity in the Church despite the diversity of race, ethnicity, culture, and economic disparity. The Parish Sharing Program was one of the archdiocesan structures addressed in *Decisions*, a strategic pastoral planning process begun in 1993 in which over eight thousand people participated. When the program celebrated its twentieth anniversary in 1996, Cardinal Bernardin issued a pastoral statement to provide direction for the future, *Building Bridges Between Communities of Faith*. It examined the biblical and theological foundations of the program and assessed its strengths and shortcomings.

Synodal Interventions. Cardinal Bernardin was one of four representatives of the U.S. Catholic bishops to the synods of bishops held in Rome in 1974, 1977, 1980, 1983, 1987, 1990, and 1994. Beginning in 1974, he was elected five times to serve on the fifteen-member Council of the Secretariat of the Synod, serving in that capacity for sixteen years. He was again elected to the council in 1994. (He did not attend the Special or Extraordinary Synod of 1985 for which Pope John Paul II himself appointed delegates beyond the *ex officio* members, the presidents of the various episcopal conferences.)

As Archbishop of Chicago, Cardinal Bernardin attended four synods: "Penance and Reconciliation in the Mission of the Church" (1983), "The Vocation and Ministry of the Lay Faithful in the Church and the World" (1987), "The Formation of Priests in the Circumstances of the Present Day" (1990), and "Consecrated Life and Its Mission in the Church and the World" (1994).

The U.S. episcopal representatives usually met once or twice before the synod and decided what topics to address in their individual presentations or "interventions" at the synod. Usually they also consulted with others in accord with the topic of the respective synod (with laity in 1987, priests in 1990, members of consecrated life in 1994). The interventions were usually drafted in three formats, differing in length. The briefest version (about twenty lines) was submitted to the secretariat for distribution to the synodal delegates and the media. A longer version (of about eight minutes' duration) was prepared for delivery in the Synod Hall. The longest, the fullest development of the intervention, was submitted in writing to the Secretariat of the Synod, and it is this version that is found in this volume. At the 1983 Synod on Penance and Reconciliation, Cardinal Bernardin submitted two written interventions, both of which are included here.

Alphonse P. Spilly, C.PP.S.

Pastoral Letters

Our Communion, Our Peace, Our Promise

*Pastoral Letter on the Liturgy**

── *February 1984* ─────────────────────────────

Greetings and peace to all of you, Catholics of this archdiocese, faithful and catechumens, for whom I pray daily as your archbishop.

I have often written and spoken to you briefly about various aspects of our work as a Church and have asked for your support. Now I want to write at greater length, not just about our work but about our life. In speaking of the liturgy, I hope to reach and touch the spirit of prayer in your hearts—that spirit which brings us together each Sunday for the Eucharist. And I also have in mind those of you whom infirmity prevents from joining physically in the celebration: Your prayer is part of every Mass we celebrate.

In December 1963, the Second Vatican Council completed its first document, the Constitution on the Sacred Liturgy. Some of you remember that time very clearly, but others have grown up in the Church since then. In honor of the twentieth anniversary, I want to speak to both: those who, like myself, knew the forms of liturgy set 400 years ago and those who cannot remember the Mass in Latin, the "last gospel," the altar against the wall.

Most often when you and I meet, we celebrate the liturgy. As we do, I realize more and more fully the truth of that great insight of the bishops at Vatican II: "In the liturgy the whole public worship is performed by the Mystical Body of Jesus Christ, that is, by the Head and His members"

───────────────────────────────

* The pastoral letter was originally published by the Archdiocese of Chicago's Liturgy Training Publications, which reissued the letter and a study guide in 1997 as *Guide for the Assembly*.

11

(Constitution on the Sacred Liturgy, no. 7). The liturgy is the action of God's assembled people.

In the past we often spoke as if the bishop or the priest alone celebrated the liturgy. But the evidence and the bishops' words at Vatican II are strong and definite: Whenever we gather as the Church—for Sunday Mass, for anointing the sick, for burying the dead—we celebrate the liturgy together. The General Instruction on the Roman Missal puts it simply: "The celebration of Mass is the action of Christ and the people of God . . ." (no. 1).

We call this gathered Church "assembly." It is you and it is I. Bishops, priests, and deacons have unique roles in celebrating the liturgy, but they act as persons who serve the assembled people.

It is good theology and also good common sense, a matter learned not so much from documents and textbooks as from experience, that the assembled Church celebrates the liturgy. I learned this saying family prayers in my home and at evening devotions in my parish church. I learned it also in these last two decades which have been a time of renewal, making it more clear that the liturgy, while Christ's action first, of course, is also the action of God's people, who sing, listen to the scripture, praise and thank God, greet one another in peace, and share in the Holy Communion of Christ and the Church.

This letter about the liturgy is sent to all of you, for you are the people who celebrate our liturgy; you are the assembly. In writing it I take for granted observance of all the Church's liturgical norms, which provide a positive framework encouraging us to engage in creative, authentic celebration of the liturgy.

Twenty years is very little time for so profound an experience to take hold, but at this point it is useful for us to ask ourselves how we are doing. I am going to ask you that, and ask it in a number of ways. I am going to chide a bit and challenge a lot. But I must say three things by way of introduction.

INTRODUCTION

First, thank you. I say that to all those who have labored to make the liturgy strong and beautiful: ushers, artists, musicians, writers, planners, lectors, cantors, deacons, servers, communion ministers, priests, sacristans—all who have accepted any ministry of service to the people of the parishes. Thanks especially to you who simply come to take your places and celebrate the Mass week after week.

The church in Chicago is known throughout the United States and even beyond for liturgical leadership which began long before Vatican II. In 1940 the first of those national gatherings that became known as

"Liturgical Weeks" was held at our cathedral. Priests, religious and laity who studied and worked through these years helped prepare the way for the renewal that came from the council. Over the years, outstanding members of the Chicago church have shown by teaching and example what parish liturgy can be. I am thankful for all this work and zeal.

A second thing I must say simply to be certain we have a common foundation, a shared understanding of the liturgy. I understand the liturgy to be those rituals in which the Church assembled expresses its very life. In our rituals we give thanks to God—for thanksgiving is the day-in, day-out attitude of the baptized; we intercede—for we are baptized to hold up all creation's needs to God; we read our sacred book, the Bible, and sing from our prayerbook, the psalms—for those words and prayers accompany us from childhood to old age.

From our parents and grandparents we have received the rites by which we give thanks, intercede, anoint and confirm, marry and bury. We do them over and over, and we teach our children to do them. Thus do we discover what it is to be a Christian and a Catholic. We learn this in hearing the word of God, in the hymns and acclamations, in the genuflections and the kneeling, in the greeting of peace, in sharing the consecrated bread and wine at the holy table. The liturgy is not an "extra," something nice that may give us good feelings. It is our life, our very spirit. It is the source of our identity and renewal as a Church.

When we let the liturgy shape us—from the ashes of Lent and the waters of baptism to the broken bread and poured out cup at every Sunday's Mass—then we shall find what it is "to put on Christ."

Yet liturgy is also a humble reality, and participation in liturgy does not exhaust our duties as Christians. We shall be judged for attending to justice and giving witness to the truth, for hungry people fed and prisoners visited. Liturgy itself does not do these things. Yet good liturgy makes us a people whose hearts are set on such deeds. Liturgy is our communion, our strength, our nourishment, our song, our peace, our reminder, our promise. This singular meeting with the Lord Jesus leads us to make all the events and circumstances of our lives occasions for meeting him. Liturgy is for me the bedrock of all my prayer and the measure of all my deeds.

My last introductory note is this: Over and over the council stressed that the great goal for liturgical renewal is our "full, conscious and active participation in liturgical celebrations which is demanded by the very nature of the liturgy" (Constitution on the Sacred Liturgy, no. 14). Since those words were written we have only begun. The liturgical books have been revised so that the liturgy may indeed be celebrated in this way. But revising books and changing language does not make it happen. There is need for excellence on the part of all who minister at the liturgy, with all the artistry and hard work that entails. And yet even that is pointless until all who assemble to celebrate the liturgy have it in mind to participate together in this sacred deed.

The commitment I envision must be in our Catholic bones: the need to assemble each Sunday, to make common prayer in song, to hear the Scriptures and reflect on them, to intercede for all the world, to gather at the holy table and give God thanks and praise over the bread and wine which are for us the Body and Blood of our Lord Jesus Christ, and finally to go from that room to our separate worlds—but now carrying the tune we have heard, murmuring the words we have made ours, nourished by the sacred banquet, ready in so many ways to make all God's creation and all the work of human hands into the kingdom we have glimpsed in the liturgy.

In 1978 the U.S. bishops reminded us that "God does not need liturgy, people do" (*Environment and Art in Catholic Worship*, no. 4). It is not an option, nor merely an obligation, not a bonus but a need—like food and drink, like sleep and work, like friends. "God does not need liturgy, people do." We need to gather, listen, give praise and thanks, share communion. Otherwise, we forget who we are and whose we are; we have neither the strength nor joy to be Christ's body present in today's world.

It is true of course—and indeed, this is a central truth about the Mass and sacraments—that the action performed is first and foremost Christ's. It is he who renews his act of perfect fidelity to the Father's will, he who welcomes new members into the community of the Church, he who forgives and reconciles. In that sense, even liturgy "badly" celebrated is efficacious. Nevertheless, the quality of *our* participation, of *our* action, is also important; that quality, in fact, enhances our participation in the action of Christ. Liturgy is not magic; we must bring to it the very best of which we are capable.

Although the liturgy expresses our whole life—our birth in baptism, our growth and forgiveness in reconciliation—here I shall speak only of the Sunday Eucharist because it is our usual and regular way of gathering. How do you and I celebrate the liturgy each Sunday? If the liturgy is something done by the assembled people of the parish, how are we doing this task of ours?

I ask you to read what follows in a very practical spirit, thinking of your own parish and the Sunday Eucharist there, and especially of your own participation in that Mass.

ON SUNDAY, HOW DO WE GATHER?

Everything that happens before the first Scripture reading is meant to help us assemble. That means gathering together many individuals as one

community at prayer, but it also means recollecting ourselves personally—not by leaving behind the cares and distractions of home and work,
but by bringing them into the gospel's light.

So we gather, one by one, household by household, passing through the
doors of this parish church of ours, greeting one another, taking our
places. This building called a "church" is a kind of living room of the family of God—it is *our* room when we assemble as the Church. Here we are
at home.

Its style differs from parish to parish. Its architecture and decoration
may be in one tradition or another. What matters most is that the room
allows us all to gather closely, see one another's faces, be truly present to
one another. The common focus is the holy table and near it the chair of
the presider and the stand where the Scriptures are read. But liturgy is
not a performance, and we are no audience. Liturgy is an activity, and the
room itself should help this happen. Many directives make it clear that in
building new churches and renovating old ones it is important to bear in
mind our need to see and hear one another, even as we see and hear the
priest, the reader, the cantor.

But even the best architecture can only invite us to come together and
pray together. That invitation must be accepted. Certainly there are
times for praying alone, seeking privacy, but the Sunday liturgy is not one
of these. The first task of each one who comes on Sunday for liturgy is to
take the open place nearest to the holy table. Let our churches fill from
the front to the back, and if there are empty places, let them be the ones
farthest from the altar. The open places near the doors are then available
for those who may hesitate to draw closer because of some private need
or sense of alienation. Let them feel welcome whenever they come to the
church.

Every parish has members who care for the beauty of the church building and the physical well-being of the assembly. Sacristans keep this house
for the Church clean and beautiful. Working with artists, they prepare
the room for special feasts and for the seasons. Ushers help people find
places, and are truly servants of the assembly. They are models of the hospitality we should all have as we greet one another.

One last note about these important moments before Mass. As members of the assembly, we should be there—we should be *assembled*—before the liturgy begins. Coming late or at the last minute, if that can be
avoided, says we are only spectators dropping in to see a performance.
But the liturgy is ours. To come late or leave early breaks the very spirit of
the assembly. Come early instead, to greet others, to pray quietly, to center your thoughts on the Lord to whose table you have been invited.
Come early and bring the concerns and problems that occupy you, all the
people you carry in your heart.

How we begin the liturgy will vary somewhat from season to season and place to place. Always we make the Sign of the Cross, respond to the greeting of the one who presides, priest or bishop, and join in the opening prayer of the Mass. Usually we sing either an opening hymn or the "Lord, have mercy" or the Gloria. The familiar and lovely routine leads us into community prayer.

The Sign of the Cross should be made with reverence and attention. By this simple gesture we identify ourselves as Christians. This sign marked us even before baptism and will mark us even after death.

We respond to the presider's greeting and give him our full attention. When he extends the invitation, "Let us pray," we welcome the silent time to gather ourselves in stillness, so that we can enter fully into the opening prayer, unique to each Sunday, which places us in communion with the Church throughout the world.

Singing within the entrance rite is a wonderful way for us to realize that we are a *community* at prayer. Cantors and those who play musical instruments select and gradually teach people those compositions which will draw forth their song. Here, and throughout the liturgy, music is not a decoration but part of the central action itself. What we do in liturgy is too vast and too deep to be left to our speaking voices. We need music so that we can fully express what we are about.

As the one who presides over the assembly, the priest has an important service to render in these introductory moments. Standing by his chair, he gives us his full attention as he leads us in the Sign of the Cross, greets us, and invites us to join in the opening prayer. Additional words, if any, should be very few, so that the cross, the greeting, and the prayer stand out and are not rushed.

How the entrance rite gathers us and prepares us for word and Eucharist will vary from one liturgical season to another. Art, music, and words themselves tell us that we are again in Advent or Christmastime, in Lent or Eastertime, or in the Sundays of Ordinary Time. Commentaries and explanations should be superfluous.

If we gather as we ought—singing together, being silent together, responding together—we will be a community praying, and know that we are such.

HOW DO WE LISTEN TO THE WORD?

From the first reading through the prayers of intercession we are engaged in the Liturgy of the Word. Most of our "doing" at this part of the Mass is listening. On Sundays we listen to three readings from the Scriptures and the homily.

This kind of listening is not passive—it is something *we do*. At these moments in the Mass the liturgical action is not just reading and preaching, *it is listening*. Readers and homilist are servants to the listening assembly.

Often, though, we do not listen very well. Listening is a skill that grows dull in the barrage of words one hears all day long. Yet we have no substitute for it. In the liturgy we are schooled in the art of listening. What we do here, we are to do with our lives—be good listeners to one another, to the Lord, to the world with all its needs.

We usually have a reading from the Hebrew Scriptures, one from the writings of the New Testament, and one from the Gospels. Every three years the Church reads through most of the four Gospels, much of the New Testament, and scattered selections from the Old Testament. The scripture selections themselves shape the liturgical seasons of Advent, Christmastime, Lent, and Eastertime. During the rest of the year we generally read straight through the gospels and letters, picking up each week where we left off the week before.

The council used the image of a pilgrimage in speaking of the Church. We are on a journey, not only as individuals but as a Church living out corporate life down through the centuries. On this journey we carry a book, our Scriptures. Each week we gather, and in our midst the book is opened and read. Its words are heard over and over again. They have come down to us through dozens and even hundreds of generations. We in turn read them to another generation and so entrust the book to our children. In these stories, visions, poems, letters—all sorts of writing—we Christians find again and again the meaning of our own journey, the Lord who is our way and truth and life.

Our listening, then, is not like listening to a lecture, not like listening to a play. It is listening with the whole self, mind and heart and soul. We do not expect to be entertained or to learn new facts, but to hear God's word proclaimed simply and with power: the word of God spoken again to the *Church*.

What helps us listen? Several things are important.

First: Lectors, deacons, and priests must read as the storytellers of the community. Entrusted with a sacred possession, our Scriptures, they must live and pray with their Scripture reading during the week before, practicing over and over, making it their own. They need to be capable of holding the attention of the assembly through their mastery of technical skills and also through their deep love for God's word and his people.

It is a delight and an inspiration to me when I hear good lectors, women and men faithful to their task and trying to improve their skills. They truly struggle with God's word. Story and storyteller become one. Deacons and priests, as readers of the gospel, must work just as hard. The lives of all who read publicly should embody the words they proclaim.

The second element for good listening is this: Unless you have difficulty in hearing, I suggest that you give full attention to the reader and not rely on a booklet or hymnal containing the Scripture texts. A reader lacks inducement to read as well as possible if others are following their own texts, for then the bond of communication is broken. We should fix our eyes on the reader and give full attention to the living word.

Third: It would be well if all of us who listen to the Scriptures on Sunday prepared by reading Scripture at home during the week—especially by studying and reflecting on the texts we will hear on the following Sunday.

Fourth and last: At the liturgy, the readings are to be surrounded with reverence, with honor. This means many things: reverent use of a beautiful Lectionary, a period of silence after the first and second readings and after the homily, singing the psalm between the first two readings, a sung acclamation of the gospel. These are to be part of the normal pattern for Sunday Mass in our parishes.

The psalm is especially important. As we chant its refrain, we are learning the Church's most basic prayerbook. The cantor is the minister who leads this sung prayer. While singing the psalm is perhaps not yet possible at all parish Masses, we can strive with all urgency to train parish cantors. The reintroduction of this ministry is one of the finest developments of the last two decades. The Lectionary permits use of the same psalm over a number of weeks so that people can become familiar with it. Gradually learning the psalm refrains by heart in the Sunday assembly, we can make them part of our morning or evening prayer each day.

We all recognize how important the homily is. You want good homilies; you need good homilies; you deserve good homilies. As parishioners, then, you must give your priests the time to prepare. Priests and deacons must both ask for that time (allowing others to take on various ministries in the parish) and then use the time well.

The homily is the assembly's conversation with the day's Scripture readings. Only by respecting both Scripture and the community can the homilist speak for and to the assembly, bringing it together in this time and place with this Sunday's Scriptures. Good homilists must be familiar with the community's needs, pains and hopes. They must challenge and encourage. And they must seek out and listen to parishioners' comments. Those who preach should make frequent use of seminars and classes on homiletics and Scripture.

Except for the most serious reason, the homily should not depart from the season and the Scriptures. Homilies flow from the Scriptures just heard, not from some other series of topics or themes. This is not a limitation on the content of homilies, for homilists who pay close attention to the cycle of readings will find ample opportunity to preach on the whole breadth of the gospel as it relates to contemporary life.

The reforms which followed Vatican II reintroduced the prayer of the faithful (the general intercessions) into the Roman Liturgy. This prayer is a litany: One after another the needs of the world and the Church are brought before the assembly, and to each we respond with prayer. When the intercessions are sung and the assembly responds to each with the singing of "Lord, hear our prayer" or "Lord, have mercy," it is clear that the intercessions are made by the people. Many of us remember how beautiful and strong a litany prayer can be when sung. The repetition of the chanted response reinforces the urgency of our appeal, and we realize our common priesthood in Jesus Christ, placing constantly before God all the troubles and needs of this earth.

How do we give praise and thanks?

Between the Liturgy of the Word and the Liturgy of the Eucharist we have some rather quiet, practical moments. The collection is taken and the gifts and table are prepared.

The collection itself is, according to the General Instruction on the Roman Missal, "for the poor and the church" (no. 49). Bread and wine are brought by the faithful, but so are gifts of money. This is a true part of the liturgy. In this way we place what we have earned by our work within the holy time of Mass. Unwilling ever to separate our lives from our prayer, we bring something for the poor and the Church from our wealth or our poverty.

Now for the first time in the liturgy, our attention is focused on the altar. We bring bread and wine to be placed there along with the book of prayers. The unleavened bread is obviously not our usual bread but a simple bread, a bread of the poor. In this bread we cast our lot with the poor, knowing ourselves—however materially affluent—to be poor people, needy, hungry. Unless we acknowledge our hunger, we have no place at this table. How else can God feed us? Ideally, because the bread is so important, enough should be brought forward and consecrated each time for all the people at that Mass.

We also bring forward wine. Like bread, it is "fruit of the earth and work of human hands," something simple, something from our tables, a drink of ordinary delight.

When the table has been prepared, we stand and are invited to lift up our hearts to the Lord and give him thanks and praise. Thus begins the Eucharistic Prayer in which we do indeed give thanks to God our Creator for all the work of salvation, but especially for the paschal mystery, that passover of Jesus whereby dying he destroyed our death and rising he restored our life. The priest proclaims this prayer, but "the whole congregation joins

Christ in acknowledging the works of God and in offering the sacrifice" (General Instruction, no. 54).

So this Eucharistic Prayer, too, is the work of the assembly. That must be clear in the way we pray it. There is an immense challenge here. Centuries of practice shaped the assembly as spectators rather than participants. We who are older grew up understanding ourselves as lone individuals deriving what we could from prayer and adoration while the sacred action took place at the altar. But we are a holy people, called to praise God actively for his saving action in our lives.

In every Eucharistic Prayer the whole assembly joins the proclamation of praise led by the priest. By singing the "Holy, holy," the memorial acclamation, and the "Amen," we claim the prayer as our own. These acclamations are so important that even if we sing nothing else at the Mass, we sing these affirmations of faith. Every parish should have a number of melodies for them which everyone can sing by heart.

Nine texts for the Eucharistic Prayer have been approved in English. Priests and liturgy planners should be thoroughly familiar with them, so as to choose the prayer best suited to each season or Sunday.

These Eucharistic Prayers express in words the action we perform. All of us are becoming familiar with them. In the words of the old Roman Canon (now the first Eucharistic Prayer), Christ is present "for us," to bring us "every grace and blessing." In our newer prayers "every grace and blessing" is spelled out in clearer detail. We thank God "for counting us worthy to stand in your presence and serve you," and ask that "all of us who share in the body and blood of Christ be brought together in unity by the Holy Spirit" (Eucharistic Prayer II); Christ is present upon the altar so that we may be filled with the Holy Spirit, "and become one body, one spirit in Christ" (Eucharistic Prayer III); we pray that we ourselves will become "a living sacrifice of praise" (Eucharistic Prayer IV). Renewed by the Holy Spirit, we lift up all the elements of life in praise and offer ourselves to be spent in sacrifice.

We are called to the Lord's table less for solace than for strength, not so much for comfort as for service. This prayer, then, is prayed not only over the bread and wine, so that they become Christ's Body and Blood for us to share; it is prayed over the entire assembly so that we may become the dying and risen Christ for the world. Participation in this great prayer of praise, as meal and sacrifice, transforms us. By grace, we more and more become what we pray.

The voice and manner of the priest should show that he offers this prayer as spokesman for everyone present. It is a *prayer* addressed to the Father. Not a homily or a drama or a talk given to the assembly, it embraces remembrance of God's saving deeds, invocation of the Holy Spirit, the narrative of the Last Supper, remembrance of the Church universal and of the dead, and climaxes "through Him, with Him, in Him. . . ."

For all our devotion to the Body and Blood of Christ present on our altars, we Catholics have hardly begun to make this Eucharistic Prayer the heart of the liturgy. It is still, to all appearances, a monologue by the priest, who stops several times to let the people sing. We seem as yet to have little sense for the flow, the movement, the beauty of the Eucharistic Prayer. How are we to make our own this prayer which is the summit and center of the Church's whole life? How are we to see that this prayer is the model of Christian life and daily prayer? Does this prayer of thanks and praise gather up the way we pray by ourselves every day? When we assemble on Sunday, we help one another learn over and over again how to praise and thank God through and with and in Christ, in good and bad times, until he comes in glory.

Are we a thanks-giving people? Do we give God praise by morning and thanks by night? Do we pause over every table before eating, as we do over this altar table, to bless God and ourselves and our food? The habit of thanksgiving, of praise, of Eucharist, must be acquired day by day, not just at Sunday Mass. In fact, it is at Mass that our habits of daily life come to full expression in Christ.

WHAT IS OUR COMMUNION?

The Communion rite begins with the Lord's Prayer and the peace greeting, continues through the "Lamb of God" as the consecrated bread is broken, moves into the Communion procession, and concludes with silent and spoken prayer. Here it is clear that the assembly performs the liturgy; all of us pray the Lord's Prayer, exchange the sign of peace, and join in the litany "Lamb of God," and all are invited to partake of Communion.

In their recent letter on *The Challenge of Peace: God's Promise and Our Response*, the bishops of the United States wrote that "we encourage every Catholic to make the sign of peace at Mass an authentic sign of our reconciliation with God and with one another. This sign of peace is also a visible sign of our commitment to work for peace as a Christian community. We approach the table of the Lord only after having dedicated ourselves as a Christian community to peace and reconciliation." So let it be in our parishes. When we greet those around us, let our words and manner speak of Christ's peace.

In the first decades of the Church the Sunday gathering was known simply as the "breaking of the bread." That gesture seemed to say everything. The loaf was divided and shared so that many might eat and become one. After our peace greeting has signified how we stand with those around us and with all the Church, we attend to the priest as he lifts up the large host and breaks it.

Following the invitation to the table and the response ("Lord, I am not worthy . . ."), the Communion procession begins. The Communion of priest, deacon and Communion ministers should never take so long that the Communion of the people cannot follow directly on the invitation.

In most of our parishes now auxiliary ministers of Communion assist the priest and deacon in taking Communion to the people. This helps make it clear that we are *together* at this table, that this Communion is the very image of the Church and of that kingdom for which we live and die. Ushers contribute to the dignity and reverence of this sacred moment by helping the assembled community form a true procession and by offering assistance to those who may need it, such as the elderly, the infirm and the very young.

At this table we put aside every worldly separation based on culture, class, or other differences. Baptized, we no longer admit to distinctions based on age or sex or race or wealth. This Communion is why all prejudice, all racism, all sexism, all deference to wealth and power must be banished from our parishes, our homes, and our lives. This Communion is why we will not call enemies those who are human beings like ourselves. This Communion is why we will not commit the world's resources to an escalating arms race while the poor die. We cannot. Not when we have feasted here on the "body broken" and "blood poured out" for the life of the world.

Let that be clear in the reverent way we walk forward to take the holy bread and cup. Let it be clear in the way ministers of Communion announce: "The Body of Christ," "The Blood of Christ." Let it be clear in our "Amen!" Let it be clear in the songs and psalms we sing and the way we sing them. Let it be clear in the holy silence that fills this church when all have partaken.

Before coming forward we say, "Lord, I am not worthy." We are never worthy of this table, for it is God's grace and gift. Yet we do come forward. This is "food for the journey" that we began at baptism. We may eat of it when we are tired, when we are discouraged, even when we have failed. But not when we have forgotten the Church, forgotten the way we began at the font; not when we have abandoned our struggle against evil and remain unrepentant for having done so. Let us examine our lives honestly each time before approaching the Eucharist. "Worthy" none of us ever is, but properly prepared each one of us must be. Christ, present in the Eucharist and in us, calls us to be a holy communion, to grow in love and holiness for one another's sake.

When the priest is seated and the vessels have been quietly put aside, then stillness and peace are ours. Only after the meaning of the life we share has entered deeply into our souls does the presider rise to speak a final prayer.

WHAT DOES OUR DISMISSAL MEAN?

The concluding part of our Roman Liturgy is very brief: the blessing and the sending forth. A procession through the assembly and a concluding song are usually part of this, but these are things the local parish needs to design for its own needs. Whatever is done in these final moments, including any announcements that have to be made, should help us pass from the moments of community ritual to less formal time together and then back to our own lives and daily prayers.

We are sent from the eucharistic table as a holy people always in mission. (The word "Mass"—in Latin *Missa*—means "sending" or "mission.") The spirit which fills us in the liturgy inspires us to re-create the world and in doing so to prepare ourselves for fulfillment in heaven.

In all we have done at Mass we have been uttering promises to one another, creating visions for one another, giving one another hope. Our hymns proclaim that faith is worth singing about. Our repentant prayers not only confess our own unworthiness but praise God's mercy and affirm our pledge to be merciful and seek reconciliation with all people. Our voices united in the acclamations express our willingness to be counted as witnesses to the gospel, with a mission to the world.

There is nothing narrow, selfish or blind in our Sunday worship. We give thanks not so much for personal favors from the Lord as for the earth itself, for the goodness of creation and the wonder of our senses, for the prophets and the saints and for our sisters and brothers throughout the earth, for God's saving deeds recorded in our Scriptures and visible in our world. Only in such thanksgiving can we look on this world, embrace its sorrows and troubles, and confront the mystery of evil and suffering.

To give praise to God in such a world is to proclaim our own baptism into the death and the resurrection of Christ, a baptism that marks us for continuing conversion, the work of Christ's Spirit in us. We have seen and will continue to see sorrow and evil, yet we go on struggling, with songs of praise to God on our lips. This is, as Paul knew, nonsense to the world, but it is the way we have chosen. We are a people who lift up songs of thanks over bread and wine which become for us the true presence of Christ. His coming was proclaimed in Mary's Magnificat, a coming marked by the removal of the mighty from their thrones and the lifting up of the lowly, by the hunger of the rich and the satisfaction of the hungry. Only those who live out that proclamation daily discover finally why it is not a dirge that we sing when we gather but praise.

The dismissal of the assembly is like the breaking of the bread. We have become "the bread of life" and "the cup of blessing" for the world. Now we are scattered, broken, poured out to be life for the world. What happens at home, at work, at meals? What do we make of our time, our words, our deeds, our resources of all kinds? That is what matters.

OUR PROGRESS IN LITURGY

I cannot reflect on the Eucharist without being aware of other concerns: how our celebration of Sunday Mass embodies our love for young children, our solidarity with the handicapped, our response to catechumens. I think, too, of that justice which we celebrate and to which we commit ourselves at Mass. How can we—in liturgy and in life—show the world a community where old age is loved and respected, where the sufferings of the poor are known and remedies are sought, where we can say with Paul that among us "there does not exist male or female but all are one in Christ Jesus"? I am conscious, too, of many matters of liturgical practice, among them: the unnecessarily large number of Sunday Masses celebrated in some parishes and how this adversely affects the quality of the liturgy; my encouragement for Communion under both kinds as prescribed by liturgical norms; my strong support for the cultural diversity in the liturgies of Chicago's parishes—in language, music, and other expressions where it truly manifests the Christian spirit of the people.

All of these things are important to me. I will look for opportunities to speak of them in the future.

Whether you remember back before Vatican II or not, you know that these have not been easy years. We have had our problems in the liturgy. Where the Spirit of God breathes, there can be human excess, either of enthusiasm or reluctance. Liturgical renewal, like any other renewal, would be inauthentic without the mystery of the Cross. Some have seen our liturgy as a mere means to teach or propagandize, some have trivialized it with unworthy songs and themes and needless comments and explanations, and some—perhaps saddest of all—have taken the renewed liturgy only as a set of directions, a kind of operating manual. One result of this last attitude has been to make the liturgy something mechanical and lifeless; the songs and words and gestures and the whole flow of the Mass fail to convey that this is indeed the action of the assembly.

Perhaps all that had to be. But now we need to ask: Are we ready for a deeper and more lasting approach to our Sunday Mass? Are we priests ready to work at presiding, to work at being members and leaders of the assembly?

Are we all, priests and parishioners, ready to say that the parish's commitment to liturgy may mean spending time and money? How else can we train good liturgical ministers? How else can we support staff people as coordinators of liturgy? How else can we pay just salaries to trained musicians who work with all aspects of liturgical music—with choirs, instrumentalists and organists, cantors and groups specializing in one or another style of music? How else can we build or renovate places of worship to make them truly "the house of the Church," fitting places for us to assemble, listen, give thanks, and share communion?

During these twenty years, much of the liturgical renewal seems to have been concerned with external changes. The approach was practical. The revised books that have followed from the Constitution on the Sacred Liturgy have given us a marvelous form for our prayer. Now we need to make this liturgy ours, to be at home with it, to know it deeply, to let it shape our everyday lives. Further changes in rubrics and wording may indeed come, but our present task is to make beautiful and make our own the tradition we have received.

I encourage all of you, especially the clergy and all others involved in various ministries at the liturgy, to mark the twentieth anniversary of the Constitution on the Sacred Liturgy in one very special way: Read it, read it again. When I go back to that initial work of Vatican II, I see what came from the liturgical movement, the courage of Pope John XXIII and the determination of the world's bishops—and the Holy Spirit working in all of them.

CONCLUSION

You know by now that I love the liturgy and find my own identity there, as well as yours and that of the whole Church. How glad I would be to see all of us delighted and inspired by every Sunday Mass in every parish! But good liturgy cannot be created out of a bishop's letters or rules. I can only call you to be what Christ has already called you to be. I can only invite you to serve God and one another in the beauty and depth of Sunday Mass. I can only hold up some goals and ideals, and pledge my own best efforts and the support of the archdiocese. I can only keep you and the liturgy of your parishes in my own prayer.

Above all else, you must know, as I do, that we learn to pray by praying. Can we take the treasure of prayer that is ours and begin—alone or together—to pray as the Church each morning and night? Can we keep Sunday holy? Can we take the Sunday Scriptures and other passages of Scripture into each week and even each day? Can we heed the bishops' call in our letter on peace—the call for prayer and fasting and abstinence on Fridays? Can we keep the great seasons of Advent and Christmas, Lent and Eastertime, not only in our churches but in our homes? Only in these ways will we gradually become active members of a Sunday assembly of the baptized who know how to gather, how to listen to the word, how to give thanks and praise, how to share in Holy Communion, how to take leave of one another for the weeklong and lifelong work of building the kingdom of kindness, justice, and peace.

Joseph Cardinal Bernardin
Archbishop of Chicago

In Service of One Another

*Pastoral Letter on Ministry**

───── *Pentecost, 1985* ──────────────────────────────

My sisters and brothers in Jesus Christ:

We Christians are called to serve one another. In doing so, we live out Jesus' great commandment: love one another as I have loved you.

In his abundant kindness, the Lord has blessed his Church with many gifts which come alive in people. These gifts enable the Church to carry out its mission through an apostolate in which all members of the Church share. As the Second Vatican Council has stated: "by its very nature the Christian vocation is also a vocation to the apostolate" (Decree on the Apostolate of the Laity, no. 2). Some members of the Church also receive the vocation and accompanying gifts of service or ministries. And recent years have witnessed a revival and renewal of ministries within the Church universal and within our local church.

All good gifts must be received from the Lord with gratitude. As the People of God, we need to acknowledge in faith the ways both familiar and new in which the Lord works among and through us. In using his gifts we need to ensure that they work together to build up the body of Christ. We need to instruct and support those who minister in the Church and those who receive this service. We need to be open to the promptings of the Holy Spirit who leads us in the path of truth and love.

In reflecting on these matters—the promptings of the Spirit, the overall goal of building up the body of Christ, the gifts at work in the Church— we are doing nothing particularly new. St. Paul's letters to the Church in

* Also published in *Origins*, vol. 15, no. 9, August 1, 1985, pp. 132–138. It was later reprinted by The Liturgical Press as *Ministry of Service* (no longer in print).

Corinth describe the very same process at work. In fact, it would be possible to trace throughout the history of the Church the various expressions of care and concern for ministries in particular eras, situations and cultures. *My* reflections are based primarily on our experience as a church in the Archdiocese of Chicago.

Three words sum up my intent: *affirmation, coordination,* and *direction.* I want to *affirm* what exists and is now developing. Many good things are happening in the Archdiocese of Chicago, especially in the ministerial life of our church. As bishop and fellow believer, I want to promote and encourage these good things. I also want to encourage the *coordination* of ministries in this local church and offer some *direction* to them.

We shall find affirmation, coordination, and direction for ministry in the measure that we move toward *clarification.* Having first acknowledged current questions and tensions regarding ministry, I shall then offer reflections aimed at clarifying three things: the general concept of ministry; the current situation of ministries in the Archdiocese of Chicago; and the understanding of ministry in light of our historical tradition and the faith of the universal Church.

SERVICE IN CHICAGO

From the very beginning, the church in metropolitan Chicago has benefited from the generous service of many men and women. In times past, people may not have spoken of "ministry," but the reality was there, embodied in the countless teachers, both lay and religious, who have staffed our parish schools, in the dedicated sisters, brothers and laity who have provided health care in a variety of institutions, and in the priests who have served faithfully in the many churches and institutions which reflect the diversity of the archdiocese.

Chicago has been and remains a center for many different kinds of apostolic movements—the Christian Family Movement (CFM), Cana, the Young Christian Workers (YCW), the Young Christian Students (YCS), the St. Vincent de Paul Society, the Legion of Mary and many others.

In the last twenty years new approaches to service in the Church have emerged and others, familiar in earlier times, have been recovered. These are often called "new ministries." For example, some serve the community in liturgical capacities as special ministers of Communion, leaders of song, and readers. Other people, trained and committed to the spiritual welfare of the sick and elderly, function as ministers of care.

In some parishes men and women serve as youth ministers, employing their natural gifts and special training to reach young people and assist in their religious formation. Religious educators—directors of religious education, teachers, and catechists—have also come to understand their role as a ministerial one, oriented toward service of the larger Church. Among the more noteworthy (and perhaps not fully assimilated) developments in our local church are the ministerial functions performed by permanent deacons and their wives and by women, especially religious, who serve in parishes as pastoral associates with priests.

QUESTIONS ABOUT MINISTRY

Candidly, though, some people are perplexed by new ministries. I and others who share my responsibility for providing leadership in the archdiocese receive many questions.

For example: "What *is* 'ministry'? What does the word mean? It has a 'Protestant' ring to it, and now Catholics seem to be using it. What is its precise meaning?" One might suppose that a trip to the dictionary would answer this question, but it is not that simple. For "ministry" is now used by different people to signify different things.

Another question concerns *priests* and ministry. "Why don't we just concentrate on getting more vocations to the priesthood? Then we wouldn't have to use extraordinary ministers of this and that." The question assumes that ministries have arisen as stopgaps to meet the decline of priestly vocations. It likewise seems to assume that priestly ministry is the only *true* ministry in the church—other "ministries" are less than the real thing. I do not share these assumptions.

Some questions concern *women* in ministry. For instance: "Why can't women be priests?" Or: "Why can't women have more say in the direction and development of the Church and thereby have a greater share in the Church's ministry?" Or: "Why can't my granddaughter serve Mass?" But other questions have a different slant: "Why are women allowed to do the things they do in the Church today? Is this really what the Second Vatican Council said and what the Holy Father wants? Haven't we gone too far?"

Still another set of questions comes from *professional lay* ministers—for example, youth ministers. "Who needs me? Who will hire me? Why am I not received well by other lay people? How can I support a family on the kind of salary offered for my services—services which I received extensive training to provide and which require a heavy investment of time and energy on my part? Perhaps I can enter into 'Church work,' but is there any opportunity for upward mobility? Can I ever achieve a position of 'influence'?"

Other questions are perhaps not as common but are of considerable import. Careful observers of what is happening in ministry may ask, "With the proliferation of different ministries, what are the criteria for screening, selecting, training, and certifying ministers? Shouldn't we insist that certain standards be met before people are publicly designated ministers?" To which others might reply: "Who are we to try to control the movement of the Spirit? Must a heavy institutional hand be involved in designating all the ministries in the Church?"

Another sort of question is of particular importance at this moment in history: "How can we affirm traditional forms of service and ministry in the Church while also welcoming the new forms of ministry which are emerging?" Surely we should be able wholeheartedly to affirm and encourage both groups of people—those in traditional ministries and those in new ones.

Finally, a whole series of questions can be raised on the level of *ecclesial understanding*. "How is our present, local experience linked to our history as a Church? Where does it fit in the universal Church? How is what is happening here similar to—and how is it different from—what is happening elsewhere in the Church? What can we learn about ministry from ecumenical dialogue? Are there elements which we can draw from other ecclesial traditions? Do we have something to share with them in return?"

From questions to tensions

These are not speculative questions. They touch people deeply. They are not unlike the questions that come up in a family. People who are so close to each other, who share so much in common, often experience tensions in living and growing together. Sometimes there is a strong emotional charge in the air. So our shared experience of ministries has not only raised questions but, sometimes, generated tensions.

Rather than sweeping them under the rug, I want to explore some of these tensions. Let's begin with the tensions *priests* experience, since, in many ways, their position has become that of a lightning rod for recent ministerial developments. For many years, priests were *the* ministers of the community. Now, the emergence of various ministries may find a priest asking questions about his ministerial identity. "If people who aren't ordained can do many of the things I do, what is the meaning of my priesthood? How am I different? What difference does ordination make?" Reasonable as they are, such questions bespeak a deep-rooted tension centering on priestly identity. A kind of competitive spirit can creep in. The priest may begin to see other ministers as competitors rather than collaborators.

For other priests, the tensions connected with the development of ministries can be quite different. Welcoming toward ministries and at home with them, they see a significant part of their priestly service as enabling, facilitating, and coordinating various ministries. The tension for *them* concerns the slowness of people and institutional structures in developing new ministries. Sometimes they feel they lack support for implementing new ideas and seeking new directions.

Another kind of tension arises for priests who are uncomfortable with collaboration in ministry. Because of their backgrounds and, perhaps, their personal dispositions, their commitment to an individual style of ministry may make it difficult for them to work with other people—other priests, but particularly religious and laity.

I want to focus for a moment on the difficulty some priests find in collaborating in ministry with women. In many professions women are emerging as professional partners with men. While for some this is a welcome cultural shift, others are uncomfortable with the change and resist it. The present historical moment is filled with possibility and also with awkwardness. Life in the Church is not immune to the impact of such cultural shifts, with their promise and tensions.

Women have played an indispensable role in the overall ministry of the Church. This is notably the case in the Archdiocese of Chicago. In the past, however, that ministerial contribution was stylized and limited. Now it is expanding. Women, especially religious, are working side by side with priests, deacons, and others. Some tensions can arise when the men-ministers are not yet comfortable working with women. The reverse can also be true. In any case, the current "unease" is a fact of life—a fact of ministry—for a number of people.

Another kind of tension which can arise for priests and those who work with them is rooted in educational insecurity. While many priests worked long, hard years, their continuing educational and personal development did not always receive the support and encouragement it deserved either from the Church or the people they served. On the other hand, many of the new ministers—religious and lay—have had a postconciliar education. Thus the priest may have the advantage of years of valuable experience and community support as the established religious leader, while some who work with him have less experience but more recent education and formation. This is a formula for the emergence of predictable professional tensions.

A major tension has to do with *women* in ministry. Some women ministers experience considerable frustration. They view the fact that only men can be ordained as diminishing their potential for ministerial service. While no man or woman can claim a "right" to ordination, the unbroken tradition of the Church has permitted only men to be ordained. The Church does not consider itself authorized to change this normative practice. Nevertheless some women consider this unjust, especially since they may possess ministerial skills—such as theological knowledge, compassion, a talent for communication, a sense of mission—at least on a par with those of ordained men.

Even if they are not personally interested in priestly ordination, as many are not, they find themselves in an atmosphere which they believe does not value their service, welcome their talents, or deal with them as equal partners in a community of discipleship. The result is tension highlighted by anger, hurt, disappointment, and disillusionment.

At the same time, many *brothers* and *sisters* share the same tensions and bewilderment as some priests and laity. They, too, struggle to find their appropriate role in the Church's life and ministry.

Many *laypersons* also experience a number of tensions concerning ministries. Some see extraordinary ministers of the Eucharist, men and women, as a sign that the Church is moving farther and farther away from its familiar roots. Why can't the Church be as they remember it? Are priests really so busy that they can't even distribute Communion or help with youth programs? They find it difficult to fathom all the new demands laid on people simply because they want to get married or have their children baptized.

Their questions reveal their tensions: "Why must we go through programs led by people just like us? Why can't priests be more involved?" "Why do parishioners have to vote on so many things?" "If lay participation and lay ministry have really enhanced the laity's role, why do we still feel powerless to shape the direction of the Church?" "Why must the parish budget so much money for a 'youth minister,' when the priest used to take care of the young people?" Perhaps the most important question is one which is seldom asked aloud: "Will the Church remain a place where I feel at home?"

Other lay people ask, "Aren't we focusing too much attention on lay ministry within the Church and neglecting the importance of the lay apostolate—bringing Christian values into the world?"

SEEDS OF HOPE

If the reality were limited to these questions and the tensions they reveal, it would be bleak indeed. And in fact there really are many difficulties which lead to confusion among people and frustration among those who want to serve the Church. I shall return to them. But I also want to share a message of hope and enthusiasm with you, for hope and enthusiasm are also part of the reality—a very important part.

There are many positive signs of an appreciation of ministry and a generous response to it. Many of our young people, who give us a glimpse of the future, recognize the need to live their faith not merely as passive "consumers" but as persons who care for others and find the means to express their caring. Peer ministry on college campuses and volunteer programs which give young people an opportunity to care for the poor are good examples of this.

There is considerable movement toward ministry and service among other age groups as well—for example, religious education programs conducted for the elderly by their peers and parochial support groups for the unemployed. In some places, people help families grieving over the death of a loved one in simple but effective ways—"house sitting" during the wake and funeral or preparing food for the family.

This is why, despite the existence of problems, tensions, and questions, I am confident that the balance falls on the side of positive development. The present pains are signs of growth, capable of purifying us and preparing us for a more vibrant Church where people will serve and be served with a greater sense of the provident care of God in our midst.

But we must be realistic. To realize the promise of the future, we must confront our situation as it is, not as we might want it to be. With this in mind and with the assurance that the Spirit is at work among us, I want now to offer some reflections which will give affirmation, coordination and direction to our efforts to serve one another in the Church.

WHAT IS MINISTRY?

"Ministry" is not a clear-cut term with well-defined meanings. Theologians are currently studying the biblical background and historical development of the concept. I do not propose to utter the last word on the matter, but simply to call attention to a few basics drawn from our tradition and practice.

The best place to begin is the ministry of Jesus. In him we find the basic pattern of all other forms of apostolate and ministry. Both derive from him.

Jesus' life demonstrates how he understood his mission and carried it out. A double proclamation initiates his ministry: The kingdom of God is at hand—be converted and believe the Good News! The Gospels tell how he continued to proclaim and act upon that basic message throughout his public life.

St. Luke's Gospel speaks of him as fulfilling words from the book of Isaiah: "The Spirit of the Lord is upon me; therefore, he has anointed me. He has sent me to bring glad tidings to the poor, to proclaim liberty to captives, recovery of sight to the blind and release to prisoners, to announce a year of favor from the Lord" (Luke 4:18-19). Jesus' words and

deeds seek to bring people into new, reconciled, and redeemed relationships with God and with one another. These relationships mark the coming of the reign of God.

The Church continues the mission of Jesus. Its words and deeds invite
people to share in the new life of the reign of God—a healed, reconciled,
and redeemed life with God and with one another.

All who embrace discipleship with Jesus Christ and join the efforts of
the Church to continue his saving work are active participants in the
Church's mission, the continuation of the mission of Jesus.

As we consider these elements—the mission of Jesus, the mission of
the Church, discipleship of those who follow Jesus in the Church—we
begin to see that the common thread is the kingdom or reign of God. The
reign of God is both the starting point and the goal of the mission of
Jesus, of the Church, and of each disciple.

"Ministry" refers to specific means for accomplishing the mission, which
is to foster the emergence of God's reign. All ministry, as I have said, finds
its model in the ministry of Jesus, as sketched, for example, in Peter's
address to Cornelius' household: "God anointed him with the Holy Spirit
and power. He went about doing good works and healing all who were in
the grip of the devil, and God was with him" (Acts 10:38).

More decisive still is Jesus' example: He came "not to be served but to
serve and to give his life as a ransom for the many" (Mark 10:45). His
service or ministry is ultimately an expression of the free gift of himself
to us in love. And not only does it provide a model for our service, it also
enables and empowers us to serve.

Viewed in this perspective, ministry appears to have two essential dimensions, *relational* and *functional*. In understanding them, we appreciate more fully the meaning of ministry and ministerial identity.

Ministry involves activity. Usually a person *does* something for someone. The activity may be explicitly religious—prayer, liturgy, preaching.
Or it may be less explicitly religious yet grounded in faith and signifying
hope in the coming of the kingdom of God—feeding the hungry, giving
shelter to the homeless, working for justice, reconciliation and peace.

Activity or function does not exhaust the meaning of ministry, however, nor does it essentially define ministry. Ministerial activity is ultimately directed toward establishing a life in communion with God and
with one another, a way of life which manifests the kingdom of God in
our midst.

At the same time, although ministry is directed toward life in relationship with other persons, it is not simply a matter of "being with" others.
Even in human terms, without a manifestation of concern and communion, merely being with someone means very little. The goal and the essence
of ministry thus consist in efforts to foster healing, reconciling, redeem-

ing relationships—communion with God and with one another in his kingdom—by tangible expressions of love.

Let us now consider ministry from a different angle, the perspective of our own experience. Reflecting on how we have *received* ministry from others will help us understand what ministry is. And all of us have been beneficiaries of such service.

When someone ministers to us, we are enabled to *be* more or to *do* better: more readily to accept the loss of a loved one, to give witness to our faith more clearly and convincingly in the circumstances of our work, to continue the ordinary routines of life with hope. The one who served us has not simply done us an isolated favor. Rather, as a consequence of ministry, we are better able to live and act in the future.

Certain patterns emerge in reflecting on our experience of ministry and the accompanying circumstances. First came a *need* on our part, though one we may not initially have perceived. Sometimes, of course, the need is quite obvious, as at a time of sickness or a season of loss. But there may have been other times when we simply needed to know something about our faith, needed a word of encouragement as we struggled with a problem, needed a way to celebrate the presence of God.

Again, we may or may not have recognized the explicit dimension of *faith* in the moment of ministry. But whether it was then or later, at some time we sensed in the care we received the presence of God, communicated through a word, a touch, a prayer, a sacramental celebration.

Another element which may have been more or less explicit at the moment was a sense of the *Church*. As someone ministers to us, we may be conscious of being joined to a larger communion of faith, hope and love; but it may also be that this awareness emerges only over a period of time.

Here, too, we find confirmation of the fact that there is more to ministry than activity. At the heart of ministerial activity is *service which discloses and supports* our relationship with God in Jesus Christ by the power of the Holy Spirit, even if this is not explicitly grasped at the time. Although ministry serves the emergence of the kingdom, it is not its full expression. Yet in the end we are destined to live in communion with God and with one another.

In addition, ministry involves an *empowering* of the recipient. He or she is disposed for fuller life with God and with other people, greater participation in the reign of God. We find a model in the account in St. John's Gospel of Jesus' washing of the apostles' feet. At first Peter demurs, but Jesus tells him he can have no part with Jesus until he allows the Lord to wash his feet. Once Peter has received Jesus' ministry, he can do for others as Jesus had done for him.

Finally, formal ministerial activity is not performed simply on the basis of one's personal initiative. It is always carried on *in communion with* the larger Church, the community of faith which supports and inspires particular service.

We can summarize our description of ministry in this way: *Ministry is a specific activity supported and designated by the Church, which discloses the presence of God in some way in our human situation and empowers us to live more fully in the mystery of God—in communion with God and with one another.*

This description moves us away from an understanding of ministry which is either purely functional or purely relational. Ultimately, ministry does open us to a relational reality—to our communion with God and with one another in God—but this happens through the concrete circumstances of our lives and through the particular activities of those who minister or serve.

This has a number of important implications. One is that it is not enough for a parish—or a cluster, a vicariate or even the archdiocese itself—simply to sponsor a number of programs or activities. Each of them must contribute to building up the whole community. Competition among programs or groups within a parish does not give witness to authentic ministry. Individual programs and activities must contribute to the bonding of parish members into one community. For example, the choir and the liturgy committee must work together to prepare and celebrate prayerful Eucharists with the entire community.

Another implication is that it is not enough simply to belong to a particular parish group with a specific focus. Parish associations must avoid exclusiveness and narrowness of perspective. A parish should evaluate activities not only by their specific objectives but also by their impact on the entire parish community. For example, although a school board may concentrate on the administration of the parish school, it should not ignore the school's impact on the whole parish.

Moreover, it is not enough to have a comfortable sense of belonging to a group without actually *doing* something—reaching out to serve others.

We could trace other implications of this understanding of ministry, but let us turn to another important issue.

THE COMMON FOUNDATION OF ALL MINISTRY

We find the foundation for all ministry, as for all apostolic service, in the Church in the sacraments of initiation—baptism, confirmation and Eucharist. In baptism, we are united with Christ in his paschal mystery. We are linked to his dying and rising. We are joined to his Mystical Body. We enter into a life of communion with God and with one another.

In confirmation we receive the fullness of the gift of the Spirit. Whereas in baptism we received the Spirit as God's children, in confirmation that same Spirit is given to empower us to participate fully in the Church's mission. Through the confirming gift of the Spirit, we are enabled to serve the communion of the Church and of the entire human family. "Moreover, through the sacraments, especially the Holy Eucharist, there is communicated and nourished that charity toward God and man which is the soul of the entire apostolate" (Dogmatic Constitution on the Church, no. 33).

It is essential that we understand our common rootedness in the sacraments of initiation. For on this level—that of incorporation into the body of Christ as his members and disciples—we find our true power and dignity. We become truly "a holy nation, a royal priesthood, a people set apart." On this foundation, the Lord adds specific gifts of ministry or service in the Church.

The Second Vatican Council has stated clearly: "Though they differ from one another in essence and not only in degree, the common priesthood of the faithful and the ministerial or hierarchical priesthood are nonetheless interrelated. Each of them in its own special way is a participation in the one priesthood of Christ" (Dogmatic Constitution on the Church, no. 10).

Although it is not my intention to treat the nature of the sacrament of orders at this time, this conciliar statement underlines the fact that there *is* an essential difference between ordained and nonordained ministry, even though both share in the one priesthood of Christ.

Next I shall briefly consider some of the ways in which we have come to distinguish the various ministries at work in the Church. But these distinctions make little sense and, indeed, can lead to considerable confusion, unless we keep in mind that all ministries are related, that all are rooted in the ministry of Jesus, and that we, for our part, are introduced to participation in the mission of the Church through the sacraments of initiation.

THE DIVERSITY OF MINISTRIES

Ministry has a single goal: the emergence of the reign of God. Yet we speak of "ministries" to signify that there is no such thing as "generic" ministry any more than there is "generic" human experience.

We human beings move successively and diversely through struggles and triumphs, needs and their fulfillment, pain and celebration. Ministries must correspond to this reality. The disclosure of God and the service of people leading to the emergence of the reign of God *demand* a diversity of ministries rooted in concrete human circumstances.

Saint Paul explained the diversity of gifts to his beloved community at Corinth: "There are different gifts but the same Spirit; there are different ministries but the same Lord; there are different works but the same God who accomplishes all of them in everyone. To each person the manifestation of the Spirit is given for the common good" (1 Cor 12:4-7).

Saint Paul goes on to explain how the different ministries and gifts function in a way resembling the different members of the human body. No one member constitutes the whole body; all are necessary and important. Then he tells the Corinthians: "You . . . are the body of Christ. Every one of you is a member of it" (1 Cor 12:27).

Saint Paul sought to help the Corinthians understand their life together as a people enriched by God with different ministries rooted in and serving the one God. That is why he underscores the unity and diversity of ministries. He speaks of their differences, but also of the need for collaboration. Above all, he insists that all good gifts are to be received with gratitude. There is to be no rivalry, no competition among those with different gifts, for everyone belongs to the body of Christ. All gifts are meant to contribute to that body.

These words of Saint Paul speak to us today with special force and challenge. We are re-awakening and rekindling the ministerial life of the Church. For many years, ministry was identified almost exclusively with priesthood. Now, as we return to a broader understanding of ministry, we need to heed Saint Paul's words and let them take root in our hearts. When we maintain a balanced perspective, we come to understand the common roots and linkage among diverse ministries. This does not diminish the importance of priesthood; rather, it heightens the significance of the priestly role by bringing its uniqueness into clearer focus.

The point I wish to emphasize is this: Diverse ministers and diverse ministries are gifts given to the Church by God to respond to different needs and different situations. Some needs are constant in the life of the Church—teaching the Word of God, for example. Others arise in response to specific historical circumstances—for instance, contemporary ministry to the separated and divorced.

I underscore the reasons for diverse ministries to avoid "ranking" service in the Church. For, when we "rank" ministries, we separate ourselves from one another and cause disharmony and discord within the body of Christ. Tensions can and have arisen because "different" can easily be misunderstood as "better." Differences may imply, in the popular mind, ranking or a superiority of certain forms of ministry over others. Paul's image of the one body with different members cautions us against setting diverse ministries in contrast or competition with one another.

This discussion of diverse ministries becomes clearer if we consider some of the ways in which ministries and ministers can be differentiated. In this way we can understand more fully the diversity with which the Church has been blessed. Basically, ministries and ministers can be grouped according to five categories.

1. Ministers can be differentiated by different forms of *ecclesial recognition and designation*. Deacons, priests, and bishops are designated as ministers of the Church in virtue of their ordination. Others are designated for ministry by receiving a canonical mission. The Church in some official way "sends" a person to carry out a particular task—for example, teaching in a specific faculty of theology. The Church designates others by instituting them for a particular ministry. At this time in the universal Church, there are two such ministries, that of lector or reader and that of acolyte or minister of the altar.

Others exercise a particular ministry because they have ecclesiastical approval for their service—for example, the official assignment of religious and lay people to offices of the archdiocese or their assignment as associates in parishes. The Church, in effect, supports the service they render and attests to the fact that it is an approved way of witnessing to the reality of the presence of God and building up the body of Christ. Finally, some are ministers in virtue of the supervision exercised by the Church over their particular service. This may occur, for example, when a parish commissions certain people as catechists.

2. A second way in which ministers are differentiated is according to the *amount of time* they devote to their ministry. For some, ministry is a full-time task; for others, it is part-time because of the nature of the service rendered, other obligations, or financial considerations. It should be clear that the depth of an individual's commitment to ministry is not to be measured by the amount of time devoted to the service. The same applies to differentiation on the basis of compensation. Volunteer ministers are in no way inferior to those who receive compensation for their ministry—and vice versa.

3. A third way in which ministers are differentiated is through the *specification of their activities*. The activities may be wide-ranging, as in the case of many priests and bishops who exercise multiple roles as teachers, celebrators of sacraments, and community builders, or they may be specifically targeted, as in the case of a religious educator who prepares children for the sacraments.

4. A fourth way in which ministers can be differentiated is according to the *background required* to carry out their particular ministries. Some ministries—such as the diaconate, religious education and music ministry—require considerable preparation, including formal education, personal formation, and certification. Others require a more limited kind of preparation and depend more on the particular charism of the minister.

5. Finally, a fifth way of differentiating ministers is according to the *setting* in which the service is carried out. People minister in many different settings: parishes, schools, college campuses, correctional facilities, health care facilities, soup kitchens, shelters for the homeless. Virtually no human

setting is excluded from the list of places where ministry can be and is found.

Unfortunately, the emphases in our culture on competition and status influence our thinking, attitudes and mode of operating in regard to ministry. We need to be mindful of what Jesus said: "You know how among the Gentiles those who seem to exercise authority lord it over them; their great ones make their importance felt. It cannot be like that with you. Anyone among you who aspires to greatness must serve the rest; whoever wants to rank first among you must serve the needs of all" (Mark 10:42-44).

In light of this, we must listen to one another very carefully in order to discover the same Spirit of the one Lord at work in all of us. This has been a continuous task of the Church from the time of Jesus until our own day, in which we seek to effect and respond to a renewal of ministerial life.

DIRECTIONS FOR THE FUTURE

We can anticipate continuing development in the understanding and practice of ministries. As a Church, we need to continue searching prayerfully for the most appropriate ways in which God can be revealed and his people served. We must learn from one another. I wish therefore to encourage certain directions for the future in our archdiocesan dialogue about ministry.

1. *All ministries are good and necessary for upbuilding the body of Christ.* The implications of this foundational understanding need further elaboration. It is a challenge for catechesis to grasp and better communicate this fact.

2. *At the same time we must continue to discern and encourage in our midst vocations to the priesthood and religious life.* Priests and religious provide unique witness to living gospel values. These traditional ways of serving and witnessing are as essential as ever and more challenging than before.

3. *All ministries and ministers require and deserve development, support, enabling, enrichment, and encouragement.* This is imperative because these ministries are gifts of the Lord for which we are grateful and responsible as stewards. Our challenge is to discover effective ways of caring for all ministries and ministers.

4. *In developing ministries, we need to be attentive and faithful to the experience and teaching of the universal Church.* This implies an appreciation of various historical developments and different cultural milieus. Although, at times, we may experience this requirement as a limitation, it can also stimulate our creativity.

5. *We need to be astute in identifying and assessing the contemporary needs of our society and responding to them in appropriate ways.* Historically, this is how new ministries have developed in the life of the Church. That is why Pope Paul VI, in his letter *Ministeria quaedam*, invited the local churches to develop their own ministries. This is a call to exercise our God-given creativity in finding new ways to disclose God and serve his people, new ways to facilitate the emergence of the reign of God in our midst.

6. *While vigorously fostering and supporting ministries, we must at the same time give greater visibility to the truth that all members of the Church have an authentic vocation to the apostolate.* Not all receive a calling to service in formal ministry, but all, by reason of the sacraments of initiation, are called to participate in the Church's apostolic work, carrying on the mission of Jesus and spreading the Good News of the kingdom according to their circumstances. I recall again, as I did at the outset of this letter, the words of the Second Vatican Council: "By its very nature the Christian vocation is also a vocation to the apostolate" (Decree on the Apostolate of the Laity, no. 2).

CONCLUSION

In this pastoral letter I have examined both the satisfactions and the tensions we experience in ministry in today's Church—the ecstasies and agonies, as it were. I have also given some guidance and directions for the future. It is critically important, however, that we see ministry in the broader context of the Church's mission.

The work begun in the Second Vatican Council continues. The Church has come to a new self-awareness through the conciliar deliberations. But it takes time for the impact of what was done at the council to be woven into the ordinary fabric of church life at the local level.

May I invite you, therefore, to join me in a vision of the Church which will provide us with the direction and motivation needed as we prepare for the third millennium of Christianity? In that vision I see a community of faith over which the risen Lord truly presides; a community which continues to incarnate, in our contemporary context, the life and ministry of the members of the first Christian community who "devoted themselves to the apostles' instruction and the communal life, to the breaking of bread and the prayers" (Acts 3:42-43).

It is a community in which all members, in virtue of their incorporation into Christ through baptism and confirmation, witness to his saving deeds before the entire world and work for the emergence of the kingdom he proclaimed. It is a community whose designated ministers—laity, religious, priests, deacons and bishops—understand and accept their uniquely different but complementary and necessary roles, working together for the good of all.

It is a community whose faith in Jesus is far more compelling than any human consideration; one which honors truth more than idle speculation and bias; a community in which respect for persons rules out pettiness, unfairness and mean-spiritedness, promoting instead dialogue, reconciliation and unity. It is a community in which Jesus' love and mercy, his justice, his compassion and healing power are tangibly evident each day.

As your bishop and fellow pilgrim, I challenge you to join me in shaping that kind of community for the church of Chicago. Help me make the vision come true!

Your brother in Christ,

Joseph Cardinal Bernardin
Archbishop of Chicago

The Family Gathered Here Before You

Pastoral Letter on the Church

─── *Autumn 1989* ──────────────────────────────

INTRODUCTION

My sisters and brothers in Jesus Christ, called by God to be holy and to be witnesses to our hope in the power of the Holy Spirit: May God's peace, wisdom, and love be yours!

For some time, I have wanted to write to you about the Church. We already have many official statements on this topic, of course, including the documents of the Second Vatican Council, especially the Dogmatic Constitution on the Church and the Pastoral Constitution on the Church in the Modern World. Moreover, theologians have made considerable efforts to deepen our understanding of the mystery of the Church. I will rely here in part on these resources, especially the conciliar documents. But my letter's purpose is also more specific and pastoral.

In writing of the Church, I want to rekindle our hope and provide a broader perspective for our archdiocesan priorities. To do this, I will speak of the Church partly from my own perspective and experience. The word "Church" means many different things to different people, and I wish to tell you what it means to me. But I also want to explore our shared understanding of the Church as a reality transcending our diverse perceptions. This letter, then, offers basic understandings of the Church and fundamental visions of our future, shaped both by our traditions and our current experience, particularly in the Archdiocese of Chicago.

In my personal reflection, the guiding question, which I invite you to make your own, is this: *How does our God-given hope move us to envision the Church in the future?* Our response to that question will determine how much we give of ourselves to the Church today and what we will hand on to our children. In looking to the future, we have a twofold responsibility: to be faithful to our origins and our tradition, and to be creative and responsive to the life-giving movements of the Spirit in our midst.

My more immediate hope for this letter is that it be read, discussed, and used throughout this local church. It has significant implications for archdiocesan and parish priorities, evangelization, liturgy, preaching, religious education, parish pastoral councils, the identity and respective roles of ministers, the Church's social involvement, ecumenism, and many other dimensions of Church life and ministry.

When Pope Paul VI opened the second session of the Second Vatican Council, he challenged the Church to a greater self-awareness. I pray that we, too, will come to greater awareness of *who* we are as the Church of God. It will not come easily. We must first examine and evaluate our experience. Then we must link our experience with the broader traditions and history of our faith. Finally, we must work to rekindle our hope and creativity as we look to the future. Our self-awareness as the Church embodies our past, our present, and our vision of the future. And all three help shape this letter.

It is not a complete treatment of the Church. Nevertheless, if it is read in the context of other documents, such as the Dogmatic Constitution on the Church and the Pastoral Constitution on the Church in the Modern World, it will provide a good basis for our dialogue about the Church, indeed, about ourselves as the Church, as the People of God.

This pastoral letter is addressed to all Catholics in the Archdiocese of Chicago—women and men, lay and clerical and religious, young and old, people strongly attached to the Church and those who feel somewhat distant from it. Although primarily addressed to Catholics, it may also help others to understand who we are. May our shared reflection and prayer draw us closer to one another and to greater fidelity to Jesus Christ, who is forever the light of all nations.

THE EXPERIENCE OF THE CHURCH

I will first explore our experience of the Church, especially some of our diverse feelings about it and the various places where we encounter it. Although we sometimes speak as if the Church were something outside of ourselves, *we* are the Church in the world today, and our experience of the Church is in large part an experience of ourselves as God's people.

How We Feel About the Church

Much that is written about the Church tends to focus on ideas, to deal almost exclusively with what we think and know about it. But whether we are Catholics from birth or converts to the faith, we also have feelings about the Church which in many cases predate our ideas.

This should come as no surprise. Belonging to the Church has always meant more than accepting certain beliefs, ideas, and customs, as essential as that is. Being members of the Church engages us in our totality as persons, including our feelings, and the reason for that is quite clear.

We have access to the mystery of Christ—his saving life, death, and resurrection—through the Church. Jesus' mission—to heal, to reconcile, to gather people in unity, to establish God's justice in the world—continues in the Church. These are not simply intellectual matters. They also touch the human heart.

This is why the experience of belonging to the Church stirs up many feelings, some positive and some negative. Different feelings often co-exist within the same person. The complexity of our experience of, and our feelings about, the Church and ourselves in the Church can be compared to the situation of a family. Both as members of a family and as members of the Church, we are in communion with others. We do not associate with them merely as a matter of convenience or to serve a utilitarian purpose.

Moreover, in both instances, the experience touches the very core of our being: our need to discover our true identity, our dignity and worth, our vocation and mission in the world, our destiny. Is it surprising, then, that we have such diverse feelings about our experience of the Church on its various levels?

I will first identify some of these feelings and then offer some thoughts on what to do with them.

For many people, membership in the Church stirs up feelings of *pride* and *gratitude*. The goodness manifested by dedicated Catholic persons and institutions in such areas as education, health care, and social service makes us proud and grateful. So do the truth of the faith, proclaimed continuously for nearly two thousand years, and the sacraments and rituals of the Church. We are also proud and grateful for the Church's support and encouragement of the arts—for example, in beholding a beautiful, religious painting or sculpture, hearing great church music, or seeing inspiring church architecture.

For many, the experience of the Church stirs up a sense of *being at home*. It is a familiar place where we feel at ease. This feeling often accompanies our experience of the local parish community, especially if we have long been involved in its life and ministry.

Some, however, feel *alienation* from the Church, a sense of not being at home, often accompanied by anger and hurt. These include some women, some homosexual persons, and some who feel that their efforts to promote social justice have not been adequately supported by the Church.

For others, the Church stirs up a sense of *being supported*. Many immigrants and migrants have often found in the Church a comforting link with the past and a helpful port of entry into a new life. Often, people making difficult personal transitions—the recently widowed, for example—find compassion and comfort in the Church.

In the wake of the renewal initiated by the Second Vatican Council, some have felt great *disappointment* in the Church. They feel the renewal has undercut much they had learned to treasure. So, for instance, worship and forms of devotion widespread before the council seem to have been hastily, and perhaps ill-advisedly, taken away, while the new forms of worship do not satisfy their deeply felt needs. They experience a vacuum, an emptiness where once there was much vitality, spirit, and nourishment. From this stem feelings of disappointment, discouragement, and even anger.

Still others are very *impatient* with the seemingly slow pace of renewal. The council raised expectations of a wholly revitalized community of faith, but some perceive that the changes have been more cosmetic than substantial. They are impatient with ecclesiastical structures, with the cumbersome process of consultations, meetings, reports. They ask why we cannot "read the signs of the times" as the council challenged us to do.

Others are quite *happy* with the Church's renewal to date and have a sense of shared responsibility for what still needs to be done. They experience an excitement about the Church's future, its contribution to the world, and their involvement in its renewal. At times, though, they may also feel somewhat apprehensive, wondering and even worrying about how things will work out.

Some feel a certain *resentment* when Church leaders address issues that are not distinctively religious but, nevertheless, are intimately connected with our faith commitments. How, they ask, can bishops talk about national defense, the economy, or the international debt? They feel that Church leaders have neither the mission nor the specific competence to deal with such matters.

Some are *sad* and *depressed* by the shortcomings, failures, and inconsistencies of Church life, the seeming triumph of sin over grace. Others are *joyful* for the positive steps that have been taken, the victories, even small ones, over sin, ignorance, and human limitation that are also a part of the Church's daily experience.

These are some of the diverse feelings that people have about the Church. In the face of this bewildering mix, one can be excused for wondering what to do with so much emotional energy, positive and negative.

This complexity and diversity does not allow me to respond directly here to all of these feelings. Nevertheless, I will offer a few observations in an attempt to provide a context for them.

It is easier to characterize feelings on paper than in real life. Still, we need to recognize and articulate our feelings about the Church and one another, lest feelings become obstacles to our living and working together.

Constructive criticism is helpful and desirable, but Church leaders—the pope, bishops, priests, and other ministers—at times become targets or "lightning rods" for the negative feelings of others. Among God's people the norms of justice and charity must prevail and keep us from such mean-spirited behavior.

Expressions like "She really speaks her mind!" and "You really know where he stands!" are often used in reference to persons on both ends of the ecclesiastical spectrum who freely and readily share their negative judgments or feelings about Church life and ministry. But authentic truth and candor require that one express not only the negative but also the positive. In particular, the criticism of other persons must always be accompanied and balanced by affirmation and appreciation. To express only negative feelings, while keeping the positive ones to oneself, leads to misunderstanding and a distortion of reality.

What, then, can we do with our feelings about the Church? There are a few simple but very important steps to take. We can acknowledge and accept both our positive and negative feelings. We can think and talk about them. We can decide whether and how we will act on them. Most importantly, because we believe in and hold fast to the mystery of the crucified and risen Lord, when appropriate we can—and must—deal with our feelings in light of our God-given call to live with patience, hope, and forgiveness.

In sum, our experience of Church is not merely a matter of the head. We cannot understand our life together simply in terms of ideas about the Church. The day-to-day reality of Church in all its dimensions deeply touches the human heart, and this is good. It reflects the human heart of Jesus who felt compassion, righteous anger, passionate enthusiasm, and great love.

Where We Encounter the Church

Another reason why "Church" means different things to different people is that we encounter the Church on several levels. In briefly describing them here, I will draw on our experience as well as on Church teaching and canon law.

I will speak of seven places in which we encounter the Church. No one, of course, experiences the Church simultaneously in all seven, but each of them is part of our overall understanding of the Church.

The Church in the Home

Family life provides our earliest, and perhaps most enduringly powerful, experience of the Church. While this function of the family has received less recognition and support than it deserves, it is here that most of us first hear the word of God, learn to pray, prepare for the sacraments, discover how to live in conformity with the gospel, and see that there is something special about our relationship with God and with others who share our faith.

The Dogmatic Constitution on the Church briefly sketches this "family" dimension of the Church. It speaks of the family as a "domestic church" in which "the parents, by word and example, are the first heralds of the faith with regard to their children" (no. 11). Other small Christian communities of various kinds also possess much the same character as familial settings for the nurturing of faith and charity, such as older couples whose grown children have moved away, single brothers or sisters who live together, single or widowed parents with children, small religious communities, and other groupings of people.

The "domestic church," whatever its particular shape, contains in a very simple form many of the essential ingredients of ecclesial life in the Catholic tradition: proclamation of God's word, sacramental life, works of service, forgiveness and reconciliation, worship, and the impetus to mission in and to the world. It leads its members naturally to live the fullness of ecclesial life in the larger community of the Church.

We need to encourage and strengthen this dimension of our experience of the Church. This requires dialogue, research, and coordinated efforts.

The Church in Small Groups

Small group experiences in the Church are not a new phenomenon. Currently there are many valuable witnesses to the vitality of this form of ecclesial life, including parish renewal groups, Cursillo, Marriage Encounter, Bible study groups, and support groups for the bereaved, widowed, separated and divorced, and homosexual men and women—all of whom try to live in conformity with the Church's faith and moral teaching. Many national and international organizations also link people in small groups to help them live a deeper Christian life, participate more fully in the Church's mission to the world, or take part in special ministries within the community of faith.

Small-group experiences of this sort are a proud part of the Church's history in metropolitan Chicago. Among others, we may list the Arch- diocesan Council of Catholic Women, the Holy Name Society, the Legion of Mary, the St. Vincent de Paul Society, the Christian Family Movement, the Young Christian Students, the Young Christian Workers, Opus Dei, and the Focolare Movement. These groups are *formally* recognized and organized. Many Catholics also belong to *informal* groups in which they share faith, study the Bible, and collaborate in works of justice, peace, and charity.

Today, then, as in the past, the experience of the Church includes for many people their participation in groups in which they can render a form of service or engage in a specific apostolate tailored to their state in life and particular gifts. Often these small group experiences are powerful manifestations of the priesthood of all the baptized. Here people pro- claim the word of God to one another, live out their sacramental com- mitments, especially baptism, confirmation, Eucharist, penance, and marriage, and inspire one another to commitment, action, and service. Here they are drawn together and sustained in community by the risen Lord, who said, "Where two or three are gathered in my name, there am I in their midst" (Matt 18:20).

Considering the significance and the great potential of small-group ec- clesial experiences, it is important that we explicitly recognize and sup- port them. We need also to ensure that they remain linked with the other levels of the Church, both for their own benefit and that of the larger ec- clesial community, so as to avoid the dangers of elitism and exclusiveness.

The Church in the Parish

A parish is a community of believers. Usually it embraces a geographi- cal area and, within that area, it is a kind of community of communities. The parish is a center of worship, instruction, and mission. There the word of God is proclaimed, the sacraments, especially the Eucharist, are celebrated, and people are empowered to bring God's transforming hope and love to the world. The parish is also a stable institution which enjoys the leadership of a pastor and other ministers and is an integral part of the diocesan church which is led, in turn, by its bishop.

Although accurate as a theological and canonical description of a parish, the account just given does not express the vital impact which a parish has on its parishioners. For most people, the parish provides their main continuing experience of the Church and is recognized as doing so. Ask most Catholics where they encounter the Church, and their answer will be "my parish."

While there are many kinds and degrees of participation in a parish, a common thread is the deliberate decision to belong. This implies, for example, that people register in the parish, attend its services, provide for its financial support, and take part in its various activities. In other words, belonging to a parish requires an active commitment, not a merely passive response.

The parochial experience of the Church varies for different people. Four examples illustrate this diversity.

For some, the parish is the pivot and center of their lives. It is a place where they are known by name. These people have a real, tangible sense of belonging to the parish. They have made a praiseworthy investment of themselves in the life and well-being of the parish that means so much to them.

For others, the parish has a certain importance, but they are not very active in its life. They are not necessarily known there by name, and they do not feel that as a loss. The parish for them is the place where the sacraments are celebrated, where their children are educated, and where special occasions in their lives are blessed. Such people come to church regularly, but their presence tends to be passive. The parish is more a "resource" which supports their personal relationship with God than a real community and a gathering of people who know one another and share a common ecclesial vision.

For still others, the parish is a more or less familiar reality, but, most of the time at least, not really significant in their lives. They go to church irregularly and infrequently. Their presence in the community is often rather anonymous and invisible. Still, at certain moments of their lives, the parish may take on great importance for them.

Finally, there is another group of people whose parochial experience is quite different from the rest. Their parishes reflect and respond to their special cultural, linguistic, or educational needs. For example, the Archdiocese of Chicago has a long tradition of national parishes, established to meet the cultural, linguistic, and social circumstances of various groups of immigrants. Again, university parishes serve the students and faculty of institutions of higher learning. Often these special parishes foster strong bonds among their parishioners. At times, this kind of ecclesial experience shares some of the qualities of the small-group experience considered earlier. And, for the most part, the experience is a very positive one, though care must be taken to ensure that a "special interest" parish remains linked to the larger local church.

From another perspective, how people experience the Church within a parish is closely bound up with its ministers. Church buildings provide space for worship and education and are a tangible sign of the stability and focus of the community of faith. So, too, parish ministers, while rendering

particular services, are also focal points and symbols of stability and continuity within the parish community. They sacramentalize, as it were, God's
faithful presence there. And, as our experience makes clear and the Code
of Canon Law confirms, the role of the pastor is of paramount importance.

Before the Second Vatican Council, the task of providing ecclesial focus
in the parish belonged primarily to the pastor, his associates, and the religious who taught in the parochial school. Their presence was a clear sign
of stability and direct care, especially in education, administration, and
sacramental celebration. Today, the presence of a pastor and, if they are
available, associates and religious remains a powerful and critically important sign of the Church's stable care in a community. At the same time,
the recovery and development of other forms of ministry (which I discussed in my earlier pastoral letter, *In Service of One Another*) have
broadened the range of people who provide for the needs of the local
parish community in an ongoing, stable way.

Although the parish is not the only setting in which people experience
the Church, it is a touchstone for all the other ecclesial experiences. It
supports and sustains the domestic church. It is a point of reference for
small groups. It unites its parishioners with the diocese and the universal
Church. Its significance must not be underestimated, even as we seek to
appreciate and develop other ways of experiencing the Church.

Parish life today is complex. Here many ecclesial efforts and expressions intersect. People find spiritual nourishment in liturgical and devotional prayer as well as personal, faith-filled care, especially at critical
moments in their lives. Here education for renewal and justice takes
place, and many other needs and expectations are met.

The parish needs the best available resources—the best ministers possible, the best structures for collaboration, the best means for meeting
people's diverse needs. Archdiocesan programs serving priorities like
evangelization, ethnic and racial harmony, the encouragement of vocations, and stewardship will only achieve their goals if they are parish-
based. Archdiocesan planning will be effective only to the extent parishes
participate in it and make its objectives their own.

The Church in the Diocese

The Second Vatican Council's Decree on the Pastoral Office of Bishops
(no. 11) and the revised Code of Canon Law describe a diocese from a
theological and spiritual perspective: "A diocese is a portion of the people
of God which is entrusted for pastoral care to a bishop with the cooperation of the presbyterate so that, adhering to its pastor and gathered by
him in the Holy Spirit through the Gospel and the Eucharist, it constitutes a particular church in which the one, holy, catholic and apostolic
Church of Christ is truly present and operative" (Canon 369).

It is essential to think of a diocese in personal terms. Both the council and canon law indicate that "a diocese is a portion of the people of God." In the Archdiocese of Chicago, the sheer variety of people, with their racial, ethnic, linguistic, cultural, economic, and educational diversity, witnesses to the inclusiveness of the Church. It makes our local church a realization and experience of the universal Church of Jesus Christ, to which all people are called.

The council and canon law specifically state that the office of bishop, along with that of priests, is central to diocesan identity and experience. My own experience confirms this. Episcopal ministry is directed primarily toward pastoral service and care, not the exercise of power.

Although this way of speaking may sound somewhat ideal, it is in fact realistic. Our experience as a local church is primarily that of people interacting—very different people brought together by the power of the Holy Spirit working in the gospel and the Eucharist.

Yet this great diversity among the Catholics of the Archdiocese of Chicago can also lead to separation and even division. Indeed, division is a sad dimension of our experience in metropolitan Chicago. Instead of enriching us, racial, ethnic, and cultural differences sometimes divide us. We are not a "perfect" or exclusively "holy" local church. Our lives, individually and as a community, are marked by sin, especially sins of intolerance, impatience, lack of understanding, sins against the unity of the Church, indifference to the poor, self-righteousness, the abuse of authority, the failure to forgive, even meanness and vindictiveness against fellow Christians.

But despite our limitations and sinfulness, we have achieved a degree of harmony and communion. That is truly a gift from God. How else can we explain the ecclesial gathering of people so different from one another? Ultimately, it is God's work and gift.

All archdiocesan offices and diocesan-wide organizations have an underlying, common purpose. They are to serve the mission of this local church. No office or agency can or should exist merely for itself. In the end, all diocesan structures must preserve and foster the gift of unity. They are meant to encourage, support, and sustain our efforts to grow as a community of faith and love.

The Church's unity is promoted and symbolized in many of our archdiocesan experiences. For example, when two communities become "sharing parishes"—sharing material and financial resources as well as spiritual support—the Church's unity is "sacramentalized," that is, it is both effected and symbolized. Unity is also served by our generous support of Catholic Charities, a bridge between those who have and those who lack. Liturgical celebrations can also express and build ecclesial unity when diverse cultural and ethnic components are incorporated into the ceremonies. The difficult, delicate, and often painful process of consolidating parishes or schools to serve new needs and bring about better stewardship of available resources is another example of diversity struggling to become a more widely embracing and enriching unity.

The primary pastoral challenge, then, is to ensure that all ministerial efforts serve the mission of the diocesan church. As "a portion of the people of God," the diocese is a concrete realization of the Church of Jesus Christ. It receives loving care from its bishop, its priests and deacons, and its other ministers. It finds its unity in the gospel and the sacraments, especially the Eucharist, by the power of the Holy Spirit. Let us rejoice that the mystery of the Church is present and alive here.

The Church in the Nation

Many people resist speaking of the so-called "American Church." They correctly perceive that, from an authentic Catholic perspective, there is no such entity. Still, there is the "Church in the United States." It is not merely a matter of semantics. An "American Church" could suggest separation and disunity, but to speak of the "Church in the United States" respects the Church's universality and its tradition, while also acknowledging the unique historical and cultural context which helped shape the faith and life of Catholics in this country.

The Second Vatican Council pointed out that local churches—dioceses—naturally have common bonds rooted in a shared culture. Far from threatening the unity of the faith and the unique structure of the universal Church, these relationships among dioceses within a nation give witness to the catholicity of the undivided Church and foster a spirit of collegial mission. (See Dogmatic Constitution on the Church, no. 23.) The purpose of reflecting on the experience of ecclesial life from a national perspective is thus to understand the special gifts and limitations of the Church in the U.S. context, without isolating it from the Church universal.

Obviously, then, the Church in the United States faces particular concerns, issues, and challenges. Documents of the National Conference of Catholic Bishops (NCCB) and the United States Catholic Conference (USCC), including some now in preparation, attest to this fact and reflect the application of the gospel and Church teaching to the realities of U.S. society.

In recent years, the bishops' conference has issued or begun to prepare documents on such issues as peace and nuclear arms, abortion and other life issues, the economy, the role of women, racism, immigration law, and U.S. foreign policy toward Central America. There has been a consistent effort to distinguish between foundational principles of morality, which apply to everyone, and the concrete application of those principles in terms of particular political and social options. These documents reflect the fact that we are a Church in dialogue with our nation and indeed the world.

There are nearly fifty-five million Catholics in the U.S., more than one-fifth of the total population. Some are affluent, educated people who occupy important positions of leadership; others are middle-class workers and consumers; and still others are among the poorest in the land. We can be a powerful force for constructive change and renewal in our country.

Catholics do not have divided loyalties—conflicting allegiances to their Church and to their nation. Viewing our national experience in the light of faith, we see our country as a providential blessing. God has been good to us Americans, and for this we are grateful. What may be more difficult for us to see, in faith, is our need as a nation for conversion and repentance, a purification of heart so that we can "do the right and . . . love goodness, and . . . walk humbly with . . . God" (Mic 6:8).

The experience of the Church in the U.S. has been influenced by various factors. Six stand out: immigration, pluralism, our brief history as a nation, our abundant economic resources, the ideal of a free democracy, and the firm belief in the value of the individual.

Immigration has substantially shaped our national and ecclesial life. Waves of immigrants came to these shores in the last century and the early part of this one. My own background and that of countless other U.S. Catholics is rooted in this immigrant experience. Although European immigration has now subsided, and children and grandchildren of those who came from the Old Country are now well established here, immigration itself continues, especially from Latin America and Asia. While Catholics may no longer be considered primarily an "immigrant Church," we continue to be shaped by the immigrant experience. Receiving the stranger, the exile, the refugee, the economically deprived continues to be an important national and ecclesial task.

In speaking of immigration, the free movement of people to our nation, we cannot forget those who were here before us, the Native Americans. Their land was often unjustly seized, their way of life deeply disturbed, and their very lives savagely taken. Many Native Americans belong to the Church and, indeed, hold a special place in it. They witness to the values of the land and our need of conversion. Their characteristic spirituality, evoking the closeness and majesty of God, enriches us immensely.

African-Americans came here in slavery. Some died along the way, and all were unjustly uprooted, separated from their homes and families, and shamefully exploited. Racism and injustice cast a shadow upon our national history and linger into the present. Sadly, this is also true in metropolitan Chicago, whose reputation for subtle racism in housing, education, employment, and health care is a cause for deep concern. It is also a stimulus for action on behalf of justice, long delayed and denied.

In this difficult context, black Catholics give extraordinary witness to deep faith. They remind the rest of us of our need for continual conversion and renewal. In their liturgy and community life, they demonstrate a spirituality of hope and joy in the midst of suffering and oppression. We see clearly the dying and rising of Jesus in the lived faith of our African-American brothers and sisters.

The *pluralism* of religious affiliation and philosophical conviction has profoundly affected our experience of the Church in the United States. Although numerous, Catholics remain a minority. From the start, we have had to reckon with the blessings and challenges of an ecumenical and interfaith environment. As a minority, we have also had to come to grips with secularizing forces which are indifferent or even hostile to our religious convictions.

Our experience as a Church in this pluralistic society has been greatly enriched by fidelity to our own religious tradition together with willingness to dialogue with others. By remaining faithful to our convictions, while simultaneously pursuing honest and sustained dialogue with people of other traditions and convictions, we have both expanded our original vision and deepened our faith.

This commitment to fidelity and dialogue has yielded impressive results. We have learned not only about others but about ourselves—for example, the centrality of the Word of God for our lives and the importance of patient tolerance in a democratic society. Fidelity and dialogue have enabled us to communicate our faith and convictions, thereby inviting others to join our community of faith.

Fidelity and dialogue have also helped us effectively to address various public issues—for example, to maintain and promote our deeply held pro-life convictions, without being excluded from public discourse, pressured into politicizing the issues, or reduced to silence. Moreover, they have enabled us, as a community of faith, to contribute to the social transformation of our pluralistic nation. The Church's voice is clearly heard as an advocate for peace and a more just economic order.

The relatively *brief history* of our country has also affected our experience as a Church. Although the United States is more than two hundred years old, we are still a comparatively young nation. Our national traditions are still fluid, still being formed. As a nation, we continue to dream and build toward the future. We are not solely, or even primarily, concerned about preserving the past. We are still developing a constitutional style of government based on liberty and justice for all.

The Church has an important role to play in helping shape the future of this nation. Based on its immigrant experience, for example, the Church has promoted a vision of hope in the United States as a land of opportunity. Efforts to educate for justice through pastoral letters, preaching, and teaching in our schools have helped fire the national dream with a vision of God's kingdom—"a kingdom of truth and life, a kingdom of holiness and grace, a kingdom of justice, love, and peace" (Preface of Christ the King).

A fourth influence on our experience as a Church here is the *abundant resources* and wealth of our nation. Not everyone is personally rich, and wealth and resources are not evenly—and sometimes not justly—distributed. Still, we are a country of wealth and material prosperity.

Because of this and the generosity of our people, the Church has been able to accomplish many good things, especially in education, health care, and the service of human needs. That experience also involves a challenge to faithful stewardship, the insistence that our resources be used in an effective and accountable way. The needs of the poor, in this country and elsewhere, must have priority. We also need to address economic disparities within the Church. While "preferential love" or "special option" for the poor, an expression often used in Church documents, may sound strange to many ears, "giving poor people a break" is a familiar value in this country which we need to keep alive and functioning.

In this land of abundance, the Church has long supported workers in their organized efforts to obtain just wages and gain the social benefits and security due them in light of their human dignity and the worth of their labor. In these and other economic matters, the Church speaks as a moral, not an economic or political, authority. Because economic issues have moral dimensions and are subject to moral evaluation, the Church has both the right and the duty to address them.

Especially in recent years, the Catholic Church in the U.S. has found itself in a position of singular responsibility. The universality of the Church encourages a global consciousness on the part of Catholics. This has led us to ask how the U.S. economy affects, and is affected by, the rest of the world, particularly poorer countries. No doubt the problems and their solutions are complex. Still, to be a Catholic in a wealthy nation like ours compels one to raise questions of economic justice throughout the world.

A fifth factor that affects our experience of the Church here is the American political ideal of a *free democracy*. A vision of people freely determining their own destiny and shaping the structures which govern them gave birth to this country and has remained its enduring foundation. The Church has profited from the democratic experience, from processes of consultation, from the concept of shared responsibility, and from practical insights into the meaning of equality and human dignity. The best social and political ideals of this nation complement our Catholic ecclesial values.

Over the centuries secular models have often influenced the Church. But no political or social paradigm, process, or structure is fully adequate to express ecclesial reality, which is a gift and a mystery of God's grace.

The sixth significant factor in our national experience which has had an impact on our understanding of the Church is a firm belief in the value of the *individual*. Historically, the settling of this country depended to a great extent on a "rugged individualism." While the historical context has shifted, individualism remains a strong value in U.S. society, as indeed respect for the dignity and rights of the individual human person is a central element in the Judeo-Christian moral tradition.

Respect for the individual, especially each person's right to life, is at the heart of the pro-life movement in this country. Firm belief in individual dignity and rights moves us also to denounce racism, sexism, and any other reductive approach to the human person.

At the same time, an exaggerated individualism has become widespread in the U.S. In its most extreme form, it amounts to an assertion of radical independence and autonomy from others and even from God. It assumes that we are self-made people, each self a law unto itself. And even short of this extreme position, there are lesser degrees of individualism which are incompatible with human community and Christian faith. Such individualism is out of step with the teaching of the Church which affirms that

> God has . . . willed to make men holy and save them, not as individuals without any bond or link between them, but rather to make them into a people who might acknowledge him and serve him in holiness (Dogmatic Constitution on the Church, no. 9).

Exaggerated individualism has sociopolitical analogues. Isolationism is one. It cuts off groups from one another, and even entire nations from others. Our U.S. experience includes historical and contemporary examples of "internal" isolationism: racial segregation, pockets and ghettoes of poverty, exclusionary clubs and organizations, and a growing inability to respect the demands of the common good. There have also been strains of isolationism in our foreign policy. Isolationism of any kind has no place in the Church or in Catholic thinking. It runs counter to our identity as an inclusive community, which has the obligation to reach out to all.

We are justifiably proud to be Catholics in the United States, fully American and profoundly Catholic. Our national tradition and our religious heritage complement and challenge each other, and each is thereby enriched. For this, we are deeply grateful.

The Experience of the Universal Church

Our experience of belonging to the universal Church has three dimensions—geographical, cultural, and historical. We belong to a community of faith which extends throughout the world and, potentially, embraces all people. Universality means that the Church crosses cultural boundaries. The Church respects and cultivates particular cultures, linking them together in the mystery of Christ.

We are, moreover, aware that we are only the latest members of a historical people of faith, whose traditions and customs, some essential and others peripheral, are part of our religious inheritance.

The universal Church is not remote from our local experience, for, when we come together for worship, service, and mission, we ourselves are its realization and manifestation. This is true also of other local churches, all united by bonds of common faith, sacraments, charity, mission, and authority. While retaining their particularity, they are in communion with one another. They form a communion of communities which manifests the universal Church.

Peter's ministry, exercised today by the Pope, serves the unity of the universal Church. By the power of the Holy Spirit and the designation and promise of Jesus, the Holy Father is a visible and efficacious sign of unity in faith and service, strengthening his brothers and sisters and ensuring faithful adherence to Jesus Christ and his gospel.

The pastoral ministry of the Holy Father makes the experience of the universal Church present and concrete for us. While he has "supreme, full, immediate and universal power in the Church" (Canon 331) and "over all particular churches" (Canon 333), his specific task is not to govern or administer the particular churches, which are entrusted to the bishops. Rather, the great and unique task of his ministry is to preside over the whole assembly of charity, protect legitimate variety, and at the same time see to it that differences not hinder unity but rather contribute to it. (See Dogmatic Constitution on the Church, no. 23 and no. 27, and the address of Pope John Paul II to the U.S. bishops at Los Angeles, 1987.)

Here in Chicago we have been blessed with many experiences which reinforce our sense of the universal Church. Pope John Paul's visit in 1979 contributed remarkably to our awareness of the Church's universality. The continuing incorporation of immigrants from all parts of the world into this local church gives us an ongoing experience of this universality. And our generous response to requests for prayerful and financial support of programs like Peter's Pence, the Propagation of the Faith, Catholic Relief Services, and various missionary endeavors reminds us of our communion with the larger Church.

In a sense, too, our experience of the universal Church is a joyful anticipation of the full unity for which Jesus prayed. We know what it is like for diverse people to be one in faith and love. We have an intimation of the power of the Holy Spirit to bring unity from diversity.

In belonging to this great communion of particular churches we are accountable to a community larger than our own. We have a responsibility for handing on the faith we have received. Perhaps we question the pace or the direction of change in some other local churches. To belong to the universal Church, however, means not only receiving the gift of communion but being called to put aside excessively narrow perceptions limited to our own experience. We are sustained as members of the universal Church by our realistic hope for the fulfillment of Jesus' prayer that we may all be one as he is one with the Father. Indeed, universal unity is already a reality to some degree.

Considering its traditions, its commitments, and its universality, the Catholic Church now has an opportunity enjoyed by no other community or organization in the world. It is the opportunity to influence for the better the values, attitudes, and structures of the whole human family. Communication, economics, and even the threat of global nuclear or chemical holocaust make the peoples of the world increasingly interdependent. As the earth continues to "shrink" and becomes a "global village," the Church has an important role to play, bringing the message of Jesus Christ to bear upon a new era in human history.

The Communion of Saints

Our experience of the Church involves more than mere interaction with our contemporaries. We are united with those who have gone before us marked with the sign of faith.

The seventh chapter of the Dogmatic Constitution on the Church is entitled "The Eschatological Nature of the Pilgrim Church and Her Union with the Heavenly Church." This title describes the Church as a people on the move toward a goal: fulfillment in God. The pilgrim Church on earth is linked with the heavenly Church—those who, in truth, "have arrived" at their eternal destiny. The Church believes and teaches, furthermore, that there is a continuity between our human efforts on earth and the final coming of the kingdom (see Pastoral Constitution on the Church in the Modern World, no. 39).

In a preeminent way, Mary, the mother of the Lord, is the great sign of our hope. Her life points to the future God has prepared for us. As Jesus' first disciple and the mother of all his disciples, she helps unite us with the heavenly Church. She herself has been assumed into heaven. We experience her as both with us and ahead of us. And with her, countless others have gone before us, yet still are present to us. We still enjoy their love, support, and inspiration in our lives.

Among those who have gone before us are the saints who are formally recognized by the Church and whose virtuous lives we honor and strive to imitate. We also remember, indeed in a special way on the feast of All Saints, the multitude of others, especially our beloved family and friends, who are part of the heavenly Church. In addition, not only on the feast of

All Souls but throughout the year, we remember and pray for all those who have died in grace and in the friendship of God, but still undergo purification and preparation before entering the glory of heaven.

It is natural to feel loss and sadness when loved ones die, but, beyond our grief and loss, we remain united with them. The first Preface for Christian Death expresses this in a beautiful way:

> In him, who rose from the dead, our hope of resurrection dawned. The sadness of death gives way to the bright promise of immortality. Lord, for your faithful people life is changed, not ended.

That sense of ongoing union with those who have died is an experience of the Church as the communion of saints.

It mirrors, even sums up, our other experiences of the Church. Domestic church, small groups, parish, diocese, the Church in our nation, the universal Church—all these embrace both struggle and hope: struggle because we are pilgrims, people on the way, who have not yet arrived at our full destination; hope because we look with faith-filled confidence to something yet to come, our ultimate destiny of complete communion with God and one another.

THE MYSTERY OF THE CHURCH

Up to now, in reflecting on our experience of the Church, we have examined our current situation. But the Church is by no means limited to our contemporary experience of it. It has a history, a past which includes its origin and a future in which God's promise will be perfectly fulfilled.

We need, then, to reflect on how we understand the Church today, how the Church has been given to us as a gift, and how, as a Church, we are to move responsibly into God's promised future.

The Church and the Trinity

With a few brief words, the Pastoral Constitution on the Church in the Modern World describes a radical vision of what it means to be human, to be social, and to belong to the Church:

> [T]he Lord Jesus, when praying to the Father, "that they may all be one . . . even as we are one" (John 17:21-22), has opened up new horizons closed to human reason by implying that there is a certain parallel between the union existing among the divine persons and the union of the sons of God in truth and love. It follows, then, that, if man is the only creature on earth that God has wanted for its own sake, man can fully discover his true self only in a sincere giving of himself (no. 24).

Our life in the Church has its origin in the Trinity. We believe in God who is Father, Son, and Holy Spirit. God's inner life is one of community. The words of Jesus in the Gospels, the proclamations of the Church, especially in the early centuries, the teachings of theologians, the witness of mystics—all speak of the trinitarian life as shared knowledge and mutual love. That communion of truth and charity, as the conciliar document describes it, is our origin as a Church, the model of our life, and our goal not only as individuals but as a people.

Our understanding of and reflection on the Holy Trinity is nevertheless fairly minimal for many of us. We believe in the revealed truth, yet belief may have little discernible impact on our daily lives. Still, we live and act in the mystery of the Trinity. Indeed, that mystery lives within us, because "sanctifying grace" is the indwelling of the Trinity within us—our participation in divine life. We can echo St. Paul's words: "All of us, gazing on the Lord's glory with unveiled faces, are being transformed from glory to glory into his very image by the Lord who is the Spirit" (2 Cor 3:18).

This means, among other things, that our life together in the Church is a life of shared knowledge and mutual love. Even now, though imperfectly, we are beginning to mirror the shared knowledge and reciprocal love of the Father, Son, and Spirit. In other words, both our origin and our destiny are tied to the very inner life of God as one and as a community of persons.

It is well beyond our intellectual powers, even beyond our imagination, to grasp how this can be. Rather, it is "the Lord Jesus . . . [who] opened up new horizons closed to human reason," as the Pastoral Constitution on the Church in the Modern World (no. 24) points out. Paul's letter to the Ephesians expresses it this way: "Jesus came and 'announced the good news of peace to you who were far off, and to those who were near'; through him we both have access in one Spirit to the Father" (Eph 2:17-18). Thus, to understand more deeply our origin and destiny as a people in the Trinity, we must consider the mission of Jesus Christ, who gives us access to the very life of God.

Before exploring the Church in the light of Jesus' mission, it is helpful to recall that the experience of the Church on its various levels is fundamentally an experience of community—life in a communion of shared knowledge and mutual love. The Church's origin in trinitarian life and its destined fulfillment there are reflected in this experience.

The Church and the Mission of Jesus

In its opening chapter on "The Mystery of the Church," the Dogmatic Constitution on the Church summarizes God's initiatives in reaching out to the human family to heal, reconcile, and redeem us. These initiatives find their culmination in the sending of the Son, Jesus Christ, and the Holy Spirit.

Jesus' mission is continued in the Church. We must always look first to him; we must continually return to him as our point of reference. As the Church of God, we continue Jesus' mission when we teach as he taught and live as he lived. Most profoundly, however, our participation in his mission transcends any program for action. As the body of Christ, we continue his mission when we share in his own life, death, and resurrection, that is, when we proclaim the word, praise God, and work for the transformation of the world.

In Jesus we have access to the very life of God, and we must turn to him constantly to deepen our understanding of and participation in the divine life to which we are called. Study, reflection, and prayer centered on the Trinity are no mere luxury but an essential component of our self-understanding and our life as God's people and of our fidelity to the mandate given us by Jesus to continue his mission in the world and in history.

These observations have practical import for our lives. If, following the pattern of trinitarian life, we wish to pursue a path of greater knowledge and love of God and of one another, we must adopt the necessary means. It is no small thing to know and love God and others. It can be costly. It inevitably demands sacrifice.

To continue Jesus' mission faithfully, we must commit ourselves to a wholehearted search for him who has first reached out to us. This is the passionate commitment which Saint Paul expressed in his letter to the Philippians:

> But those things I used to consider gain I have now reappraised as loss in the light of Christ. I have come to rate all as loss in light of the surpassing knowledge of my Lord Jesus Christ. For his sake I have forfeited everything; I have accounted all else rubbish so that Christ may be my wealth and I may be in him, not having any justice of my own based on observance of the law. The justice I possess is that which comes through faith in Christ. It has its origin in God and is based on faith. I wish to know Christ and the power flowing from his resurrection; likewise to know how to share in his sufferings by being formed into the pattern of his death. Thus do I hope that I may arrive at resurrection from the dead (Phil 3:7-11).

Later I will develop the theme of fidelity to Jesus' mission at greater length. Here I merely note the foundations in faith of our existence in the Church—namely, the Trinity, the mission of Jesus, and the mandate given us to continue that mission in the power of the Holy Spirit. These foundations call for our commitment to pursue full knowledge and practical love.

The Church as God's Gift and Our Response

The Church's existence, we firmly believe, is rooted in God and the divine plan of salvation. It is not something which we construct on our own but is freely given to us by Christ in the Holy Spirit, without our having earned or merited it. But we have the responsibility of building up the Church and sustaining it. It is a gift from God which continually calls for our response.

The history of the Church is the history of the interaction of God's grace and human freedom. Despite human sin, infidelity, and ingratitude, God's presence always sustains and protects the Church. There have also been seasons of renewal, heroism, and creativity. Each generation—including ours—must receive the gift with gratitude and make the choices required to build up the Church.

Practically speaking, to receive the Church as God's gift means to be faithful to it. Fidelity is not mere static preservation, as if the Church were a museum piece, simply for viewing and admiring. Fidelity means maintaining, with integrity and reverence, the Church's essential identity revealed in Jesus' death and resurrection and the sending of the Spirit. It also means engaging our faith with the human condition, applying human and graced intelligence and love to circumstances which lead into the future.

One word especially captures this complex act of creative fidelity: *tradition* which "comes from the apostles and makes progress in the Church, with the help of the Holy Spirit" (Dogmatic Constitution on Divine Revelation, no. 8). The tradition of the Church is both constant and living. Without constancy and consistency, we lack a stable foundation or, for that matter, any assurance that we are in touch with Providence. Without vitality, we are immobilized in a kind of historical vacuum, incapable of bringing faith to bear upon our time, place, and culture.

Tradition in its best sense, then, is that dimension of the Church which assures our connection with the mystery of God and with the unfolding of human history. Tradition is an active "handing on": We gratefully receive tradition, creatively appropriate it, and faithfully hand it on to others.

Several questions immediately arise. What elements of ecclesial life and identity are essential for our faithful reception of God's gift? What major themes can we draw from the gospel account of Jesus' mission to guide our creative response to God's gift today? Which issues require our special attention? In examining these areas of constancy, fidelity, and contemporary concern, we will grasp more fully the gift we have been given in the Church.

Constant Elements of Church Life: Fidelity to the Gift

I will explore five elements of Church life in this section. This is not an exhaustive list, of course, but it does reflect our experience, especially in the Archdiocese of Chicago, of essential activities and functions without which we cannot be true to our identity as God's Church. While they are part of our contemporary experience, they can also be traced back through centuries of Spirit-guided ecclesial life and are part of the Church's tradition itself.

a. The Word Is Proclaimed. The Second Vatican Council insists that a primary and fundamental dimension of our ecclesial identity is the proclamation of the word of God. This task does not belong exclusively to bishops and priests, although proclamation is to be their first task (Dogmatic Constitution on the Church, no. 25, and Decree on the Ministry and Life of Priests, no. 4). Proclamation pertains to all the baptized. In the words of the council:

> The baptized, by regeneration and the anointing of the Holy Spirit, are consecrated to be a spiritual house and a holy priesthood, that through all the works of Christian men they may offer spiritual sacrifices and proclaim the perfection of him who has called them out of darkness into his marvellous light (cf. 1 Pet 2:4-10). Therefore all the disciples of Christ, persevering in prayer and praising God (cf. Acts 2:42-47), should present themselves as a sacrifice, living, holy and pleasing to God (cf. Rom 12:1). They should everywhere on earth bear witness to Christ and give an answer to everyone who asks a reason for the hope of an eternal life which is theirs (cf. 1 Pet 3:15) (Dogmatic Constitution on the Church, no. 10).

The foundational characteristic of this activity is clearly expressed by Saint Paul in writing to the church in Rome: "But how shall they call on him in whom they have not believed? And how can they believe unless they have heard of him? And how can they hear unless there is someone to preach?" (Rom 10:14). Proclamation of the word is also the Lord's mandate: "You will receive power when the Holy Spirit comes down on you; then you are to be my witnesses in Jerusalem, throughout Judea and Samaria, yes, even to the ends of the earth" (Acts 1:8).

In carrying out this task of proclamation, we join the whole Church, including the communion of saints. We are linked, for example, with Mary, Mother of the Lord, who says, "My being proclaims the greatness of the Lord" (Luke 1:46).

To be faithful to our identity as God's Church, we must be steeped in the word of God, and its proclamation must be our first task. We are encouraged to grow in our understanding and love of sacred Scripture by Vatican II, as well as by our appreciation of the revered place the Scriptures occupy in other Christian churches and communions.

In the Archdiocese of Chicago, this means that all of us—bishops, priests, and people—must strive to understand, contemplate, and find ways of proclaiming effectively God's word. The proclamation of the Word must be our first priority.

But what does it actually entail? *Where* are we to proclaim it? *What* are we to proclaim? And *how* are we to do it?

Where? The word is to be proclaimed *everywhere*, not only in church and school, but also in homes, factories, the marketplace, the media, and every other place where people gather.

What is the message? It is a proclamation of God's sovereignty in a world full of idols, an announcement of healing reconciliation in Jesus Christ to people who are wounded and sinful, and an invitation to share new life now in a community of faith, worship, and service.

How is this proclamation made? Authentic and effective proclamation assumes that we have come to understand God's word as a saving message to the human family and that we thoroughly know the human condition with all its joys and sorrows. The proclamation of God's word is an invitation to enter freely into a covenantal relationship with him. It expresses the living, loving faith of those who make the proclamation.

In a word, we are to be an *evangelizing* Church—proclaiming Jesus Christ and inviting others to share our life of faith, service, and worship. At the same time, we also need constantly to be evangelized, so as to grow in faith and love. Evangelization is a continual task of announcement, thanksgiving, and invitation, something we never outgrow. As Pope Paul VI said so eloquently:

> The Church is an evangelizer, but she begins by being evangelized herself. She is the community of believers, the community of hope lived and communicated, the community of brotherly love; and she needs to listen unceasingly to what she must believe, to her reasons for hoping, to the new commandment of love. She is the People of God immersed in the world, and often tempted by idols, and she always needs to hear the proclamation of the "mighty works of God" which converted her to the Lord; she always needs to be called together afresh by him and reunited. In brief, this means that she has constant need of being evangelized, if she wishes to retain freshness, vigor and strength in order to proclaim the Gospel (*Evangelii nuntiandi*, no. 16).

b. The Sacraments Are Celebrated. As I said above, the Church itself is the great sacrament. The Dogmatic Constitution on the Church expresses it this way: "[T]he Church, in Christ, is in the nature of sacrament—a sign and instrument, that is, of communion with God and of unity among all men" (no. 1). The seven sacraments, celebrated and lived, are specific points of interaction with Jesus' saving death and resurrection and with his life-giving Spirit.

As a kind of sacrament, the Church has the task of being an instrument of salvation and also making it manifest to the world that this is so. We who are the Church must express the implications of God's word and the seven sacraments in the way we live. United with Christ in baptism, reconciled in penance, strengthened for apostolate in confirmation, we are called to live like people who are truly in union with Jesus, experience his forgiveness for our sins, and accept our mission to the world.

The Eucharist, in particular, provides a sacramental grounding for our life as God's Church. The Second Vatican Council says of the Eucharistic Liturgy that it is

> the summit toward which the activity of the Church is directed; it is also the fount from which all her power flows. For the goal of apostolic endeavor is that all who are made sons of God by faith and baptism should come together to praise God in the midst of his Church, to take part in the Sacrifice and to eat the Lord's Supper (Constitution on the Sacred Liturgy, no. 10).

These reflections on the Church and the sacraments will have only a superficial bearing on our lives unless we understand how important this sacramental dimension is for our life as Church.

In the sacraments we participate, in tangible, audible, visible ways, in rituals which disclose and effect our union with Jesus in his saving mysteries. As he was the visible, audible, tangible presence of God among us—the one who himself bridged the gulf between the divine and the human—so now the Church continues to make him present to us in the sacraments. The Church will continue to celebrate the sacraments until the entire world is completely transformed and "God is all in all" (1 Cor 15:28). Then, and only then, there will be no further need for sacraments.

Sacramental celebration is therefore the lifeblood of the Church. This, in turn, calls for a commitment—on the part of all in the Church—to celebrations which are reverent encounters with the saving Lord, alive to the human needs of the worshipers, manifest signs of God's gracious presence. To celebrate the sacraments in this way means making them the very center of our lives by giving them a priority of time, energy, and resources. Above all, because the celebration of the sacraments is part of our response to the gift of the Church, we are to cultivate an attitude of openness and the disposition of a faithful heart.

c. The Church Works for the Unity of All Christians and for Union with All People of Good Will. In the past it was not clearly understood that working for the unity of the Church is an essential part of our ecclesial identity. Since the Second Vatican Council, however, we have grasped that ecumenism means much more than occasional friendly encounters with other Christians. The Lord's prayer for unity (John 17:21-23) is our mandate. The divisions of the Church of Christ are a scandal, a stumbling block. The pace of ecumenism is slow but deliberate. The paths are often uncharted. But commitment to unity is part of our very identity.

Through interfaith dialogue, we also seek to develop bonds with all those who do not share our Christian faith but sincerely "look to their different religions for an answer to the unsolved riddles of human existence" (Declaration on the Relation of the Church to Non-Christian Religions, no. 1). In a special way, we desire to develop a deeper appreciation of the spiritual bond linking us with our Jewish brothers and sisters who share with us faith in the one true God and his promises. We also share our monotheistic faith with the sons and daughters of Islam.

As a practical matter, here in the Archdiocese of Chicago our commitment to unity means ongoing dialogue and cooperation. We need to speak, and, with equal attention, we need to listen. The structures already in place for ecumenical and interfaith dialogue and cooperation must be sustained and strengthened. Continual attention to our internal renewal as a Church and to that growth in holiness which opens us to the gift of unity is another very important dimension of our commitment to unity.

d. The Church Dialogues with and Works in the World. Fidelity to its true identity also requires that the Church be in dialogue with the world, without intruding on areas that belong to secular competence and authority. This relationship has been examined in great detail in the Pastoral Constitution on the Church in the Modern World and most recently in Pope John Paul's encyclical, "On The Social Concern of the Church." It is instructive that the Second Vatican Council chose to write *two* ecclesiological documents, one dealing with the Church from an inner perspective and the other with its relationship to the world.

Plainly the Church cannot despise the world, since "God so loved the world that he gave his only Son" (John 3:16). At the same time, the world needs to be transformed by God's saving love, mediated by Jesus' followers through their proclamation of the gospel and their deeds of service. Listen again to Jesus' prayer at the Last Supper:

> I do not ask you to take them out of the world, but to guard them from the evil one. They are not of the world, any more than I belong to the world. Consecrate them by means of truth—"Your word is truth." As you have sent me into the world, so I have sent them into the world (John 17:15-18).

The Church does not want to run the world, but we would be unfaithful to our ecclesial identity if we ran *from* the world and withdrew into our own internal affairs. We must be in dialogue with the world and its social structures concerning the moral dimensions of such vital issues as justice and peace, the economy, the role of women, abortion and other life issues, capital punishment, the criminal justice system, immigration, human rights, foreign policy, and much else.

Sometimes the Church speaks as a community of conscience, sometimes as a voice of affirmation, sometimes as a partner in social concern. And sometimes, when others are silent, the Church may be obliged to assume a countercultural and prophetic stance.

In his encyclical on the social concern of the Church, Pope John Paul reaffirms the Church's right and duty to speak on social issues. He acknowledges that the pastors of the Church do not have "technical solutions" to social questions. But he affirms that the Church as a community of faith is an "expert in humanity," as Pope Paul VI put it. Social issues involve more than merely technical questions. They affect human beings and therefore have moral and spiritual dimensions. The Church has the right, the expertise, and the duty to speak from its spiritual and moral perspective.

Moreover, the vocation of the laity is to be salt, light, and leaven in the world. Lay Catholics are called to be evangelizers, to bring the gospel into the home, the workplace, the public arena. As Pope John Paul pointed out earlier this year in his Apostolic Exhortation on the Laity, *Christifideles laici,* there are eight basic ways for lay people to do this: promoting the dignity of every human person, respecting every individual's inviolable right to life from conception to natural death, recognizing the religious dimension of human life, strengthening the family, serving others in love, participating in public life, placing the individual at the center of socioeconomic life, and evangelizing culture and the cultures of humanity.

e. Direct Service Is Rendered in Love. In St. Luke's Gospel, Jesus describes his mission in an opening discourse in the synagogue at Nazareth. Quoting from the book of Isaiah, he says,

> The spirit of the Lord is upon me: therefore he has anointed me. He has sent me to bring glad tidings to the poor, to proclaim liberty to captives, recovery of sight to the blind and release to prisoners (Luke 4:18).

To be faithful to Jesus' mission, the Church must care for people, especially those most in need. Its service to humanity includes instruction, healing, peacemaking, and authentic and full human liberation. These activities are not peripheral to the Church's mission, but are at its very heart. We read in St. Matthew's Gospel that the care of the least of Jesus' brothers and sisters is the ultimate criterion by which we shall be judged (Matt 25:31-46). That responsibility belongs both to individuals and to the Church community.

In the Archdiocese of Chicago, we have responded to this dimension of Jesus' ministry by serving others in many ways. Our past and present commitment to education is part of our concrete, loving response. Fidelity to this dimension of our ecclesial identity requires that, even under great financial pressure, we strive to maintain our educational services.

The Catholic health care system expresses our commitment to continue Jesus' healing mission. The services of Catholic Charities and other organizations offer relief and assistance to people who fall "between the cracks" of public social assistance. The Church cannot substitute for governmental programs, but its mission requires it to help anyone in need, just as Jesus did.

Education, health care, and social services are complex and costly enterprises in our society and in the archdiocese. We are challenged to make sacrifices to sustain them while ensuring that these efforts are integrated with the larger vision of our ecclesial identity and reflect our commitment to continue Jesus' mission.

Major Themes for the Church's Creative Response Today

Throughout the Church's history and also in our own day, the elements we have just considered have been essential to the faithful reception of God's gift of the Church by Catholics. And now as in the past this gift calls for a creative response by its recipients in the light of contemporary circumstances.

To be faithful and creative, we need to make our own certain basic themes derived from the gospel and from Jesus' mission. Let us see what some of these are and how we can incorporate them into our archdiocesan response to God's gift of the Church.

a. Inclusion. Jesus' ministry is inclusive. He invites into fellowship with him the educated and the ignorant, women and men and children, observers of the law and public sinners. The early Church continued this inclusive approach and, in fidelity to the risen Lord, reached out to the Gentiles.

Jesus gathers around him an open community. It transcends even blood ties. All are called, and all are welcomed. But within the community he requires complete dedication to himself and fidelity to his gospel. It is an inclusive community united by an exclusive commitment to God's kingdom.

The Church today must also be an inclusive community. Readiness to incorporate all people into our community of faith is a measure of our creative fidelity in continuing Jesus' mission. Inclusiveness, however, involves more besides accepting "outsiders" into our community. It also pertains to how we deal with one another.

In the Archdiocese of Chicago, we need to address this question in practical ways. Many people are affected—for example, divorced and separated individuals, those who have special cultural and language needs, African Americans and Hispanics, handicapped people, and, perhaps especially, women who feel excluded from the inner life of the Church. Of course, these and other groups all present very different situations calling for very different responses. But they also share the experience, or in any case the perception, of having been excluded, and so challenge us to seek ways, consistent with our Catholic teaching and heritage, of including them fully in the Church.

Resolving issues of inclusion and exclusion depends, at least in part, on how we understand equality and hierarchy in the Church. Our attitudes and values about either may enable, or make it impossible, for us to be truly inclusive. When we view equality and hierarchy in conflict or even in contradiction with one another, we cannot be truly inclusive. But they need not be in conflict, even if they are often in tension. In fact, they can harmonize quite well with each other.

There is an astonishing and radical equality among Jesus' disciples gathered in the intimate common life of a family.

> He said in reply, "Who are my mother and my brothers?" And gazing around him at those seated in the circle, he continued, "These are my mother and my brothers. Whoever does the will of God is brother and sister and mother to me" (Mark 3:33-35).

St. Paul picks up this theme of radical equality in his letter to the Galatians: "There does not exist among you Jew or Greek, slave or freeman, male or female. All are one in Christ Jesus" (Gal 3:28).

At the same time, the hierarchical structure of the Church is no less real. Indeed, it is a constitutive element of the Church. "Hierarchy" is a "holy ordering" of the Church for *service*, not for domination (see, for example, Mark 10:35-45; Matt 20:20-28; Luke 22:24-27; John 13:1-20). It is based on Jesus' teaching about pastoral leadership: "Feed my lambs . . . tend my sheep . . . feed my sheep" (John 21:15-17). It is similar to Paul's understanding of how different gifts are to be used on behalf of the community of faith:

> There are different gifts but the same Spirit; there are different ministries but the same Lord; there are different works but the same God who accomplishes all of them in everyone. To each person the manifestation of the Spirit is given for the common good (1 Cor 12:4-7).

The challenge facing us in the church in Chicago is how to affirm and support both our fundamental equality and our hierarchical structure. It is not a question of choosing one or the other but accepting both. This requires basic changes in our relationships and attitudes. We need to develop new ways of relating to one another in order to reflect both values faithfully. Even more important, we need a conversion of heart and mind which will help us respect and live both simultaneously.

b. Material Possessions. Creative fidelity to the gift of the Church includes attention to stewardship, that is, appropriate care of the material goods of this world, a world that is good, created by God.

Jesus' words and deeds make this clear. In the Gospels we read of individuals called to leave everything to follow Jesus. He tells us not to worry about material possessions, to determine where our heart's true treasure is, to use material goods to help the needy. The prophetic tradition, which he incorporates into his own preaching, frequently points to the need for justice in human society. Moreover, Jesus speaks of love of neighbor in such a way that it demands practical charity.

These evangelical themes are of special importance to us today, especially in the Archdiocese of Chicago. Our metropolitan area has considerable resources. Yet, while some are quite wealthy, others must struggle to get by, and still others, caught in a vicious cycle of poverty, barely survive.

Rich or poor, we all are prone to being driven by the desire for more money and material goods. Of course this is understandable in the case of those who truly do not have enough. But what of those who do? Without belaboring the point, there is a great danger of becoming obsessed with the desire for excess material goods to such an extent that it comes to rule one's life.

Membership in the community of faith calls us to reexamine and realign our values in accord with the gospel. We must hear and act on the demands of justice and practice generous charity. As individual Christians and as a community of faith, we are to use what we have prudently, wisely, justly, and charitably.

Our approach toward material possessions is often complex and deserves detailed analysis and balanced discussion. Here, I have simply identified it as a basic theme for our life in the Church.

c. Witness to Transcendence. This motif is quite simple and very close to the basic needs of people. "Witness to transcendence" means that we are a community which points to the deepest realities underlying human existence. This witness, so desperately needed today, says there is more to life than the here and now. We participate in the reign of God breaking into our world. We are caught up in the very mystery of God who calls us to fulfillment.

This theme takes on added importance as we take a close look at our contemporary world, including metropolitan Chicago. Many people today set and work for goals that will bear fruit quickly. This "short term" mentality can dominate our lives and lead to an obsession with wealth, power, fame. Trying to control and manipulate the forces of the marketplace or nature, we may actually deceive ourselves into imagining that we are the ultimate masters of our lives and that this is all there is to life. This can happen even in regard to something as beneficial as medical technology, by causing us to think that life, as we know it, is all that there is.

Witnessing to transcendence is thus an essential element in the Church's faithful and creative response to its identity. The Church gives powerful witness to the realm of spirit—the human spirit and God's Spirit. The Church, as a community of witness, insistently proclaims "that beneath all that changes there is much that is unchanging, much that has its ultimate foundation in Christ, who is the same yesterday, and today, and forever" (Pastoral Constitution on the Church in the Modern World, no. 10).

This may sound obvious. Today, however, the voices and forces of human reductionism deeply and, at times, subtly insinuate themselves into our lives. Media, politics, and a host of cultural influences tell us to get and enjoy all we can in this life for that is all there is. This is a great distortion of reality and not easily corrected.

Worship "in spirit and in truth" is an essential means of giving an external witness to transcendence. It is expressed most fully in our liturgical celebrations, when we proclaim to the entire world that the true center of our lives is in God. The church in Chicago will truly witness to transcendence to the extent that we live together in faith, acknowledge our belief in transcendence, and proclaim it in authentic worship.

Theological and spiritual writers point out that there is a deeply rooted human drive to worship. We need to adore—either God (authentic worship) or someone or something less (idolatry). Our ecclesial theme of worship "in spirit and truth" has its origin in this basic human need.

Our acts of worship—either the true worship of God or the secularized rituals of civil society—determine the practical center of our lives: the loving mystery of God or the illusory idols of the age—power, pleasure, status, money, fame, uncommitted freedom.

For our worship to be truly "in spirit and in truth," it must correspond with our other actions. It cannot be detached from the rest of our lives. It must be the key to everything we do. Its authenticity and holiness are measured and expressed by how we live. For example, if we praise and thank God in worship for his justice and his vindication of the poor, our actions must reflect this by our pursuit of justice for the poor. Quite simply, then, being a member of the Church involves more than "getting to church" once a week.

d. Loving, Reconciled Human Relationships. For years this has been a special concern of mine. Jesus' teaching calls us to relate to one another in a unique way, one that is more in accord with our true selves as redeemed by him. For without the gift of redemption and healing, hurt would beget only a visceral response of vengeance, violence, or war; sexual drives would move merely on an instinctual track apart from God's plan which calls for care for the other and a sense of the sacredness of generating life; life issues—including abortion, care of the terminally ill, care for the young, the poor, and the elderly—would be resolved primarily by a search for the most convenient path.

Jesus is quite clear. He teaches us to relate to one another in freedom and love, not out of mere instinct. When we do so, hurt dissolves into forgiveness and reconciliation, sexuality is inseparably connected with love and the generation of life, and the approach to life issues protects and enhances human life and dignity.

There is a profound need for loving, reconciled human relationships, a need which extends to married couples and families, relationships between men and women, neighborhoods and economic classes, ethnic and racial groups. In all these areas the Church wishes to be a leavening agent for society—to be a kind of sacrament, to engage in outreach, to practice social dialogue, to give witness.

Our capacity to bring about loving, reconciled human relationships is conditioned by our holiness as members of the Church and by the degree to which we are marked by limitation, imperfection, and sin. We live in a loving, reconciling, and forgiving way in the measure that we seek holiness and struggle to overcome our sinfulness.

The Church is holy because it is of God and the Spirit dwells within it and guides it. It is also holy because it proclaims the word of God, celebrates the sacraments, and hands on its apostolic structure. Nonetheless, we who belong to the Church are also the sinful People of God. Our lives manifest not only unavoidable human limitation but also avoidable sin. Our failures—to be an inclusive community, to work for justice and charity, to promote loving and reconciled human relationships, to be faithful witnesses to God's kingdom, to worship in spirit and in truth—highlight our need for repentance and conversion of heart.

How are we to identify those aspects of the Catholic Church in Chicago which are true scandals or stumbling blocks to those outside our family of faith? How are we unfaithful to our true ecclesial identity? How do we express hardness of heart? We must address these questions both as individual Christians and as a community of faith.

We need God's forgiveness and must accept it when it is given. For Catholics, "reconciliation" especially means regular celebration of the sacrament of penance, where we receive God's pardon and find strength to foster healing with others. When this occurs, we become instruments of healing, reconciliation, and forgiveness. It is very important for us to do so in Chicagoland at this time, for our community suffers from the divisions of racism and ethnicity, economic and social disparity, lack of welcome for new immigrants. The authenticity of our life as a Church depends on our capacity to forgive, heal, and bring people together.

e. The Communion of Our Local Church with Other Local Churches and the Universal Church. Catholicity or universality is a gift from God to the Church, but it is not a simple one. We must be in communion with other local churches and with the universal Church—in a special way, with the church of Rome and its bishop, the Holy Father, who is also pastor of the universal Church. This involves honest communication, mutual understanding, firm fidelity, and great patience. We live together as a single People of God in communion with one another.

In the Archdiocese of Chicago, we need to examine our communion with other local churches. We have, for example, special bonds with persecuted churches, with young churches where the gospel has only recently been proclaimed, and with poor churches. We also have an essential bond with the church of Rome. We need to renew our affection for and our loyalty to the Holy Father who represents apostolic traditions and, "as the successor of Peter, is the perpetual and visible source and foundation of the unity both of the bishops and of the whole company of the faithful" (Dogmatic Constitution on the Church, no. 23). As pastor of the universal Church, he presides over the communion of particular churches, a communion of charity.

Our partnership in mission with the Diocese of Chilapa in Mexico offers us an opportunity to expand our pastoral vision. The many missionaries—priests, women and men religious, and lay people—who have left metropolitan Chicago to proclaim the gospel elsewhere also help keep us in communion with other local churches and the universal Church. We need to continue to explore ways in which we can better appreciate and deepen our communion with the Church and the churches beyond the boundaries of our archdiocese.

THE FUTURE OF THE CHURCH IN CHICAGO

Up to now we have explored our experience of, and feelings about, the Church. We have examined our history and our traditions, in order to deepen our understanding of the Church as God's gift. We have considered elements of Church life which are essential if the Church is to remain faithful to its identity. And we have reflected upon themes related to our creative response to the gift of the Church.

Now let us turn to our future. I will briefly share my hope and dreams for the Church, particularly for the church in Chicago, as we prepare to enter the third millennium of Christianity.

This is a decisive moment in the Church's history. What happens during the next decade or two will have great impact. The renewal begun by the Second Vatican Council will continue. Earlier periods of ecclesial renewal extended over many decades. Although we are now in the third decade of the renewal initiated by Vatican II, the process is likely to continue for some time to come. I hope that many things will have happened, especially in the archdiocese, by the time we begin the third Christian millennium.

1. I hope we will have found a way, expressed both in structures and in attitudes, to keep our focus fixed on *essentials*. Life today is very complex and fast-paced; it can be difficult to distinguish what is trivial from what is important. Without bad will or ignorance on anyone's part, we can lose sight of our authentic identity and essential mission in the clutter of details and particular problems. That is why we must keep returning to essentials. I trust this letter will help, as will our prayer together.

2. I hope the church in Chicago will be a source of *unity and reconciliation* in the city and the suburbs. Fragmentation, division, and suspicion, often centering on racial issues, afflict our community today. I hope the Church will help bring people together, not fearful of the cost, not impatient with slow progress, not discouraged by prophets of doom, not intimidated by those who foster division.

3. I hope the church in Chicago will continue its search for *Christian unity* as it develops its covenantal relationship with the Lutheran and Episcopal churches and deepens its dialogues with all Christian churches and communions. I hope, too, that its commitment to interfaith dialogue, especially with the Jewish community, will bear fruit in our common effort to enhance the life and spirit of all people. And may the Church in Chicago be a willing cooperator with all people of good will.

4. I hope the church in Chicago will be known as a community which *reaches out* to others, especially the unchurched and unaffiliated and those alienated from the Church. This is a responsibility of every member of the Church, not simply of priests and other ministers.

While reaching out, of course, we also must develop welcoming, hospitable communities to receive people. In practice, this means such things as effective RCIA programs, support groups for those who are searching for faith, and a warm and welcoming attitude in the entire community. To reach out and to welcome are indispensable elements of evangelization.

5. I hope we will be successful in welcoming our most recently arrived *immigrants* who share the Catholic faith with us, especially Hispanics and

Asians. I hope, too, that this welcome will be based in part on our pro-found gratitude for the welcome extended by the Church in the U.S. to our own immigrant forebears as well as for the ways in which newcomers enrich our community of faith with their cultural and religious values and practices.

6. I hope that, within the context of our Catholic faith and the Church's living tradition, we will come to a better awareness of the gifts of *women* in the Church and that this deepened appreciation will be reflected in our structures and ways of relating to one another. For this to happen, there must be mutual commitment to ongoing dialogue. If men or women—or groups of men and women—decide to separate or cut themselves off from dialogue, this hope will not be realized.

Even so, it will not be realized without pain. It is difficult to revisit hurts and feelings of disappointment, to take a fresh look at how things could be. The dialogue of which I speak requires wisdom, courage, and perseverance, so that there will be no winners, no losers, but only people confirmed in their shared discipleship to Jesus Christ.

7. I hope we will continue to speak out clearly and persuasively about the *life issues* which are central to our national public policy debate. This means standing firm on the issues themselves while making our defense of the sacredness of human life more convincing and credible to others.

I firmly believe that the gospel calls us to embrace what I have termed a "consistent ethic of life." This ethic is based on the belief that life is a precious gift from God which must be protected and nurtured from the moment of conception until natural death. The direct taking of innocent human life—whether of an unborn child through abortion, an aged per-son through euthanasia, or noncombatants in war—is always disordered and immoral. Moreover, whatever diminishes human life—for example, prolonged poverty, inadequate nutrition and health care, chronic unem-ployment—is also a moral challenge.

True, these are distinct issues which cannot be collapsed into one. Not every violation is as grave as every other, and each question requires its own moral analysis and response. Also, because of circumstances at any given moment, a greater priority may have to be given to one than an-other. For example, the evil of nearly unrestricted abortion in our country requires special attention at this time. As long as the lives of the unborn are considered expendable, all life is in jeopardy. The recent decision of the Supreme Court in the *Webster* case, by seemingly giving greater re-sponsibility for legislation restricting abortion to the states, has set the stage for a new public debate on this topic.

Yet all these life issues are linked. Each in its own way involves threat-ening or diminishing God's gift of life. As a community of faith which seeks to live in accord with the gospel, we cannot ignore any one of them.

8. I hope the quality of our *worship*, especially the Sunday Eucharist, will grow greatly. Bringing this about will require hard work, time, and energy. We should be able to look forward to celebrations of the Eucharist in the knowledge that, in the proclamation of the word, the praise of God, and the memorial of Jesus' self-giving sacrifice, we will be inspired, strengthened, and nourished for daily life.

In my pastoral letter on the liturgy, *Our Communion, Our Peace, Our Promise,* I reflected on

> how our celebration of Sunday Mass embodies our love for young people, our solidarity with the handicapped, our response to catechumens. I think, too, of that justice which we celebrate and to which we commit ourselves at Mass. How can we—in liturgy and in life—show the world a community where old age is loved and respected, where the sufferings of the poor are known and remedies are sought, where we can say with Paul that among us "there does not exist male or female but all are one in Christ Jesus"?

9. I hope we will find more effective ways of handing on the faith to our young people and that *catechesis* will be a priority not only for priests and professional religious educators but for the entire Catholic community. All of us must strive constantly to educate and form young people in ways faithful to the Church's tradition and sensitive to contemporary needs.

Our young people face a bewildering set of options. We may not let them drift, simply allowing them—in the name of a misunderstood "liberty"—to remain ignorant of the truths God has revealed. They have a right to know the teaching of our faith as it is articulated by the Church's teaching authority. They also have a right to the riches of our traditions of prayer and spirituality.

This hope will not be realized, however, by indoctrination. The religious formation of the young requires that, while listening to them sincerely and patiently, we give clear and forthright witness to the importance of faith in our own lives. Unless we are faith-filled, unless we believe and live what we teach, unless we form communities where gospel values are visible, our efforts will not be successful.

10. I hope the Church will be home to rigorous *intellectual inquiry* and to creative explorations of imagination. More personally, I hope the Church will welcome, support, and benefit from scientists, writers, artists, musicians, and all people committed to higher education and intellectual pursuits. The laboratory, the studio, the classroom, and the theater are places where human spirit and holy mystery can touch each other.

11. I hope we will teach one another to *pray* better. May the future bring to fruition the present-day signs of a renewal of prayer. For this to occur, we must put aside our shyness about speaking of prayer and enrich

one another with our experiences of God. We must also create "contemplative spaces"—both physical places like chapels, prayer centers, houses of prayer, and times of renewal, retreats, and other programs of spiritual formation.

12. I hope we will be effective in recognizing, encouraging, and supporting all *ministries*. In my pastor letter on ministry, *In Service of One Another,* I gave six directions for the future which I wish to reaffirm now:

a) All ministries are good and necessary for building up the body of Christ. The implications of this basic understanding need more reflection and elaboration.

b) We must continue to discern and encourage vocations to the priesthood and religious life. Priests and religious provide a unique form of witness to gospel values. These traditional ways of serving and witnessing are not only as needed now as ever, but more challenging than may formerly have been the case.

c) All ministries and ministers require and deserve development, support, enabling, enrichment, and encouragement.

d) In developing ministries, we need to be attentive and faithful to the experience and teaching of the universal Church.

e) We need to be astute in identifying and assessing the contemporary needs and aspirations of our society and responding to them in appropriate ways. Historically, this is how new ministries have developed in the Church.

f) While vigorously fostering and supporting ministries, we must at the same time give greater visibility to the truth that all members of the Church have an authentic vocation to the apostolate, that is, everyone in virtue of baptism is called to bring the gospel to the home, the school, the workplace—any place where life is lived.

13. I hope we will find practical ways to appreciate and more effectively support the experience of the Church on all levels, especially the *domestic church* and the *parish.* As places of initiation in the life of faith, these are the building blocks for the other experiences of the Church. In the past they have often been taken for granted rather than cultivated and nourished. In the future they must receive deliberate and effective support and encouragement.

14. I hope we will develop and assimilate a deeper understanding of *stewardship,* a commitment to the Church's life and mission which leads us to acknowledge that we share responsibility for its welfare. This Christian understanding of stewardship is grounded in the belief that there is an inner human need to give. This giving involves our time, our talents, and our treasures. In practical terms, this means making wise and effective use of ecclesial resources. Our archdiocesan planning efforts are intended to promote and support stewardship.

While I have many other hopes for the future of the church in Chicago, I have listed these because they are particularly important. Everyone who believes in and loves the Church has dreams for its future. I will have accomplished a great deal in sharing mine with you if this serves to unleash your own dreams and hopes. In such sharing, we have already begun to work with God's grace and, under the promptings of the Holy Spirit, to move into the future.

Conclusion

When I preside at the Eucharist in the archdiocese, especially before very large assemblies, I am deeply moved as I see you gathered with me in prayer.

I see faces young, old, middle-aged, black, white, yellow, red, and brown, and read in them histories of struggle and pain mixed with joy and hope. In my mind's eye I picture those forebears in faith who came here from Africa, Asia, Europe, and Latin America.

When I look at you, who are both my flock and my brothers and sisters, I am often deeply moved. For I love you very much and, uniting myself with Jesus, the Good Shepherd, I am ready to lay down my life for you.

As I look at the liturgical assembly, diverse as it frequently is in Chicago, I see a future promise taking hold. In deep and mysterious ways, God's reign breaks in upon us—a kingdom of truth, justice, mercy, and peace.

This is my deepest experience of the Church: people gathered together with a rich heritage of the past, with present struggles and celebration, with a future hope. The Church is not an abstraction for me. It is a community and a way of life which depends totally on God's grace and our free human response.

During the third Eucharistic Prayer, I pray on your behalf: "Father, hear the prayers of the family gathered here before you." That is my fundamental understanding of the Church, the one that inspires, energizes, draws me to love: a family gathered before the Lord.

We are gathered, we are called, we are assembled. Our present experience as the Church is provisional, temporary. In the heavenly kingdom, when we stand together before God's throne and share in his glory as human members of the divine family, it will be forever.

Your brother in Christ,

Joseph Cardinal Bernardin
Archbishop of Chicago

A Sign of Hope

Pastoral Letter on Health Care

— *October 18, 1995* ————————————————————

During my entire ministry as a bishop, especially during the past two years, I have invested considerable time and energy on issues related to Catholic health care. When health care reform became part of the public policy debate last year, I made several contributions to that discussion—pointing out, for example, the importance of the not-for-profit status of Catholic health care institutions. In all of my efforts I have expressed my appreciation for the past and current dedication to, and service in, the ministry of Catholic health care by the religious women and men who sponsor this ministry and the dedicated laymen and women who collaborate with them.

Several months ago, I decided to write this pastoral reflection on Catholic health care to bring together several of my concerns and to give some direction to health care ministry in the Archdiocese of Chicago. However, before I was able to begin the project, I was diagnosed with pancreatic cancer. After surgery at Loyola University Medical Center in Maywood, Illinois, and a brief period of recuperation, I underwent nearly six weeks of radiation therapy and chemotherapy.

Now I return to this project not only as a bishop with an abiding interest in, and commitment to, Catholic health care, but also as a cancer patient who has benefited greatly from this competent, compassionate care in the model of Jesus the healer.

When I entered the Loyola University Medical Center last June, my life had been turned completely upside down by the totally unexpected news that what I had been experiencing as a healthy body was, in fact, housing a dangerous, aggressive cancer. The time since the diagnosis, surgery, and postoperative radiation and chemotherapy has led me into a new dimension of my lifelong journey of faith.

I have experienced in a very personal way the chaos that serious illness brings into one's life. I have had to let go of many things that had brought me a sense of security and satisfaction in order to find the healing that only faith in the Lord can bring.

Initially, I felt as though floodwaters were threatening to overwhelm me. For the first time in my life I truly had to look death in the face. In one brief moment, all my personal dreams and pastoral plans for the future had to be put on hold. Everything in my personal life and pastoral ministry had to be reevaluated from a new perspective. My initial experience was of disorientation, isolation, a feeling of not being "at home" anymore.

Instead of being immobilized by the news of the cancer, however, I began to prepare myself for surgery and postoperative care. I discussed my condition with family and friends. I prayed as I have never prayed before that I would have the courage and grace to face whatever lay ahead. I determined that I would offer whatever suffering I might endure for the Church, particularly the Archdiocese of Chicago. Blessedly, a peace of mind and heart and soul quietly flooded through my entire being, a kind of peace I had never known before. And I came to believe in a new way that the Lord would walk with me through this journey of illness that would take me from a former way of life into a new manner of living.

Nevertheless, during my convalescence I found the nights to be especially long, a time for various fears to surface. I sometimes found myself weeping, something I seldom did before. And I came to realize how much of what consumes our daily life truly is trivial and insignificant. In these dark moments, besides my faith and trust in the Lord, I was constantly bolstered by the awareness that thousands of people were praying for me throughout the archdiocese and, indeed, the world. I have been graced by an outpouring of affection and support that has allowed me to experience ecclesial life as a "community of hope" in a very intimate way.

I have also felt a special solidarity with others facing life-threatening illness. I have talked and prayed with other cancer patients who were waiting in the same room for radiation or chemotherapy. I have been contacted by hundreds of people seeking my advice and prayers on behalf of family or friends suffering a serious illness, often cancer.

This experience of the past four months plays an important role in shaping this pastoral reflection on Catholic health care. I have reason to believe that my reflections on my illness as well as on the state and future of Catholic health care will help and interest others who are struggling either with illness itself or with the delivery of health care services in a rapidly changing social, economic, and political environment.

In this statement I will first reflect on my recent experience of both illness and Catholic health care in the light of Scripture. Then I will share some of the key concepts that I have articulated in recent years regarding

Catholic health care—especially my attempt to define more clearly what is distinctive about Christian health care ministry. Finally, I will outline some directions for the future of Catholic health care in the archdiocese.

A BISHOP'S REFLECTION

With people of all faiths throughout every age, Christians value physical and emotional life and health. We value all human life as a gift from God and, therefore, stand as ready stewards to respond to the reality of sickness in the world. We do so as individuals when we expend personal resources to prevent illness and find the best, affordable medical care available when we or someone we love becomes ill. We also do so as a Catholic community when we establish a variety of health care services, especially for the poor and most vulnerable in our society. Indeed, Catholics as a group are the largest provider of health care under single sponsorship in the United States today. Catholic health care continues Jesus' healing ministry and reflects a consistent ethic of life, which requires of us a commitment to preserve, protect, and promote the physical health and well-being of all people.

How do we do this as Catholic Christians? What is the distinctively Christian vocation in caring for those who are ill? What do we need to do when, as Christians, we care for those who are ill?

A Promise of Life in the Midst of Chaos

Let us begin this reflection on the Christian vocation of helping the sick and the suffering by asking, "What is God doing in the world?" We begin to find an answer in the very first chapter of Genesis. The first creation narrative was written at a time of great turmoil in the history of the Hebrew people. The nation had been attacked by the Babylonians; their temple, the center of their life as a community, was destroyed; and many of the people were forced to leave their homes to live in exile. Against this background the narrative speaks of God as doing more than creating life in the world. In fact, in its emphasis that God looked at creation and "saw that it was good," we are reminded that God gives order, meaning, and purpose to the chaos that at times surrounds or invades our lives.

It should be noted, however, that the biblical narratives do not portray God as conquering and doing away with chaos. Genesis does not describe a cosmic battle in which order triumphs over chaos once and for all. Instead, chaos itself is ordered through God's creative activity. But chaos continues to exist. It is a part of life. At times, it can seem to get the upper hand and overcome the order, purpose, and sense of meaning in our lives.

But God's creative work is ongoing. God continues to order the chaos we encounter, making it possible for us to live our lives under his protection.

This is an important lesson for us who live in a world where disease and tragedy can shake the foundations of our faith, of our very being. In its own way, illness is a kind of human exile, a feeling of not being "at home," of being cut off from our former way of life. Depending on the seriousness of the illness and our own resources, we may be separated from our homes, our family or loved ones, our source of income or sustenance. Some are abandoned in their illness by those who are unable or unwilling to care for them. At times, family and friends feel abandoned by the sick person on whom they had depended, or by others who do not share the care of the sick person.

People who are ill sometimes speak of being attacked and ravaged by a disease that slowly but inexorably conquers them. They may even speak of their own body betraying them, as they begin to lose control of simple bodily functions, or become weaker, frailer, and more dependent on others. Illness can bring people to question if God has punished or abandoned them. Recently, a thirteen-year-old girl who has cancer asked her parents, "I go to church every Sunday, and many of my classmates don't. Why do I have cancer, and they don't?"

We begin to ask: How can we live with Alzheimer's disease, cancer, heart disease, a disability, or an HIV-related disease? A life of illness or disability may seem to be, for the ones who are ill and/or for those who care for them, virtually impossible to live. And in this desperation some seek a solution in euthanasia or assisted suicide. The question that believers and nonbelievers alike have often faced is: How can I continue to live like this?

None of this is new. Believers through the ages have faced the desperation that sometimes accompanies the chaos of illness and suffering. The many laments in the book of Psalms give eloquent expression to this pain, panic, and desperation. However, the laments also express a firm belief in the power of God to make it possible for us to live our lives despite the chaos. The first chapter of Genesis lays the foundation for this comforting reminder that God's creative activity includes the promise that we are able to live our lives, even in the face of the chaos of illness and death. God's promise of life is the basis for Christian hope.

Hope and the Christian Life

Why does God make such a promise? Because God loves us. And how do we know of this love? St. Paul tells us that we can see God's love for us in the suffering, death, and resurrection of Jesus. "God proves his love for us in that while we were still sinners Christ died for us" (Rom 5:8). As the apostle also says, we are called to trust that neither death nor life, angels nor principalities, nothing already in existence and nothing still to come can separate us from that love that comes to us in Christ Jesus (Rom 8:38-39). This event of God's love, revealed to us in Christ Jesus, is the basis for our hope in the midst of life with all its health and sickness, joy and suffering, birth and death. Trusting in God's love from which we can never be separated, we are confident that it is always possible to continue with life despite the chaos we encounter along our pilgrim journey. This, St. Paul tells us, is our hope (Rom 8:25).

Let me be clear what I mean by "hope." It is not a hope for something. It is not the expectation that something will happen. Although some people hope for a physical cure, not everyone does. Often people believe that a cure is not possible, or they are too tired to hope to be restored to their former state of health. But, even when a cure is not to be expected, one can still hope. The hope of which I speak is an attitude about life and living in God's loving care. Hope, rooted in our trust of God's love for us in Christ, gives us strength and confidence; it comforts us with the knowledge that, whatever is happening to us, we are loved by God through Christ. So, we need not grieve or despair in the same way as those who do not share in this hope (1 Thess 4:13-18). Illness need not break us. Even if we remain ill, even if we are to die prematurely, we can still be courageous and confident of God's enduring love for us (2 Cor 5:6-10).

Some might think that the primary reason for our hope in time of sickness is the fact that Jesus physically cured in his ministry. It is true that Jesus did cure people of their illness, and it is certainly appropriate for us to hope and pray for cures. However, as Christians, we recognize that Jesus does more than offer a physical cure. More central to his mission is the strengthening of people's faith so that they may live as a people of hope. This is the fuller meaning of Jesus' healing miracles. In the miracle accounts, the central point is not so much that someone is cured, but, rather, that his or her relationship with God is restored and/or deepened through their trust in Jesus' love. It is people's faith in Jesus' love for them that saves them from the despair that can overwhelm people when they encounter chaos in their lives. Jesus helps us see that he is someone we can trust in the midst of chaos, someone through whom we can be filled with hope for the future. If we trust in Jesus' love for us, all life, even a life of sickness or disability, is worthwhile.

Health Care as a Ministry of Hope

In light of all this, I will now share several basic convictions about the ministry of health care.

As Christians, our hope relies on the fact that God's love for us in Christ Jesus is permanent and unchanging. Trusting that we are so loved, we face life, with all its sorrows and joy, with hope. However, it is not enough that we be comforted in our affliction. St. Paul tells us that our own consolation enables us to bring comfort to others in their need:

> Blessed be the God and Father of our Lord Jesus Christ, the Father of mercies and the God of all consolation. He comforts us in all our afflic- tion and thus enables us to comfort those who are in any trouble, with the same consolation we have received from him (cf. 2 Cor 1:3-4).

As Christians, we are called, indeed empowered, to comfort others in the midst of their suffering by giving them a reason to hope. We are called to help them experience God's enduring love for them. This is what makes Christian health care truly distinctive. We are to do for one another what Jesus did: comfort others by inspiring in them hope and confidence in life. As God's ongoing, creative activity in the world and the love of Christ make it possible for us to continue to live despite the chaos of ill- ness, so too our work in the world must also give hope to those for whom we care. Our distinctive vocation in Christian health care is not so much to heal better or more efficiently than anyone else; it is to bring comfort to people by giving them an experience that will strengthen their confi- dence in life. The ultimate goal of our care is to give to those who are ill, through our care, a reason to hope.

Our witness to hope is increasingly important in today's commercial- ized health care environment. There are strong economic pressures to pursue income at the expense of the patient and, in fact, to reduce the patient to a commodity. In this context one of the ways in which we wit- ness to Christian hope is through fidelity to our charitable mission within the health care industry. Our primary service to those who come to us cannot be for sale. We can sell pharmaceuticals and surgical services, it is true, but these are secondary. Our distinctiveness cannot be turned into a commodity and sold. The moment we shift our motive to one of profit, we will, in fact, undermine our primary mission. Few will find hope in God's love for them if others make a profit from such care.

More importantly, we must recognize the absolute necessity of being present as a community to others in their need if they are to gain confi- dence in life. Human life is not meant to be lived in isolation. To be fully human, we must live in community. It is very important that a person who is ill have others with whom to communicate. Those who are ill can experience God's enduring love for them through the loving care and concern of the Christian health care community. We also serve as a com- munity of conscience for the rest of health care.

We are also to give people an experience of God's enduring love for them through a nonjudgmental approach to illness. We do not make a theological or moral distinction between health and sickness. We do not, as Jesus did not, suggest that illness is a punishment for sin (John 9:2-7). Our nonjudgmental welcome of the person who is ill, like Jesus' nonjudgmental welcome of the Samaritan leper (Luke 17:11-19), gives people an experience of hope by delivering them from the isolation or abandonment that the sick fear most. A judgmental attitude toward illness and disability cuts people off from community and erodes or even destroys hope. Our hospitality saves people from such isolation. Like Jesus, we strive through our hospitality to give people the strength, comfort, and consolation of hope.

We seek to do more than merely cure a physical illness. Like Jesus, we heal the whole person. We care for people in such a way, that, whether or not we can physically cure their illness, they find strength and comfort in knowing God's abiding love for them, despite their experience of chaos.

To illustrate this point more fully, let us reflect briefly on two biblical accounts of illness: that of Job in the Old Testament and that of a paralytic in the Gospel of Mark. The contrast of the roles played by the sick persons' friends in these two accounts gives us a powerful insight into the kind of approach we Christians are called to take toward those who are ill.

You will recall that, as the book of Job opens, Job is faced with several disasters, including the loss of his livelihood, his children, and his health. As a man of great suffering, he is in need of comfort and hope, but he does not get it from the three friends who come to talk with him. Instead, they accuse him before God, telling him to repudiate the sin that he must have committed. Job, who knows of his innocence, is left alone, abandoned by those who ought to have offered him comfort and hope. At the end of the book, after God has spoken to him, Job acquires hope sufficient enough to continue living, but his suffering, his experience of chaos, remains a deep mystery to him.

The approach of Job's friends stands in stark contrast with that of the friends of the paralytic (Mark 2:1-12). While Jesus is teaching in Capernaum, so many people come to hear him that there is no room for anyone else in the house. Then a paralytic, carried by four friends, arrives.

Unable to get in through the door, they climb to the roof, make a hole in it, and lower the paralytic down before Jesus. We know from the context of the story that the paralytic is seeking forgiveness for sin. But unlike Job's friends, the paralytic's friends do not accuse him before Jesus. Far from abandoning him in his illness or suggesting that he was in some way responsible for his plight, these four devote themselves to caring for their friend. They save him from isolation, and their friendship gives him a reason to have hope, even in the midst of his paralysis.

Jesus sees the man lowered before him, but takes particular note of those who lowered him. We are familiar with Jesus' words to other individuals who are ill: "your faith has saved you." In this text, however, we read that Jesus saw the four friends' faith (Mark 2:5). He commends their faith, not the paralytic's. The four friends believe in God's enduring love for them revealed in Jesus, and they find their hope and comfort in him. It is this deep faith and comfort that enables them to console the paralytic, remaining with him as a reason for him to hope. This is the heart of Christian health care: caring for people in such a way that they have hope.

Although illness brings chaos and undermines hope in life, we seek to comfort those who are ill, whether or not they can be physically cured. We do so by being a sign of hope so that others might live and die in hope. In this we find the Christian vocation that makes our health care truly distinctive. It is the reason we are present to believers and nonbelievers alike.

A BISHOP'S MINISTRY

One of the benefits of reflection is that it allows us to see reality in a new, fresh way. Although the object of our reflection stays the same, our understanding is deepened or enhanced. Speaking of the Catholic health care ministry as a sign of hope enriches an already fruitful ministry. It also serves as a source of motivation and inspiration, especially when we seem to be "losing control" of the ministry. Likewise, it is a powerful standard against which we continually evaluate all that we do.

As we know, however, the health ministry is situated in an environment that is evolving rapidly as a result of technological change and institutional forces. Today, health care delivery is no longer centered in the free-standing, acute care hospital. There are several reasons for this. Increasingly, health care is focused not only on curing illness but also on preventing illness and building "wellness." Similarly, health care is no longer focused solely on the patient but also attends to the overall health of the community. Further, the provision of health care is understood as an integrated process that involves many in the community: physicians, nurses, social workers, therapists, ambulatory care sites, physical therapy and rehabilitation centers, long-term care facilities, hospice programs, home nursing, local parishes, chaplains, pastoral care ministers, and individuals as well as the more traditional, community-based, acute care hospital.

Concurrent with these more "philosophical" changes, health care has experienced many external challenges. Over the years changes in the administration of federal entitlements (such as Medicare and Medicaid) and the concerns of those who purchase health care insurance have sought to constrain the escalating cost of providing health care. These realities precipitated a discussion at the national level about the possibility of systemic reform of the provision and financing of health care in the United States.

As followers of the Lord Jesus and as citizens of this nation, the U.S. Catholic bishops participated in that debate and articulated several principles that should guide health care reform. I personally participated in the discussion through my address at the National Press Club in Washington, D.C., in March 1994, where I highlighted several key concepts. The points I made then remain relevant today, even though the context has changed somewhat (see Appendix A).

The same forces, and others, that precipitated the national debate unfortunately were insufficient to overcome the resistance that emerged from many sources. Although the systemic reform that I and many others advocated has not been realized, the debate did require us as a Catholic community to step back and reflect on why and how we continue the Lord's healing ministry as a sign of hope. Assisted by the many significant contributions of the Catholic Health Association (CHA), as well as by the efforts of the many religious congregations that sponsor Catholic health care and countless individuals in the ministry, we have renewed our dedication to Catholic health care. I certainly have done so.

In the context of these national and ecclesial movements I developed a protocol to inform and guide the making of important decisions by Catholic health care institutions in the Archdiocese of Chicago. Central to that protocol (issued in August 1994) is my belief that health care is a ministry of the entire community of faith, the Church. Indeed, it is an essential ministry. Therefore, each health care institution or system should see itself as part of the whole Church, sensitive to the needs of Catholic health care and the other institutions within the archdiocese. So, it is very important that we have both a vision and the strategies necessary to ensure that this essential ministry:

- Is available throughout the archdiocese and especially to the poor and marginalized, women and children, the aged and the disabled;

- Adapts to changing conditions so that it can provide quality and cost-efficient care;

- Is carried on in such a manner that the decisions of the individual Catholic health care institutions contribute to the well-being of the entire ministry and not bring undue harm to other Catholic institutions;

- Is faithful to our beliefs and values when entering into relations with other than Catholic organizations.

The last point is included because, in the future, health care will increasingly be provided in the context of what is often described as "integrated delivery." As a result, Catholic health care will find it necessary to enter into relationships with organizations, systems, and businesses that may share some but not all of our values. Of itself this is not bad. The Second Vatican Council taught us about the goodness that can be found in secular culture as well as about our responsibility to be present to culture and society as a leaven of transformation. In fact our mutual collaboration with other people of good will could help us bring about national health care reform.

However, as we seek to realize the above goals, two obstacles stand in our way. One is *internal*, and the other is *external*.

Let me begin with the *internal*. The strength of Catholic health ministry has been grounded in the charisms of the many religious communities that have carried on the Lord's healing ministry. In a way, diversity of background, heritage, and religious sensitivities were the energizing forces that made possible the establishment of Catholic health care ministry across this nation in response to unique needs, whether they were ethnic, geographic, or other. Today, however, that historical diversity at times seems to get in the way of the future.

What do I mean? The various forces that are propelling change in what is often called the health care "industry" are requiring greater collaboration, as I noted earlier. From a strictly business perspective it would seem obvious that those health care institutions which share a common value and vision would want to enter such increased collaboration from a position of strength. They would want to ensure:

1. That there would always be "space" for their religiously based "product" in the "evolving market," and

2. That, insofar as possible, they would have the ability to influence the community and others in a positive manner.

And it would seem this would also be the desire of institutions whose "product" is the healing comfort and hope of Jesus.

Often, however, this does not seem to have been the case. The diversity of the past seems to be an impediment to developing the type of collaboration on a local, regional, or national level that will allow us to adapt, as needed, to current trends in order to ensure our ongoing presence as well as our ability to influence the national culture of health care delivery. Indeed, at times it has been easier for religious-sponsored institutions to join with nondenominational entities than with other Catholic institutions.

As a bishop, I have responded to this obstacle in several ways. On the local level, I have been committed to the development of a network of Catholic health care institutions that will meet the goals and objectives I have mentioned. At the national level, I have encouraged my brother bishops and Catholic health care leaders to take the steps necessary to prepare for the future. It would be a tragedy if we did not have the courage to move beyond the past and have the creativity to address the future. I hope that:

- Religious congregations will continue to deepen their trust of one another as they ask themselves how they can ensure the future of the entire ministry as well as the future of their own respective institutions;

- Local boards, medical staffs, administration, and employees will enhance appropriate institutional or financial self-interest with a more "Catholic" perspective responsive to local, regional, and national health ministry;

- Diocesan bishops will experience "collegiality" in a new way as integration and consolidation challenge the divisions or isolation sometimes caused by diocesan boundaries.

Now to the second, *external* obstacle. We are experiencing a troubling trend in our nation: viewing health care primarily as a business commodity. The most evident manifestation of this is the movement to transform health care delivery from a not-for-profit to an investor-owned status. I reflected on these concerns in an address to The Harvard Business School Club of Chicago on January 12, 1995 (see Appendix B). In quite strong terms I urged that all involved in the Catholic health ministry join with others to ensure the continued viability of not-for-profit health care in our nation.

The primary focus of that address, however, was on the status of health care delivery, whether it be sectarian or non-sectarian in nature. While I remain convinced that the reasons outlined in that address apply in a special way to Catholic health care, serious questions have recently been raised within the Catholic community about the compatibility of the Catholic health care ministry and investor-owned enterprises.

Because of these questions and other forces, we must carefully identify again that which makes the Catholic health care ministry truly distinctive and which organizational structures best preserve and nurture that distinctiveness. As a person of faith, I believe this time of challenge is a "happy fault" that will give us the opportunity to understand better the health care ministry as a sign of hope. As the Jewish theologian, David Hartman, reminded our group during my recent pilgrimage to Israel, when we confront another who is different from ourselves, we can better discover our particularity, our distinctiveness.

Overcoming these obstacles will not be easy. While confronting the demands of the changing reality of health care, we continually will have to ask ourselves two questions:

1. Can we make a successful transition to the new way of doing the "business" of health care?

2. Does this new way lend itself to our Catholic mission and values, especially our being a sign of hope? Most secular providers, including the not-for-profits, have to address only the first question.

As we strive to answer these general questions, we Catholics will also face some more specific questions:

- As the focus of health care moves from acute care to the organized practice of medicine within integrated delivery networks, how can we become "sponsors" of this form of health care?

- How can we sponsor HMOs, or own vehicles for providing insurance or other forms of securing adequate access to health care services?

- Can we ever sponsor investor-owned organizations?

- Can we work closely with or engage in joint ventures with investor-owned organizations or organizations whose mission and value base are possibly not compatible with our religiously based tradition?

In light of my earlier reflection, I suggest that, as we work to answer these questions, we do so keeping in mind that our ministry is distinctive because it is a sign of hope.

In what follows I cannot address all of these issues. They will have to be answered collaboratively by all who are involved in health care ministry. To that end I am encouraged that Catholic health care leaders are coming together at this crossroads for health care and fully support the "New Covenant" initiative sponsored by the National Coalition on Catholic Health Care Ministry, the Catholic Health Association, and Consolidated Catholic Health Care.

A BISHOP'S PROPOSALS

In anticipation of that process I now will offer some pastoral guidance on several matters pertaining to the Catholic health care ministry. I will speak as a bishop who, with his brother bishops, is responsible for addressing moral and ethical issues that confront us as a nation as well as for engaging those pastoral concerns that are common to the life of the Church in the United States. In this larger context I will also speak as pastor of this local church about the health care ministry in the Archdiocese of Chicago.

Social Issues

I was deeply disappointed by our inability as a nation to move forward with systemic reform of our nation's delivery of health care. While now is not the time to attribute blame, I am troubled that our constitutional process for decision-making seems increasingly incapable of addressing fundamental issues. We have become a nation of "sound bites" and "special interests." More recently, we have also become ever more comfortable with an "ethic of punishment," which seeks to replace an ethic of personal and social responsibility.

As persons of faith, we believe that these trends require that we become more and more involved as voices of conscience within the political process. In a very special way we must become more adept at challenging the "what-am-I-going-to-get-out-of-this" mentality. We can do this by sharing some Catholic insights. First, we must share with others our Catholic vision of the human person as someone who is ultimately grounded in community. The vision of human solidarity of which I spoke earlier is the best antidote to a sense of alienation and isolation that ironically often expresses itself in an exaggerated attention to personal needs and desires.

Second, while encouraging the movement toward a greater sense of personal accountability and personal responsibility, we must share with others our convictions about the need for compassion, the existence of the common good, and the responsibility of society and government to promote the common good. An unbalanced attention to personal responsibility can become the excuse for neglecting our social responsibilities. While we can never condone or endorse personal irresponsibility, such irresponsibility does not destroy a person's innate dignity or our social obligations to ensure that all citizens are able to realize their basic human rights.

A third Catholic insight—one that is more difficult for some to accept—is our responsibility toward the poor. Our Catholic tradition tells us that those who are poor or marginalized have the first claim on us, as individuals and as a society. While this expectation is grounded in a deep faith conviction, it also flows from a Catholic understanding of social justice. This philosophy of society says that the state has two responsibilities. Many agree with the first, that government should do nothing to impede or violate fundamental human rights. In regard to the second responsibility, that government is to create those conditions necessary to realize those rights, people of goodwill may disagree on how to define such rights and are even more likely to argue over how one describes those conditions. Such a debate and discussion are healthy for a nation.

However, it seems to me that today the real debate, especially in the current discussion about welfare reform, is about whether to affirm or deny the second responsibility. In fact, in certain quarters I sense a mean-spiritedness that, under the guise of encouraging responsible living, is, in fact, judging the poor and the marginalized as a class or social group who are responsible for their situation. The logical conclusion of this judgment is that society need do nothing. And because we are now in the realm of so-called "personal failure," some have concluded that the not-for-profit sector of society, and in particular religious institutions, and not the government, should care for the needs of such people. After all, it is argued, it is religion that helps people to achieve a moral conversion.

In addition, while it is true that much of what presently exists as welfare programs can and should be improved, our efforts at reform cannot ignore the reasons why current programs or entitlements were created in the first place. Over the last half-century, we have come to recognize certain human and social needs, which, as a nation, we could not ignore. In effect, we concluded that in these areas the demands of the common good required action. Attempts to eliminate inefficiency and ineffectiveness must be carefully evaluated to ensure that, intentionally or unintentionally, they do not result in our walking away from these communal and social responsibilities.

Obviously, we must do all in our power to ensure a proper ethical foundation for public policy in this and other aspects of our common life.

I make note of all this in a pastoral reflection on the ministry of health care for two reasons. First, the decisions the federal and state governments make on welfare reform will have an immense impact on the provision of Catholic health care. Because we consider the provision of health care as a social good, we are present where others will not go. That presence, however, has been assisted in recent years by state and federal entitlements. If that assistance is eliminated or significantly reduced, many people, especially the vulnerable, will not be served. In particular, many of our "disproportionate share" hospitals (those that serve a large number of patients who have no insurance or personal means of paying for health care) will find it extremely difficult to continue. While we will do all we can to preclude such closings, the suggestion that religious organizations should be able to replace government dollars with charitable dollars is, at best, naive. It is not realistic to assume that parishes, churches, and synagogues will be able to offset through their charitable activity the withdrawal of government support.

Second, if such regrettable decisions are made, we will have to find new ways of meeting the health care needs of those who are being abandoned by society. The poor, who will come to us because of a governmental retreat, must become the occasion for a new creativity on our part. While our presence will be different, we must still be there for those in need. How we achieve such solidarity will require the involvement of the entire community of faith.

Catholic Health Care

I now would like to address my sisters and brothers who exercise positions of leadership in the health care ministry. We are at a turning point, at a critically important moment. While some have concluded that this is "the beginning of the end" of Catholic health care as we have known it, it can be a time of "refounding." Previously I noted some of the changes that would help this "refounding" to occur: developing greater trust and more effective collaboration among religious congregations, moving beyond institutional self-interest that excludes the common good of Catholic health care, and entering into a new sense of episcopal collegiality.

These seem so self-evident that one immediately begins to wonder why it appears so difficult for them to be realized. I offer one possible explanation for this difficulty: Catholic health care has become more of a business than a ministry. As health care has become increasingly expensive, quite complex, and ever more sophisticated, we necessarily have had to become more focused on economic, technological, systemic, and complex medical realities in a predominantly acute care setting. Could it be that, despite our best intentions and efforts, these forces may distract us from an interiorization of the vision of health care as a sign of hope? To say it another way, how can we revitalize the "Catholic imagination" of health care that sustained and challenged those who went before us? Unless we attend to this spiritual and formational vision, we will not be able to experience the rebirth we all desire. Economic, technological, systemic, and medical realities are not enemies. Rather, it is also to them that we bring our ministry of Christian hope.

The Archdiocese

Now I will address the church in Cook and Lake counties, Illinois, and indicate some directions we need to pursue as a local church. In order to realize them, we must work together as one family of faith.

First, I challenge the parishes of the archdiocese to become more vigorously engaged in forming people and communities of hope. As Jesus himself lived and taught, it is in the midst of the Christian community that God's word of hope is proclaimed and people of hope are formed and nourished. The parish is a vital place for education and formation, for bringing the resources of our faith to bear on how we interpret and respond to the experiences of aging, illness, and dying in the local community. Historically, the parish community has responded to the spiritual needs of its sick and elderly. The parish needs to reclaim its sacred responsibility by calling forth and training leaders and groups to provide a powerful witness of God's care for those suffering sickness or struggling with the process of aging. Our unique vocation in health care will not be fully achieved unless it is rooted first in our parish communities, and our parish communities, in turn, collaborate more effectively with other ecclesial institutions, such as Catholic Charities.

Second, I encourage Catholics to take advantage of Catholic health care. In saying this, I realize that often the first decision people make is about which physician they will consider "their doctor." They then go to the hospital at which their doctor serves or one that is most convenient geographically. For others, the choice is more restrictive, depending on the type of health care coverage or plan that is offered by their employer. Nevertheless, I encourage individuals and employers to consider and support Catholic health care systems and institutions. I say this not out of an outdated sectarianism but because of a profound belief that Catholic health care can and should provide an environment of faith-filled hope in face of the chaos that accompanies serious illness. Catholic health care envisions working in partnership with parishes and others to develop healthy communities. And a vibrant Catholic health care will have the resources necessary to carry on our ministry to those in need. I strongly encourage pastoral leaders in our parishes and agencies to add their own encouragement.

Third, we must ensure that the vision of the Catholic health care ministry outlined in my meditation is truly present in our Catholic health care institutions. To achieve this end, I ask the Catholic Health Alliance of Metropolitan Chicago (CHAMC) to develop a joint committee representing sponsors and management as well as representatives of the archdiocese. The task of this committee, using work already done by the Catholic Health Association and others, will be to propose ways to identify and implement standards for evaluating the Catholic character of our health care institutions and programs. I do not envision these standards as punitive. Rather they will raise up the best of who we already are in order to ensure that what we proclaim is what we provide. They will complement the necessary movement within Catholic health care to ensure the existence of high-quality, cost-effective, community-based services by guaranteeing that our services are also value-based.

Fourth, because the leadership of our Catholic health care institutions is more and more the responsibility of dedicated laypersons, we need to ensure the ongoing theological and spiritual formation of all levels of health care leadership in the archdiocese. While primary responsibility for such formation belongs to the particular institution, we need to explore how we can ensure that this is done effectively. I therefore ask that CHAMC, in conjunction with the Center for Development in Ministry, research what is currently available, including the resources of the Catholic Health Association, and how this formation can be enhanced.

Fifth, I have a direct responsibility for overseeing the pastoral or spiritual care of patients in Catholic health care institutions. I know that our health care facilities are committed to providing this important service and that they see it as essential to their identity. I am asking that the Archdiocesan Office for Health Affairs bring together representatives of pastoral care departments in our facilities, along with skilled pastoral practitioners whom I will appoint, to review the issues confronting the provision of effective spiritual care and to make appropriate recommendations for its ongoing transformation. Such care must attend to the manner in which physical, emotional, and spiritual needs intersect in a person whose life is lived in the environment of family and friends, as well as business, social, and other relationships. Consequently, this spiritual care, while respecting the conscience and privacy of those it serves, must be better integrated with parish pastoral services. In this way it can become an effective catalyst for health care being a ministry of hope to all it touches.

Sixth, I again express my support for the creation of an effective archdiocesan Catholic health care network. While such a network is but a first step in what I hope will be a process of increased collaboration, it is a very important step. I commend those who have already decided to participate. Unfortunately, at this time, not all of our Catholic acute care institutions have decided to participate in the network. I will continue my discussions with those institutions with three goals in mind: achieving effective collaboration within the Catholic ministry; avoiding actions that will bring unjustified harm to others who share in the Catholic ministry; and preserving Catholic integrity and identity.

Seventh, because our health care ministry continues Jesus' healing work, the archdiocese will initiate discussions with other institutions and systems in the Chicagoland area that also carry on the Christian mission of health care. Our commitment to developing effective avenues of ecumenical cooperation, as well as the common needs we share as faith-based organizations, requires such dialogue. This is particularly true of the Episcopal and Lutheran communities with whom we have entered into covenantal relationships.

Eighth, we must review our own archdiocesan and parochial ministries to those who experience permanent or transitory health care challenges, in particular, those who experience mental or emotional illness. Often these persons and those who care and support them have not felt the support and encouragement of their brothers and sisters in faith. I ask that the Office of Health Affairs review these efforts and make appropriate recommendations for consideration by the Archdiocesan Pastoral Council and Presbyteral Council. This review also should pay attention to the manner in which we provide for the spiritual and sacramental needs of those who are homebound or in other than Catholic institutions.

Finally, I ask that all those who share in the responsibility for carrying on Jesus' healing ministry join me in resisting efforts to make health care in our nation or our own ministry merely another commodity, simply another item to be sold.

Personal Thoughts

Now, I will close with some personal thoughts.

As I said at the beginning of this pastoral reflection, I have recently experienced personally the chaos that accompanies illness. I have had to let go of some things that I thought brought me security in order to find the healing that only faith in the Lord can bring. I have been graced by an outpouring of affection and support that has allowed me to experience the Church as a community of solidarity and a sign of hope in a very intimate manner. I am grateful for this because it has strengthened my confidence, my hope that in Christ life can be lived, even with pancreatic cancer.

In the context of this new moment in my own pilgrimage I offer this pastoral reflection to the Church. May it be for all who encounter it an opportunity for personal reflection and rededication. May we always be a people "who comfort those who are in any need with the same consolation we have received" (2 Cor 1:4) from the Lord.

Joseph Cardinal Bernardin
Feast of St. Luke

A PPENDIX A

Key Concepts of Address to National Press Club
(March 1994)

1. In this current debate, a consistent ethic of life requires us to stand up for both the unserved and the unborn; to insist on the inclusion of real universal coverage and the exclusion of abortion coverage; to support efforts to restrain rising health costs; and to oppose the denial of, or retrenchment in, providing needed care to the poor and vulnerable.
2. We have been drawn into a discussion of fundamental values and social convictions. And these convictions find their origin in a vision of the human person as someone who is grounded in community, and in an

understanding of society and government as being largely responsible for the realization of the common good.

3. Health care is an essential safeguard of human life and dignity, and there is an obligation for society to ensure that every person be able to realize this right.

4. The only way this obligation can be effectively met by society is for our nation to make universal health care coverage a reality. Universal access is not enough.

5. Universal coverage is not a vague promise or a rhetorical preamble to legislation, but requires practical means and sufficient investment to permit everyone to obtain decent health care on a regular basis.

6. If justice is a hallmark of our national community, then we must fulfill our obligations in justice to the poor and the unserved first and not last.

7. If real reform is to be achieved—that is, reform that will ensure quality and cost-effective care—then we must do what is necessary in order to ensure that our health care delivery system is person centered and has a community focus.

8. Our objective must be a healthy nation in which the mental and physical health of the individual is addressed through collaborative efforts at the local level. The poor, vulnerable, and uninsured persons cannot be denied needed care because the health system refuses to eliminate waste, duplication, and bureaucratic costs.

9. In light of these concerns, the nation must undertake a broad-based and inclusive consideration of how we will choose to allocate and share our health care dollars. We are stewards, not sole owners, of all our resources, human and material; thus, goods and services must be shared.

10. The U.S. Catholic bishops continue to insist that it would be a grave moral tragedy, a serious policy mistake, and a major political error to link health care reform to abortion.

11. Fundamentally, health care reform is a moral challenge—finding the values and vision to reshape a major part of national life to better protect the life and dignity of all.

A PPENDIX B

Key Concepts* of Address to
The Harvard Business School Club of Chicago
(January 1995)

1. The health care delivery system is rapidly commercializing itself, and, in the process, is abandoning core values that should always be at the heart of health care delivery.
2. Health care by its nature is not a mere commodity. It is fundamentally different from most goods and services.
3. The primary goals of medical care are wellness, a cured patient, and a healthier community—not to earn a profit or a return on capital for shareholders.
4. A not-for-profit structure is better aligned with these "noneconomic" ends and is more compatible with the essential purpose of health care.
5. There are four essential characteristics of health care delivery that are especially compatible with the not-for-profit structure but less likely to occur when health care decision making is driven predominantly by the need to produce a return-on-equity for shareholders: access to care for costly and hard-to-serve populations; medicine's patient-first ethic; attention to community-wide needs; and volunteerism.
6. Each of us and our communities have much to lose if we allow unstructured market forces to continue to erode the necessary and valuable presence of not-for-profit health care organizations here in Chicago and throughout the nation.

* Excerpted from *Making the Case for Not-for-Profit Healthcare*. For a copy, call the Archdiocese of Chicago, 312-751-8233 or CHA, 314-253-3463.

Pastoral Reflections

"Christ Lives in Me"

A Pastoral Reflection on Jesus
*and His Meaning for Christian Life**

―― *1985* ―――――――――――――――――――――――

Foreword

My dear brothers and sisters in Christ:

> The grace of the Lord Jesus Christ, and the love of God, and the fellow-
> ship of the Holy Spirit be with you all! (2 Cor 13:13).

I invite you to reflect with me on the most important person in our
lives, both as individuals and as a community of faith. That person is Jesus
Christ.

I have thought a great deal in recent years about the meaning Jesus has
for you, for me and for all men and women. I have also tried to enter into
closer communion with the Lord through prayer, so that no part of my
life, no part of myself, would be excluded from my relationship with him.
This search for union has been an exciting, life-giving experience. But it
has brought pain and frustration, too.

Pain, because the closer we are drawn to Jesus, the more conscious we
become of our shortcomings and sins. Jesus is the Light of the World. As
we approach that Light, it brings ever more sharply into relief the defects
in ourselves which we thought, or at least hoped, did not exist!

* The book was originally published by the St. Anthony Messenger Press in
Cincinnati, Ohio.

Frustration, because growth in intimacy with the Lord intensifies my desire to proclaim him and his gospel, and often I feel unequal to the task. There are so many things to do for the Lord, so many people to awaken and encourage, so many initiatives to take. And, more often than not, my efforts fall short of the mark and have little visible effect!

Like Paul, I tell myself not to be anxious to see the fruits of the soil I have tilled, for it seems to be of evangelization's very nature that the person who sows the seed is usually not the one who reaps the harvest. Yet I am left with the uneasy feeling that I have not done as much, or done it as well, as the Lord deserved of me.

But I do not despair, and in this, too, I seek to be like Paul. He was so caught up with Jesus, so much in love with him and convinced that his strength was in the Lord, that he never surrendered to discouragement. His many trials only confirmed his faith and strengthened his resolve to preach the gospel to all people, whatever the cost to himself.

As Paul told the Corinthians, "It is not ourselves we preach but Christ Jesus as Lord, and ourselves as your servants for Jesus' sake" (2 Cor 4:5). He saw Jesus as a great treasure. So certain was he of Jesus' presence and power in his life, that he could assure the Corinthians without fear or hesitation:

> We are afflicted in every way possible, but we are not crushed; full of doubts, we never despair. We are persecuted but never abandoned; we are struck down but never destroyed. Continually we carry about in our bodies the dying of Jesus, so that in our bodies the life of Jesus may also be revealed (2 Cor 4:8-10).

In that spirit, I want to share with you some of my hopes and aspirations as well as my anxieties and sorrows. I hope these can become for you words of encouragement as you seek to know, love and follow Jesus Christ in the circumstances of your lives. And I ask your prayers for me as I seek to do the same.

Introduction

THE IMPORTANCE OF CHRISTOLOGY TODAY

The *Church* has been the dominant theme of theology in this century, both inside and outside Roman Catholicism. One of the Second Vatican Council's most important documents was the Dogmatic Constitution on the Church *(Lumen gentium)*.

Perhaps the term for the Church most identified with the council in Catholics' minds is "People of God." This is a rich biblical image found in both the Old and New Testaments. The council referred to those baptized into Christ as the "new People of God." It said we are a messianic people:

> Established by Christ as a fellowship of life, charity, and truth, [this people] is also used by him as an instrument for the redemption of all, and is sent forth into the whole world as the light of the world and the salt of the earth (cf. Matt 5:13-16).[1]

Another important document of the Second Vatican Council is the Pastoral Constitution on the Church in the Modern World *(Gaudium et spes)*. Whereas *Lumen gentium* considers the Church's inner nature as established by Christ, *Gaudium et spes* speaks of how the Church should address the challenges and problems of the concrete temporal situation in which it finds itself. It deals, therefore, with such questions as social and economic justice, war and peace, marriage and culture.

Today, however, the study of Jesus and his meaning for people of our day (christology) is replacing the study of the Church (ecclesiology) on center stage. That is logical—perhaps inevitable—for not only was the Church founded by Christ, it is also the Mystical Body of Christ, Christ *present* in the world. To reflect upon the Church leads naturally to reflection upon him.

Furthermore, it seems clear that the internal and external problems and tensions confronting the Church today cannot ultimately be solved on the level of ecclesiology alone. We must have recourse to christology to understand the inner reality of the Church and to work for its authentic renewal.

This renewed study of Jesus is important to anyone who wants to follow him. To know who *we* are as human beings and as Christians, and to know what it means to live as Christians, we must know who *Christ* is and what meaning his life holds for us. Such knowledge does not come exclusively or even primarily from theology; its best sources are prayer, the sacramental life of the Church and the practice of Christian piety. But theological reflection is also important in deepening and enriching our relationship with Christ.

St. Paul's life and ministry support this view. His letters are rich sources of christological doctrine. They express the theological reflection on Christ up to that time and carry it dramatically forward. They are crucially important to our own efforts to learn more about Jesus.

Paul's primary intention, however, was not to write a book of theology. He had a simple, practical end in view: to help the early Christians know

---

[1] Dogmatic Constitution on the Church *(Lumen gentium)*, *The Documents of Vatican II*, 1964, no. 9.

the Lord better and respond more generously to his expectations, to move them to make Jesus Christ the Lord of their lives.

That is why Paul gave such compelling witness to Jesus' marvelous presence and power in his own life and ministry. Consumed with love for Jesus, Paul found meaning only in the service of his gospel:

> None of us lives as his own master and none of us dies as his own master. While we live we are responsible to the Lord, and when we die we die as his servants. Both in life and in death we are the Lord's. That is why Christ died and came to life again, that he might be Lord of both the dead and the living (Rom 14:7-9).

Paul's vision lives on today. In *The Redeemer of Man (Redemptor hominis)*, the first encyclical of Pope John Paul II, the Holy Father says:

> The Church wishes to serve this single end: that each person may be able to find Christ, in order that Christ may walk with each person the path of life. . . . Jesus Christ becomes, in a way, newly present, in spite of all his apparent absences, in spite of all the limitations of the presence and of the institutional activity of the Church. Jesus Christ becomes present with the power of the truth and the love that are expressed in him with unique unrepeatable fullness. . . .[2]

What does Jesus Christ mean for you and me? What does he offer for our spiritual growth? How does he enrich our understanding of the Church he established and of our role in this community of faith? Where does he fit into our relationships with other people, our evaluation of the critical issues of our times? These are the questions we must consider.

I fervently hope these reflections will help bring us all closer to the Lord Jesus. But any good effect they may have will not finally be due to our efforts, but to Jesus. Finding in us even a small desire to follow him, Jesus is ready to fan our flickering commitment into the flame of an ardent love.

Chapter 1

THE PASTORAL RELEVANCE OF CHRISTOLOGY

Christology and christological dogmas sometimes seem very abstract, to the point that they appear to have little or nothing to do with actual Christian living. Yet Catholic piety and liturgy have always focused on Jesus as the center of Christian life. Now there is a particular need to show how christological doctrine is equally relevant to our lives as Christians.

---

[2] Pope John Paul II, *The Redeemer of Man (Redemptor hominis)* 1979, no. 13.

A point made in the Introduction bears repeating here. In Christ (and therefore in christology, which seeks to tell us more about him and his expectations of us) we learn who *we* are and how *we* live. Jesus is our model, and a Christian's life is essentially an "imitation" or "following" of Christ, as we know from Scripture and from our history as a Church.

Peter made this clear on Pentecost, when he addressed the thousands of people in Jerusalem who had witnessed some of the visible manifestations of the Holy Spirit. Having heard Peter's forceful discourse on Jesus' saving deeds and their significance for the human family, the people asked what they were to do. Peter answered: "You must reform and be baptized, each one of you, in the name of Jesus Christ, that your sins may be forgiven" (Acts 2:38).

In other words, Peter was saying: Unite yourselves with the Lord in his death and resurrection and, in doing so, adopt a radically new way of life. We are told that "those who accepted [Peter's] message were baptized; some three thousand were added that day" (Acts 2:41). From that moment on, as they shaped their lives according to the teaching and example of Jesus, they became a "new" people whose values and way of life were recognized as different by their neighbors.

> The community of believers were of one heart and one mind. None of them ever claimed anything as his own; rather, everything was held in common. With power the apostles bore witness to the resurrection of the Lord Jesus, and great respect was paid to them all (Acts 4:32-33).

In saying that Jesus is the "model" for Christians, we mean much more than when we say, for example, that Abraham Lincoln, Florence Nightingale, Babe Ruth and Helen Keller are models for young people. People aspire to be "like" other people they admire, but Christians are to be more than just "like" Jesus. They are to *put on* Christ, as Paul told the Corinthians; in a sense, they are to *become* Christ, to be *other* Christs. They are to carry on Christ's work and help bring it to completion.

Although our modeling of Jesus, rooted in union and identification with him, is absolutely central to our lives as Christians, it is exceedingly difficult to explain in human terms. It is unique, part of the Christian mystery which we will never fully comprehend in this life.

Still, some light is shed on it by a common human experience—the process by which members of a family come to resemble one another, psychically as well as physically. This happens not so much by self-conscious imitation, as by a much more profound and organic process involving both genetic factors and personal interaction. We become like those whom we live with and love. As Christians, we are members of God's "family"— adopted sons and daughters of God, brothers and sisters of Christ. And in a real sense we come to resemble Jesus, to be like him, by living with him and loving him.

Jesus himself gave us an image which tells even more about this profound reality:

> I am the vine, you are the branches.
> He who lives in me and I in him,
> will produce abundantly,
> for apart from me you can do nothing.
> A man who does not live in me
> is like a withered rejected branch,
> picked up to be thrown in the fire and burnt (John 15:5-6).

Plainly this signifies no superficial identification or union. We are affected in our very being—Jesus' life becomes our own. Separated from him, we simply cannot live: We wither spiritually and ultimately die.

Paul understood this; throughout his letters he emphasizes the changes that occur in him as his union with the Lord deepens. He becomes a new creation, his very powerlessness a source of spiritual power because it permits Jesus to work in and through him. So great is this identification that he can say, "In my own flesh I fill up what is lacking in the sufferings of Christ for the sake of his body, the church" (Col 1:24). And to the Galatians: "the life I live now is not my own; Christ is living in me. I still live my human life, but it is a life of faith in the Son of God, who loved me and gave himself for me" (Gal 2:20).

What is true of the individual Christian's identification with Jesus is also true for Christians collectively. The Church is Christ's Mystical Body; it is Christ present in the world. It would literally make no sense to separate Christ from the Church and say one accepts the former but rejects the latter.

Further light is shed on these realities when we reflect on the main themes of christology: for example, on the fact that Jesus is both God and man (the incarnation); on his redemption of the human family through his death and resurrection; on his triple mission of sanctifying, teaching and governing which continues in and through the Church. Let us consider these themes under two headings: first, the incarnation and its significance for the human family; second, Jesus as the Way, the Truth and the Life. I shall note the doctrinal points involved, then suggest some of their implications for our lives.

The Incarnation and Its Significance for the Human Family

Our race is fallen but redeemed; we have glimpsed an eternal destiny. In the heart of every human being is an irrepressible desire for union with the Creator. Not even sin cancels this desire, for even in sinning we still have in view some limited aspect of a good which reflects, however dimly, the perfection of God. Our longing for him does not end, and to suffer eternally this unsatisfied longing is the greatest tragedy imaginable.

Yearning for God was deeply rooted in the Israelites. Despite their disappointments and periodic disloyalty, they never forgot their identity and special dignity as God's people. The human urge to reach out to the Transcendent is beautifully expressed in Psalm 42:

> As the hind longs for the running waters,
>   so my soul longs for you, O God.
> Athirst is my soul for God, the living God.
>   When shall I go and behold the face of God?
> My tears are my food day and night,
>   as they say to me day after day, "Where is your God?" (Ps 42:2-4).

Among the writers of the Christian era, St. Augustine gave particularly poignant expression to this longing. His spiritual pilgrimage and ultimate conversion from a wayward life made him keenly aware of the soul's anguish when it is not in communion with its Lord. "We were made for you, O God," he said, "and our hearts will be restless until they find their rest in you."[3]

It is God who plants this desire in our hearts and God who satisfies it. Conscious as we are of our broken, sinful condition—conscious sometimes even to the point of despairing—we may find this hard to believe. Yet we should not. Having created us in his image and likeness, God loves us so much that he wishes to share his own divine life with us. From the moment humankind first rejected him through sin, he determined to reconcile us with himself, to make us whole again so that we could enjoy the intimacy of his loving friendship. Since then, human history has been at its heart the story of God's self-revelation to his creatures and of our response—faithful at times, unfaithful at other times—to him.

This relationship, in which God and his creatures reach out to each other, is the context of the incarnation; there is no other way to understand its full significance. Although it was unthinkable to the Israelites that the transcendent God should actually become a part of the human scene by taking on human form, the unthinkable occurred in the mystery of the incarnation. God became man in Jesus of Nazareth. In Jesus, he identified fully with humanity. John's statement in the first chapter of his gospel is simple and definitive: "The Word became flesh and made his

---

[3] St. Augustine, *Confessions.*

dwelling among us" (John 1:14). The incarnation constitutes an unbreakable link between God and the human family.

The immediate result of the incarnation, as it unfolded in the life, death, resurrection and exaltation of Jesus, was our redemption. Paul told the Galatians:

> But when the designated time had come, God sent forth his Son born of a woman, born under the law, to deliver from the law those who were subjected to it, so that we might receive our status as adopted sons. The proof that you are sons is the fact that God has sent forth into our hearts the spirit of his Son which cries out "Abba" ("Father!"). You are no longer a slave but a son! And the fact that you are a son makes you an heir, by God's design (Gal 4:4-7).

The incarnation established a new relationship not only between us and God but also among us human beings. We adopted children of the Father are Christ's brothers and sisters and, in him, brothers and sisters of one another. Jesus made very clear the inseparability of love of God and love of neighbor: "This is the first" of all the commandments, he said:

> "Hear, O Israel! The Lord our God is Lord alone!
> Therefore you shall love the Lord your God
>   with all your heart,
>   with all your soul,
>   with all your mind,
>   and with all your strength."
> This is the second,
> "You shall love your neighbor as yourself" (Mark 12:29-31).

To follow Jesus one must love all those whom he loves. There is no other way.

It is of crucial importance that we understand and appreciate the incarnation's significance for the human condition in its many dimensions. That God redeemed us through the *humanity* of his Son has tremendous implications for how we understand ourselves and the meaning of our lives.

For example, the incarnation rules out any kind of dualism which would radically separate the human body and soul. Such dualism sets body and soul in opposition as if they were essentially separate entities, with the soul considered to be what is properly human in a person, while the body is thought to be subhuman, inferior, of scant value. In such a view the body's role is limited to housing the soul for a short time, so that what happens to the body has little or no impact on one's real self.

The incarnation rules out this view because to become truly human; the Word became *flesh*. (Hence, too, the necessary truth that Jesus rose *bodily* from the dead. Conquering death involved for him, as it will for us, not the attenuated existence of a disembodied spirit but true, resurrected bodily life.)

Thus, in redeeming us through his death and resurrection, Jesus redeemed the whole person, body and soul. Evidently, then, the incarnation teaches us that bodiliness is an integral part of our own identity, as it was of the Word-become-flesh. It is not something "out there"—something removed from our personhood to be abused or manipulated without harm to our real selves. A human person is a bodily person. And this substantial unity of the material and the spiritual in the human person has important implications for the moral life, helping us to make ethical judgments about such "bodily" things as our sexuality and some current and future projects of biotechnology. To violate the integrity of the human body is to violate the integrity of the human person.

There is tremendous significance for the human family in Jesus' appearance among us and the continued presence of the risen Lord in the world. Above all, Jesus is the sign and cause of our redemption. Because he became flesh and redeemed us through his death and resurrection, we are now "new creations," as Paul told the Corinthians: "This means that if anyone is in Christ, he is a new creation. The old order has passed away; now all is new!" (2 Cor 5:17).

We are a people called to a new intimacy and friendship with God; a people with an eternal destiny, who even now have begun to experience the treasures of the heavenly kingdom. We are a people who reflect, with new brightness and beauty, the image and likeness of God; a people who, in the totality of our humanity, are expected to express the values which Jesus realized in his own life. We are a people to whom much has been given and from whom much will be expected.

There can be no dichotomy between the material and the spiritual, between flesh and spirit, between the divine and the human. They are distinct, of course, but not opposed. In becoming man, Jesus brought into a new and higher harmony these diverse elements whose original harmony had been fractured by sin.

The only absolute dichotomy or division—a fatal one, spiritually—is that between Jesus and the forces opposed to him. But as Jesus triumphed over sin and death, we also can overcome evil and death by being united with him in faith and love. We "overcome" evil, of course, precisely as he did—by redemptive suffering. The Cross is central to Christian life. That is because sin, both original and personal, and its consequences are still very much with us.

In sum, the incarnation puts us and the kind of life we are expected to live in a totally new perspective. As Christians, we are fully human and also in a true sense, divine; for what we call "grace" is our participation in the divine life. To be fully and authentically human, therefore, means striving for the highest sanctity. One who sees this simply cannot be satisfied with being a mediocre or marginal Christian.

As a people redeemed by Jesus' blood, we are called to a radically new way of life in which the criteria of success are totally different from the world's criteria. Now that the Word has become flesh, we cannot be overly concerned with ourselves—our petty vanities and prejudices, our hostilities and fleeting attachments. We have a higher calling. To be sure, we see now as in a glass darkly; yet, seeing with the eyes of faith, we begin even now to discern the "new heavens and a new earth" (Rev 21:1) which are to come fully into being through Christ's power at the end of time. Our vision must not be limited. We have work to do—our share in restoring all things in Christ. We must take off the blinders, so that we can see "the splendor of the gospel showing forth the glory of Christ, the image of God" (2 Cor 4:4).

Jesus Is the Way, the Truth, and the Life

Only through Jesus can we fully approach the Father and come to know him.

> I am the way, and the truth, and the life;
> no one comes to the Father but through me (John 14:6).

Impossible though it is to plumb the depths of this statement, its meaning for us is nevertheless clear enough: In and through Jesus we come to God.

Jesus is the Way. In what sense is Jesus our *way* to the Father? First, by his death and resurrection. Through the events we call the "paschal mystery" Jesus reconciled us with his Father. As Paul told the Romans, Jesus "was handed over to death for our sins and raised up for our justification" (Rom 4:25).

The Lord's death and resurrection are not just historical events which happened in a particular time and place; they are life-giving events whose power permeates our lives. Their impact will never cease. More than that, those who seek to follow Christ are called in a mysterious way to participate in these events and reenact them. Paul expressed this when he told the Corinthians:

> Continually we carry about in our bodies the dying of Jesus, so that in our bodies the life of Jesus may also be revealed. While we live we are constantly being delivered to death for Jesus' sake, so that the life of Jesus may be revealed in our mortal flesh (2 Cor 4:10-11).

Our duty as Christians is to continue Jesus' redemptive mission in the world today.

Jesus is also our way to the Father through the Church which he established to continue his saving mission. He made it clear from the very beginning that his mission had a communitarian dimension. Certainly there was a deep personal relationship between him and each of the disciples, as there is between him and each of us today. But he was also related to them, and is related to us, as to a community united by faith in and commitment to him. The Gospels tell us how he formed this community, teaching and challenging its members, encouraging and even correcting them when necessary.

Before returning to his Father, Jesus took steps to ensure the continued stability of the community of his followers. Not even their fear and despondency during the terrible events of Good Friday robbed them of their identity and unity as believers in the Lord Jesus. After the resurrection, when the Holy Spirit came to them, they emerged as a courageous and determined group, ready and indeed eager to begin proclaiming Jesus and his gospel to a hostile world. The Acts of the Apostles tells us:

> The community of believers were of one heart and one mind. None of them ever claimed anything as his own; rather, everything was held in common. With power the apostles bore witness to the resurrection of the Lord Jesus, and great respect was paid to them all (Acts 4:32-33).

They gave this witness by devoting themselves to "the apostles' instruction and the communal life, to the breaking of the bread and the prayers" (Acts 2:42). Acts, as well as the epistles, also tell us of the suffering and martyrdom which so many members of the early Christian communities willingly suffered for Jesus' sake.

Plainly, then, the Church is no mere organization; it is a community of faith over which the risen Lord presides and through which the baptized make their pilgrim way to the Father. Nor is the Church something optional, a kind of religious club to which one can belong or not, according to individual taste and temperament. The Church cannot be separated from Christ. Christian life, which is essentially communitarian, is to be lived in the community Christ founded. As I remarked before, it makes no sense to say, as some do, that one accepts Christ but rejects the Church.

Why, then, do people take this attitude? In some cases, I believe, because they wish to avoid the obligations which accepting Christ in his Church would entail. But others are sincere—they find it hard to see Christ in a community which in the past and also today has at times fallen tragically short of the high standards proclaimed by Christ.

The Church is not an impersonal institution; it is made up of people. Jesus himself warned that there would always be wicked and insensitive people among us. Even those who were privileged to be in Jesus' immediate company during his life on earth often bickered among themselves, misunderstood his message, fell short of the standards he set for them. One betrayed him, and their chief, Peter, denied him.

Today, too, all of us can recognize failings in ourselves which dim Christ's image in the Church. The presence of weakness and evil in the Church—that is, in us who *are* the Church—is simply a reminder that we are all sinful and always in need of forgiveness and healing. But Jesus does not reject the Church because of our sinfulness. Rather, he acts continually

> to make her holy, purifying her in the bath of water by the power of the word, to present to himself a glorious church, holy and immaculate, without stain or wrinkle or anything of that sort (Eph 5:26-27).

We must cooperate with him in this work, purifying the Church by purifying ourselves.

A clear pastoral imperative flows from all this. Not only have we been redeemed by Christ, we are to *continue* Christ's redemptive mission in the world, individually and together with the other members of Christ's Church. This requires striving to be absolutely faithful, as he was, to the Father's will and to overcome evil primarily through redemptive suffering.

Jesus is the Truth. Jesus is also the way to the Father because he reveals to us his Father's *truth*. But this Son does more than just tell us about his Father; he *is* the Father's revelation to us.

> In times past, God spoke in fragmentary and varied ways to our fathers through the prophets; in this, the final age, he has spoken to us through his Son, whom he has made heir of all things and through whom he first created the universe. This Son is the reflection of the Father's glory, the exact representation of the Father's being . . . (Heb 1:1-3).

First of all, Jesus reveals the Father to us in his very being and life—that is, precisely in his humanity, which our senses can perceive and our minds can grasp. The opening words of the first epistle of John declare this truth and convey the wonderment Christians have always felt in contemplating it:

> This is what we proclaim to you:
> what was from the beginning,
> what we have heard,
> what we have seen with our eyes,
> what we have looked upon

and our hands have touched—
we speak of the word of life.
(This life became visible;
we have seen and bear witness to it,
and we proclaim to you the eternal life
that was present to the Father
and became visible to us) (1 John 1:1-2).

Above all in his death and resurrection Jesus reveals to us his Father's great love and his plan for the human family.

There is no greater love than this:
to lay down one's life for one's friends. . . .
I no longer speak of you as slaves,
for a slave does not know what his master is about.
Instead, I call you friends,
since I have made known to you all that I heard from my Father
(John 15:13, 15).

Jesus also reveals his Father to us through his teaching. He constantly taught his followers about his Father and what he expected of them. As we know from the Gospels, he taught in a very simple, down-to-earth way, especially in parables. So compelling was his personality that people were eager to hear what he had to say, even though he called them to a way of life not always to their liking. His miracles testified to the credibility of his words. "They were spellbound by his teaching," Luke tells us, "for his words had authority" (Luke 4:32).

Jesus' teaching mission did not end with his public ministry. He promised to send the Holy Spirit, who would instruct us in everything and remind us of all Jesus had told us while he was on earth (cf. John 14:26). As Paul said,

The Spirit we have received is not the world's spirit but God's Spirit,
helping us to recognize the gifts he has given us (1 Cor 2:12).

This teaching mission of Jesus is carried on through his Spirit *in the Church*. Jesus promised the Church special assistance so that his followers would never have to be in serious doubt or error concerning the essential elements of his teaching.

Learning more about the truth Jesus has revealed to us and growing in fidelity to that truth are essential to our relationship with him. That relationship is of questionable authenticity if we have little regard for what he has revealed to us—if we do not feel obligated to seek the truth and shape our lives by it. Furthermore, his doctrine is essentially self-revelation: Not to believe what he teaches is not to believe in him. Hence the importance of the Church's teaching mission and our duty to be faithful to what the Church teaches in his name.

Pope John Paul II emphasized the importance of truth when he spoke to the Mexican bishops in 1979 about their teaching role:

> As pastors, you have the vivid awareness that your principal duty is to be teachers of the truth. Not a human and rational truth, but the truth that comes from God, the truth that brings with it the authentic liberation of man: "you will know the truth, and the truth will make you free" (John 8:32).[4]

He then spoke about the truth concerning Jesus, the Church and its mission, and ourselves. Only if we know the truth about all three can we have a correct understanding of what we are about today, together with a clear vision of our destiny and the means of attaining it.

Jesus is the Life. Finally, Jesus is our way to the Father because in and through him we are restored to grace and grow in supernatural *life*. In and through Jesus we are "reborn" in the spiritual order—we become a new creation:

> [Y]ou must lay aside your former way of life and the old self which deteriorates through illusion and desire, and acquire a fresh, spiritual way of thinking. You must put on that new man created in God's image, whose justice and holiness are born of truth (Eph 4:22-24).

Jesus—and only he—is the source of spiritual regeneration.

Jesus breathes his divine life of grace into us through the sacraments. Yet today, even within the Church, some tend to downplay their importance. Why not encounter Jesus directly, they ask, instead of approaching him through sacraments? This sadly misses the point.

For one thing, Jesus instituted the sacraments for our benefit. He expects one who knows this and has access to the sacraments to take advantage of them. A person who accepts Jesus but at the same time rejects his precious gifts is not acting consistently.

The crucial thing about these gifts of the Lord is that, far from being alternatives to a direct encounter with Christ, they *are* our life-giving means of encountering him. It is Jesus who cleanses us and welcomes us into his Church in baptism. Similarly, it is Jesus who strengthens us in our apostolate in confirmation, Jesus who forgives our sins in penance—

---

[4] Pope John Paul II, Address to Mexican Bishops in Puebla de Los Angeles, Mexico, January 28, 1979. *Messages of John Paul II* (Daughters of St. Paul, 1979) p. 261.

Jesus who is present and active in each of these seven signs of his great love for us.

To grasp fully the significance of the sacraments it is necessary to see them from an incarnational perspective. Jesus redeemed us in a very *human* way. He became man; he suffered and died for us; after he rose from the dead, his disciples saw him and ate and talked with him—indeed, he even invited Thomas to place his hand in the wounds of the crucifixion in order to dispel his lingering doubts about the reality of what had happened on Easter Sunday.

Jesus has chosen, for our sakes, to remain present and active among us in a way equally suited to our human, bodily condition. Knowing how eager we are to see and tangibly experience whatever most affects our well-being, he gave us the sacraments, which are both signs and occasions of his saving presence and grace. In the sacraments, constituted by simple elements and familiar words, we truly encounter the Lord who shares with us his divine life and prepares us for the important moments of this life as well as the next. In celebrating the sacraments we experience a foretaste of the peace and joy of his kingdom which will be ours in their fullness when we are united with him in the next world.

Chapter 2

OUR RESPONSE IN FAITH TO JESUS

Having spoken of who Jesus is and of the significance of his presence in the world, I wish now to reflect more deeply on the personal response which he expects of us. And it must be a *personal* response. For we profess faith in a person, Jesus Christ, Son of Man and Lord of all creation. St. Paul says of him:

> Though he was in the form of God,
> he did not deem equality with God
> something to be grasped at.
>
> Rather, he emptied himself
> and took the form of a slave,
> being born in the likeness of men.
>
> He was known to be of human estate,
> and it was thus that he humbled himself,
> obediently accepting even death,
> death on a cross!
>
> Because of this,
> God highly exalted him

> and bestowed on him the name
> above every other name,

So that at Jesus' name
  every knee must bend
  in the heavens, on the earth,
  and under the earth,
  and every tongue proclaim
  to the glory of God the Father:
  JESUS CHRIST IS LORD! (Phil 2:6-11).

This Jesus is not a myth, an abstraction or a mere memory. He is alive and close to us—now, at this very moment. He is brother, he is lover, he is friend. He cares about us, about our well-being and needs, about our joys and sorrows. Like all those who love us, he expresses his love through concern and service and support.

But he also has more to give than the rest of our friends. He invites us to share, through the mystery we call grace, his own life—that unending, vibrant, glorified life he received from the Father. As St. John tells us:

> Yes, God so loved the world
> that he gave his only Son,
> that whoever believes in him may not die
> but may have eternal life (John 3:16).

Faith, then, is our response to the person of Jesus; it is a personal and individual response to his personal presence in us and in our world. Certainly faith has an intellectual content, truths we must hold and profess because they are part of God's self-revelation in Jesus. But in the end, to use the words of Thomas More in *A Man for All Seasons*, "It isn't a matter of reason. . . . Finally, it's a matter of love."[5] The only fitting response to love is love.

Unfortunately, some people feel that they attend adequately to their spiritual lives by participating in religious exercises in a more or less unreflective and perfunctory way. They have no sense of being personally challenged to surrender themselves completely to Jesus.

But unless we see at the center of Christianity a personal relationship with God through Christ and in the Holy Spirit, we risk reducing our religion to a philosophy of life, a set of principles, a code of conduct—all of which we can master and manipulate. Christianity does involve those things, but it is also infinitely more. Essentially, it is a personal, loving relationship with a living person, Jesus Christ.

---

[5] Robert Bolt, *A Man for All Seasons* (New York: Random House, 1962).

For this relationship to flourish and deepen, we must be open, attentive and ready to grow. I am so convinced of this personal dimension of Christianity that in 1977, in my last address as president to the National Conference of Catholic Bishops, I stated:

> The most important task of a bishop—and the supreme reason for which his leadership is sought in the Church—is to proclaim Christ Jesus and his Good News in such a way as to elicit a deep, personal commitment to him and acceptance of his message. Like St. Paul, "We must preach not ourselves, but Jesus Christ as Lord. . . . For God who commanded light to shine out of darkness, has shone in our hearts to give enlightenment concerning the knowledge of the glory of God, shining on the face of Jesus Christ" (2 Cor 4:5-6). This is the work of evangelization, which aims at conversion.[6]

I went on to explain how, as bishops, we should be evangelizers. I also pointed out that proclaiming Christ and his gospel is a responsibility of the entire Church, not just the bishops.

This talk elicited a greater response, from all parts of the country, than any other I gave as president of the bishops' conference. Why? Surely the Church has always known that its primary responsibility is to preach the Lord Jesus, to continue his saving presence in the world so that people will come to know and love him and enter into intimate relationships with him.

One reason for the extraordinary response, I believe, is this: We are emerging from the first, immediate phase of the intense renewal of the Church called for by Vatican Council II. During these years much time was spent developing new structures and new ways of doing things, so that the Church would be in a position to fulfill its mission more effectively. With this work nearing completion, many people now perceive more keenly than before that renewal's basic purpose is not structural change but better, more zealous proclamation of the Lord and his gospel. And that requires changing much more than structures; it requires changing minds and hearts.

I believe there is also another reason why the talk attracted attention. Our world is dominated by secular and material values. God is simply not the most important person in many people's lives. As a result, more and more people experience apathy and indifference, alienation and hostility toward the Church, even to the point of no longer practicing their religion and falling away from the faith.

---

[6] Joseph L. Bernardin, Address to the National Conference of Catholic Bishops, November 14, 1977.

At the same time, those who remain committed to the Church are more aware than ever of the need to make the Lord known to those who have turned away from him. They desire to show in a concrete and credible way that the Christian faith is as relevant as it ever was—that, without faith in the Lord, even the greatest of human accomplishments have little lasting value. And these committed Catholics realize that, as things now stand in the Church and the world, they cannot sit back and do nothing. While the grace of conversion and faith comes from God, *we* are the human instruments he uses to draw people to himself. Jesus' mandate to the apostles is meant for us, too: "Go into the whole world and proclaim the Good News to all creation" (Mark 16:15).

Our most urgent need, as individuals and as a community of believers, is total commitment to the Lord and all he has taught us. We must put him first in our lives and give priority over everything else to his message of salvation, as handed on by the Church. To do this we must abandon ourselves completely to him, placing ourselves in his hands and letting him make us instruments of his saving presence in the world. To put it simply, we must let go, so that there will be no obstacle in our lives separating us from the Lord.

This turning to Jesus is conversion. Initial conversion may be a sudden event, but thoroughgoing conversion—sanctity—is the work of a lifetime, a work to which we all are called. John the Baptist, who prepared the way for the appearance of Jesus, cried out to the people of his day: "Reform your lives! The reign of God is at hand" (Matt 3:2). St. Paul, after Jesus' appearance, told the Corinthians: "We implore you, in Christ's name: be reconciled to God!" (2 Cor 5:20). That call to conversion is as valid today as it ever was. "If we say, 'We are free of the guilt of sin,' we deceive ourselves; the truth is not to be found in us" (1 John 1:8). No matter who we are, no matter how much we think of ourselves, no matter how much God may have blessed us—we are sinners. We need conversion.

Conversion means turning away from the evil in our lives and more and more making our own the mind and heart of Jesus. It means transforming our lives into his so that he can live in us. Paul said it best, I think: "[T]he life I live now is not my own; Christ is living in me" (Gal 2:20).

Few, if any, of us are Christians of Paul's stature, but a real personal relationship with Jesus is nevertheless possible for us as it was for Paul. Jesus wants us to have such a relationship, and he can and will bring it about if we cooperate with him.

Such a relationship with Jesus is not reserved for mystics, nor is it exclusively the result of a highly emotional "experience" of Christ. It is true that in many cases the experience of conversion does seem to be very intense and emotional; but, even so, that ordinarily passes in time, and one is left with the everyday challenge—a welcome one—of maintaining and deepening the relationship which began with the conversion experience. This is not unlike the familiar process where, having met a person by whom one is deeply impressed, one goes about taking the continuing and often not very exciting steps required to build up and enrich the relationship over a period of time.

How then are we to establish, maintain and deepen a personal relationship with Jesus? There are two basic and indispensable ways: prayer and participation in the sacramental life of the Church. Union with the Lord through personal and liturgical prayer and the sacraments in turn releases within us a great force, which shapes not only our own spiritual growth but our relationships with others. Let us see more closely what this means.

Chapter 3

THE FOLLOWING OF CHRIST

We saw earlier that the sacraments are encounters with Jesus. Now let us probe more deeply how union with the Lord is strengthened and enriched through participation in the sacramental life of the Church. Then we shall consider prayer, for it, too, is essential to establishing and maintaining a relationship with God. Finally, I hope to show how prayer and the sacraments shape our behavior as Christians in the world.

The Eucharist and Penance

I shall focus here on the Eucharist and penance. These are the sacraments we celebrate regularly throughout life. How we use them makes a great difference, for better or worse, in how we relate to the Lord and also to one another.

Our encounter with Jesus in the Eucharist. Jesus is truly present—body, blood, soul and divinity—in the Eucharist, under the appearances of bread and wine. We cannot fathom this great mystery of faith, but the Church has always taken quite literally what Jesus said at the Last Supper:

> During the meal Jesus took bread, blessed it, broke it, and gave it to his disciples. "Take this and eat it," he said, "this is my body." Then he took a cup, gave thanks, and gave it to them. "All of you must drink from it," he said, "for this is my blood, the blood of the covenant, to be poured out in behalf of many for the forgiveness of sins" (Matt 26:26-28).

Earlier in his ministry Jesus had intimated to his disciples that he would give himself to them in the Eucharist. The miracle of the multiplication of the loaves and fish, recounted by all four evangelists, has traditionally been considered a sign not only of Jesus' power as God's Son and his compassion for the hungry people who had followed him, but also as a foreshadowing of something far greater—the Eucharist. Through the Eucharist, Jesus' redemptive act is continued through time in a way that makes it possible for us to participate in it.

The Eucharist is a dynamic reality. Jesus' presence in the Eucharist is active, not passive, capable of making a tremendous impact on our lives as individuals and as a community of believers.

A meal was an important occasion for the people of biblical times, as it is for us. In the Old Testament, the Passover, one of the most sacred events for the Jewish people, was celebrated each year by a religious rite which took the specific form of a family meal. This is natural: A meal shared with family or friends is a sign of human intimacy. To invite a person to one's table is a mark of trust, confidence and affection; to accept the invitation is to return these sentiments. Thus a meal shared in a religious context, such as the Passover meal, is a sign of the intimacy among the participants as well as their intimacy with God.

It was at a meal, the Last Supper, that Jesus gave his disciples his greatest gift—himself. In doing so, he expressed his great love for them and also for us. As part of his total redemptive act, completed on the cross the next day, the Last Supper had a sacrificial character: It was a forceful sign of his gift of self for our salvation. Moreover, by commanding the apostles and those who came after them to continue to celebrate this sacred meal until the end of time and by promising that whenever that was done he would be truly present under the appearances of bread and wine, Jesus perpetuated his saving presence among us, while also making the celebration of the Eucharist not only his action but the Church's.

The Eucharist both memorializes and truly reenacts the great mystery which is central to our salvation: Jesus' sacrificial death on the cross and his resurrection. Now, however, we share in Christ's action. Celebrating the Eucharist in union with Jesus, we worship the Father, giving him thanks for all he has done for us. We join in Jesus' offering and offer our lives in union with his. In this sacred meal we receive Jesus, the Bread of Life, who nourishes and sustains us spiritually. The Eucharist is moreover a sign of and an initial participation in the heavenly banquet where we will be in total communion with God—Father, Son and Holy Spirit.

Thus, we believe as Catholics that the Mass is at the same time and inseparably

> a sacrifice in which the Sacrifice of the Cross is perpetuated; a memorial of the death and resurrection of the Lord . . . ; [and] a sacred banquet in which, through the communion of the body and blood of the Lord, the people of God share the benefits of the paschal sacrifice,

renew the new Covenant which God has made with the human family once for all through the blood of Christ, and in faith and hope foreshadow and anticipate . . . the banquet in the Kingdom of the Father, proclaiming the Lord's death "till his coming."[7]

The Eucharist has still another dimension. No one can partake sincerely of the sacred banquet while remaining indifferent to his brothers and sisters. The Eucharist unites us in the love of Christ, and this is a love to be shared with others, a love that commits us to their devoted service.

In this way the Eucharist, properly understood and celebrated, is a source of social consciousness and of moral imperatives for the life of the Church as a whole and for each of its members individually. Not a purely private action, affecting only the individuals who directly participate in it, the Mass is instead a celebration of the entire Church, calling the faith community to foster the well-being of the human family by bringing Jesus' love, mercy, justice and compassion to bear upon its earthy pilgrimage. The Second Vatican Council expressed this with succinct eloquence in calling the Eucharist "a meal of brotherly solidarity."[8]

No wonder, then, that the Mass is at the very heart of Catholic life and worship! Nothing else so well expresses what we believe and are as baptized Christians, completely dedicated to the Lord. In celebrating the Eucharist, the Church experiences the presence of its risen Lord in a unique way and unites itself with him in his saving action. Truly the sacred liturgy, especially the eucharistic sacrifice, as the council told us, is the source and summit of the Church's worship, mission and life.[9]

For one who grasps this, participation in the Eucharistic Liturgy is no mere external ritual but an experience intimately related to conversion to the Lord and life with him. But let us be honest. We know that it is possible—even easy—for our participation in the Eucharist to be slack and indifferent.

This is so when, unresponsive to God's grace, we raise barriers to Jesus and refuse to reflect in our lives his goodness and truth, his love and mercy, his justice, his understanding and compassion. As Paul told the Philippians, our thoughts and our actions must always be "directed to all that is true, all that deserves respect, all that is honest, pure, admirable, decent, virtuous, or worthy of praise" (Phil 4:8). If it is otherwise with us, we may "go to Mass" but we remain unchanged.

---

[7] Instruction on Eucharistic Worship, 1967, no. 3; cf. also the "General Instruction" of the new *Sacramentary*, 1974, nos. 1–15.

[8] Constitution on the Sacred Liturgy *(Sacrosanctum concilium)*, *The Documents of Vatican II*, 1963.

[9] Ibid., no. 10.

Sometimes people say they have stopped going to Mass because they get little out of it; the Mass is not a "meaningful experience." Often they blame the Church and its liturgy. True, poorly planned and poorly celebrated liturgies can present obstacles. But in some cases the real obstacle lies elsewhere. Not failures by the Church and its representatives, but individual failure to live by gospel values may lie at the heart of the problem. Those whose lives are not faith-filled and whose priorities are not gospel-oriented will hardly be able to see and experience the Lord in the sacred rites.

One of my favorite gospel stories tells of the encounter of the risen Jesus with the two disciples on the road to Emmaus (cf. Luke 24:13-35). We all know it well. Traveling from Jerusalem, the disciples were reviewing the recent events. A stranger approached and asked them what they were talking about so animatedly. Their answer was slightly condescending: "Are you the only resident of Jerusalem who does not know the things that went on there these past few days?" The stranger simply asked, "What things?"

The two men then related all that had happened to their friend Jesus. They began with his trial, told of his crucifixion and death, and concluded with the report of the empty tomb. They seemed not to have been altogether persuaded on the latter point. Yes, witnesses had returned from the tomb saying they had seen angels there who told them Jesus was alive. And the tomb was certainly empty. But where was Jesus himself? Their keen disappointment was evident when they added, "We were hoping that he was the one who would set Israel free."

The stranger's response was surprising—and impatient. "What little sense you have! How slow you are to believe all that the prophets have announced! Did not the Messiah have to undergo all this so as to enter into his glory?" Then—now very patiently, as Luke tell us—"beginning . . . with Moses and all the prophets, he interpreted for them every passage of Scripture which referred to him."

By the time they reached Emmaus, the two disciples were so fascinated with the stranger that they begged him to stay and have supper with them. He agreed. Luke tells us that "when he had seated himself with them to eat, he took bread, pronounced the blessing, then broke the bread and began to distribute it to them. With that their eyes were opened and they recognized him; whereupon he vanished from their sight."

In an instant the two disciples changed radically. They came alive. "Were not our hearts burning inside us as he talked to us on the road and explained the Scriptures to us?" Hurrying back to Jerusalem, they enthusiastically told the apostles and all the others who were with them: "The Lord has been raised! It is true!" Never again would they doubt. Their beloved Jesus was alive. All their time and energy would go to proclaiming the risen Christ to the world. The work of evangelization had begun.

Whenever we celebrate the Eucharist, Jesus speaks to us in the Scriptures and he "breaks bread" and shares it with us. Do we see him with the eyes of faith? Do we recognize him and welcome him into our lives, so that, loving us, he can share with us the graces of redemption? The two disciples were slow to recognize him, but at last they did—in the breaking of the bread. Do we? Or do we fail even then to grasp his presence among us? While hearing his words and participating in the breaking of the bread, do we yet remain unchanged by Jesus' saving power because we do not wish to change? Does pride or an attachment to someone or something stand between us and the Lord, blinding us to his presence and preventing us from responding to his love?

May we open our hearts wide to Jesus in the Eucharist. May we not be afraid or hold back. In the powerlessness of the crucified Jesus we find our power as a redeemed people. In the triumph of the risen Christ we find our life and glory.

Our encounter with Jesus' forgiving and healing power. On the evening of the day that Jesus rose from the dead, the apostles gathered fearfully behind locked doors. Suddenly Jesus was with them. After bestowing his peace upon them and, just as the Father had sent him, sending them forth to continue his work, he breathed on them and said:

> Receive the Holy Spirit.
> If you forgive men's sins,
> they are forgiven them;
> if you hold them bound,
> they are held bound (John 20:22-23).

These words refer very directly to the sacramental ministry of reconciliation—that is, to penance.

Today this sacrament is in eclipse for many. Not that penance has lost its wonderful power, but fewer people feel the need for it. Any parish priest can confirm that the number of confessions has radically decreased in recent years.

This is unfortunate, even tragic. The need for reconciliation is as great now as it ever was. Perhaps the "sense of sin" has dimmed for many, but despite exaggerated statements one sometimes hears about the near impossibility of committing sin, deep down most of us know better. We know we are weak and sinful, and Scripture testifies to this.

> If we say, "We are free of the guilt of sin,"
> we deceive ourselves; the truth is not to be found in us.

But if we acknowledge our sins,
he who is just can be trusted
to forgive our sins
and cleanse us from every wrong.
If we say, "We have never sinned,"
we make him a liar
and his word finds no place in us (1 John 1:8-10).

Aware of our sinfulness, we instinctively feel the need to be forgiven. We crave to open up to someone, admit our shortcomings and then be told that we are loved and pardoned. Above all, we crave to hear this from the Lord. And that is what the sacrament of penance or reconciliation is all about. Here we encounter the Lord Jesus and experience his forgiving, healing love.

The new rite of penance encourages us to avoid a rote and unreflective use of the sacrament. Penance is much more than a mechanical recitation of sins. We must tell our faults, fully and honestly, but in doing so we should also probe more deeply, seeking the sinful attitudes and habits that underlie our sinful deeds and striving to uproot them. The Lord stands ready to help. Jesus offers himself to us not as a condemning judge but as a redeeming savior, eager to embrace us with his love and healing if only we ask.

Furthermore, by providing for communal penance services, the new rite helps us experience the social dimension of both our sinfulness and our forgiveness in the Church. Sin disrupts our relationship both with God and with our brothers and sisters. This point is crucial to grasping the connection between personal sin and the disorders and injustices of society.

Today, too, the sacrament's link with baptism and the Eucharist needs to be brought into clearer focus, while the integral relationship between repentance, penitential practices and an authentic Christian life also is emphasized. Relationships broken by sin must be restored; the sacrament of penance is therefore a necessary element of spiritual growth. We must approach the sacrament humbly and sincerely, acknowledging that we are sinners who, needing God's forgiveness, wish to repent, to change, to be converted. Perhaps most of all, we must have deep confidence in God's love, in his willingness to forgive and his power to heal and change us.

It would be a mistake to think of penance only as a kind of emergency remedy, a way of obtaining pardon for serious sins and no more than that. This sacrament is indispensable for *anyone* striving to make progress in the spiritual life. Its frequent reception can make a world of difference in how we relate to God, to others and even to ourselves.

That has surely been my experience. The sacrament of penance is an essential part of my spiritual life. As time passes, this becomes more and more clear to me. How alone, discouraged and even helpless I would feel at times if I did not approach Jesus in this sacrament; if I did not tell him of my personal faults and weaknesses along with my concerns, my hopes, my aspirations; if I did not receive from Jesus, through the priest-confessor, assurance of his forgiveness and his love—assurance that, if I try to do my part, he will always be at my side to help me. Approached in this spirit, penance provides a rich experience of Jesus' love and mercy and serves as a source of true joy and consolation.

The Role of Prayer in Christian Life

Like the Eucharist and penance, prayer also brings us into closer union with Jesus. In doing so, it helps us know ourselves better and relate more lovingly and intimately to others. In each of these aspects it can transform us.

Today there is much evidence of renewed interest in spirituality and prayer. Despite material and secular pressures, people are praying. Here we have a reaffirmation of a tradition that goes back to the beginnings of faith.

Jesus was a man of prayer. The Gospels tell us he prayed before all the important events in his life. Before beginning his public ministry, he went into the desert to fast and pray for 40 days. And what intense prayer he experienced in the garden of Gethsemane the night before making the supreme gift of himself to his Father on our behalf! Similarly, St. Paul speaks often in his letters of his own need for prayer and the need of those to whom he writes. "Never cease praying," he tells the Thessalonians, "render constant thanks; such is God's will for you in Christ Jesus" (1 Thess 5:17-18).

Christ's followers must be people of prayer. But it is important to know what prayer involves. What kind of prayer were Jesus and the apostles talking about? What should be prayer's effect on us?

The answers which follow, flowing from my own spiritual journey, are meant to be of help and encouragement to you in yours. I may not be able to shed much light on the dark areas you have encountered, but perhaps just knowing that you are not alone will encourage you to persevere.

These reflections, which specifically concern personal prayer, take for granted the centrality in Christian life of communal, liturgical prayer. Personal prayer and liturgical prayer are not competitors; they complement each other. Personal prayer is, among other things, a way of preparing for liturgical prayer, while liturgical prayer is, among other things, a source of inspiration and nourishment for personal prayer.

If I speak here mainly of personal prayer, that is because of the growing interest in the subject which I noted above, and because, alongside the interest, many people have genuine questions, even doubts, about their ability to undertake and continue this admittedly difficult but enormously important spiritual practice.

Prayer as discovery of self. Prayer can change our lives. Authentic prayer does not insulate us from the real world, nor is it a crutch on which to lean in order to avoid facing up realistically to life. Rather, prayer which brings us into intimate, loving union with God influences deeply and for the better, how we perceive and deal with others and with ourselves.

To pray effectively requires practice, engagement and regularity—the constant doing of it. Even someone whose faith is weak or sporadic can pray in a crisis; but as good as that may be it is much better that prayer be a regular, continuing part of our lives. Love can hardly grow and flourish without communication. And prayer is the dialogue of human and divine lovers. Thus the saints of every age have insisted, as Christ did, on the need to "pray constantly" so that the heart may know its beloved and the Lord may become as present to us as our very breathing.

But considering the typically overextended schedules which most of us struggle to maintain, how can we pray—and constantly—in season and out, when convenient and inconvenient? Too often we pray only when we feel like it and find it convenient. That is a formula for praying seldom. We must find time for prayer not in the rare lulls in our schedules, but despite our "busy-ness," alongside it, in its very midst.

No matter how little or how much we have, we will be moved to pray if we are truly in love with Jesus and yearn to be with him; if we long to hear him speak what we most need to hear: "Repent and believe the Good News. . . . Follow me. . . . Come aside and pray with me awhile. . . . As I have done, so also must you do to your brothers. . . . I am with you. . . ."

The absolute necessity of making time for prayer came home to me very forcefully a few years ago. My schedule was unbelievable. For several days in a row I was sure I simply did not have time to do more than celebrate Mass and pray a small part of the Liturgy of the Hours. Suddenly it dawned on me: "My life for many years to come will probably be as busy as it has been the past several days. Therefore, never again will I have the time to pray as I should." Immediately I saw the absurdity of the situation and determined to make prayer a real priority in my life. Doing so has required constant discipline but, happily, it has made a great difference in my life.

Spiritual writers tell us there are many kinds of prayer. All can be described as conversation or dialogue with God which begins in hearing, accepting and responding to his revelation. But this "conversation" can and does take various forms. The four classical forms of prayer are vocal (that is, prayer expressed in words, either a fixed formula or one's own words), meditative, affective and contemplative. The terms are somewhat strange and ponderous, but the experience to which they refer is direct and simple—as direct and simple as any exchange between two persons who love each other.

Today many people are rediscovering and using an ancient method called "centering prayer." This is really a form of contemplative prayer. One of its advantages is its simplicity, for the techniques involved make it accessible to everyone.

Centering prayer does not require keeping up a constant flow of words. Rather, with mind and heart open to any insight or manifestation of love the Lord may care to send, one simply acknowledges his presence and quietly enjoys it. Some call this "wasting time" with God, but the time is wasted only by worldly standards, which measure an investment of time by its tangible payoffs and rewards. In reality, this wasting of time in prayer nourishes and celebrates love. It demands "time out," timelessness, patience with one's whole life, patience to be with God.

Whatever method we use and however well or badly we use it, prayer, if it is genuine, must move us to a greater knowledge of ourselves. St. Teresa of Avila holds that one cannot grow closer to God without constantly growing in self-knowledge. Precisely for this reason, real growth in prayer involves a movement toward greater simplicity, that is, fewer words and thoughts. Both St. John of the Cross and Teresa say our own words and thoughts may lead us in the wrong direction; they may distract us from what God wants to show us about ourselves.

I hasten to add that prayer is not simply a process of introspection and self-analysis. Yet God cannot help us if we are unwilling to present ourselves to him as we are. Much of our time is spent pretending, trying to persuade others and even ourselves that we are someone other than we truly are. When we turn to God in prayer, however, we must present our real selves, candidly acknowledging our strengths and weaknesses and our total dependence on him. We should not be afraid to tell him all about our failings, our infidelities, our sins. To experience true conversion, we must first honestly face our innermost self which exists independently of external circumstances and pressures.

Let us consider some practical implications of self-knowledge. To know the truth about oneself in prayer includes honestly knowing one's motives. What do I want out of life? Why do I choose and act as I do? What guides me in my relationships with others? How important to me are acceptance and recognition? What roles do competition, fear, insecurity and resentment play in my life? Honest self-examination may lead us to conclude that, although our motives are not all "bad," they are frequently quite imperfect and, as such, can lead away from Jesus and his way of life.

In his letter to the Galatians, Paul describes forms of conduct arising from motivations which are of the Spirit, along with conduct arising from inclinations which are not. His description gives a good yardstick—that of external behavior—for judging our inner selves. It leaves no room for the notion that one can habitually do evil deeds yet be a good person at heart:

> It is obvious what proceeds from the flesh: lewd conduct, impurity, licentiousness, idolatry, sorcery, hostilities, bickering, jealousy, outbursts of rage, selfish rivalries, dissensions, factions, envy, drunkenness, orgies, and the like. . . . In contrast, the fruit of the spirit is love, joy, peace, patient endurance, kindness, generosity, faith, mildness and chastity. . . . Since we live by the spirit, let us follow the spirit's lead. Let us never be boastful, or challenging, or jealous toward one another (Gal 5:19-23, 25-26).

As we draw closer to God, that within us which is not of God is increasingly disclosed. But if we close our eyes to motivations or movements within us which are not of God, if we refuse to recognize the evil in us, that refusal itself becomes an obstacle to closer union with the Lord.

Often, of course, we are not fully conscious of what motivates us. We easily fool ourselves. That is why we need a spiritual director who, along with other vital, positive assistance rendered to us on our spiritual journey, can help us make objectively correct judgments about what is going on inside us.

Discovering our true selves can be a very painful experience. When we confront our ugly side, we tend at first to rebel. That is to be expected. But the suffering entailed in humbly acknowledging our own weakness and imperfection can itself be redemptive. We have been told to expect the Cross in our lives, and sometimes the Cross comes not from outside but from within. Did not Jesus say: "If a man wishes to come after me, he must deny his very self, take up his cross, and begin to follow in my footsteps" (Matt 16:24)? The letter to the Colossians goes further, saying that our suffering completes the process of purification required for our redemption: "In my own flesh I fill up what is lacking in the sufferings of Christ for the sake of his body, the church" (1:24).

Emotional satisfaction in prayer is not the necessary and exclusive sign that God loves us and is pleased with us. On the contrary, spiritual writers tell us that even for those who have committed themselves to prayer, the prevailing experience over long periods of time is not satisfaction but "dryness." In part this is our human reaction against the discipline of prayer; in part—and more significantly—it is God's way of teaching us to rely entirely on him.

That certainly has been my experience. I remember once complaining to my spiritual director about the dryness troubling me. He asked how often I experienced spiritual satisfaction in prayer. Without giving it much thought, I said about half the time, perhaps a bit more. He smiled and told me that, if so, I was quite advanced spiritually; most people, even those very committed to prayer, experience satisfaction in praying far, far less often than that! I realized, of course, that I had exaggerated. The point is that we are being spiritually selfish in supposing that because we have put in our "time," we have a right to expect a "return" in the form of satisfaction. Authentic prayer is concerned not so much with getting as with giving.

Despite the dryness, however, if we are people of faith and fidelity, we will feel a certain restlessness or hunger calling us to communion with the Lord in prayer. For God never abandons us—he is always present, calling us to him. And hunger for communion with the Lord in the midst of dryness is actually the *gift* by which God calls us to himself.

This gift implants in us the desire to grow spiritually, to abandon ourselves completely to the Lord, to risk encountering him in prayer. And "risk" it is, for a true encounter with God in prayer may well provoke a crisis in our lives. His demands can be overwhelming—embarrassing, even devastating, in human terms. We may find ourselves called to make a radical, painful response. We secretly fear that if we hold back nothing and do just what the Lord wants of us, we will stop being the charming, witty people we are (or think we are) and turn into really odd people—as though God might cast an evil spell on us! And all the while God calls us to trust enough in his love and his power to risk knowing ourselves and encountering him.

Prayer as discovery of others. As I have said, however, self-discovery in prayer is not a sort of self-regarding spiritual narcissism. Why, after all, do we wish to know ourselves better in this way? First, as I have suggested, in order to present ourselves more honestly and openly to the Lord. But also in order to recognize more clearly our obligations to others—family, friends, neighbors, fellow workers—all those with whom we live and work and come in contact in the course of our lives.

To say this is to say that the goal of self-discovery in prayer is a clearer grasp of and stronger commitment to one's personal vocation. What does God ask of me in the unique circumstances of my life? What practical implications does this have for my relationship with him and my efforts to serve my brothers and sisters in the Lord? Exploring personal vocation in the context of prayer necessarily involves a movement toward greater intimacy with others: with God first, of course, but also and in a particular way with other men and women.

The testimony of Scripture supports this view. Jesus made it very clear that love of God cannot be separated from love of neighbor.

The incarnation adds a new and special dimension to this inseparable link between love of God and love of neighbor. The Father so loved us that he sent his Son to redeem us. Jesus became flesh and lived among us. So close and intimate a relationship does the incarnation establish between us and God, and also among us human beings, that we can now call ourselves sons and daughters of the Father and brothers and sisters of and in the Lord. To follow the Lord, we must love all those whom he loves. There is no other way.

That is why, for example, racism so fundamentally contradicts our Christian faith. Racism rests on a denial of the essential equality of all human beings, based on our relationship to God as Creator and to Jesus Christ as Redeemer. One who refuses to accept the fundamental unity of the human race in its origin and destiny rejects, knowingly or unknowingly, the truth that God created us all and Christ died for us all. Racism is thus an attack on Christianity at its roots. So is any other attitude or behavior whose basic thrust toward others is discriminatory or exclusive. This is not the way of Jesus and the community of friendship with God which he founded.

Though we may often experience tension between love of God and love of others, we know that ultimately the two things cannot be separated. In his great parable of the Last Judgment Jesus makes this unmistakably clear:

> Then the just will ask him: "Lord, when did we see you hungry and feed you or see you thirsty and give you drink? When did we welcome you away from home or clothe you in your nakedness? When did we visit you when you were ill or in prison?" The king will answer them: "I assure you, as often as you did it for one of my least brothers, you did it for me" (Matt 25:37-40).

The implications of Christian intimacy. Our faith and everything that flows from it—including our prayer—must be understood in its incarnational perspective. That includes not only our new relationship to God as redeemed people but also our new relationship to all of God's children. Part of this relationship is the God-given capacity to love others.

Any consideration of love inevitably touches the area of sexuality. Unfortunately, many people understand sexuality in too limited a way, identifying it almost exclusively with sexual intercourse. While that is certainly a dimension of it, sexuality is a much broader concept. Human sexuality is part of our God-given natural power or capacity for relating to others in a loving, caring way. From it flow the qualities of sensitivity, warmth, openness and mutual respect in interpersonal relationships.

If God's love lives in us and we nurture it by prayer, it will be manifest in our ability to love others, to be present to them in a caring way. The intimacy of which I speak is not primarily genital, although love obviously can and should be expressed in this way by two persons joined in the covenant of marriage. Rather, for all people, married or single, this intimacy means at least two things.

First, it means willingness to disclose oneself to others, to become somewhat vulnerable with them by being honest about oneself. That is hard for many of us. We think we look weak when we reveal our weaknesses or needs—and pride or fear blocks our self-revelation. So we hold things inside while pressures build within us until, in some cases, we can no longer cope successfully with them.

In the sacrament of penance the Lord has given us a wonderful way of dealing with such pressures. Even humanly speaking, people need opportunities to open up, to get things out of their system. They need a way to be honest about their inner self—including the evil within—and then to hear the words, "I forgive you." I am not suggesting that the sacrament is primarily a form of therapy; its operation and benefits are essentially spiritual. But that in no way excludes the natural benefits which it also confers.

Admittedly, the forum of the confessional is special—both sacred and limited. Generally speaking, we do not reveal ourselves even to close friends as we do to our confessor, and that is as it should be. But many matters outside the realm of the confessional cause us confusion, anxiety, depression and other negative feelings. Such matters can and should be shared with those who are close to us. More often than not, we will find that our friends experience the same difficulties. That discovery itself deepens the mutually beneficial bond of solidarity and understanding.

Second, intimacy involves willingness to let others become a part of and an influence on my life even as I become part of theirs. This is an important element of commitment and fidelity. Not only do I accept responsibility for those whom I love, care for and try to help—I strengthen the bonds of responsibility by allowing them to love me, care for me and help me in return. My life and my decisions are no longer simply my own; having let others into my life, I cannot fail to take them into consideration.

Precisely this willingness to assume responsibility for others is often missing in our world today. We have all heard accounts of people who were injured, even killed, because bystanders did not want to "get involved." These may be extreme cases, but a similar refusal to get involved with others often manifests itself in failure to say a kind word, to extend a helping hand, to show some tangible sign of understanding and concern, even when the other person is a friend or associate.

Intimacy, as I have described it, obviously involves the risk of self-sacrifice. That should not be surprising. As we have seen, any intimate encounter—with God, with a fellow human being or with oneself—is dangerous, for it can demand radical changes of us. It can shake us from our lethargy and require us to make peace with God, our neighbor and even ourselves. To reach out and relate to others in a way that fosters well-being and growth in them and us requires courage and self-discipline. One risks being rejected or feeling foolish. But the fruits of authentic Christian intimacy are worth the risks.

Paul is a model of such intimacy. We know from his letters that he had close human relationships:

> Give my greetings to Prisca and Aquila; they were my fellow workers in the service of Christ Jesus and even risked their lives for the sake of mine. . . . Greetings to my beloved Epaenetus; he is the first offering that Asia made to Christ. My greetings to Mary, who has worked hard for you. . . . Greetings to Ampliatus, who is dear to me in the Lord; to Urbanus, our fellow worker in the service of Christ; and to my beloved Stachys . . . (Rom 16:3-6, 7-8).

But the prime model for Christian intimacy is Jesus. The Gospels speak of his close relationships with many men and women. He often risked his reputation and even his life for those he loved. Eventually, he gave his life to enter into the ultimate intimacy with us—the intimacy of the Redeemer who frees us from sin, the Mediator through whom we are reestablished in God's friendship and love.

Following Christ in Today's World

For each of us individually and for the entire human family, the incarnation of Jesus and the risen Lord's continued presence in the world have tremendous significance. As we have seen, the incarnation has established a new relationship not only between us and God but also among us human beings. Because he became flesh and redeemed us through his death and resurrection, the old order has passed away; now, as Paul told the Christian converts, we are a "new creation" (2 Cor 5:17).

Paul's language may seem poetic, but it has literal, practical meaning. Although I alluded earlier to the communitarian aspect of Christianity, I focused mainly on the individual dimension of Christian faith—how we are expected to shape our individual lives according to the gospel. Now I want to reflect on some of the implications of that new relationship with our neighbors. While outreach to others takes many forms, I shall highlight three: being "present" to friends and neighbors, helping the poor by promoting justice, and living as peacemakers. What I say is meant merely to illustrate how following the Lord Jesus leads one to become involved in these and other social issues.

Presence to others. In order to be "present" to others Jesus gave of himself; so must we. Many people today are suffering, have empty lives, search vainly for meaning. We find them all around us: They may include members of our families, our closest friends, people with whom we work. We see this emptiness and despair, for example, in a betrayed spouse; in a person whose zest for life has been eroded by serious illness or loneliness; in those who have lost control over their destiny because of drugs or drinking; in those whom life's difficulties and disappointments have made cynical or bitter; in those on the verge of despair because the material values in which they placed their trust have failed them.

As believers in the Lord Jesus, people intimately united with the Lord who have experienced his love, mercy and forgiveness, we can bring joy, consolation and hope to those who are suffering. We cannot remove all the pain and frustration which are part of the human condition. But we can help people cope better with their trials by encouraging them to see their sufferings in the light of the Transcendent, which assures them that a new and better life exists beyond this vale of tears, and to find meaning in their suffering here and now by identifying themselves with the sufferings of Christ (cf. Col 1:24).[10]

Something I said on another occasion to priests applies, I believe, to all Christians. Usually, what people need and want from us is much less difficult to discern and give than we tend to suppose. People do not expect solutions to all their problems or answers to all their questions. Often they know the answers already, or know that their problems have no immediate solutions. But more than anything else, people look to us—to you and to me—for our *presence* as loving, caring and forgiving persons. They want our help in their efforts to handle pain and frustration. They turn to us for understanding; they seek a sensitive and consoling response to their hurt feelings; they need the spiritual comfort we can bring them. They want someone who will pray with them, whose presence will remind them that, no matter what difficulties they face, God loves them, cares for them, will never abandon them. As faith-filled people who live in close union with Jesus and reflect his qualities in our lives, we can give them this assurance.

Our obligation to the poor. The Gospels depict Jesus' great sensitivity to the poor and oppressed. He was criticized for openly associating with them and acting as their advocate. Fidelity to his teaching and example demands that we show the same concern for the poor and suffering people of our day by promoting justice. In times of economic crisis, for example, we must not allow the heaviest burden of adjustments in social

---

[10] Cf. Pope John Paul II, *Apostolic Letter on the Christian Meaning of Human Suffering (Salvifici doloris)* February 11, 1984.

and fiscal policy to fall on those least able to help themselves. We must seek to have their voices heard and their needs considered in the arena of public policy.

This was the thrust of Pope John Paul's message to the American people in his homily at the Mass in Yankee Stadium in 1979:

> Social thinking and social practice inspired by the gospel must always be marked by a special sensitivity toward those who are most in distress, those who are extremely poor, those suffering from all the physical, mental and moral ills that afflict humanity, including hunger, neglect, unemployment and despair.

The Pope made it clear that such sensitivity (which the Latin American bishops have described as a "preferential option" for the poor) is a real obligation. It is a matter of justice and not simply of charity:

> The poor in the United States and of the world are your brothers and sisters in Christ. You must never be content to leave them just the crumbs from the feast. You must take of your substance, and not just of your abundance, in order to help them. And you must treat them like guests at your family table.[11]

The reality of poverty in the world at large and even in our wealthy United States is startling and scandalous. For its victims, poverty means ignorance, helplessness, fear, hunger, illness and even death. Poverty erodes human dignity by withholding the conditions which make it possible for people to live in dignity and self-respect. How those of us who do not suffer from this scourge respond to the poor is a test of our humanity and also of our Christianity.

There is a sense in which we need the poor in our lives. I do not mean this in an exploitative sense—not even the subtly exploitative "Lady Bountiful" sense which views the poor as fortunate beneficiaries of our largesse. I mean instead that we need the poor to challenge our complacency and selfishness, to force us to open our eyes and our hearts, which we might not otherwise do. Faced with the fact of poverty, we must acknowledge the sinful structures and systems which oppress people and set about correcting them. Faced with the poor themselves, we must cultivate a spirit of sharing, generosity, hospitality and service, and put it into action through appropriate, personal deeds.

---

[11] Pope John Paul II, "Open Wide the Doors for Christ," Homily for Mass in Yankee Stadium, New York, October 2, 1979, *U.S.A. The Message of Justice, Peace and Love* (Daughters of St. Paul, 1979).

The quest for peace. The gospels portray Jesus as a man of peace. Whenever he spoke of his kingdom, he made it clear that justice and peace were to be among its essential hallmarks. He wanted people to live together in harmony, working to build up the human family, not destroy it.

For nearly two millennia the message of the Prince of Peace has been preached to the world, yet seldom has the world enjoyed authentic peace. Today peace seems more elusive than ever. Instead of turning instruments of war into plowshares, as the Scriptures admonish us to do, nations are building not only more weapons but increasingly destructive ones.

What folly! Even as a method of deterrence, the arms race, especially the escalation of nuclear arms, is a treacherous way to preserve peace. As Pope John Paul II told the United Nations in 1979:

> The continual preparation for war, demonstrated by the production of ever more numerous, powerful and sophisticated weapons in various countries, shows that there is a desire to be ready for war, and being ready means being able to start it; it also means taking the risk that sometime, somewhere, somehow, someone can set in motion the terrible mechanism of general destruction.[12]

The Pope pleaded for a reduction in nuclear arms and their eventual elimination, a plea repeated by the bishops of the United States in their pastoral letter on war and peace.

In light of all this, there is a moral imperative for nations to do everything possible to prevent any use of nuclear weapons under any conditions. But why speak only of "nations"? As Christians and citizens, we are obliged to do all we can to create a climate conducive to ending the arms race and eliminating all nuclear weapons and other weapons of massive destructive force. No opportunity must be lost to take those steps, no matter how small, which will halt humankind's rush toward self-destruction.

It is true that nations have a right to defend themselves and that national leaders must be prudent in safeguarding their people's interests. But the interests of nations and peoples today require leaving no stone unturned in the search for peace. Let us reject the idea that the only, or the best, way to peace is through unremitting preparation for war. Let us seek urgently for alternatives to war as a means of resolving conflicts and injustices. Not to do so would be immoral negligence.

To speak of social issues may seem to have little to do with the theme of prayer and participation in the Church's sacramental life as bases for our relationship with Jesus. But there is a direct and necessary connection.

---

[12] Pope John Paul II, Address to the XXXIV General Assembly of the United Nations Organization, October 2, 1979, ibid.

As prayer and the sacraments are the foundation of our relationship with Jesus, so that relationship is—or should be—the ground and context for our lives, including our efforts to address and remedy the social evils of our times.

I have said of prayer—and could as well say of participation in the sacraments—that if it is authentic it leads, among other things, to a clearer understanding and more wholehearted acceptance of one's personal vocation, and so to greater knowledge of self and greater intimacy with others. Loving the Lord and living in communion with him have a profound effect on our personal growth and our relationships. While growth in sanctity—which comes about preeminently through prayer and the sacraments—is an interior phenomenon, it is inseparable from how we live and manifest love for others.

Paul describes the manifestation of Christian love in these words:

> Love is patient; love is kind. Love is not jealous, it does not put on airs, it is not snobbish. Love is never rude, it is not self-seeking, it is not prone to anger; neither does it brood over injuries. Love does not rejoice in what is wrong but rejoices with the truth. There is no limit to love's forbearance, to its trust, its hope, its power to endure. Love never fails (1 Cor 13:4-8).

True, love of this kind is oriented to heavenly fulfillment, but it also has the power to change the world. If we only tried to love consistently in this way, our families, our communities, our places of work and recreation and indeed all our enterprises would be well on the way to becoming models of Christ's love and peace, witnesses before the entire world of how people who accept Christ's lordship live together in mutual respect and love.

Perhaps this sounds like a simple, even simplistic, solution to the many complex problems of families, communities, nations and the world at large. I do not mean to be simplistic. Certainly the solutions required call for much thought, skill and hard work—they must be as complex and sophisticated as the problems. In the final analysis, however, sophistication, skill, hard work and the rest will accomplish very little to change the world or our lives—lastingly and for the better, at least—unless they are energized and directed by the power of love. And we best learn to love in prayer and the sacraments, by turning to love's model and source—Jesus, who is Love.

CONCLUSION

Jesus himself is the supreme model and best guide for living the Christian life. But we also need and seek other guides and models—men and women who, in their own times and places, responding to their own personal vocations, showed what it means to follow Christ. These men and women are the saints. Preeminent among them is Mary.

One cannot speak long about Jesus without speaking of his mother. It saddens me to hear, as I sometimes do, that mistaken notions of "renewal" have diminished her role in the lives of Christians. It is sad, too, to hear it said that this is somehow what Vatican Council II had in mind. Do people who say this really know what the council said about Mary? It spoke of her in its most important document, the Dogmatic Constitution on the Church, precisely in order to bring into sharper focus her role in the Church and, therefore, the ecclesial significance of devotion to her.

Only in the context of the incarnation, which expresses God's unbelievable love for us, can we really understand Mary's role and her greatness. It is right that we extol Mary and her many privileges, but not in isolation from the mystery of Christ and the Church. Unfortunately, the latter tendency sometimes existed in the past. The council sought to correct that by situating Marian doctrine and devotion very clearly in God's plan of salvation.

When this is done, we see more clearly Mary's place in relation to the central doctrines of the incarnation and redemption. Quite simply, her relationship to Jesus becomes much clearer, and we perceive how Mary's various titles or prerogatives illuminate the one fundamental truth of God in Christ. For example, her title of *theotokos* (the one who gives birth to God) is rightly understood and treated in relation to christology; the setting for the dogma of the Immaculate Conception becomes the doctrine of grace and redemption, of which it is an element; the title "Virgin" is seen from the viewpoint of a theology of covenant; and the dogma of the Assumption is viewed from the perspective of Christian eschatology, telling us not only of Mary's destiny but of ours. Mariological doctrine, like christological doctrine, is not abstract but is intensely related to Christian life.

Aside from the theological significance of Mary and her role in the plan of salvation, there is also a very important practical consideration bearing upon an authentic appreciation of and devotion to the Blessed Virgin: Mary has a great deal to say to us now in our contemporary setting, because she is an outstanding model for a Christ-centered spirituality.

It has been said that all spirituality, no matter what specific form it takes, is ultimately Marian. When I first heard that, I was somewhat startled. But upon reflection, it makes much sense. For what do we mean by spirituality? What is its basis? In the final analysis, all spirituality is rooted in the fundamental orientation of the individual and the community to the demands which the gospel makes—namely, that we hear and accept the Word and manifest the glory of the Word in our lives. Of all human persons, Mary has done this most perfectly; her spirituality is thus the model for the entire Church.

The incident in Luke's Gospel where Gabriel told Mary of God's plan for her bears this out. In response she asked: "How can this be since I do not know man?" I do not think this expresses doubt or hesitation, but only a reasonable human desire to understand. When she learned that she would conceive by the Holy Spirit, Mary had no more questions. "I am the servant of the Lord," she said. "Let it be done to me as you say" (Luke 1:34, 38). Because Mary heard God's word and responded to it, the Word became incarnate in her.

Shortly afterwards, she hastened to visit her cousin Elizabeth, who had also conceived a child in extraordinary circumstances. On that occasion Mary sang her song of praise in which she testified to the power of God's Word in her:

> My being proclaims the greatness of the Lord,
>   my spirit finds joy in God my savior,
> For he has looked upon his servant in her lowliness;
>   all ages to come shall call me blessed (Luke 1:46-48).

Mary truly heard the Word, allowed it to become incarnate in her and witnessed to its glory and power in her life. That is why she is the model for our own relationship with the Word. Like Mary, we must see the Word not as something external to us but as the most profound mystery in our lives. Like Mary, too, we must cherish this mystery within us as a precious gift which God gives us not only for our own personal well-being but for that of the entire human family.

I encourage you to read and prayerfully reflect on the late Pope Paul VI's Apostolic Exhortation on Marian Devotion. In this wonderful document the Holy Father explained why Mary's example is so relevant to the contemporary Church:

> The Virgin Mary has always been proposed to the faithful by the Church as an example to be imitated, not precisely in the type of life she led, and much less for the socio-cultural background in which she lived and which today scarcely exists anywhere. She is held up as an example to the faithful rather for the way in which, in her own particular life, she fully and responsibly accepted the will of God, because she heard the word of God and acted on it, and because charity and a spirit of service were the driving force of her actions. She is worthy of imitation because she was the first and most perfect of Christ's disciples.[13]

[13] Pope Paul VI, Apostolic Exhortation on Marian Devotion *(Marialis cultus)* February 2, 1974.

Mary is a wonderful model and a source of inspiration for us as we seek to meet the challenges of today's Church and society. She did not run away from life and its demands. She accepted life freely and eagerly. She stood up, declared herself and made decisions. Never in the history of the human family has there been a freer, more responsible and more far-reaching decision than Mary's acceptance of the invitation to be the Mother of the Savior.

So we can truly say, as Pope Paul VI did, that Mary was a perfect Christian whose example can give direction, strength and inspiration to our efforts to respond to the Lord's call. Indeed, I believe it is correct to say that Mary's true greatness rests not so much on the privileges and honors which were bestowed on her in virtue of her special calling—and which we have no reason to expect for ourselves—as on her own free, generous and unreserved acceptance of God's will—which we have at least some capacity for emulating.

Our Catholic tradition has always given a prominent place to Mary. From the very beginning, we have taken to heart that wonderful woman who gave her flesh to our Savior and who, together with her husband Joseph, nurtured and cared for him during his early years. There is no doubt that she loved her son intensely and that he loved her. To be close to Jesus we must have a special place in our hearts for her. There is no other way.

Earlier I spoke of the significance of the incarnation in its implications for us personally. In the intimate relationship between Mary and Jesus we see better than any other the communion of the divine and the human. No relationship this side of heaven tells us as much about God's love and tenderness toward the human family. And it is the model of our own intimacy with the Lord!

The Fondness of God

Father Edward Farrell, a well-known spiritual writer, begins one of his books with a touching story. A priest visiting Ireland some years ago was walking one evening along a country road near the place where he was staying. He met an old man who also was out for an evening stroll. They walked and talked together until a sudden shower caused them to take shelter nearby. As they waited for the rain to stop, they continued chatting for a while, but finally they ran out of conversation. The old Irishman took out his little prayerbook and began to pray, half aloud. The priest watched him for a long time. Then quietly he said, "You must be very close to God." The old man simply smiled and, without embarrassment or self-consciousness, answered, "Yes, he is very fond of me." That reply became the title of Father Farrell's book: *The Father Is Very Fond of Me.*[14]

Indeed, the Father is very fond of us all—so fond that he could not bear for us to be separated from him. He therefore sent his Son to redeem us. Through his death and resurrection, Jesus offers us a new kind of life, radically different from the life of unredeemed humanity. As Paul told the Corinthians:

> [Christ] died for all so that those who live might live no longer for themselves, but for him who for their sakes died and was raised up. . . . If anyone is in Christ, he is a new creation. The old order has passed away; now all is new! (2 Cor 5:15, 17).

In this pastoral reflection I have tried to say what this new life means to us in practice, what actually happens to us when we accept Jesus in faith and turn over our lives to him. As I conclude, I wish to do three things.

First, I want to profess my faith in the Lord Jesus and all that he has taught us. I believe in the Lord, and I wish to love him with all my mind and heart and soul. The great desire of my life—one which becomes stronger as I grow older—is to be intimately united with him so that I can experience in the very depth of my being his great love for me, so that his life will be mine.

I understand, of course, that this will not happen without effort on my part. I must avoid those things which separate me from the Lord. When I sin, I must repent and seek forgiveness. I must always follow the Lord's example, trying each day to shape my life and ministry according to his. I must constantly seek to grow spiritually, to develop an ever greater intimacy with him through personal prayer, through participation in the Church's sacramental life and through my ministry—especially to the poor and forgotten people of the world. I must work tirelessly to proclaim Jesus and his gospel to the entire human family.

I know very well that, because of human weakness, I do not always measure up to what is expected of me. As I said in the beginning of this pastoral letter, my failures cause me pain and frustration. Still, like Paul, I do not despair or give up, for I know the Lord loves me and will never abandon me. He will make his strength mine if I let him. I take this occasion to reaffirm my faith and my determination to place myself totally in the hands of the Lord.

Second, I wish to affirm and encourage you as you search for the Lord and seek to grow in intimacy with him. Do you ever feel misunderstood,

---

[14] Cf. Edward Farrell, *The Father Is Very Fond of Me* (Foreword), (Denville, N.J.: Dimension Books, 1975).

lonely, discouraged, wounded, abandoned? So did he, and there is meaning in our painful experiences when we understand and accept them as a way of sharing in his sufferings. More than that, in our moments of pain we can and should turn to him as a friend. What other friend has won for us victory over death itself? He is very close to us, only waiting for us to turn and place ourselves in his hands so that he can help us.

Mark's Gospel tells of a man whom Jesus cured of leprosy. The leper put himself at Jesus' mercy and asked to be cured. Mark tells us: "Moved with pity, Jesus stretched out his hand, touched him, and said, 'I do will it. Be cured'" (Mark 1:41).

You and I are like that leper. We are spiritually ill, and we need to be healed. Often we are reluctant—even afraid—to approach Jesus. Will he understand? We have sinned so often—will he believe the sincerity of our repentance now? I urge you to put aside such embarrassment and anxiety. Place yourself at his mercy and he will take pity on you, touch you, heal you. He will shower on you his love and understanding. He will pierce through the dark cloud hanging over you, so that, seeing the radiance of his glory and saving power, you can take heart.

Finally, I ask you to join me in prayer for all those who are not close to the Lord, the many people who desperately need to experience his love but who, for whatever reason, have not sought his mercy. They are all around us: perhaps a spouse or child, another relative or a friend, a neighbor or fellow worker. Pray that they will have the courage to reach out to Jesus and experience his healing power. And to our prayer let us join personal gestures of love and concern, since often it is through us that Jesus wishes to reveal himself to others, using us as instruments to mediate his saving graces.

Together we are called to do the work of the Lord. May the love, joy, peace and hope which are the fruits of fidelity to Jesus be with us always. I make Paul's prayer for the Ephesians my own prayer for you:

> I pray that [the Father] will bestow on you gifts in keeping with the riches of his glory. May he strengthen you inwardly through the working of his Spirit. May Christ dwell in your hearts through faith, and may charity be the root and foundation of your life. Thus you will be able to grasp fully, with all the holy ones, the breadth and length and height and depth of Christ's love, and experience this love which surpasses all knowledge, so that you may attain to the fullness of God himself (Eph 3:16-19).

Your brother in Christ,

Joseph Cardinal Bernardin
Archbishop of Chicago

Appendix

THE DEVELOPMENT OF CHRISTOLOGY TODAY

Theologians today are actively discussing a number of christological questions. In itself, this is healthy. But publicity and popular writing sometimes leave the impression that our basic understanding of Jesus and his mission is changing radically, that the creeds which have been such an important part of our lives no longer mean what we thought they meant. This, of course, is not so.

What, then, are the theologians doing? What is the purpose of their research and writing? What is their relationship to the Church's magisterium and the bishops?

Bishops and Theologians: A Creative Tension

Let me begin with the last question first. The bishop bears the responsibility for presenting the teachings and the person of Christ to the People of God in his own diocese and to the world at large. In part, this implies ensuring that the contents of revelation remain undistorted by any human error. Together with the Holy Father and all the bishops, he has final authority over what is presented as the teaching of the Church.

Another aspect of the bishop's role as a teacher is to cultivate an ever-increasing understanding of divine revelation. For this reason the bishop must encourage and promote further study and deeper penetration of God's word to us as well as better formulations of God's truth in the context of contemporary social and intellectual realities. In other words, while the bishop's responsibility is to see that the basic content of the revelation remains constant, he must also see that it is pertinent and meaningful to his people.[15]

The bishop carries out his responsibility to further penetrate the meaning of revelation primarily through promoting study and reflection by theologians. They look to the past, they look to present realities, they look to future possibilities in order to provide a deeper understanding of what God is saying to us. In the vast region of God's message to us, they are the explorers.

Because their work implies searching, they must have a certain amount of freedom. At the same time, we must expect that their searches will not always be successful, that there are going to be some mistakes. In

[15] Cf. Dogmatic Constitution on the Church, no. 25, and Decree on the Bishops' Pastoral Office in the Church, nos. 11–13, in *The Documents of Vatican II* (1966).

conducting these explorations, however, the theologian provides a great and necessary service to the Church. The theologian keeps the Church intellectually alive, in touch with the realities of the world in which it exists, as well as in touch with its own roots and basic realities.

Insofar as theologians are dealing with revealed truth, they are subject to the judgment and the teaching of the Church's bishops. What this means, in essence, is that there must be collaboration, cooperation and support among theologians and bishops. There is a necessary creative tension built into this relationship, and through it the Church continues to grow in her witness to Christ.

Developments in Biblical Studies

To explain what contemporary theologians are doing and what the purpose of their research is, it is first necessary to understand that the way in which we study the Bible has undergone significant developments in recent decades.

After the Council of Trent, Catholic biblical studies were primarily apologetic in character—that is, focused on defending the biblical origin of Catholic dogma. From the middle of the last century, however, biblical scholars have developed more learned and scientific approaches to the Scriptures. For the most part, the purpose of these new methods of interpretation has been to grasp the meaning of biblical texts in light of their literary, historical, and canonical contexts. Of special importance for this task has been the discovery of the function of various literary forms or genres in ancient Jewish and Christian literature.

Although the Church was understandably hesitant about new methods of interpreting the sacred texts of Scripture, Pope Leo XIII and Pope Benedict XV wrote encyclicals encouraging biblical studies and providing guidelines for scholars.[16] The Pontifical Biblical Commission was established in 1902 to oversee these developments. In 1943 Pope Pius XII, in his encyclical *Divino afflante Spiritu*, gave a major impetus to scientific biblical studies, initiating a new era in Catholic exegesis.

Another important development took place in 1964 when the Pontifical Biblical Commission issued an *Instruction on the Historical Truth of the Gospels*.[17] It counseled Catholic biblical scholars to use the historical-critical method as well as form criticism with circumspection in order to gain a fuller understanding of the Gospels.

---

[16] Leo XIII, *Providentissimus Deus* (1893), and Benedict XV, *Spiritus Paraclitus* (1920).

[17] *Catholic Biblical Quarterly* 26 (1964) 305–12.

In 1965 the Second Vatican Council promulgated its Constitution on Divine Revelation. This document made two important points which provide a framework for the work of Catholic biblical scholars. First, the council reaffirmed what Pius XII had said in *Divino afflante Spiritu* about the importance of distinguishing literary forms as a way of determining the intention of the human author of a biblical text: "[T]he interpreter of Sacred Scripture, in order to see clearly what God wanted to communicate to us, should carefully investigate what meaning the sacred writers really intended, and what God wanted to manifest by means of their words. Those who search out the intention of the sacred writers must, among other things, have regard for 'literary forms.' For truth is proposed and expressed in a variety of ways, depending on whether a text is history of one kind or another, or whether its form is that of prophecy, poetry, or some other type of speech."[18]

The other point made by the council was that the responsibility for the final judgment about how Scripture should be interpreted rests with the official teaching authority of the Church. "The task of authentically interpreting the Word of God, whether written or handed on," the Constitution on Divine Revelation stated, "has been entrusted exclusively to the living teaching office of the Church, where authority is exercised in the name of Jesus Christ. This teaching office is not above the Word of God, but serves it, teaching only what has been handed on, listening to it devoutly, guarding it scrupulously, and explaining it faithfully by divine commission and with the help of the Holy Spirit; it draws from this one deposit of faith everything which it presents for belief as divinely revealed."[19]

It is within the framework of these norms that biblical scholars and theologians are to probe anew the mystery of Christ, not in order to change what we believe about Jesus but to enrich our understanding and belief. They are studying the revelation about Jesus in the Scriptures and his universal significance for the human family.

Questions in Contemporary Christology

This brings us back to the question posed earlier: What is the meaning of contemporary biblical and theological study about Christ? This can best be answered by focusing on six questions in contemporary christology.

1. The meaning of the "historical" Jesus. Using all available biblical methods, it is important that we find out all we can about the "historical" Jesus, the God-man who lived and died in a concrete geographical, cul-

---

[18] Constitution on Divine Revelation, no. 12, in *The Documents of Vatican II* (1966).
[19] Ibid., no. 10.

tural, religious, and historical setting. The primary goal of this research, however, is to discover the *meaning* of Jesus for humanity.

The Scriptures situate the life and mission of Jesus in the larger context of God's plan of salvation. The evangelists are less concerned about providing *historical details* about his life than presenting, under divine inspiration, a *theological understanding* of his ministry, death and resurrection. As the International Theological Commission stated:

> The New Testament does not intend to convey mere historical information concerning Jesus. It seeks above all to hand down the witness which ecclesial faith bears concerning Jesus and to present him in the fulness of his significance as "Christ" (Messiah) and as "Lord" (Kyrios, God). This witness is an expression of faith, and seeks to elicit faith. A "biography" of Jesus in the modern sense of this word cannot be produced, if it were taken to entail a precise and detailed account.[20]

It would be wrong to suppose that research is needed to discover the "real" Jesus as though we had not known him up to now. Rather, as the Theological Commission says, there is a "substantive and radical unity" between the historical Jesus and the Christ of faith, a unity which "pertains to the very essence of the Gospel message."[21] The Jesus of history is also the Jesus whom we know in our creeds and celebrate in our liturgy. Historical research on Jesus, understood correctly, does not undermine christological dogma but deepens our knowledge of Jesus and enhances our acceptance of him in faith.

2. Restating christological truths. Another aim of the current renewal in christology is to address difficulties which dogmatic statements of the early councils can present for people today because of their language or the philosophical concepts they employ. Not only do the dogmatic statements themselves pose such a difficulty, so does subsequent theology which was itself aimed at a better understanding of the dogmatic statements and their implications.

During the first several centuries of the Church, there were a number of serious christological controversies. Basically, they arose from the effort to explain how Jesus could be both fully divine and fully human, with the exception of sin. Some explanations were heretical because they ended by denying Christ's divinity (for example, Arianism). At other times the error lay in undermining or denying the full humanity of Jesus (for example, Gnosticism and Docetism).

---

[20] International Theological Commission, *Select Questions on Christology* (USCC Publications, 1980) 2.

[21] Ibid., 3.

Several ecumenical councils dealt with these controversies. In dialogue with one another, they reshaped christological terms and definitions. The Council of Nicaea (A.D. 325) affirmed Christ's divinity by defining that the Son is consubstantial *(homoousios)* with the Father. The Council of Ephesus (A.D. 431) affirmed the real unity of the divine and human natures in the person of Christ. The Council of Chalcedon (A.D. 451), in an effort to uphold Jesus' humanity, considered how both the divine and human natures can be united in one person. It stated that the two natures exist within the person of Christ:

> Following therefore the holy Fathers, we unanimously teach and confess one and the same Son, our Lord Jesus Christ, the same perfect in divinity and perfect in humanity, the same truly God and truly man composed of rational soul and body, the same one in being *(homoousios)* with the Father as to divinity and one in being with us as to humanity, like unto us in all things but sin. . . . The same was begotten from the Father before the ages as to the divinity and in the latter days for us and for our salvation was born as to his humanity from Mary the Virgin Mother of God.
>
> We confess that one and the same Lord Jesus Christ, the only-begotten son, must be acknowledged in two natures, without confusion or change, without division or separation. The distinction between the natures was never abolished by their union but rather the character proper to each of the two natures was preserved as they came together in one person *(prosopon)* and one hypostasis. He is not split or divided into two persons but he is one and the same only-begotten, God the Word, the Lord Jesus Christ, as formerly the prophets and later Jesus Christ himself have taught us about him and as has been handed down to us by the Symbol of the Fathers.[22]

Several other important christological councils followed Chalcedon. While firmly rooted in the teaching of the Fathers of the Church and the Councils of Nicaea, Constantinople, Ephesus and Chalcedon, they clarified a number of questions which had arisen. In doing so, they further enriched the Church's understanding of Christ and his meaning for the human family. The Third Council of Constantinople (A.D. 681), in particular, gave a "better perception of the place occupied in the salvation of mankind by the humanity of Christ, and by the various 'mysteries' of his life on earth, such as his baptism, his temptations and the 'agony' of Gethsemani."[23]

---

[22] Quoted in Richard P. McBrien, *Catholicism* (Minneapolis: Winston Press, 1981) 456.

[23] International Theological Commission, 8.

Contemporary difficulties with the dogmatic statements of these councils do not concern the *truth* they convey, which can never change, but some of the philosophical terms and concepts they use. For example, words such as *substance, nature* and *person* are not generally understood by people today in the same sense in which they were used by the early council fathers. Theologians are, therefore, attempting to restate the christological truths in language and concepts which are understood and accepted today. The main concern is "to show how the dogma 'true God and true man in one person' was to be understood in faith today, and how it could be interpreted and adapted with the aid of modern philosophical methods and categories."[24]

This is laudable. The International Theological Commission states: "As history takes its course, and cultural changes occur, the teachings of the Council of Chalcedon and Constantinople III must always be actualized in the consciousness and preaching of the Church, under the guidance of the Holy Spirit." This, it adds, is "an obligation binding both upon the theologians and upon the apostolic solicitude of shepherds and faithful."[25] But great care must be taken to ensure that the essential truth contained in the dogmatic formulations is not changed. Therefore, both biblical scholars and theologians must be sensitive to the teaching authority of the Church, which was instituted by Christ and is assisted by his Spirit in its work of ensuring fidelity to revelation.

3. Jesus and his mission. In the past, christology has sometimes focused more on the person of Christ than on his mission (soteriology). As a result, Jesus' person and his work tended to be separated in people's minds.[26] One aim of modern christology, therefore, is to examine more deeply Christ's mission and his ministry. This will enrich our understanding of Christ and his meaning for us.

The International Theological Commission has expressed support for this effort to bring about a better synthesis of the person of Jesus and his work of redemption. "Some theological speculations," it said, "have failed to adequately preserve this intimate connection between christology

---

[24] W. Kasper, *Jesus the Christ* (New York: Paulist Press, 1976) 17.

[25] International Theological Commission, 11.

[26] Father Gerald O'Collins, s.j., states: "Too often Christology simply lapsed into a mass of abstract and cliche burdened teachings about the divine-human constitution of Christ. It simply slipped out of view that not just 'Saviour' but all the other titles used of Jesus in the New Testament express aspirations for salvation. It was likewise forgotten that behind the Christological statements of the early Church we find soteriological themes." *What Are They Saying about Jesus?* (New York: Paulist Press, 1977) 11.

and soteriology. Today, it is always imperative to seek ways to better express the reciprocity of these two aspects of the saving event which is itself undivided."[27]

4. Christ's preexistence. As the earthly life of Jesus has been examined rather closely in modern christological research, this has led to a reexamination of his preexistence (the person who becomes human as Jesus Christ was always in existence beforehand) and the role that reality plays in the New Testament and early Church Fathers.

The International Theological Commission has also addressed this issue. After referring to Jesus' resurrection, the commission states, "In the light of this exaltation the origin of Jesus Christ is openly and definitively understood: sitting at the right hand of God in his post-existence (that is, after his earthly life) implies his pre-existence with God from the beginning before he came into the world."[28]

The same report goes on to say, "Jesus Christ's origin from the Father is not a conclusion of subsequent reflection but is made clear by his words and the facts about him, namely that Jesus took it for certain that he had been sent by the Father."[29] Later the commission acknowledges that "the concept of the pre-existence of Jesus Christ has acquired greater clarity as Christological reflection has evolved."[30]

5. Searching for a compassionate God. Closer attention to the Scriptures and especially to the doctrine of the Cross has led us more deeply into another mystery of our faith. The Scriptures often speak of God's "suffering" or of his "compassion." In the New Testament we encounter a Jesus who weeps, who gets angry and who feels sadness. How are these expressions to be understood in the light of doctrine about God's immutability (his unchangeableness) and his impassibility (being beyond the reach of suffering)?

The International Theological Commission has stated that affirming God's impassibility "is not to be understood as though God remained indifferent to human events. God loves us with the love of friendship, and he wishes to be loved by us in return. When this love is offended, sacred Scripture speaks of suffering on the part of God. On the other hand, it speaks of his joy when the sinner is converted." It goes on to say, "there is undoubtedly something worth retaining in the expressions of Holy Scrip-

---

[27] International Theological Commission, 12.

[28] International Theological Commission, *Theology, Christology, Anthropology* (USCC Publications, 1983) 14.

[29] Ibid.

[30] Ibid., 16.

ture and the Fathers, as well as in some recent theologies, even though they require clarification."[31] This fits in well with our contemporary desire and search for a God who is all-powerful but also compassionate towards us in our sufferings, a God who in some way suffers with us.[32]

6. Jesus' knowledge. A number of themes and issues in contemporary christology come together in discussion of a question which has received a good deal of recent scholarly and popular attention: the question of Jesus' knowledge. There are several dimensions to this question. One relates to his knowledge of the ordinary affairs of life: his knowledge of religious matters (for example, of the Scriptures and contemporary religious concepts) and his knowledge of the future (for example, of his passion, death and resurrection, the destruction of Jerusalem, the parousia or Second Coming). The other dimension, in a sense more sensitive and important, is Jesus' awareness or consciousness of himself as Messiah, Son of God, and of his salvific mission.

Our questions about Jesus' human knowledge and human consciousness of his unique relationship to the Father stem from the fact that he is truly man as well as God. In his humanity, he was like us in everything except sin. As the letter to the Hebrews states: "[T]herefore he had to become like his brothers in every way that he might be a merciful and faithful high priest before God on their behalf, to expiate the sins of the people. Since he was himself tested through what he suffered, he is able to help those who are tempted" (2:17-18).

That being the case, how could he have had knowledge of all things from the very beginning of his earthly existence? In what sense are we to understand Luke's statement that, after his parents found him in the Temple, "Jesus, for his part, progressed steadily in wisdom and age and grace before God and men" (Luke 2:52)? Does this imply that, initially at least, he lacked full knowledge of all things, including his unique relationship to the Father and his salvific mission? If so, how do we explain that limitation, since, in the one person of Christ, his human nature is united with his divine nature (the hypostatic union)?

If, in trying to resolve this problem, unlimited knowledge is attributed to Jesus (because of his superlative gifts and mission), one might fail to respect the truth of Jesus' real share in our limited humanness. But, by going too far in the other direction and denying all special knowledge in

---

[31] Ibid., 19–20.

[32] Cf. John Paul II in his apostolic letter *Salvifici doloris*, no. 16: "In his messianic activity in the midst of Israel, Christ drew increasingly closer to the world of human suffering . . . above all . . . through the fact of having taken this suffering upon his very self."

Jesus, one might fail to respect the exigencies of his mission and the reality of his gifts as a prophet.

For many centuries the Church has held that Jesus had unlimited knowledge. In order to explain how Jesus, even in his humanity, had unlimited knowledge, the theologians of the Middle Ages attributed to him different types of extraordinary knowledge including *beatific knowledge* (in his immediate vision of the Word the human soul of Jesus knew all that God knows and knew it in the same way in which God knows it) and *infused knowledge* (Jesus' intellect was gifted with special knowledge from God similar to the knowledge traditionally attributed to angels).

In this century there have been several official Church pronouncements concerning Christ's knowledge. In 1918, for example, the Holy Office declared as "unsafe" for teaching in Catholic seminaries and universities the opinion that Christ may not have had the beatific vision during his lifetime, that he would not have known "from the beginning . . . everything, past, present and future, that is to say, everything which God knows with the knowledge of vision."[33]

In 1943 Pope Pius XII declared in his encyclical on The Church as the Mystical Body of Christ *(Mystici corporis)* that Jesus enjoyed the beatific vision "from the time he was received into the womb of the Mother of God." Consequently, "the loving knowledge with which the divine Redeemer has pursued us from the first moment of his Incarnation is such as completely to surpass all the searchings of the human mind."[34]

With the new era in biblical studies initiated by Pius XII in 1943, Catholic scholars have made an intense effort to come to a better knowledge of the historical Christ. Understandably, this effort has focused attention again on the question of Christ's human knowledge. The International Theological Commission has supported this. "Theologians," it said, "must also devote their full attention to perennially difficult questions: for example, the questions relative to the consciousness and knowledge of Christ. . . ."[35] More recently, the commission has indicated a hope to bring this issue to a satisfactory conclusion.[36]

From what has been described above, it should be clear that the theological endeavors of orthodox and responsible scholars about christological questions are not intended to downplay or deny either Jesus' divinity or his humanity. Rather, the precise intent of scientific scriptural interpretation and theological reflection is to probe and ground the revealed truth

---

[33] Denziger-Schonmetzer, *Enchiridion,* ed. XXXVI, pp. 3645, 3646.

[34] Pope Pius XII, *Mystici corporis;* Denzinger-Schonmetzer, p. 3812.

[35] International Theological Commission (1980) 11.

[36] International Theological Commission (1983) 13.

believed and taught by the Church: that in the one person Jesus Christ the divine and human natures are united without confusion or division.

These efforts by scholars are not infallible; they can be one-sided and they can be mistaken. But they are aimed at helping us understand better the mystery of Christ, the God-man. Ultimately, of course, to be sure that efforts to understand the mystery of Jesus do not deviate from the truth God has revealed, faithful Catholics, scholars and nonscholars alike, seek guidance from and are faithful to the magisterium.

In the latter months of 1984, the Pontifical Biblical Commission published a document, *Bible et Christologie*, to guide christological research.[37] It first examines eleven contemporary approaches to the biblical text, pointing out the advantages of each as well as their limitations. The second part is a brief summary of biblical witnesses relevant to christology, including the expectations of salvation and of a Messiah (in the First or Old Testament) and their fulfillment in Jesus Christ (in the New Testament). The document insists on the importance of moving toward an integral christology which includes promise and fulfillment and takes into consideration the totality of the biblical witnesses to Jesus the Christ. Biblical scholars and theologians will find valuable guidance in this latest document from the Holy See.

The relationship between the magisterium and theologians is one of mutuality. Theologians look to the magisterium for guidance. The teaching authority of the Church, through such vehicles as the International Theological Commission and the Pontifical Biblical Commission, responds to the work of theologians and biblical scholars and evaluates them in the light of the Church's traditions regarding faith and morals.

The goal—understanding the mystery of Jesus—will never be fully achieved in this life. In the meantime, however, theological reflection is an exciting endeavor, one that can deepen our faith and bring us closer to Jesus, God's only Son.

---

[37] Pontifical Biblical Commission, *Bible et Christologie* (Paris: Les Editions du Cerf, 1984).

Reflections on Religious Life
—*March 1986* ——————————————————————

My dear sisters and brothers in religious life:

I am very grateful for this opportunity to share some reflections with you as we begin the second phase of our study of religious life. Once again, I wish to express my gratitude and that of the entire archdiocese for all that you have done and are doing in our midst. Without you we simply could not serve God's people as fully and as capably as we are doing today. In your roles as leaders, as leaven, and as animators; in your witness to Christ Jesus and his gospel through your consecrated life, you are a precious gift, a blessing to this local church. Thank you!

The basic context for this study of religious life in the U.S. is the long tradition of the Church, as well as the teaching of the Second Vatican Council and the ecclesial experience of the past two decades. In particular, the Dogmatic Constitution on the Church, *Lumen gentium*, has had a profound impact on every aspect of Church life and ministry. It has encouraged all of us—clergy, religious, and laity—to situate ourselves within the larger Church, and it has given us helpful insights regarding our respective charisms and roles.

The Second Vatican Council and the subsequent Instructions which flow from it have called for a renewal of religious life. These documents, especially *Mutuae relationes*, have also called for closer collaboration and cooperation between bishops and religious and, in particular, have highlighted the bishop's role of pastoral service to religious within the local church. This was certainly the intent of the Holy Father when he asked us to undertake this study. I personally welcome these developments. I trust that you do also.

As you will recall, the Holy Father specifically asked that this study of religious life be undertaken for three basic purposes: (1) that the bishops

might be better able to teach the faithful about the significance and importance of religious life—that it is a gift to the *whole* Church, not a private
"possession"; (2) that we might encourage men and women religious to
embark with us pastors upon a path of continual conversion which involves
self-criticism for all of us; and (3) that we might deal constructively and
sensitively with any departures from the essential norms of religious life.

The first phase of this study consisted primarily in listening to the lived
experience of women and men religious and responding briefly to that experience. Basically we dealt with two dimensions of that experience: (1)
how religious life is understood and lived today in the United States and
(2) how it is understood and lived in the Archdiocese of Chicago.

This proved to be a beneficial experience for this local church. Many
men and women religious participated, sharing with one another and their
bishops both their enriching and their problematic experiences of religious life during the past twenty years. They also identified areas of concern which need further attention, especially in the archdiocese. After
listening, I responded briefly at the two celebrations of religious life on
April 9 and 11, 1984.

Based on what I heard during this first phase, I have subsequently initiated such changes as the reorganization of the Office for Religious, the establishment of an Advisory Board for that Office, and the establishment
of Placement Services for nonordained ministers. Moreover, the Center
for Pastoral Ministry is now offering in-service programs designed for religious. Through these structures and programs, as well as meetings with
the leaders of various religious communities and visits with many religious congregations throughout the archdiocese, I am continuing to listen
and respond to your concerns.

In this second phase of the study, we are called to come to grips with
the essential elements or values of religious life which must be present if
religious life is to be authentic. To do this, we must consider both your
lived experience in the light of your approved constitutions and the teaching of the Church, in particular, the documents of the Second Vatican
Council and the postconciliar Instructions.

To open this next phase of exchange, I will offer you my reflections on
the six important dimensions of religious life which the Pontifical Commission chaired by Archbishop John Quinn has asked us to consider:
identity and charism, community, obedience, structures of authority, consecration and mission, and public witness. I will do so in light of the
Church's teaching and my own experience.

First, however, I wish to acknowledge that I am very sensitive to the
tensions which exist within and among some religious communities, as
well as between some religious communities and their bishops or the
Holy See. In the reflections which follow I do not come before you as one

who has all the answers; neither do I present these reflections to you on a "take-it-or-leave-it" basis. I am, indeed, a brother who is walking, with his sisters and brothers in religious life, on a journey which will bring all of us to a greater understanding of our respective roles in the Church and which will enable us to respect and support each other more effectively.

It is precisely because we journey together that I want to share my reflections and ask you to consider them prayerfully, personally, and communally. I invite you to gather with me and our auxiliary bishops during April and May so that we can discuss these points and thereby deepen our mutual understanding and strengthen our collaboration in service of the Church.

Of course, I walk with you on this journey—I participate in this exchange—in fidelity to my role as bishop of this local church. I accept my ecclesial responsibility for discerning and affirming its charisms, building up its harmony and unity, and implementing its mission and ministry. Moreover, I realize my obligation to carry out this responsibility in communion with the Holy Father and the college of bishops, as the Second Vatican Council has so clearly indicated.

In keeping with these responsibilities, I intend to reflect accurately what the Church teaches about certain elements pertaining to religious life. On some points, I will share with you my own personal understanding of how these elements or values might be lived in the present-day circumstances of the archdiocese. Finally, I will indicate some challenges which flow from these reflections—challenges which might be fruitful areas for our continuing dialogue.

I have no hesitation about candidly expressing my own convictions because I do not do so in a vacuum: You will be listening and will offer your responses. Indeed, I hope that you will not hesitate to express your convictions in the sessions which begin in April. It seems to me that, if we accept this context and establish this kind of atmosphere, we will be able to enter into an honest dialogue which will be mutually respectful and enriching. This will be beneficial both for us and those whom we serve.

Before reflecting on the six dimensions of religious life to which I referred, I wish to make three *overall* comments. First, in reflecting on the documents of Vatican II and the postconciliar era, we must read, understand, and apply their teaching and insights to the *particular milieu* in which we live. It is understandable that these essential elements of religious life will be lived out in different ways in diverse parts of the world. The situation in Chicago is quite different from that in San Salvador, Calcutta, or Nairobi. Nonetheless, what we must ensure is that the essential values which these documents identify are kept alive and in focus in our local church. We need to ask: In this particular context, what needs to be done to protect and nurture these values?

Second, I am aware that these values may be understood and lived out in diverse ways within a local church because of the *inherent differences* among religious communities—contemplative, monastic, and apostolic. This needs to be kept in mind as we study your lived experience and the teaching of the ecclesial documents.

Third, it is important that you and I—as well as religious and bishops throughout the United States—work toward a *common understanding* about how the essential elements of religious life should be lived and that we *communicate* our local experience to the Holy See. This will give the Holy Father and the Congregation for Religious and Secular Institutes a clearer understanding of religious life in the United States. This, in turn, may be expected to influence the drafting of any future instructions which may be issued with regard to religious life. This kind of mutuality will be constructive and helpful to us.

1. Charism and Identity

"Charism" is crucial to understanding the fundamental identity of religious life. The particular charism of a religious community determines its identity, way of life, spirit and spirituality, structures, and mission. However, it is difficult to define what is meant by charism. The term, especially in its biblical sense, is dynamic rather than static. Because it describes the action of God's Spirit, it is also a term which connotes mystery. This helps explain why ecclesial documents use the word in several ways.

Lumen gentium, for example, notes that the Holy Spirit "distributes special gifts among the faithful of every rank. By these gifts he makes them fit and ready to undertake various tasks and offices for the renewal and building up of the Church" (no. 12). The same dogmatic constitution distinguished "hierarchical" from "charismatic" gifts, noting that the bishops' proper role is to distinguish authentic charisms from counterfeits.

In *Evangelica testificatio* Pope Paul VI specifically applied the term "charism" to religious life: "In reality, the charism of the religious life . . . is the fruit of the Holy Spirit who is always at work within the Church. . . . It is precisely here that the dynamism proper to each religious family finds its origin" (no. 11). In other words, charisms have their origin in the Holy Spirit. A charism is a special enabling gift for a way of life or a specific ministry, both within and for the Church. Its basic purpose is to renew and develop the Church. Because of its ecclesial orientation, the bishops have a responsibility for evaluating and judging it, always in dialog with the religious congregation involved.

The postconciliar Instructions treat both the charism of the founder or foundress and the charism of the religious community.

Initially the charism is given to the founder or foundress. It enables that person to perceive the needs of the people whom he or she is called to serve and to respond to those needs. In other words, it is primarily the God-given capacity both to *discern* and to *decide*. The effectiveness of the person's work is brought about by the power of God working in and through him or her—and recognized as such by the Church's pastors.

When a newly founded religious community is approved by the Church, the existence and authenticity of its specific charism is officially and publicly recognized. The charism, in turn, provides the dynamic which defines the new community as well as a certain "constancy of orientation" as the community adapts to changing circumstances.

The foundress' or founder's followers in an approved religious community also receive the charism of the respective institute. This gift of the Spirit is exercised when the community comes together, especially to discern the needs of the people whom they are called to serve and to respond to those needs in appropriate ways. (I am distinguishing communal discernment and decision-making from purely personal discernments and decisions.) In discernment and decision-making, the community is to remain faithful to the charism of the founder or foundress.

Pope Paul VI addressed this concern: "For while the call of God renews itself and expresses itself in different ways according to changing circumstances of place and time, it nevertheless requires a certain constancy of orientation" (*Evangelica testificatio*, no. 12). In other words, reading the signs of the times and remaining faithful to one's charism are complementary responsibilities. This implies that charism involves both *stability* and *change*.

The main responsibility of fidelity to the charism and docility to the Spirit dwells in those who have received that gift and call. Communities are endowed with an internal authority, which is recognized by the Church. But, because the charism is given to the religious community for the service of God's people and because the individual institute's discernment and decisions affect the larger Church, the bishops must judge the quality of the evangelical witness given by religious, their response to the needs of God's people, and the harmonious insertion and integration of their ministries into the pastoral plan of the diocese.

Throughout the Church's history, as well as in our own times, there have been tensions between "charismatic" and "hierarchical" gifts, between religious life and ecclesial structures. Because these tensions can, at times, become strong, there may be a tendency to treat these gifts as independent realities. The Congregation for Bishops and the Congregation for Religious and Secular Institutes, in their joint Instruction, *Mutuae relationes*, indicate that this would be a mistake, that these two entities *"form one,* even though *complex reality"* (no. 34).

They are, in other words, interdependent. Both the institutional and charismatic dimensions belong to the one Church, and both are needed if the Church is to grow and become a more effective servant and witness in the world. The natural tension which exists between the two can be positive and life-giving.

Discernment is never an easy process—whether undertaken by religious or by bishops. The bishops may err by quenching or stifling the Spirit at work in the Church when they are not attentive enough to the distinctive nature of the various charisms and calls. A religious community may err by resisting the bishops in the legitimate exercise of their leadership in the Church.

Nevertheless, bishops and religious communities can engage in beneficial, joint discernment by prayerful reflection, dialogue, and effective channels of communication. Moreover, in carrying out their role of pastoral service to religious, bishops will find it helpful to become familiar with a community's charism through a study of its constitutions and through personal contact with its leaders and members. Religious will find it helpful to become more familiar with the bishop's pastoral role through a study of the pertinent ecclesial documents and through personal contact with their bishops.

How can an authentic charism or its legitimate exercise be judged? Primarily by (1) the manifestation of the signs of the Spirit, (2) the witness provided by the lives of the members of the religious community who model their lives on, and ground their actions in, Christ Jesus, and (3) a constructive love of the Church (cf. *Mutuae relationes*, no. 51a,b,c).

The challenge facing religious congregations at this point in the Church's history is to discern—and develop—their unique charism and the ways in which it should be expressed in a rapidly changing Church and world. Further, we need to develop procedures and patterns of interchange that will effectively incarnate the interdependence of the charism of the religious congregation and that of the Holy Father and the bishops.

2. Community

The Second Vatican Council's decree on the renewal of religious life, *Perfectae caritatis*, describes religious community life as patterned on the model of the early Church in which the members come together with a common sense of mission and share their resources. Such a community provides support for its members in their way of life and creates an environment favorable to the spiritual progress of each. This, in turn, enables them to minister more effectively to those in need. The unity of such a community—manifested to all—is essential to its effectiveness in carrying out its mission, especially evangelization.

In other words, religious community life promotes the spiritual discipline of its members, enables them to carry out their mission and service, and provides healthy, intimate relationships which give support to each member. Contemplative, monastic, and apostolic communities may emphasize one or more of these dimensions, but, in some way, they are all important.

At the same time, community is not a one-way street. Each member is expected to share her or his gifts and resources with the community to enable it to carry out its service and ministry to God's people in accordance with its charism.

Historically, apostolic communities were founded first as an answer to some need in the Church, and they became religious communities in order to foster and give greater stability to their ministry. A similar thing is happening today. With a renewed awareness of their respective charisms and in response to the gospel mandate to espouse a preferential option for the poor (a concept supported by recent popes as well as the Extraordinary Synod of Bishops), many apostolic religious communities are focusing on their specific mission and developing the way of life needed to support it.

This implies that they will differ in lifestyle, as well as spirituality, from contemplative or monastic communities and even—in view of their diverse ministries—from one another. For example, since the Second Vatican Council many of these communities have developed smaller local houses because of their desire to live closer to the people they serve—especially the poor—and to make possible deeper relationships among the religious who live together.

The challenge in adapting to new understandings of religious life and mission, as well as to new circumstances, is to preserve what is essential to community life, as outlined by Pope Paul VI:

> [W]hatever their size, communities large or small will not succeed in helping their members unless they are constantly animated by the Gospel spirit, nourished by prayer and distinguished by generous mortification of the old man [or woman], by the discipline necessary for forming the new man [or woman], and by the fruitfulness of the sacrifice of the Cross (*Evangelica testificatio*, no. 41).

Community life is meant to be a support and a sign of evangelical unity. Nonetheless, many religious experience the same human difficulties of living together as all other people. Community life, simply stated, is a constant challenge. Differences in age, outlook, emphases placed on values, forms of ministry or service all contribute to the diversity of members. While this diversity bespeaks a richness of human experience, it can also cause divisions and alienation within the community.

Religious who live together in a spirit of forgiveness and reconciliation, in peace and harmony, give witness to the Church and the world that, with God's help, it is, indeed, possible for human beings to live together as sisters or as brothers. Indeed, living in community in this way contributes to the healthy development of the individual.

3. Obedience

Every Christian is called to imitate the example of Jesus, as Mary his mother and the men and women who were his first followers did, unconditionally submitting to the saving will of God.

How is a Christian to discern God's saving will? While prayer, reflection and spiritual direction are essential elements, discernment is not a purely personal matter. It has a communal, ecclesial dimension as well. All Christians are to be obedient to the gospel message transmitted within the community of believers. Moreover, each is called to be obedient to the Holy Father and the bishops of the Church, who, in turn, have the responsibility of authentically interpreting the word of God (cf. The Dogmatic Constitution on Divine Revelation, no. 10).

The obedience of religious, based on gospel obedience, has more precise connotations since, in order to enter into communion with others, they make it the object of a special gift of their own will through their vow or promise, and thereby limit their range of choices. Pope John Paul II has highlighted the significance of religious obedience in this way: "By living out the evangelical counsel of obedience, [religious] reach the deep essence of the entire economy of the Redemption" (*Redemptionis donum*, no. 13). In other words, religious, through their exercise of obedience, enter into the mystery of the redeeming obedience of Jesus.

Religious communities understand and exercise religious obedience in accordance with their basic self-understanding and mission. For good order and the coordination of individual gifts, it is important that there be recognized leaders who exercise authority in the religious institute. The religious vow or promise includes obedience to these leaders. At the same time, the exercise of leadership through consultation and collaboration helps ensure that all members' insights are heard and their values respected as the community discerns and makes decisions.

In the United States, given our traditional respect for democratic processes and our emphasis on the role responsible adults play in shaping the decisions which affect their lives, it is natural that obedience will often be understood in a more communal or participative way. This sometimes is confusing to the faithful and of concern to the bishops and the Holy See because lines of authority and accountability, at times, seem to be less clear than in the past.

It is important, therefore, that religious, together with their bishops, clarify the essential role which obedience plays in religious life and the legitimate ways in which it may be exercised. While tensions will inevitably occur, there is no inherent contradiction between religious obedience, correctly understood, and human dignity.

Admittedly, this is a sensitive topic, but it cannot be swept under the carpet. If obedience is essential to religious life, there must be agreement on what it means and how it is to be accepted and exercised. Certainly no one favors a "blind" obedience which is demeaning and inconsistent with human dignity and freedom. At the same time, if obedience is understood in purely subjective terms, it becomes merely an empty word and does not provide for the common good as discerned by chosen leaders in consultation with the community. I envision our searching together for a clearer understanding of obedience as lived in a religious community.

4. Structures of Authority

Both creativity and order are essential to the Church's mission. Structures of authority are not to stifle, but to channel, connect, expand, refine, and otherwise serve the dreams, resources, and energies of the Church—and the religious community—so that each can carry out its mission and ministry effectively.

Authority which is *external* to the religious community has two dimensions. Like all Christians, religious look to the gospel as the highest norm. Like all Christians, they also owe respect to the authority of the bishops, in communion with the Holy Father, "both because these exercise pastoral authority in their individual churches and because this is necessary for unity and harmony in the carrying out of apostolic work." The hierarchy, on its part, has the responsibility of using "its supervisory and protective authority to ensure that religious institutes established all over the world for building up the Body of Christ may develop and flourish in accordance with the spirit of their founders" (*Lumen gentium*, no. 45).

As for *internal* structures of authority within religious communities, *Perfectae caritatis* sounded a note which has had profound influence in all areas of religious life:

> The manner of living, praying and working should be suitably adapted everywhere . . . to the modern physical and psychological circumstances of the members and also, as required by the nature of each institute, to the necessities of the apostolate, the demands of culture, and social and economic circumstances (no. 3).

While some religious communities retain a more hierarchical structure of authority, other institutes have moved towards a more participative model, understood as more in keeping with the apostolate, culture, and needs of their members. Whatever the specific structure, religious leaders also serve as animators of the community.

As I noted earlier, the charism of a religious community enables it to discern the needs of the people whom it is called to serve and to decide how to respond in faith to their needs. This task requires forms of government and structures of authority which are consonant with the community's charism and enable it to carry out its mission. It is important today that religious be mature, responsible people and that structures and leaders recognize the gifts and talents of their members so that these can be coordinated in the work of the Church and the religious community.

Similarly, leaders of religious communities are expected to fulfill their office "in a way responsive to God's will. They should exercise their authority out of a spirit of service to [their members], expressing in this way the love with which God loves their [members]" (*Perfectae caritatis*, no. 14). As with any office of authority within the Church, leaders are to serve the others, not lord it over them.

This interplay between members and leaders of a religious community is most visible in communal structures such as chapters and councils where the members of the religious institute, in accordance with their constitutions, formally exercise the responsibility for maintaining fidelity to the community's charism, reading the signs of the times, carrying out the institute's mission, building its unity, and ensuring a healthy relationship with the local church.

Just as congregational leaders sometimes need to challenge, temper or correct their members, so too bishops sometimes need to question, advise or admonish those—including religious institutes—in their care. This is an integral part of the service rendered by those in authority.

Because of the tensions inherent in such situations—tensions enhanced, in the view of some, by the fact that bishops are usually not members of religious institutes or participants in a community's charism—and given the human condition, things will go wrong at times; abuses will occur. And because both bishops and the leaders of religious institutes are usually involved and responsible in these instances, there is potential for conflict.

Such situations, therefore, call for the Christian "practice [of] the truth in love." *Mutuae relationes* acknowledges the potential conflict and counsels both bishops and leaders of religious communities to proceed in a spirit of mutual trust and dialogue, in fulfillment of the obligations incumbent upon each, in keeping with the exercise of each one's responsibility, acting decisively and with clear dispositions, always in the spirit of charity but also with due resoluteness (cf. no. 43).

Lest such legitimate actions of bishops be counterproductive, it is imperative that they be preceded by prayerful and honest dialogue among the religious community, the diocesan bishop, and the Holy See. Proper canonical procedures must be followed, and, of course, external intervention should be rare and utilized only in the most serious of situations.

It is painful to talk of these conflictual moments in human and ecclesial life. Fortunately, they are the exception, but they do happen and they hurt. I share these thoughts with you, invite your response, and look forward to our gatherings in April and May as a means by which we may avert or at least minimize such conflict and pain. Processes such as the one in which we are now engaged can build our mutual trust, expand our common understandings, clarify issues of concern among us, and contribute both to our friendship in the Lord and to our service of his people.

Structures of authority, as I indicated earlier, channel resources and facilitate the achievement of each institute's purpose and mission. Religious in the U.S. have been creative in seeking, adapting, or designing structures that enhance their life and service to the Church.

Nonetheless, as we continue to assimilate the teaching of the Second Vatican Council and to adapt to changing circumstances, bishops and religious face an ongoing challenge: We seek a common understanding of the place and balance between authority and freedom, between obedience and dissent, within the Church. We must seek this understanding together in theological study and in reflection on our lived experience, always in fidelity to the constitutions of the religious institutes and the teaching of the Church.

5. Consecration and Mission

Today there is considerable discussion—even debate—among religious about the relationship of *consecration* and *mission* to the nature of religious life. Because they are "two facets of one reality" (*Essential Elements*, no. 23), they are intimately interrelated and closely interdependent. Problems arise over the emphasis or priority to be given to each, and different understandings exist among religious institutes as well as bishops. We need, therefore, to take a closer look at the conciliar and postconciliar documents which reflect these distinct emphases.

Pope Paul VI indicated that religious, through profession of the evangelical counsels, move beyond their baptismal commitment to follow Christ "more freely and to imitate him more faithfully, dedicating [their] entire lives to God with a special consecration rooted in that of Baptism and expressing it with greater fullness" (*Evangelica testificatio*, no. 4).

The most recent document of the Congregation for Religious and Secular Institutes *(Essential Elements)* envisions consecration as the basis of religious life and understands it as an act of being set apart from the world. "The apostolate of all religious," the document states, "consists first in the witness of their consecrated life which they are bound to foster by prayer and penance" (Norm §29). It continues, "The essential mission of those religious undertaking apostolic works is the proclaiming of the word of God. . . . Such a grace requires a profound union with the Lord . . ." (Norm §31).

Some interpret these norms to mean that mission is primarily to be understood as a subsequent reality, flowing from consecration and nourished by it. Apostolic religious have found difficulty with this interpretation. Historically, they begin, instead, with their mission and understand consecration in terms of the condition (i.e., a profound union with God) which makes it possible for them to pursue their mission more fruitfully.

Many apostolic congregations believe that they have arrived at this understanding by being faithful to the teaching of the Second Vatican Council and the earlier Instructions of the Holy See. In identifying the particular character of their respective founders or foundresses and in adapting to the understanding of the Church's posture toward the world found in *Gaudium et spes*, they have committed themselves to living in the world even as they commit their lives totally to God and the Church.

I wish to stress here that consecration involves the public profession of the evangelical counsels and the public commitment to devote one's life totally to God and his people. This implies embracing a life of asceticism necessary to grow in holiness and to live the gifts of poverty, chastity and obedience, which are expressed in the vows or promises which religious make. Understood in this way, consecration enables one to carry out the mission of the religious institute and receives its particular shape from that mission. As I noted earlier, consecration and mission are "two facets of one reality."

Nevertheless, the challenge before us—as bishops and religious—is to acknowledge the importance of *both* concepts, consecration and mission, and to recognize the various legitimate ways in which they can be understood and lived out. In pursuing this matter, our dialogue must include the Holy See because we are dealing with values which are crucial for religious life and the Church as a whole.

6. Public Witness

Pope Paul VI summed up the testimonial value of religious life when he wrote: "The evangelical witness of the religious life clearly manifests to [all] the primacy of God's love; it does this with a force for which we must give thanks to the Holy Spirit" (*Evangelica testificatio*, no. 1).

By their *personal holiness*, religious are to manifest to all the goodness of God's gifts and the gifts of redemption which transform human life and bring it to its fullness. By their *community life*, they are to manifest to the Church and the world God's plan for peace, harmony and unity among all people. Through their *apostolic service*, religious are to show to all—especially to the most vulnerable in our midst—the love and care of God for each of his creatures.

Everyone seems to agree that religious are called to give public witness to Jesus Christ and gospel values. Beyond the three aspects mentioned above, however, there is disagreement about how this public witness is to be given as well as which gospel values are to be emphasized. This question is related to the previous one about consecration and mission. How one understands that issue—whether religious are to be "separated from the world" or "immersed in the world"—affects how one regards the appropriate manner and means of religious' public witness. Whether religious work with members of their own institute or collaborate in team efforts with other religious, clergy, and/or laity also affects how one assesses what is appropriate witness and what is not.

In particular, the question of housing and dress arises most clearly in this context. This, I know, is a neuralgic topic for many. For some it is a litmus test for judging the authenticity of religious life. We should avoid giving a central role to this matter because, as important as symbols are, the greater need is to focus on the more substantive issues confronting religious life today.

Still, bishops and religious need to arrive at a common understanding of the appropriate ways of giving public witness in this local church and in our U.S. culture. This will greatly enhance understanding both at the level of the local church and that of the Holy See. In so doing, we need to delve beneath the surface so that we can identify and understand the deeper realities which are present, that is, the underlying thinking and motivation.

On this matter of public witness, the Instruction, *The Contemplative Dimension of Religious Life*, raises another concern: "Religious, on their part, must give witness that they effectively and willingly belong to the diocesan family" (no. 22). *Mutuae relationes* (no. 38) points out that this implies that major religious superiors need to know not only the talents and potential of their members but also the pastoral needs of the local church. This, in turn, implies the need for an ongoing dialogue between the local bishop and leaders of religious communities.

For my part, I am eager to do whatever is necessary to enable women and men religious to participate more fully in the life and ministry of this local church. I take this stance not because it is pragmatic—we need your help—but, rather, because I believe, as did Pope Paul VI, that the authentic renewal of religious life is essential for the renewal of the Church and the evangelization of the world (cf. *Evangelica testificatio*, no. 52).

Our challenge with regard to the public witness of religious life, then, is twofold: (1) to arrive at a common understanding of what such public witness entails and (2) to discover ways by which religious can be more clearly involved in the life of the local church.

Underlying these reflections on religious life is my deep love for the Church and my own understanding of the Church's nature and mission. Today we speak about different "ecclesiologies" or "models" of the Church. These do exist. The Church is ultimately a mystery, a multifaceted reality which brings together both the divine and the human. As we study the Church and deepen our understanding of it, it is inevitable that at different times we give more or less emphasis to one or another particular aspect. In this sense, it is legitimate to speak about different "ecclesiologies."

Nevertheless, we must also acknowledge this truth: The Church is *one*. We do not have many different churches, and in no way may we allow our discussion about different ecclesiologies to give the impression that we are talking about different churches. This is true in our exchange of ideas about religious life as well as all other areas of Church life. We will not resolve some of the deep-seated tensions in our contemporary Church until we share a common understanding of the Church's nature and mission.

At its very heart, therefore, whatever problems or ambiguities there are about religious life can be understood and resolved only within the framework of an accurate ecclesiology. Faulty ecclesiology, whatever the cause, can only lead to faulty notions of religious life. It is in this broader context of the important study of the Church's nature and mission that we face the challenges which I have outlined in these reflections.

Discussions about the nature and mission of the Church and appropriate responses to the challenges I have noted above will not be easy. That is why I indicated at the outset that I do not intend these reflections to be a "last word." Knowing that your diverse experiences will enrich our discussions, I look forward to hearing your thoughts and your responses to these reflections.

Hopefully, the very complexity of the realities with which we are dealing will motivate all of us to listen carefully during our spring consultations. To listen attentively is to learn and to proceed toward greater mutual understanding—not merely between religious and bishops but also among different religious institutes. Because of diversity among congregations and because intercongregational opportunities have been limited, our spring gatherings offer a valuable opportunity for men and women of various institutes to learn more about how these congregations understand the essentials of religious life and why they live and work as they do.

Thus, we will continue to work together towards a common understanding of the issues we face. Those I have identified in this paper are far from being our sole concerns. I have some other questions that I can answer only in dialogue with you.

How, for example, can we establish collaboration among religious, laity and diocesan clergy as a normal mode of contemporary apostolic action? How can we develop a vision for the future that will include creative options and apostolic risk when vocations are growing fewer? How can I encourage a community to develop in such a way as to be securely identifiable and attractive to young candidates? How can I support you in maintaining high standards for admission to your communities when decreasing numbers tempt us to take more chance with personal needs of applicants?

These are compelling questions of immediate need, but they can only be answered in the context of those I have elaborated earlier in this paper. And in the process we must deepen our mutual love and respect, aware always of our interdependence in carrying out the Lord's work. Only in this way will we be able to fulfill the Church's mission effectively in the archdiocese and in the world.

The Challenges We Face Together

Reflections on Selected Questions
for Archdiocesan Religious Educators *

—— *Autumn 1986* ————————————————————————————

My dear brothers and sisters in Christ:

Even before coming to serve you as archbishop, I knew how important the religious education programs of the archdiocese were and how talented and dedicated were those serving in them. I commend the many women and men—priests, religious, and laity—who taught in Catholic schools and CCD programs before the Second Vatican Council. They gave many young people the basics of the faith, and they taught them well.

This spirit of fidelity and service has continued to the present day in all those who currently assist in the religious education and formation of the young people of this local church. I have met many of you in my visits to the parishes and institutions of the archdiocese. I have been impressed by your sincerity and your faith-filled dedication to the Lord, to his Church, and to the young people you teach. I deeply appreciate your ministry, and I often pray for you.

I am also grateful to those who have served in the various archdiocesan offices responsible for religious education ministry since the Second Vatican Council. They have been responsible for the development of new programs suited to the teachings and spirit of the council and the needs of the times.

* Also published in *The Priest*, vol. 43, no. 1, January 1987, pp. 13–20.

Purpose of this letter

Why am I writing to you now? Your task is important, but it is not easy. You must continually struggle to educate and form young people in ways at once faithful to the Church's tradition and sensitive to the needs of today's youth.

You are not alone in that struggle. I share it with you. Differing opinions exist in our community regarding both the substance and methods of religious education. Both you and I, as teachers and catechists, may often feel "caught in the middle." As your bishop, I desire to reach out and help you to meet *the challenges we face together*.

During the past year, some of you have shared with me your dilemmas and frustrations, as well as your commitment and great desire to communicate the treasures of our faith to your students. When I spoke of my own concerns and said I was thinking of writing a pastoral letter to express my support and clarify some of the issues, you encouraged me to do so. I hope these reflections will help you and your colleagues.

Some general observations

As pastor of this local church, I must see to it that what Jesus handed on to the apostles is faithfully shared with our young people and passed on to the next generation. You are my collaborators in this important ministry.

Along with parents, who are the primary educators of their children, we must be creative, forward-looking, diligent, and enthusiastic about our task of religious education and formation. Most of all, we must be faith-filled. We must believe and live what we teach, for we proclaim a living Person who is at the center of *our* lives as well as the lives of our students. We must work as hard to nourish our spiritual lives as to develop our professional lives.

It is a privilege to proclaim the Lord and his message, but it is also demanding. We are not called to teach personal opinions or theological speculation. We are charged with teaching the faith entrusted to the Church, particularly as proclaimed and articulated by the pope and college of bishops (the magisterium).

The manner of our teaching must be appropriate to the age and maturity of our students, while its setting and style should encourage acceptance of and growth in the Church's faith. More is needed than unstructured "rap sessions" or efforts to win personal affirmation. At times the lack of understanding and response leaves us frustrated and discouraged. Then we must turn to the Lord who is the source of our strength and courage.

As I listen to many of you and read letters from parents and others concerned about religious education, certain questions continually emerge. Here I shall address three of them: (1) Does the Church's faith change? (2) Where is its faith expressed? (3) How should we deal with disagreement or dissent within the Church?

1. Does the Church's Faith Change?

If a Catholic Rip Van Winkle were to reawaken today after a twenty-year doze, he would find the Church much changed. English in the liturgy, altars facing the people, congregational singing and musical accompaniment with guitars and flutes, lay people proclaiming the Scriptures and distributing the Eucharist, a new emphasis on simplicity in Church decor—such things would confuse him greatly. But if a time machine then carried him back through the years, he would also be confused by a third-century Eucharist in the catacombs or a tenth-century Mass in a monastic church. The Church *does* change in externals—in language, in gesture, in custom, and in ritual. But there is no substantial change in the Church's *belief*.

Still, external changes do manifest some new emphases and a deeper awareness of certain beliefs—for example, the centrality of the Eucharistic Liturgy in the Church's prayer life, rightful participation of the laity in worship, and the importance of relevance and intelligibility in worship. But even such emphases and insights do not represent something essentially new; they are the fruit of decades of serious efforts at renewal within the Church.

As the Second Vatican Council began its solemn deliberations, Pope John XXIII reminded everyone that there is a difference between the mystery of faith that remains constant and the way we express that mystery. He spoke about the tension between the changing and unchanging elements in the life of the Church. He said that "certain unchangeable doctrine, to which faithful obedience is due, has to be explored and presented in a way that is demanded by our times. One thing is the deposit of faith, which consists of the truths contained in sacred doctrine, another thing is the manner of presentation, always, however, with the same meaning and signification" (*Acta Apostolicae Sedis*, 54, 1962, p. 792).

The mystery in which we believe is eternal and infinite, but we are finite, limited persons. We must study continually how to express and proclaim the mystery of our faith in the most accurate, understandable, credible way possible. This prayerful study and reflection is a responsibility for all believers. Some, however, because of their office or because of their training and expertise, have a special responsibility to assist the faith community in its reflection. This is true, for example, of theologians.

The efforts of theologians and scholars do not alter the substance of the mystery of faith, whose source and foundation is the Lord Jesus. Theologians are explorers who look to the past, as well as to present realities and future possibilities, in order to provide a deeper understanding of revelation. They do not create the faith, but help us to comprehend, assimilate, and apply it.

Because theologians are explorers, their work implies searching—casting about for deeper understanding of the mysteries of faith, new approaches to old realities. They need, in turn, some leeway in this effort, and we should not expect that their search will always be successful or free from error. Theirs is a great and necessary service to the Church, keeping it intellectually alive; but they are not the official teachers of the Church. Therefore, their opinions are subject to the oversight and judgment of the Church's pastors—the bishops in union with the Holy Father—who share in the ministry entrusted by Jesus to the apostles and their successors, to be the official, authoritative interpreters and teachers of the Church's tradition.

The distinction between the mystery of faith and its expression, together with the complementary responsibilities of theologians and bishops, helps us better appreciate what has taken place in the last twenty years. We can be sure that theological developments accepted by the magisterium in the name of the community of faith have not substantially altered the faith which the apostles received and which is passed on to all believers.

What is the precise role of the religious educator in this process? Because the education and formation of youth is a participation in the Church's official ministry of passing on the faith, religious education is supervised by and accountable to the Church's official teachers, the bishops in union with the Bishop of Rome. It is their duty and their charism to determine that what is communicated in religious education programs is in accord with the faith of the Church. Speculation and exploration appropriate in schools of theology or theological journals are not appropriate in programs of religious education.

As religious educators we must make it clear to those we teach that the authentic faith of the Church, in which we truly come to know the Lord Jesus and his gospel, has not changed. We invite them to accept the same faith embraced by the apostles. We affirm the reality of a loving Father whose creation is a sign of his love. We proclaim that Jesus is God and man and that, by his redemptive actions, the power of sin has been overcome. We declare that the Spirit of the Lord has been sent to us and lives in the Church. That same Spirit graces the community of faith when it celebrates the Lord's Real Presence in the Eucharist, when it experiences

God's healing forgiveness in the sacrament of penance, and when its faith is shielded from error through the charism of infallibility which preserves it pure and undefiled.

Nevertheless, it is a fact that some today are confused. This is understandable in light of the striking changes in the Church's contemporary articulation of the faith and its emphasis on certain aspects of it. Confusion has also been caused by those who sometimes present theological opinion as if it had the same standing as Church teaching.

I know that you are sensitive to your responsibility of teaching the faith. I thank you for the wonderful way in which you continually share the Good News so that those you teach might truly grow in their faith.

2. Where Is the Church's Faith Expressed?

Another question often asked flows from the concern of some that the *true* faith is not being taught. It also arises because of your sincere desire to communicate the Church's belief clearly and faithfully.

The question is this: Where can we find the faith expressed in a manner faithful to the Lord's gospel and suited to our times? To put it another way, where can we find authoritative direction regarding what should be taught in our programs of religious education?

One important place is the documents of the Second Vatican Council. The council provided us with a broad charter of renewal rooted in the gospel. The council fathers reflected upon many of our central beliefs—as found in the Scriptures as well as in our creeds and other statements of our Catholic heritage—and showed their relevance to the needs of our time. Of particular value to those in religious education are the Dogmatic Constitution on the Church, the Pastoral Constitution on the Church in the Modern World, and the Dogmatic Constitution on Divine Revelation.

The council did not, however, publish a complete synthesis of Catholic faith or a contemporary catechism. That was left for the postconciliar period. In 1971 the Congregation for the Clergy published the *General Catechetical Directory* to assist national bodies of bishops in preparing their own catechetical material. After a period of national consultation and review, the U.S. National Conference of Catholic Bishops, with the authorization of the Congregation for the Clergy, published its National Catechetical Directory, *Sharing the Light of Faith*, in 1979.

More recently, the bishops attending the Extraordinary Synod of Bishops in 1985 recommended the development of a universal catechism or compendium of Catholic doctrine. Pope John Paul II has established a commission to carry out this recommendation. Working in consultation with the bishops of the world, this commission is to complete its work in time for the 1990 Synod of Bishops.

Even if we are familiar with the documents just mentioned, it would be well to reacquaint ourselves with the rich treasure of doctrine and guidance they contain. Pope John Paul II's invitation last year to the bishops of the world to reflect on the work of the council and its contemporary application is an invitation to the entire Church. I encourage religious educators to initiate such studies at every level—archdiocese, vicariate, deanery, cluster, and parish. Just as when reading a book or seeing a movie for a second or third time we discover things we have missed or forgotten as well as new dimensions of things we already know, so through continued study of the conciliar documents we better assimilate their content and more fully imbibe their spirit.

As teachers of the faith, we also must present the Church's moral doctrine. Faith is intended to transform our daily lives and activities. Christians seek a continual change of mind and heart—a conversion—by which to live more fully human and Christian lives.

The Church, with a wisdom grounded in the Spirit, helps us reach that goal through its moral teaching. People have always needed this guidance, but the need is particularly urgent today, in light of the attitudes and values communicated to our young people through the public media and the contemporary youth subculture.

In addition to the section on "The Moral Life" in *Sharing the Light of Faith* (pp. 57–63), the U.S. bishops in recent years have presented the moral teaching of the Church, especially in three well-known pastoral letters: *To Live in Christ Jesus*, a 1976 pastoral reflection on the moral life; *Brothers and Sisters to Us*, a 1979 statement on racism; and *The Challenge of Peace: God's Promise and Our Response*, published in 1983. Currently as you know, the bishops are working on another pastoral letter of great importance: *Economic Justice for All: Catholic Social Teaching and the U.S. Economy*. All of these documents are of significance to us as religious educators.

The Holy See has also recently issued two important documents on moral issues. The first is Pope John Paul II's "Apostolic Exhortation on the Family" *(Familiaris consortio)* which persuasively outlines the Church's moral teaching about marriage and family life. In 1983 the Congregation for Catholic Education presented Catholic teaching on the Christian understanding of human sexuality and sex education in its document, *Educational Guidance on Human Love*. These documents have not yet received the attention they deserve. This is unfortunate because they contain so much that is of value; they are part of a long series of teaching documents that present Catholic moral teaching for our times.

As you know, I have personally sought to contribute to the articulation of our moral teaching. I have a profound belief that the gospel invites us to embrace a "consistent ethic of life." Such an ethic is based on the belief that life is a precious gift from God which must be protected and nurtured from the moment of conception until natural death. This is why the direct taking of innocent human life—whether of an unborn child through abortion, an aged person through euthanasia, or noncombatants in war—is always grievously sinful. This is why those actions or situations that diminish life—such as poverty, inadequate nutrition and health care, chronic unemployment—are also moral issues. True, these are distinct issues which cannot be collapsed into one. Violations are not all equally grave, and each question requires its own moral analysis and response. But these issues *are linked* because each in its own way impinges upon God's gift of life. As followers of Jesus who seek to live by his teaching, we cannot ignore any one of them.

The consistent ethic of life, I am convinced, gives us unique perspectives on *such* matters as international justice and peace, economic justice and business ethics, civil and human rights, the family and interpersonal relationships, the protection and nurturing of human life, and stewardship of the environment. The consistent ethic provides both the vision and the norms needed to guide and direct individual and communal behavior in a multitude of contexts.

The Church's moral teaching is not a superfluous burden but something we desperately *need*. The values it embodies are capable of enriching and transforming our lives and our world. Each of us experiences the weakness and limits of our personhood, feels the forces that oppose what we affirm and encourage us to be less than we would like to be. We know that sin is real—not merely in others but also in ourselves. But we also know that we dream of becoming the full persons God intends us to be and living in a better world.

To realize that dream, in ourselves and in those we teach, we must be clear about fundamental values and moral principles. For that reason I invite you to return to the documents that present the Church's moral teaching and give them your serious attention. Though some elements of the Church's teaching may have engendered controversy and may be difficult to understand or accept, they *are* part of the teaching of the Church, our family of faith. It is important to share them with those for whom we are responsible. I trust that this is your concern as it is mine.

3. How Do We Deal with Disagreement Within the Church?

Today we all recognize that in the Church there is disagreement with some aspects of its moral teaching, as well as other elements of its doctrine. We must not be surprised, therefore, when we encounter disagreement and dissent in the classroom.

Some disagree with *what* we say, others with *how* we say things. But such disagreement—no matter how painful—should not deter us from proclaiming the faith. I share the following reflections as one who stands with you as a brother in faith.

Disagreement is not necessarily bad in itself. There cannot be growth without some sort of questioning and conflict. The process of education in particular involves more than memorization and blind acceptance. We *want* those whom we teach to probe and search so that they can make the wisdom of the Church their own. For that to happen, there must be room for dialogue.

Disagreement becomes a problem when it goes beyond raising questions and *attacks* the fundamental identity of a family, society, or fellowship of faith, such as the Church. For the Church, this is especially true when the unique ministry of its pastors, as the authentic interpreters and teachers of the gospel, is questioned or challenged. Disagreement also becomes destructive when it fails to respect those with whom one disagrees. The Spirit of truth is ultimately the Spirit of love.

Let us now consider the subject matter of disagreement. Over the centuries Catholic teaching has made a distinction between universal moral principles and the application of these principles. This distinction is particularly applicable in regard to the Church's social teaching.

According to this distinction, when the Church teaches universal moral principles, it speaks with the expectation that the guidance given will be accepted and utilized in the formation of the conscience of each believer. However, in the application of these principles the Church recognizes that there is room at times for honest differences of opinion. In other words, the moral authority of the application is different from that of the principles themselves. This is true, for example, in determining matters of public policy in the social and political fields. This distinction needs to be communicated to those we teach.

It is important to note, however, that in certain moral matters the Church teaches that there is *no* distinction between the principle and its application. The principle itself is a moral norm which must always be respected and observed. This is true in matters regarding human life in its origins and its protection.

Having made these preliminary points, we can now deal more directly with the reality of disagreement or dissent in the Church, a phenomenon most evident in regard to the Church's teaching on human sexuality.

My analysis of the tension related to certain moral issues within the Church prompts me to believe that one of the difficulties is that, at times, we fail to understand the complexity of the disagreement. I suggest that there are three distinct, but interrelated, areas of disagreement. Let me address each of them.

a) Ecclesial Authority

In recent years considerable controversy has surrounded the Church's teaching on a number of moral issues, especially in the area of sexual morality. Even though the magisterium has spoken clearly and consistently (for example, on the question of birth control), disagreement or dissent from its teaching continues. Such disagreement ultimately raises questions about the meaning of ecclesial authority itself and the demands it makes on us as believers.

Most participants in the discussion seem to agree on certain items. They acknowledge, as our Catholic tradition has always affirmed, that the ecclesiastical magisterium (the pope and the bishops) is a gift of the Spirit to the Church. It serves the gospel by proclaiming Christ's teaching "in season and out." The Spirit is present in the Church to assist, guide, and guard that proclamation.

Second, all acknowledge that this ministry of teaching can be exercised in different ways. For example, a particular teaching can be presented as divinely revealed and taught unanimously throughout the Church. In this instance such teaching is guaranteed by the charism of infallibility, and our response must be that of faith.

Such teaching is done either by the "extraordinary" magisterium (the pope alone when he solemnly and explicitly defines a matter of faith and morals, or the bishops united with the pope at an ecumenical council) or the "ordinary" magisterium (the pope alone, or the bishops of the world united with the pope but apart from the two instances noted above). Historically, such infallible teachings have dealt primarily with dogmatic truths. When the magisterium teaches infallibly, it is expected that the individual will accept its teaching internally and externally as a matter of faith.

The ecclesiastical magisterium can also present to the community of faith "authoritative" teachings on dogmatic and moral questions. Although such teaching is not guaranteed by the charism of infallibility, it is presented authoritatively by those responsible for teaching in the name of the Lord. In so doing they are assisted by the Spirit. This is why such non-infallible teaching of the ordinary magisterium is assumed to be correct and is to receive what the Second Vatican Council called "religious assent of mind and heart" (*Lumen gentium*, no. 25). Specifically, in matters of morality it is expected that such teaching will be accepted for the formation of one's conscience. It is not simply one more source alongside others; it is a privileged place where Catholics encounter authentic values rooted in the faith.

Today there is much controversy about dissent from authoritative, non-infallible teaching. Although this question is important, I shall not explore all its dimensions at this time. However, I do want to emphasize an important point. It is essential that we, who teach in the name of the Church, present clearly and without ambiguity what the magisterium teaches. I ask you, therefore, to join me in affirming the Church's moral teaching as containing the normative principles for a fully human and Christian life.

Still, as we know, people sometimes question the Church's moral teaching. Some even consider it wrong. How do we respond? As brothers and sisters in faith, we must reach out to them—with integrity in regard to our responsibility as teachers, but also with compassion and understanding. We know that often such people sincerely struggle to accept the Church's teaching and experience pain when they reject it. Let us invite them to continue their search and to be open to the truth and beauty of our moral teaching.

b) Moral Methodology

Today the Church is experiencing a tension between two different ways of approaching contemporary ethical issues, two different methods or schools of moral analysis. This is also an issue which I shall not address in detail, but I do wish to describe the two positions in general terms, so that you will better understand the difficulty and be able to deal with it more effectively.

One perspective, often called the "traditional" view, has been articulated by moral theologians and accepted by the Church for centuries. Although this approach to morality, in accord with the teaching of the Second Vatican Council, has experienced its own reform, it continues to affirm that there are certain actions which, in and of themselves, are always wrong.

While the circumstances or intention involved in a particular case may mitigate (or aggravate) the immorality of such an action, they will not make it moral. For example, the artificial separation through contraceptive means of the life-making aspect of sexual intercourse from its celebration of human love is an example of an action that the traditional view sees as never morally justified, no matter what the circumstances or intention of the persons involved.

The other approach to morality is given various names and is sometimes called "proportionalism" or "consequentialism." In fact, as in any general theological system, there are areas of disagreement within it. In general, however, it can be said that this perspective *does not deny* that some human actions are morally wrong. But it denies that this judgment can be arrived at without an evaluation of all that it considers to be relevant ethical issues. By identifying all the values and disvalues present in a moral situation and using them all to determine the morality of the action, this approach finds it possible in some situations to conclude that actions, which the traditional view would always consider morally wrong *in an objective sense*, could be morally justifiable.

The ecclesiastical magisterium has never accepted this latter methodology. While some aspects (such as its attention to the person performing the action) are commendable, this methodology can lead to incorrect conclusions in certain areas (such as abortion and sexual morality).

Therefore, as persons commissioned by the Church to teach, we cannot present proportionalism or consequentialism as an equally valid alternative to our traditional moral methodology. Nonetheless, it is important that there be dialogue in theological circles between proponents of the two methodologies. There should also be more dialogue between the bishops and all moral theologians. Theological conflict is not unusual in the life of the Church. My hope is that respectful conversation and prayerful study will help us avoid caricatures that inhibit understanding and the search for truth. Above all, we must accept guidance in this search from the Church's teaching authority.

While theological conflict is not appropriate matter for religious education, it is sometimes appropriate and, indeed, necessary to acquaint students with the theological debate concerning various moral issues. This must always be done in a way that respects their age and maturity. Thus, they will be better prepared to evaluate what they might read or hear in this regard. As teachers commissioned by the Church, however, it is our task to present the Church's moral teaching with clarity. We are not to teach dissent.

In responding to the specific questions that students ask, more than "answers" are needed. We must help them appreciate the human and Christian values that underlie our teaching. We must also help them understand how to make good decisions in the many complex areas of their adult lives. Inculcating these values and developing these skills at the different stages of growth is a challenge. I pray that the Spirit will guide us as we face that challenge.

c) Meaning and Purpose of Human Sexuality

Because there has been much controversy and disagreement about the meaning and purpose of human sexuality, I would like to share with you some further thoughts about this matter. It is important that our approach to sexuality be positive; we must encourage our young people to see and accept sexuality as a gift that brings richness and fulfillment to our lives when used in accord with God's plan.

The Church's norms of behavior flow precisely from its understanding of sexuality as an expression of personhood and the human call to intimacy. Such norms neither exist for themselves nor were developed in a vacuum. Rather, they articulate and give us insight into certain values which are essential to integral human fulfillment.

Using this criterion, the magisterium has concluded that certain forms of behavior are contrary to the purpose of human sexuality. Thus, the Church opposes contraception, premarital and extramarital sex, homosexual acts (as distinguished from homosexual orientation), and sexual indulgence in thought and deed by oneself. It does so because it is convinced that such behavior vitiates God's creative love as reflected in the bodies of man and woman who, in Christian marriage, become "one flesh" for mutual and life-giving love; such behavior is contrary to the values inherent in the gift of sexuality.

I emphasize this relationship between *values* and the *norms* that express and protect them because it can help us present the Church's moral teaching in a more credible way, one that elicits assent rather than dissent. I believe that many young people are open to learning more about the values inherent in personhood and sexuality; indeed they often share them. With those values as a starting point, it will be easier to show why certain forms of behavior are consistent with them and some are not. The concrete norms of behavior then become more "believable." They are seen not simply as a list of "do's" and "don'ts," but as a call to live in a way that is in accord with God's plan for the human family.

This effort to identify the true meaning and purpose of human sexuality is not new. Especially since the time of the Second Vatican Council there has been a growing desire among bishops and theologians to find a way of speaking about these values that utilizes the wealth of contemporary learning about personhood and sexuality. Some of the most creative work along these lines has been done by Pope John Paul II. The importance of this search is increased by the unfortunately lingering impression among some Catholics and others that the Church takes an unrealistic and negative view of human sexuality.

A careful reading of the recent writings of Pope John Paul should put any such impression to rest. One of his central insights is that sexuality is not simply "an attribute" of the person but *intrinsic* to human personhood; it is a constitutive element of our humanity and our identity.

As educators of youth, it is important that we understand and appreciate this positive, rich concept of human sexuality. Some time ago I sought to bring this perspective to the fore in five weekly columns in *The Chicago Catholic* under the title "What the Church Is Saying About Sex." I also spoke of the need for such an approach at the 1980 Synod of Bishops in Rome.

Sexuality belongs to human persons made in God's "image and likeness" and striving for a wholeness of personhood despite the reality of sin. Made in the image of a God who is a community of Persons, the human person is called to intimacy, that is, to loving relationships with others. Sexuality is an aspect of our personhood which expresses this innate tendency to self-giving and dynamic openness to others. Genital activity, then, must correspond to this meaning and purpose of human intimacy and sexuality if it is to be authentically human and to witness effectively the kingdom.

In this context, human sexuality and its genital expression are esteemed as gifts from God. We make good use of these gifts when we use them as God intends—when they incarnate and support other God-given human values, such as fidelity in love, the propriety of pleasure, the place of discipline, the significance of parenting, the challenge of naturalness, the complementarity of genders, the legitimacy of social concern, and the necessity of human growth.

We must communicate this full spectrum of values to those whom we teach. While we may agree about their importance, we also know that others in our society see things differently and communicate an understanding of sexuality that would separate the life of the body from that of the spirit, sex from love and fidelity, and love-making from life-making.

It is critical that these values to which I have briefly alluded be clearly presented at every stage of the religious development of those we teach. I ask you not to present the Church's teaching simply as a list of things "not to do." Although we must clearly articulate the Church's moral teaching—integrity does not permit us to be ambiguous or misleading—rules of behavior without the values that undergird them will make little sense to those whom we educate.

I have still another reason for encouraging you to follow this approach. I am convinced that, if people truly seek to make these values their own, they will come to understand why it is necessary to their fulfillment to live in accord with the specific norms proposed by the Church. In other words, with the assistance of the community of faith and the power of the Spirit, they will begin to live in a certain way because they are convinced it is the *right* way, not just because they have been told to do so.

Some may consider this naive or unrealistic. I disagree! If we challenge youth—if we candidly and credibly present the values we affirm as a community of faith and the norms of behavior that protect and enhance those values—they will respond. They will be motivated to live as the Church invites them to live. Quite simply, I believe in the basic goodness of young people and their inner yearning, however inadequate it may sometimes be expressed, to live full and authentic lives.

Final thoughts

I hope these reflections will help you personally and as religious educators. I value your service. I am eager to support you. The questions I have addressed affect both you and me. I welcome your reaction. Have these reflections been helpful? Are there other ways in which I might assist you? I look forward to hearing from you and invite you to take advantage of the Department of Educational Services to facilitate that communication.

My prayer for you is this:

> Blessed are you, Lord God of all Creation!
> Through your goodness we have
>   been gifted with
>   the beauty of your creation,
>   the presence of your Son, and
>   the ministry of your Church.
> We thank you especially for those who
>   serve in our communion of faith
>   as religious educators.
> Watch over them and guide them.
> Give them strength and wisdom.
> Make them images of your love and
>   communicators of your freeing message.
> In those they teach and in their services,
>   may you be praised forever and ever.
> Amen!

Devotedly yours in Christ,

Joseph Cardinal Bernardin
Archbishop of Chicago

Pastoral Statements

A Challenge and a Responsibility

A Pastoral Statement on the Church's Response to the AIDS Crisis*

—— *October 24, 1986* ————————————————————

Dear Sisters and Brothers in Christ:

In recent times we have been confronted with a new and fatal disease, AIDS. Some time ago I appointed a task force to study how we might best minister to the growing number of people with AIDS in the Chicagoland area. I thank its members for their concern and their generous investment of time and energy in this project.

I have now prepared a pastoral statement in light of the task force's recommendations. It is my hope that this statement will help us all, as a community of faith, to respond in a compassionate and helpful way to our brothers and sisters who are afflicted with this disease, as well as their family and friends.

It is important that AIDS be seen as a *human disease* that deserves the same care and compassion as any other disease. This is the context in which this pastoral statement was developed and must be understood.

Nonetheless, I know that in the Chicago area 89 percent of the AIDS cases have been homosexual and bisexual men. As a result, AIDS has had a significant impact on the gay community; it is indeed a community of grief.

This grief is intensified for some because they feel alienated from the Church. At times this is due to a certain bias which exists among some members of the Church. It is also due at times to a misunderstanding or rejection of the Church's theological position. Unfortunately,

* Also published in *Origins*, vol. 16, no. 22, November 13, 1986, pp. 383–385.

in our efforts to teach the wrongness of homosexual acts, at times all that has been "heard" is the sound of condemnation and rejection. What is missed, then, what is not heard, is the Church's teaching that people with a homosexual orientation, like everyone else, are created in God's image and possess a human dignity which must be respected and protected. With vigor and clarity we must proclaim the love of Christ and his Church for every individual so that this message can be *heard* by members of the homosexual community and the broader community.

Now is the time for all of us to put aside whatever alienation or fear or prejudice we may have. Now is the time for all of us—ever faithful to the Church's teaching—to reach out to one another in a spirit of understanding and reconciliation because this is what Jesus asks of us. It is only in this context that we can respond effectively and compassionately to the challenge that AIDS presents to our community today.

Devotedly yours in Christ,

Joseph Cardinal Bernardin
Archbishop of Chicago

Recently I was told the story of Stephen, a young man who died of AIDS. His story is not unique.

Stephen, a young man in his early thirties, was a computer specialist. He was good at his work, enjoyed it, and was making new friends. This had not always been the case, for Stephen's acceptance and personal integration of his homosexuality had not been easy for him, causing him to drift away from his hometown and family. Now, however, he had started a new job which was going well, and his life seemed to be pointed in a much more positive direction.

This was not to last, however. Rather quickly, Stephen found it increasingly difficult to perform satisfactorily at work. He did not understand why he was making mistakes he had never made before. Concentration and accuracy, so necessary in computer programming, became more of a problem. Although his first job review had been positive, his second was devastatingly negative. He was warned, and, a short time later, he was fired.

Although unemployed, he was able to support himself out of his small savings. But soon, as his condition worsened, his landlord urged him to see a doctor. He responded that, without the insurance which he lost when he was fired, he could not afford to seek professional medical help. He hoped whatever he had would soon go away on its own.

That did not happen. Several days later his landlord took the then-incoherent Stephen to a public hospital. Because he tested positive for the HTLV-III virus, his encephalitis was diagnosed as being an AIDS-related disease.

Stephen lapsed in and out of consciousness and, when conscious, was seldom coherent. That is why it took the hospital several days to locate his family. When informed of his terminal condition and its cause, his family reacted poorly: They abandoned their dying son. Perhaps it was fear or ignorance or alienation, but Stephen died alone. A social worker later informed Stephen's friends of his death. When they inquired about his possessions, they discovered that they had been stolen.

What a sad story! The death of a young person is tragedy enough, but Stephen died of a new and virulent disease, without insurance and penniless. He died without family and friends to comfort him, without the ministry of his Church. And after death, he was violated a final time in the theft of his belongings.

In this tragic and true story it is easy enough to identify with *some* aspects of its emotional impact. The possibility of contracting some new and fatal disease, for example, is terrifying. We can understand the devastation of dying alone. We can sympathize with another's fear, alienation, and suffering. Even so, it is so tempting to say that this is not *our* problem, that we don't want to get involved.

But we cannot allow ourselves to identify with only *some* of the aspects of the AIDS phenomenon. We are called to examine more closely *all* its implications. Quite simply, Stephen's story confronts us all. We may wish that it would go away or that it will never touch anyone close to us, but the reality is that AIDS is a growing threat to our society which will not disappear soon. Our response to such a threat cannot be fear, ignorance, or alienation. As followers of Jesus, we have learned a different, better way. He has taught us to show compassion for the sick and suffering, no matter what their background or social standing. He has called us to be ministers of reconciliation so that our wounds and alienation may be healed.

This is the purpose of this pastoral statement. We are called, as a community of faith, to confront courageously and compassionately the suffering and death which AIDS is bringing to our world in 1986. To do this, we must put aside our fears, our prejudices, and whatever other agendas we may have in this regard.

AIDS AND THE GOSPEL

Hearing Stephen's story, some may respond by saying that AIDS is a divine punishment for what they describe as the "sin of homosexuality." Without questioning their sincerity, I disagree with this assessment.

First, medically speaking, AIDS is not a disease restricted to homosexuals. In fact, it appears that originally it might have been spread through heterosexual genital encounters. In the United States many people have been exposed to AIDS or have contracted it through the use of IV-drugs, tainted blood transfusions, and heterosexual genital activity. Consequently, even though a large percentage of those in the United States who have been exposed to the AIDS virus are homosexual, AIDS is a *human* disease, not a specifically homosexual one.

Second, God is loving and compassionate, not vengeful. Made in God's image, every human being is of inestimable worth, and the life of all persons, whatever their sexual orientation, is sacred and their dignity must be respected.

Third, the gospel reveals that, while Jesus did not hesitate to proclaim a radical ethic of life grounded in the promise of God's kingdom, he never ceased to reach out to the lowly, to the outcasts of his time—even if they did not live up to the full demands of his teaching. Jesus offered forgiveness and healing to all who sought it. And when some objected to this compassion, he responded: "Let the one among you who is guiltless be the first to throw the stone . . ." (John 8:7).

That is why we who are followers of Jesus see the AIDS crisis as both a *challenge* to respond in a Christlike way to persons who are in dire need and a *responsibility* to work with others in our society to respond to that need.

AIDS IN OUR SOCIETY

If we are going to respond adequately to the AIDS crisis, we must begin with some facts.

—As of September 15, 1986, 24,430 persons with AIDS have been diagnosed in the United States. 13,442 of them have already died. In Chicago, 430 cases were diagnosed by the same date; 254 are dead. Nationally, AIDS cases are *doubling* every eleven to thirteen months and in Chicago every ten months.

—Contrary to some assumptions, AIDS is not just a disease in the white community. Twenty-six percent of AIDS cases in Chicago are among blacks not of Haitian origin. And one in ten cases is in the Hispanic community.

—Although the percentage of intravenous drug users with AIDS is lower in Chicago (5.6%) than in the nation (17%), it is expected that this form of transmission will increase in the Chicago area. Also, there is some indication that the percentage of women with AIDS will increase in the future. There is also a projection that the number of heterosexual AIDS cases will increase among intravenous drug users and those with multiple sexual partners.

These facts are cited not to frighten, but to highlight the seriousness of the challenge we face as a civic and religious community.

In light of these facts, it is understandable that this disease, which spreads so quickly and is invariably fatal, would occasion misunderstanding, fear, prejudice and discrimination. Quite frankly, people are afraid that they may contract it. This is not a new phenomenon. Recall, for example, how we used to isolate tubercular patients and discriminate subtly (and sometimes not so subtly) against cancer patients. So also, for different reasons, we spoke with moral righteousness and indignation about the "sin" of alcoholism. In time, however, scientific advances and growth in human awareness and understanding helped us to see things in a new light and to develop better ways of relating to those suffering from these diseases.

Similarly, we are now called to relate in an enlightened and just way to those suffering from AIDS or from AIDS Related Complex (ARC) as well as those who have been exposed to the AIDS virus. While it is understandable that no one wants to put himself or herself in a vulnerable position, we must make sure that our attitudes and actions are based on facts, not fiction.

At the present time, there is no medical justification for discrimination against these people, and, in fact, such discrimination is a violation of their basic human dignity and inconsistent with the Christian ethic. To the extent that they can, persons with AIDS should be encouraged to continue to lead productive lives in their community and place of work. Similarly, government as well as health providers and human service agencies should collaborate to provide adequate funding and care for AIDS patients. Moreover, people with AIDS have a right to decent housing and landlords are not justified in denying them this right merely because of their illness. While acknowledging that special precautions may be needed, funeral directors should not refuse to accept or prepare the bodies of deceased AIDS patients for burial. Finally, the quarantine of persons with AIDS, the use of the HTLV-III antibody test for strictly discriminatory purposes, and the "redlining" of certain classes of people by insurance companies are deplorable practices.

I also affirm and commend the concern that so many professionals and volunteers have shown toward AIDS patients. The increasing seriousness of the problem, however, requires that more be done. I therefore join my voice with the many others who have called upon civic, governmental, religious, and community leaders to intensify their efforts to respond to the many human and religious needs caused by AIDS. No one segment of our community can do it alone. It requires the full collaboration of all.

But what can we do? A number of specific objectives for this collaborative action come to mind:

—that acute and long-care health facilities be encouraged to expand their services where needed to be able to care for more persons with AIDS and ARC;

—that all hospitals be encouraged to provide adequate in-service education of their personnel and to develop sufficient patient advocacy procedures to ensure respectful and compassionate care of persons with AIDS;

—that hospice programs be developed to address the unique needs of persons dying from AIDS;

—that educational programs, utilizing the media, be developed to help reduce prejudice and discrimination towards persons suffering from AIDS;

—that programs and services be developed to assist the families and friends of AIDS patients while the patients are alive and to support them in their bereavement;

—that the leaders of the black and Hispanic communities, as well as the community as a whole, be attentive to the special needs of blacks and Hispanics with AIDS.

This is indeed a large agenda, but I believe that it can be realized if we all work together.

THE CHURCH AND AIDS

The Church also has a specific role to play in ministering to those suffering from AIDS, their families, and their friends. As noted above, the Church should collaborate with others as it seeks to fulfill its own responsibilities. To that end, I pledge that we will work with public, private, and religious groups to achieve the above-mentioned objectives. We will continue to support interfaith efforts in exploring such possibilities as opening a chronic care facility (similar to a hospice) to care for those with AIDS, providing temporary housing for families and friends unable to afford other accommodations who are visiting people with AIDS, and establishing an Interfaith Pastoral Counseling Center to assist surviving families and friends in their time of grief.

As I intimated earlier, one of the obstacles to an effective ministry to AIDS patients is fear and prejudice. One of the best ways to lessen such fear and prejudice is to communicate the truth in a straightforward way. To assist other civic and religious groups in this important task of communicating the facts about AIDS, I have given two directives to archdiocesan agencies.

First, I have asked the Center for Development in Ministry, in collaboration with others, to develop programs that will help achieve the following objectives:

—provide priests, religious and lay leaders of the archdiocese with accurate information about the medical, psychosocial, and pastoral issues related to AIDS and ARC so that they can communicate such information in a manner that is best suited for their particular community. Such information should include a list of resources and support systems available to AIDS or ARC patients and their families and friends.

—assist in the development of training programs for those who minister to those affected by AIDS or ARC, e.g., hospital eucharistic ministers, visitors to the sick.

Second, I have asked the Archdiocesan Department of Educational Services to make accurate information about AIDS available to our schools and religious education programs. I leave it to the judgment of our educators as to how this information might best be used in educational programs to assist students in forming a correct, compassionate, and healthy attitude toward persons with AIDS and their families.

Another critical concern is the employment of persons who have contracted the AIDS virus, ARC, or AIDS itself. As in other areas, the Church has a responsibility to give good example in such situations. Accordingly, our Department of Employee Services has developed a general employment policy for all employees with life-threatening illnesses, including AIDS. Further, since at the present time the HTLV-III blood screen test is neither wholly accurate nor diagnostic nor predictive of AIDS, it is not to be used as an instrument for hiring persons working at any level of the archdiocese or seeking admission to our schools or other Church institutions.

To ensure that our response to the many dimensions of the AIDS crisis is effective, I will soon appoint a Pastoral Care Coordinator for AIDS Ministry. Working within the Archdiocesan Department of Community Services and, specifically, in conjunction with Catholic Charities, this person will oversee and coordinate present and future initiatives in our AIDS ministry. This person will also serve as liaison with the other public, private, and religious groups with which the archdiocese will collaborate.

I also call upon the parishes of the archdiocese to open their doors and their hearts to those touched in any way by AIDS.

There is a final point I wish to make in regard to our AIDS ministry. When we minister to persons with AIDS, like Jesus, we do so with love and compassion. It is not our task to make judgments but to call ourselves and those to whom we minister to a deeper conversion and healing. It would be a mistake to use our personal encounters with AIDS patients only as an occasion to speak about moral principles of behavior.

Nonetheless, as persons concerned about the well-being of all our sisters and brothers, we should do all we can—as we minister to the broader community—to encourage people to live in a way that will enhance life, not threaten or destroy it. It seems appropriate, therefore, to remind ourselves of the call to use God's gift of sexuality morally and responsibly, as well as the obligation to seek help when problems with drugs or other substances develop. In addition to being the correct thing to do, it could do a great deal to prevent the spread of the AIDS virus in the future.

CONCLUSION

As the archbishop of Chicago, I call upon the members of our faith community to join me in reaching out to and caring for those suffering from AIDS as well as their families and friends. It is our Christian responsibility to provide for the physical necessities of our suffering brothers and sisters in a context of spiritual support and prayer. As the Introduction to the Rite of the Anointing and Care of the Sick reminds us, "the one who is seriously ill needs the special help of God's grace in this time of anxiety, lest she (he) be broken in spirit and subject to temptations and the weakening of faith."

I know that the fear and pain can be great, but we are a community whose Master's love was so pervasive that it broke through all barriers—those created by society as well as those built up in the human heart. Our responsibility and challenge is to overcome ignorance and prejudice, to become a community of healing and reconciliation in which those who are suffering from AIDS can move from a sense of alienation to one of unity, from a sense of judgment to one of unconditional love. I personally commit myself to praying and working to achieve this goal. Please join me!

I began this Pastoral Statement by telling the tragic story of Stephen. I would like to conclude with another—a story of hope.

Once a leper came to Jesus and pleaded on his knees: "If you want," he said, "you can cure me." Feeling sorry for him, Jesus stretched out his hand and touched him. "Of course I want to," he said, "Be cured." And the leprosy left him at once and he was cured (Mark 1:40-42).

At the very start of his ministry, Jesus broke through the religious and social barriers of his day and dared to touch the pain of a fellow human being. His touch brought healing and life.

At this moment of the AIDS crisis, we come before the same Lord in need of healing. Healing is needed in our society, within the Church, within families, and by individuals and communities directly affected by AIDS. Today our prayer is the same as the leper's: "If you want to, you can cure us." Already his hands are stretching through the barriers, and he is saying, "Of course I want to."

In faith we know that we are not alone as we face our *challenge* and fulfill our *responsibility*.

"Come, Holy Spirit"

A Pastoral Statement on the Catholic Charismatic Renewal

—*Pentecost, 1988* —————————————————————

My dear friends in the Lord:

In the Acts of the Apostles (1:14), Jesus' disciples are described as "devoting themselves to constant prayer" until the Holy Spirit came upon them. At Pentecost the Spirit filled their incomplete lives, freed them from fear, and gave them the courage to proclaim "Jesus is Lord!" Their new awareness of God's power in their lives drew them into communities of loving service and witness to the world, and inspired them to be willing to lay down their lives for the kingdom.

The Holy Spirit continues to play an important role in the Church's rebirth and renewal in our day. As members of the Church, we are all called to let God's Spirit work in and through our lives, as we enter into an intimate relationship with the Lord Jesus and proceed prayerfully on our pilgrim way to the Father.

The mystery of Pentecost has a special place in the charismatic renewal, which provides a way for Catholics, led by the Spirit, to experience some of the freshness, newness, and enthusiasm of the early Church. And so, this is an appropriate moment to share some reflections with you about the Catholic charismatic renewal.

This Pastoral Statement is dedicated to the loving memory of Father James Jakes, the former liaison between the charismatic renewal and myself. He was a man of deep prayer, gentle persuasion, unshakeable faith, and fidelity to the Gospel. He helped many members of this local church—laity, religious, and clergy alike—in innumerable ways, and we continue to miss him greatly.

He had urged me to issue a statement like this and helped me prepare its first draft. At his funeral I promised that I would complete this

Pastoral Statement and issue it in his honor. Since then, as this document reflects, the liaison structure between the renewal and my office has undergone some significant changes. I have also invested additional time in developing this statement because the Catholic charismatic renewal deserves such care and attention from its bishop.

My hope is that this statement will strengthen the Catholic charismatic renewal and help bring about a new Pentecost in the Church of Chicago.

With cordial good wishes, I remain

Devotedly yours in Christ,

Joseph Cardinal Bernardin
Archbishop of Chicago

"Come, Holy Spirit" has been the fervent prayer of Christians throughout the centuries. The Spirit of God has always been present and active in the Church, and continues to guide and enliven it today.

"Come, Holy Spirit" is, in part, a prayer for spiritual renewal. In preparation for the Second Vatican Council, Pope John XXIII led the whole Church in praying, "Renew your Church as by a new Pentecost in our time." The conciliar and postconciliar years have focused Catholics' attention on personal and ecclesial renewal as well as the Church's role in the modern world.

The charismatic renewal has been an authentic part of the Church's spiritual renewal, supported by both Pope Paul VI and Pope John Paul II. In 1984 the Administrative Board of the National Conference of Catholic Bishops issued a Pastoral Statement on the Catholic Charismatic Renewal. That national document provides the basis for this archdiocesan statement, which is intended to complement, not to repeat, what the U.S. bishops have already said.

The Catholic charismatic renewal has been and is a *wonderful blessing* to the church of Chicago. The "charismatic" and the "institutional" dimensions of the Church are complementary and, as St. Paul himself acknowledged, sometimes in tension with one another. Christians need the freedom to allow the Spirit to "blow where it may" as well as certain regulations or guidelines to preserve the good order of the community, and to establish an appropriate climate in which they can carefully discern the Spirit's authentic presence and activities.

In this Pastoral Statement I will (1) clarify certain issues associated with the renewal; (2) explain why it deserves our support; (3) point out certain challenges which all of us in the Church, including members of the renewal, face; and (4) describe the current resources and liaison structure of the renewal within the archdiocese.

CLARIFICATION OF CERTAIN ISSUES

Conversion

Authentic Christian conversion is not a single, once-for-all event but rather a lifelong effort. Christians strive to walk in Jesus' way, and that means a continual struggle to allow the Spirit to deepen the faith they have received in baptism. We all need to turn from self-centeredness towards openness to the gift and beauty of life itself and towards the service of God and neighbor.

Nevertheless, there are occasional moments when individuals experience fundamental spiritual changes in their lives. About ten years ago, for example, I personally came to realize that to be a truly effective pastor—one who would walk with his people in the valley of darkness—I had to put Jesus first in my life, both in theory and in practice. Personal prayer became an essential part of my daily life, and, since that time, everything has changed! I have let go of myself and put my life in the Lord's hands. I retain my human weakness, but there has been a fundamental spiritual difference in my life, a deepening of my faith, a new intimacy with the Lord that gives meaning and perspective to all that I say and do.

Many members of the Catholic charismatic renewal have had similar experiences of spiritual change or conversion. They often refer to such a moment of transformation as "baptism in the Spirit."

"Baptism in the Spirit"

Many people have been Catholics since birth. The charismatic renewal offers them a way, among others, to experience and maintain an adult commitment to Jesus and his Church. Participation in the renewal nurtures an internal desire to let God work more freely in their lives. During an initial "Life in the Spirit" seminar, they pray and receive instruction. This process culminates when members of the prayer group encircle and lay hands upon them. This moment is called "baptism in the Spirit."

For many, it is a moment of special grace when they experience a release of certain charisms of the Spirit, gifts which often were received earlier in baptism and confirmation. This event does not compete with, discount, or ignore the effects of sacramental baptism or the other sacraments; instead, it builds upon them. The experience of gifts simply means that the persons being prayed over may become more aware of the newness and freshness of the Spirit's presence through a peace, joy, and trust that lead to generous service of others. Beyond this moment of spiritual transformation, claiming Jesus as Lord takes on a deeper meaning during their pilgrim journey through life.

"Charisms"

The spiritual gifts or "charisms," from which the renewal takes its name, are understood as gifts from God to be used for the good of the Church. This implies that, when individuals use these gifts in the service of others, they allow the Lord's power to work in and through them. For good order and the Church's well-being, the community and its pastors are to test these gifts and encourage their expression so that the whole Church might grow "perfect in holiness." Two particular "charisms" require some clarification.

Speaking in Tongues

Speaking in tongues, often quite prominent in the charismatic renewal, may seem strange or mysterious at first to those who are not familiar with it.

However, have you ever wanted to speak to God, but did not know exactly what to say? The gift of tongues—what appears to be speaking or singing in unintelligible sounds—is simply a way of praying, a form of contemplative prayer. Specific words with precise intellectual content are set aside to allow for a deeper union of one's heart with the Lord. Spoken words may also have the same effect, but a certain freedom comes with the gift of tongues and allows for new possibilities of communication with God. In some instances, this prayer may be interpreted for the community by someone with the particular gift of interpreting tongues. Many within the renewal experience the gift of tongues as a way of allowing them to let go of their inhibition and hesitancy, to risk living a fully committed Christian life.

It is important to keep the gift in its proper perspective. In his correspondence with the church at Corinth, St. Paul pointed out that the gift of tongues is not the most important of the Spirit's gifts and should not draw undue attention. Moreover, when individuals are prayed over and do *not* receive this gift, it does not imply that they have not experienced the Spirit's presence or that they are resistant to God's grace or gifts. God's Spirit is not bound by our expectations.

What *is* essential is the presence of the Spirit of love, for love, as St. Paul has said so beautifully, is "the way which surpasses all others" (1 Cor 13:1).

Healing

As the Gospels frequently attest, healing the sick was an important dimension of Jesus' ministry. Through the centuries it has continued to be a vital part of the Church's mission—for example, by celebrating the sacrament of the anointing of the sick, sponsoring health care facilities, maintaining special places of pilgrimage.

Healing—spiritual, psychological, or physical—may also take place within a charismatic prayer setting. Healing is God's work and makes manifest the presence of his kingdom. The Church rejoices in this and praises God for his goodness and compassion.

At the same time, healing is to be placed in its proper perspective. The episode of the healing of the leper in Mark's Gospel (1:40-45), like similar healing narratives, affirms that God works through those who heal the sick. The passage also implies that Jesus is more than a miracle worker. His followers rejoice in God's healing power whenever and wherever it is truly manifested. Nevertheless, healing is not to be viewed as a spectacle to gather crowds or to promote the popularity of the healer.

When a serious question arises about the authenticity of a healing, the matter is to be resolved by the discernment of the community and its pastors. Failure to experience healing does not, of itself, mean that the afflicted person is sinful or lacking in faith. When nonsacramental anointing is used in healing services in the archdiocese, the group is to be reminded that this action is different from the sacrament of the anointing of the sick.

Prayers of deliverance are part of the healing ministry. As the U.S. bishops' Pastoral Statement on the Charismatic Renewal indicates, "deliverance addresses some form of inordinate control being exercised over a specific aspect of a person's life" (pp. 19–20). Such control is more than an ordinary temptation and less than full demonic possession. That is why prayers of deliverance are not to be confused with exorcism. As the U.S. bishops also counseled, when a group uses prayers of deliverance, "wise pastoral guidance and discernment of spirits are absolute requirements" (p. 19). Moreover, if such prayers are to be offered vocally, they should be done by a team whose ministry is recognized by the local community and its pastors. "Excessive preoccupation with the demonic and the indiscriminate exercise of deliverance ministries are based upon a distortion of biblical evidence and are pastorally harmful" (p. 20).

Support for the Charismatic Renewal in the Archdiocese

Pope John Paul II has called the Catholic charismatic renewal "a very important component of the entire renewal of the Church" (December 11, 1979). And as the renewal's leaders constantly remind us, participation in the renewal is not an end in itself, but a "means" of renewal, a help toward personal conversion, a valuable way of renewing the Church in our day.

The Catholic charismatic renewal is alive and well in the Archdiocese of Chicago! There are more than 150 prayer groups throughout Cook and

Lake counties. More than 10,000 people, representing every age, ethnic background, racial origin, socioeconomic state, and career belong to the renewal. Their weekly meetings are times of shared prayer and praise, instruction in spirituality, and response to the needs of the Church and the world.

Members of the renewal, like many other members of the Catholic community, reach out to alienated youth, the disabled, the homeless, the hungry, prisoners, gang members. They give assistance to broken families and to those troubled by unwanted pregnancy. They work toward justice, peace, and charity. All these activities, moreover, are to be integrated into an active parish life, especially in the fervent, joyful celebration of the Eucharist.

Speaking about the charismatic renewal, Pope John Paul II has pointed out the "unique and indispensable role" of priests in the renewal. He has encouraged the priest "to adopt a welcoming attitude toward it, to embrace it, based on the desire he [the priest] shares with every Christian by Baptism, to grow in the gifts of the Spirit" (March 23, 1980).

Members of the Catholic charismatic renewal in the archdiocese have often indicated that they greatly desire the ministry and guidance of priests. Realistically, this does not imply that every priest need agree with or feel drawn toward all the aspects of the renewal. But it does invite priests to be willing to minister to its members, to assist them in their discernment, and to help them in difficult moments as individuals and as a group.

I encourage pastors and all those in positions of ecclesial leadership to welcome Catholics within the renewal into their faith communities, to open parish doors for their prayer meetings, and to support and foster their activities. I am grateful that many do precisely these things. Moreover, I urge priests and other pastoral ministers to do them out of a genuine concern for their people, responding to their authentic pastoral needs and desires.

I also encourage renewal members to participate fully in the life of the Church by supporting parochial life and worship. I am delighted that so many do precisely this. I urge them to share with their parish what they have learned about the joy of the Lord, and not to give into the temptation to pull away. All members of the Church deserve to share the Lord's peace and joy. This fosters new hope and trust among all members of the Church and helps eliminate unwarranted negative criticism and judgment. At the same time, I ask members of the renewal to be willing to exercise prudence in their zeal and enthusiasm when it may be detrimental to the development of the renewal or to the harmony of their local parochial community.

This collaboration between the renewal and parish life is mutually beneficial. Priests provide appropriate spiritual direction and the kind of

Scripture study and theological reflection that deepen faith. Catholics in the renewal, in turn, use their gifts to help carry out the parish's mission, evangelizing those who are distant from the Lord, praying for the whole parish community, and assisting in its ministries and services. By mutual collaboration a healthy sense of the Church will flourish, and the total community will more ably manifest to the world "how these Christians love one another."

CERTAIN CHALLENGES TO BE FACED

Mutual trust, support, and collaboration between pastors and the members of the Catholic charismatic renewal are essential if the entire Church, including the prayer groups, is to face certain challenges as well. The specific challenges I raise here, while not by any means unique to the renewal, are, nonetheless, of special concern to renewal leaders and all others who seek to be faithful to the Church's tradition and teaching and who devote their lives to building up the body of Christ.

I will discuss three specific challenges here: (a) reading the Scriptures in an authentic Catholic way, (b) balancing an intimate relationship with Jesus with service to the community, and (c) integrating groups into the larger ecclesial community. Stated negatively, they imply avoiding (a) biblical fundamentalism, (b) spiritual narcissism and quietism, and (c) separatism and elitism.

Catholic Reading of Scripture

Renewed interest in sacred Scripture is a manifestation of God's providence in our day. Hearing and heeding God's word is at the heart of all authentic spiritual renewal, including the Catholic charismatic renewal. All members of the Church, all disciples of Jesus, are called to respond to the proclamation of God's word by reflecting upon it prayerfully, studying it carefully, and putting it into practice faithfully.

In accord with the teaching of the Second Vatican Council, Catholics esteem Scripture as part of the Church's tradition, as essential and normative for the community of faith. Both Scripture and tradition "make up a single, sacred deposit of the Word of God" (Dogmatic Constitution on Divine Revelation, no. 10). That is why "both Scripture and Tradition must be accepted and honored with equal feelings of devotion and reverence" (9).

Catholics approach sacred Scripture in the same spirit in which it was formulated, namely, a fervent response to God's marvelous deeds. They pay close attention to the literary, historical, theological, and canonical context of the biblical text. This helps ensure that the fullness of divine revelation will be an effective force in their personal lives and in the life of their communities. It also helps ensure avoidance of fundamentalism, a literalist interpretation that does not take into adequate consideration a text's fuller context and thereby distorts its intended meaning.

Familiarity with the Bible is an essential dimension of Catholic spiritual renewal. Yet, it is not an easy task. Each of us reads the Scriptures with personal presuppositions and selectivity. This means that we often approach and interpret the biblical text in a subjective manner. While the local assembly plays an important role in interpreting the Bible, the New Testament itself describes the larger Church as a network of local communities under the leadership of the apostles and their successors. That is why Catholics must look to the Church's teaching authority, which is in continuity with previous generations of believers and under the ongoing inspiration of the Holy Spirit, for an authentic interpretation of Scripture.

Balance of Personal Spirituality and Service

Because of the peace and joy associated with spiritual renewal and religious experiences readily found in the charismatic renewal and other vehicles of renewal, we are sometimes tempted to devote as much time as possible to activities which foster and nourish these gifts. This is quite understandable, but, unfortunately, it may also lead to neglect of important responsibilities associated with marriage, family, priestly ministry, religious life, work.

In extreme cases, it may lead a person to withdraw from the world— not in order to join a monastic community or to adopt a contemplative lifestyle but to avoid involvement with the concrete reality of daily life. It may also prompt an individual, with a sincere intent to acknowledge utter dependence upon God, simply to place everything in God's hands *without* doing anything personally or making any efforts to implement gospel values in the world.

Spiritual narcissism and quietism are contrary to Jesus' own criterion of spiritual discernment: "By their fruits you will know them" (Matt 7:16-19). The proof of authentic spiritual renewal is how we carry out our individual responsibilities at home, at work, and in the world—by the way we work for social justice and peace, caring especially for the most vulnerable among us.

Integration in the Local Ecclesial Community

During the Church's history it has often experienced a natural human tendency to form elitist groups which separate themselves from other members of the community and look upon the "uninitiated" as inferior to themselves. Although this may not be a conscious attitude on their part, it is often expressed in subtle ways and may cause considerable harm to a parish community.

I wish to emphasize that charismatic groups may not experience this tendency any greater or more often than others. Nonetheless, as I noted in the previous section, it is vital to the Church's harmony and development that all groups within a parish community be fully integrated with the local community of faith. All who are truly attuned to the Spirit's promptings must relentlessly seek ways and means for contributing to building up the whole body of Christ, the Church. They will find their legitimate place in the pluriformity of Church life and participation today.

RESOURCES FOR THE RENEWAL IN THE ARCHDIOCESE

The archdiocese has several resources to assist the development of the Catholic charismatic renewal. First, there are the liaisons, my delegates to the renewal, its groups, its ministries, and all its members. Presently, Father Paul Burak is the Archdiocesan Liaison to the Renewal.

It is my expectation that every Catholic charismatic prayer group and ministry be affiliated both with its respective parish or ecclesial institution and with the Catholic Charismatic Renewal Center for Chicago. This implies mutual responsibilities. As the U.S. bishops pointed out in their Pastoral Statement on the Charismatic Renewal:

> Those in the Renewal should look to the bishop for guidance, keeping him informed, asking his suggestions, maintaining contact with the diocesan liaison. On the other hand, bishops need to take personal pastoral responsibility for the Renewal, especially for the formation of leaders (9).

The Catholic Charismatic Renewal Center for Chicago (CCRCC) is the representative body of Catholics involved in the renewal in the archdiocese. The ministry of CCRCC is promoted by a Service Team made up of the Archdiocesan Liaison and seven other people, all of whom are appointed by the archbishop. The ninth member of the team is the director of the center, who is chosen by the team. The Service Team is developing an Advisory Board which will reflect the variety and diversity found within the renewal. The center and the Service Team have my full support as they strive to unify the diversity that exists in the Catholic charismatic renewal within the archdiocese.

With the assistance and support of the Liaison's Office, the CCRCC has established a center to meet the needs of anyone interested or involved in the renewal by providing information, communication, conferences, teaching seminars, and other events and services to "build the Body of Christ." *The Vine,* CCRCC's monthly newsletter, provides news, teachings, testimonies, and a calendar of coming events. Visitors and volunteers are always welcome at the center.

The renewal transcends the Church's ethnic and racial dimensions. Nevertheless, I would like to commend in a special way the work of the charismatic renewal in the Hispanic community. It is organized under *Renovacion Carismatica Catolica Hispana* (RCCH). Its special liaison is Father Richard Simon. Because of the diversity of Spanish-speaking nationalities—Cubans, Mexicans, Puerto Ricans, Central and South Americans—these prayer groups form a unique meeting place where spiritual ties overcome social, political, and other barriers.

Hispanic evangelistic ministries are an important part of the renewal. "Alabare," a weekly television program is coordinated by the deacons and the laity of the Hispanic Catholic charismatic community. Like CCRCC, evangelistic teams minister in retreat work, music ministry, youth ministry, healing, and MAPA (ministry for those affected by abortion).

I warmly encourage continuous efforts toward unity in the midst of the diversity present within the Catholic charismatic renewal throughout the Archdiocese of Chicago.

CONCLUSION

The spiritual renewal of ourselves and the Church is at the heart of a new Pentecost. While not everyone is called to be "charismatic," all are encouraged to let God's Spirit work in them. While not everyone is outgoing and expressive of his or her deepest feelings, all are called to enter into a personal and intimate relationship with the Lord Jesus. While not everyone speaks in tongues, all are called to yield to the prayer of the Spirit that comes from the heart.

While not everyone may be comfortable with a particular style of prayer, all are called to "pray in the Spirit . . . constantly and attentively for all in the holy company" (Eph 6:18). While each Christian responds to God's grace in a particular way, all belong to the one body of Christ in which each part is joined to and needs the others. All Catholics must heed the Spirit's universal call which constantly urges us to change our lives and yield to spiritual growth.

Openness to the work of the Spirit is a challenge of our times. The good effects of the Catholic charismatic renewal manifest a wonderful sign of this openness. An authentic way of life in the Church today, it is a gift to the body of Christ in innumerable ways.

It brings a voice of praise and joyful worship to our communities. Its proclamation that "Jesus is Lord!" reminds every Christian of the importance of an intimate relationship with Jesus, "who inspires and perfects our faith" (Heb 12:2). The renewal invites us to acknowledge our utter dependence upon the Father for all we are and do. The renewal is also a prophetic voice, challenging all women and men to give themselves over to God's power and grace.

To say it quite simply, the Catholic charismatic renewal is a vital part of this local church.

Together with Mary, the Mother of the Church, a model of openness to the Spirit, I pray with the Catholics in the charismatic renewal and the entire family of the archdiocese that we might all be true sons and daughters of God.

> Come, Holy Spirit,
>   fill the hearts of your faithful and
>   enkindle in them the fire of your love.
> Send forth your Spirit,
>   and they shall be re-created,
>   and you shall renew the face of the earth!

The Call to Service

Pastoral Statement on the Permanent Diaconate *
——*Autumn 1993* ————————————————————————

The order of deacon can be traced back to the early Church. The Eastern Churches have ordained permanent deacons through the centuries. But in the West, since the fourth or fifth century, the diaconate was generally conferred only as a sacred order preliminary to ordination to the priesthood and restricted primarily to liturgical functions.

The possibility of restoring the permanent diaconate to the Western Church was considered by the Council of Trent in the sixteenth century, but nothing was done to implement the idea. At the Second Vatican Council, a large number of bishops expressed a desire that the permanent diaconate be restored for the Latin Rite. Statements to this effect in both the Dogmatic Constitution on the Church (art. 29) and the Decree on the Church's Missionary Activity (art. 16) also add that the decision of whether and where it is opportune that the permanent diaconate be restored would pertain to each episcopal conference, subject to papal approval.

Accordingly, in 1967, Pope Paul VI reestablished the permanent diaconate in the Latin Rite, and placed the decision regarding its local restoration in the hands of each nation's episcopal conference, subject to papal approval. On May 2, 1968, the U.S. Catholic bishops petitioned the Holy See for permission to establish the permanent diaconate in our country. They received a favorable response on August 30, 1968.

So, this year we mark the 25th anniversary of the permanent diaconate in the United States, and that celebration provides the specific context

* Also published in *Deacon Digest*, vol. 11, no. 2, March/April 1994, pp. 14–15.

for this pastoral statement. After a quarter-century, we celebrate the fruits of the vision shared by the fathers of the Second Vatican Council and Pope Paul VI.

In the Archdiocese of Chicago, the first candidates began their preparation in 1970 and were ordained in 1972. Presently, 628 deacons serve this local church in parishes, hospitals, archdiocesan agencies, prisons, and wherever the needs of people call for their ministry. We currently have the largest number of deacons of all the dioceses in the world.

In this pastoral statement, I will clarify what diaconal ministry is; examine diaconal identity and explore how it sheds light on the relationship of deacons to others in the Church; explain how deacons are selected, prepared for, and assigned their ministry; and look toward the future of the permanent diaconate in the archdiocese.

Before I do this, I want to add a special word at the very outset about the wives of the permanent deacons. We all owe them an enormous debt of gratitude. By Church law, a married candidate for the permanent diaconate cannot be ordained without the written consent of his wife. The wives of our deacons have very generously given their consent, not without personal cost to their married and family life. Moreover, these wives have gone through the full three-year program of preparation with their husbands and have become aware of the unique gifts which they, too, bring to the ecclesial community. Many assist their husbands in serving the Church. The success of the collaboration of the deacons and their wives is a hopeful sign to the larger Church and society. Our celebration of 25 years of deacons' dedicated service to the church in the United States is, therefore, also an affirmation of, and an expression of deep gratitude for, the service which their wives have provided to the Church.

DIACONAL MINISTRY

There has been considerable misunderstanding about the nature of diaconal ministry. This is quite understandable. When the permanent diaconate was restored in the Latin Rite, we lacked any recent experience which could help shape its development. Moreover, this restoration occurred at a time when the council had also given a new impetus to lay ministry, and the number of priests had begun to decline.

From our centuries-old experience with the transitional diaconate, we initially placed a heavy emphasis on the permanent deacon's liturgical roles. Indeed, most Catholics encountered a permanent deacon only at Sunday Mass, where, wearing liturgical vestments, he looked like a "mini-priest." However, deacons in the U.S. do not normally wear clerical garb. In order to distinguish permanent from transitional deacons, some incorrectly conceived of the permanent diaconate as a "lay ministry" and referred to them as "lay deacons." So, the question naturally arises: Is the deacon a lay person or a cleric—or someone in between?

Deacons themselves have struggled with their identity and the essential nature of their ministry. Some have found themselves drawn to one aspect more than to another. Others report that one or two areas of responsibility prevent them from carrying out other important dimensions of their ministry. And still others continually search for new forms of diaconal ministry.

Let us return briefly to what the Second Vatican Council and the post-conciliar Popes—Paul VI and John Paul II—have said about the diaconate, because that is the starting-point for understanding and evaluating diaconal ministry today.

Threefold Service

The terms "deacon" and "diaconate" derive from the Greek word *diakonia* which means "service" or "ministry." A deacon, then, is ordained by the Church for *service*. But what kind of service? The conciliar and papal documents point to three traditional forms, whose roots reach back to the first Christian centuries and which encompass the three great areas of Church life: the transmission of the word, the celebration of the sacraments, and the community's loving service.

The *service of the word* is quite far-ranging and may include—besides proclaiming the gospel and articulating the Church's needs in the general intercessions at the liturgy—preaching, offering catechetical instruction, counseling, instructing catechumens, giving retreats, conducting parish renewal programs, and reaching out to alienated Catholics. There is also an informal dimension to this ministry of the word. Deacons have many opportunities to speak about Jesus and his gospel as they carry out their ministry of charity and justice, and as they live at home, work in the marketplace, and participate in civic life.

The *service of the altar* centers, above all, on the Eucharist, but includes other sacraments as well. The deacon's role in the Eucharist—in addition to proclaiming the gospel and articulating the Church's needs in the general intercessions—is to prepare the gifts and distribute Communion at the Lord's table. Moreover, the deacon may solemnly baptize children or adults, witness marriages in the name of the Church, bring viaticum to the dying, and preside over wakes, funerals, and burial services. He may also preside over Liturgies of the Word, the Liturgy of the Hours and exposition and benediction of the Blessed Sacrament. He may lead non-sacramental reconciliation services, conduct prayer services for the sick and dying, and administer certain of the Church's sacramentals.

The *service of charity* is as extensive as are human needs. Deacons minister in prisons and in hospitals, serving prisoners and the sick. They visit the homebound and people in nursing homes. They serve the mentally ill, the chemically dependent, the abused and the battered, the old and the young, the abandoned, the dying and the bereaved, immigrants and refugees, and the victims of racial and ethnic discrimination. In the Archdiocese of Chicago, they also assist the homeless at shelters and the hungry through the SHARE/food program, as well as other food distribution efforts. There are more than enough opportunities in metropolitan Chicago for our deacons to carry out their ministry of serving the poor and the needy. In doing all this, they carry out the biblical mandate to feed the hungry, clothe the naked, and give relief to all in need.

Nonetheless, in modern society, it is no longer sufficient merely to help someone in need. The root causes of such needs must also be addressed. As Pope John Paul pointed out to U.S. permanent deacons in Detroit in 1987,

> The Second Vatican Council reminds us that the ministry of charity . . . also obliges us to be a positive influence for change in the world in which we live . . . so that society may be renewed by Christ and transformed into the family of God.

This means that deacons, like other disciples, are to be a "leaven" in the world. They are to bring the values of the gospel to bear on marriage and family life, U.S. culture, economic and social life, the trades and professions, and political institutions. Today, the potential for the deacon's involvement in efforts to bring about structural change through economic, political, and legislative strategies is virtually unlimited and sorely needed. This means that working for social justice—striving to overcome such evils as abortion, euthanasia, and racism, to name only a few—is an integral, vital part of the deacon's ministry of charity or love today.

Interconnectedness of Three Forms of Service

These three dimensions of diaconal service—ministry of the word, the altar, and charity—are intimately interconnected or, in Pope John Paul's words, "inseparably joined together as one in the service of God's redemptive plan." What does this mean? "The word of God," the Holy Father explains, "inevitably leads to the Eucharistic worship of God at the altar; in turn, this worship leads to a new way of living which expresses itself in acts of charity." He also offers this corollary: "By the same token, acts of charity which are not rooted in the word of God and in worship cannot bear lasting fruit." Another way of saying this is that the deacon's ministry at the altar needs to be an extension of the ministry of service he has given in the community. He brings the needs of the poor to the altar and takes from it the wisdom and the strength to minister to the poor.

In short, if a deacon is to be an authentic sign of the Servant-Christ—who is prophet, priest, and king—his diaconal ministry must include all three dimensions. However, that does not mean that he must give equal time to all three. The needs of the community, the deacon's own specific competence, and the guidance of the Church's pastors will help him decide how to use his resources wisely and effectively.

DIACONAL IDENTITY

At this point, one may legitimately ask: What is unique about diaconal ministry? Looking at the three areas of the Church's life and the deacon's various responsibilities necessarily raises the question because some of the functions—e.g., reading the gospel at the Eucharist—may also be carried out by priests. Others—such as working for social justice—rightly pertain to any baptized Christian. What makes a deacon different? And to return to a question raised earlier: Is the deacon a cleric or a layperson?

The Sacrament of Orders

The answer is found by examining the nature of the sacrament of orders. The diaconate is a distinct order within the ordained ministry of the Church. Deacons are clerics, not laypersons. The grace of the sacrament of orders strengthens them and makes their ministry fruitful. Because the deacon is an ordained minister, he must always minister in union with and for the Church. He no longer acts on his own or in his own name. Neither is he meant to be a substitute for either a priest or a layperson.

All Christians, by reason of their baptism, receive their own gifts from the Holy Spirit, but not all receive the same gifts. Likewise, each member of the Church shares a responsibility for its mission, but not all receive the same charism. There is a unity of mission but a diversity of charism and ministry. Central among all the ministerial gifts which are given to the Church are the ordained ministries of the bishop, the priest, and the deacon. The essential role of these ordained ministers is to lead the Church in carrying out its mission by coordinating all its other ministries and services. Canon 1008 of the Revised Code of Canon Law explains the nature of the sacrament of orders in this way:

> By divine institution some among the Christian faithful are constituted sacred ministers through the sacrament of orders by means of the indelible character with which they are marked; accordingly they are consecrated

and deputed to shepherd the people of God, each in accord with his own grade of orders, by fulfilling in the person of Christ the Head the functions of teaching, sanctifying, and governing.

When we say that a deacon is ordained specifically for *service*, that does not mean simply that he is to serve the bishop or the parish priests. All three orders—which constitute one full office in the Church—serve the People of God, but in three different ways. By reason of ordination, the deacon is to serve as a sign or sacrament of Jesus himself, who "came not to be served but to serve." Because Jesus was a servant, his Church must also be a servant. Pope John Paul II has said that the service of deacons "is the Church's service sacramentalized"—that is, made visible. They are to be "living signs" of the servant dimension of the entire Church.

This does not mean that the deacon has a monopoly on service in the Church. Many of the tasks he performs can be carried out by others in the community, and his ordination is not intended to exclude others from performing those tasks. *All* in the Church are to serve others. But by liturgical consecration and the empowerment of *some* among us—that is, the deacons—this call and response to serve is made visible and effective. So, the deacon is a sign and instrument of that manifold service without which the Church cannot be the sign and instrument of the risen Lord Jesus.

In other words, when the deacon assists at the Eucharist—or when he serves in the soup line, the prison, or the hospital—he is meant to be an eloquent reminder to each of us of what we, too, should be doing, what we must continually strive to become, in accord with our own God-given gifts.

Relationship with Priests

As I stated above, the deacon shares ordained ministry with the bishop and the priest. Unfortunately, because of our limited vision of the nature of the permanent diaconate twenty-five years ago, the deacon's ministry has often been defined in terms of what he can or cannot do in comparison with the priest or bishop. After a quarter-century of experience, we are beginning to move beyond that. Deacons are not called to be replacements for priests, even though they may share responsibility for ministry within a parish or other ecclesial institution. While the priesthood and the diaconate are distinct orders, they are not in competition with one another. Deacons are not "mini-priests," but they must exercise their ministry in communion with priests, complementing priestly ministry with diaconal service.

This implies that permanent deacons must respect the office of priest and collaborate with him and the parish staff. Deacons have a corresponding right to be fully respected and accepted as ordained ministers by the priest and parish staff, as well as the parishioners.

Relationship with Laity

A fundamental aspect of the deacon's ministry is to model and encourage the development of the servant ministry of all the baptized. The deacon's task is to inspire, enable, and prepare the laity for the service of others. How faithful the deacon is to his call will be evident to the extent that others are inspired, welcomed, and led to engage in the ministry of service as a result of his presence and ministry.

The fundamental role of the deacon, then, is to perceive the presence of Christ in the needy, the helpless, and the poor—and to reveal this presence to the rest of the People of God, including the bishop. Then the deacon's responsibility is to call all of us to respond to that presence—and to do something about it.

This is most visible in the deacon's liturgical role, in his assistance at the Eucharist. When someone who works with the poor also proclaims the Good News, calls on the people for prayers of compassion, prepares the gifts and distributes Communion, people can recognize the connection between a deacon's ministry of charity and his ministry of the word and the altar. The people's participation in the liturgy also forms them for Christian service. The laity are the hope and future of the Church; permanent deacons can be the catalysts, working with them to address particular needs.

Distinctive Role: Married Clergy in the World

There is another special dimension to the permanent diaconate: Most of our permanent deacons are married men who also work in the world. This means that the deacon has a special witness to give. As Pope John Paul has pointed out, "the fact that he is an ordained minister of the Church brings a special dimension to his efforts in the eyes of those with whom he lives and works."

While our permanent deacons and their wives have made many contributions to our lives and the Church, I would like to single out two of them, in particular, which remain important needs and continue to present significant challenges.

1. Marriage and Family Life. Since the great majority of our deacons are married, the development and nurturing of the relationship between them and their wives is essential to meaningful and productive ministry. The experience which our deacons and their wives, along with their families, bring to the Church is unique in our time. Burdened with all the responsibilities of a job, a home, and a family, they struggle, together, to maintain a meaningful and growing relationship with one another and with God—not unlike the challenge faced by the great majority of the People of God. Their life of prayer and service enriches and challenges us all. Their efforts to grow as spiritual men and women, and as a couple, have much to teach us. Since diaconal ministry and life are still relatively new to the Church, we have not yet had the opportunity to identify and reflect on the richness which their experience will add to our understanding of the sacrament of matrimony.

2. Marketplace Ministry. I have already alluded to this, but I wish to highlight its importance and potential for the Church and society because "marketplace ministry" is still a fairly rare phenomenon. There are several possible reasons for this. We may have done a better job in preparing deacons for their ministries of the word and altar than for carrying out their ministry of charity and social justice. We may have found it necessary to use our deacons more to meet parochial needs. Perhaps, we simply have not understood the importance of their ministry of charity in our local church today.

Who will ask the hard questions within our local communities, our factories and offices, our schools and neighborhoods? Why are people homeless, hungry, out of work? Why are some welcome, and others not? Why is there such violence and disregard for life? And who will do something about it? Should this not be an arena in which the deacon serves? Should not the deacon play a leading role in bringing back to his faith community a social awareness, a call to respond, a challenge to help build the kingdom of God?

By now, it is clear that being a deacon is an enormous challenge. That leads to another set of questions. Who is called to become a deacon? Who verifies that call? How are deacons prepared for their ministry? How are they assigned within the local church?

DIACONAL VOCATION, FORMATION, AND ASSIGNMENT

Vocation

The call to the diaconate is both a call from God to serve, and a call from the community of faith which is to be served. This call does not come to the individual alone, nor for his own sake. It is received in the community of faith, for the community of faith, and affirmed and recognized by this same community. Otherwise, we must question its source. An individual may feel an attraction, a "call" if you will, to a deeper spirituality, to a more permanent commitment to the Church's ministry, but it must always be discerned in communion with the faith community.

Anyone who hears such a call, who feels gifted with the charism of service, must have that gift validated by the Church. Today, while some individuals present themselves to their pastors and pastoral staffs for consideration, most of those who enter into discernment are invited to do so by those responsible for the pastoral care of the particular community. Usually through its designated leaders, the Church must discern that an individual has the God-given charism to meet a particular need, to perform a specific service. Then this local church has an obligation to assist him in further discernment, spiritual formation, and whatever theological and pastoral preparation is needed to enhance that gift for service of God's people.

A call to the diaconate must be supported by a man's lived dedication to service and compassion long before the call to holy orders is offered. The charism of *diakonia* held prior to ordination remains the same; the service he did for people, the ministry he carried out for the Church, may remain the same.

Yet, as I explained above, the celebration of holy orders, ordination, does make a difference—a twofold difference. For the *Church*, ordination is the public commissioning by the diocesan bishop of an individual for a ministry considered vital for the community's life and growth. For the *deacon*, it is the acceptance of and permanent commitment to this special call. The Church publicly recognizes that this individual has demonstrated a God-given call and gift for service and can personally be a symbol of the ministry to which we are all called. The individual, with the grace of the sacrament of orders, publicly promises fidelity to the obligations inherent in such a call to the just and compassionate service of people.

Formation: Initial and Continuing

The formation of deacons for ministry must be both ongoing and appropriate to the identity and ministry of the diaconate.

Formation is not simply a program; it is a process. It involves an openness to lifelong growth in spirituality, ministerial competence, personal accountability, and the development of community. Unless deacons continue to deepen their relationship with God, enrich their theological knowledge and pastoral skills, open themselves to valid critique or evaluation, and share both faith and ministry with others, they cannot be who they say they are: servants of the gospel. If they do remain open to the formative effect of prayer, study, and community, they will not only be servants, but also credible servants of the gospel of Jesus Christ.

A strong formation program is a program attuned to the ministry and needs of the deacons. It is pastoral in tone and direction, employs an adult-learning style of education, teaches skills in theological reflection, offers opportunities for personal and communal spiritual growth, provides experience in a variety of ministries, and is based on the theological, scriptural, and liturgical teaching and insights of Vatican II. It should also highlight the importance of social justice. By design and in implementation, a diaconal formation program should both reflect and address the needs of all people—across lines of race and ethnic origin as well as socioeconomic status. Unless the diaconal formation process itself meets these diverse needs, it will not be able to assist the larger society troubled by cultural and socioeconomic divisions.

In short, the diaconal formation program is a beginning step in a lifelong and joint pursuit of the kingdom of justice, love, and peace.

Assignment of Deacons

At the time of ordination, deacons make a promise of obedience to their diocesan bishop and his successors. They are to collaborate with the bishop in serving the needs of the people as the bishop directs, where he discerns the need. The deacon is ordained for the archdiocese and, like our priests, is accountable to the bishop. He is not the "parish deacon," nor does he belong exclusively to, or serve only, that given community.

However, since diaconal candidates come from specific parishes, our practice has been to return them to serve the communities from which they came. This has not been the practice in all dioceses. As the Archdiocese of Chicago develops structures and ministries to respond to specific local needs within our vicariates and deaneries, we anticipate a different use of the wealth of talent and experience our deacons share with us. While they may initially serve in their community of origin, we may invite them to serve in other communities where the need is greater, and their gifts are more needed. We anticipate that they will collaborate much more closely with our episcopal vicars and deans in responding to identified needs. Steps are already being taken to prepare for such an expansion of diaconal presence within the archdiocese. We believe that the great generosity and flexibility of our deacons will provide still another example of *diakonia* within the context of these new avenues of service to our people.

As the shortage of priests grows, many parishes have used deacons, among others, to meet needs and situations formerly addressed by the priest. Of course, such needs must be met. But I caution pastors, pastoral staffs, and the deacons themselves not to co-opt diaconal ministry in this way. Many permanent deacons have not been trained or formed as leaders. Moreover, others can be trained and formed to meet many of these concerns, thereby freeing the permanent deacon for his ministry of charity and justice in the larger community.

The deacon should be the one who brings to the pastoral staff an awareness of the needs of the people, not only in the parish, but also in the broader community. The deacon should be the one who is free to respond to the immediate needs and demands of the poor, the unemployed, the sick, and the neglected who are present in each of our communities. The deacon should be the one prepared to address social justice issues in the larger community, and in the workplace—bringing back an awareness and a raising of consciousness to the faith community which he also serves. This is the unique contribution which the deacon can make both to the parochial staff and community.

Other parish ministers, often overwhelmed by their growing responsibilities and the many demands on their time, are unable to be present or to respond to these needs in the world. If the deacon should become totally enmeshed in parish life alone, we would lose what is perhaps the most vital and dynamic element of his particular call to service.

THE FUTURE OF THE PERMANENT DIACONATE IN THE ARCHDIOCESE

Our Expectations and Hopes for the Permanent Deacons

We need from each of our permanent deacons a life that witnesses to prayer, service, an unwavering commitment to social justice, and building community in line with the kingdom of God. We need deacons who understand the word of God well enough to proclaim it effectively and, if properly prepared and authorized, to preach on it. We need deacons who give witness to the stability and holiness of marriage and family life.

Since they live and work in the midst of the people, permanent deacons must contribute in unique ways to building the community of faith, and to strengthening community among all people. They live and work with people of every faith and nationality. They touch lives which the more structured efforts of our Church often do not reach. They need to be conscious of this. They need to be equipped to respond with organizational, community-building, and listening skills.

As the Church becomes more and more diverse ethnically and culturally, the deacons need to focus on building unity among the diverse peoples in their parishes and communities. We are blessed with many diaconal vocations from different ethnic and cultural groups. They can and should provide leadership in such multicultural efforts.

Deacons are involved in what is by nature a gregarious and out-reaching ministry. To avoid isolation and burn-out, they must be rooted in a community of people who understand and support diaconal ministry. We realize that some of this will come from their parish staff and the people they serve. But more is needed, namely, a sense of community among deacons who gather from time to time for support and prayer.

I am encouraged by the efforts being made in this regard within our archdiocese: the Diaconate Council, the Deacons' Personnel Board, the gatherings for deanery assemblies, their annual convocation, annual retreats, and the many efforts being made to bring them together for continuing spiritual and professional growth. It is important that all of our deacons experience this sense of community in order to ensure the well-being and growth of their ministries.

The deacons have also set priorities for their ministry to and with us. They will pursue social justice and actively address issues of poverty, alienation, and oppression in our society and within the Church. They have committed themselves to spiritual and intellectual growth for quality ministry that addresses our real needs. They are committed to collaborating with everyone, regardless of status, ministerial position, diversity of race, culture, or ethnic background. In short, they have pledged to serve us where our needs are greatest.

The Expectations and Hopes of the Permanent Deacons

Of Their Archbishop. As I have stated in my previous pastoral letter, *In Service of One Another,* "All ministries and ministers require and deserve development, support, enabling, enrichment, and encouragement. This is imperative because these ministries are gifts of the Lord for which we are grateful and responsible stewards. Our challenge is to discover effective ways of caring for all ministries and ministers" (p. 22).

This pastoral statement on the permanent diaconate gives me an opportunity to declare my respect and appreciation for the permanent deacons, the uniqueness of the diaconal charism, and their ministerial contributions to the Church. I am committed to a strong diaconal formation program, helping our deacons to grow spiritually and professionally, recognizing and accepting them as collaborators in my ministry, helping the deacons bring clearer focus to their ministry, and calling them to greater involvement in archdiocesan life.

Of Their Pastors, Priests, and Parish Staffs. The deacons have demonstrated their faithfulness over these twenty-five years. The contribution they have made to building up the Church, their efforts in fashioning a new ministry, the untold hours given in unnoticed efforts to serve our people—all this demonstrates that they have proven their worth. The permanent deacons in this local church have played an important role in the service of our people. Where they work in close collaboration with our priests, religious, and laity, significant things have been accomplished! They have earned the right to expect to be included in the dynamic collaboration necessary to serve our people, our parishes, and our agencies. They should be recognized for their contribution as ministers of the gospel. They are an integral element in the mosaic of the Church. The affirmation, supervision, and calling of these ministers to accountability by the pastor and the entire pastoral staff is the linchpin of successful diaconal ministry. Where this is present, we have seen diaconal ministry flourish, and other diaconal vocations come forth. Where it is absent, the Church, the deacons themselves, and the people are poorly served.

Of the People They Serve. As with everyone who ministers to others, deacons—and their wives—need the support of our prayers. I urge all of you to respect their call; open your hearts to them; share with them your concerns, both personal and for the Church. They need your encouragement and your friendship. The relationships you form together are the heart of the Christian community. They need to know you well; they need to share in your joys, your struggles, your happiness, and your sorrows so that they may truly bring your needs to others who minister to you with them. Living as you do, and working among you, gives them a great advantage, an opportunity many of us bishops and priests do not have.

They also need you to challenge them. You have a right to expect them to be examples of prayer, witnesses of authentic service, and reliable supports for yourself. Should this not be forthcoming, for whatever reason, call for it. The great gift of deacons is their availability and their flexibility. Affirm it and strengthen it by using it in your time of need.

We congratulate the permanent deacons as they celebrate this 25th year of renewal. We thank them for what they have given to the church in metropolitan Chicago. We are grateful, too, for the wisdom and creativity which they have shared with the larger Church in developing new forms of ministry. Let us challenge them to live the commitment they have made. May God continue to bless this wonderful sign of love and care for all people!

Here and Now

Pastoral Statement on Youth

——Autumn 1994

Church doors—really open to us?

I remember hearing this message at the Youth Hearings—it came through very loudly and very clearly. There was a great desire on the part of the people who participated in those hearings to be more involved in the life and ministry of the Church. But somehow, they felt this was not happening. They feel that the doors are physically open, but they don't feel that they really belong. And, as I listened, I think they feel that, in many instances, everything that is done in the Church—or much of what is done in the Church—is geared toward adults, older people, or very young children, and that teenagers—those of you who are in the middle—are somehow overlooked. People keep telling you, "You're the future of the Church," and so, the impression is given that you don't have to do anything right now. Well, that's not true, as you know. You're part of the Church *here and now* and you have a contribution to make. You've got responsibilities in the Church. But it is up to us, who are leaders in the Church, to make sure that the opportunities are presented to you, that you are invited to take part in the life and ministry of the Church.

We feel intimidated!

I know exactly what you're saying because, when I was young, there were times when I felt intimidated. And there are times when adults take you for granted. They think that you're young; you don't know any better. And so, you kind of feel left out.

221

But there's another side to it that sometimes people don't think about: that we adults, at times, feel intimidated by young people. Now that may sound surprising to you, but why do I say that? Because I live in an adult world, I don't know at times what young people are saying, what they're thinking. I don't know, at times, for sure what their hopes and expectations are, and so I pull back because I don't want to say something that won't really be relevant to what they are about. So, just remember that, even though you feel intimidated at times, sometimes the adults with whom you work feel intimidated because they have not had the same experiences, at least in recent times, that you have had.

We should accept and love each other just as we are, and we should be able to talk with each other in a very candid way and not be afraid of saying what we think. I think that kind of open relationship is very good and very helpful, and both of us have to work at that.

We need to be leaders!

I agree totally with you. If we just let things happen, young people are not going to be prepared. We have to look to the future. But then we have to prepare for it right now. One of the biggest challenges facing us is to invite young people into the Church and to help them develop spiritually and in every other way so that, even now, they can be leaders for their peers.

This is the message that we have to bring to our parishes. We have to let our parishes know—the lay people, the priests, the deacons, and the religious—that our young people are ready and willing, but they have to have opportunities. They have to be helped; they have to be given the tools they need in order to be leaders not only in the Church but also in society.

There are leadership programs for young people, but, even beyond that, we need to invite young people to take part in what's going on in the Church now. For example, we have parish pastoral councils to help the pastor and the other pastoral ministers in making decisions that impact the well-being of the parish. I wonder how many parish pastoral councils have young people as members. Some do, but many others do not.

Another very important part of the Church's ministry is the liturgy. That's what the Church is all about. We're a community of faith, a worshiping community. But how many young people are involved in the planning and preparation of the Eucharist, of the liturgy—especially the Sunday Eucharist? There should be programs designed specifically for young people so that they will be assisted in the development of their talents and skills. Even more important than that is actual involvement, taking your place *here and now*. Using your talents. Making your talents available. Being part of the mix.

A youth program in every parish?

In all of the guidelines that we publish, policies that we articulate, we impress upon people the importance of ministry to our young people. Nevertheless, not only in the future, but also now, in order to have excellent youth ministry and excellent youth programs, we're going to have to have more collaboration among parishes. So, what we are recommending—indeed, almost insisting on—is that there be greater collaboration among our parishes so that they can share their resources. And in that way we can do much more along the lines of youth ministry than if each parish tries to do it on its own.

There has to be someone in the parish, or generally more than one person, who has a special responsibility for relating to young people and for helping them develop their talents and their skills, for helping them become better integrated in the life and mission of the Church.

There's a great deal of youth ministry that's going on now. But it is important that there be a good youth program in every parish.

Aren't priests supposed to be like friends to us?

I'd like to tell you a little story. Many, many years ago I visited Columbia, South Carolina, which is my hometown. As a priest, I was stationed in Charleston, which is about one hundred miles away. I went with my bishop to Columbia, and we decided to visit my mother, and my six-year-old niece was there. She was in first grade at St. Joseph's Grade School. And the bishop asked her, "Annamaria, do you know Monsignor Kamler?" Well, first she started talking about the young priest, the associate priest, who was always in the school and who played ball with the kids and talked to them, and she kept talking about him. So the bishop said, "Well, that's wonderful, but do you know Monsignor Kamler?" He was the older priest who was the pastor. "Oh, yeah," she said, "I know him. He owns the place, you know." So, in other words, she looked upon him as the landlord; he was the one who owned the place and ran the place. But the one she related to was the young priest who would talk to her.

To be a good pastor, you have to spend a lot of time personally relating to people. In the final analysis, what's important is people. The Church is people, not buildings. We need buildings; we need other things to carry on our ministry. But that's not the Church. You're the Church! I'm part of the Church.

Many peoples—one Church?

This is a real challenge in a diocese, or archdiocese like Chicago, where we have so many ethnic and national groups. This, of course, is part of our history. At the present time, for example, Mass is celebrated in some 20 or 21 languages every weekend. But it's not only a matter of language; it's also a matter of culture. If people are conversant only in one language, their native language, then you have to provide liturgy and other services in that language so that they can fully participate.

On the one hand you have to attend to the needs of the individual parishioners. But at the same time, you don't want each group to feel that it's somehow alienated from the rest of the parish. So, you have to find ways in order to bring the different segments of the parish together. And that can be done liturgically, for example, on special occasions. Also, you can bring together the various cultures in many of the social functions of the parish.

Racism—isn't it a sin?

First of all, I agree with you that racism is a terrible evil. It's a sin! It is extremely destructive. It's absolutely wrong to discriminate against people because of race, color, gender, or any particular thing like that. And yet, this type of discrimination does exist, and people suffer because of it. As a society, but especially as a Christian community, we have an obligation to do everything in our power, first to condemn it, but that's negative. Positively, we must do all that we can to bring people together.

Frequently, racism is based on a lack of knowledge of people, a fear of the unknown. When people get to know each other, then they begin to see each other as human beings, as children of God, and they accept each other much better.

Violence—it's killing us!

Almost everyday you read about violence. At times, it's people shooting other people; at other times, it's violence that shows up in other kinds of ways. And related to all of this, of course, is the drug problem and gangs. Eighty-five percent of the crime that takes place in this metropolitan area is drug-related. So, this is a tremendous problem. How do we do something about it? We have to educate people, and we have to give them an education that is rooted in moral values. This is one of the things that we do in our Catholic schools. We have Catholic schools in all areas of the city and suburbs. In the so-called inner city, for example, nearly 42,000 children attend our schools; 60 percent are Catholic, and 40 percent are not. We also educate people in moral values through our religious education, youth ministry, and adult education programs.

Often violence occurs because people don't have jobs; they don't have access to good jobs; they don't have access to good housing. So, there are many social ills that have helped perpetuate violence, and we must attend to them. Now, the Church can't do it all by itself. But we can be the motivators. We can show people that these social ills, which result in violence, are caused by racism and have a moral dimension. As a faith community, we need to highlight the moral dimension of these problems.

Gangs, other things distract us!

We all want to belong to something, but young people, even more so, want to belong. A gang comes along, and they say, "You can belong to us; you can be one of us and take part in all that we have to offer,"—some of which might not be so good. That desire to belong kind of impels you to go along with it.

Well, we have to do the same thing with the Church. We've got the greatest message in the world. That message basically is Jesus Christ and his gospel. There's nothing greater than that. It is a beautiful thing. So we have to offer it and offer it in such a way that people will instinctively say, "Hmm, that means something to me. I want to belong to the community that really accepts and lives this faith, this message." That's what we have to do, and then some of these other things will begin to fall by the wayside. I don't think we have done a very good job at times. We try, and in some instances we do quite well. But it's not easy at times to be a counterpoint to all of the things that are going on in society. But that's what we're all about, and that's what we have to do. But I can't do it alone. We adults can't do it alone. *You* have to do it! You have more influence on your peers than I do. If you're convinced that it really means something to be a disciple of Jesus, and if you live a life that reflects discipleship, people, young people, your peers will sit up and listen.

"See those Christians how they love one another," remember the verse in Scripture? Those early Christians were known, they stood out in their day from other people, because of the way they lived, because of the way they took care of one another. And the same is true today.

Women can do more than sing!

Have we done enough? Have we gone far enough? The answer is no. But, we *have* made some progress. And women are members of the Church as much as I am, and therefore women have a responsibility, the same as

I, for the well-being of the Church. Women have to be fully engaged in the life and mission of the Church.

Are you aware of the fact that some 60 or 70 percent of the people who work in our parishes as teachers and pastoral ministers and pastoral associates are women? And this is right, and this is just.

Those of us who are in leadership positions in the Church must do everything we can to make it possible for women to enter the mainstream of the Church's life and ministry. And this is why there are many more women in positions of leadership today than there might have been just a few years ago.

Give us guidance—give us reasons

This is a very important point. When I grew up, it was understood that I was to accept what those in authority told me, whether it was my mother (my father died when I was very young), or whether it was my teacher or whether it was the parish priest. If he said, "Do something,"—I did it. If he said, "Don't do something,"—well, I tried not to do it; at least I knew I wasn't supposed to do it. But, things have changed a great deal. People today—and this is a cultural reality that we have to take into account—want to know the reason why. And if you don't give them a good reason, then they will say, "Well, I don't know whether I really have to do that" or "I don't know whether I really have to avoid that." And so it's very important that we give good reasons for the positions that we take as a community of faith. I agree totally with you on this, and sometimes the problem is that we use a language, we use symbols, we use figures of speech that make sense to *us*, but may not make sense to *you*. This is where you can help us. As we become engaged in a discussion about the Church's moral teaching or the tradition of the Church, if you think that what I'm saying doesn't make sense, or you don't understand it, you have to say, "I don't understand that—explain it another way." Let's see if we can find a way that will be understood by young people.

Where does the Church stand on homosexuality?

We hear a great deal today about gays and lesbians. But frequently, people, not only young people, but adults as well, don't really understand what the Church's teaching is in regard to this. Everyone, regardless of sexual orientation, is a child of God. Everyone has his or her human dignity, his or her human rights. So, we should love everyone; we should respect the rights of other people. And if there is discrimination against people who are homosexual, if there is a bias or a prejudice against them, then we have to stand up and be counted. We have to say, "That's not right!" In addition to that, as a Church, as a community of faith, we have to reach out pastorally to those who are homosexual. They may have special spiritual needs that we should try to fulfill. But at the same time, we have taught that God's plan for sexuality—a sexuality that is the basis for human intimacy, an intimacy that is nourished by love, an intimacy that results in new life—that plan of sexuality as God has given it to us, is to be fulfilled in a stable union, the stable marriage of man and woman, of husband and wife. But to teach that in no way is to belittle a person who may have a homosexual orientation.

Premarital sex—why is it wrong?

We are sexual beings. Our sexuality is a gift from God. That's the first thing we have to acknowledge. Our sexuality is very much at the heart of human intimacy, which we all crave as human beings, and it's that intimacy that comes into being, that is nourished, by love. It's that intimacy also that produces new life. Once we understand that this is what sexuality is all about, then we begin to realize that the plan of sexuality that God gave us, this wonderful reality that is part of our very being, is fully realized, and is best fulfilled, best protected, and best nourished in a stable relationship in marriage between a man and a woman, husband and wife.

Too often we think of the Church's teaching about sexuality more in negative terms—you're not supposed to do this—you can't do that. And so, after awhile, sexuality becomes a list of do's and don'ts. It is very important, and this is a point that was made earlier, that you have to explain clearly the reasons why certain things are considered good and appropriate, and certain actions and others are not good and not appropriate. You have to know what the meaning of the reality is.

Teen pregnant out of wedlock decides to have baby!

In this situation, some very basic moral decisions have to be made. I certainly would support the young person involved. At the same time though, I would do everything I could to help the parents understand why this is a good moral decision. In other words, I think it would be wrong to pit a child, a young person, against his or her parents. So, what I would try to do in that instance is to bring them all together and help them see why this is the right decision.

One of the things we can offer as leaders in the Church, as priests, is to help resolve those conflicts so that there won't be that kind of adversarial situation.

Why can't priests get married?

Today when you mention celibacy, it's understood as: "You can't get married." And if that's all you see in celibacy, then you quite rightly ask the question, "Well then, why do we insist on it?" But there's a positive dimension to celibacy as well. Sometimes people don't think of this, but it's a way of loving. It's a way of loving totally and completely for the sake of the kingdom. For an individual who has made a vow of celibacy, it's a way of loving that can intensify that person's intimacy with the Lord and also intensify his dedication to and his love for the people whom he serves. That the Church expects its priests to live the celibate life is perceived by many of you as a negative reality. It is not that way for me. That's why we need to keep talking.

If you remember nothing else—REMEMBER THIS!

I'd like to sum up our gathering by making a few remarks. First of all, I have found that being a part of the Youth Hearings and a part of this discussion has been very invigorating. I'm much older than you. On my last birthday, I was 66 years old. So, in a sense, I grew up in a different world. But I can tell you that whenever I am with young people, I begin to feel young again. I begin to think young again. And this is very important to me. So, I want to thank you for what this has meant to me personally.

Secondly, I want you to know that the Church, this local community of faith, appreciates very, very much what you have to offer to the Church, and our expectations of you are really higher than you think they are. So, you are very important in that sense also.

And finally, one of my biggest concerns: One of the biggest challenges we face is the one that all of you have articulated in some way—namely: Where do you fit in the Church? How can you use your talents and gifts now? You're the Church of the future in the sense that, twenty years from now, thirty years from now, I won't be here—you will be. So in that sense, you're the Church of the future. But you are also the Church of the *here and now*. And if you don't offer your gifts and insights, if we don't accept and use to the best advantage your gifts and your insights, then the Church will suffer; the Church will lack something that is very important.

Our responsibility is to help you fulfill your responsibility, and, as I mentioned earlier, you want to belong to something. Everybody wants to belong to something. But young people especially have a great need to belong to a particular group, a particular community.

You want to belong to the Church, and we have to open the doors, not only physically, but in every other way so that you will have a tremendous sense of belonging. It's your Church as much as mine. And it's only when you realize that, when you understand that, it's only when you feel that you truly belong to this community of faith, it's only then that you're going to come alive and make the kind of contribution that you're expected to make. And so, I want you to know that I'm fully behind you, and I'll do everything I can to make it possible for you to realize the things God has in mind for you. . . . God bless you all!

Building Bridges Between Communities of Faith

Pastoral Statement on Parish Sharing

——*May 1996* ————————————————

For twenty years, the Parish Sharing Program in the Archdiocese of Chicago has built bridges between communities separated by race, ethnicity, culture, and economic disparity. Our Catholic faith has been the basis for overcoming many divisions that otherwise occur in our society. The results have transformed many peoples' lives as well as their parish communities. Faith has been nurtured, hearts have been moved, and much good has been done.

I offer these reflections on the 20th anniversary of Parish Sharing to celebrate this past, but more importantly, to advocate for a future in which every parish fully partakes in this experience of Christian community. I set the transformation of this program as a goal of *Decisions* because I have seen its positive impact on many parishes, while realizing that many other parishes participate in a marginal way.

I encourage *every* parish to do what it can to enhance Parish Sharing. For some, this will require invigorating partnerships that have had little vitality. For others, it will entail parishes' sharing their experience and expertise, gained after decades of strong and faithful relationships, with other parishes that can benefit from these examples. And for all, it will involve a commitment to invite parishioners to learn the faith dimension of this interparochial program.

Parish Sharing: Rooted in the Early Christian Church and a Means to Mission Today

Let us begin with an examination of the biblical and theological foundations of Parish Sharing. Striking parallels exist between Parish Sharing and practices of the early Church. Our program creates bonds within our local Catholic community in a way that manifests a preferential option for the poor. As such, it provides a vehicle for the archdiocese to advance its social mission.

The roots of Parish Sharing are set firmly in the early Christian communities. The early Church also experienced differences that divided it. St. Paul pointed out how important it was for sharing to occur between rich and poor, Gentile convert and Jewish convert, Hellenistic Christians and Palestinian Christians so that one communion (*koinonia* in Greek) would be realized. Paul also emphasized that different local churches possessed different resources for sharing. The material wealth of some filled needs among the poorer communities, who in turn shared their spiritual wealth with those who were in need of it.

St. Paul's second letter to the Corinthians, in chapters eight and nine, describes in detail the sharing that occurred between the churches in Macedonia and Jerusalem. In a shorter passage in his letter to the Romans, he captures the essence of the relationship:

> At present I am going to Jerusalem with aid for the saints. For Macedonia and Achaia have been pleased to make some contribution for the poor among the saints in Jerusalem; they were pleased to do it, and indeed they are in debt to them, for if the Gentiles have come to share in their spiritual blessings, they ought to be of service to them in material blessings (Rom 15:25-27).

Note that St. Paul describes a reciprocal relationship. Each partner contributes to the life of the other. This mutuality assures dignity for all, and it promotes true communion between the respective local churches. St. Paul regarded this sharing to be of such importance that he personally brought the collection of funds from Macedonia to Jerusalem, even though he knew that he would probably be arrested and imprisoned if he went to the Holy City. For him, it was not an option; it was essential to his Christian mission and ministry.

St. Paul believed that this sharing represented a concrete manifestation of the love to which Christians were called. Today, we often refer to the "preferential option of love for the poor" as one of the defining characteristics of the Church's mission.

Jesus' preaching and ministry inspire this mission. Jesus proclaims at the beginning of his public ministry: "The spirit of the Lord is upon me, because he has anointed me to preach good news to the poor. He has sent me to proclaim liberty to captives and recovery of sight to the blind, to let the oppressed go free, and to proclaim a year acceptable to the Lord" (Luke 4:16-19). We also hear this message often during his ministry, both in words and actions.

He reaches out to those on the margins of society: the poor, lepers, Samaritans, prostitutes, tax collectors. In the Last Judgment scene in the Gospel of Matthew (Matt 25:31-46), the option for the poor comes into its clearest focus. The passage vividly depicts Jesus' identification with those who are in need and declares that eternal salvation comes to those who cared for Jesus when they cared for the least of their brothers and sisters.

In this way Jesus calls us to recognize the oneness of the human family. He included people that others sought to exclude. He elevated the dignity of people whom others denigrated. He made it clear that the "least of these" were to be embraced as the Christ. He showed us how to live the virtue of solidarity through which we embody the unity that God intends for all humanity.

In Jesus' teaching and example and in the life of the early Church we find a basis and an impetus for Parish Sharing. Parish Sharing provides a very important vehicle for carrying out the Church's mission in the Archdiocese of Chicago.

In his second letter to the Corinthians, St. Paul explains that the collection taken up in Macedonia was intended to build *koinonia:* communion or fellowship. (The root of the word *koinonia* means "to share.") For us to carry out our God-given mission today, we also must build *koinonia*. In our metropolitan area, vast gulfs exist among people, even within our Catholic Church. Housing segregation remains a fact of life, separating races and ethnic groups. Economic disparities are enormous, even though the geographical distance separating some of our region's wealthiest people from the poorest can be negligible. Ethnic groups are also divided by language and customs. The Church has the mission to bring unity from this diversity, and to make possible the sharing of the gifts and talents with which God has blessed his body, the Church.

The option for the poor, which has a distinct place at the center of the Church's mission, finds an outlet through Parish Sharing. The goods and money that are shared can be regarded as symbols of the love we are called to have for one another. Yet the full embodiment of the option for the poor requires acknowledgment of the human dignity of those we serve. This is realized best when the gifts that the poor have to offer are recognized. These gifts of the Spirit hold the highest value, a truth that a materialistic culture too often conceals or disregards.

Parish Sharing also creates opportunities to nurture solidarity among people in the archdiocese. The bond of a common faith provides an essential foundation upon which strong relationships can be built. The unity we find through Jesus Christ brings us together despite the diversity of race, ethnicity, culture, and economic disparity. Parish Sharing helps us experience and nurture the solidarity that is essential to our mission and, therefore, must be part of our future.

S TRENGTHS AND SHORTCOMINGS

Twenty years' experience with Parish Sharing has shown that the kind of sharing of resources that St. Paul described in the New Testament remains possible today. It has also revealed that many parishes have not yet tapped the richness of this experience of *koinonia*. Let us consider some of the positive results:

- As many as 160 parishes interact socially and liturgically in what they describe as a meaningful, reciprocal way.
- Parish Sharing has provided a vehicle for racial and ethnic groups to come together in common purpose.
- Some relationships precede the founding of the Sharing Program and have thrived for more than 25 years.
- Parishes report that Sharing relationships bring vitality to parish life and to a full range of parish activities.
- Inner-city parishes share in significant ways with other inner-city parishes.
- Sharing partnerships make possible opportunities for faith sharing and service.
- Close to $3 million was shared between parishes over the last year alone.
- An estimated $3 million worth of goods and services also flowed from more affluent to less affluent parishes.
- The sharing of resources has helped parishes and schools remain open.
- Individuals have found their lives transformed as a result of involvement in Parish Sharing relationships.

So, the effectiveness of Parish Sharing is considerable. It is worth noting that the Archdiocese of Chicago is still the only diocese in the country to have such a program in which every parish participates in some way. However, we also need to face up to the program's shortcomings and to take the steps needed to offset them.

With such a significant amount of financial and material resources involved, an undue emphasis on these kinds of resources results, and a corresponding stress is placed on the financial and material needs of the parishes that receive them. This will always be an important component of the Parish Sharing Program, but it must be placed in proper context. We must continue to emphasize the other ways of sharing: spiritually transforming ways that build meaningful bridges between otherwise divided people. Getting to know one another through prayer, socializing, play, common projects—in order to share aspirations and disappointments, joys and sorrows—is a deeper goal of parish sharing that too easily is overshadowed by the amount of money parishes send to other parishes. As St. Paul points out, we all have gifts to share, and we all have needs to be filled. We need to address this problem of Parish Sharing: that the financial and material gifts and the financial and material needs are given primary or, at times, singular importance.

The priority given to financial and material sharing has led to the unfortunate labeling of parishes as "giving" or "receiving." At their best, Parish Sharing relationships embody a *reciprocity* in which each partner gives and each partner receives. I urge everyone to consider Parish Sharing in this way, emphasizing mutuality in our attitudes, our language, and our actions.

A second problem relates to the current alignment of sharing partners. Demographic changes in the metropolitan area over the past twenty years have shifted the boundaries of what could be called "the Macedonian" and "the Jerusalem" churches. Economic downturns in some neighborhoods and gentrification in others are the forces largely responsible for these changes. Unfortunately, negative economic trends have affected more communities than have positive developments. There is, consequently, the need to foster some realignment so that the resources and needs of partners can be shared more effectively and equitably.

Some have raised questions about the equity of the current alignment. To a certain extent, these concerns are justified, but I raise a caution in this regard. While it is true that some parishes obtain very significant resources from sharing partners, these parishes typically are located in neighborhoods with the greatest needs where some of the worst poverty in the United States exists. In some cases, they are like mission churches, providing a presence for the Church amidst the poor. Most parishes that receive substantial support from Sharing Partners have also nurtured their relationships over long periods of time. Despite the limitations of personnel, they invest the time needed to stay in regular contact with their partners and to foster reciprocity between the two communities of faith. As a result, it is common for materially affluent parishes to express the sentiment that St. Paul described when he wrote: "Macedonia and Achaia have been pleased to make some contribution for the poor among the saints at Jerusalem; they were pleased to do it, and indeed they are in debt to them" (Rom 15:26-27a).

A third problem involves unevenness of participation in Parish Sharing. I have no illusions that Parish Sharing will receive the same high priority in every parish. In *Decisions* I did, however, set a goal that every parish participate in Parish Sharing through both financial transactions and interpersonal relationships. For parishes that have enjoyed strong relationships with their sharing partners, the mutual benefits of true sharing are clear. For parishes for whom partnerships have been weak or essentially nonexistent, it will be necessary to take steps to transform them or establish new relationships.

Steps are already underway to address each of these concerns. The implementation of *Decisions* includes a plan to bolster Parish Sharing. The Parish Sharing Commission, which operates under the auspices of the Office for the Ministry of Peace and Justice, has been developing resources and sponsoring events that seek to strengthen Parish Sharing relationships. The experiences of parishes that have excelled at Parish Sharing provide the cornerstone for the materials that have already been developed and for the ones that will be created by the end of this year. The Archdiocesan Parish Sharing Mass at Holy Name Cathedral and the "Sharing with Vitality" session offer opportunities for sharing partners to deepen their relationships.

Plans for partial realignment of sharing partners have also been drawn up. A task force, comprised principally of parish staff members, has recommended an approach that calls for ten realigned relationships in each of the next three years. The group has employed several beliefs and principles in developing the plan:

- Good relationships will not be disturbed.

- Realignment will not threaten the financial solvency of parishes.

- Solutions are possible in which all parishes benefit.

- An untapped abundance exists.

Implementation of this plan has already begun on a pilot basis. It will not immediately remedy all instances of inequity in the present structure, but it will move the program in the right direction. In order to ensure continuity in this process, I will appoint a permanent committee, whose members will include pastors and parish staff members, to review and adjust the alignment, as needed, on an annual basis.

From the beginning of the Parish Sharing Program, every parish has been expected to participate. This continues to be my expectation. Without placing undue emphasis on the financial dimension of Parish Sharing, I ask *all* parishes to share financially with another parish. Inner-city pastors have said that it is important for their parishes to share financially with other inner-city Catholic communities.

I am convinced that every parish has gifts to share—and unmet needs, be they spiritual or material that can be met—through our unique Parish Sharing program. Our gratitude for the bounty with which God has blessed the Archdiocese of Chicago can express itself in many ways. The Parish Sharing Program is one very important means to do this. Indeed, through it, we imitate the example of the early Christian communities.

I pray that every parish may realize the life-giving truth found in true sharing that has been experienced from the time of St. Paul through the last twenty years of Parish Sharing in this local church.

Synodal Interventions

The Sacrament of Penance in a Sacramental Church*

World Synod of Bishops

—1983—

1. The Rite of Christian Initiation of Adults is a kind of microcosm of the life of conversion to which the entire Church is called. In the period of the RCIA called the pre-catechumenate, those who have heard Christ's invitation recognize their isolation and their brokenness, as well as the possibility of reconciliation in Christ. The Church for her part announces this message of hope and healing. Furthermore, the word of salvation which is proclaimed to inquirers must also continually penetrate the hearts of those who already belong to the community of the faithful; thus the same word which invites inquirers to *begin* their journey of conversion encourages those already on their way to the Lord to *deepen* their resolve and intensify their efforts. As inquirers come to the community of the Church to declare their first conversion, those who already belong to the community confess their subsequent experiences of sin and conversion.

Conversion must change one's way of living. Persons who experience initial conversion and desire to change their lives (RCIA, no. 5) express this externally within the community of believers. This same community, which welcomes and supports catechumens, also assists penitents and reconciles each of them to God, and to itself, always under the guidance of the ordained ministers.

* Also published in *Origins* as "New Rite of Penance Suggested," vol. 13, no. 19, October 20, 1983, pp. 324–326.

Baptism is the ritual completion of the process of conversion. Similarly, penance is the ritualization of the Father's mercy in the lives of penitents. As the Church concludes the RCIA by inviting neophytes to reflect on what it means to have begun their spiritual journey, so does the Church remind those who have experienced sacramental reconciliation in penance to renew their conversion in acts of charity and justice, penitential celebrations and practices, and especially in the Eucharist.

2. The witness of the Church's tradition, manifest in her pastoral life, and the model of the conversion process and its sacramental celebration proposed in the RCIA together suggest certain principles on which to base contemporary pastoral approaches to the ministry of reconciliation. These include the following:

a. Liturgy is the *sacramentum fidei;* that is, liturgical celebration "sacramentalizes" the faith experience of Christians. Participants must therefore have reached a level of faith sufficient to serve as the basis for their celebration of liturgy.

b. The Church's ministry has been entrusted to the entire community in a diversity of roles.

c. Consideration should be given both to the sacramental event and to the process which precedes it.

d. The journeys of conversion (initiation) and reconversion (penance) provide candidates and the community with opportunities for renewal in the life of Christ.

e. The "organization" of all sacramental processes and their culmination in the celebration of the sacraments are entirely subject to the direction of the divine initiative and always respect the situation and response of the candidate and the community.

f. In regard to penance, exclusive focus upon the moment of absolution, without appropriate attention to the previous journey of conversion, opens the door to a magical view of the sacrament.

g. However, the "moment" of the sacrament itself, while it cannot be fully significant without sufficient preparation, is not merely an affirmation of the preceding process but is itself efficacious.

h. In a very real sense, the sacramental ministry does not conclude with the sacramental celebration. In the RCIA (nos. 37–40) a time of mystagogy is envisioned. During this period, there is an opportunity for unfolding both the understanding of the sacramental celebration which has occurred and the practical consequences for daily living of the celebration.

i. Pastorally sensitive liturgy takes into account the particular moment in history and the character of a particular culture. The directives of the Constitution on the Sacred Liturgy concerning the cultural adaptation of liturgy (cf. 37–40) are always pastorally relevant.

These principles help to establish a theological, liturgical, and pastoral context for the sacrament of penance. To this it is necessary to add the ascetical context. This, too, can best be done here in the form of principles or propositions.

a. The sacrament of penance is an important element of spiritual direction; and spiritual direction, as the experience of the Church makes clear, is an all but indispensable instrument of ongoing conversion and growth in holiness.

b. While spiritual direction takes various forms and is immediately given by persons trained for the purpose, it is always an ecclesial process: it takes place within the community of faith, and the community supports and contributes to it in a variety of ways.

c. Since the parish is the institutional expression of the faith community for most Catholics, spiritual direction should be an important part of the total parish program.

d. The sacrament of penance should therefore be celebrated within the parish precisely as part of its comprehensive program of spiritual direction for its members.

3. Studies are needed to determine how the principles outlined here can become more fully operative in the present three rites of penance. I further suggest that consideration be given to a new rite of penance—not in place of those which now exist, but as a further option which has merit of its own.

Concretely, this pastoral proposal envisages four distinct stages.

Stage One: The Confession of Sins

After sufficient pastoral assistance provided by members of the community such as spiritual directors, guides, and sponsors, and through participation in events of community prayer, the well-prepared penitent approaches the priest to make a full confession of sin. At this time, the penitent is welcomed with love and compassion and receives counsel and advice for the next stage of the penitential journey. Confession of sins enables the confessor to suggest proper courses of action.

Stage Two: Doing Penance

Having received counsel, encouragement, and support from the community, and fortified by the confession of sins, the penitent sets about living a program of conversion. The community continues to offer the same kind of support, especially the counsel of a spiritual director, and welcomes the penitent to events of community prayer.

Stage Three: The Celebration of the Sacrament

When the penitent has advanced far enough so that there occurs "a profound change of the whole person by which one begins to consider, judge, and arrange his life according to the holiness and love of God" (*OP*, no. 6), the time has come for the liturgical celebration of conversion in the sacrament of penance. The celebration should be according to the approved rites of the Church as described in the *Ordo paenitentiae* (nos. 60–63) with full community participation. In many cases celebration of the sacrament may be related to the seasons of the Liturgical Year.

Stage Four: The Prolongation of the Sacramental Experience

Through continued contact with the various ministers of the Church as well as the other faithful, the penitent would continue to experience the prayerful support of the community and would have available a forum for dialoguing about the practical implications of a new way of life.

This pastoral proposal in effect provides for reinstituting the "Order of Penitents" practiced in the penitential discipline of the ancient Church. Initially at least, the option would no doubt be chosen only by a relatively small number of persons. Yet it need not necessarily be an option for an elite, provided its benefits were extended to the community as a whole.

For example, implementation of the proposal could provide opportunities for catechesis for all members of the faith community concerning the sacrament of penance. Furthermore, by potentially engaging the community as a whole in its celebration, it could serve as a means for making parishes more effective settings for spiritual direction and celebration of the sacrament of penance according to all the rites. It is possible, too, that the option would in time come to appeal to some sincere individuals who have given up the practice of devotional confession yet continue to perceive the value and necessity of the sacrament in their lives. It also offers advantages as a focal point of ecumenical dialogue and outreach.

Whether or not this particular pastoral approach becomes a reality, the Church must strive constantly to give authentic sacramental expression to the lived experience of the faithful, encouraging and helping them to undergo conversion and re-conversion. In this way she will be a compelling sign to the world of how people are reconciled with God and with one another through her ministry.

The Virtue of Penance:
The Ideal and the Contemporary Reality*
World Synod of Bishops
── 1983 ────────────────────────────────

In preaching redemption the Church must preach penance; in preaching penance she must preach the fact of sin. Have we failed to do this in recent years or to do it as well as we might? Perhaps we have been deterred by the thought that it would be unfashionable to speak of sin; perhaps we have been beguiled by a neo-Pelagian rhetoric of human perfectibility by human means. Now it is the synod's task to foster a catechesis which restores penance—the virtue and the sacrament—to a central, indispensable place in the lives of our people.

1. "In his name, penance for the remission of sins is to be preached to all the nations, beginning at Jerusalem" (Luke 24:47).

The Church's proclamation of penance is universal in its scope. It is directed to all individuals, all nations, all cultures. This proclamation is oriented toward the forgiveness of sins and new life. This proclamation is rooted "in his name," that is, in the full paschal mystery of the Lord Jesus, his death, resurrection, and the sending of the Holy Spirit.

The preaching of penance is directed both to the world and to the community of faith. Saint Paul, for example, announces that for those who believe God's reconciliation is given, "God . . . has reconciled us to himself through Christ" (2 Cor 5:18). At the same time, he acknowledges the

* Also published in *Origins* as "Contemporary Attitudes Toward Sin," vol. 13, no. 19, October 20, 1983, pp. 326–328.

pilgrim state of those who believe and he urges them: "We implore you, in Christ's name: be reconciled to God!" (2 Cor 5:20).

Penance is necessarily rooted in a sense of personal sin. Faith in Jesus Christ gives us access to the Father; it makes possible an ever-deepening grasp of God's power, love, and holiness. But with this comes a growing sense of sin, whose full weight is visible in the crucified Jesus. We see sin, furthermore, in personal terms: as evil for which we are morally responsible. Our sorrow is therefore equally personal: "I have sinned against you whom I should love above all things."

Those who responded to Jesus' call to repentance and joined him in the days of his Galilean preaching found themselves members of a community of repentant sinners. Today, too, the newly baptized are called by God into the communion of those whom Christ has forgiven; they are part of the "sacrament . . . of communion with God and of the unity of all mankind" that is the Church.

The eucharistic sacrifice of the Mass most fully expresses our baptismal dedication to our Lord. Here we immerse ourselves in his sacrifice, offering ourselves to the Father through his Son in the Holy Spirit. Our eucharistic "amen" declares our readiness to become ever more like Christ, specifically in his dying and rising. The sacrament of penance, however, is a "second baptism" in tears. Here our sorrow and determination to admit our sins meet God's merciful love and call to repentance, and we receive sacramental forgiveness. The virtue of Christian penance is constantly sacramental in its origin and reference.

The virtue of penance takes visible form in practices which manifest that change of heart which is its essence, oneness, and configuration with Christ in his dying and rising, and willingness to repair the harm done by sin. Since sin injures the sinner first, our efforts at reparation must encompass the injury we have done ourselves by sinning. But because we are baptized into the body of Christ, penance always retains its communal, ecclesial significance. The evil we do afflicts the whole body in ways which are sometimes evident and sometimes hidden. So, too, our penance is always in some way for the benefit of the whole Church. "I must fill up in my body what is wanting in the sufferings of Christ."

Penance as a virtue also involves God's gift of profound self-knowledge in faith, hope, and love. In proclaiming the self-knowledge that God offers us, the Church identifies the deep needs of the human heart: the need to be transformed into the image of Jesus Christ, the need to live in a reconciled way by the power of the Holy Spirit who is the bond of unity both of believers among themselves and with God, the need to mend the elements of personal and social life that are broken by sin, the need to grow in knowledge and love of the mystery of God in whom we live and move and have our very being.

Although regret and sorrow for the past and present as we have let them and our very selves be broken and scarred by sin are initial elements of God's gift of penance, they are ultimately ordered to draw us into new life in Jesus Christ by the power of the Holy Spirit. Thus, penance in the Gospels is consistently attached to a sense of joy, welcome, and liberation (cf. Luke 15:1-32).

2. Against this background we must look carefully at contemporary attitudes toward penance. Here I wish to suggest only some general themes and insights.

In many cultures and societies today an ethic of self-reliance predominates which emphasizes individual achievement. This is paralleled in the religious sphere when "belief" becomes a mélange of private and even idiosyncratic personal convictions rather than acceptance of a common faith grounded in the authority of divine wisdom. Against excessive reliance on self the Church proclaims Christ the redeemer. Against the tendency to privatize religion and overemphasize individual experience she offers the community of all those who "confess their sins to one another" and "wait the glorious coming of their Lord and Savior Jesus Christ."

Today, too, many see inner asceticism devalued in favor of secular activism directed to the transformation of society. In many respects the latter impulse is good and generous. Noble efforts of political and structural reform often hold out new hope to the oppressed and the poor. But as matters now stand, the gospel frequently goes unpreached and the human spirit remains unnourished. The Church for her part also seeks the transformation of society, but she remains committed to personal transformation as both the indispensable basis and the ultimate goal of positive social change. As a community, too, the Church realizes that persons are not transformed in isolation. Rather, all within the Church—indeed, all members of the human family—are called to a continual personal transformation which helps bring into being Christ's kingdom of peace, justice, and love. As Christians we acknowledge that this arises from the working of the Spirit, the imitation of Christ, and the liberating force of the gospel.

Often today authentic moral absolutes, rooted in the nature of the human person and expressly defended in the Christian tradition, are overshadowed by moral relativism and subjectivism. Along with this phenomenon, many people no longer turn to religious structures and disciplines in pursuing their search for spiritual meaning. The Church encourages and supports men and women in seeking their identity and their authentic fulfillment; but she knows that they search in vain unless their quest leads them to Christ—his wisdom, the values of the gospel, and the Christian community.

Side by side with contemporary expressions of individualism, many people today are acutely aware of the social consequences of their values and their decisions. Facing the possibility of nuclear warfare and even nuclear destruction of the planet itself, we have good reason to acknowledge the social dimensions of sin.

There is a great paradox here: At the very moment when sin clouds our perceptions and enfeebles our judgments concerning human potential and the possibility of re-creation in Christ, the universal experience of sin dramatizes our human weakness and our common need for redemption in and by Christ. Vatican II expressed the social consequences of this state of affairs in these words: "Pulled by manifold attractions modern man is constantly forced to choose among them and to renounce some. Indeed as a weak and sinful being, he often does what he would not and fails to do what he would. Hence he suffers from internal divisions, and from these flow so many and such great discords in society" *(Gaudium et spes)*.

3. How should the Church respond? On the one hand, she should not dwell too much on sin, as if it were a subject worth contemplating for its own sake. On the other hand, the Church should seek to clarify the reality of sin, as a necessary part of the process by which sinful human beings are progressively freed from the bonds of sin through conversion.

Part of this task of clarification requires emphasis on the fact that sin is not simply an act committed in isolation from other acts. Rather, sin tends naturally to vitiate other acts and undermine relationships among persons. People immersed in sin and in sinful situations tend to be blind to their condition, blind to alternatives, and blind to the possibility of change for the better. This is true whether what is in question is the sinful reality of an individual's selfish sexual life, the denial of human rights in a nation, or the nuclear arms race.

To persons suffering from this condition of spiritual impasse the Church proclaims God's fidelity and love, the victory over sin won for them by Christ, the unlimited access which they now enjoy to God's re-creating grace, and the existence of an option other than sin and sinfulness which is now available to us in Christ's Spirit.

To move in the direction of effective proclamation leading to the fruitful celebration of the sacrament of penance, the Church might follow the pattern found in the Second Vatican Council's pastoral constitution *Gaudium et spes*. Thus, the initial phase of preaching penance would be the identification of such present-day human experiences as those noted above, the brokenness which is the result of sin, the human longing for integrity and the fullness of life with God and other human beings. This would be followed by the bold proclamation of God's gift of penance, which is ultimately an invitation to forgiveness and new life. The Church would then continue its proclamation by supporting people in their efforts to accept the call to penance in the face of obstacles. Finally, proclamation finds its terminus and goal in the sacramental celebration of penance, which is the focused and effective moment of the fruit of the virtue of penance—the moment at which God's loving, life-giving, and transforming forgiveness is accepted.

The Church, the World, and the Kingdom*

World Synod of Bishops

— 1987 —

"One of the gravest errors of our time is the dichotomy between the faith which many profess and the practice of their daily lives."[1] One may rightly point out that much has been achieved since the fathers of the Second Vatican Council made that assessment. Nevertheless, it is also true that much remains to be done "to integrate human, domestic, professional, scientific and technical enterprises with religious values."[2]

In order to shed some light on the discovery of religious values within human life and work, I will first offer some reflections on the conciliar teaching about the Church in the world[3] and the experience of the Church in the United States. Then I will raise some questions for discussion at this synod with a view toward promoting a greater sense and practice of co-discipleship within our ecclesial communities.

THE CHURCH IN THE WORLD AND THE KINGDOM

As *Lumen gentium* states clearly, the Church is intimately related to the kingdom of God. The Church "is, on earth, the seed and beginning of

---

* Also published in *Origins* as "Politics, Bishops and Laity," vol. 17, no. 19, October 22, 1987, pp. 348–349.

[1] *Gaudium et spes*, no. 43.

[2] Ibid.

[3] I am using "world" in the same sense that *Gaudium et spes* does.

251

that kingdom. While she slowly grows to maturity, the Church longs for the completed kingdom,"[4] "the kingdom of truth and life, the kingdom of holiness and grace, the kingdom of justice, love, and peace."[5]

At the same time, the Church "travels the same journey as all mankind and shares the same earthly lot with the world: it is to be a leaven and, as it were, the soul of human society in its renewal by Christ and transformation into the family of God."[6]

The Church's specific mission to the world is not in the political, economic, or social order; its proper mission is a religious one. Nevertheless, this religious mission seeks to structure earthly realities in light of the vision of the kingdom. The Church communicates divine life to human persons and "casts the reflected light of that divine life over all the earth."[7] It does so especially "in the way it heals and elevates the dignity of the human person, in the way it consolidates society, and endows the daily activity of men with a deeper sense and meaning."[8]

Thus, the protection of human dignity, the pursuit of human rights, the work of justice, and the pursuit of peace are properly understood as within the scope of the Church's work.

The entire Church, through its efforts in society, sanctifies itself and makes present the kingdom of God. Moreover, the world is one of the *loci* of God's presence, and the Church is the means and source of discerning and celebrating that presence.

The Church carries on Jesus' mission of proclaiming the Good News and building up the kingdom, and all members of the Church share responsibility for this mission in virtue of their baptism and confirmation.

While all are co-disciples of Jesus, there are different roles.[9] These roles should not be allowed to disturb the unity and harmony which are characteristic of Jesus' community of disciples. As the Second Vatican Council pointed out clearly:

> Although by Christ's will some are established as teachers, dispensers of the mysteries and pastors for the others, there remains, nevertheless, a true equality between all with regard to the dignity and to the activity which is common to all the faithful in the building up of the Body of Christ.[10]

---

[4] *Lumen gentium*, no. 5.
[5] Ibid., no. 36.
[6] *Gaudium et spes*, 40.
[7] Ibid.
[8] Ibid.
[9] Cf. 1 Cor 12:4-7.
[10] *Lumen gentium*, no. 32.

In light of the Church's mission in the world, the council delineated the respective roles of the laity and the bishops, along with their priests.

The laity, in virtue of their special vocation, "seek the Kingdom of God by engaging in temporal affairs and directing them to God's will."[11] In fact, they contribute to the sanctification of the world by fulfilling their respective duties in the home, the workplace, and the public forum. They are "to animate the world with the spirit of Christianity" and "to be witnesses to Christ in all circumstances and at the very heart of the community of mankind."[12] The laity, indeed, find their salvation in and through their daily lives in the world.

The laity, then, have a primary, though not exclusive, role in the world.[13] Bishops, along with their priests, are "to preach the message of Christ in such a way that the light of the Gospel will shine on all activities of the faithful."[14] They are also to provide guidance, to the extent they can, and spiritual strength to their lay sisters and brothers so that the latter may "shoulder their responsibilities under the guidance of Christian wisdom and with eager attention to the teaching authority of the Church."[15]

Working together as co-disciples, all members—both ordained and nonordained—carry out the Church's mission in the world.

THE EXPERIENCE OF THE CHURCH IN THE UNITED STATES

I will now speak more concretely of the experience of the church in the United States. Like every local church, it faces particular cultural and constitutional conditions. Hence my reflections bear the limitations of one specific experience. Nevertheless, they may be useful in raising questions which pertain, *mutatis mutandis*, to the teaching and practice of the Church's broader life which we are examining in this synod.

Throughout the history of the church in the United States, and especially in this century, the Catholic bishops have taught the Church's social doctrine. In earlier decades, for example, they have addressed such diverse topics as abortion, labor relations, secularism, and racism. As a result, the bishops were successful in promoting human rights, in persuading the working classes to remain within the church, and in developing a significant core of lay leadership.

---

[11] Ibid., no. 31.
[12] *Gaudium et spes*, no. 43.
[13] Ibid.
[14] Ibid.
[15] Ibid.

In the decades immediately after the Second World War, many Social Action programs were developed under the supervision of the hierarchy, but with dedicated and competent lay leadership. Numerous lay organizations were established which have given effective witness to gospel values in the family and the public arena. These new ventures have played a significant role in carrying out the Church's mission within U.S. society.

Today the Church in the United States is no longer primarily a community of immigrants, even though new members continue to arrive from throughout the world. Many Catholics in our country are in leadership roles in nearly every field of human endeavor. They are well educated and deeply dedicated to the Church, but not all of them are familiar with the Church's social teaching. Especially since the Second Vatican Council, lay persons have been taking their rightful place within the Church as ministers and members of parish and diocesan pastoral councils. More recently, the laity themselves have seen the need for and have requested greater support for their vocation in and to the world.

During this decade the U.S. bishops have developed a consistent ethic of life which addresses a broad spectrum of life issues from conception to natural death, bringing the light of the gospel and Church teaching to bear on such issues as war and peace, the economy, abortion, and the concerns of women. This has also allowed us to engage both the community of the Church and the wider society in reflection, debate, and examination of the moral dimensions of public policy. As part of this effort, the bishops developed two pastoral letters, one on peace issues and the other on the economy, in close collaboration with the laity who had special expertise in those areas. At the same time these pastoral letters and other statements by the bishops will remain mere words unless the laity assimilate that teaching, develop it further in dialogue with the bishops, and make concerted efforts to implement it in the world.

One way of implementing this teaching is through the political order. I would like to address some of the opportunities and difficulties of doing so.

It has been our experience that the Church's social and moral teaching can be effectively introduced into public discussion on a wide range of political issues. It is necessary to be very clear about what is meant here: The bishops should not be political partisans, but they can specify, examine, and press in the public debate the *moral* dimensions of issues as diverse as medical technology, capital punishment, human rights, economic policy, and military strategy.

The experience of our episcopal conference in addressing the issues of nuclear and economic policies has shown us the need to give high priority to this teaching task. Our critics have said we have entered too deeply into the political order, that we are too specific in our teaching, and that we are usurping the proper role of the laity in the secular and, particularly, the political order.

It is my conviction that this is a mistaken criticism. While attributing a lesser degree of authority to our applications, we have nonetheless thought it necessary to show how principles are to be applied in our contemporary circumstances so that the principles and their implications will be correctly understood. In the final analysis, moral teaching involves concrete choices.

In truth, the distinct teaching role of bishops in addressing the political order complements the indispensable role of the laity as participants in the political process. For that teaching role to be fulfilled, the character of the moral teaching must meet three requirements. (1) It must be morally credible; that is, it must have the theoretical capacity to illuminate the human values and dimensions of political questions. (2) It must be empirically competent in its assessment of problems. (3) As noted above, it must lead toward specific recommendations and conclusions which are realizable. Teaching which combines these characteristics is a permanent mode of the Church's contribution to the political process.

At the same time, both the theology of the lay vocation and the political requirements of effectiveness demand that the Church's direct engagement in the political order be through lay people. Nonetheless, if this crucial role is to be filled well, those who undertake it need solid grounding in the vision of faith and the Church's social teaching as well as political skill and empirical competence.

Endowed with these capacities, Catholic lay men and women who enter the political process, whether by election or appointment, should have the encouragement of the bishops in undertaking this vocation. They must be addressed and treated as professionals in their sphere of competence. While commentary and critique of public debate, public policy, and specific political choices are necessary parts of the Church's social ministry, the freedom to exercise professional judgment and the virtue of prudence must be accorded those in public life. It is the task of Catholic politicians, in cooperation with others of good will and a wide range of political coalitions, to grapple with how the moral teaching should be joined with the concrete choices of the political order and the requirements of building public support for needed policies.

When we fulfill our role as moral teachers and help prepare lay people for the political vocation, we exercise a ministry of co-discipleship.

In sum, in the United States since the council we have attempted to change our understanding of the Church as entirely separate from the world to its being an active agent in society. Moreover, individual Christians are becoming more aware of their responsibility to act as leaven in the world. We are also moving away from an understanding of ministry which is primarily defined by priests and religious to one in which all the baptized accept their shared responsibility as co-disciples for carrying out the Church's mission. Lay ministry, in this context, is seen both as service to the ecclesial community and as service and support for the lay vocation in the home, the workplace, and the public forum.

Although considerable progress has been made in the development of lay ministries within the Church, the great challenge in the United States is to help lay people become more aware of their vocation and mission in the world. They are to act as leaven in society, bringing gospel values and Church teaching to bear upon societal issues, as they build up the kingdom in their home and place of work—in all they do.

QUESTIONS FOR SYNODAL DISCUSSION

I have spoken briefly about the experience of the church in the United States because it parallels to some extent the experience of the Church in other parts of the world and because it represents an example of the gospel and Church teaching taking root in a particular culture.

Certain important questions arise, whose answers require the collective wisdom of the universal Church. I would like to recommend them for our synodal discussions.

First, how can we build upon the teaching of the Second Vatican Council in regard to the Church's mission in the world? How can we move beyond entrenched notions which tend to set the Church too much apart from the world? How can we avoid false dichotomies or a dualism which confuses people, neglects their experience, and tends to invite divisions and divisiveness within the Church?

Second, how are we to discover effective ways of listening to the experience of laypersons who seek to be leaven and agents of transformation in their homes, workplaces, and the public forum? How can we help them use that experience to develop spiritualities, structures, and programs that will support them in their vocation?

Third, how can we help them and ourselves to be faithful to the gospel in cultures in which many neither understand nor appreciate its values?

Fourth, how can bishops articulate a moral teaching that speaks persuasively to the important issues of public policy?

Fifth, how can the Catholic laity, in accord with their distinctive role and legitimate autonomy, participate more effectively as agents of change in the political processes of a secular society?

The answers to these questions will provide the key to the productive realization of co-discipleship within our ecclesial communities. May the

Spirit guide us as we reflect, in solidarity with our brothers and sisters, on the many possibilities which can assist us in the fulfillment of our respective responsibilities toward the kingdom which is already in our midst but still moving toward completion.

Spirituality of Diocesan Priests and Celibacy*

World Synod of Bishops

—— *1990* ———————————————————————

It is difficult to determine accurately the *status animarum presbytero-rum*. Our viewpoints are partial, and our experiences limited. Neverthe-less, as a priest and bishop, I offer some general considerations as a prelude to my reflection on the spirituality of diocesan priests.

Our priests are good people, men who strive to follow Jesus Christ and serve his people in the Church. They have, however, fragile spirits which are weighed down by many burdens: shrinking numbers of priestly co-workers, the misunderstanding of faith and religion in contemporary so-ciety, and inadequately developed ecclesial structures of support for their ministries and lives. So, it would be both inaccurate and unfair to de-scribe priests as not engaged enough in priestly activities, as ill-willed, or as spiritually lazy.

Priests are people who thirst for the Lord, who are in need of new en-ergy and refreshment, and who long to discover the presence of the Lord who is already close at hand to them.

My reflection on the spirituality of priests does not focus on spiritual practices or exercises. Indeed, such practices, especially the Liturgy of the Hours, are an integral part of priestly spirituality, for they stimulate, support, sustain, and express the spiritual life of priests. But that spiritual life itself is lived, first of all, as a gift of God who is Love.

Since charity is the measure of one's spiritual life, the spiritual life of diocesan priests—from the perspective of their experience—refers to

* Also published in *Origins* as "Celibacy and Spirituality," vol. 20, no. 19, Oc-tober 18, 1990, pp. 300–302.

their encounter with the living God and their growth in love for God and others which results from that encounter. The essential question of priestly formation, then, is this: Where do they find God, and where does God find them?

Diocesan priests, in virtue of their baptism and confirmation, share the path of discipleship common to all followers of Jesus by the power of the Holy Spirit. But by reason of holy orders, in which they are sacramentally identified with Christ the High Priest in a special way, their spirituality also has a certain particularity, just as the spirituality of other disciples responding to other vocations is marked by a corresponding specificity.

WHERE PRIESTS FIND GOD AND GOD FINDS THEM

Diocesan priests find God, and God finds them, in three fundamental situations as they journey with the entire pilgrim people of God. I will briefly describe these three kinds of encounters. Then I will indicate how the discipline of celibacy in the Western Church enhances the spirituality of diocesan priests. Finally, I will pose several questions which address some of the practical implications of this understanding of priestly spirituality.

In Ministry and the Human Condition

Priests find the Lord, and the Lord finds them, in a privileged way within their *priestly ministry*. When, *in persona Christi capitis ecclesiae*, they proclaim the word and teach, celebrate the sacraments, especially the Eucharist and penance, or exercise their role of leadership, they meet the Lord. For the Lord is present in the people served, in the signs, symbols, sacraments, and words which he has given to his Church, and in the priests themselves who, in virtue of their ordination, serve God's people.

Unless priests are ready to receive the Lord, to meet him in these ministerial encounters, his presence—which is ever faithful and true—may in fact pass unnoticed by them, if not by the people they serve. Thus, if the encounter with the Lord is to be both consciously appropriated and transformative of their lives, priests must be alert and ready to meet the Lord. Unless they are attentive, prayerful, and reflective, they will become mere pastoral technicians.

From another perspective, priests are immersed in a unique way in the *human condition*. Their contemplation of that condition reveals God's presence. They serve men and women of all ages and all economic, educational, and social classes. They traverse the human life cycle from birth to death with their people. No single dimension of the human condition is outside the range of their care. In the human community and in all aspects of the human condition, which have been assumed in the humanity of the Incarnate Word, they contemplate and find the Lord. Similarly, in the full range of human life, the Lord finds his priests.

As I have intimated, however, this encounter with the Lord in the human community, which priests serve and to which they belong, may pass unnoticed unless their eye is trained, their heart is open, and their religious imagination is attuned.

In Solitude

Priests are consecrated or set apart to serve and lead the community of faith. In the Western Church, only those who have promised celibacy are ordained for priestly service. Both the call to lead and the commitment to celibacy involve priests in a profound experience of solitude. Moreover, this solitude is also lived and expressed in their personal prayer, obedience, and simplicity of life. They are drawn to recognize their complete dependence on the Lord. And in that solitary recognition they find the Lord, and he finds them.

Solitude, however, is true solitude—being truly present to oneself in God—when it is freely entered into and responded to positively and creatively. Indeed, only a living relationship to Christ sustained by daily prayer transforms loneliness into solitude. By contrast, if one perceives solitude as "imposed," then the experience can lead to a stultifying loneliness which drains energy and fuels resentment. Only true solitude, which is discovered and freely embraced, becomes an occasion for meeting the Lord.

In the Presbyterate Gathered Around Its Bishop

Diocesan priests are not ordained simply as individuals. They are ordained in the presbyteral order, and so, linked to their bishop in a presbyteral college. This applies *mutatis mutandis* to all priests, diocesan or religious, serving in a particular church.

The Lord promised his community of apostles that he would be present until the end of time. He sent them to preach, teach, and baptize (Matt 28:28). The presbyterate gathered around its bishop participates in this community and mission. Priests serving in a diocese are linked by multiple bonds: a common mission, a spirit of collaboration, an environment of personal support, and a shared sacramental life. In this community, they find the Lord, and he finds them.

The Lord is ever faithful to his promise to be present among those who serve him and his people—the presbyterate gathered around its bishop.

Sadly, however, we know that these communities of service can also be marked by sin, division, and a "hardness of heart," all of which obscure the Lord's presence. Hence, the bonds which unite priests need care and attention. Only then will the presbyterate be a holy gathering of priests with their bishop—a gathering which enables them to work effectively for the diocese and provides a context for a transformative encounter with the Lord.

CELIBACY

In today's society, celibacy often appears unattractive and, indeed, unattainable. Some who have made the commitment say that they did so under constraint, because it was a necessary condition for ordination. The witness value to the community, they maintain, seems minimal because of a growing openness of the faithful to a married clergy. These problems are sometimes compounded by transgressions, both public and private, of the discipline of celibacy. We must deal with these realities in a way that will positively engage the minds and hearts of our priests and people. Otherwise, there will be a further erosion, and celibacy will not be fully appreciated and embraced as a valued way for priests to develop a more intimate relationship with the Lord and his people.

The foundations for understanding celibacy as a gift to the Church are clear in our Western tradition. Consecrated celibacy expresses discipleship. It is a way of following Jesus who chose to be celibate, and it is embraced for the sake of the kingdom. It offers witness to a life oriented toward the future which God offers humanity. It expresses and expands ministerial availability. These general values apply to the celibate commitment of diocesan priests.

There are, moreover, other elements more directly and specifically connected with the dimensions of priestly spirituality which we have just considered. Celibacy—for those so gifted—offers a discipline of *attentiveness*, enabling priests to recognize the Lord's presence in their ministry and in the human community, in solitude, and in the presbyteral community. Celibacy also involves a form of *poverty* which focuses priests' attention on their dependence on God and the community of faith. Moreover, celibacy helps priests to cultivate personal *freedom* to grow in their love for others, especially through their ministry.

This positive and spiritually enriching dimension of celibacy in the lives of diocesan priests, as in the lived sacrament of marriage, demands a psychosexually integrated personality and a free embrace of the commitment, along with periodic, perhaps even daily recommitment.

QUESTIONS

It will never be enough simply to articulate general principles for the spirituality of diocesan priests. We must find ways to translate principles into practice. The following questions provide some indication of the practical paths which deserve exploration.

1. The loving and transforming encounter with God in ministry and the human community, in solitude, and in the presbyteral community requires attentiveness to God's presence. For some, ministry itself (e.g. an inordinate number of liturgical celebrations) can diminish such attentiveness. What aspects of priestly ministry and life actually enhance it?

2. How do traditional spiritual practices or exercises truly contribute to the spiritual life of priests? In what ways can this contribution be enhanced?

3. Who supports and challenges diocesan priests on their spiritual journey? Ways must be found for doing this on a continuing basis.

4. How can this vision of spirituality for diocesan priests come alive in an engaging way and not suffer the fate of other abstract idealizations which may elicit notional assent but, in reality, are often ignored?

Authenticity and Diversity in Consecrated Life*

World Synod of Bishops

—— 1994 ——

In a sense, my topic extends back to the early apostolic community which grappled with the tension between authenticity and diversity in the Christian life as well as that between the charismatic and hierarchical dimensions of the Church.

Many times throughout the Church's history, usually in times of transition, a recurrent phenomenon is detectable: New forms of consecrated life emerge to enlarge and enrich it. Periodically, the canonical structures and even the traditional names are no longer able to convey the new reality, and the Church must build some new structures and coin new names. We have passed from anchorite life, to monasticism, to religious life, and, more recently, to consecrated life. And even "consecrated life" does not cover the phenomenon of religious life today, and so we speak of institutes of consecrated life and societies of apostolic life.

We live in a time of crisis for consecrated life, but also a time of creativity. It is a time of *crisis* because of the deep tension affecting society and the Church as it prepares to pass from the second to the third millennium of Christianity. It is a time of *creativity*, as all times of crisis are, because the Holy Spirit seems to be particularly active in times of transition.

So, it is understandable that, today, we witness the same phenomenon: new, concrete ways of life among lay communities, particularly by members of already existing congregations of women religious founded for an

* Also published in *Origins*, vol. 24, no. 18, October 13, 1994, pp. 308–312.

apostolic mission. A deep change has been introduced in some of these communities, and a distinction has arisen between communities which continue in the traditional ways and communities which adopt new lifestyles. This has been, at times, the source of some misunderstanding and tension.

It is significant that diversity, tension, and divisions have affected mostly women's communities. This may be due to two causes, among others:

(a) the significant changes in the way many women perceive themselves, a fruit of a higher education and of tendencies of modern society;

(b) the fact that women's apostolic life is something relatively recent and may not yet have found its definitive place in the Church;

(c) unlike men, who had three options for an ecclesial vocation (diocesan priesthood, brotherhood, and religious life and priesthood), women have had only religious life as an ecclesial choice with all its structures and strictures.

Realistically, we must acknowledge that there has *always* been tension between the older groups and the newer ones. There are traces of discussions between hermits and cenobites in the fourth century, each one judging the other, according to one's own values: "Where is your poverty, cenobites?" "Where is your obedience, hermits?" In the twelfth century the tension was between monks and canons regular with the discussion *De vita vere apostolica*. Today, we ask, "Who lives authentic consecrated life?"

Three factors must be considered in our attempts to answer that question. The first is the role of the Holy Spirit, who gives charisms to both the communities of consecrated life and the bishops, gifts which are to be used on behalf of the Church and in service to the world. The second is the proper role of religious who possess both a special charism and a unique understanding of how that charism has been impacted by the historical-cultural context in which it has been lived out. The third is the appropriate role of ecclesial authority, whose responsibility it is to discern authentic charisms, approve the way of life of communities of consecrated life, and build up the unity of the entire Church.

CRITERIA: CHARACTERISTICS OF AUTHENTIC CONSECRATED LIFE

Church teaching, based on the gospel and articulated by the Second Vatican Council and postconciliar documents, is quite clear about the essential characteristics of consecrated life. In particular, we may identify five such characteristics which serve as criteria for determining authentic consecrated life. Religious may live these basic elements in diverse ways which call for further discernment.

1. Christocentric. Consecrated life is rooted in Jesus Christ. At the heart of consecrated life is each member's personal intimacy with the risen Lord. Every relationship requires personal contact, shared experiences, coming to deeper knowledge and love. So, too, the relationship of the man or woman religious with Christ must grow and develop through personal prayer. That is why, today, a greater emphasis is placed on following Christ chaste, poor, and obedient as he is revealed in the Gospels. To conform one's life to the Lord requires continual conversion. This is at the very heart of every Christian vocation, but religious make it their unique life work by vowing chastity lived in celibacy, as well as poverty and obedience according to the specific lifestyle of their institutes. History, tradition, spirituality, apostolate, and culture all help to shape the specific way in which the evangelical counsels are lived out in a given institute.

2. Ecclesial. Consecrated life is lived at the heart of the Church. The Second Vatican Council recognized the life of the evangelical counsels as a wonderful gift to the Church. So, the various institutes in which they are lived out are also a priceless treasure. From this fundamentally charismatic dimension of consecrated life in the Catholic Church flow other dimensions of that relationship which may be termed juridic, apostolic, and mystic. Those who have the responsibility in the Church to discern the authenticity of charisms are also charged with encouraging and fostering their growth and development. It is the role of ecclesial authority to authenticate founding charisms, formally erect institutes, and approve their constitutions. Following the nature of the Church, an institute's invisible charismatic dimension is ordered through visible structures, establishing a juridic bond with the Church. A part of each institute's proper law describes its role in the Church's mission. In the order of charity, through their profession of the evangelical counsels, religious are linked in a special way to the Church and its mystery.

3. Apostolic. Consecrated life is a sharing in the mission of Christ as that is continued in the Church. Among the various aspects of the life of each institute is its way of participating in the mission which Christ entrusted to the Church. Through women and men religious, the Church presents to the world Christ in contemplation and Christ engaged in a variety of active works on behalf of others. The Church has always recognized the apostolic fruitfulness of the purely contemplative life. And it constantly urges religious engaged in apostolic works to keep a contemplative perspective. As men and women of the Church, they integrate apostolic action and union with God. They also carry out their works in the name of the Church, by the mandate of the Church, and in ecclesial communion.

4. Prophetic. Consecrated life bears witness to gospel values. It is a witness against compromise with those values. Evangelization has been defined as bringing the gospel into every segment of humanity, transforming from within humanity's criteria for discernment, its determining values, its sources of inspiration, its designs for living. Men and women religious today can "speak clearly and forcefully to today's world which is suffering from so much consumerism and discrimination, eroticism and hatred, violence and oppression" (*Essential Elements*, no. 17).

5. Communal. As consecrated life has evolved through the centuries, it has maintained a communal identity within the Church. As noted above, consecrated life is a distinct state of life within the Church, living, working, and witnessing openly in the name of Christ and his Church. Incorporation into an institute of consecrated life means that members are no longer "private" persons. Moreover, while it has been done in different ways, religious have lived, worked, and witnessed as a *community*. The various expressions of a common life have been supportive of both their personal lives as vowed religious and the apostolate in which they have been involved.

INTERPRETATION: LEGITIMATE DIVERSITY WITHIN CONSECRATED LIFE

While certain fundamental characteristics remain essential to consecrated life in the Church, history has demonstrated the possibilities of diverse manifestations, in diverse eras, cultures, and historical circumstances. There is a broad scope for legitimate diversity, and the failure to recognize this as legitimate, indeed as a gift from the Spirit, can result in unnecessary tensions, fear, and accusations. As is the case with the initial authentication of a new charism, there is a concomitant need for prudent discernment in new expressions of diversity. The primary responsibility for this lies with the institute of consecrated life, but it may involve changes which also require the involvement of ecclesial authority.

It will be helpful to identify the sources of legitimate diversity. Ultimately, the Holy Spirit is the source of the wide variety of institutes of consecrated life in the Church. The 1983 Code of Canon Law describes what may be called the spiritual heritage of an institute. In doing so, it shows a broad understanding, which, in turn, offers criteria for evaluating diversity. Canon 578 states:

> The intention of the founders and their determinations concerning the nature, purpose, spirit, and character of the institute which have been

ratified by competent ecclesiastical authority *as well as its wholesome traditions* all of which constitute the patrimony of the institute itself, are to be observed faithfully by all.

Now, as in the time of these foundations, the Holy Spirit works within historical reality. For example, congregations originally founded in the chaos left by the French Revolution or established for the care of specific immigrant populations, have evolved as the socioeconomic and political situations around them changed. Because the Holy Spirit works within evolving historical reality, the Church—and its religious—need to read carefully "the signs of the times."

Inculturation is another source of diversity, legitimately arising—indeed, called for by the Church. Inculturation involves the incarnation or insertion of the gospel into various cultures, while also transforming and integrating into Christianity authentic cultural values. This is a slow and delicate process requiring a discernment which avoids compromising the integrity of faith. At times, there may be a lack of appreciation for the incarnational nature of the gospel. At the same time, it may be that, today, institutes of consecrated life, at least in some parts of the world, may need to focus more on firm countercultural witness than on inculturation. Again, there is need for continual spiritual discernment to know when there can be a beneficial integration of the positive values of a culture and when its values are truly in conflict with the gospel.

There is no magical formula for balancing authenticity and diversity. Rather, it takes great care, wisdom, and discernment. While legitimate diversity needs to be affirmed, protected, and appreciated in the Church, we need to acknowledge the existence of contemporary tensions and to ask why they have arisen.

Some have arisen because of imprudent experiments, practices which exceed the parameters of authenticity, unwillingness or inability to enter into mutually respectful dialogue, and negative attitudes toward ecclesial authority and canon law. Others are the result of ignorance or misunderstandings about legitimate historical diversity and fearful mistrust of supposed or alleged abuse. Examples can be found in the areas of common prayer, apostolate, government, and community life. I will now focus on the last of these.

DISCERNING AUTHENTICITY AND LEGITIMATE DIVERSITY ON A SPECIFIC ISSUE: COMMUNITY LIFE

De facto, there are multiple understandings of community. The term is an analogous, not a univocal, term. Moreover, unlike celibate chastity, obedience, and poverty, community is not an element common to all forms of consecrated life. It is not part of the eremitical life, considered by the ancient Church and still by the Eastern Church as the exemplary form of a life committed to the service of God. Nor is it considered an essential feature of secular institutes. But, as noted above, it is a necessary dimension of religious life (cf. no. 5, above).

Throughout history, community is perhaps the element that has been subject to more changes in the different forms of consecrated life: from the *lauras* of the Middle East, to the monasteries, to the priestly communities, to the mendicants, to the institutes founded for an apostolic activity, to the missionary congregations.

Belonging to an institute has its own dynamics. All the members of a province cannot live under one roof, but they have a loyalty and sense of belonging to the larger institute that is most important. Even those living alone or in small groups have to have that sense of loyalty.

Moreover, religious communities also relate to the parish in which they live. The widows in the early Church were very close to the parish and formed a part of it. Religious also relate to the larger diocesan community even if their motherhouse is in another diocese. So, again, community is not a univocal concept.

The Second Vatican Council's emphasis on understanding community as "communion" has had a profound effect on the way many religious in the United States view community life today. They rely less upon external structures and physical presence than in the past, and concentrate more on the *quality* of their mutual relationships. That is why many lay congregations, especially of women, have been building a new way of community.

They have done so for many reasons. Some are *cultural:* the higher level of education and the professional training of many contemporary women religious have opened many new areas of ministry for them and have introduced changes in the way they relate to one another. Other reasons are *psychological:* the old, very strict, and hard-working community is less attractive for some today because society places a greater emphasis on assuming more responsibility for one's life and work. But they have also changed the way they live in community for *economic* and *apostolic* reasons. Women religious often can find work only in places where there is no house of their congregation: universities, colleges, retreat houses, counseling centers, parishes, hospitals. Thus, while many continue to live with members of their own congregations, others live, at times, with members of other institutes, or, at other times, they live alone.

I hasten to add that I am referring to mature religious in the fullness of apostolic activities; junior religious begin their consecrated life living together, and retired religious again gather together. In between, women religious may pass from periods of living together to periods of physical separation. Their economic dependence on the community, part of the vow of poverty, is well protected, given the centralized administration of these congregations. The administrators usually receive the salary of their members and send to them what has been approved for their monthly expenses.

In order to keep their experience of community alive, these women religious have intensified their mutual relationships by frequent meetings, retreats, workshops, visits by their leaders, community celebrations, and visits with one another. This kind of community life is very similar to that of men's missionary institutes in the past.

In this matter, as in any other, tensions regarding "authenticity" arise when questions are raised about how far one might go in the direction of the changes noted above and still live a true "community life."

The recent document *Fraternal Life in Community* recognizes the historical and charismatic fact that different families of consecrated life with different roles in Christ's mission have different kinds of community life. Leaving aside the unique life of cloistered religious—which, moreover, differs from one order to another—the document acknowledges the diversity among "apostolic communities." Some, it notes

> are more strongly centered on common life so that their apostolate depends on the possibility of their forming community. Others are decidedly oriented toward mission and for them the type of community depends on the type of mission (n59b).

It states nonetheless that "common life in a house of the institute is essential for religious life" and therefore concludes with *Evangelica testificatio* that religious "should not live alone without serious reason, and should not do so if there is a community of their institute reasonably near" (*Fraternal Life*, no. 65). So, religious living alone is an *exception*—one for which there are legitimating norms.

But some questions still remain. Given that community life is essential to consecrated life, there are clearly differences in the way institutes have understood and lived common life in community. Today some of these differences have become more pronounced.

Which ones are legitimate? To what extent are the changes the work of the Spirit? How does one discern the limits beyond which "community life" becomes more a name than a reality? As the *Instrumentum laboris* [working paper] points out, "All are called to consider the apostle's teaching: 'Do not stifle the Spirit. Do not despise prophetic utterances. Test everything; retain what is good' (1 Thess 5:19-20)."

These and many more questions must be addressed by the institutes of consecrated life in conjunction with ecclesial authority whose responsibility is to affirm officially the validity of the institute's life and ministry in light of its charism.

The tension between authenticity and legitimate diversity is creative, necessary, and inevitable. The tensions which arise within or about institutes with regard to their "authenticity" as institutes of consecrated life can, as has been seen, arise from various sources and/or abuses. Moreover, they may arise from ignorance of legitimate diversity, a lack of openness to legitimate inculturation, or simply from a lack of accurate information about the situation being judged. Tensions are inevitable in an era like ours when there is rapid change in almost every aspect of societal and ecclesial life. For some, these are exciting challenges. For others, they are a bitter trial. In any case, where the approach to tension is one of seeking the truth together, in mutual respect and charity, there is strong hope for the achievement of deeper communion.

However, when tensions do not lead to a search for greater understanding, but result only in premature judgments, accusations, and counter-accusations, the result will be further divisions into opposing camps, each rigidly defending its own concept of the "truth." Such a situation cannot bear witness to the risen Lord, the gospel, or the Church. In such an atmosphere there is not the inner freedom which permits conversion to take place.

In order to discern authenticity amid diversity in consecrated life, we must proceed within a process of mutually respectful dialogue and prayerful discernment on the part of both religious and ecclesial authority. Only in this way can we make correct judgments about the many issues faced today.

In the spirit of promoting such a process, I pose two possible questions for further synodal discussion:

1. How can religious contribute more effectively to the development of an authentic, multicultural, theological, and pastoral understanding of consecrated life in the Church today?

2. How can we develop a better process of dialogue so that at every level—from the Holy See to the particular church—bishops may acquire a deeper understanding of the many dimensions of authentic consecrated life and the diverse ways it is continually impacted by the historical-cultural context in which it is lived?

Part Two

HOMILIES

Introduction to Part Two: Homilies

While we were vesting for Cardinal Bernardin's funeral, I spoke with some archdiocesan priests about our beloved brother, Joseph. One of them mentioned that, as he had recently read Paul's epistles, he had often thought of Joseph's own words and witness. Another said that he had had the same experience reading the Gospels, and several of us began to share some of the specific biblical passages that we associated with Cardinal Bernardin, especially in the last three years of his life. The consensus was quickly articulated that we were about to bury a truly holy man, a pastor who had had an intimate relationship with the Lord and had faithfully witnessed to the Word of God as archbishop of Chicago.

Cardinal Bernardin's homilies attest to this. In the final analysis, they flowed from his faith, his love of Christ and the Church, and his careful reading of the Scriptures, which helped shape his spiritual life and pastoral ministry as well as consoled, nourished, and challenged him on his journey.

METHODS OF SELECTION

When we decided to publish a volume including his homilies in this series, I drew up several criteria to guide the selection of the fewer than 100 texts that would be included out of his full collection of about 1,600 homilies. I discussed these criteria with a group of consultants, and we agreed that I would include homilies:

- that were given on special occasions in the cardinal's own life, in that of the archdiocese, and elsewhere in the Church;
- that used Scripture well and in effective homiletic styles;

275

- that have an interest beyond the original occasion and/or audience;

- and that provide insights into Cardinal Bernardin's personal faith, ecclesial vision, spirituality, pastoral sensitivity, and human characteristics (including his sense of humor).

My initial selections for inclusion in this volume were based on these criteria.

Alternate approach. It was later suggested that we consider publishing Cardinal Bernardin's homilies for each Sunday and major feast in all three liturgical cycles. This would have an obvious appeal if it were feasible. I again reviewed the entire collection and discovered three obstacles.

First, for several reasons there were gaps in the sequence of Sundays in each of the liturgical cycles. For example, the cardinal often dedicated new or renovated churches or celebrated major parochial anniversaries on Sundays, but the liturgical readings were taken from the selections for the Dedication of a Church. At other times, he had delivered a major address on a particular Sunday and did not celebrate a parish Mass. On still other Sundays, primarily in July, he was on vacation. Furthermore, on occasion he simply did not use a written text, and a few of the written texts appear to be missing. So, the Bernardin collection does not have a homily for each Sunday and major feast in all three liturgical cycles.

Second, when there *is* a Bernardin homily based on the readings for a given Sunday, it was usually directed to the specific circumstances of the occasion and congregation. At his request, about six to eight weeks before Cardinal Bernardin went to a particular place to celebrate the Eucharist, we sent the parish or institution a multi-page liturgical form (to be channeled back to his office through the Office for Divine Worship) and a one-page form to be returned directly to us indicating what was expected of the cardinal—merely to be present, give the homily, offer a welcome at the beginning of Mass, or offer comments after Communion. We also asked for an up-to-date profile of the congregation and suggestions about anything they would like him to mention or emphasize in his talk. Most of his homilies on these occasions were quite effective from all accounts, but their interest probably does not extend much beyond the original congregation and/or occasion.

Third, many of the homilies that I had selected in the first phase of preparing this volume had been delivered on weekdays, not Sundays or major feasts, and did not fit into this new, comprehensive format.

Final selection and organization. So, again with the agreement of my archdiocesan consultants, I returned to the original criteria and finalized the selections accordingly. In each of the six sections of this volume the homilies are listed chronologically, but, where possible, the specific Sunday or feast day is noted and the liturgical cycle identified. The first section includes homilies from his week of installation as archbishop of Chicago, and the last section includes homilies that allude to the challenges he faced the last three years of his life: a false accusation, pancreatic cancer, and approaching death. Sections two, three, and four are categorized under the rubrics of Advent–Christmas, Lent–Easter, and Ordinary Time, but, as I indicated, the individual homilies are in chronological order. The fifth section includes homilies on special occasions.

The reader will notice that Cardinal Bernardin delivered many of these homilies at Holy Name Cathedral. This is a bit misleading; it is due mostly to the criteria I used in making the selections. In fact, Cardinal Bernardin regularly visited parishes throughout the archdiocese; I doubt there were very many that he did not visit in his fourteen years as archbishop. (By the time he had served as archbishop of Chicago for five years, for example, the archdiocese reported that he had already visited 307 of the 433 parishes in the local church. Indeed, he visited some of them several times.)

I have read the full collection of Cardinal Bernardin's homilies several times. Only six of the 89 homilies included here have been published before. I did not include many other favorites of mine, but I hope that the selection offered here—as subjective as it may be—will help the reader understand more fully a holy man of God and continue to be inspired by his words.

Throughout his years as archbishop of Chicago, Cardinal Bernardin proclaimed "the Lord Jesus and his gospel in word and deed to the best of [his] ability" (Liturgy of Installation, August 25, 1982). His voice has been stilled, his presence has been taken from us, but his memory and his words remain. They retain the capacity to inspire future generations, for they derive their force from the power of God's word on which they are based and the credible personal witness of this extraordinary shepherd of God's people.

Alphonse P. Spilly, C.PP.S.
September 9, 1999

First Days in Chicago

Homily

"I Am Joseph, Your Brother"

Evening Prayer with the Presbyterate,
Archbishop-Designate of Chicago

Holy Name Cathedral, Chicago, Illinois

——*August 24, 1982*————————————————————————

Archbishop Laghi, Bishop Hayes, Bishop Abramowicz, Father Keating, my dear brothers in Christ:

PEACE BE WITH YOU

Peace be with you. This is my first greeting to you, the priests who serve this local church, the Archdiocese of Chicago. Peace be with you and all the parish communities you represent. Peace be with your families and friends. Tonight in all sincerity I embrace each of you in the peace of Christ. From the warm welcome you have given me, I already feel that the peace I offer rests upon you and that you embrace me in peace. The peace we share strengthens me as I begin my pastoral ministry among you.

When the bishop of a diocese dies the whole Church mourns and prays for his repose. When a new bishop is named the whole Church gives thanks and everyone opens his eyes and ears in curiosity about the new shepherd. But none mourn and pray more for their bishop in death, and rejoice more at the news of a new bishop, than the priests. Even as I speak you are asking: "Who is he?" "What manner of man is Joseph Bernardin?" "What does he think of us?" "What is his vision of the priesthood?" "What are his plans?" "Is he the man of faith, prayer, and compassion that a diocese needs or is he a career bureaucrat rewarded for his loyalty?"

And I, in turn, am full of questions about you. We all sense the excitement and feeling of challenge of this occasion.

WHAT AM I LIKE?

Who am I? What am I like? I am a member of the class of 1952! I know Chicago has had some remarkable ordination classes. Your ranks extend from Father Martin Schmidt, ordained in 1910, to Father Jack Clair, the youngest member of the class of 1982. But I am told that the class which Cardinal Stritch ordained on May 1, 1952, is really extraordinary in terms of the leaders it produced.

Just a few days earlier, on April 26, I was ordained a priest for the Diocese of Charleston. I look forward to meeting my Chicago classmates and celebrating our thirty-first anniversary together. Called to be the new head of the presbyterate of Chicago, I am a new member of that class as well.

My father Joseph, who came to America from the province of Trent in northern Italy, was a stonecutter. Though he died when I was only six, I remember him. With the loss of my father, I became even closer to my dear mother, Maria, and my sister, Elaine. I was very blessed to grow up in a family full of love, faith, and a willingness to work hard.

I had long wanted to be a doctor, but in 1945 I decided instead to become a priest. I have very happy memories of the years I spent in Charleston after ordination and in Atlanta as pastor of Christ the King cathedral parish. Two of the most influential priests in my life have been the late Archbishop Paul Hallinan, whom I served as chancellor in Charleston and later as auxiliary bishop of Atlanta, and Cardinal John Dearden, who was president of the bishops' conference when I was general secretary.

I have benefited greatly from my experiences as president of the National Conference of Catholic Bishops, as a delegate to several synods, and as a member of the Congregation for Bishops. But the greatest blessing in my priesthood were the ten years during which I was privileged to serve as archbishop of Cincinnati. The loyal and dedicated priests, religious, and people of that gifted archdiocese have shaped my identity as a priest and bishop. If my labors here in Chicago are fruitful, it will be due in great measure to what I learned from the church of Cincinnati.

The priests of Cincinnati were especially helpful to my spiritual growth. Several years ago, I sensed that administrative responsibilities were eating away at my interior life. I told several young priests that I felt they were praying more and better than I. I told them I wanted and needed their help. They generously took me into their lives of prayer and helped me come closer to the Lord. Theirs was a wonderful and permanent gift.

As to my personal tastes and habits, I am quite ordinary. I do like music. My favorite is classical, especially opera. I am credited with being a good cook but that is somewhat exaggerated. One of the main difficulties in recent years has been the lack of time needed to develop whatever culinary skills I might have. Also, I do not want to regain the weight I lost several years ago. My friends say I am a workaholic, but I do not think I am. If I do work hard, it is more because I like what I do than because of compulsion. Yet I do not consider myself indispensable. I do take time for recreation and refreshment. At the end of the day I enjoy a brisk walk and an easy conversation with a fellow priest.

WHAT DO I THINK OF YOU?

What do I think of you, the priests of Chicago?

Over the years I have come to know a number of priests from Chicago. I have been impressed by them. Since the announcement of my appointment I have benefited from the generous assistance of Bishop Hayes and Bishop Abramowicz, Father Keating, who has guided the archdiocese during the last four months, and many others. They have all made me welcome and helped in many ways.

While I do not know many of you personally, I feel that I know the priesthood of Chicago. It is more than just a local reality. It is a national asset. In the '40s, '50s, '60s, '70s and '80s—the years before, during, and after the council—the Church around the country has often looked to Chicago for leadership. Pioneering programs in youth ministry (the Catholic Youth Organization), family services (the Christian Family Movement), urban ministry, social justice, education, liturgical development, seminary renewal, the permanent diaconate, and many others were all developed here. Much good for the Church came from Chicago under the leadership of Cardinals Mundelein, Stritch, Meyer, and Cody. Many talented priests of the archdiocese have contributed to the Church nationally and internationally. You are loved and respected all over the country. Your good works are widely known and praised. What do I think of you? I think you are a remarkable group of men. I praise you and applaud you. It is a privilege and a challenge to be called to serve as head of the presbyterate in this archdiocese. I count on your help in meeting the challenges that lie before us.

WHAT IS MY VISION?

What is my vision of the priesthood? I hope to answer in word and deed over the months and years to come. I look forward to hearing your answers as well. I have been a priest for thirty years, and I still do not fully comprehend the mystery of the priesthood. But this much I do know. The priesthood is not a job. The priest is not a functionary, not a general practitioner, not a poor man's psychologist. True, many things about priestly ministry resemble a job. Priests ask, for example, "Where are you *working* now?" We have work schedules, organizations, a distinctive uniform. But still the priesthood is not a job.

Here in Chicago we are blessed to have one of the largest and most diverse communities of priests in America: diocesan and religious; pastors and educators, serving inner-city, suburban, and rural communities; chaplains in hospitals and jails; those in specialized ministries and those who serve at the Archdiocesan Pastoral Center, to name a few. As important as this diversity is, ours remains the one priesthood of Christ. We cannot measure our success and failure by the standards of the world. We must not think that moving from one post to another is "moving up or down in the Church," as if the body of Christ were a giant corporation. Whatever each of us is called to do as a priest, we are all building up the Mystical Body. All ministry is pastoral ministry. We are all laborers for the one Harvest Master.

The priesthood is a passionate commitment, a fiery-eyed vision, and an insatiable thirst for holiness and practical justice. The priest is called to be challenger, enabler, life-giver, poet of life, music-maker, dreamer of dreams. He must be a man of deep personal faith, conformed to Christ, a man who loves the Scriptures, draws sustenance from the sacramental life of the Church, and truly knows the community with and for whom he offers sacrifice. A priest is a man with a clear sense of his own self, one who strives to develop all his natural talents to the limit for the good of the Church. He is a man of unreasonable hopes and expectations, who takes seriously, for himself and others, the injunction to be perfect as the heavenly Father is.

Priests of this generation will see George Orwell's menacing 1984 come and go. They will witness the start of the third millennium of Christianity. Together we face a future that is familiar yet startlingly new. As we proclaim that the reign of God is at hand, none of us knows where the Church is in her pilgrimage. Some suppose she has just begun the journey, others that she is at midpoint, still others that the goal itself is in sight. We do not know. But building upon the solid achievements of the past, we must all set our faces to the future. Our lives and ministries will be the foundation stones for the Church to come.

To be good priests we must first be good men. This requires that we seek to understand the mystery of our whole humanity. We must make provision for our physical, emotional, and psychological health. We cannot hide from life. Our vocation is not a matter of "easy hours and no heavy lifting." Only by living life in all its complexity will we be able to serve our people with compassion. Our genuine interest and authenticity should be manifest. If we are truly comfortable with ourselves and have a deep appreciation of our celibate commitment, we should not fear opening ourselves to others in love and lasting friendships. Like everyone else, the priest needs affection.

Our priesthood must also be fed by an inner silence, a spiritual tranquility, public and private prayer, and an abiding joy. Without prejudice to the important social mission of the Church, the basic thrust of our efforts as priests must be spiritual. That is what is unique about our ministry. Indeed, only a radical spiritual commitment can sustain us in our efforts on behalf of the poor and downtrodden. To understand and appreciate this we must turn to Jesus himself, seeking in him the wisdom, guidance, and strength we need to fashion our priestly ministry. Any attempt to explain the priesthood apart from the mystery of Christ and his Church is fruitless. Any attempt to tear the ministerial priesthood from its roots in Christ and in the Church will bring disillusionment and failure. The effort to explain the priesthood in purely human terms, though often well intentioned, has in fact caused confusion and pain among the best of us. Such efforts rob the priesthood of its essentially spiritual task of reconciling all people to one another and to God through the power of Christ and the Holy Spirit.

As the Holy Father reminds us, the Eucharist is the very source of our identity as priests and the source, too, of our ministry to Christ's priestly people. In the Eucharist, God reveals who he is to us in Christ, and we reveal who we are. In liturgy we seek to be men of public prayer, men of transparent, tangible faith, in order to inspire and encourage prayer in others. We can proclaim the gospel convincingly only if we have heard its echo in the stillness of our own hearts. We can break the Bread of Life only if we ourselves have been broken and given, and found life in the giving. As Pope John Paul tells us: "Our whole priestly existence is and must be deeply imbued with this service, if we wish to effect in an adequate way the eucharistic sacrifice *in persona Christi*" (Letter to All the Priests of the Church, Holy Thursday, 1979).

Liturgical spirituality is not something we can put on or take off like a chasuble. It must be real. It must flow from who we really are. It arises from an intensely intimate relationship with Jesus, a relationship which can exist and be nourished only through prayer. Like it or not, we reveal our own prayer life—or lack of it—to those we would lead in prayer.

This is why prayer cannot simply be a part of our lives. It must be everything. It must be, as Teresa of Avila writes, the heavenly rain that waters the garden of our soul. Such prayer gives meaning to our priesthood, foundation to our liturgical ministry, clarity to our pursuit of justice, and strength for our perseverance. It is the beginning of our external union with the Lord who is the greatest lover we will ever know.

WHAT ARE MY PLANS?

What are my plans? Do I have a program in my suitcase to make the church of Chicago the living announcement of the nearness of the kingdom of God that Christ calls it to be? No, I have no such program. But I do have the advice of the many people who have told me in one way or another that Chicago is a big city, take your time, get to know the place and the people, and most of all, listen. Listen to their joys and sorrows, hopes and aspirations. Listen to their stories of the Church. That is very sound advice, and I intend to try to follow it.

To aid my listening, I am reconstituting the Senate of Priests as of this evening. In the months and years ahead may it become a vital force in the life of the archdiocese. I accept the suggestion of the senate for a series of regional gatherings at which I can learn about the human family and the Catholic Church in Chicago from you, the priests. I look forward to visiting with the leaders of the Association of Chicago Priests. With your help, I hope to bring together the senate, the association, and the Board of Consultors in more efficient structures of consultation and collaboration. In time—but soon—I intend also to explore an Archdiocesan Pastoral Council, so that I can better learn the needs of the religious and laity of the archdiocese.

I intend to give special priority to visiting with priests in key positions in various offices, agencies, and programs in the archdiocese. I hope to learn firsthand how the archdiocese is organized and to form an assessment of its practical needs. This is a necessary step in developing an effective team which I consider essential. As part of this process, it may be that, where ordination is not required, laypersons, sisters, and brothers will be invited into positions traditionally associated only with priests. Among other things, this will help us who are priests to become more open to the talents and legitimate aspirations of lay people in the Church. In any case, the overriding motivation of all our work in the central offices must be to serve the parishes.

I know very well that I cannot do alone all that must be done. None of us can do anything without Christ, and I can do very little without you. I am very human, subject to the same shortcomings and limitations as you. So I need all of you. I need your great talent, energy, collaboration, faith, loyalty, challenge, and honest counsel. One area of great importance where I shall seek your counsel in the months ahead is the recommending of worthy candidates from the presbyterate of Chicago for the office of bishop. A diocese of this size must have more auxiliary bishops. There are many reasons for this, but among them is the danger that otherwise people will lose their sense of "church" as something more than the local parish. Personal contact with bishops is necessary to counteract this tendency. In this regard, too, I am very aware that you have asked that recommendations for auxiliaries show appreciation of the rich ethnic and racial diversity of our Church.

It goes without saying that in all my efforts as your new bishop, I shall be guided by the teachings, disciplines, and practices of the Church in collegial communion with our Holy Father, Pope John Paul II, pastor of the universal Church. I believe deeply that this is the will of Christ for the well-being of the Church and all its members. I am honored this evening by the presence of Archbishop Laghi, the Holy Father's personal representative in the United States. I ask you, archbishop, to convey to the Holy Father our best wishes and our promise of prayers and support. Like the Holy Father, I, too, look in a special way to our Blessed Mother for guidance and assistance; pray for her intercession on my behalf and on behalf of the archdiocese.

CONCLUSION

I cannot conclude without speaking of Cardinal Cody. I was four years old when the cardinal became a priest, and he was archbishop of Chicago longer than I have been a bishop. Thus we are men of different generations and different experiences of Church and episcopal ministry. I was saddened by the pain, suffering, and conflict that seemed to cloud his final years. He was called to leadership in the Church during years of unprecedented change and turmoil. The achievements of his fifty years of priesthood are real and lasting. By any objective measure, Cardinal Cody did many good things for Chicago which make my work easier. If any hard feelings, bitterness, or anger—toward the cardinal or among yourselves—remain in your hearts for any reason, tonight is the night to cast off the burden and purify your hearts. Let us continue to pray for Cardinal Cody. May he be with God even as we speak.

One of the cardinal's great achievements was the restoration of this historic and beautiful Holy Name Cathedral. I have been admiring the magnificent bronze panels by the contemporary Italian artist, Attilio Selva, above the cathedra of the bishop. The last panel on the far right of the chair portrays the holy name and priesthood of Jesus. It shows our Lord in priestly attire at the altar of sacrifice presenting the chalice of salvation to humanity of all races. We, the priests of Chicago, continue to offer that chalice both at Mass and throughout the day. When you pray now at the altar for the leaders of the Church, you will add my name to that of our Holy Father. And when you call my name, may we be united in a special way through the Eucharist.

As our lives and ministries are mingled together through the breaking of the Bread and the blessing of the Cup, I hope that long before my name falls from the Eucharistic Prayer in the silence of death you will know well who I am. You will know because we will work and play together, fast and pray together, mourn and rejoice together, despair and hope together, dispute and be reconciled together. You will know me as a friend, fellow priest, and bishop. You will know also that I love you.

For I am Joseph, your brother!

Homily

"It Is a Spiritual Event"

*Liturgy of the Solemn Installation
of the Seventh Archbishop of Chicago*

Holy Name Cathedral, Chicago, Illinois

———*August 25, 1982*————————————————————————

PROLOGUE

The biggest movie hit of the season here and around the country is
E. T.—The Extra-Terrestrial. The story deals, as you know, with an amaz-
ingly intelligent and endearing creature from another planet and his
struggle to understand the strange world of suburban America. Imagine,
if you will, that E. T., having wandered to the near north side of Chicago,
looks into Holy Name Cathedral and sees this ceremony in progress.

Full of curiosity, he asks a policeman what is going on. After learning
that it is the installation of the new archbishop of Chicago, E. T. goes off
to continue his exploration. He stops in a short-order cafe down the
block and tells a man who seems to have had a bit too much to drink and
too little to eat about the installation. "So what?" he replies. "Is that going
to change the price of a bottle of wine?" He visits a number of fancy ho-
tels and restaurants and asks their managers if they have heard the news.
They have, they are disappointed. They thought the installation might
generate more business.

Strolling out of the lobby of the Drake Hotel, he makes his way to the
Oak Street Beach. Young people are working on one of the last good sun-
tans of the summer. When they take their Walkman earphones off, he

asks them about the new archbishop. "It doesn't make that much differ-ence to me," one answers. "I used to be a Catholic, I mean, I guess I still am. But it's my parents who are really into religion. They're at home now, watching the ceremony on TV."

On his way back to the cathedral, E. T. stops to chat with a young black man who is the custodian in an exclusive apartment building. He is glued to his television set watching the ceremony. Why is it so interesting to him? "Because this is history," he declares. "I've been a Catholic since grade school, and this is important to me. I really love the Church. When most people think about Catholics in Chicago, they think of those who are Irish, Polish, German, Italian. But there are all kinds of Catholics here—black, Hispanic, Oriental, Haitian, and many others. With all our different backgrounds, we are all one in the Church. I'm watching this in-stallation because it's a spiritual event."

Returning to the cathedral, E. T. tunes in on the thoughts of some of those present. A retired pastor muses: "I was in this cathedral seventeen years ago yesterday, when Cardinal Cody was installed. It's a big job, being archbishop here. I hope people will be realistic, give the new man a chance." A few leaders of the civic and financial communities are asking themselves whether the new archbishop will be a friend or a foe of City Hall and La Salle Street. A member of the interfaith and ecumenical dele-gation is hoping the years ahead will be marked by substantial cooperation and concrete steps toward unity. Still others are asking themselves what the media mean in saying the new archbishop is "moderately conservative" on doctrinal matters and "moderately progressive" on social ones.

Finally, E. T. decides he might just as well find out the meaning of this event from the archbishop himself. Taking a seat in the back pew, he pre-pares to listen.

My dear brothers and sisters in the Lord:

I HAVE COME TO CHICAGO WITH ONLY ONE DESIRE

I am deeply moved and challenged by the confidence our Holy Father, Pope John Paul II, has placed in me by appointing me archbishop of Chicago. I wish to thank him publicly in the person of his representative, the apostolic delegate, Archbishop Pio Laghi, for this new opportunity to serve the Church. I pledge to the Holy Father my prayers, obedience, and support. As I told the priests last evening, all my efforts will be guided by the teachings, disciplines, and practices of the Church in collegial union with the Holy Father as pastor of the universal Church.

My heart is full at the sight of all who are gathered around this great altar of Christ to pray with me and for me and the Archdiocese of Chicago. You are civic leaders, educators, leaders from other Christian traditions, and friends of the Jewish faith as well as other religions. You are my brothers in the college of bishops. I acknowledge especially the bishops of the suffragan sees of the province of Illinois whom I am now called to serve as metropolitan. As I acknowledge the cardinals, archbishops, and bishops who are present, I wish also to pay tribute to my predecessors, especially Cardinal Cody.

You are dear personal friends and coworkers from Columbia, Charleston, Atlanta, and Washington. You are my closest collaborators from the Archdiocese of Cincinnati, which I love dearly and shall truly miss. You are my relatives and family members, whose support and affection I have always cherished—my beloved mother, Maria, who gives me love each day, and yes, my dear father, Joseph, whom I remember with love and gratitude. And, of course, you are the bishops, priests, deacons, sisters, brothers, and Catholic people of the Archdiocese of Chicago. I make my own the words of Saint Augustine, bishop and doctor of the Church, whose feast we celebrate on Saturday:

> For you I am a bishop, but with you I am a Christian. The first is an office accepted, the second is a grace received. The first is a danger, the second, salvation. . . . I am happier by far to be redeemed with you than I am to be placed over you.

As my voice goes beyond this cathedral, I greet in a particular way the retired sisters, brothers, priests, and laity. So much that is great in the archdiocese is due to you. I thank you not only for what you have done but for what you are still doing through your prayers and good works.

I wish especially to embrace those in hospitals, nursing homes, and homes for the handicapped. I also extend my hand and my heart to those who do not believe in God, to those who follow no religion, to those who are disenchanted, angry, alienated and hurt, and to those in prison.

I have come to Chicago with only one desire: to do all in my power to proclaim the Lord Jesus Christ and his gospel in word and deed. In the reading from Jeremiah just proclaimed, the Lord said to the great prophet, "To whomever I send you, you shall go; whatever I command you, you shall speak. Have no fear because I am with you to deliver you. See, I place my words in your mouth!" (Jeremiah 1:7-9).

I am but a shadow compared to the prophet, but I take these words to heart this day. They are addressed not only to me, but to all who collaborate with me in serving the People of God in Chicago. A bishop in the Church is called to teach, to govern, and to lead his congregation to holiness of life. Every good teacher knows that the best instruction begins in silence. The first and most profound silence is that of reflective prayer, listening to the word of God and responding to it in one's heart. The second is the silence of listening to those one is to teach, in order to know them.

Saint Paul tells us of the words which God places in our mouths in silence. "It is not ourselves we preach but Christ Jesus as Lord and ourselves as your servants for Jesus' sake" (2 Cor 4:5). Paul was well acquainted with human nature. Against our self-righteousness, vanity, and ambition he makes it clear that the surpassing power of the message we preach comes not from us but God. "Earthen vessels" that we are, we bear within us a great treasure.

In the gospel our Lord tells us that the Good Shepherd knows his people and lays down his life for them. In a church as large as that of Chicago this is—in one sense—far from easy. It will take a long time for me to get to know all of you. Indeed, to do so may be impossible. I am not an immediate part of the daily joys and sorrows of your lives. I do not baptize your children, hear your confessions, witness your marriages, counsel you in times of pain, bury your dead. For so much of this I count instead on my principal coworkers, the dedicated priests of the archdiocese.

I intend, nevertheless, to go from one end of Chicago to another, to the northern, western, and southern suburbs, to the many communities that make up Lake and Cook counties, in order to meet you. It may be difficult, even impossible, for me as your shepherd and father in Christ to know each one of you and call you by name, yet already we enjoy a true and profound unity—the bond of our common baptism and the unity of the breaking of the Bread and the blessing of the Cup. Our kinship in the Blood of Christ is as real to me as the bonds that join me to my own family.

Moreover, Jesus tells us that the Good Shepherd is one who lays down his life for his people. Some live this calling literally, shedding their blood as martyrs. Others live it in the unstinting giving of their time, their energy, their very selves to those they have been called to serve. Whatever the future holds for me, I pledge this day to live as a Good Shepherd who willingly lays down his life for you.

THE RECOVERY OF THE SPIRIT

I shall gladly spend my life in service of the spiritual mission to which the Church calls me this day. The reaffirmation of the spiritual nature and destiny of the human person may be the most challenging task of these times. Everyone knows that today's world is split, threatened by the arsenals of world powers capable of destroying each other and all humankind. But in truth there is a division in the world still more profound, a rift in the human condition that threatens manifold disaster for us all. I speak of the tendency of modern culture to alienate men and women from their divinely given spiritual nature and destiny.

Here is the central challenge facing religion in our day—that cultural myopia which narrows human horizons by denying life's transcendent dimension. Social, educational, and political systems all imply that physical well-being and the accumulation of material goods constitute our highest purpose. And what is the result? It is, as Pope John Paul II tells us in that remarkable document, his first encyclical, *Redemptor hominis*, that "man lives increasingly in fear" (no. 15).

For if the "theology" of television commercials and our consumer society is correct—men and women are born only to seek pleasure and amass material possessions—what possible meaning can there be in the fact that ultimately we die? Without faith, death is both obscene and absurd. Since we *are* doomed to die, however, our sojourn on earth and the fact of our death call out for an explanation that transcends these experiences themselves. If life has a meaning, it must lie in the fulfillment of lasting vision, an eternal joy. Life itself must be an experience of moral growth, so that we come to its end on earth spiritually richer and better than we began. Only this spiritual vision can lift life above the banality of materialism and the meanness of self-indulgence.

For those of us who cherish the name Christian, there is a further dimension to this reality, the dimension of Jesus Christ. As the Holy Father says, "Unceasingly contemplating the whole of Christ's mystery, the Church knows with all the certainty of faith that the Redemption that took place through the Cross has definitively restored his dignity to man and given back meaning to his life in the world . . ." (*Redemptor hominis*, no. 10).

In his Harvard commencement address several years ago, Alexander Solzhenitsyn challenged the West, declaring that the world has come to a turning point in history, equal in importance to the transition from the Middle Ages to the Renaissance. Facing the challenge of this transition requires of us a spiritual response. And in light of this we have some hard questions to face, as a Church, as a city, as a nation, and as the human family. Must the quality of human life and social activity be measured by material expansion? Can we responsibly promote such expansion while ignoring, even violating, our spiritual identity? Relying on a vision of the human person bereft of the spiritual dimension, can we find authentic solutions to such problems as sexism and racism, social violence, and family disintegration, global poverty, and threat of nuclear extinction? I think not. Never has there been a more urgent need for those who believe in God to discern what faith truly means, for those who believe in Christ to proclaim who he really is and what he means to human life.

INTERFAITH AND ECUMENICAL COOPERATION

I am committed to this witness. I join hands with all who respect the dignity and value of the human person, all who believe in God, and all who believe in Christ. Whatever our differences as believers, we all bow our heads and cover our faces before the same God. Whatever our differences as Christians, they are differences among Christians. And there is only one Christ. As for the work for Christian unity, I rededicate myself this afternoon with renewed hope to every level of ecumenical activity. I am not discouraged by the smallness of our steps. For we are moving. When we think of the previous centuries, it is remarkable how far we have come in recent decades on the road to the unity which Christ wills. As Pope John Paul himself has asked, "Have we the right to turn back? Dare we to turn back simply because the road is difficult?"

In the face of the spiritual crisis facing our society, it is my hope that, as I come to know the many religious leaders of Chicago, we will often be able to speak and act jointly, drawing on the resources of our respective Christian, Jewish, and other traditions to promote the commonweal of our community.

MY PERSONAL FAITH

In the context of this liturgy of installation, I wish to share my belief in the mystery of God and the spiritual nature and destiny of the human person. I wish to profess my personal belief in the Lord Jesus and all that he has taught us. I believe in the Lord, and I love him with all my mind and heart and soul. The great desire of my life—a desire which intensifies as I grow older—is to be intimately united with him, so that I can experience in the depth of my being his great love for me; so that I can allow his life to become my life.

I wish also to affirm and encourage each one of you as you search for the Lord and seek to grow in intimacy with him. I ask you to join with me in prayer for all those who are not close to the Lord, for the many people who desperately need to experience his love, but have not placed themselves at his mercy. I am confident that Christ, the Good Shepherd, will answer our prayers.

CONCLUSION

If God gives me the strength and grace, I shall preside in charity over the church in Chicago from the bishop's chair of this cathedral for many years. When, in the year of my retirement, the archbishop's crozier is passed to my successor, we shall have reached the year two thousand plus three. A sobering thought for me and for you as well. Together we may cross the threshold of the third millennium, a milestone for civilization and for Christianity. For however many years I am given, I give myself to you. I offer you my service and leadership, my energies, my gifts, my mind, my heart, my strength, and, yes, my limitations. I offer you myself in faith, hope, and love.

I have long admired the beautiful restoration of Holy Name Cathedral as one of Cardinal Cody's many achievements during his long years of service in Chicago. On the wall above the bishop's chair are a series of beautiful bronze panels, the work of the contemporary Italian artist, Attilio Selva. The central panel, right over the cathedra, portrays the names of Jesus and the central mystery of Christianity. At birth Christ received the name Jesus in accord with his mission as savior. At the moment of his resurrection he received a second name: Lord. The bas-relief illustrates the investiture of the risen Christ in his sovereign dominion over all creation.

That same risen Christ is with us this day.

And he continues to need each one of you.

He needs your eyes to continue to see.

He needs your strength to continue to work.

He needs your voice to continue to preach.

He needs your hands to continue to bless.

He needs your heart to continue to love.

And he needs your whole being to continue to
build up his body, the Church.

As we believe, so let us live.

Homily

"Christ Calls Us Who Are Many to Be but One"

Mass of Greeting and Thanksgiving for the People of the Archdiocese of Chicago

Grant Park, Chicago, Illinois

—— *August 29, 1982* ——————————————————

INTRODUCTION: WE ARE GOD'S HUMAN FAMILY

My dear brothers and sisters in the Lord:

Our Mass today brings us together in a family festival and makes it possible for me to greet more members of my new archdiocesan family than I could last Wednesday afternoon. My first words to you, the priests, religious and so many of the laity of the Archdiocese of Chicago, can only be: I am glad to be among you, glad to be one of you. I am a newcomer in Chicago, but you have made me feel like a neighbor, an old friend, indeed a family member.

To be a family member is a beautiful human experience. But to us who are the family of the Church, it is that and more. The whole human race is called by God's Holy Spirit and the needs of the world to be one family. And our rebirth in the waters of baptism, our redemption through the Blood of Christ, and our ongoing pilgrimage to the Father as members of the Church bind us together as a family of faith in a real and lasting way. This is more than a metaphor, a figure of speech. We share through God's grace in the intimate trinitarian life of God himself. We who are the Church are God's human family. Let us believe this, and let us live as we believe!

The portion of this great Christian, Catholic family which is the Archdiocese of Chicago is not a nuclear family, consisting only of parents and children. It is an extended family that encompasses the most diverse members: priests, deacons, religious, and laity; black, white, Hispanic, and Oriental; rural, suburban, and urban; parishes, hospitals, schools, universities, administrative offices; parents and children, childless couples, the single, the widowed, the separated, the divorced; those who give all of their energies to the Church and those who are all but inactive. Today we celebrate the unity of us all.

One of the finest results of the Second Vatican Council is the fact that Catholic people everywhere have come to a deeper appreciation of their ecclesial identity and baptismal dignity—their membership in the family of God. The People of God do not come to the sisters, priests, deacons, and bishops to receive services from "the Church" as if it were some sort of dispensing agency. Rather, all the baptized, sharing in the royal priesthood of Christ, are prompted by the Holy Spirit to gather *as* the Church in order to proclaim and live their faith. We who serve in the Church as sisters and brothers, deacons, priests, and bishops are by no means the "real Church" while the rest are only spectators.

WE NEED ONE ANOTHER

As archbishop, called to preside in charity over the family of the church in Chicago, I have publicly dedicated myself to the well-being of this great family. But I know I cannot do it all. I cannot do it alone. Nor can the sisters and brothers, the priests and deacons. We all need each other. Lay people have a right to expect much from bishops, clergy, and religious. But the Lord expects much from all of us who are his human family. Enlightened by Christian wisdom and the teaching of the Church, lay people must more and more assume their distinctive role—in the Church and also as Christians in the world.

For if you do not bring Christ into your homes, neighborhoods, offices, businesses, factories, shopping centers, schools, hospitals, prisons, nursing homes—who will? I know how much you have already done, how much you now do, and I thank you for it. I praise God for the leadership you have had from bishops before me. We must build together on the foundations they have laid, so as to proclaim Jesus Christ in words that truly speak to the minds and hearts of men and women in our day.

The Scriptures of today's Mass offer us guidance in doing this. We must be faithful to the message of God. In the book of Deuteronomy, Moses warns that we must not add to or subtract from the commandments God has given us. In the letter of James we learn that by fidelity to

God's word we can become the first fruits of God's creation. We must humbly welcome the word that has taken root in us, with its power to save us. Listening is not enough; we must act on this word.

And in the gospel our Lord confronts all of us in the Church. We must never pay God our Father mere lip service, while keeping our hearts far away from him.

WE MUST OPEN OUR LIVES TO CHRIST

All this amounts to a great challenge. In meeting this challenge we must open our hearts to Jesus Christ. We must not hold back any part of ourselves from the power of God's Holy Spirit. If we open wide the doors of our whole lives, holding nothing back from God, Christ will surely enter. Then we will be fitting heralds to announce God's saving word to others.

As a priest and bishop I have continued to try to open wide the doors of my heart to Christ. I have found again and again that, when I stopped resisting, stopped trying to be completely in charge of my life and placed my trust in the Lord, things have gone better for me. As your new archbishop, I want each of you to know how important Jesus Christ is to me. I believe in him and all that he has taught. He is the Way to my salvation. I love him with all my heart, and the central desire of my life is to be intimately united with him. Then will I experience his great love for me in the very depths of my being. I know that in this way my life will become one with his.

I wish to affirm and encourage you, as you also search for the Lord in your daily lives and seek to grow in intimacy with him. Do you ever feel misunderstood, lonely, discouraged, wounded, abandoned? Then you need to experience Jesus' love, compassion, and healing power. He is not far away. He is right there beside you, waiting for you to turn to him and place yourself in his hands.

I ask you to join me in prayer for all those who are not close to the Lord, for the many who desperately need to experience his love but who, for one reason or another, have not sought his mercy. They are all around us. Sometimes it is a spouse or child; it may be some other relative or a friend; it may be someone with whom we work. Pray that they will have the courage to extend their hands, and touch Jesus, and receive his healing power. And to our prayers we must join our own personal gestures of love and concern, because often it is through us that Jesus reveals himself to others.

If each one of us continues to strive for union with Jesus, we can go forth from this, our first Mass together, "as those who serve." We can build bridges of faith and love between ourselves and all those around us.

In this way we will know the joy of true community and friendship. Saint Augustine, the great bishop and doctor of the Church whose feast we celebrated yesterday, spoke movingly of this Christian fellowship: "We loved each other with all our hearts, and these marks of friendship that were shown on our faces, by our voices, in our eyes and a thousand other ways, were among us like ardent flames that fused our souls together, and of many made but one."

Dear brothers and sisters in Christ: We are God's human family. What a grace it is for us to be together today to worship the Lord, to express our deep appreciation for his great love for us, and to renew our commitment to return that love through our fidelity to his will. May the sentiments of peace, joy, and hope which fill us remain with us always. May we always live up to our calling as sons and daughters of God and brothers and sisters of his Son, Jesus.

Advent–Christmas Season

Christmas Midnight Mass

Holy Name Cathedral, Chicago, Illinois
— *December 25, 1986* ————————————————

Her name was Julia. They said she was past eighty, but no one really knew. Her wrinkled face had seen both triumph and tragedy in her lifetime. Her physical strength had waned considerably in recent years, but she was still full of life, determined, at times even feisty.

But on this Christmas morning, she was like a little child, looking and waiting for someone with great expectation. No one or no thing could distract her or talk her out of what she was determined to do. You see, for some years now her only son had not visited her. But every Christmas she really believed that he was coming to the home for senior citizens where she lived and take her out for Christmas dinner. So every Christmas morning she went through the same routine of putting on her best dress and waiting in the lobby, ignoring completely the Christmas festivities in which the staff and other residents were engaged.

But he never came. Usually around three o'clock in the afternoon she would give up and sadly eat the dinner which the nun who was in charge of her floor saved for her.

My dear friends, this is a true story. I once asked the nun, a friend of mine, why she let this lady sit in the lobby so long, just to be disappointed. She said that even if she tried to stop her—which she did when she first came—she would not listen to her. "But then," she added, "why not let her have a few hours of joyful expectation?" It was only at the end, when she finally realized that her son was not coming, that she became sad. Then the sisters and residents did all they could to cheer her up and help her forget her disappointment.

As I reflected on the significance of the feast of Christmas, it occurred to me that the Lord is very much like that lady. He loves us so much that he became one of us and gave his life for us. Not only on Christmas day, but every day, he stands in the wings, waiting for us to turn to him; waiting to shower his love on us in so many wonderful ways.

Did you have some hostile feelings toward the son who forgot his mother on Christmas day? I did when I first saw the lady and heard her story. But, you know, you and I are very much like that son. Even though the Lord has made himself available to us and is eagerly waiting to embrace and love us, we often fail to respond. We give priority to whatever happens to be important to us at the moment. Everything else, including the Lord, takes a second or third place or is forgotten altogether.

Whatever the cause, to ignore God in whose image we were created and to ignore Jesus through whom we have become a new creation, is to condemn ourselves to a life that lacks vision, a life of hopelessness, one marred by sin and its demeaning, devastating effects. To reject God and our redemption through his Son, is to exchange darkness for light, hatred and greed for love and generosity, violence and war for tranquillity and peace, despair for hope, alienation for intimacy. It is precisely this rejection, this unwillingness to place ourselves in the hands of the Lord and enjoy his intimacy, that lies at the heart of so many of today's difficulties.

At times the number and magnitude of these problems cause us to lose heart: in our own land, the injustices, the racism, the erosion of moral values which are the bedrock—or should be—of our lives; and the religious, political, social, and economic ills that have created serious disturbances in other parts of the world such as Northern Ireland, the Middle East, Central America, South Africa. This Christmas, too, our attention is drawn in a very special way to the human suffering experienced by the countless thousands of refugees who have fled their homelands—whether for economic or political reasons—and are trying to start a new life in strange and often hostile lands.

So enormously complex are the problems, we wonder what individuals might do to resolve them. But remember that the world is made up of individuals and will change only when each of us changes. Little will be accomplished if we spend most of our time looking for others to blame but refuse to put our own houses in order.

But there is *good* news! There *is* a remedy, and its name is *Jesus*. Each Christmas, when we retell the astonishing story of how God entered into the history of the human family through Jesus, we are reminded that the possibilities of new life are not only creative and exciting, but endless. If we wish, we can allow God's Word to take flesh in us. And he will do so, everyday, in ways that are original and fresh, ways that will deliver us from the pain and despair of sin and from all that is stale and debilitating.

If we let him, he will help us fashion a world that will have purpose and meaning. His presence will brighten our lives, driving away the gloom and fear that blur our vision, and cause us to see only the troublesome trivia of the moment.

If we let Jesus come into our lives, the greatest romance we will ever experience is God's passionate love. Our greatest adventure will be the journey into his kingdom. Our greatest achievement will be to live as a faith-filled brother or sister of the risen Lord. Our greatest challenge will be to carry on Jesus' mission and ministry, bringing his healing presence and saving love to the entire world.

It is because I personally believe in Jesus with all my mind and heart that I find so much hope and joy in this Christmas celebration. It is because I really believe that he is the Lord of life who can make all things new again that I am excited and eager "to tell his glory among the nations." It is because I love him more than anyone or anything else in the world that I vow never to stand him up, as Julia's son did to her on Christmas day.

Won't you join with me, on this Christmas day of 1986, in proclaiming the Lord Jesus, and his great love for us, from the housetops? Won't you join with me in becoming a sacrament of Christ's presence so that all who are hurt or wounded or disenchanted might find him? We can do this if we make our own the life and message of Jesus. Together, let us make this our Christmas gift to our friends and, indeed, to the world.

Homily

600th Jubilee of Christianity in Lithuania

First Sunday of Advent
Holy Name Cathedral, Chicago, Illinois
—*November 29, 1987* ——————————————

The church of Chicago rejoices today as we celebrate the 600th jubilee of Lithuania's definitive "Yes!" to God's call to believe in Jesus Christ and to become a worshiping community of faith within the universal Church. In my own name and in that of the entire archdiocese, I warmly welcome all who have come here this afternoon from the neighborhoods of Chicago, the metropolitan area, and other dioceses to celebrate this joyous occasion.

Today we also enter the liturgical season of Advent, a very special time to renew our trust in the Lord's faithfulness to us, a season of increased awareness of the great need to wait actively and expectantly for the Lord.

Blessed George Matulaitis, the Lithuanian archbishop beatified at the jubilee Mass in Rome on June twenty-eighth, has written the following in his spiritual diary:

> A person becomes truly free with the freedom of the children of God only when the vesture of self-centeredness is discarded and the clothes of the grace of Christ are put on. Only then does the mind become clear, the spirit alive, the heart attentive. The love of God for us opens up our hearts to provide ample room for all people, without regard for social or ethnic privileges.

God has called us to accept Jesus Christ personally—in our families, communities, and nations. Indeed, the Lord invites all humankind to his

306

kingdom of justice and peace. This invitation reached the Lithuanian people in the late Middle Ages, long after the rest of Europe had become Christians. In their own name and on behalf of their nation, the rulers of Lithuania freely and without foreign imposition said "Yes!"—initially King Mindaugas in 1251, and, definitively, King Jogaila and Grand Duke Vytautas in 1387.

The customary diplomacy of the time required formal negotiations and included political, cultural, and social motives. But, after the coming of our Lord Jesus Christ, there is no barrier between the people and God. This is because free acceptance of faith is the willingness to receive from God and to share in the universal Church's support and concern for each and all.

Today, on this First Sunday of Advent, God's people pray in the words of the book of Isaiah: "O Lord, you are our father; we are the clay and you the potter: we are all the work of your hands."

This very beautiful image of clay in a loving potter's hand is an apt expression of the Lord's care for his people. It prompts us to reflect on the ongoing development and growth of faith. God first molded the Lithuanian people through millennia of natural religion with its high value on tolerance for all, closeness in the family, honesty and generosity in human relationships, respect for nature as the human home, and the land as the source of livelihood. During this period of growth the Lord provided a sound foundation for the fuller revelation of life in Christ.

Coming from the ancient religion in which daily life in community was the measure of faithfulness, Lithuanians were able to see and understand that we respond to God's fidelity and trust in us with our daily lives, and that the privileged expression of this ultimate relationship between God and his people is the celebration of the Eucharist.

As we gathered with Pope John Paul at the tomb of St. Peter in Rome five months ago, we heard the voices of faith spoken in diverse languages by people of many lands. The Holy Father's warmth towards all, and his specific concern for the faithful of Lithuania, made us more keenly aware of the more than six centuries of the heritage of faith celebrated that day in the capital cities of Rome, Vilnius, and Washington.

The church in Lithuania has grown through periods of human freedom and harsh oppression, abundant harvests and fearful famines, tragic wars and devastating plagues, vigorous Christian education and flagrant denial of basic human rights. We believe that the Lord is a faithful father, a skillful potter. That is why we trust in his handiwork and desire to be pliable in his loving care throughout our lives and in the spiritual growth of the Church.

Advent is a special time of active and expectant watchfulness as we are molded for the future. In their pastoral letter for this jubilee, the bishops of Lithuania remind us: "A person alive with the Spirit sees widely and is always prepared to respond to another person's cry, even to the most inaudible call, knows how to understand others and to communicate effectively." To this cry and hunger for faith, justice, and community we answer with our own contributions to the Church, and through the Church to the world.

Lithuanians have always been active in their parishes and concerned for the future of the Catholic faith in their families and community. We see this responsible involvement in the past 120 years in Chicago, and in the vital role the laity play in the persecuted church in Lithuania.

The 1974 Synod of Bishops emphasized that all of us—clergy, religious, and lay people—are gifted with the call to evangelize—to believe deeply ourselves first and then to share with others our faith in Christ. The 1983 Synod of Bishops called upon us to be reconciled among ourselves within the community of faith and to be bearers of forgiveness and reconciliation in a wounded world. And this year's synod on the laity brought out more forcefully the opportunity and, indeed, the responsibility of every Christian to be involved actively in building up the body of Christ in the concrete circumstances of each culture and historical period.

Active watchfulness for the Lord involves the care of others. Many have been involved, for example, in urging the restoration of basic human and religious rights to all the oppressed faithful, especially in Lithuania. And, it seems that our efforts may be taking effect—for example, with the promised return of the confiscated Klaipeda church to the faithful.

I wish you to know that I stand in solidarity with you and with all your people who still live in Lithuania. We must never forget them or abandon them. And we will not! We must be their voices in the world demanding the recognition of their rights.

Active waiting for the Lord means not allowing ourselves to be lulled into purely private interests in our homes and apartments, but donating our attention, time, and talents. It implies sharing our strengths and accepting our weaknesses in our parishes, schools, Catholic societies, community work, and in society at large.

By being attentive to our own and others' gifts and needs, our parishes and small communities become living signs of watchful waiting for the Lord who is ever faithful. "By being led by the Spirit, we express this blessed fruit of its activity among us," say the bishops of Lithuania, "attentive to holy inspiration, encouragement, and guidance as we immerse ourselves in the meaning of the Gospel of Christ."

As we celebrate the 600 years of Christianity in Lithuania, as the Eastern Church is about to commemorate 1,000 years of faith, and as we look forward to the 500th anniversary of the evangelization of the Americas five years from now, let us pray and work so that the words of the apostle

Paul can truly be applied to the community of faith gathered here this afternoon:

> I continually thank my God for you because of the favor he has bestowed on you in Christ Jesus. He will strengthen you to the end, so that you will be blameless on the day of our Lord Jesus Christ. God is faithful, and it was he who called you to fellowship of his Son Jesus Christ, our Lord.

Simbang Gabi

Holy Name Cathedral, Chicago, Illinois
—*December 23, 1987* —————————————————

How easy it is to bring tears to the eyes of Filipinos at this time of the year! When you think of going to the *Simbang Gabi* very early in the morning for those nine days preceding Christmas, you see the colorful, illuminated *parols* on all the homes, the warm sweet *puto-bumbong* eaten with your friends after the Mass. And what else do you and your friends discuss except the *noche buena* party after Midnight Mass when everyone eats *bibingka*?

The closeness of the Filipino family is legendary, and Filipino families are never so close to each other as they are at Christmas. To be able to be with their families, many made reservations for international flights months ago. In the Philippines, tickets for the domestic airlines, buses, and trains are no longer available. During this festive season many of you here this evening will spend hours at the telephone, trying to get a line to talk to your family back home.

For Filipinos—especially those like you who are so far away—Christmas is a time of nostalgia. Because of the precious memories of your homeland and the deep love for your families, you long to be back in the Philippines during this holy season. But you also know that the homeland of your memories is not the same as it once was; it is not the same country which the rest of the world knows today—especially through news reports. Political unrest and serious economic problems have brought about an instability that has caused many Filipinos to be unwilling to invest money back home, and many tourists to be afraid to enter the most thoroughly Christian country in the Orient.

With their strong faith in God, Filipinos long for another peaceful Epiphania de los Santos (EDSA) Revolution similar to that in February 1986 which thrilled all who watched television during those perilous and exciting days. Filipinos believe that God sustained them and their compatriots during the February revolt when millions came to sit and pray on the superhighway so that the military could not engage in battle the soldiers at Camp Crame. Filipinos believe that God has always sustained them and will never let them down.

Our Mass this evening is filled with that same hope. We are celebrating our *Simbang Gabi*, of course, a day early so that you may celebrate Midnight Mass in your home parishes, in the local communities to which you belong.

In the first reading, the prophet Malachi tells us that God's Messenger is on his way to purify his people in a way similar to the refining of silver and gold. Selfish politicians and warlike militarists must not be allowed to gain control of a people's destiny. No one can resist God's Messenger. Hope, not despair, is as precious for the Filipinos as is the Messenger for whom Malachi tells us to prepare.

As with problems throughout the world, those presently confronting the Philippines are fundamentally human ones. God will do his part in solving them, but we must cooperate. St. Paul tells us in his letter to the Ephesians that God gives us power through his Spirit, that God will make his home in our hearts through faith. Through faith, we know that our prayers for the Philippines, and our aid for this wonderful nation, will be matched by God's power and help coming through the Holy Spirit.

The gospel this evening reveals the hand of God at work in the naming of John the Baptizer. John's relatives have chosen a name for the new baby, but by God's intervention the baby is given another name, John. God chose the name for the precursor of the Savior, and, as always, God's will is accomplished. Zechariah is God's instrument: because he is open to God's plan, he declares that his son will have the name which God himself has chosen.

God wants to be an intimate part of the life of all his children. However, he will not force himself upon us. He challenges us and sends us his empowering Spirit so that we might do our part in fulfilling his will. All Catholics believe that God works in and through us in this way. We are partners with God in the fulfillment of his plan for the human family. This is certainly true of Filipinos. Your expression *"bahala na"* expresses beautifully your devotion to God's will and his work.

We may think that the political and economic problems in the Philippines are the only issues confronting Filipinos. However, we know this is not the full reality. Let me identify three issues which you will undoubtedly recognize, issues that the Filipino community in our own local church must attend to.

First, in the United States nearly one out of two marriages ends in divorce. This phenomenon affects immigrants of all cultures, even those with traditional strong family ties and support systems. If the Filipino community here is to preserve its cultural and religious values regarding family life, it will have to develop support systems equal to the task. I urge you to do this.

Second, children and adolescents in the Philippines are esteemed because of the respect they show adults. In the United States, American-born children and teenagers often listen to one another but not to their elders. It would be tragic and scandalous if Filipino young people were to lose a proper respect for their elders here. My dear young people, never let this happen!

Third, there are many professionals in the Filipino community here. Their gifts are God's blessings, and they have a responsibility to use these gifts with integrity and to share their talents and other resources with others, especially with the poor. I beg you: always live up to your responsibility!

These issues highlight the need we all have for redemption, for strength and direction, for Jesus our Savior. I am sure they make you appreciate and long for the strength of the Filipino family back in the Philippines.

We often hear that the members of the Filipino-American family would be closer, and that there would be fewer problems, if the family situation in America were similar to that back home. But how can you achieve such unity and harmony? There are many ways. For example, you can adopt for your Filipino-American families certain values and traditions which were and still are practiced in the Philippines. I would like to remind you of two such traditions.

The first is the family religious shrine. In the Philippines, the poorest home in the barrio and the richest in the city have a shrine to Jesus, Mary, and the local patron saint. Your children should have the opportunity to participate in this wonderful custom. The family shrine can inculcate religious values in a child which will last for a lifetime.

The second custom is the family recitation of evening prayers in front of the shrine. Isn't it true that even the *butiki* bow their heads to pray at evening devotions with the family? And after the prayers come the greeting of all the family members to one another and the *magmano* to the adults.

Our lifestyle in the United States may be busier or more hectic than in the Philippines. But if every family joined together in prayer, if only for a few minutes each day, your families here in America would experience the same solidarity and spirituality as the families you knew in the Philippines.

Today's gospel highlights the theme of family unity. Zechariah cannot speak during the religious ceremony which takes place on the eighth day after the birth of his son, but he and his wife are *one* in naming the child as they are one in everything else. As home life in America becomes stronger through unity and prayer, so will concern for your beloved homeland and your bond with those who live in the Philippines.

You can also help the Philippines by praying through the intercession of the new Filipino saint and martyr, Lorenzo Ruiz. Some of you were in Rome two months ago when Pope John Paul II declared this layman, a family man from Manila, a saint—someone we can venerate and whose intercession we can seek on behalf of your homeland. Prayers to St. Lorenzo Ruiz will be especially efficacious.

During this special Marian year, let us also turn to Mary, the Mother of Jesus and our Mother, for her assistance. Let us pray that God may bring about that unity and prosperity which will keep the Philippines free from political and economic disasters and human exploitation.

Christmas is nearly upon us. We celebrate the birthday of Emmanuel, which means "God-is-with-us." May this Emmanuel—who is as present among us today as he was in the stable at Bethlehem nearly 2,000 years ago—bring peace, unity, and prosperity to that land which gave so many of you birth, culture, and education. Pray for the Philippines where everyone still celebrates the *Simbang Gabi* at 4:00 A.M. with prayerful smiles.

Our prayers, the intercession of St. Lorenzo Ruiz and the Blessed Virgin Mary, and strong Christian family life can save this Pearl of the Orient and the only thoroughly Christian nation in the Far East.

I wish all of you:

Maligayang Pasko!

at

Mabiyayang Bagong Taon!

Christmas Midnight Mass

Holy Name Cathedral, Chicago, Illinois
— *December 25, 1988* ————————————————————

How did God slip in? How did God infiltrate our closed ranks, there to subvert *our* plans and substitute his own instead? How did we not recognize him on our night watch so as to be ready? Surprisingly, God came into the world in a form we could never have expected, in the very form that he had given each one of us. Grace entered our world as we all do—in the painful joy of birth. And with his child's cry, he awakened us to the glory to be found in fragile human flesh when it is quickened by God's Spirit.

How frail our flesh to be called to bear eternal light! God seems to delight in the incongruity of it all. He saw that we are all shepherds who have made an uneasy peace with the darkness of our day. He understood that we have become confused creatures, fearing the light, while at the same time longing for it. He looks upon us still as we listen to the now-silent sky for some good news which will be a cause for great rejoicing. How hard it is at times to believe that this same mute sky once rang with the angels' song of glory! God seems so far away at times from our prayers, from our struggles, from our ordinary, daily living.

But then there's the *child*. There's the child who was born into this same world where *we* pray, struggle, and live. This child held heaven in his eyes. And those who had the good sense to come close and gaze into his eyes could witness how close heaven had drawn to earth in him. But one does have to draw *very close* to see this.

For it is not God who remains aloof. He has drawn dangerously, scandalously near. It is *we* who keep our distance, who have, at times, not

314

dared to come to Bethlehem to see the wondrous child. To Bethlehem came the unexpected, uninvited guest. Although he was offered no home or place to rest, he made himself at home. An unheated stable became the gathering place for as disparate a lot as shepherds and kings.

The gentle story of Christmas becomes like a shepherd who leads us. The story is familiar to us, and so it calls us by name. It leads us out of warm, well-lit, beautiful cathedrals into other pastures, into darkened hovels where the pangs of God's birth continue to be felt. It shepherds us beyond the big city to the small town where a personal God may be more easily noticed.

We are guided through dark valleys where dwell our fears and doubts, dark valleys where we face what is despised and rejected in ourselves. And we come to know that God is present even there, and, perhaps, *especially* there. Slowly, those of us who had walked in darkness—and all of us *have* walked in darkness—suddenly, we rejoice to see a great light, a glory found even here, *especially* here in our human flesh.

So we allow this "kindly light" to "lead us midst the circling gloom," to borrow a phrase from Cardinal Newman. We open ourselves to the deep joy brought by the story we retell tonight. Such joy continues to surprise us—like a flower in winter, a sense of peace in sickness, a certain calmness in time of danger.

In his book *Will and Spirit*, Gerald May has pointed out that

> [J]oy is altogether beyond any consideration of pleasure or pain and, in fact, requires a knowledge and acceptance of pain. Joy is the reaction one has to the full appreciation of being. It is one's response to finding one's rightful, rooted place in life, and it can only happen when one knows, through and through, that absolutely nothing is being denied or otherwise shut out of awareness.

Finding our "rightful, rooted place in life . . ."

Again, it seems to involve displacement from where we have *wandered* from the Shepherd's watchful eye, and a kind of "replacement" to where we *belong*. "Coming home" is what so many do at Christmas. "Coming home" to the flock is a cause of real joy. For, if there is a distance between ourselves and God, guess who moved? The story which gathers us also feeds us with the Good News that God wants to draw close to us, that he wants to be a part of our lives—as messy or as glorious as they might be. We warm ourselves over the fire of that truth on this winter-cold night. Tonight the light absorbs our attention. It is beating back the darkness.

It gives me great joy to celebrate this story with you again. I do it in full awareness that, oftentimes, I feel like a shepherd on night watch, sometimes fearful of the "circling gloom" of our day. The gloom is real, and it is powerful.

And yet, we find our rightful, rooted place in the story of Jesus' birth. And in that rooting, there is joy, and there is power. Sometimes our Christmas focus on the helpless child in the manger makes us forget that, in some marvelous, inexplicable way, that child is the all-powerful God for whom *nothing* is impossible. His powerful light shows us that, today, there still is homeless poverty, still people seeking lodging in our crowded, lonely, anonymous world.

Jesus is a strengthening food which empowers us to make room for the wanderer, the unwed mother, the harried father, the rejected child. He is a thunderous word which shatters all pretense and illusion. He is God who comes dangerously near to us at Christmas and in every Eucharist, a powerful God come to save us. Let us draw near and become radiant at what we see!

Homily

Christmas Day Mass

Cook County Jail, Chicago, Illinois
— December 25, 1988 ─────────────────────

It's good to be here. I really mean that. As you may know, I celebrated Midnight Mass at Holy Name Cathedral last night. It was a wonderful event with a big crowd and beautiful music. The cathedral was decorated with wreaths and poinsettias. But, as impressive as all those things are, they can be distractions from the simplicity of that first Christmas so long ago in Bethlehem.

That's why I say to you very sincerely that it's really good to be here with you. Because, in a sense, this is closer to what it was like for Jesus, Mary, and Joseph in that stable on that silent night.

Sometimes we glamorize Christmas. We romanticize the stable. To put it in modern terms, being born in a stable would be like being born in a garage out behind someone's house along one of Chicago's back alleys. It wasn't first-class treatment. It was hardly even second best.

And the shepherds weren't well-dressed people like those we might encounter at Water Tower Place. They were more like the outcasts of society. They were rough, undereducated men. They smelled of sheep. They were shunned by polite society. And yet, those were the first people whom God selected to hear the announcement of the birth of his Son, Jesus.

And so, God, who made those choices, might be quite comfortable here at this Mass today—with us at the Cook County Jail. That may sound strange to you, but remember: he chose a stable, not a palace, for the birth of Jesus. He chose shepherds, not aristocrats, to be the first to hear the Good News. There was no room in the inn for his Son, so he had to find a birthplace in a most unlikely spot.

317

What does all of this tell us about *God?* What does this tell us about *Christmas?* What does this tell us about *ourselves?*

It reminds us that God sees things quite differently than we do. He sees deep beneath the surface appearances of life. He sees into the very heart of things. Whether a person is well dressed or poorly attired, whether a person is highly educated or never finished grade school, whether a person celebrates Christmas in a mansion or in prison—none of that, in itself, is important or impressive in God's eyes.

What makes a difference is what is to be found deep down within our human hearts. Is there violence, greed, anger, jealousy, lust within us? Or is there goodness, gentleness, forgiveness, and hope? God sees beauty in the stable, and he can see beauty in this place too.

Moreover, God does not want to intimidate, frighten, or overwhelm us. If he wanted to behave in that manner, he could have sent his Son as a mighty warrior at the head of a vast army, conquering all that stood in its way. But God's ways are not our ways. Instead of an army, he sends a carpenter, Joseph, and his young wife, Mary. Instead of a mighty warrior clad in armor, he sends a newborn baby wrapped in swaddling clothes and laid in a manger. Instead of forcing us to bow down in fear, he inspires us to rise up in love.

Is it too good to be true? Can we really believe that God loves us with all of our flaws, faults, and shortcomings? Yes, that is the message of Christmas. That is the message of the stable. That is the message of the star and the angels. God loves us more than we can imagine! God loves us even when we don't love ourselves!

Today's gospel describes Jesus as the light of the world, a light which shines in the darkness, a darkness which was not able to overcome it. If there's darkness in your mood today, please allow the light of Christ to enlighten you with love, hope, and goodness—at least for this one special day, if not longer.

Today's gospel also says that Jesus is the fullness of God of which we have all had a share. If you feel empty today, please allow God's goodness and strength to fill you—at least for this one special day, if not longer.

Today's gospel announces further that Jesus is the Word-made-flesh who pitched his tent among us. If you feel alone, lonely, forgotten, or forsaken today, please allow the Lord to pitch his tent with you as your friend, your companion, your brother—at least for this one special day, if not forever.

I'm here this morning because I *want* to be here—with you! Last night's Midnight Mass at the cathedral was truly wonderful, but here is where the simplicity and beauty of Christmas is also to be found in a very special way. Thank you for allowing me to share it with you.

I ask God's special Christmas blessings upon all of you.

Homily

Cathedral of St. Patrick

Second Sunday of Advent
New York City
—— *December 9, 1990* ——————————————

"What in the world are you waiting for?"

How often we hear that phrase. A motorist in busy holiday traffic on Madison Avenue trying to maintain equilibrium as the car ahead hesitates in making a left turn. A spouse nudging his partner to make a decision about which of two dresses she should pick to wear at their daughter's wedding. A high-school senior urging a good friend to choose one of the four universities which have accepted her application. A person with AIDS waiting for doom to descend.

"What in the world are you waiting for?" A hawkish adviser urging a head of state to give up on a political solution to a crisis, and start a shooting war. A business leader knowing that a big deal might evaporate if a risky decision isn't made within the next hour. A couple wanting to sign a contract for a new condo, but fearful that, in this slow market, they may not be able to sell the home they already have. A cancer patient waiting for the test results which will reveal whether the tumor has metastasized or not.

So many examples. So much waiting. So many decisions great and small. We wait on many levels, some profound, some inconsequential. We wait in many ways, some in our control, some beyond us. We wait for many things—the latest news, the right time, more information.

December is a time of waiting *par excellence*. Thousands of years ago, our ancestors waited for the deepening of the darkness as the winter solstice drew near. Lacking electricity, their lives were diminished and circumscribed by the encroaching danger of darkness. They also waited as the weather grew *colder*, wondering if they had stored away enough food to last until spring. Many New Yorkers and Chicagoans share that deep uneasiness with impending winter, even though we have climate-controlled homes, heaters in our cars, access to well-stocked grocery stores, and the possibility of a vacation to Bermuda, Florida, or the Caribbean.

But some among us especially dread waiting for winter to take its icy hold on their lives. The poor whose windows leak heat, whose furnaces are balky. The homeless who huddle in stairways or shelters. The unemployed who are uncertain about their future and that of their families. As people of faith, we are called to wait with them, to share their dread, to do what we can to alleviate their burdens as best we can.

"What in the world are the poor, the homeless, the unemployed waiting for?" For someone to notice, to care, to understand, to help—not in a condescending manner, but with respect, sensitivity, compassion, and effective action.

December is a special time of waiting for the children among us and for the child within each of us. The faces of children are lit by excitement as Christmas draws near. "What in the world are they waiting for?" For a special toy advertised on television. You know, the one they "have to have" this year. The one for which you search in eleven different stores, only to learn each time that they just sold the last one ten minutes ago. And the children wait for Santa Claus, wondering how seriously they must take the familiar song which warns, "You'd better watch out, you'd better not pout, you'd better not cry, I'm telling you why . . ."

Sometimes we adults want a new toy—a car, a coat, a sound system, a painting, tickets that are hard to get. And sometimes we might think of God as a sort of supernatural, omnipotent, omniscient Santa Claus. "You'd better watch out, you'd better not pout. . . . He's gonna find out who's naughty or nice."

Sometimes we adults are too smart for our own good. We think we've already been there. We've gone through the drill so many Decembers. Sure, it's a beautiful story, but it's been told to death. The ornaments get dusty, tarnished, a bit shopworn. And so does the story of Christmas. How many times can you tell the story of the shepherds and wise men and really come up with a new angle? Christmas cards are a chore. Instead of shopping for gifts we wonder if gift certificates might be enough. There are so many parties, but we'd prefer a quiet night at home.

"What in the world is the child within us waiting for?" Perhaps the willingness to invest ourselves in beauty. Perhaps the willingness to be fascinated by lights and sounds and touch. The touch of a child, any child, the Christ Child. The touch of God in the depths of our being. The touch of the panhandler near Grand Central Station who is both a derelict and the messenger of God's grace. The touch of memories and dreams in the noise, excitement, and busyness of this hectic season.

"And what in the world is our planet waiting for as we move through this final decade of the twentieth century towards a new millennium of Christianity?" Scientists and environmentalists warn us about the greenhouse effect, global warming, and the rapid disappearance of the rain forests throughout the world. We ask ourselves, "Are they alarmists or prophets?" In return, they trouble us with the uncomfortable question, "What are we bequeathing to our children, grandchildren, and those to come beyond them?" Are we squandering their future? Are we mortgaging their rightful inheritance? After the Berlin Wall came tumbling down, we were dismayed to see the profound degree of pollution in some of the Eastern European countries and the Soviet Union, done in the name of expansion, quotas, trade, and what have you. How do we balance the legitimate needs for jobs and development with the limited resources of our beautiful planet?

"What in the world is the world waiting for?" The human family seems to have a penchant for flipping from the frying pan into the fire. No sooner do we achieve an end to the forty years of the Cold War, no sooner is the Iron Curtain torn down, no sooner do we declare a "peace dividend," than we find ourselves embroiled in a confrontation with Saddam Hussein in the Persian Gulf. We discover that we Americans are an impatient people. We are not good at waiting. We like to move decisively to clean up a mess and get on with our lives.

So, frankly, Advent is a difficult season for us. Each year we seem to start Christmas earlier and earlier. It used to begin the day after Thanksgiving. Now decorations appear in stores soon after Halloween. But then they disappear the day after Christmas, as we frantically prepare for Valentine's Day—not Epiphany! We are not good at waiting for so many things.

Perhaps Advent's waiting has more to teach us than we realize. Life has a rhythm. Plastic poinsettias can be stamped out, fully bloomed, in a moment by a machine. But live plants take time and care. They bloom and grow and change and die. Advent teaches us that a pregnancy takes nine months, whether the life unfolding in the womb is a prince or a pauper, a potential millionaire or a welfare baby—or the Son of God.

Are the ancient texts in today's Scripture readings mere museum pieces, relics of a former age, quaint quotations from an age of parchment and papyrus, irrelevant in an age of fax machines and word processors?

Isaiah proclaims the coming of the Lord to his people in Exile. In Babylon they have experienced disillusionment, confusion, anxiety, and a profound test of faith. The prophet announces the comforting Good News of God's great tenderness, compassion, and mercy. The time is short: prepare in the desert a way for the Lord. What do *we* need to do to prepare for his coming at Christmas? In our personal lives? As a family? As a Church? As a nation? As a world?

And then comes the psalmist's plea, "Lord, let us see your kindness." And God responds by proclaiming his peace, justice, truth, and salvation. But how do we experience the deep, quiet safety and security of God's presence among us? Paradoxically, in the face of that poor child in the feeding stall in Bethlehem two thousand years ago. And in the faces of poor children in the inner city who yearn for quality education. And in the anxious faces of Mary and Joseph knocking upon door after door, desperately seeking a place of shelter into which they can bring new life. In the memories of the countless immigrants, like my own mother and father, who passed through Ellis Island in times past. And in the contemporary faces of the thousands of migrant people, displaced people, wandering people in the refugee camps of our world.

St. Peter tells us that God shows us "generous patience." And this leads me to ask a final question, "What in the world is *God* waiting for?" Might he not be tempted, at times, to give up on the world, as in the days of Noah? Might he not be tempted to weep over our city, as Jesus once wept over Jerusalem? Might he not be tempted, as the astronomers are increasingly fond of reminding us, to abandon this weary planet and transfer his affection to some distant place in the vast panoply of galaxies?

"What in the world is God waiting for?" The voice of Mark bids us cease idle speculation and wasted effort. His voice bids us fan into flame even the smallest morsels of hope. For Mark describes John the Baptizer who has come to prepare a way for the Lord—in our personal lives, in our homes, in our churches, in our nation, throughout the world. When the Lord comes, he will bring to fulfillment God's reign of justice, truth, and peace. This is why we wait; this is why we hope. May he find a warm welcome among us.

Homily

50th Anniversary of the Cana Conference

Second Sunday of Advent
Holy Name Cathedral, Chicago, Illinois
—*December 4, 1994* ————————————————

"Restoring the poetry which is the divine idea of man and woman and marriage"—that is how Father Walter Imbiorski described the function of the Cana Conference, "restoring the poetry which is the divine idea of man and woman and marriage."

My dear brothers and sisters, we gather this afternoon to celebrate the restoration of that poetry through the efforts of the thousands of people who have worked in the various Cana programs in our local church during the past half century. In the name of the hundreds of thousands of couples who have benefited from these programs and in my own, I thank you for this wonderful, loving work. You have helped the Church to articulate a new theology of marriage—one that helps couples maintain the divine poetry of their intimate relationship.

We observe the fiftieth anniversary of the Cana Conference during Advent, a liturgical season that looks both to the past and to the future. We look back to that marvelous moment when the Word of God "became flesh and made his dwelling among us" (John 1:14). And we look forward to the day when the Son of Man will come "on a cloud with great power and glory" (Luke 21:27).

Significant anniversaries are a bit like Advent. The fiftieth anniversary of Cana encourages us to use the present moment to look both to the past and to the future.

In a sense, the Cana Conference in the archdiocese began quite simply in 1944, when Edwin and Marge Kirwin invited some friends of theirs,

323

including Pat and Patty Crowley, to attend a Family Renewal Day and hear Jesuit Father John Delaney speak about the value of Christian marriage and family. The new theological vision of marriage caught on, and others were greatly attracted to it. By 1946, thanks to the dedicated efforts of dozens of couples, Father James Voss, and Father Julian Marhoefer, the Cana Conference of Chicago received its name, and Pre-Cana Conferences began.

The next year Cardinal Stritch appointed one of Msgr. Reynold Hillenbrand's students—an energetic, young Father Jack Egan—as Cana's first director. If his work with Cana were Msgr. Egan's only claim to distinction as a priest of the archdiocese, it would have been enough! For eleven years, with the generous help of his many friends among the laity and the clergy, together with his associate directors, Father Lawrence Kelly and, later, Father Walter Imbiorski, he laid a solid foundation for the Cana Conference. He and his friends also traveled widely with their "Cana Road Shows," which introduced many dioceses throughout the nation to the importance, the potential, and the excitement of Cana.

Yes, the roots of Cana are deep in Chicago Catholic tradition. The concept that couples could be prepared for Christian marriage in a group of their peers, rather than during individual meetings with clergy, was creative and innovative. Participation by lay people in marriage enrichment was also novel—and very effective. The participation of the laity in Cana and Pre-Cana was one of the earliest examples of ministry performed and led by lay Catholics. The opportunity to lead marriage preparation groups was an opportunity for those pioneering couples to examine and strengthen their own marriages and to enhance their own Christian values.

As the needs of each generation have changed, the Cana Conference has responded in creative, pastorally effective ways. For example, when the Second Vatican Council spoke of marriage as a covenant, the Cana ministers worked hard to integrate the conciliar insights into its programs. Moreover, Cana's programs have been adapted for the growing number of Hispanic couples, for African-American Catholics, and for older couples preparing for marriage.

The primary mission of the Cana Conference has become the preparation of couples for Christian marriage. What better way can there be to build up the body of Christ, the Church, than to equip young people with the motivation, understanding, and skills they need to live in a strong Christian marriage?

The Cana Conference also responds to the call to teach, by training couples who go back to their parish communities and do marriage preparation at the local level. Another response to the call to teach is the publication of materials that are used in marriage ministry throughout the United States and Canada.

The world exerts severe pressure on Christian marriage. The need for a solid foundation is greater than ever. We applaud and support the volunteers and clergy who, under the current direction of Mr. Frank Hannigan, labor with great diligence to build and maintain this foundation.

And what of the future? The trends we see in regard to marriage and family life in our society are not encouraging although there is a rising tide of concern about restoring "family values"—a phrase that often carries more rhetoric than substance. We must do all we can to preserve and enhance the Christian vision of married and family life, and the values associated with it.

The readings for this Second Sunday of Advent help us prepare for the future with a sense of hope and mission.

In the first reading, the prophet Baruch speaks to people who are in exile, far from their homeland. He urges them to set aside darkness and gloom and to be joyful, for they will return to Jerusalem, the Holy City, the site of God's holy Temple, where they will feel and experience God's special presence. The word of the Lord calls us to have *hope*, for God never abandons his people.

John the Baptist appeared on the scene at a crucial and precise moment of human history. His task was to make ready the way of the Lord, to prepare the people for the coming of the long-awaited Messiah. In his providence, God has placed *us*—you and me—in this particular place at this precise moment. Without claiming the greatness or uniqueness of John the Baptist, we should see our own Christian vocation in light of John's. God calls us, too, to prepare the way of the Lord. Through our prayer, our deeds of goodness, our fidelity to the gospel, our efforts to prepare for and enrich marriage and family life, we clear a straight path for the risen Lord to enter people's lives so that all can see the salvation of God.

In its 150 years, the Archdiocese of Chicago has enjoyed many *blessings* and faced many *challenges*. Among the greatest of its *blessings* has been the Cana Conference, which anticipated the teaching of the Second Vatican Council and elicited lay collaboration with the clergy in a vital area of the Church's ministry. This local church has been and remains a leader in this ministry.

One of our greatest *challenges* is to continue preserving and enriching marriage and family life in a climate that often is not supportive. Given Cana's past and present achievements, I am confident that, with God's help, we can and will meet the challenges that lie before us. My dear brothers and sisters, there is still a great need for those who are able and willing to restore "the poetry which is the divine idea of man and woman and marriage." May God who began a wonderful, good work among us bring it to completion!

Homily

Mass of Healing

Third Sunday of Advent
Our Lady of Angels School Fire (1958)
Chicago, Illinois

—*December 11, 1994* ——————————————————

At first, today's readings may seem somewhat inappropriate for this occasion, especially the exuberant ones from the prophet Zephaniah and the apostle Paul. After all, we have gathered for this Mass of Healing because of the painful memories, the suffering, and the scars that resulted from a tragic fire thirty-six years ago at Our Lady of the Angels School. We have come together to remember the ninety-two young students and three B.V.M. sisters who died in the blaze as well as the nearly one hundred others—students, staff, firefighters, and civilians—who were injured. Our assembly includes survivors of the fire and their families, firefighters and police who fought the fire, medical personnel who cared for the victims, parents and siblings of the dead, friends and families of Our Lady of the Angels parish, including current and former parishioners. We are here because that catastrophe has deeply affected each of your lives in some way.

At second glance, today's readings could have been written precisely for this occasion.

In the first reading the prophet Zephaniah addresses the people of Jerusalem, who were alienated from God. Many of them had stopped worshiping him, and others felt abandoned by him. In the reading we heard a few moments ago, we learn that God has *not* abandoned his people. He cares passionately for them. God is with us, so we no longer need to fear or be discouraged. This is consoling news, if we accept it in faith.

In the second reading St. Paul urges his beloved Philippians to "Rejoice!" and "dismiss all anxiety" from their minds. He does not offer them "pie in the sky." Paul is not a Pollyanna. He is in *prison*, and he knows that the Philippians face many difficulties. But Paul also knows what is most important in his life—his relationship with the Lord. Nothing else matters to Paul—not even his freedom or his very life. He tells the Philippians to pray with gratitude. "Then God's own peace, which is beyond all understanding, will stand guard over your hearts and minds, in Christ Jesus."

My dear brothers and sisters, *all of us* greatly desire that kind of inner peace and tranquillity. I can only imagine the depth of *your* desire for such peace because of what you have suffered since the fire. But, you may ask me, after all we've gone through, is it really possible to live without anxiety—without the kind of fear that paralyzes us? Is it reasonable under such circumstances to pray always with gratitude rather than out of a sense of helplessness? Is it realistic to search for inner peace, that special serenity that can withstand what time has to offer, including the loss and trauma of so many of ourselves and our loved ones? Is authentic Christian joy both possible and realistic, despite suffering and painful memories?

If it were simply up to us, it probably would *not* be realistic. But, ultimately, it's not what we do that matters, but what God does. Today, we are reminded of his care for us—made forever visible in the love, care, and peace of Christ Jesus. We have only to open our hearts to receive his healing and his love.

In today's gospel John the Baptist invites people to the desert where they will prepare for a new chapter in the story of their relationship with God. In the wilderness they will renew their covenant with God. John tells the crowds that it is not enough to claim to be Abraham's children; they must also be faithful to their religious heritage, especially by striving for social justice and sharing with the poor.

If he were with us this afternoon, what might John the Baptist advise, if we were to ask him the same question as the tax collectors and the soldiers: "What are we to do?"

I suspect that John might give us three suggestions.

First, remember that you are not alone. You have gathered from many places because you endured the same debilitating catastrophe many years ago. You have come here in order to participate in this Mass of Healing. You stand in solidarity with one another—not only in pain, but, especially, in your desire for healing and inner peace. And I stand with you as your brother.

Second, trust that God is with us and loves us more than we can ever imagine. While we may not be able to heal ourselves or one another fully, God's healing power is infinitely greater than any hurt and pain, no matter how deeply these are rooted in our lives. God's healing may not come in an instant, but it will come to you if you sincerely, earnestly, and perseveringly ask him for this gift.

Third, ask God to give you peace of mind and to help remove any residual anger that may still plague you, help you to be reconciled. This may be the most difficult task of all, but, with God's help, I know that reconciliation is possible.

How do I know this? From my personal experience. Let me tell you a true story. Some years ago, when I was archbishop of Cincinnati, a great tragedy struck a small parish in the northern part of that archdiocese. One evening, a group of eight teenagers was standing next to their car in the middle of a country road, just beyond a small hill. A car came down the road at a fast pace and ran through a stop sign at the top of the hill. Only after running through the stop sign did the driver see the young people. But then it was too late. All eight teens were killed. To make it worse, they were all students in the same high school—including the young man driving the car!

I went to the parish church to preside at the joint prayer service for all eight the evening before the funeral. As you can imagine, the entire community was devastated by the accident. In particular, the families, classmates, and friends of the eight teens were overcome by grief and all the emotions that go with it—denial, confusion, anger. Needless to say, the driver of the car was also overcome by emotion and guilt, because the accident was his fault, the tragedy was his fault—he had run through the stop sign at a high speed.

During the prayer service, the driver and his parents were in the sacristy. Just before the service, the parents of the eight young people told me they wanted to be reconciled with the young man because they knew him, and they also knew that any one of their children could have done what he did. So, one by one, I personally brought each family to him for reconciliation. This was the most powerful experience I have ever had of God's reconciling power. Because the driver and the families relied on God's grace, healing began to take root in that community. Their grief did not suddenly evaporate. The loss of those eight lives continued to affect everyone involved. But they were able to go on with their lives and experience some inner peace and tranquillity.

My dear friends, it has been very good for us to be here this morning. We may not yet be able to rejoice like St. Paul, but I pray that all of us will experience a deeper sense of God's presence in our lives, a stronger trust in his healing, reconciling power, and a greater sense of inner peace. My prayer for you is that the healing that has already taken place in your lives will continue until "God's peace, which is beyond all understanding, will stand guard over your hearts and minds, in Christ Jesus."

Christmas Midnight Mass

Holy Name Cathedral, Chicago, Illinois

——*December 25, 1994* ————————————————

At the heart of Christmas is a sublime joke. "And on that sacred jest," G. K. Chesterton said, "the whole of Christianity doth rest." A joke is the unexpected and surprising coming together of opposites, a playful juxtaposition of contraries. What makes us laugh—at an image, a story, or a play on words—is incongruity. The incarnation is the greatest incongruity of all, and the world has not yet stopped laughing with delight.

"While they were there, the days of her confinement were completed, and she gave birth to a son." They say that the stable of Bethlehem was, in fact, a sort of subterranean cave, a place where the shepherds sometimes drove their flocks in time of storm. It was there, under the earth, that the Lord of Heaven was born, a tiny infant. In that strange reversal, heaven and earth embraced; highest and lowest came together; infinite and finite met. In that moment, the unknowable and incomprehensible God became as familiar and vulnerable as any child. In that moment, the one who had formerly inspired awe and wonder, now awakens something like pity. In a totally unpredictable leap of love, God has become one of us in order to show us, as dramatically as possible, that we are never alone.

"[A]nd she wrapped him in swaddling clothes." The power that brought the universe into being, the one who strung the stars and hung the moon, the God who spins the galaxies and the planets is now wrapped in the swaddling clothes of our frail humanity. The Lord of the world, the creator of all that is, enters his creation as one too weak to raise his head, as one dependent and afraid. The artist who formed all the living creatures of the world now has hands too small to reach the huge heads of the cattle that surround him. In the swaddling clothes of the Christ Child, we may see God's embrace of all our weakness, all our anxiety, all our failure, all our sickness and suffering. In the frailty of this divine child, we have the blessed assurance that nothing human is alien to God.

Many before this moment had sung the glory, the power, the wisdom, and the majesty of God. But no one before this night, not even the greatest poets and prophets, ever dared to imagine that this majesty would express itself in the weakness of a baby wrapped in his mother's arms. Yet, it is this divine jest that we have gathered, some two thousand years later, to hear once again. And my dear friends, like so many others, this joke has a dark edge. The swaddling clothes that envelop the Christ Child are an ominous foreshadowing of the burial shroud that will one day enfold the body of the crucified Jesus. The divine condescension, begun in Bethlehem, will move to its awful conclusion on Golgotha, for nothing can stop the momentum of God's self-forgetting love.

"[A]nd she laid him in a manger." The helpless child is put in a manger, the place where the animals eat, for he is destined to be food for the world. The shepherds stand for the hunger of the heart that longs for love, and the Magi represent the hunger of the mind which yearns for the truth, and both will find the bread that satisfies in this child, the embodiment of God's abiding truth and love. What is beautifully foreshadowed here is, once again, Jesus' passion and death. On the night before he died, the one who was once placed in a manger gives his flesh and blood to a hungry world, laying himself out as a banquet. On this Christmas night we remember that the Incarnate God comes, not as a king to be idolized, not as a prince to be honored, but as food for the journey of life. The one to whom sacrifice had long been offered, now offers himself as sacrifice for us.

"[T]here was no room for him in the place where travelers lodged." The irony here is striking. An artist feels particularly at home in his studio, among the paintings that he has created. The gardener is at home among the plants that he has planted and nourished. And the father is at peace among his children because they are his own. But the creator of the world is not at home in the world. The maker of the universe, when he comes as a traveler, finds no room in the place where travelers stay. The world had grown so old and tired and alienated from God that, when God himself appeared, he was seen as an outcast, an exile, someone not acceptable in polite society. The overcrowded inn stands for our hearts overstuffed with pride and worldly distractions, our souls so cluttered that God finds no room there. But the message of Christmas is not one of condemnation or judgment; rather, it is, as we have seen, that gentle divine joke. When he finds no place to stay, the judge of the world quietly takes his place among the homeless, among the forgotten, among the poor.

The Incarnate God will lure a world grown cold through the power of his own humility, gentleness, and love.

"The angel said to them: 'You have nothing to fear! I come to proclaim good news to you.'" My dear brothers and sisters, our lives are often so dominated by fear. Indeed, ours has been described as the age of anxiety. We are beset by fear of the unknown, fear of the future, fear of the darkness within us and around us. The simple message, proclaimed by the angel of Christmas and contained in the sublime jest of the incarnation, is that we no longer have to be afraid. In the baby, wrapped in swaddling clothes and lying in a manger, we have Immanuel, God-with-us. Fear is useless because God, on this Bethlehem night, has taken on all that frightens us.

And so, good Christian people, laugh and rejoice tonight! God has become a little child—and the joke is, wonderfully, on us.

A happy and blessed Christmas to you all!

Christmas Midnight Mass

Holy Name Cathedral, Chicago, Illinois
── *December 25, 1995* ─────────────────────────

My dear mother, Maria, who is ninety-one, lives in the wonderful home for the elderly run by the Little Sisters of the Poor here in Chicago. Mother's memory is fading, and frequently we do not know whether she is fully aware of what is going on around her. But periodically she says things that are profound and moving. Recently, for example, the nun who cares for her asked her how she felt. Mother looked up and said: "I'm so full of love, and I want to share it with everybody!"

My brothers and sisters in the faith, is this not the very heart of the message of Christmas? God is so full of love—and so desirous to share it with all his creation—that he sent his beloved Son into the world. As St. John's Gospel reminds us, "The Word became flesh and made his dwelling among us, and we have seen his glory: the glory of an only Son coming from the Father, *filled with enduring love*" (1:14).

God's infinite and eternal love for us is reflected in the Virgin Mary's tender love for her infant. Words fail us as we try to describe or measure such love. As a beautiful Christmas carol by John Rutter points out:

> How do you capture the wind on the water?
> How do you count all the stars in the sky?
> How can you measure the love of a mother,
> Or how can you write down a baby's first cry? . . .
> Nations proclaim him their Lord and their Savior,
> But Mary will hold him and sing him to sleep.

My friends, it is easy for you and me to remain near the crèche, to be charmed by the Christ Child, to be warmed by his mother's love. But we know that the story goes on. The child grows into a man—a man who teaches, who heals, who touches hearts and challenges them. And the mother who, today, tenderly cradles the infant Jesus in her arms will one day hold his crucified body after it has been taken down from the cross.

While the event of Jesus' birth was hidden away in a humble cave—far away from the palaces of the rich and mighty—the entrance of God's beloved Son into the world has reverberated through two millennia, revealing God's enduring love for each of us. What we celebrate, then, is much more than a nostalgic remembrance of a past event that now has only historical significance. We come together at this midnight hour, in faith, to worship a living God who is present among us *now,* a God who lovingly sustains us along every step of our pilgrim journey. We proclaim that Jesus, the child of poverty and a sign of contradiction, is also the messenger of hope, the light shining in the darkness, the pledge of God's love for us, and the author of our call to love one another.

And that makes all the difference in the world—especially when we face suffering, trials, and tribulation. During the past six-and-a-half months I have learned in a very personal way that, when people who have cancer or other serious illness realize that God loves them, they do not perceive their physical condition as a sign that God has abandoned them. Their awareness that God loves them becomes a source of great comfort, consolation, and inner peace. Their faith is deepened, and their experience of Jesus, the Prince of Peace and the crucified Lord, becomes very intimate, indeed.

Faith-filled prayer becomes especially important at such times—prayer for ourselves and prayer for others in need. In the past two months I have received many requests for my prayers, for example, from:

—a mother whose three children have, respectively, multiple sclerosis, cerebral palsy, and epilepsy;

—the parents of a young mother who was beaten to death by her husband a year ago, leaving behind a four-year-old daughter;

—a mother whose thirty-year-old daughter has advanced terminal cancer;

—a widower whose young wife died recently, leaving him alone with two children, six and eleven years old;

—a pregnant mother whose unborn child, according to ultrasound tests, has two cysts on its brain, increasing the risk of brain damage;

—a mother addicted to crack cocaine for eight years despite four treatment programs, who is desperately trying to become "clean" so that the lives of her ten-year-old son and elderly mother will not be such a "hell," as she described it.

As these and so many other requests for prayers have made clear to me, many people have a deep faith in God, and they trust in his love for them, especially when they are lonely and frightened, desperate and panicky, when they are forced to live one day or even one hour at a time, not knowing if the future will be better or worse.

This morning, as we contemplate the marvelous mystery of the incarnation, the angels announce a message of peace and joy to everyone everywhere—to everyone who is searching for some meaning in the trials and dilemmas of life. The angels give us a glimpse of the powerful realm of heaven from which God's enduring love descends into our world and enters into our lives, totally transforming every fiber of our being.

And that is precisely the most precious gift we can share with others at Christmas: God's love that has filled our hearts. Yes, my dear mother had it right. May we share God's love not only on this blessed day, but throughout the year with all our brothers and sisters—especially those who are the most vulnerable, those who are in the greatest need. May the peace, love, and serenity of Jesus and his Blessed Mother be with you always! A blessed Christmas to all of you.

Lent–Easter Season

Homily

Passion (Palm) Sunday

Holy Name Cathedral, Chicago, Illinois

——March 27, 1983 ————————————————

> As he was now drawing near, at the descent of the Mount of Olives, the whole multitude of the disciples began to rejoice and praise God with a loud voice for all the mighty works that they had seen, saying, "Blessed be the King, who comes in the name of the Lord! Peace in heaven and glory in the highest!" And some of the Pharisees in the multitude said to him, "Teacher, rebuke your disciples." He answered, "I tell you, if these were silent, the very stones would cry out" (Luke 19:37-40).

If these were silent, the very stones would cry out!

At some point, this man on the donkey comes riding into all of our lives. There is no keeping him out. Oh, it is true, there are forces, life-denying powers, which would keep him on the outskirts—this Lord of life—but they are doomed to fail however much they may seem to succeed for a time.

What are those forces? Some of them, the less powerful finally, are outside ourselves: natural disaster, social displacement, economic oppression, famine, war. The really *strong* ones are those within: selfishness, pride, ambition for riches or reputation at the cost of personal integrity.

But he rides into our midst anyway. And even though our welcome may sometimes be less than enthusiastic, still he warns us that if we fail to recognize him for who he is, the lifeless stones themselves will cry out in greeting. Perhaps the reason our cheers sometimes ring hollow is that we recognize deep down the reality of our situation, that as Lord of Life, he has sway over every aspect of what we do and are. Nothing is excused.

337

Nothing is exempt. Nothing is locked to his entry. Politics, economics, human endeavors of every kind: all are unbarred to his gaze. And this means that those voices which would limit the man on the donkey to what is specifically "religious" understand neither who he is nor what he claims.

The blessed King who comes in the name of the Lord is not decked out with the usual trappings of public people: well-tailored clothes, hovering assistants, splendid means of conveyance. No, he comes poor but *not* unnoticed.

Why? Because he is the Lord of all life. And those who believe in life and love life know him for the ally that he is.

At the very moment of his triumphal entry, there were waiting little groups of the rich and the powerful and the elite who saw what must be done. Their stock-in-trade was not the enhancement of life but cruel oppression, a living death for all but their own small number. And here came this upstart, this countryman, proclaiming freedom and Good News to the poor, even—so it was rumored among the ignorant—raising the dead to new life.

The rest is plain. They marshalled their forces, surely sufficient to snuff out a single, insignificant human life. And that they did, without any room for doubt. The man on the donkey was, within a matter of days, the man on a cross. For our sakes, he was, in St. Paul's terrible words, made sin for us and, at a certain time, on an afternoon, during which the same sun that shines on us now shone on him, during which birds sang, and the breath of a hundred breezes came down the hillsides, and infants were brought forth from their mothers' wombs and old men died in their beds, during three hours that could have been measured on a clock, the man who had ridden in triumph on a donkey, his body wrenched and his blood spilt, died the death of a slave. But even at that moment he was no less the Lord of life.

After a little time he was buried, all that remained of him lovingly placed in a tomb by those who followed him. It was finished, or so thought the guardians of public order. But for those who believe, the man on the donkey is not dead. Even death could not hold him long in its embrace. And still he comes into each of our lives and will not be kept out, for that man on a donkey is God, the Lord of *all* life.

Homily

Sage Chapel

Second Sunday of Lent
Cornell University, Ithaca, New York
——*March 3, 1985* ——————————————————

Listening to this mysterious gospel—with its striking visual and auditory features—we encounter the elusive presence of God. As we enter into its mystery, our response might well be that of Peter who wants to prolong such a wonderful experience. But—also like Peter—we have to learn the lesson of the Transfiguration—that we cannot settle down prematurely, basking in the warmth of the kingdom before the victory has been fully achieved.

Three occasions in Mark's Gospel give rise to confessions of faith in Jesus. The first is his *baptism*, during which the Father proclaims Jesus his "beloved Son," thereby revealing Jesus' true identity. At this beginning of his public ministry, he stands before the world—full of great promise.

The second occasion is the *transfiguration*, during which his identity is confirmed for the inner circle of Peter, James and John—again by a heavenly voice: "This is my Son, my beloved. Listen to him!" This midpoint in Jesus' ministry joins the promise of glory with predictions of suffering.

The third is the *crucifixion*—almost the antithesis of the transfiguration! Jesus dies in full obedience to the Father's will, giving witness to steadfastness despite feelings of utter abandonment. This time a Roman army officer confesses: "Clearly this man was the Son of God."

These three narratives combine to teach us about hope despite great human suffering. The immediate context of today's narrative is also key to understanding its fuller meaning.

Immediately preceding the transfiguration are a number of interrelated events. After Peter confesses his faith in Jesus as "Messiah," Jesus predicts his passion and death for the first time. Peter then chides Jesus for talking nonsense, and Jesus responds with very sharp words: "Get out of my sight, you Satan!" He goes on to explain that there is a cost to being his disciples: we must take up our Cross and follow him.

The transfiguration narrative itself projects us into the future beyond the Cross, into the glory of the kingdom where the risen Christ reigns. But after we have experienced this vision of the future, we must come down the mountain with Jesus to face the power of demons and to listen a second time to his prediction of passion and death. Jesus and his disciples must return to an earthly road—one which leads to rejection and death, to Calvary. Easter is not yet upon us!

The underlying themes of this part of Mark's Gospel make it clear that we cannot rightly understand who Jesus is until we have seen him suffer, die, and rise again. Moreover, there is a cost to being his disciple. It is not enough to sing alleluias because we have heard Good News. As disciples, we must learn that taking up *our* Cross is the way, the only way, to true glory. Although we glory in his resurrection and our deepest yearning is to share new life with him, we cannot arrive at that point unless we embrace the Cross as Jesus did.

We cannot understand Jesus without the Cross just as we cannot understand the Cross without the resurrection. But, like the disciples, we are slow to realize this truth. Peter wants to settle down prematurely. The others are bewildered and do not understand. Like them, we, too, would like to avoid pain and suffering—if at all possible. Do you remember the television commercial which used to prompt us to seek immediate relief from pain: "When you hurt, even a little bit, time counts!" Avoidance of pain is one of the characteristics of our society!

So, perhaps you wonder, as I do at times: why is the Cross necessary? Why didn't God save us in some other—less painful—way? Why do *we* have to accept suffering as a necessary cost of following Jesus?

The first reading this morning, from the book of Genesis, provides a clue. The story of Abraham's willingness to sacrifice Isaac is one of the most powerful and poignant narratives in all of Scripture. It is easy to identify with Abraham's agony as he takes his only son, his *beloved* son, to the site of sacrifice.

The story focuses on his response to Isaac's problematic question about the lack of a sacrificial animal. When Abraham says, "God himself will provide the [animal] for the sacrifice," he does not yet know how the story will end! What he says, in effect, to his son is "I don't know, but I believe and trust God—he will provide. . . ." This is the man of faith *par excellence* in the Old Testament—trusting in God in the face of human pain and suffering despite God's elusive and mysterious presence.

Some people are bothered by the image of God they seem to find in this story. To them he seems cruel and demanding. However, the story is written to highlight Abraham's faith and trust in God rather than to tell us what God is really like.

As we read this story in the context of today's liturgy, we come to realize that the *same* God who asks Abraham to be *willing* to sacrifice his son does not withhold his own beloved Son from us, nor does he spare him from the sacrifice of the Cross. In this he shows us the depth of his love. "There is no greater love than this: to lay down one's life for one's friends." And that is what we are—God's friends.

The transfiguration gives us glimpses of God's loving presence and of the glory awaiting us at the end of our struggle. The story of the transfiguration is a story of hope—of trust in God's love—despite human pain and suffering. It takes root in the lives of Christians wherever Jesus' disciples encounter the Cross in their lives.

As you undoubtedly know, I returned to the United States yesterday from a weeklong visit to Central America. A number of bishops, staff people, and I visited Nicaragua and El Salvador and met with the bishops' conferences of all the Central American nations in order to update the policies and positions of the National Conference of Catholic Bishops in regard to Central America.

We encountered firsthand what we already knew—the extreme poverty, civil strife, and military turmoil of these countries. We heard so often about the struggles of these people, but also their triumphs, of their fears and, above all, of their hope for the future. They are true disciples of Jesus. They not only carry their Crosses with courage and dignity, they are a *hope-filled people*. They trust in the Lord and in their solidarity with one another and with their bishops.

Their poverty is simply overwhelming! The average family income in Honduras, for example, is about $200 a year and more than 30 percent of the population are unemployed. Civil strife takes a *daily* toll in the life of the people in a country such as Nicaragua, where the people must face each day the consequences of social unrest and political instability. Human rights violations are common throughout the region, perhaps nowhere worse than in Guatemala.

We have much to learn from their courage, but even more from their trust in God and in one another. Despite intense suffering, continuing deprivation, and numbing fear, they remain a hope-filled people. Their very survival may well depend upon this hope for the future. It enables them to face each new day.

Yes, ours is a broken world. There is so much human pain and suffering! The issues which threaten or diminish human life are manifold and exceedingly complex. But we need not be discouraged. We dare not be!

The challenges are enormous, but we are *capable* of meeting them. As Pope John Paul II said to young people recently: "The time we are living in is not just a period of danger and worry. It is an hour for hope. . . . The present difficulties are really a test of our humanity. They can be turning points on the road to lasting peace, for they kindle the boldest dreams and unleash the best energies of mind and heart" (World Day of Peace Message, 1985).

These words are not simply wishful thinking or chanting of slogans. They are not a pep talk to encourage a team which has little or no chance of winning. The fundamental reason for such deep hope is that God is close to us. It does not matter that we may experience his presence at times in elusive and mysterious ways. The world is not only the product of God's creative work, it is also the object of his love. He is not indifferent to what happens to us. After all, he has not withheld his own beloved Son from us. He sent him into our midst, "filled with enduring love!"

Trust in God leads to faith in the human person. If we acknowledge God as creator, we are led directly to reverence the pinnacle of God's creative work, the human person. Every person of every culture reflects the wonder and the mystery of God. We are made in his image and likeness.

If we are to have hope in the task before us of building a just and peaceful world, of healing a deeply divided human community, we must have confidence in the God-given genius of the human spirit. The astounding beauty of physical creation pales before the wonder of human intelligence. As free, thinking people we inherit the world and its history as raw material which we can shape anew in each generation. God gives us all we need to build up his kingdom!

Admittedly, there are many constraints on our activity, rooted in the events of the past and the realities of the present, but none of this can suppress the potential of human intelligence, individually or collectively, to shape a better future. In short, our effective involvement in building a peaceful world will be measured in part by the possibilities we believe are open before us and our capacity to be creative.

Besides hope and creativity, we need compassion in serving our neighbor—*all* our brothers and sisters, especially those most vulnerable among us. Taking up our Cross implies standing in solidarity with our crucified brothers and sisters. Standing with them means sharing in some way in their pain—investing time and energy to learn about their plight. Standing with them means forming public opinion within our nation to support life-giving aid to poor nations and to bring to an end the ever-escalating arms race which is strangling all of us. Standing with the most vulnerable among us means being advocates on their behalf.

It is not enough to recognize our Cross in the personal crises or problems we face. Focusing all our attention on our own problems can be a form of narcissism if all we embrace is ourselves! Have you ever tried to embrace Jesus as he hangs on the cross? It's impossible to do unless you also embrace the cross. The reverse is also true: we cannot embrace the cross without also taking into our arms Jesus, our suffering brother who is nailed to it.

My dear brothers and sisters in the Lord: it is so good for us to be here together—in the presence of Jesus. We have gathered in peace and fellowship to give thanks to the Lord for all he has given us. God shares his own word and food with us. Perhaps you and I would like to prolong this time together—even to stay here forever!

But it is not yet the time for that. With Jesus, as his disciples, we must go down from this mountain to walk with him in the ordinary journey of this world—bringing healing to those who approach us with their needs, giving voice to those who are so weary from suffering that they have nearly lost their own voices, proclaiming to all the world the Good News that God loves us, witnessing to the hope that is ours as his people.

We have hope for the future because we believe in the resurrection and new life. We are Easter people—ultimately. But, as we walk with Jesus and our brothers and sisters, we cannot deceive ourselves: the road first leads to Calvary. Let us walk together with the Lord!

Chrism Mass

Holy Name Cathedral, Chicago, Illinois

—April 14, 1987 —————————————————————

> The spirit of the Lord is upon me. . . .
> He has sent me to bring glad tidings to the poor,
> to proclaim liberty to captives,
> recovery of sight to the blind . . .
> to announce a year of favor from the Lord.

The prophet's joyous, hope-filled song—echoed by Jesus in the synagogue at Nazareth—resounds through the ages, and we must pass it on to our own generation as well as the next.

> A new day is dawning—it is always dawning!
> Salvation is at hand—it is always at hand!
> People are sharing good news with one another.
> They are experiencing healing and consolation.
> Those who have drained the bitter cup of captivity
>   now savor liberty.
> The word is being fulfilled in our midst. And we say, "Thanks be to God!
> Glory to you, Lord Jesus Christ!"

These words are true of all of us because, through baptism, we are all members of Christ's body; together we are a priestly people. But this afternoon I'd like to speak to the priests because the Chrism Mass highlights in a special way the ministerial priesthood. It is very appropriate, nonetheless, that lay people hear what I have to say to their priests because these dedicated men need and deserve the support and love of the people they serve.

My dear brothers in Christ:

The new day announced by Isaiah and Jesus arrives amidst clouds. Darkness covers the earth. Thick clouds cover the peoples. They cast the shadow of war and poverty, dissension and confusion.

Priests are quite familiar with clouds. You often find yourselves in the middle of diverse, and sometimes conflicting, expectations from your people. At times you feel that you are in the middle, trying to hold the parish or institution together, striving to make everyone feel valued and respected. You are frequently tired physically and drained emotionally because of the many individual, family, and community problems you must deal with. There is more work to do and fewer, less energetic priests to do it.

Unfortunately, sometimes we bishops may become so preoccupied with crisis intervention that we take for granted or unwittingly neglect the vast majority of our priests who function effectively but need—and miss—our direct, personal support and encouragement.

Because of this—and many other factors as well—priests sometimes ask "Does anyone care? Is it really worth it? Is it really worth being a priest?"

There is no reason, however, to be depressed or fearful or to feel abandoned because, in faith, we know that the Lord Jesus is present in those clouds. Indeed, he usually comes to us in the midst of clouds! Clouds, we must remember, are often the harbingers of something new. They bear within themselves the power of transformation. The eyes of faith permit us to see Jesus Christ in their midst, taming them through and with us, riding them with great gracefulness. The essential thing is that we keep our eyes fixed on the Lord. "Is it really worth it?" you ask. Yes—as long as we place our total faith and trust in Jesus and let him take over.

Jesus bursts like a spring shower onto our sometimes barren lives and ministries. His warmth causes us to shed the heavy trappings of winter's discontent. He clothes us with a sunny mantle of glory.

Like soothing, fragrant oil, the Divine Word flows luxuriantly into what is listless and broken. It seeks to penetrate and loosen what is bound. It anoints us. It leaves its gleaming mark on us.

If it is true that Jesus arrives surrounded by clouds, it is also true that he arrives amidst suffering. Where there is suffering, there is the healing, life-giving Word. Perhaps that is why we love the Lord so much. Perhaps that is why we believe in him so profoundly. The crucified Jesus is no stranger to us. Jesus' heart was moved to pity at the sight of the crowds who hungered for a word, a promise of life. He was moved to pity by the plight of the sick, the blind, and the sinner. He was no stranger to our suffering. To see it made him weep. To see it made him angry.

And yet, things did not remain there, at the level of a compassionate, but ineffectual, emotional response. In the power of the Spirit, he transformed suffering. Hurt calls for healing. Blindness yearns for light. And this was the mission he had been given—to heal, to bring light, to proclaim Good News. He remained faithful to that mission even when failure and personal suffering seemed to be the only outcome of his efforts.

We are asked to contemplate and celebrate this Suffering Servant today. He is the model of the priesthood. He has drawn near to his people with his healing touch. The oils we bless today will be the means by which he will continue to touch, heal, and send forth many people. It is the great privilege of the priest to participate in this way in Jesus' healing power and ministry. You are the instruments he has chosen to continue his saving mission.

Your hands will touch infants and adults with the oil of catechumens, through which God's power will penetrate and raise them up as his beloved people. Your hands will touch those who are ill with the oil of the sick, bringing both to body and soul God's healing and saving power. Through the anointing with chrism, God will send forth women and men to live confirmed lives of faith and service. Chrism will also be used to anoint those called by God to serve in the ministerial priesthood.

This celebration, in fact, anticipates a year full of service to God's people. You who have received the anointing of ordination have the privilege of carrying on Jesus' mission for and with the local church here in Chicago.

Priests often have a special awareness of being the instruments of God's healing, reconciling grace. It is an awesome thing to be so used by God—but it is not without its share of suffering. On Friday we will recall in a vivid way that Jesus was both priest and victim—for the salvation and new life of others.

"Is it really worth it?" you ask. When the dust has settled and the clouds have disappeared, if only for a moment, we see more clearly the truly important difference that priests make in the lives of their people. And then we can say, "Yes, it is worth it!" This is why I cherish my priesthood.

My brothers, our recommitment today is an expression of our willingness to participate in Jesus' mission with renewed fidelity and enthusiasm. The oils have long since dried since our ordination day. We have known periods of questioning and doubt. We know the pain of loss as some of our friends have chosen to leave the active ministry. We have walked through the valley of darkness with our people—the dark valley of moral dilemmas, of physical and spiritual sickness, of injustice and oppressive structures. So, the question, "Is it worth it?" may still haunt us.

In all this, the Church asks us today to keep our eyes fixed on Jesus as he comes upon the clouds of darkness, suffering, and doubt. We are to watch him with great hope and love as he embraces all who need his care. The transformation that our eyes behold in this Eucharist—the transformation we see and experience each day in our ministry—evokes a promise that we will sing forever of the goodness of God.

In conclusion, my brothers, I want to assure you—in the presence of your people—that I do *not* take you for granted. I respect and love you more deeply than you will ever know. If, during the past year, I have offended any of you or caused you pain in any way, I ask for forgiveness. Such offense or pain was surely not intended. I pray each day for you, as I know you do for me. Let us continue to love and support one another even as we deepen our faith in and love for the Lord, whose priesthood we share.

And now, let us renew our priestly commitment.

Pro-Life Pilgrimage

Fifth Sunday of Lent
Mission of Nombre de Dios, St. Augustine, Florida
——*March 20, 1988* ——————————————————————————

"Sir, we should like to see Jesus."

That's all the Greek visitors to Jerusalem said—a simple request to see the Master. And see Jesus they did. What did they expect to see? A dazzling orator perhaps? A powerful healer? A prophet of God? They came looking for Jesus and found a man preparing to meet his death. What they saw was Jesus in agony.

"Sir, we should like to see Jesus."

Josephine used to dance the Tarantella at weddings, in the VFW hall, at block parties, and at parish dances. She used to dance the Tarantella, and no one could keep up with her—so graceful and strong was her body.

But that was long ago when she was young, when she could move freely. Now all her partners had died. Her neighbors had moved away, seemingly overnight, and only she was left—an old woman whose fingers were like gnarled oak tree limbs, whose legs were stubborn, stupid, and fairly useless. But she used to dance the Tarantella, and the stories she could tell if there were only someone to listen!

But she is forgotten. She has no one to talk to. Not even the walls listen to her. At times she feels that even God has forgotten her. How else could she explain why he had not sent her a visitor? So she waits to die, sometimes talking to the TV, most of the time staring into space thinking about the Tarantella she would never dance again.

"Sir, we should like to see Jesus."

Since the U.S. Supreme Court legalized abortion in 1973, more than 21 million lives have been destroyed in the womb. An estimated 1.5 million abortions are performed in the United States every year—one every 21 seconds. A third of all pregnancies in the U.S. end in abortion; and nearly one-third of all abortions are performed on teenagers.

Lisa is a young woman in Chicago who conceived a child at the end of her sophomore year in high school. Under tremendous pressure from her peers and those who should have known better, Lisa aborted her unborn child in October. She thought it would be a "quick fix" to a problem that should never have happened. But instead, it has turned out to be a long-term nightmare. Lisa has trouble sleeping nights because she keeps waking up in the middle of the night; she keeps hearing a baby cry—and that cry will never stop.

"Sir, we should like to see Jesus."

What did the Greek visitors to Jerusalem expect to see in the quest for Jesus? A strong, powerful king? A powerful figure comfortable with wielding great power? A self-assured, confident leader? They came looking for Jesus and found a man preparing to meet his death. They saw Jesus in agony.

The gospel does not say, but we may imagine that it was difficult for the disciples to see Jesus hurting so. Perhaps it was similar to our coming upon the scene of a serious accident and, in spite of our curiosity, feeling impelled to turn away our eyes. It is not easy to watch or listen to the Lord when he is in agony.

But watch we must. "Sir, we should like to see Jesus."

My sisters and brothers, the Lord is *still* in agony, and the challenge of today's gospel is *not* to look away. To watch Jesus in agony is to identify those areas of our lives and our society where sin still has the upper hand, where oppression is the rule, where the sanctity of human life is ignored or violated.

Even as we mourn the death of the unborn, efforts are openly being mounted today to place the lives of the elderly and the infirm in jeopardy. "Euthanasia" is no longer an unspeakable word. There are those who would have us believe that it is an act of mercy. However, this heinous disregard for the sanctity of human life is, in reality, nothing other than murder or assisted suicide.

But the specter of death haunts not only the unborn and the elderly and infirm. Suicide is the second highest killer of our *teenagers* in this nation. What shall we say about a society in which teenagers choose the oblivion of an early grave over the continued pain of living? The Lord is still in agony.

Never before have people of this country been so assaulted by the tragic insertion of pornography into our airwaves, our television and movie screens, our books. The temples of the Holy Spirit, our human bodies, have been turned into objects of lust for easy money. Virtue is reduced to a quaint, old-fashioned ideal, and human dignity—and indeed, at times, human life itself—becomes a casualty. The Lord is still in agony.

Ethiopia is one of the poorest countries in the world, a nation where the average annual income is $110 and where 17 out of every 100 babies die before they are two years old. In that country today at least 6 million of its 46 million inhabitants face imminent starvation. Think the unimaginable—imagine your own son or daughter, grandson or granddaughter starving to death before your very eyes. The Lord is still in agony.

Even as we deplore the present assaults on human life and its dignity, we continue a nuclear arms race which not only devours a disproportionate share of the resources needed for integral human development, but also holds hostage our children's future. As Pope John Paul told the diplomats accredited to the Holy See this past January: "The stockpiling of these arms in itself constitutes a threat to peace as well as a challenge to the nations that lack the essentials for survival and for development." Yes, the Lord is still in agony.

It is in this context of the need to protect human life and promote its dignity that the bishops of the U.S. have opposed capital punishment. I know that your bishops in Florida have been very vocal on this issue. While Catholic teaching holds that the state has the right to use capital punishment, we are convinced that that right should not be used at this time when assaults on life have become so pervasive in our society. Capital punishment contributes to the myth that life is cheap, expendable. In justice, we must surely address the evil of crime—especially the plight of its victims—but there are other, more effective ways of doing this—ways that will not undermine respect for life. While all may not agree with this position, it is an issue which demands careful reflection by everyone who is truly committed to protecting and enhancing the gift of human life.

The historical moment of Jesus' crucifixion occurred nearly 2,000 years ago. We are not witnesses to the terrible passion of that first Good Friday. But the Lord's agony continues. Wherever life suffers, Jesus suffers. And the gospel narrative today summons us to stand with Jesus—wherever and whenever he suffers. "Where I am, there my servant will be."

The only place worse than being *on* the cross itself is standing at its foot. It is not easy to watch Jesus in agony. But that is where we are called to be. We must not give up and walk away, trying to avert our eyes from the threats to and the destruction of innocent human life. Like Mary, the other women, and the beloved disciple, we must stand beneath the cross—full of courage and faith.

From my personal experience I know that working to defend, protect, and nourish the sanctity of human life is a difficult task. Sometimes it seems that, for every step forward we take, the world takes five steps backwards. Life has so many enemies, so many threats today that we may feel overwhelmed, isolated, frustrated, and exhausted.

If that has been or is your experience, today's gospel reading has a special message for you. We are called to trust that our agony will bear fruit, to trust that God will use our suffering, love, and service on behalf of the gift of life. We are to trust that the seed of our sacrifice will, in God's hands, bear much fruit. There is no easy path to salvation. The only way for "this world's prince" to be driven out is for us to risk ourselves the way Jesus did.

The anguished cry of Jesus on Golgotha, "My God, my God, why have you forsaken me?" continues today in all those persons and situations where life is threatened, diminished, or destroyed. Yes, the passion of the Lord persists today wherever the sanctity of human life is belittled or violated. Although they are not all the same, and they may not all be equally urgent at any given moment, *all life issues are linked*. Because of that linkage, no one of them can be eliminated from our overall vision of life and our responsibility toward this great gift.

But one in particular requires special attention at this moment in our history as a nation. The anguished cry of Jesus continues in a poignant way in the silent screams of unborn children who are denied their right to live. The Scriptures tell us that, when Jesus died, a darkness covered the earth. This darkness now envelops our world. No matter how much we try to lift this darkness, we will never succeed unless we first decide, as individuals and as a nation, that we will protect the life of the unborn, that we will not deprive the most vulnerable of God's creatures of the gift of life which he has given them.

Let us return to our homes this evening determined to defend life at every stage of development and in all circumstances from the moment of conception to natural death. The one issue is *life* in all its manifestations. So let us be consistent in our support of all life issues. To ignore one is to place all in jeopardy. It is that very consistency, I submit, that demands that we be absolutely uncompromising in our defense of the life of the unborn.

My brothers and sisters, my prayer for us today is that we will always see Jesus, especially as he suffers, that we will never give up or lose heart in our struggles to defend and promote the sanctity of life, and that we will always believe that our own personal sacrifice and struggle glorifies God.

Let us follow the example of Mary, who heard God's word and responded to it. She did not run away from life and its demands. She stood up, declared herself, and made decisions.

She still stands at the foot of the cross—with great love and sorrow because of the suffering of her children, but also with deep faith and hope in the resurrection and new life that some day will be ours.

"Sir, we should like to see Jesus." May that request to Phillip be our daily prayer, and may our prayer always and forever be answered. Let us stand in solidarity with Jesus and Mary and our suffering brothers and sisters—at the foot of the cross.

Easter Sunday

Holy Name Cathedral, Chicago, Illinois

——*March 26, 1989* ————————————————————————

Easter Sunday has its share of wonderful stories. This morning I'd like to share with you a favorite of mine.

A second-grade teacher decided to put on an Easter play. All of the children were given parts, although some of the parts were quite insignificant. One boy, for example, was given the part of the *stone* that was placed in front of Jesus' tomb. The teacher told this child that when it was time for the stone to be rolled aside so that Jesus could rise from the dead, all he needed to do was to move his hands in a circle and then step to the side.

The first time they had a rehearsal, the boy got a running start and began to do a series of somersaults at the end of which he knocked down several children. The teacher took him aside and told him that it simply was not necessary to be so dramatic. It would be sufficient for him merely to move his hands in a circle and then step to the side.

At the next rehearsal, the boy did the same thing—knocking the other children aside as he did his somersaults. The teacher decided that, rather than try to reason with him, she would offer him a different role instead. First she offered him the part of one of the *soldiers*, but he replied that he wanted to be the stone! Then she offered him the part of *Peter*. He thought a little longer about this possibility; but again he refused, insisting that he wanted to be the stone!

Finally, in exasperation, she offered him the highly coveted role of *Jesus* himself. The boy gave this careful thought before telling her that he still wanted to be the stone! When she asked him why he insisted on being the stone, he proudly replied: "Because when I let Jesus out of the tomb, it feels so good!"

There is profound Easter wisdom in the little boy's words. For the forty days of Lent, through *prayer, fasting,* and *almsgiving,* we invited God to roll away from our hearts the stones that keep the new life of Jesus and the gifts of his Spirit entombed within us.

In lenten *prayer,* we asked God to remove from our hearts the stones of blindness that prevent us from seeing Christ's light that shines forth from inside ourselves and others. We asked him to remove the stones of deafness that prevent us from hearing his word which he continually speaks within us. We asked God to remove the stones of dumbness that prevent us from proclaiming the Good News that is to be shouted to all the world.

In lenten *fasting,* we sought to surrender to God all the disordered attachments in our lives, all the things to which we have become addicted, all the rubble that has accumulated around our hearts, preventing us from developing a deeper relationship with him.

In lenten *almsgiving,* we asked God to roll back the stones that hinder the gifts of the Spirit within us from finding expression in our lives through our generosity and compassion toward those less fortunate than we.

And if we have been conscientious, disciplined, and repentant during these forty days of Lent, then we believe that God's healing power and saving grace are at work in our lives. We believe that, even now, he is rolling back the stones of sin and selfishness that entomb the life of Jesus within us, just as he rolled back the stone that entombed the body of his beloved Son, Jesus.

This Easter Sunday, then, we celebrate like the little boy—with great enthusiasm and joy—because Jesus' resurrection is Good News and his life continues to be released within our hearts and within our world.

In today's gospel, we heard that the stone in front of Jesus' temporary tomb has been rolled away. Mary Magdalene, Peter, and the other disciple arrive, and all three see the same things—an empty tomb, "the wrappings on the ground," and "the piece of cloth which had covered [his] head." Yet all three react in quite different ways.

Mary Magdalene assumes the worst. In panic, she concludes that the Lord has been taken from the tomb by Roman soldiers or by members of the Jewish Sanhedrin. *Peter* appears to be stunned, confused, and paralyzed by what he sees, not knowing what to think or say or believe.

But the *other disciple* both sees and believes. Although, like the others, he does not yet understand the full significance of what he sees, he nevertheless believes that Jesus has risen from the dead. Why? Because he is the disciple whom Jesus loved. There is an intimate connection between *loving* and *believing.* Having been loved by the Lord and having loved him in return, he was given by God the gift of faith by which he was able both to see and believe.

This Easter morning, we stand before the tombs of our own hearts. And as we look within, how do *we* respond?

Do we allow Jesus' sacrificial love to move us beyond Mary Magdalene's fear and panic? If not, they will prevent us from seeing and recognizing God's presence and glory within ourselves and others, as well as in the places and events of our world.

Do we allow Jesus' wondrous love to move us beyond Peter's stunned, confused silence? If not, it will paralyze us and prevent us from living out the gifts of God's Spirit.

Do we allow Jesus' intimate love to enable us, as it did the other disciple, to see and believe? If we do, we will see and believe that Jesus' death and resurrection have removed from our hearts the stones of our original sinfulness, and revealed to the light of day our original goodness.

In other words, we must first believe in the power of Jesus' love to transform our hearts and also in the beauty of our original goodness. Then we can begin to respond in faith and commit ourselves to live out all that he taught by his word and example.

That is why the renewal of our baptismal promises is the most appropriate response we can make to this Easter celebration. It gives each of us the opportunity to respond in faith to the Good News of the resurrection. The promises are our way of saying "No!" to sin, "No!" to all that would lead us into sin, to all those stones that block the manifestation of the new life of the risen Lord within us. Indeed, through these baptismal promises, we say an unqualified "Yes!" to him and indicate our willingness to rededicate ourselves to his mission of salvation.

I assure you, if we renew these promises with sincerity and fidelity—to use the words of the little boy—it will feel very good to let Jesus out of the tomb!

Homily

Third Sunday of Easter

Old St. Patrick's Church, Chicago, Illinois

—*April 9, 1989* ─────────────────────────────

As the weather warms, and spring flowers burst into bloom, our thoughts easily and naturally extend beyond the opening of the baseball season to anticipated, delightful summer activities. Capitalizing on such daydreams, supermarkets and mini-marts alike have begun to display such summer staples as barbecue grills and bags of charcoal.

Our daydreams about summer may help us enter into today's gospel narrative, which, at first glance, seems to be a relaxed cookout on the beach of the Sea of Tiberias. Let us gather around the charcoal fire with Jesus, and listen to what transpires between him and his disciples, especially Peter.

Recall that Peter had originally been a fisherman. On an earlier occasion—as described in St. Luke's Gospel—Jesus had arranged a similar miraculous catch of fish for him. Peter, the professional fisherman, was quite perplexed at that time, for he knew that fishing was best at *night*. If you didn't catch fish then, it would be useless to fish during the *day!* Nonetheless, on that occasion, Peter put his trust in Jesus and followed his command. The result was a marvelous catch of fish!

When Peter got over his initial shock, he became aware, at a deeper level, of the great difference between himself and Jesus, between a sinner and a God-sent worker of miracles. So, he wanted to pull away from the Lord. But Jesus had come to *invite* sinners to open their hearts to *receive* the Father's forgiving love—not to *drive* them *away!* His response to Simon Peter was a call to be a fisher of *people*—despite his unworthiness.

Now, on this occasion as described in today's gospel, as Peter and his companions confront the risen Lord on the beach, does Peter recall that earlier meeting with Jesus on the seashore? Does this latest encounter also remind him that, as fishers of men and women, Jesus' disciples can catch *nothing* without the Lord's assistance?

John's Gospel frequently identifies Jesus as the Light of the world, a light that darkness can never snuff out. In the presence of the risen Lord, in the daylight, Peter and his companions again miraculously catch an enormous number of fish. And they do so because they listen to the Lord's command and obey it, even before they recognize him.

As on other occasions after the resurrection, the Beloved Disciple is the first to discover that the seeming stranger on the beach is, in fact, Jesus. Knowing Peter as we do, we are not surprised when he impulsively jumps out of the boat and wades to the shore to greet the Lord.

We might assume that Peter is overjoyed to be with Jesus again, and re-assured by his invitation to breakfast. But the charcoal fire on the beach triggers other memories, painful ones. Not long before this incident, Peter had warmed himself at another charcoal fire—in the high priest's courtyard. There he had said—not once, not twice, but three times—that he was *not* one of Jesus' disciples. Despite his protestation at the Last Supper that he was ready to lay down his life for the Lord, a few hours later Peter denied that he even knew him!

But now in this peaceful setting on the beach, Peter has nothing to fear. This is the same Jesus who washed his feet in the upper room. He is the Servant who prepares a table for his people and serves them bread (and fish). Moreover, he has come to invite sinners to enjoy the Father's heal-ing, forgiving love.

In a beautiful dialogue, Jesus affords Peter an opportunity publicly to profess his love for him—not once, not twice, but three times. Peter's re-pentance flows from his love for the Lord. And because of that love, Jesus gives him charge of his flock. Peter becomes a shepherd.

Centuries before, the prophet Ezekiel had announced that God him-self would be the shepherd of his people—taking care of their every need, guiding and protecting them, nourishing them and giving them rest in gentle pastures. More recently, Jesus had proclaimed in Jerusalem that he himself was the Good Shepherd who takes exceptional care of his flock, even to the point of giving his life for it.

Now the shepherd's staff is passed on to Peter—an impulsive, sinful person who has been cleansed and transformed by God's power and his own faith and love of the Lord. Peter's faithful pastoral care will cost him his life also. In imitation of Jesus, Peter will eventually be crucified be-cause of his great love for and fidelity to the risen Lord.

The Acts of the Apostles give us glimpses of Peter the shepherd at a later date, *after* Jesus has returned to his Father. And how he has changed! Now he is fearless, articulate, brave, and courageous. When the religious authorities of Jerusalem, who constitute the Sanhedrin, forbid him and the other disciples to preach and heal in Jesus' name, Peter retorts that he will obey God instead. The power of God's Spirit has, indeed, made him a very effective fisher of men and women.

The lesson in this gospel is quite simple—and profound. Despite obstacles, opposition, and persecution, the Church continues Jesus' mission which was first entrusted to Peter and the other apostles. But *you and I* are the Church. Although we, too, are unworthy, God's power works through *us*. While our roles might be different, we are the instruments he uses to bring his healing, forgiving love to everyone.

To be effective instruments, we must place our full *faith* and *trust* in the Lord, as did Peter, confident that his power will overcome our weakness and sinfulness. This knowledge—this conviction that the Lord Jesus will prevail—will give meaning to our lives; it will give us the strength and courage needed to face up to the often conflicting realities of daily life.

My brothers and sisters, I am delighted to have this opportunity to worship with you this morning. I am very impressed with what you have accomplished here at Old St. Patrick's in the past few years—with the leadership of Father Jack Wall, your pastor, and Father John Cusick, and the support of thousands of Chicagoans who have helped bring this historic parish back to life. You are the instruments through which the new life of Jesus has become a reality in the minds and hearts of the many people who now form this community of faith. You are the instruments through which the risen Lord will continue to reach out to all people.

Today is a special day because after this Mass we will announce publicly that in the fall Old St. Pat's will open a preschool and kindergarten which hopefully will develop into a full school—from preschool through the eighth grade. I commend you for this. I have come today to give my own personal, moral support to your effort.

Like Peter, let us open our hearts this morning to Jesus' caring, forgiving, and healing love. Let us join the heavenly choirs in their hymn of praise to the Lamb that was slain. And as we leave the charcoal fire on the beach this morning, let us take its light, its warmth, and its reassurance with us, and share it with everyone whose lives we touch.

Homily

Mass for the Newly Initiated

Ascension Thursday
Holy Name Cathedral, Chicago, Illinois
— *May 4, 1989* —

In the summer of 1982, I received the call from the Holy Father to serve as the archbishop of Chicago. Naturally, I was very grateful for the opportunity to embrace this ministry. The church of Chicago has such a proud history. I had long been impressed by its powerful witness to the presence of God's Spirit among you. The thought of being a part of the life of this vibrant local church filled me with indescribable happiness.

Well, frankly, it *partially* filled me with indescribable happiness. It also deeply saddened me, for the call to come to Chicago meant leaving Cincinnati. I had invested ten years of my life among the people of that archdiocese, and, during that time, they became family to me. I was quite willing to spend the rest of my life as their pastor. So, as excited as I was to accept the call to serve among *you*, leaving Cincinnati was one of the hardest things I ever had to do.

Undoubtedly, everyone here this evening could tell a similar story of the happiness of a new beginning in life that was a bit tainted with the sadness of an ending. New beginnings for us mean that we must end something else. For example, if we were to walk into any high school in metropolitan Chicago during the next month, we would find scores of seniors eager and excited about the new beginnings that await them after graduation. But we would also notice an abundance of tears associated with leaving friends and familiar surroundings behind.

This evening, the Liturgy of the Word reflects similar competing emotions about the Lord's ascension into heaven. As a community of faith, we

359

tell two stories of that same experience from two different perspectives. And both are written by the same author, the evangelist Luke.

The version of the story presented in the Acts of the Apostles clearly celebrates the joy of a new beginning. The version presented in Luke's Gospel, on the other hand, seems to capture the other dimension of starting anew. While the evangelist tells us that the "disciples returned to Jerusalem filled with joy," they must also have felt some sadness when they realized that a particular way of relating to the Lord Jesus had just come to an end.

Luke's Gospel describes the ascension as an occasion for saying "good-bye." The story is told primarily from the perspective of looking back to what has already occurred. It celebrates the completion of Jesus' earthly ministry. He reminds the disciples that he had accomplished his messianic mission in Jerusalem where he had suffered, died, and rose from the dead. They must now return to Jerusalem to await a new moment in God's saving acts.

The story of the ascension in Acts looks more to the future. It celebrates the inauguration of a new epoch in salvation history: the era of the Church. The disciples are challenged not to stand looking toward the sky, but to take up Jesus' ministry and mission and to extend them to the very ends of the earth.

So, one narrative about the ascension celebrates an ending, the other a new beginning. But both call Jesus' disciples and all believers to rejoice in God's saving power.

This evening, we call one another to celebrate God's saving power at work among us. We gather to remember and to give thanks for all that has happened among us as you, the newly initiated, journeyed through the Rite of Christian Initiation of Adults. We also look forward in hope to the wonders which God will continue to accomplish in and through our communion with one another.

This evening, then, is an occasion for us to remember what has happened in the past, to proclaim an end to a particular moment in our lives, and to say "good-bye" to one way of relating to the risen Lord and to one another. It is also an opportunity for us to find nourishment to meet and embrace the challenges that lie ahead. As with any new beginning, we are somewhat sad that an end has come. But we also rejoice in the possibilities of the future.

My brothers and sisters, we give thanks and praise to God for all that has taken place during your time of preparation for the Easter sacraments. So much good has already happened among us because of you. During your period of inquiry, we were compelled to examine again the importance of our own identity as believers. In your period of the catechumenate, we were challenged to present the truths of our faith in creative, exciting ways. Breaking open the treasures of God's word with you made the Lectionary come alive for us, too. During the period of enlightenment and purification, the powerful prayers of the scrutinies moved the hearts of all to give thanks to God for rescuing us from sin and evil. And celebrating the Easter sacraments with you lifted us up in joy and renewed us in our commitment to our baptismal faith. Mystagogy has been a wonderful time for all of us to celebrate the wonders of God alive in us!

Yes, so much good has happened among us in your time of preparation for the sacraments of initiation. Assemblies of believers throughout the archdiocese have been renewed in faith because of you. Your journey through the process of Christian initiation has brought us all into a greater awareness of the mystery of God's love for his people. Thank you, my dear brothers and sisters in the Lord.

I would also like to express my gratitude to all who have ministered to the newly initiated. First, I wish to thank the parish communities who themselves are the primary ministers in the catechumenal process. It is the vibrant response to God's call, as evidenced in the life of our parishes, that draws and nurtures catechumens. I would also like to thank all who exercise a particular ministry in the RCIA. May God bless you for your deep faith and generous love.

While we remember and give thanks for the wonderful things that have already taken place, we also proclaim an ending to what has been! Our newly initiated friends, you have risen from the baptismal bath. You have been anointed in the Spirit's power and have shared in the banquet of the Bread of Life. Mystagogy has enabled you to reflect more deeply upon the power of these Easter sacraments.

Now, you stand at a new moment in your lives as believers. It is time to say "good-bye" to the womb experience of the RCIA. The process has served the Spirit in giving birth to you as fully initiated members of the Church. We may experience a tinge of sadness in proclaiming an end to this enriching experience, but, like the disciples at the ascension, we also rejoice, for we know this is also a new beginning for you.

The mission of giving witness to the Lord awaits all of us who approach this Table. No longer do we dismiss you from the assembly at the completion of the Liturgy of the Word. We gratefully share in the Eucharist with you. We promise you our continued support and love. We look forward to future opportunities to share stories of God working among us. We join with you in the Church's mission and work, as, together, we proclaim the reign of God!

Homily

Pentecost Sunday

Holy Name Cathedral, Chicago, Illinois
—*May 14, 1989* ———————————————————

Wind and fire have mysterious qualities. A poet, Christina Georgina Rossetti, captured this sense of mystery when she wrote:

> Who has seen the wind?
> Neither you nor I.
> But when the trees bow down their heads,
> The wind is passing by.

Both fire and wind can be wonderfully beneficial or tragically destructive for the human family. They may appear as a great power unleashed upon the world in lightning and hurricane, or as a restrained power that lights the pilgrim's way and cools the earth. Traditional proverbs from around the world reflect the tension between the potential benefit and destruction of wind and fire. They wisely advise: embrace the wind, but beware of it. Kindle the fire, but handle it with great caution.

On Pentecost, God sends a mighty wind rushing through the streets of Jerusalem and the upper room. His fire burns ardently in the hearts of Jesus' disciples, giving them courage, strength, and boldness for the sake of the kingdom. God's wind and fire set in motion a mighty evangelistic effort, a proclamation of the Good News throughout the world. They help launch the early Church to continue Jesus' mission and ministry.

Never have fire and wind been more mysterious than they are on Pentecost. They change simple fishermen into fearless evangelists. They transform mere Galileans into articulate missionaries who irresistibly sweep through the Roman Empire. In a single generation, Jesus' disciples develop an obscure Jewish sect into a world-embracing religious movement.

On Pentecost the "wind" of the Spirit of God and the "fire" of the Power of God break down barriers of language and give witness to the gospel's reconciling power. The primordial curse of Babel—the inability of people to communicate with one another because of their arrogance in building the Tower of Babel—is reversed by the "gift of tongues" granted to the apostles. Incredibly, visitors to Jerusalem from throughout the Roman Empire understand the apostles' babble, and the Word of God begins to take root in the hearts of converts to Jesus and his new way of life.

Jesus gave his disciples a similar gift of the Spirit in the same upper room on Easter. Rather than unleashing a mighty wind, however, he gently breathed upon them. And their fear was transformed into joy by his presence in their midst. They had been imprisoned in the upper room by their own shortsighted feelings and vision. They were in a kind of spiritual *rigor mortis*, unable to move ahead.

Now, however, Jesus sends them forth, commissioning them to carry on his mission and ministry throughout the world. He also empowers them to forgive and to withhold forgiveness on behalf of his Father—a weighty task, indeed, but one that is much needed in the world. And they have learned from Jesus that they are to use these powers as he himself did: with compassion, sensitivity, and love.

My brothers and sisters in the risen Lord, God's wind and fire are also part of *our* lives. God has brought us together this morning to celebrate the presence of the risen Lord and his Holy Spirit in the Church throughout the world, in this local church, and within the heart of each one of us.

Now, you may object that *you* chose to attend this particular Eucharist this morning. As mature adults, we are accustomed to making decisions and choices; we exercise our freedom as we will. So we freely chose to come to Mass this morning. Nevertheless, in our common faith, we must also affirm that God, in his providence, has also brought us together—not by circumventing our freedom, not by manipulating us, or imposing his will upon us—but by *drawing* us, irresistibly, to the upper room so that we, too, can experience God's fire and wind as did the first disciples.

Because of our baptism, you and I share responsibility for the Church's mission and ministry. We are the disciples of today. We are God's eyes and ears and hands and mouths. In a certain sense, without us he can do nothing—because he does not impose himself on us or on our world.

At times, we are quite like the first disciples. We may keep our religious faith and values hidden in the upper room while we go about our daily life and work. We return to the room on a regular basis, but our fear and timidity hinder us from taking our religious and moral values with us when we return to our homes, the marketplace, or the public arena.

God invites us to the upper room on Pentecost so that we may rejoice in the presence of the risen Lord among us, recommit ourselves to our baptismal responsibilities in regard to the Church's mission, and allow the Holy Spirit to engulf us with wind and fire, thereby empowering us to live out our vocation in the world.

As we join the other disciples in the upper room, we will discover that Mary, the mother of Jesus, has a special place there. She first encountered the Holy Spirit at the annunciation when she accepted the invitation to become the mother of God's Son. And the same Spirit guided and empowered her thereafter to live in accord with her decision. As mother of Jesus, she also became Mother of the Church, our Mother.

Today, we honor Mary and our own mothers in a special way. This is Mary's month and Mother's Day.

On Mother's Day, it is natural to recall fondly our mother's constant love, uncomplaining sacrifices, authentic joy in our successes, unfailing support in our failures, humor and strength, discipline and wisdom, patience, and, above all, faith in God and in us. Our mothers protected and cared for us. They guided our early development in all its dimensions—physical, emotional, mental, and spiritual. We have truly been blessed!

I am happy that my own mother is with me today. I say to her and to all of you mothers who are present: thank you! There are so many reasons to be grateful. But the greatest of all is the *life* and *love* you have given us. And in so doing, you have made it possible for *us* to share in *God's* life and love. What greater gift could anyone give us? So, again, thank you!

Easter Sunday

Holy Name Cathedral, Chicago, Illinois

—April 15, 1990 ─────────────────────────

Anna was an old, old woman. Crippled. Blind. Nearly deaf. Some said she was senile. Others who knew her better insisted that she was perfectly clear of mind, but chose to give a different impression so that others would leave her alone. In either case, Anna spent her days and nights in the solitude of her room, and the quiet of her own thoughts.

Her family often visited the nursing home where she lived. They brought her cookies and presents and news, but it seems as though she didn't care. The cookies crumbled in her shaking hands and fell in pieces to the floor. The presents remained unwrapped, set aside and forgotten. The family news—of babies born, weddings celebrated, and graduations pending—passed between them with barely a nod of interest from Anna.

It was as if she had locked herself up in the tomb of her private thoughts and secret pain, and then rolled a stone in front of the only opening. It seemed clear that this self-imposed tomb would soon give way to one more real. But one day something happened, something quite simple but almost miraculous.

Her grandson Steve visited Anna. And as he looked at her, he saw more than a feeble old woman; more than a sickly patient in nightgown and robe; much more than a cranky, withdrawn, unmanageable burden. He saw his *grandmother* and remembered who she really was.

So he began to tell her of his fond memories:

> "Do you remember, Grandma . . . ?" he began. "Do you remember the times when we built snowmen on cold winter days and then warmed

our toes in front of your hot stove? Do you remember how you taught me to plant seeds in your garden and to gather beautiful bouquets of flowers on warm summer days?

"Do you remember the times when we picked blueberries together and baked delicious pies? The times when we had ice cream feasts in the middle of the afternoon?

"Do you remember the time when you taught me how to dance? Or the time when we stayed up late and watched a scary movie on television? Do you remember the time when you let me drink some wine?

"Do you remember, Grandma?" he asked. "Do you remember?"

And then, with a slow, unquenchable smile, Anna admitted what she had long forgotten, but could no longer deny: "I *do* remember, Steve," she said, beaming, "all except the wine!"

And with that, something was shaken. A stone rolled away. Love surged forth once again, and with it—new life!

Like Anna, there are times in most of our lives when we feel entombed. Times when we feel buried by the difficulty or pain of a given situation. Times when we lose our sense of perspective. Times when we forget where we have been, where we are going, who we are.

There are times when we forget the *real story* of our lives—when we forget that our lives are "hidden with Christ in God." And so we spend these days of Easter remembering the story.

It's not that we will hear so much that's new. Rather, the story is quite familiar: a story of betrayal, capture, and trial; a story of denial, panic, and despair; a story of a body crucified and laid in a tomb—and of disciples terrified, hidden in an upstairs room.

But it is a story of more than that, for *we* remember it. We remember how on that early morning—that *first* morning—in the midst of a darkness that filled their hearts, they looked into the tomb and found it empty! And so today, as we remember, *we* become the ones running alongside Peter—outrunning him, in fact, in our haste to reach the tomb—to see the stone rolled back—to peer within—to *believe* as the Beloved Disciple believed, to love as he loved the Lord.

My dear sisters and brothers in Christ: It is Easter! Let the light of this new day dispel any darkness in our hearts. Let the remembrance of Jesus' life, death, and resurrection bring new life to our souls.

Let us understand that, as we have been buried together with Christ, so we will rise with him—and that his promise of life is the power that can unlock the gift of love within us, so that we too may be the living witnesses of the risen Christ.

Although each of our stories is unique, we have much in common. We share burdens of uncertainty and fear, concerns about health and safety, worries about the well-being of children and parents. We share, too, the risk of taking all our fears and burdens into the seclusion of our hearts, and hiding there in the darkness of our self-imposed tomb.

But Easter pulls us back into the light. The Easter story reminds us of who we truly are. It restores our identity as living witnesses, and challenges us both to live in the light and to bring others the life-giving news that will roll away their darkness as well.

Do you remember the story? Do you remember the love? Then join me in the sacred meal Jesus left us to call us back together as one. Join me in the Bread that is life, in the Cup that is promise. Join me in recognizing the risen Lord in flesh and blood again—in our bodies, our hearts, our spirits.

Join me in giving voice to the words that, in darkness, seemed too much to believe—the words that, in light, cannot be held back: "He is risen! I believe! Alleluia!"

First Sunday of Lent

Holy Name Cathedral, Chicago, Illinois
— February 17, 1991 —————————————————————

Airports are hectic, exciting, but generally well-ordered places. Thousands of people come and go each day, directed, in part, by the loudspeaker reports of arrivals and departures. Most people, however, pay little or no attention to the announcements. Some simply are not listening; most have reservations on flights other than those being called. Certain destinations—Tampa, Phoenix, San Diego—may catch one's fancy for a moment, leading to daydreams about a winter vacation in the Sun Belt, but this soon passes. Ultimately, when passengers hear the announcement of the particular flight for which they are waiting they head for the gate.

In today's gospel, Jesus announces the coming of the reign of God. Are we listening? Do we have other destinations in mind, perhaps a place less demanding? Are we ready to follow him? Are we ready to enter fully into the lenten preparation for Easter?

Lent is very much a *desert* experience. For most of us, the desert may not be an appealing place. It is faraway from State Street or Michigan Avenue both in distance and character. Its remote, harsh environment tests one's courage, one's capacity for survival. In the Scriptures, the desert is described as a place of chaos, far removed from the order of the city and inhabited by wild beasts and Satan.

The desert, of course, has a more immediate connotation for us this year. Today, the Arabian Desert haunts us; it is a place of great danger, chaos, and violence. And so we enter into the lenten desert this year in solidarity with our relatives, friends, and fellow citizens who are at great risk in the Persian Gulf—and with all our brothers and sisters in the Middle East who suffer from the threat or the reality of war, destruction, and death. In the lenten desert this year, we pray as never before that the peace of God's kingdom will take hold in the world, that the violence and bloodshed of war will be discarded as a means of resolving conflicts.

Today's Scripture readings establish a broader context for understanding the meaning of Lent and of the contemporary events which impact our lives.

The first reading, from the book of Genesis, is both striking and consoling. After the great destructive flood, God makes an irreversible commitment, an everlasting covenant, with his creation. "Never again" will he destroy the world by the "waters of a flood." Despite the evil which continues to mar and distort his marvelous handiwork, he will not reject the work of his hands. Sin, death, and destruction have not been eradicated from creation, but God will not be swayed from his healing, saving work. Despite the human obstacles, he will establish his kingdom of justice, harmony, and peace!

God's promise, his covenant, still exists today. It is essential that we believe this and allow its truth to permeate our being. "Reform your lives and believe in the Good News," Jesus said. It helps us survive the chaos which surrounds and threatens us. Indeed, it draws us closer to the source of all life and love.

The first letter of Peter focuses our attention on the paschal mystery—Jesus' death and resurrection—which inaugurated God's kingdom of justice and peace. The purpose of his death, as we heard, is to "lead us to God." Through baptism, we experience salvation and become Jesus' disciples.

This, too, is compelling and comforting. We have a place in God's kingdom which already exists among us. We have only to develop eyes of faith to recognize its presence. The kingdom draws near whenever the gospel is faithfully proclaimed. The kingdom is in our midst whenever we reach out to one another in compassion and love, whenever we share our blessings with those less fortunate than ourselves, whenever we work for civic and racial harmony in our city, whenever two or three of us gather to pray in Jesus' name. The reign of God is, indeed, at hand whenever we work for justice and peace in our community and throughout the world.

But today's gospel also reminds us that building up the kingdom is not easy. Discipleship has its costs and risks. The passage we just heard about the forty days he spent in the desert follows immediately after Jesus' baptism in the Jordan. When he was baptized, God's Spirit came upon Jesus, his divinity was proclaimed, and he was commissioned to do his Father's work. Today's passage shows us briefly, but clearly, that being commissioned to do God's work also involves suffering and conflict, that being God's son or daughter means struggle.

The same Spirit which empowered Jesus at his baptism now leads him into the barren wilderness for forty days. There, in the realm of the wild beasts, Satan tests Jesus' strength. But he is not alone. God's angels minister to him, giving him the strength to resist Satan. By winning this battle, Jesus definitively overcomes the powers of evil for himself and for us. He has already established God's kingdom. And its New Covenant will be sealed in his own blood.

My dear brothers and sisters, the Word of God consoles and challenges us. It assures us that everything is ultimately in God's hands, but it also points out that *we* ourselves are meant to be God's hands. He wants to work through us, through human instruments, as he has always done.

But, as Jesus points out in the gospel, this means that we have to do two things: (1) believe the Good News and (2) reform our lives in the light of gospel values. Both comprise the underlying agenda of Lent. We are invited into the desert where our faith and strength will be tested. We will wrestle with demons who try to lure us away from the Lord and his gospel. But God is always with us to make us strong and to confirm us in faith, hope, and love.

The announcement—that the kingdom of God is at hand—has been proclaimed again today in this holy assembly and throughout the Christian world. It is the time for each of us to make a decision. Will we follow Jesus or not? Will we embrace the gospel and its values, or like travelers in a busy airport, will we wait for another flight? Jesus is waiting for us to answer—not tomorrow or next week, but now. I pray that our answer will be yes. For only then will our lenten journey into the desert lead us to the joy and new life of the resurrection!

Passion (Palm) Sunday

Holy Name Cathedral, Chicago, Illinois
—— *March 24, 1991* ——————————————————

In his poem, "The Wild Dog Rose," John Montague describes a brutal story he heard from an old woman. It was, he said, "a story so horrible, I try to push it away, my bones melting."

"A story so horrible, I try to push it away, my bones melting."

In many ways, the story we have just heard, the Passion of Our Lord Jesus Christ according to Mark, is a story like this. It is a soul-searing, bone-melting story which many of us would prefer to push away. Understandably so. After all, who wants to hear about the persecution of innocence, the betrayal of truth, the attack on integrity, the crucifixion of love?

Yet, horrible as it may be, it is also very familiar. We know it well, almost by heart—not because we've memorized it, but because we know it from the inside! We've experienced it as it is played out in our lives—individually, communally, and globally. It is not simply a story about what happened to an innocent person two thousand years ago. We recognize it because it is a story of our own time; it is *our* story.

It is the story of the helpless addict, in unbearable pain, who hits rock bottom and cries out to God from the depths of his being, that he might "take this cup away."

It is the story of the Kuwaiti man, holding his infant child in his arms, who is forced to leave the child on the sidewalk in front of his home, when, without warning, he is carried off as a hostage.

It is the story of the lonely, isolated child, who does not "fit in," and is forced to endure the ridicule, scorn, and rejection of classmates.

Yes, it is a horrible, but familiar, story; as common as the story of our own sin and suffering and brokenness. That is why it is crucial that we resist the impulse to push it away and refuse to listen to it, or even to deny it.

Instead, we need to embrace the story of the Lord's passion, entering it so deeply that we can see the stories of our lives and our world reflected in it. When we do that, we will feel both its pain and its familiarity. We will realize that we aren't very different from Peter, Judas, Pilate, Caiaphas, or any of the other individuals in the story. Their hopes and dreams, their fear and confusion, their betrayal and hatred, their suffering and sin are similar to our own. Indeed, that is why it is not easy to sit with this story.

But, terrible as the passion narrative may be, it is not only or even primarily a story of *human* suffering and sinfulness. At its heart, it is the story of *God's* irrevocable commitment to us. It reminds us that God embraces our suffering and absorbs our sin, not because he likes or wishes to glorify them, but simply because he loves us and, rather than abandon us, he will take unto himself the very worst we have to offer.

That is the real power of this story. That is why we need to embrace it, painful and repulsive as it may seem. By receiving this story into our hearts, we experience the love of God who is *faithful* to us even in our infidelity; *gracious* to us even in our pettiness; *committed* to us even in our idolatry; *present* to us even in our pain.

My brothers and sisters, as we begin this holiest week of the year, let us participate, once again, in the familiar story of Jesus' passion, death, and resurrection. Let us allow the sacred narrative to shape and change our lives. Let us move beyond the pain of our own suffering and the confusion of our own sin so that we may experience the power of God who loves us despite our sin, who loves us in and beyond our brokenness. Let us allow ourselves to be embraced by God who transforms our suffering and death into peace, joy, and everlasting life in his presence.

Homily

Mother's Day

Seventh Sunday of Easter
Holy Name Cathedral, Chicago, Illinois
——*May 12, 1991* ——————————————————

Not so long ago, a friend of mine, a mother of four, commented on the dangers of attending Mass on Mother's Day. "One runs the risk of having some Barry Fitzgerald type of priest waxing on interminably about his sainted mother from County Mayo."

Well, my friends, be at ease. My sainted mother hails from the Trentino region of Italy, not County Mayo. Although I continue to grow in an ever deepening admiration for the wonderful life she has led and gratitude for her generous love for me and my sister, I will not spend these precious moments extolling her virtue.

Instead, as my mother would have it, I ask you to focus your attention on Jesus. While the presence of so many mothers and their families among us today reminds me of the need to celebrate motherhood, we are here primarily to enter more deeply into the mystery of Jesus Christ. It is *his* story which we have gathered to hear. It is *his* meal which we share.

But celebrating Mother's Day and gathering to celebrate the risen Lord are not at odds. Mother's Day provides us with an occasion to celebrate what some have observed as a maternal dimension of the mystery of the Lord. We recall that some of our predecessors in the faith, Julian of Norwich and St. Thérèse of Lisieux, for example, found it helpful in prayer to liken Jesus to a mother. We also remember the trend among our medieval ancestors to use the image of the mother pelican, piercing her own breast to feed her young with her life's blood, in depicting the mystery of the Eucharist.

373

One of my favorite gospel passages presents Jesus, lamenting the future of Jerusalem (Matt 24:37): "Jerusalem, Jerusalem, you kill the prophets and stone those sent to you. How many times I yearned to gather your children together, as a hen gathers her young under her wings . . ."

This particular image appeals to me, who, as pastor of the archdiocese, longs to gather under our wings those who feel alienated from the Church.

The portion of John's Gospel, assigned by the Church for this seventh Sunday of Easter, serves as a window which enables us to gaze into the prayer life of Jesus. He is about to depart from this world and enter into the glory of his Father. In a manner reminiscent of a mother praying for a child as she or he is about to enter a world beyond her immediate control, Jesus intercedes for his disciples. He asks the Father to protect the family he has gathered and to keep them one. He summarizes his ministry among them. He has kept careful watch. He has entrusted to them the Father's word. Now, he is sending them out into the world, consecrated in truth.

The first reading provides us with an insight into the experience of the fledgling early Christian community as it ventured out into the world after Jesus' ascension. The Acts of the Apostles shares with us stories of power, as the first Christians began to carry out the Church's mission. These stories stir up feelings similar to those associated with listening to the stories of young people starting college or beginning their careers. One can feel the power, the enthusiasm, the thrill. One can also sense the fear, the uncertainty, the worry.

It must have been exciting for the disciples to begin the process of calling forth new leadership. Yet, Peter may well have spent a few anxious moments before assuming his role as leader and standing up among the 120 disciples, calling the church to order.

Today's post-Ascension, pre-Pentecost liturgy captures something of the mystery of the disciples' connection with, and separation from, Jesus. It is the mystery of his presence within his absence. It is the mystery of the Holy Spirit. Reflecting on this mystery, St. John writes in today's second reading:

> No one has ever seen God.
> Yet, if we love one another
> God dwells in us
> and his love is brought to perfection in us.
> The way we know we remain in him and he in us
> is that he has given us of his Spirit.

We share in the mystery of connection with, and separation from, the Lord. We share in the mystery of his presence within his absence. Here, again, reference to motherhood may assist us in our contemplation of this essential mystery of our faith. I say "essential" because the Church's whole life—its preaching, its sacraments, its ministry, and its structures—have their foundation in the Lord's presence within his absence.

In my own experience, I have found my mother strangely present to me even when she is physically absent. When confronted with a painful decision, I can hear her voice speaking within the depths of my conscience. When feeling overwhelmed by a particular task, I can envision her assuming the difficult responsibility of taking care of two small children after the death of my father. When I become too busy to pray, I can see her quietly saying her prayers, and I remember to keep my priorities straight.

The example falls short in helping us savor the mystery of Christ's Real Presence in his absence. But it may help in our celebration of Jesus, who now lives at the right hand of the Father, but is also here, among us, and will one day return to bring us the fullness of the kingdom.

I began with a promise not to spend this Mother's Day homily extolling my own mother. However, I cannot talk about Jesus on Mother's Day without making some reference to the woman who has been so instrumental in bringing me to him. Many of you have gathered here today with the woman who has played the same role in your lives. Others gather here in spiritual communion with their mothers, who may live across the miles or who have gone home to God's kingdom in heaven. And we also recall the woman who played such an important role in Jesus' life—his mother, Mary, whom we all honor and call blessed among women.

My own mother loved to set before us a table filled with an abundance of good food. The Lord, like a good mother, invites you to this table of the Eucharist, where we taste the abundance of his love. At special meals, there are always toasts for honored guests. Ladies, as we come to this Table of the Lord, in the name of the Church, I salute you. Thank you and bless you for your motherly love. And now, to all, in the Spirit of Jesus, I say, "Come to the Table of the Lord Jesus who, in the consecrated Bread and Cup, shares with us his Body and Blood as a memorial of his death and resurrection and as a pledge of future glory."

Homily

Ash Wednesday

Holy Name Cathedral, Chicago, Illinois
——February 24, 1993 —————————————————————

Perhaps you saw the news item that in France, for the last fifteen weeks, the number-one-selling single record is a rap song by a young Frenchman who has attained the ripe old age of five. The title of the song is: "It's Tough to Be a Baby." Apparently things are tough all over because the record is also topping the charts in Hong Kong, Greece, and Spain.

Of course, things aren't really tough for the young singer, especially as he piles up hundreds of thousands of francs. But sometimes children's songs—the anonymous, heard-in-the-street kind—strike a more ominous note. There's an old children's song, for example, that has the line, "Ashes, ashes, all fall down." Like many so-called children's songs, that one seems to have an underlying sentiment that is quite adult. The song faces a reality that should not haunt children, but often does.

Because of a fall, as it were, everything comes down to ashes. There's a realism in the line about the end of things that is both childlike and chilling. No matter how solid and lasting things seem, they pass away, barely leaving more than a residue.

The line from the song may in fact describe the fate of the universe. Scientists who study life, the universe, and everything, have a name for this phenomenon: entropy. Entropy is happening when the battery in your watch runs down or a belt in your car's engine snaps or a star collapses. Someday, the whole universe will burn itself down to a heap of ashes. End of tale.

We believers, though, don't think that's quite the whole story. Today we begin a season of forty days which culminates in a Holy Week. Because of the hope-filled, supreme message of that week, we have a different way of beholding ashes. In fact, we bless them.

We bless ashes today and put some on our foreheads because there is another side to the story. These ashes were gathered from burning the palms used to celebrate the Lord's entrance into Jerusalem on Palm Sunday. That triumph would end in the defeat of Christ's death. However, that death leads to the most important triumph of all.

Others may look upon ashes as a symbol of loss. For us they are a sign of our confident hope that life can rise from death. At the beginning of Lent, the ashes remind us of the season's end: through death to life; through the crucifixion to the resurrection. So we present ashes as an offering, to stand for all about us that passes away. In these next few weeks, we want to join more closely to the Lord Jesus and his passage through death to life. Through his death and resurrection all that passes away will be reborn into a new and everlasting creation.

The gospel's call to give alms, pray and fast in secret so that only God knows about it finds us Americans in a time when the word "sacrifice" is being bandied about as something all of us should do. And we're being asked to do it today to save our country's future, the children's future, from a dangerous flirtation with entropy. But in the end, it will be a matter of obeying the laws and curbing our consumption.

As the prophet Joel says, fasting and prayer are the way back to God, a way to return. Ashes are a good symbol for a season of fasting and praying. When we fast or pray we are aware of how tied we are to things that do not matter. We get used up and burned out and stressed out over nonessentials. The call to return to God reminds us of how far away we can get.

We forget that all good things come from God. We begin to think that we ourselves are the source of all good. Certainly, our daily routine finds us doing worthwhile things. But we have become dependent on much else that gets in the way of our steady achievement to God's love and power in our lives. All those things and worries that don't really matter, on which we spend so much time, amount to less than the ashes we bless today. We need to clear a space in our lives for the Lord Jesus, the only lasting source of peace.

The ashes on our foreheads will be a sign that we have taken a step. They signify our willingness to start now, not to put off our return to God another day. As Paul says, "See, now is the acceptable time; see, now is the day of salvation!"

Some people think that people who put things off are lazy. But that's not the case. In fact, procrastination is caused by fear. When we put something off again and again that we know we should—and could—do, it's because we're afraid that what we do won't be perfect. We're afraid that we won't be able to match our idealized picture of what we hope to accomplish.

The ashes we will wear today remind us that if we wait until we're perfect to return to God, we'll never do it. This is a season of forgiveness and grace. We forgive ourselves for not being perfect, because God has already forgiven us. We allow God to heal us and build us up with the power of his love. He created us for a more perfect life. Our reconciliation with one another and with God already gives us a hint of what that better life will be like. As Paul says, in Christ we can become the righteousness of God. That is, we become representatives, ambassadors, of Christ to the world that needs to be reborn from the ashes.

The sacrifice of almsgiving, prayer, and fasting during Lent has a special purpose. Through these experiences God will change us. As God showed when he made us, the ashes of our lives are a worthy place for God's creative power to shape and sustain us. Once again this Lent we are offered an invaluable opportunity to let ourselves be prepared to stand on the threshold of resurrection of life. If we do this, we can be sure that through us Christ can raise others from the ashes.

In this Eucharist, let's pray for one another, that we may, through this special season, abstain from what we do not really need and help our brothers and sisters who need our help. Let's pray that we will be loving not only in great and exceptional moments, but above all in the ordinary events of daily life. With God's help, we will find that it is not so tough to be God's children.

Mass for the Newly Initiated

Ascension Thursday
Holy Name Cathedral, Chicago, Illinois
——*May 20, 1993* ———————————————

"And know that I am with you always, until the end of the world."

Some of you may know that my parents came to this country from northern Italy before I was born, and settled in Columbia, South Carolina. Compared with some of the states of the north and the northeast, there aren't a great many Italian-Americans in South Carolina. Nor are there a great many Polish-Americans or Hispanic-Americans or Asian-Americans for that matter; again, compared to a city like Chicago. In a place like South Carolina, it is easier to forget that most of our forebears came from somewhere else. It is easier to forget that the United States, along with all of the other countries of the Western Hemisphere, was once known as the "New World."

I still have family in Italy; as a matter of fact, I plan to visit them this coming summer. And from time to time, they have come to visit me here in Chicago. To return to the home of one's parents, to look into the faces of one's aunts and uncles and cousins and observe traces of one's own face, is to retrace the path of one's heritage.

In a more subtle way, when I listen to an aria from a favorite opera, or lift a fork full of pasta to my mouth, I am reminded of the place from which my parents came. I suspect that the same is true for many of you: whether your forebears came from Europe or Africa or Asia or Latin America, you carry in yourselves vestiges of their language, their customs and beliefs. Their blood flows in your veins.

379

To reminisce in this way is disagreeable for some people. Perhaps they had to flee from their ancient homes, or perhaps they were brought to this country against their wills. "We are *Americans*," they like to say. This is understandable. Perhaps their memories of their homelands are too full of pain and loss, and what they have found here is too important. In their memories, at least, they have to make a break.

And there are dangers in misplaced ethnic pride. One need only think of the troubles in Bosnia, or Northern Ireland, or the Middle East to recognize that when people's identity is rooted more deeply in what distinguishes them from others than in what they have in common, hostility and belligerence are bound to follow.

Rather, the value of looking back toward the horizon from which one came is to situate oneself more intently in the present. The value of looking back is to claim one's place in the world, and then turn around and press forward.

We gather this evening to look back together. Forty days ago, on the vigil of Easter, all of you came, as pilgrims, to a new world. The paths that led you to that night were many and varied. Some of you came after years of wandering and searching. For others, the journey was less wearisome. Some of you had not practiced any religion for many years. Others traveled less far, from other Christian churches. Some of you came here to join the rest of your family who were already settled in the Church. Others of you, painfully, had to leave family behind.

But for most of you, I trust that the experience of the Easter Vigil was not unlike an arrival. After months or years of traveling, after the experiences of the catechumenate and election, you arrived, at last, at the doors of the church and were baptized or received into the embrace of the Church. You were anointed with the oil of redemption and you feasted with us at the Lord's own table. I pray that the memories are marked by joy and thanksgiving.

If you will remember, the Scriptures of that night retold the stories of another journey, one of which you are now a part. We heard the story of the journey's beginnings, in Eden, at the creation of the world. Next we heard about Abraham, "our father in faith," who had left his father's home to wander to a land that God would show him. And then we heard the account of Israel's escape from Egypt, their "passing over" through the Red Sea on their way to the Promised Land.

Finally, we heard the account of another passage; it is the turning point of the story. From this point on, we are on our way home.

[T]he angel spoke, addressing the women: "Do not be frightened. I know you are looking for Jesus the crucified, but he is not here. He has been raised, exactly as he promised. Come and see the spot where he was laid. Then go quickly and tell his disciples: 'He has been raised from

the dead and now goes ahead of you to Galilee, where you will see him.'
That is the message I have for you."

They hurried away from the tomb half overjoyed, half fearful, and ran
to carry the good news to his disciples . . .

The Scriptures tell us that for forty days more he appeared to them,
teaching and comforting them. Finally, he gathered them on a mountain-
top, and as we have just heard, he said to them:

> Full authority has been given to me both in heaven and on earth; go,
> therefore, and make disciples of all the nations. Baptize them in the
> name "of the Father, and of the Son, and of the Holy Spirit." Teach them
> to carry out everything I have commanded you. And know that I am
> with you always, until the end of the world.

Then, as St. Luke tells us, "he was lifted up before their eyes in a cloud
which took him from their sight." Christ, God-made-flesh, truly human
and truly divine, returns to paradise to open the doors, to "make a place
for us," to prepare a home for us in heaven. Having wandered from the
time of Adam and Eve, we have been given Christ—Christ the Path, Christ
the Guide, Christ the Journey's End—who now goes ahead to show us
the way, to write the map in our hearts, so that where he has gone, we
may follow.

It is a paradox that, as pilgrims, you journeyed along diverse paths to
enter at Easter the company of the Church; and having been received,
you became, along with us, pilgrims once again. For that is who and what
we are: a pilgrim Church, eyes fixed on the horizon, tracing the footsteps
of the Master.

But ours is not an immigrant group, fleeing, frightened, worried eyes
cast over our shoulders. No, ours is a joyful company, calling out to others
along the way, "Join us! Come along! Go up with us to the city of the
Lord, where Christ awaits us at the banquet of heaven!"

And having passed over the frontiers of death, paradoxically, he who
awaits us is with us still, with comfort and calm, urging us on. "Know that
I am with you always," he says, "until the end of the world."

Pilgrim sisters, pilgrim brothers, it is good to have you with us; to share
with you his blood, flowing in our veins; to share with you the memories
of the land from which we came; to share with you his promise, a promise of life that never ends.

Forty days ago, do you remember, on the night of your rebirth, a fire was
lighted, a flame was kindled, and a voice sang out in the receding dark:

> Jesus Christ yesterday and today
> the beginning and the end

Alpha and Omega;
all time belongs to him
and all the ages;
to him be glory and power
through every age for ever. Amen.

. . . All time belongs to him and all the ages; to him be glory and power through every age forever. Amen!

Fifth Anniversary of AGLO (Archdiocesan Gay and Lesbian Outreach)

Trinity Sunday
Our Lady of Sorrows Basilica, Chicago, Illinois
——*June 6, 1993* ——————————————————

My dear friends in the risen Lord:

On Trinity Sunday we celebrate in a special way the source of all that is good for us: the one God who exists in a unity of three Persons. Liturgically, Trinity Sunday invites us to look back over the whole year and recall how we celebrate the great gifts of the Holy Trinity. Advent prepares us for the Christmas season, when we celebrate the Father's gifts to us. Lent prepares us for the Easter season, when we celebrate the great gifts of his beloved Son. Finally, Pentecost reminds us of all that we receive through the Holy Spirit. From the moment of our birth, we have been watched over by the unique and threefold love of the faithful and eternal God.

Love is the thread that connects all the Scripture readings today. To Moses, God proclaims that his name is love: "The Lord, the Lord, a God merciful and gracious, slow to anger, and abounding in steadfast love and faithfulness." The five rapid orders that St. Paul gives to the Corinthians all revolve around the theme of mutual love: "rejoice, put things in order, encourage one another, be of one mind, live in peace." The Corinthians should make love of God and love of neighbor their daily project. Then the "God of love and peace," the God of Moses, will be with them. In the gospel, Jesus tells Nicodemus how great is God's love for us. God gave his only Son so that we might be saved.

If this is true—and it is!—that means that there is a mysterious depth to our lives. There is a wonderful, marvelous dimension residing just below the superficial and the ordinary. Our search for that mystery brings us here to worship. As we began our prayer, we made the Sign of the Cross. With that act, we placed ourselves before the mysterious presence we seek. So, what we do here, we do in the name of the Trinity.

The noted author, Monica Furlong, tells how she encountered the mysterious presence of the Trinity. She was twenty, and the event led her to convert to Catholicism. One rainy day she was standing at a bus stop. All around her were people and stores and cars. At her side was a friend with whom she was traveling downtown. I will quote her own words about what happened next:

> All of a sudden, for no apparent reason, everything looked different. Everything I could see shone, vibrated, throbbed with joy and with meaning. I knew that it had done this all along, and would go on doing it, but that usually I couldn't see it. It was over in a minute or two. I climbed on the bus, saying nothing to my friend—it seemed impossible to explain—and sat stunned with astonishment and happiness.

Ms. Furlong experienced one of those moments of coming into contact with the mystery of God's love for the world. The Trinity of Father, Son, and Spirit is present in the deepest dimensions of our lives. He loves the world so much, that he sent his only Son to save us.

Of course, as St. Paul reminded the Corinthians, the real test is in our daily lives. Someone recently told me the story of a young man who attended a Pentecostal service for the first time. It was in a small country church in the South where he was visiting his aunt. He was surprised and a bit turned off with everyone jumping around and shouting. "Don't worry, honey," his aunt said. "It ain't how high they jump that matters. It's what they do when they come down!" Our encounters with the Trinity in worship and prayer are really only part of the picture. Our worship is only as good as the quality of our love for one another—what we do when we return to our so-called ordinary lives.

What about those times when we face difficulty or even death? Even then, when we seem most alone, somehow we know that we are not really alone. For the God of steadfast love is with us: the Father, the Son, and the Holy Spirit.

Today we dedicate a new shrine honoring St. Peregrine, whose intercession over the centuries has been especially helpful for those who suffer from cancer and other serious, life-threatening diseases. Many miraculous physical cures have been attributed to this saint's intercession.

Our suffering reminds us of the greatest need we have for the power of the Trinity in our lives. Living with ourselves and others can be hard enough. What can be hardest of all is learning to live with cancer or a similar problem—personally or in the case of a family member or close friend.

Should we simply "grin and bear it"? The British author and Catholic convert, G. K. Chesterton, once said that "there is a vital objection to the advice to grin and bear it. The objection is that, if you merely bear it, you do not grin." Trying to bear our suffering alone can lead to a grudge against God. Or, perhaps, self-pity will eat away at us until our problem becomes twice as bad as it was. And there's always the temptation simply to give up.

"Why me?" we may cry out to God. But since our birth, the Holy Trinity has watched over us, whether or not we recognize or acknowledge this. Yes, we find it easy to assume that God is with us when good things happen. But when bad things happen—things we certainly do not deserve, like disease and misfortune—God's steadfast love is *still* with us.

There are limits to our own resources. If we are to be creative and courageous in our suffering, we cannot rely on ourselves alone. We need another source of energy, strength, and courage. That is the power of the Holy Trinity which works through us. Jesus said that he is with us always, until the end of the world. He also said that we do not have to fear the world, for he has conquered it. Moreover, he sent the Holy Spirit to comfort and help us. So, we have available to us the inner power of the Trinity to meet the difficulties and hardships of life.

We add St. Peregrine's prayers, and the prayers of countless believers, to our own as we seek that healing power in our lives. On this occasion I thank the Servite Friars of the Order of Servants of Mary for their compassionate service in the Archdiocese of Chicago. We are especially grateful that you have relocated this National Shrine of St. Peregrine here at Our Lady of Sorrows Basilica. May all who come here, especially those with cancer, find peace of mind and heart, spiritual comfort, and a source of grace.

My friends, on this Trinity Sunday and on every day of the year, let us be open—especially in unexpected times and places—to encounter the Holy Trinity of compassionate love. And let us pray that the love we celebrate here this morning will have a powerful effect in our lives!

Ash Wednesday

Holy Name Cathedral, Chicago, Illinois
—*February 16, 1994*

Our memories have recently been seared by visual images of glowing ashes—around Los Angeles and Sydney, Australia—as fires raged out of control and wreaked havoc and destruction. Our consciences have been repeatedly scorched by the images of the flashes of explosions and the resulting injuries and deaths of innocent civilians in Sarajevo and Mogadishu.

Ashes—both real and symbolic—have a bad reputation. They symbolize jobs lost, opportunities missed, marriages shattered, reputations lost, lives burned out, children murdered. Eventually the ashes—the residue of loss in our lives—lose their glow, become cold and lifeless and seemingly useless.

But is that true? Are not ashes also used as fertilizer? Do they not contain nutrients which can nurture new life? As a matter of fact, their usefulness reminds us that, as Christians, we understand the ashes we wear today primarily as a sign of *hope*. They remind us that there is more to the story of the Christian life than loss or death or failure.

Yes, the ashes we bless and put on our foreheads today have a deeper meaning. They were gathered from burning the palms used last year to commemorate Jesus' entrance into Jerusalem on Palm Sunday. As we know, the crowds who acclaimed him were fickle; within days they clamored for his crucifixion. However, the ashes remind us that his death led to the most important victory of all—his resurrection. The risen Lord overcame death itself!

So, for us believers, ashes are a sign of our belief that new life can rise from death. On this first day of Lent, they focus our attention on what awaits us at Easter, forty days from now—the new life in Christ which we have been invited to share.

May the ashes we wear today help us remember the age-old lenten agenda of prayer, fasting, and almsgiving. In order to share in the new life of Easter, we must draw closer to the Lord in prayer. We must fast in order to reach the deepest hungers of our heart and to stand in solidarity with the poor, the hungry, the homeless. We must be willing to share our blessings—whether they be great or small—with those among us who are vulnerable and needy.

In short, our wearing of the ashes on our foreheads today—a very public gesture—must be matched by an interior commitment to spiritual renewal. Let us begin right now! Listen again to St. Paul's words: "Now is the acceptable time! . . . Now is the day of salvation!"

Easter Sunday

Holy Name Cathedral, Chicago, Illinois
——*April 3, 1994* ——————————————————————

When Mary Magdalene arrives at the tomb, it is still dark. This is the darkness of the abyss at the beginning of time. This is the darkness that covered Egypt before the Exodus. This is the darkness into which Judas slipped on his mission of betrayal. Shadows stand in the Scripture for the power of sin and evil, the oppressive weight of fear, the burden of hopelessness.

Mary Magdalene had been liberated by the words, the gestures, the love of Jesus. He had mediated to her the forgiveness of a God who is friend, especially to sinners and outcasts. In Jesus, she found something she thought she had lost permanently: a reason to live. But now life and hope are gone. The one who was everything to her had been handed over to sinners, condemned to death, crucified as a common criminal, and laid in a tomb recently hewn from a formation of rock. A great stone had been rolled across the entrance of the tomb, sealing off the body of the one she loved, and stifling her hope. Yes, indeed, it is dark when Mary comes to the tomb.

Do you see how the Magdalene speaks to and for all of us? As we make our way through life, we taste beauty and pleasure. We savor friendships. We know what it means to love and to be loved. We sense God's mercy. In short, we encounter moments of grace, rumors of angels. But even the richest experiences, even the greatest accomplishments, even the most intense joys are, we know, eventually swallowed up in death. Death is the enemy that threatens us, the ghost that haunts us, the abyss into which all of our hope is finally drawn. Do we not, like the Magdalene, ultimately face that terrible tomb with the unmovable rock before it?

But upon arriving at Jesus' sepulcher, Mary is shocked to see that the stone has been moved away. Her first instinct is to think that grave robbers have been at work, that Jesus' body has been spirited away to another place. There is a lovely irony here, for a grave robber has, indeed, been at work, and Jesus' body has, indeed, been taken elsewhere. The Father, the Creator of the world, the God of life, the One who promised the prophet Ezekiel that he would bring his people from their graves, has robbed and despoiled a tomb. He has thrown away that terrible stone, symbolic of the finality of death. He has opened the door that was thought to be permanently closed!

The Father of mercies has taken the body of his Son—that body which had gone down into the utter silence and powerlessness of the grave, that body which had been enveloped by death—and has raised it up to share in his glory. In this wonderful "grave robbery" we see that God hates death. We see that hope and trust and life have the final word. We realize that the rumors of angels are more than rumors. In the vacant tomb of the risen Christ, we see that our wildest hopes are not wild enough, that our most extravagant dreams are not extravagant enough, that our deepest joy falls infinitely short of the joy that God holds out for us!

Full of fear and confusion, perhaps just beginning to understand, Mary Magdalene races to inform the disciples that Jesus' tomb is empty. Peter, the leader of the Twelve, and the disciple whom Jesus specially loved, run to the tomb. It is wonderful that they run! The news of resurrection is something that all of us, in our heart of hearts, long to hear. Many of the giants of our theological and mystical tradition concur in saying that all of us are made for God, that our deepest longings are disguised yearnings for union with God.

Resurrection from the dead means that the most powerful obstacle to that union has been overcome, that nothing can finally separate us from what we most desire. So, when they hear that Jesus' tomb is empty, the disciples begin to suspect the great truth. The idea that captivates and attracts all human beings begins to take hold of them. And, thus, they run, hoping against hope. And all of us run with them, equally eager to hear the news, to see the empty tomb. The disciples, hurtling themselves toward their goal, stand for all of us, pressing forward with enthusiasm towards God's promise.

The Beloved Disciple soon outdistances Peter and races ahead of him toward the sepulcher. It is a beautiful detail worth pondering. He outruns Peter, not only because he is younger, but also, at a more symbolic level, because he represents the power and the energy of love. Remember that this is the disciple who entered into a specially intimate relationship with the Lord, the one who leaned on Jesus' breast at the Last Supper. The Beloved Disciple, the father of all mystics, listens to the Lord's heart, is attuned to the movements and inclinations of his soul. Perhaps, therefore, more than the Magdalene, and more than Peter, the Beloved Disciple strongly suspects *what* the news of Jesus' absence from the tomb means. Perhaps more than anyone else, the Beloved Disciple is filled with fire—and thus he runs with special fury.

When he arrives at the tomb, he stares into the emptiness. He sees and believes. In seeing *nothing at all*, in appreciating Jesus' absence, the Beloved Disciple truly sees. He realizes that the risen Lord has not, like Lazarus, simply returned to this world and this life. Contemplating the empty tomb, he knows that Jesus has gone to the Father, has entered into the infinite richness and beauty of God.

My dear brothers and sisters, like the Beloved Disciple, we stare this morning into the vacant sepulcher of Jesus Christ and are lost in wonder and praise. We see in faith that we are invited to share in the very life of God, that we are called beyond the frustrations, anxieties, fears, and sufferings of this world to an adventure of discovery, to a journey into God. The *emptiness* of Jesus' tomb is an *opening* to fullness of life.

On this day of days, on this Easter morning, we see, with Magdalene, and with Peter and the Beloved Disciple, that God is nothing but enduring love. And our response is *Alleluia!* "Praise God!"

Annual Archdiocesan Charismatic Conference

Pentecost Sunday
Holy Name Cathedral, Chicago, Illinois
—*June 4, 1995*

Praised be Jesus Christ! My dear brothers and sisters in the Lord, I am delighted to have this opportunity to address you this afternoon. Seeing so many of you, from all parts of the archdiocese, representing diverse cultural backgrounds, speaking a variety of languages, and all filled with God's Holy Spirit, I cannot help but think of that exhilarating scene described in the first reading from the Acts of the Apostles.

The disciples of Jesus, that ragtag band of uneducated, rather cowardly, and altogether ordinary men, stand in the heart of Jerusalem, the Holy City, and boldly proclaim the Good News of Jesus Christ to people from many nations. Not afraid of arrest or persecution, not fearing the taunts of the crowd, not cowed by their own unworthiness, these simple men hand themselves over to the fiery Spirit of God and allow that power to seize them and speak through them.

My friends, this surrender to the Spirit, this fearless proclamation of the gospel, is the responsibility and the joy of every follower of the Lord Jesus, but it is your special mission in the Church to remind us of this call and this task. It is my firm conviction that one of the greatest fruits of the Second Vatican Council was the rise of the charismatic renewal in the Catholic Church. Over the past several decades, you and your predecessors have imitated the risen Lord who said, "I have come to light a fire on

391

the earth." Through your preaching, your witness, your enthusiasm, your celebration of the gifts of the Spirit, you have enlightened the Church, stirring her to greater life. The charismatic renewal has been like that "mighty wind" that shook the upper room on Pentecost morning and, in time, rocked the entire world. My friends, always remember what you as a community continue to offer to the whole Church of Jesus Christ and to a society so desperately in need of the fire of God's love.

Friends, on this great feast of the Holy Spirit, let us reflect on One whom some have called the most overlooked of the divine Persons. In the classical theology of the Church, the Holy Spirit *is* the love shared between the Father and the Son or, in St. Bernard's loving image, the kiss or embrace of the Father and the Son. As such, the Holy Spirit is not so much a thing or a substance as an activity, a passion, a shared energy. The Father and the Son go out of themselves in a sort of mutual ecstasy, and that ecstasy *is* the Spirit. St. Thomas Aquinas speaks of the Third Person of the Trinity as the "spiration," the breathing back and forth of the Father and the Son, the heartbeat, the living rhythm of God. The power that seized the apostles on Pentecost, the wind and flame that animate your lives and ministries, is this divine "breath" or "wind."

This is not simply an abstraction; it is at the very heart of the Christian life. What we announce to the world, and what we strive to embody in our lives, is this message of love, this message of ecstasy; the Spirit is the pearl of great price, the meaning of life, the only sure path to joy. When we forget ourselves in love—as the Father and Son forget themselves in mutual love—we come to fullness of life; we discover who we are. When we imitate the very being and energy of God, allowing ourselves to be caught up in the wind of the divine Spirit, we find that happiness that God wishes, above all, to share with us.

Psychological research has confirmed that, when people forget, transcend, go out of themselves, they are most content. This could involve reading a book, climbing a mountain, engaging in a lively conversation, playing a complex game, or performing an act of love or charity. This also corresponds to what the Christian spiritual tradition has always taught— that we human beings are happiest when we look beyond ourselves; when we love God and one another because then we imitate God who *is* love.

My dear friends, this is why Jesus, in our magnificent gospel reading, *breathes* the Holy Spirit on the disciples. The risen Lord wants them to share *in God's very inner* being and energy! He wants them to participate in the "spiration," the breathing back and forth of the Father and the Son in the Spirit. He wants them to experience some of the ecstasy of the Godhead. In his intimate conversation with his disciples the night before he died, Jesus summed up his life, his message, his teaching in a very simple command: love one another. He did not mean, simply, be kind to one another or be ethically upright; no, he meant "be who God is." He urged his followers—and that includes all of us—to live in the self-forgetting love of the Holy Spirit.

After breathing on his disciples, Jesus, of course, sends them out to proclaim, to live, to embody this Spirit. All of us Christians—including you members of the charismatic renewal—have this great task of bearing the breath of God to a world that is dying from selfishness and fear. To the violent streets of the city of Chicago, and indeed its metropolitan area, you must go; to families torn apart by dissension and hatred, you must go; to young people in the grip of despair, you must go; to your friends and colleagues caught in the trap of materialism and careerism, you must go. In a word, to all those who have forgotten how to lose themselves in love, you must carry the breath of God's Spirit.

Wind, breath, flame, energy, life in the Holy Spirit of God: this is our beginning and our end! This is our mission and our task! This is our hope!

Homily

Chrism Mass

Holy Name Cathedral, Chicago, Illinois
——April 2, 1996 ———————————————————————

During this holiest of weeks we focus our attention on the saving events that culminated Jesus' life: his passion, death, and resurrection. That is why it is rather striking that the readings for this Chrism Mass take us back momentarily to the *beginning* of his public ministry, back to Nazareth, his home town. In its synagogue he adopts the program of an earlier prophet: to bring glad tidings to the poor, liberty to captives, and recovery of sight to the blind.

As we walk with Jesus from Nazareth to Jerusalem, we see the many ways in which he fulfills his mission—always showing great compassion toward people and offering faithful praise to his Father. He embraces little children, frees lepers of a debilitating and enslaving disease, teaches his listeners about the things of heaven. Along the way to Calvary, Jesus also prepares his disciples to carry on his mission after his death and resurrection. He promises to give them all they need to continue his creative and saving work in the world.

We have gathered here this afternoon to remember Jesus' mission and, as his disciples, to recommit ourselves to it. As we do so, we bless the oils we use in our ministry. In particular, we bless chrism, the oil used in the sacramental celebrations of baptism, confirmation, and ordinations of priests and bishops. In each of these sacraments the chrism symbolizes both a moment and a life of *consecration*.

When we are baptized, confirmed, or ordained, we are anointed with chrism and consecrated in that sacramental moment for the rest of our lives. From then on we exist for the Lord and his work. We are set apart to bring compassion to others and offer praise to God.

When we are consecrated for *compassion or service*, we are moved by God's Spirit to *bring Good News to the poor:*

—to both the materially and the spiritually poor;

—to all those who have exhausted their own human resources;

—to the child of divorced parents who worries that he has caused the rift between his mother and father and feels that no one in the world cares for him;

—to the well-to-do widow who sits by her apartment window, watching the world pass by, feeling deeply the pangs of loneliness, the ache for human companionship.

The poor need to know that God is with them and for them. They need to know, to be convinced, that God will never abandon them, no matter how difficult life may be.

We are also moved by God's Spirit to *proclaim freedom to captives:*

—to people entrapped by ignorance or sin or oppressive social structures;

—to victims of alcohol and drug abuse weighed down by the chains of their addiction;

—to those obsessed with a single issue, closing in on themselves and becoming alienated from their neighbors.

Captives need to hear the truth of God's enduring and liberating love. They need to know that, with God's help and their own courageous efforts, they can be set free.

We are also moved by God's Spirit to offer *recovery of sight to the blind,* to offer light:

—to those who live in the valley of dark death, hopelessness, depression, violence, greed, or exploitation;

—to racial bigots who stumble along life's highways and alleys, reaching out to attack others or defend themselves rather than to embrace brothers and sisters who can walk alongside them and make the going easier;

—to those whose sole preoccupation is making money, who miss the sheer enjoyment of life itself.

The blind need the light of Christ to guide them out of darkness into the fullness of God's warmth and love.

When we are consecrated for *praise or worship*, we are moved by God's Spirit to make a bold proclamation of our gratitude for the mysterious work of God even when we do not see it clearly—or even dimly. We are challenged to believe in the Lord's presence and care for us—especially when things go badly in our lives. Acknowledging that, of ourselves, we can do nothing, we take the risk of entrusting our lives to God in praise and thanksgiving. We are moved to say with the early Church: "To him who loves us and freed us from our sins by his own blood, who has made us a royal nation of priests in the service of his God and Father—to him be glory and power forever and ever! Amen!"

To accept and live our consecration for service and worship, for compassion and praise, requires deep faith. It calls for times such as this, when we gather around the symbols of our tradition and remember our consecration, and support one another in our growth in faith. Let us use our creativity and courage to proclaim Good News, to speak of true freedom, to offer sight and perspective, to proclaim what God has done for us. We have all been consecrated for God's work. We are salt, leaven in this world. We are truly "a royal priesthood, a holy nation, a people he claims as his own."

My brothers in the ordained priesthood, consecrated and set apart for God's holy and priestly people, I urge you to join me in renewing our consecration for compassion and praise. Let us mobilize all our intelligence, let us call on the Lord with all our hearts, let us stretch our spirits, so that we can continue to offer a leadership of faith to our people.

This afternoon—as laity, religious, and clergy—we have come together in harmony and unity. But sometimes tensions exist in the Church between clergy and laity. As we understand more clearly the role and responsibility of the laity, and promote and celebrate their increased participation in the life and mission of the Church, some tend to downplay the importance and unique charism of the ordained priesthood. Even priests occasionally begin to lose sight of the great gift of the priesthood to the Church.

To build up the body of Christ and to achieve the Church's mission—a mission inherited from the risen Lord—both laity and clergy are called to work together harmoniously, respecting and affirming the gifts of both. Only in this way will we be a community of faith over which the risen Lord truly presides, a community in which all members—in virtue of their consecration through baptism, confirmation, and holy orders—witness to Jesus' saving deeds before the entire world and work for the emergence of the kingdom he proclaimed, a community whose members—laity, religious, deacons, priests, and bishops—understand and accept their uniquely different but complementary and necessary roles, working together for the good of all.

May the blessing and Eucharist we celebrate this afternoon, and the saving events we celebrate later this week, renew us in mind and heart, prepare us to rediscover, with the freshness of spring and Christ's risen life, the greatness of our consecration.

Ordinary Time

150ᵗʰ Anniversary Mass

Old St. Mary's Church, Chicago, Illinois

—*May 7, 1983* ——————————————————————————

We gather this evening to celebrate the 150ᵗʰ anniversary of the establishment of this parish dedicated to Mary, the Mother of God, under the title of the Assumption. An anniversary is a time to look at the past and to reflect on the many blessings God has given us.

Eighteen thirty-three. It was the year that Chicago was chartered as a city. It was 150 years ago this past Thursday. It was the first Mass to be celebrated in a city that was to become in many ways a center for Catholicism in the New World! The priest, Father St. Cyr; the place, a log cabin near the so-called Sauganash Hotel. For the staggering cost of $400, a church was soon built—at the corner of State and Lake. And so St. Mary of the Assumption came to be.

Somewhere in its migration to Madison and Michigan, to Madison and Wabash, to 9ᵗʰ and Wabash, it became known as "Old St. Mary's." Somewhere in that migration, the Diocese of Chicago was officially established. Somewhere in that migration, the Sisters of Mercy opened a school in connection with the parish. Christian Brothers followed suit—and somewhere, too (in 1845, to be specific), St. Mary's was consecrated as the first cathedral of Chicago.

When the fire of October 1871 destroyed our city, it took with it St. Mary's Cathedral, the bishop's residence, Mercy Convent, and the schools. Though the *title* of cathedral moved north of the river with the dedication of Holy Name in 1875, the *spirit* of St. Mary's as the mother church refused to die. Like the city and the diocese, St. Mary's, too, rose from the flames.

What a rich history, with the first black priest ordained in America ministering especially to black Catholics; with business and offices and shops reshaping the neighborhood and turning it into a "cosmopolitan traveling community." These were the words of Archbishop Quigley, my predecessor, who affectionately dubbed St. Mary's as "the Church of the Stranger." Sensitive to the special needs of this unique community at the turn of the century, he invited the Paulist Fathers to minister here. In their Christ-like hospitality, they have seen to it that no one who comes to worship here need feel a stranger.

I express my gratitude to the staff here today—and to all who went before them: to all who extended a welcoming hand, a warm word to the traveler, to the stranger—to the Filipino, the Mexican, the office worker, the shopper; to all who have labored to make the Loop a circle of love, a symbol of Jesus Christ who embraces everyone and to whom no one is a stranger.

God's praise has been sung here. And in the presence of Father O'Malley, we express a special word of gratitude to him and all who made the Paulist Choir a world-recognized expression of that praise.

God's word has been proclaimed here by the priests of the parish, the guest lecturers and preachers.

And God's Mother has been honored here—both in the eloquent sermons of the late Archbishop Fulton Sheen, a favorite friend of Old St. Mary's, and in the quiet prayers and intercessions of countless thousands who have worshiped here in the past 150 years.

I said earlier that an anniversary is a time to look at the past and to reflect on our rich heritage. But an anniversary is also an occasion to look forward to the future. While this parish community should remember its great heritage with gratitude and with pride, it cannot simply rest content with that heritage. The really important question is: how can this heritage—the lived experience of the past—help you to understand and to be more sensitive to the needs of the present and future? The anniversary of Old St. Mary's is significant only to the extent that it reminds us, as St. Paul did the Corinthians many centuries ago, that it is the people of the parish who are really "God's building"—not the brick and mortar we see around us. As the parishioners of St. Mary's today, you are expected to continue building on the foundation laid by those who went before you. I believe that Mary, the patroness of this church, has a great deal to tell us about how we should go about this—now, in our contemporary setting—because she is an outstanding model for Christians of all ages. She can show us how to grow spiritually; to deepen our intimacy with the Lord. Let me explain.

A well-known theologian and spiritual writer has said that ultimately all spirituality, no matter what specific form it takes, is Marian. When I

first heard that, I was somewhat startled. But as you reflect on this statement, it begins to make more sense. For what do we mean by spirituality?
What is its basis?

In the final analysis, all spirituality is rooted in that fundamental orientation of the community and the individual to the gospel's demands of us,
namely, that we be *hearers* of the Word, that we *incarnate* the Word in
ourselves, and that we *manifest the glory* of the Word in our lives. If this
is the norm, then Mary is the perfect example and her spirituality can
become the model for the entire Church. Luke's account of Mary's response to God's invitation to be associated with him in his plan of salvation clearly substantiates this.

When the angel Gabriel told Mary of God's plan, she did ask: "How
can this be since I do not know man?" But when she learned that she
would conceive by the Holy Spirit, she hesitated no longer. "I am the
maidservant of the Lord," she said. "Let it be done to me as you say." Because Mary heard God's Word and responded to it, it became incarnate in
her. Shortly afterwards, as we heard in today's gospel, she hastened to
visit her cousin Elizabeth who had also conceived a child in extraordinary
circumstances. On that occasion, Mary sang her song of praise in which
she witnessed to the power of God's Word in her: "My soul proclaims the
greatness of the Lord," she exclaimed, "my spirit rejoices in God my Savior for he has looked with favor on his lowly servant . . ."

So Mary truly heard the Word, allowed it to become incarnate in her,
and witnessed to its glory and power in her life. This is why she is the
model for our own interaction with the Word. For, like Mary, we must see
the Word not as something external to ourselves but as the most profound mystery within our own being. And also, like Mary, we must cherish this mystery within us as a precious gift which God gives us both for
our own personal well-being and that of the entire human family.

Just as this interaction with the Lord profoundly affected Mary's life,
so will it make a powerful impact on our lives. It will radically influence
the way we go about our task of witnessing to Jesus in a world which all
too often has stopped listening to him and his Church. May Mary intercede for us and, by her intercession, help us to live up to our responsibilities as believers in the Lord and members of his Church. In the final
analysis, this is what Old St. Mary's is all about. And this anniversary
loses its significance if it does not call us to a greater commitment to the
Lord in the future.

In conclusion, I simply want to tell you, from the heart, how happy I
am to be your bishop. This visit and Mass today is just the first of many
occasions that we will come together to worship, to grapple with the
many matters which will concern us as members of the Church, to discuss ways in which we can join with all men and women of good will, no

matter what their religious convictions may be, in helping to make this a better world, a more just and more loving world.

In order to accomplish our task we need, in addition to our common faith and commitment, a great deal of mutual trust and confidence. Only if this trust and confidence exist will we be able to accept each other as we are; only then will we be able to understand and accept our weaknesses and imperfections and build on our strengths and talents. Only then will we be able to forget ourselves and focus our attention on Christ, our Savior. I promise, with the help of God, to be the kind of bishop whom you will trust and in whom you will have confidence. And I know from all that I have heard about you that I can trust and have confidence in you.

Let us, therefore, pray for one another so that—like Mary—each of us may realize the wonderful things that God has done for us, and how much he has enriched us with his love and mercy. May we receive from our faith in Christ and this Eucharist the strength and grace to continue our work of service in and for the kingdom of God. For only to the extent that we do continue this work does this celebration today assume meaning and relevance. May we never tire of witnessing to the power of God in our lives; may we never cease to be the body of Christ.

Homily

Thanksgiving Day Liturgy

SS Faith, Hope and Charity Church,
Winnetka, Illinois

―*November 24, 1983*―――――――――――――――――

This is a difficult day on which to pray. It is not that we lack things for which to offer prayers of thanksgiving. We have been given so much! There is an embarrassment of blessings for which to give thanks. It is just that it is so hard to concentrate on Thanksgiving morning. While our hearts should be flying to God in prayer, our stomachs are growling in anticipation of the feast to come.

Food is the problem.

Some of you may have heard that I like to cook. I do not have much time to do it any more but, when I do, it is a great relaxation. I know well the dangers of a good recipe. How difficult it is to concentrate on prayer today when our noses have already sniffed the product of good recipes: steaming sweet yams covered with marshmallows, brown sugar and butter; rich brown gravy spilling over snow-white mounds of potatoes; tangy cranberries on tender dark turkey; pumpkin pie smothered in whipped cream. All melting in our mouths.

See what I mean? The dangers of a good recipe.

These Thanksgiving treats, however, are not the only recipes in circulation today. I would like to tempt you with another, more important recipe. It is a "recipe for holiness"—one suggested so beautifully by the Scriptures today.

Why a recipe for holiness? Well, what is it we bring to God today? What can we bring to the God who has so abundantly blessed us? How can we begin to show him our thanks for the many undeserved blessings in our lives? What can we give him?

Thousands of those rams we heard about in the first reading? Ten thousand streams of oil? Our children and our children's children? Or maybe our credit cards?

The prophet Micah suggests that all God asks of us today is that we do right, love goodness, and walk humbly with him. That's all: that we do right, love goodness, and walk humbly with God. That, my friends, is a succinct definition for holiness. It is so clear, precise, and simple. Yet you and I both know that the doing of right, the loving of goodness, and walking humbly with God are difficult in our complicated world. We need more help. We need more specific recommendations. In short, we need a recipe for holiness.

And so we look to today's gospel. I would like you to think of the Beatitudes as a workable recipe for holiness in our world. Life as envisioned by Jesus in his Beatitudes—the Lord's own holiness lived out in our lives—is the most perfect gift we can bring to God. It is the best prayer we can offer.

What are the ingredients of holiness? What does the Beatitude recipe call for?

It calls for a *poverty of spirit:* for lives less cluttered with needless possessions, for hearts hungry for the important things of life; for a stripping away of our endless luxuries, our chemical abuses that numb and insulate, our lust for the nonessential. It asks that we spend less time filling our many wants so that we might better know our singular need of God.

The recipe calls for *sorrow*. This would seem to be the least desirable of ingredients. Yet sorrow simply asks that we open our hearts to the risk of love, that we be vulnerable to the sacrifice and sometimes hurt that love demands. The prerequisite of a sorrowing heart is a heart that has known love; a heart that has loved and has been loved. In an age that emphasizes the need for looking out for "number one," and attaches great value to insulating oneself so as not to be hurt, this recipe calls for the risk of love and the vulnerability that comes with love.

Another ingredient is *humility*. Egos inflated by a consuming self-love have no room for someone else. It is the lowly, the humble, the selfless among us who show us the meaning of life. For life is fullest when we give it away, rather than when we clutch it exclusively for ourselves. A generous helping of humility and lowliness ensures that we might die so that Jesus might more fully live in us and among us.

The recipe also calls for a strong dash of *peacemaking*. Peacemaking does not mean simply reaching some general agreement that peace is a good thing. It is much more than merely expressing a vague hope that peace might come some day. This recipe, instead, calls for concrete, practical peacemaking; for the doing of deeds that will promote peace with justice in our relationships, neighborhoods and world, deeds that will prevent war in our time. This is one of the most important ingredients in the recipe for holiness. Sad to say, it often seems to be in short supply today.

The final ingredient for which the recipe for holiness calls is *mercy*. Mercy knows that the finger we point at the accused also points back at us, the accusers. Mercy knows that no one is without sin, no one is clean enough to cast the first stone. Mercy knows that judgments leveled against others are miserly things; but that compassion offered is balm. Mercy gathers the peripheral, the broken, the wounded walking among us. Mercy knows that when we sit on our hands we are actually tying up God's hands because God works through us; our hands are really his.

These ingredients are generously spiced with singleheartedness and a passion and a thirst for the right. But there is a cost for these ingredients and spices. No money can buy them. There is no fixed price tag. It is only our willingness to lay down our lives for God and his kingdom that will make these ingredients available. We must be willing to sacrifice ourselves. This is a most necessary price to pay, because the presence of holiness always seems to bring out the enemies of life in our world. The forces of darkness will take measure of us and do their worst. So one must be willing to suffer if one wants to be holy. It has always been so, as we know from the Scriptures, and will always be so.

My brothers and sisters, there are recipes and there are recipes. Some push the limits of our waistlines. Some push our human limits as we discover all we can be in God.

Today I proclaim a simple message to you. I speak as your brother and shepherd, struggling in my own life to find ways to give back to the Lord a fraction of the goodness God has given me. What God asks from all of us in return on this Thanksgiving Day is that we do right, love goodness, and walk humbly in holiness. What God asks is that we fashion our life to the fullest extent possible around his Beatitudes. Let that be our Thanksgiving.

Know, too, my friends, that I give thanks for you today. I know of your goodness, your generosity, your great desire to follow in the footsteps of the Lord. Today I promise you my energies and indeed my very life which I give in service to you, for the sake of the Lord.

Happy Thanksgiving to all!

ry, Mundelein, Illinois
— *September 7, 1984* —

My official relationship with this seminary, as you know, is determined by a number of awesome—and sometimes burdensome!—titles, like chancellor and archbishop. But today I come to you in a very personal and loving way; I come simply as Joseph, your brother.

I first want to welcome each of you. In a special way, I want to welcome all the new students and faculty who begin a new phase of life at St. Mary of the Lake Seminary. May God bless your time here and make you aware of his presence among you. I also want to welcome back students from other years, as well as veteran faculty. It is good to be with friends, and my prayers are with you all.

Like the poor, we always have with us the students of the archdiocese. You are obviously dear to me. I am your bishop, and I think that over the past two years I have shown you, in many ways, how much I care for you and what you mean to me.

But there are also so many of you here from other dioceses. If it should happen that you feel overwhelmed by the city or by this giant archdiocese, please know that I also share these feelings on occasion. After all, I came here from Charleston by way of Atlanta, Washington, D.C., and Cincinnati. I want you to know that your presence enriches this seminary and our local church. To the extent that you will permit me, I'd like to be your brother and spiritual father. Your own bishop won't mind, as long as you ultimately go back home! I pray that your experience here will help you to serve your own local churches well.

408

This afternoon I want to share some thoughts about you and me and Jesus and the Spirit. The link, the thread, is *discipleship*. For you and I are disciples of Jesus by the power of his Holy Spirit. This is your formational theme for the year. You have already heard Bishop Morneau's eloquent words on this topic. But as we celebrate the Mass of the Holy Spirit, I want to add my own reflections about the *cost* of discipleship, its *joy*, and its *future*.

First, the *cost* of discipleship. Dietrich Bonhoeffer, the German Lutheran pastor and seminary professor who was martyred by the Gestapo in 1945, often emphasized this theme in his writings. He lived and died in such a way that we are all reminded that to follow Jesus is no simple or easy matter. It is costly. It is also suffused by his truly amazing grace, made possible by his precious blood.

Many of you, whether new or returning students, know that there is a cost in following Jesus. Some have given up a promising career by the world's standards. Each of you gives up the ordinary pattern for young men—marriage and family. And, in all candor, I have to tell you that responding to our very normal craving for love and intimacy as men committed to celibacy is not without its pain, no matter how sincere and noble our motive.

Moreover, there is a cost in following Jesus in terms of our ministry, our outreach to others. And my experience tells me that in the future—when you will be exercising your priestly ministry—the cost will grow. I can personally testify to that. For example, I have faced keen opposition—in the form of innuendoes, slanted or false interpretations of what I have said, the impugning of motives, etc.—as I have worked for peace, as I have proposed the need for espousing a consistent ethic of life, as I have tried to witness to the values of the gospel and the teaching of the Church in the face of indifference and hostility. Just recently, too, in my visit to Poland, I saw firsthand the cost of discipleship in a nation subjected to a Godless, totalitarian government.

This really should not surprise us. Remember Jesus' warning in this afternoon's gospel? "Remember what I told you: no slave is greater than his master. They will harry you as they harried me. . . . When the Paraclete comes, the Spirit of truth who comes from the Father—and whom I myself will send from the Father—he will bear witness on my behalf. You must bear witness as well. . . ." So we have a promise of suffering, a promise of the cost of discipleship.

I hasten to add, however, that the situation is not totally bleak; quite the opposite. We also have a promise of the Holy Spirit. And so, alongside the cost of discipleship, there is its *joy*. In a way that no one can fully explain unless he has shared the reality, we simply *know* that to follow Jesus and to be close to our brothers and sisters who follow him is a great joy.

The essence of happiness is to break out of our sad or lonely isolation and become a part of the mystery of God and the mystery of one another. In Jesus, this is possible. His Holy Spirit is our bond of unity with the Father and the Son, and with one another. When we pray in the unity of the Holy Spirit, we pray as the Church, the community of disciples.

Again, I would like to tell you something about myself. As the cardinal archbishop of Chicago, I receive considerable news coverage. People recognize me wherever I go. My life for the most part is very public. But, beneath all that, I am simply a human being like yourselves. Sometimes, like you, I become discouraged. I wonder where it is all going to end. I often feel inferior. And I worry that people might not like me or accept me; their criticism really hurts. Moreover, despite all my busyness, I am subject to the sense of loneliness that is so much a part of the human condition.

However, as I get older, I become more and more aware of another reality, far better and greater than all the rest: my *real joy* is to be near the Lord, to be his disciple. My joy is sustained and nourished and supported when I stand before and with the community of his disciples and celebrate the sacraments, when I preach the word, when I am able to extend the Lord's compassionate care to those who are needy or hurt. My joy is particularly nourished when I turn to him in personal prayer; when I stop all I am doing and enjoy a little relaxation with him; when—by the world's standards, at least—I am willing to "waste" time with him.

So the joy of my discipleship is to be *with him* and to be *with you*. And, in both of these moments, it is the Spirit that binds us to him and to one another.

Besides the cost of discipleship and its joy, I want to say a word about the *future* of discipleship. Let me state it boldly: the future of discipleship is *here*—in this room—this afternoon. No matter how the Church changes in the next forty to fifty years, right now *you* are the ones who will exercise special spiritual leadership in the Church, the community of disciples. You will have more responsibility for shaping the future than you can imagine, perhaps more than you would care to know about just now. But the responsibility is there. What *you* do academically, formationally, spiritually, pastorally will have an impact on the future discipleship of millions of people. This is not just rhetoric; it is a fact!

Let me hasten to add a word of thanksgiving to that somber pronouncement. Thank God that the future does not depend on us exclusively! As we heard in this afternoon's first reading, it is really the work of the Holy Spirit. As the prophet Joel proclaimed: "Then afterward I will pour out my spirit upon all mankind. Your sons and daughters shall prophesy, your old men shall dream dreams, your young men shall see visions; even upon the servants and handmaids, in those days, I will pour out my spirit. And I will work wonders in the heavens and on the earth."

Join with me in praying for an abundant outpouring of that Spirit. And then don't be afraid to dream dreams, to see visions, to prophesy, to plan, to create, to do something new! We are approaching the end of a century that perhaps has had more shadows than light. We have a chance to enter into a new era.

But the kind of era it will be depends on the kind of vision the world will have; the kind of vision that people will choose to live by. As priests, as disciples of the Lord Jesus, you will have a lot to say about that.

My prayer is that you will have the courage to face the challenge creatively, to allow yourselves to be flooded by the Spirit so that, like a rushing river, you can help to shape and cleanse and water the land, helping new life break forth from what was once parched earth. Know that in responding to the call of discipleship, I am with you. Know that your brother, Joseph, shares with you both the agony and ecstasy of discipleship.

By the Spirit, may we be his disciples at all cost!

By the Spirit, may we rejoice in his love and the love of one another!

By the Spirit, may we dream and build a future that rests in his hands!

Homily

Scouting Mass

Church of St. Dismas, Waukegan, Illinois
—September 22, 1984 ————————————————————

My dear sons and daughters, peace be with you all!

Something great is taking place here this evening. For the first time, Boy Scouts, Girl Scouts, Explorers and Webelos, Camp Fire Girls, and Junior Daughters of St. Peter Claver from all the councils in the Archdiocese of Chicago are gathering to pray and play together. "Kumbaya," the theme you have given this weekend, means "be with us." At this special moment, God is certainly with us. One look at your shining faces and this beautiful night is proof of that.

Let me tell you a secret. I have never earned a merit badge! So, I am greatly honored that you, the finest scouts in our entire archdiocese, should invite a tenderfoot like me to celebrate this Eucharist with you.

Immediately after Mass we are going to have a great campfire. There is something very special about a campfire. Campfires are scouts' best friends. When your boots and socks are wet and you are shivering with the cold, there's nothing like the warmth of a campfire. When you're frightened—by stories of ghosts or the Cricket Man, or all those scary, crawling, snarling things in the dark—there's nothing like a campfire to reassure you. When your stomach is growling with hunger, a campfire is the next best thing to your mother's kitchen. And, when you're homesick and lonely, there's nothing quite like a campfire to turn a group of people into a family. There's something almost magical about campfires. They always seem to draw the best songs, worst jokes, loudest giggles, and tightest circles out of us. God loves us best when we are at our best around campfires. I suspect

412

that Jesus liked campfires. In fact, there is something holy about a camp-fire, for God's heart is like a campfire—it warms, it comforts, it nourishes, it brings us together in a special way as brothers and sisters.

I am going to ask a special favor of all you scouts and leaders. We need more campfires in our world. I would like *you* to build more campfires in our world. Now, before you decide to start setting fires in your homes or schools—and tell the police "Cardinal Bernardin told us to do this!"—let me be more specific about the kind of campfires I have in mind. I want you to build "kingdom campfires"—campfires of God's kingdom.

Any good scout knows that the first step in building a campfire is choosing the proper location. You must find a spot that has some shelter from the weather and a good place to store firewood, a spot that will pose no danger to the surrounding campsites and that, nevertheless, is close to your tents.

In building our "kingdom campfires," how do we find the right spots? Look for places *where God's people are hurting*. Build your campfires wher-ever there is loneliness, poverty, or need—places where people are ex-cluded. Do you know someone in your school who is a loner, someone who is always mocked and laughed at, left out or ignored? That person needs to share your campfire. Do you know someone in your neighborhood who is shut-in and isolated, lonely or needy? That person needs to share your campfire. Wherever people are hurt by rumors or rejection—wherever people are discarded because they don't seem to fit in or don't have the right clothes, color, or witty comments—wherever people carry broken hearts or bruised spirits, it is *there* you need to build "kingdom campfires."

Okay, so now we know *where* to build the campfire. Now, *how* do you start a good campfire? Any good scout knows that you can't have a camp-fire unless you collect all the essential ingredients: matches, kindling, and firewood. Without these elements, you won't have much of a fire, if any at all!

What is the necessary ingredient you need to start "kingdom camp-fires?" We will need *charity or love*. We need to decide to live our lives, not for ourselves, but for others. We need to be people who are willing to serve others. Without the daily, concrete practice of love and service, we will never build the campfires the world needs. Your hand can be used as a fist—but charity can make it into a hug. Your talents can be used to make you "number one," but charity can make you first in God's king-dom. Your eyes can be used to watch your beautiful reflection in the mir-ror, but charity can help you see beyond your heart—and help you notice the God-given beauty of the people around you.

Practice charity. Do something for others every day. The more you practice charity, the better you become at it. Charity is as important to "kingdom campfires" as kindling is to scout fires.

Now we know how to *start* these campfires, but how do we *keep them burning?* Regular fires need logs. Your "kingdom campfire" will need *courage.* Some people leave God on the doorstep as they leave church. While they are inside, they listen to the Lord's gospel and think about it. But once they leave, they leave empty-handed and empty-hearted. I hope you won't be like that. To keep the campfire burning, you will have to have the courage to live your faith all week long. As the Holy Father, Pope John Paul II, has said this past week in Canada as he addressed young people like yourselves: "Have the courage to resist the dealers in deception who make you pay dearly for a moment of false paradise—a whiff of smoke, a bout of drinking or drugs."

Have the courage to pray and to get involved with your parish even though some might say you're "not so cool" for doing so. Have the courage to hold on to your Catholic morals and sexual values when the world around you tries to offer you lust instead of love, easy pleasure instead of a lasting relationship. You will need a lot of courage to show everyone who you really are—a Catholic who lives faith in all the moments of life. If you can burn with this courage, people will be drawn to the warmth of your campfire, just as we are all drawn to our campfire tonight.

My brothers and sisters, scouts and leaders—all of you have earned merit badges. You are skilled in something—camping and hiking, swimming and cooking, woodcraft or other arts. This evening I'm inviting you to begin working on a very special merit badge—one awarded for building "kingdom campfires." Let me sum up the requirements for the badge. (1) Look for God's lost and lonely people. (2) Bring them the best of your love. (3) Live your lives of service and charity with courage.

Tonight, after Mass, as we sit together around our campfire in that special magic of closeness and love, remember that we are called to build kingdom fires throughout our lives. You are not going to do this alone— we will do it together. You will do it with God's love and mine as well.

Homily

25th Anniversary

Church of St. Alexander, Palos Heights, Illinois
—September 23, 1984 ———————————————

My dear brothers and sisters in Christ! I am very happy to be at St. Alexander's this afternoon, celebrating this twenty-fifth anniversary with you. I want to thank Father Crosby, Father Murphy, and all of you for your kind invitation.

There are some moments in life which are pure prayer. It seems that no matter what we might be doing or what postures our bodies might be taking, our hearts and souls are kneeling in prayer. A parish anniversary is such a time—a frozen moment of thanksgiving for all we have been for one another and of petition for all we want to be in the future. The presence of our gracious and loving Father in our midst is the silver thread that is woven through the fabric of the past twenty-five years. It is the theme which gives focus, significance, and beauty to the story of St. Alexander's.

The parable of the workers in the vineyard in today's gospel is a perplexing story. It seems to offend our notion of getting a fair day's wage for a fair day's labor. What is Jesus trying to tell us? What does he want us to learn? What does this parable mean for you as a parish as you stand on the threshold of the next twenty-five years?

My friends, let me tell you a contemporary parable. Once upon a time there was a skinny, little seventh-grade boy who played football on the local team. Actually he hated football, but he played on the team to please his father. During the first game of the season, the boy failed miserably at every play. It wasn't that he wasn't trying, but he dropped the ball, missed tackles, and literally ran away from the real action. After

415

every mistake, he looked to the sideline and saw his father's face. Each time he saw a barely concealed disappointment. And, finally, the game ended. The son walked in utter despair and utmost anxiety back to his father, fearing that he would be disowned! But the father greeted him with a hearty hug and invited him to share a deep-dish pizza. The son, incredulous and blinking back tears, blurted out, "But, Dad, I was awful!" His father, blinking back some tears of his own, answered, "Son, you'll never start for Notre Dame, but I never want you to forget—you'll *always* be my son, I love you!"

How much like that seventh grader we are at times! We can so easily misunderstand the true nature of God's grace and love, thinking that we have to *earn* them! Don't we sometimes view life as a complex of merit systems through which we earn love and acceptability? Don't we feel that rewards should be exactly proportionate to achievement, punishments to failures? Don't we feel that we have to be good to be loved, worthy to be graced by God? And don't we feel sometimes that people's pain and misfortune are just what they deserve?

If we have answered "yes" to any of these questions, then this parable is clearly meant for us. Jesus' point is precisely that our legalistic, merit-reward understanding of life can lead us to misunderstand the very nature of God's grace and love. They are *free gifts* of God. Grace is the unexpected, amazing, awesome entrance of God into our lives—something that we *do not* and, in fact, *cannot* earn, deserve, or merit.

The tragedy in Jesus' parable is that some workers could not see and rejoice in the fact that there is great, unexpected grace in life. Not understanding this, they run the risk of excluding themselves from future opportunities to enjoy it. God's gracious dealing with us shatters our understanding about how things are ordered in our world. Any substantial growth in faith and maturity depends upon whether we can notice and accept God's immense generosity. He is generous with his love and mercy even though we are sinners. It *does* matter how we live our lives, of course. We are expected to live as he has taught us to live. We can close ourselves off from his grace and love because he does not impose his gifts upon us. But the point of the parable is that we simply do not earn or merit God's love.

What concrete meaning does this have for our lives? Let me suggest some possibilities. How many young children, like the seventh grader in my story, feel they have to earn their parents' attention and love? How many teenagers feel they have to wear the right clothes, say the right things, listen to the right music in order to be considered accepted? How many people feel that inward beauty is not nearly so important as outward beauty? How many feel that their basic worth and value lie in the work they produce—that they are only worthwhile to the extent that they are productive? When any of us lives with these presuppositions about our basic value and worth, we are ill at ease and ultimately dissatisfied. All of these attitudes are examples of our attempt to earn love, self-worth, and personal value.

The Good News in today's parable is that we are endlessly loved and utterly precious. We simply cannot earn love or worth. It is beyond us to do so. We can only trust Jesus' word that we *are* loved, precious, and always forgiven when we repent and are willing to try to do better. Actually, the fact that we cannot earn God's love makes the gift of it so much more precious! That is the reality about God and the truth about human life.

How many of us feel we have committed an unforgivable sin or that we are only loved by God when we are good? How many of us feel we aren't worthy to be a lector or eucharistic minister? How many of us feel that we are too ordinary to be called to special service in the Church? The gospel today calls us to move beyond these feelings, beyond a mere merit-reward understanding of life. If we believe that we have to earn God's love, that grace is the proportionate reward for our achievements, we risk missing all of the graced moments of life and the very presence of God among us. We will continue to live with hungry or paralyzed spirits.

My brothers and sisters, what does this mean for you as a parish beginning your next twenty-five years? My hope and prayer is that the incredible expanse of God's love will empower you to expand and enrich the scope of your parish life.

When we reflect on this parable deeply, with our hearts as well as our minds, we begin to sense the almost unbelievable, loving reality of God that Jesus knew so well. Jesus knew that God's love for people is endless. Jesus knew that, rooted in God's power and healing love, the lame could run again, the dead could rise, and Satan would fall like lightning from the sky. Jesus knew that God's infinite capacity to forgive could transform a sinner like Mary Magdalene, a fisherman like Peter, a persecutor like Saul, making them heroines and heroes in the faith. Jesus knew God. Can you, the people of St. Alexander's, come to know, experience, and proclaim this same God more deeply?

Many people helped lay the physical and spiritual foundations of this parish. But, now that there are no more buildings to erect, what will you do to build up this parish? Will you build this parish community into a living church, a breathing tabernacle where God is present and worshiped?

This archdiocese needs parishes with depth of faith and breadth of vision. We need models for what it means to be Catholics and a Catholic community in the 1990s and beyond. How can we have an impact upon our culture with our gospel values in ways that liberate and transform? How can we best use our priestly and lay resources in parish leadership? In a society that is becoming increasingly fragmented and polarized, how can St. Alexander's be a loving, unified sign of what it means to be the People of God, a Catholic-Christian community? This is the vineyard in which God, with great urgency, calls us to work. With God, all things are possible. With each other in God, you will continue to write the history of your parish, the story of your faithfulness to God and to one another.

The ultimate meaning of life lies in coming to terms with God's gracious dealing with us. To understand and experience that love is to be created anew. My prayer for you all is that you experience the depth of God's love and that you become the light of the world he has created you to be. Know that I too search in faith, engaged in the same enterprise with you.

As you go into the next phase of your parish history, go with God's love as you go with mine.

Homily

Catechists' Annual Resource Day

Chicago, Illinois

——November 3, 1984 ————————————————————

It had been a very long, frustrating day! Jesus was exhausted. First he had crossed the Sea of Galilee. Then the usual crowds had gathered and pushed in on him. He had climbed the mountain with his disciples. The crowds had followed close behind. Then he had fed the multitude, and they had misunderstood its meaning and his motivation. Finally, he had been forced to flee from everyone to this secluded spot—at last, alone with his thoughts, his feelings and his Father. And so he prayed . . .

"Abba, Father, may we talk awhile? I need to talk with someone who understands me, someone who cares. I need to unburden my heart. Being a Messiah is not an easy task! Did you see all those people today? Why do they keep coming to me, pressing in from all sides? What more can I do for them? They seem so hungry, so thirsty for something better in life. They are like sheep without a shepherd, wandering to and fro, afraid but bold, defenseless and yet trying to live independently of everyone—even of you. They need healing—not simply of their bodily illnesses, but even more of the ache in their hearts, the anxiety in their minds. They are so needy!

"I did what I could for them today. As always, I talked with them about you and your love for them. I tried to show them you continue to care for them by feeding them. But I don't think they understood very much of what I was saying or doing. They're bombarded by so much bad news that they seem incapable of digesting much Good News at one sitting. If they are going to follow me, I will have to stay close to them and they to me. But I really can't do it all. There are so many of them. They are going to have to help me. What I teach them, they will have to teach one another. Yet, somehow I know I'll have to stay in close touch with the teachers to make sure they understand what they are teaching and live according to the gospel.

"As you remember, the plan has been to continue my mission and ministry through the apostles. But did you see how they acted today? Sometimes I wonder if I picked the right people! Philip once again demonstrated he doesn't understand me. I have to admit Andrew was a bit better today. At least he found some food that I could start with. Nevertheless, his efforts today still don't offset his introducing his brother to me! Peter! I love him, but you know what he's like. One minute I think he may have some leadership qualities, the next he says something impulsive and stupid. And did you see the doubting look on Thomas's face when I prayed over the five loaves and two fish? I couldn't help but smile when he saw what was happening during the distribution of the food. His eyes got very big, but I don't think he understood very well the significance of what I was doing. I could tell Judas was already calculating what a profit we could make by my multiplying food as I did today. Sometimes I feel the only ones I can count on to stand with me are my mother and Mary of Magdala.

"I know you sent me to usher in a new age, a new creation, to make a new beginning. But people seem so accustomed to the old ways even though it dulls their senses, keeps them in chains, makes them think poorly of themselves. It's going to take a lot of work to change all that—despite the power you have given me. Frankly, it's sometimes easier to multiply loaves and fishes than to transform peoples' minds and hearts! I'm not questioning your wisdom or how you created human beings—so full of mystery, freedom, and the capacity for independence. But even you must have shuddered when the crowds tried to make me king this afternoon! Things nearly got out of hand! (pause)

"I think you're right. I'm going to have to stay very close to my disciples and all the people, especially the teachers. They need my presence, my support, and challenge. They will need to be brought together as a community and nourished frequently. I will have to teach them how to care for one another, how to serve one another. I will have to instruct them how to celebrate and implement your Word, how to receive and enjoy your nourishment.

"Actually, I've been thinking a lot recently about what lies ahead for me and my disciples. It probably would be wise to begin telling them about Jerusalem. I saw their enthusiasm—especially Zebedee's sons—when the people wanted to make me king today. I simply have to tell them about Jerusalem! They really can't hear me when I tell them about the future, when I warn them about the costs and risks of being my disciples. I'll have to emphasize this more when I'm with them.

"I also want to arrange some special way to say good-bye to them before I am arrested—some special way for them to remember me. I'm wondering if today's events offer a clue. Maybe I could prepare a special supper for them and share my innermost thoughts and feelings with them on that occasion. It has always been special to sit in fellowship with them at table. It would be a wonderful occasion to tell them how much I love them. Maybe you and I could think this over, and we could discuss it sometime later."

"Thank you, Father, for your understanding presence, for your listening heart."

At this point, Jesus abruptly jumped up and looked toward the setting sun. He had just remembered that his disciples had decided to set sail just before sunset. They didn't know where he was! He had fled from them also! Perhaps they would think he had deserted them! Jesus began to run down the mountain, tripping over boulders, dodging obstacles, slipping on loose pebbles. As he ran, he caught sight of Peter's boat in the distance—leaving the shore. Jesus realized he would not be able to catch up with them, and they could not hear his voice at this distance! He suddenly became deeply aware of how much he loved them despite their weaknesses—how much they needed him. He kept running until he reached the shore out of breath.

Then he gasped one additional prayer: "Father, I hope you won't mind if I do something extraordinary to catch up with Peter, Philip, Andrew, and the rest." And then he walked on the water . . . !

Religion Enrichment Day

Chicago, Illinois

──*March 5, 1985*────────────────────────────

It *will* happen!

Unexpectedly, perhaps. At the beginning, in the middle or at the end of the day. In the corridor between math class and science—or on the playground during recess—or at lunchtime somewhere in between peanut butter sandwiches and granola bars. I don't know when or where, but I *do* know: it *will* happen!

Suddenly your routine will be broken by a question:

"Teacher, why did my mom and dad get divorced?"

"Teacher, why did my grandma have to die?"

"Teacher, why do people hate and kill one another?"

"Teacher, why am I different from everyone else?"

A question—a simple, innocent question. But, whether or not you attempt to offer an answer, you know deep within that you've suddenly stumbled into deeper waters, that you've unexpectedly plunged into the mystery of life. And, at that moment, everything is different.

It *will* happen! It might be with a fellow teacher, a parent, or a student. It may happen in the middle of a conversation, during a midyear conference, or right in the middle of your lesson plan. I don't know when or where, but I do know: it *will* happen!

Suddenly you'll find yourself caught up in something more profound, something more important, than your present task. It may be an awareness of the meaning of friendship. It may be a realization that what you thought you were teaching to *others* is really meant for *your* ears, *your* heart, *your*

422

life. It may be a moment of letting go of a worry or anxiety and allowing someone else—even God—to share a burden you thought was yours alone.

A moment of insight. A simple, quiet, private revelation. But whether you completely understand it or not, you sense that something has shifted: the flow of learning and insight from you to others has been reversed. Now *you* are the learner, *you* are the recipient of God's grace.

It *will* happen!

Maybe it will happen while you're repeating the same instructions for the hundredth time—maybe as you're enforcing rules which have been ignored once too often or stretched just a bit too far—maybe on a day when you're struggling with a head cold, lamenting the lack of progress indicated by semester grades or just ready to surrender to the fatigue brought on by a winter that lasts much too long. I don't know when or where, but I *do* know: it *will* happen!

Suddenly, one, two, or even an entire classroom of students will begin to change and learn. Suddenly you'll sense that they're more aware of the presence of God in their lives, more thankful for their blessings, more willing to share or to serve, more caring towards one another—or even toward you.

A sign of movement, of progress. A tiny step, perhaps, but enough to give you hope. But, while you're too surprised to appreciate it fully, too wise to expect it to last, too humble to take much credit—you can't help but feel a surge of joy, of pride, of hope. For, you are witnessing the phenomenon of faith taking root in human hearts.

It *will* happen! It *does* happen! It *must* happen!

When it occurs, experiences such as these become the ground—the fertile soil—for your vocation as a teacher, your growth in faith, your unique spirituality. Experiences such as these help you remember that you, too, are loved—by the One who has called you to discipleship, service, and evangelization.

It *will* happen! But God knows—it won't happen *every* day! Some days—perhaps most days—it may seem as though *nothing* is happening—nothing to give you a sense of accomplishment, to strengthen your faith or to keep you going. Some days it may seem as though you are giving far more than you are getting back—and yet, so many need so much more than you can give.

On those days, you might well feel as Jesus must have felt in today's gospel—pressed in on every side by those who want to be taught, healed, fed—who want to be loved! Pressed so much that he finally needs to get away from it all—to find a quiet place, a hillside, where he can be alone with his friends. But, even there, they find him!

And they'll find us also—just when we're most tired. When we have the least to give, they'll find us and want the little we have at the moment.

My dear brothers and sisters, that is why we must have a faith rooted in a deep, personal relationship with the Lord. That is why our spirituality—our way of living out our faith—must be designed for the long term.

It is your special challenge to communicate God's love to the child who struggles to learn as well as to the brightest student. Your challenge is to proclaim Jesus' compassion towards the child who disrupts your class as well as to the "little angels" who cooperate in every way. It is challenging to share your faith in God who loves us as mothers and fathers love their children. Realistically, you share this with young people whose families are torn by divorce, whose homes are burdened with the disease of alcoholism, whose lives are filled with the loneliness of a parent's death—as well as with happy children who return home each night to the warm embraces of mom and dad.

If you're going to be able to meet these challenges, you must truly believe that the Lord is *with you*. On days when your energy has run low, you must believe this and turn to him, acknowledging your need. On days when all has gone well, you must believe it and run to him, sharing your joy. On days when you feel alone, you must seek him—even in silence. On days when you're overwhelmed by others' love, you must remember that he is the source of *all* love.

On days when you're confused, anxious, or frustrated, you must believe it and remember that he too experienced these moments of life. On days when everything seems clear, you must believe it and give your heart to him who is calling you to himself. You must believe that he is *with you!*

We've gathered together this morning to pray and learn more fully what it means to be "disciples for a new age." But what is this "new age," really? Do we mean the twentieth century with its new impressive technology and ever-increasing advances in science? Do we mean more recent decades which have witnessed so many changes in society, religion, and morality? Do we mean the '80s with our particular challenges of racism, poverty, and threats to life on many levels? Or do we mean the age that is always just around the corner—still unknown, full of surprises?

We mean all of the above! Throughout this day, in many workshops and discussions, each of you will have many opportunities to explore ways you can better live out your faith and effectively share that faith with others in the midst of this "new" age.

In another sense, the "new age" of our discipleship began long ago—in Jesus Christ. It was through him that everything "old" was made "new," that we were called to discipleship and sent to proclaim his "new" Word to this "old" world.

This "new" Word is at the heart of the mystery of the incarnation; we heard it proclaimed in the reading from the book of Revelation at the beginning of our prayer service.

It is simply this: God—our God—lives with us. His very name is "God-with-us." Our every concern is his concern. Our every breath is filled with his Spirit. To find him, we need only look around us: in *this* city, in *this* person. Remarkable as it is, he is present even in *this* heart, even though it is mine!

To be a disciple of the new age is really a very simple task. All we need do is recognize that everything, including our hearts, belongs to him and acknowledge his presence as we discover his love all around us.

That is why, my friends, I can say with such certainty: it *will* happen! Because I truly believe in the living presence of Jesus Christ. Because I have experienced his love through people like you. Because I have witnessed his hope in what you give to others.

That is why I truly believe that the simple questions, the moments of insight, the tiny signs of progress offer us the strength and meaning we need to go on with our lives and our vocations—because these simple signs are indications of his love.

In today's gospel, as Jesus tries to flee the pressures of the world by climbing a hillside with his disciples, needy people press in on him once again. His disciples acknowledge that nothing more can be done, that the demands—now for food—are insurmountable.

At that moment, humanly speaking, Jesus could easily have given in to further flight or even despair. Instead, he acts as if a "new age" is dawning! He tells his disciples to find out if anyone has *any* food to share. They find only one—a little child—with only a child's portion to share. But, in the new age, even a little child can give us more than enough to begin again! In the new age, a child's portion in the Lord's hands can feed the multitude!

My dear friends, I want you to know how much I care for you. Even more, I want you to remember how much the Lord loves you. In your vital ministry as teachers, you are called to do all you can to know him, to love him, to serve him. If you need to find him, simply look around, for he is with you! He will be there to provide for you—in the guise of a question which leads you to deeper meaning—in the form of an insight—in the manner of some little progress—or, maybe, simply in the face of a little child with only a child's portion to share. The Lord will provide all you need for nourishment, because we're living in the "new age"!

Memorial Day Mass

All Saints Cemetery, Chicago, Illinois

—*May 27, 1985* ————————————————————

My brothers and sisters, Memorial Day demands a simple eloquence because the real homilies have already been preached! The true sermons have already been proclaimed by the men and women we honor today: those who gave their lives for our country and, indeed, all the faithful departed. Their pulpits were not in churches but on the battlefields of Europe, North Africa, and Asia. Their sermons did not last a few minutes—they perdured through long years of struggle and sacrifice on behalf of their families and friends. Their message was not so much spoken as lived out in countless deeds of quiet heroism. They were ordinary men and women who loved in an extraordinary way.

Today we look back in loving memory to those who have gone before us. We pray in gratitude for seeds sown in the agony of war or in the fidelity of family life—seeds which have blossomed for us in the fruit of freedom and love. We also look forward to the future with hope and trust in God.

Memorial Day is a day of promises—promises made and kept. All of us make important promises to people we care about. We make promises to take a son to a ball game, to make a favorite dinner for the family, to love in good times and in bad. When we make promises to significant people in our lives, we do everything in our power to fulfill them. Not to keep a promise to someone we care about would be a terrible thing, a breach of love, a damaging blow to a close relationship.

My friends, today we pray in thanksgiving because God has made and will keep his promise with those who have gone before us, the promise he makes with each of us: "No one who comes will I ever reject. Everyone who looks upon the Son and believes in him shall have eternal life."

God has promised us *eternal life*, if we believe. If we, in all of our sinfulness, can keep the promises we make to our loved ones, how much more will God fulfill his promises to us, his precious sons and daughters! Nevertheless, isn't belief something we *live*, not merely *speak* about? Isn't the belief of our hearts and spirits translated into action through the deeds of our arms and hands?

Today we honor people who lived their faith, sometimes in unimaginable difficulty, but with utmost generosity. We honor people who died to protect and preserve freedom. They gave their lives for people they didn't know and for generations they would never meet. They died to end threats to the goodness and sacredness of life in the human family. We remember others because of the intimate ways they touched and shaped our lives, our beliefs, our values. Those we honor today were true believers, and we proclaim that God will keep his promise to them.

The first reading this morning calls us to pray for the dead in view of the resurrection, for we believe the dead will rise again. We pray "with a view to the splendid reward that awaits those who have gone to rest in godliness." We pray that they may be released from their sins. We pray confident that God will keep his promise to them.

There are others whose memory we cherish today—those who may not have had an opportunity to perform heroic deeds or to sin. We remember in a special way the *children* and *infants* whose bodies are buried here. Their passing often seems so great a mystery to us because of the dreams we had for them, the opportunities we wished to create for them. But with them, above all, God is faithful to his promise, loving and compassionate. He is their creator; he has called them to live with him in peace and love forever.

There is yet another dimension to this day of promise. There are some promises *we* need to make today. We best honor the memory of those who have preceded us by carrying on their dreams, beliefs, and values.

They believed in the preciousness of life. Let us carry on their dream. Let us promise to root out all callous disregard for the sanctity of life in our society and world. Let us dismantle the structures and change the attitudes which hurt and threaten human life in all its forms. From racism to abortion, from Cambodia to Cabrini Green, for the poor and elderly, the sick and well—let us pledge ourselves to defend and foster human life.

Those we honor today believed in and loved the family. Let us carry on their dream. The fundamental premise of world order and a key component of the Christian vision is the unity of the human family. Let us acknowledge that we are joined by a common creation and destined for the same kingdom. Let us build new structures of cooperation and interdependence between the peoples and nations of our world. Let us strive to build a united family of peoples.

Many of those we honor today gave their lives because they believed in peace. Let us summon the moral courage to say "no" to the weapons of mass destruction. As Christians, let us assume our responsibility of being peacemakers.

Memorial Day is a day of promises made and kept. We rejoice in prayer, grateful to God who keeps the promise of eternal life made to true believers. In honor of those who have gone before us, let us promise to respect life, to build the human family and to build a peaceful world.

My prayer today is that we will deepen our trust in God who is faithful to his promises. May the Lord bring eternal rest and peace to all our loved ones.

Homily

St. Benedict's Home for the Aged

Niles, Illinois
— *July 3, 1985* —

My dear brothers and sisters in the Lord,

I'm very happy to be with you this morning in this home which gives so much glory to God. He always seeks human arms to communicate his infinite love and care to us. This is a truly blessed place because there are so many arms held out in love here.

Perhaps you're like me whenever you hear this morning's gospel: I feel sorry for Thomas. I really do! When I think of all the mistakes I made last week, I'm grateful that there was no evangelist following closely behind, waiting to record my blunders for posterity's sake. We call St. Thomas "the Doubter"—as if doubting were something he invented or he were the only person who ever doubted!

But let's be honest. Isn't there doubt in us all? Perhaps Thomas's great gift to us on his feast day is the permission to admit that, at times, we, too, persist in unbelief. Unbelief is the spirit-killer. Unbelief compromises and scales down Christ's presence within and among us. Unbelief paralyzes our great potential as sons and daughters of God. Perhaps St. Thomas will stand less isolated in his doubt today if we honestly acknowledge the ways *we* persist in our unbelief—even here in the community of St. Benedict's Home.

Sometimes we persist in unbelief when we can't move beyond the limits of our suffering. I know that for many of you life is a burden. Advancing years have brought a painful physical fragility for some and losses of important loved ones for others. Each of us has a particular Cross to bear.

We persist in unbelief when our suffering makes us selfish. If all we do is complain about our pains—if all we can shout is "Why me, Lord?"—

429

if all we can see is our own neediness, our own hurt, our own agenda, then we persist in unbelief. This, in turn, closes us in on ourselves in loneliness.

My brothers and sisters, today the Lord calls us—along with Thomas, our friend—to faith, to belief. Instead of asking, "Why me, Lord?" we might try praying, "Yes, Lord, your will be done." Instead of seeing our pain as a burden, we might try to see it as an opportunity. After all, the person of faith knows that the crosses of Good Friday always give way to the empty tombs of Easter.

Suffering can sensitize us to the pain of others. Suffering can provide the occasion for others ministering to us. We do great service when our limitations give someone else a chance to perform acts of charity. When life gives us trouble, God gives us each other. When our suffering becomes intense, we have the opportunity to join ourselves with the suffering Christ. We can join in his sacrifice on behalf of those who are oppressed and lonely, those who experience war and injustice rather than the peace of Christ. When we do this, our suffering becomes redemptive.

We also persist in unbelief when we feel that we're no longer productive, useful or worthwhile. You might not have the energy you did thirty years ago. You no longer hold a forty-hour-a-week job. Many of the major tasks of your lifetime are behind you, but this does not mean that your value as a human person has declined! We persist in unbelief when we feel all used up, when we think there's nothing more we can do, when we assume that, as life gets older, it gets less precious.

My brothers and sisters, the Lord calls you to faith today. He invites you to see yourselves as the wonderful gifts you are and to share your gifts with others. You have special gifts of wisdom. You've learned a lot about life during your years. You can share that with your loved ones and with one another here at St. Benedict's Home. The insight you share might make an important difference in someone else's life.

You have the gift of time for prayer. You are at a time in your life when you can exercise a ministry of prayer for our troubled world. More wonders are wrought by prayer than we dream of. Pray for our Church, for the suffering, for young people, for leaders in the Church and the world. Pray for *me!* Perhaps it will be your prayer that one day will bring peace to the hearts of the people of this world.

You also have the opportunity to inspire us. The examples of courage, sanctity, and deep faith you can set are very precious to us. The goodness of your lives speaks louder than you will ever know. Everyone needs an example. You can be a model for us. And, in doing so, you will discover the great value of your lives. You will realize that you're making a significant contribution to our world—to peoples' lives—a contribution that fits your present state of life.

It's easy to point a finger at poor Thomas the Doubter. It's more difficult to realize how much we are like him. But, when we acknowledge the ways in which we persist in unbelief, we can allow the Lord to bring healing and faith into our hearts. We who have not seen the Lord but have yet believed—even if imperfectly—we are blessed. May the risen Lord help you persist in the belief that will lead you to his kingdom.

Homily

Pro-Life Mass

*National Shrine of the Immaculate Conception,
Washington, D.C.*

─── *January 21, 1986* ───────────────────────

Her name is Lisa, and her story is typical, though nonetheless tragic for
being so. Lisa is having trouble sleeping nights. Once upon a time, Lisa
was in love. She gave away her heart and her soul the way teenagers have
always done. But she was more in love with the *idea* of being in love than
with the person she thought she loved, and she began to make some bad
decisions. She chose to love in the easy ways but in none of the real. And
soon Lisa found herself seventeen years old and pregnant.

Because commitment was not something taken to their bed, Lisa's
boyfriend ran. Besides, he had a deeper interest—working on a football
scholarship. And Lisa, all alone and pregnant, decided to take care of a
problem that should never have happened.

One terrible afternoon, for $250, she bought what she thought would
be a short-term solution. Instead, it became a long-term nightmare. You
see, she is having trouble sleeping nights. Lisa sometimes wakes up to the
sound of a baby crying, and she wonders how so much love could end in
so much hurt. And God weeps in heaven. He weeps for his two precious
children—for the baby that will never cry—and for Lisa who will always
hear that silent cry.

My brothers and sisters in Christ: listen once again to the words of Jesus
proclaimed in this evening's gospel: "I have come that they might have
life and have it to the full." The Lord is talking about all the Lisas of our

432

land, about all the babies who will never cry, and all the babies yet to come. He is talking about us!

Life—life in all its fullness—is God's great and wonderful gift to us. Tonight we gather in this special church seeking to appropriate more deeply the preciousness of God's gift of life and the great responsibilities it entails.

Think of your favorite baby. Picture that son or daughter, that niece or nephew, that little child who is endlessly precious to you. The miracle of that little life is nothing less than sacred. The spontaneous love we have for our children affirms that fact.

Human life is not abstract. It is *real!* It is *tangible!* It is a source of inexpressible joy and awe. We feel this when we pick up a crying infant, when we share the joy of a baby at play, when we applaud the achievements of a growing child. We also know it, in a different way, when we experience the graciousness, vitality, and wisdom of the older members of our community.

For each of us, then, human life is our most precious gift but also, in many ways, our most fragile possession.

The fragility of human life lays claim upon us for nurturance, sustenance, protection. At best, our hold on life is rather tenuous. We are ever more aware of this in the contemporary world where the arms race is a constant threat to peace and security—indeed, even to human survival! We see it in the wake of famine, natural disasters, and diseases which quickly reach epidemic proportions.

The recognition that life is a precious, but also fragile, gift generates both a sense of responsibility and specific obligations. Human life is not meant to be lived in isolation from others. In our increasingly interdependent world, no one truly lives alone. Rather, we live on various levels of human community, called both to defend our brothers' and sisters' right to life and to work towards enhancing the quality of their lives.

Society expresses its esteem and respect for human life by protecting the life of each person through laws and social institutions. No life is of inferior value—beyond protection or sustenance. The law is the guardian of each person's life and rights, and it must apply equally to all of us.

But beyond the protection of the law, we must create an atmosphere within society, a climate in which the value and sanctity of human life are acknowledged, affirmed, and defended. Moreover, we must be consistent in our respect for and protection of human life at every stage and in every circumstance. A commitment to human dignity and human rights requires protection of human life from conception until natural death. It also requires a constant effort to assure every person a fullness of opportunity and a legitimate share in the material benefits and advantages of the modern world. This is a special challenge in the United States.

Our hold on life is only as strong as the most vulnerable member of our society. We can gauge our success in defending and respecting all human life by examining the plight of the most vulnerable in our midst—especially the unborn.

Human life usually begins quietly, almost mysteriously, in intimacy and love. Man and woman join in loving embrace, and God calls forth new life. This is the unending mystery of creation. In the earliest weeks and months after conception—quietly hidden in the mother's womb—the infant develops those physical characteristics by which each person is recognized: eyes, ears, head and limbs, heart and brain.

But the hold on this precious new life is tenuous, and the threats against it are frightening. Respect for the developing life of this newest member of the human family requires physical and emotional care of both mother and unborn infant. Nutrition, medical care, personal support, and encouragement are necessary to enhance life and to create the atmosphere of hope and promise after birth when life will continue to develop through its various stages.

Unfortunately, at the very moment in human history when we have the greatest capacity to sustain unborn life and enrich the experience of pregnancy, we have also developed an attitude of callousness and the technological tools to destroy the life of the unborn. Since the 1973 Supreme Court abortion decisions, the unborn child's right to life is frequently ignored or denied.

The incidence of abortion grows annually and, in far too many cases, the reason is human convenience. We must not allow this to go unchallenged, just as we cannot acquiesce to any diminishment of the full range of human rights. To do so would be to fail in social responsibility and moral integrity.

We are here this evening to witness to the fact that the tragic 1973 Supreme Court abortion decisions will not be forgotten or allowed to settle comfortably into our societal subconsciousness. We come together at this time each year to remind the nation, and particularly our elected representatives, that there can be no silent acquiescence to the errors of the Court's opinions. We are here to proclaim to all that we will continue the struggle to have those errors erased from our juridical system and from our historic consciousness. There can be no acceptance or toleration of any erroneous reasoning that strikes at or undermines our understanding of the value and dignity of the human person.

Through the years many Americans who do not share our faith convictions have taken an increasingly active and visible role in their support and protection of the unborn. This is a hopeful and promising sign to the pro-life movement. It is also an added incentive for us Catholics to continue our pro-life efforts and to widen and deepen our perception of the sanctity and value of all human life.

Most of all, we gather in prayer during this vigil to beg of God a renewal of commitment, energy, and perseverance so that we may fulfill what the Second Vatican Council described as "the surpassing ministry of safeguarding life." We derive wisdom from praying together so that we might more effectively convince our governmental leaders that the constitutional protection of the right to life, liberty, and the pursuit of happiness must extend to every human being from conception to natural death.

And we derive our strength from praying *here*. It is no accident that we gather this evening in the National Shrine of the Immaculate Conception. There is no radar so finely tuned as the ears of a mother to the cries of her children. Mary, our mother, surely hears us, and in that hearing there is hope. She has known the pain and anxiety of bringing a child into the world. She has known the horror of the Holy Innocents' death. She has stood beneath her Son's cross. There is no pain we have encountered that Mary has not already withstood. Let us take our strength from her.

We gather this evening in love, not in hatred, for "love never wrongs the neighbor. Hence love is the fulfillment" of the gospel and the law. May the God of love, the creator of life, continue to show his care for us. May the Lord Jesus walk with us in our efforts for justice and peace. May he give us the very fullness of life. May our loving embrace of one another this evening reach out to include all our brothers and sisters in all stages of human development and in all circumstances.

Homily

Old St. Patrick's Church

St. Patrick's Day
Chicago, Illinois
——*March 17, 1986* ——————————————

There are three things which newcomers to Chicago learn rather quickly. First, distances in the metropolitan area are measured in traveling time rather than miles. Second, Catholics tend to refer to their places of residence in terms of the parish to which they belong. Finally, despite the great ethnic diversity here, nearly everyone claims to be Irish—to some degree or other—on St. Patrick's Day!

Chicago's celebration of this feast day is a part of its folklore and local color. Does any other city celebrate March 17 in quite the style of Chicago—with green milkshakes, green beer, and a green river? On St. Patrick's Day we expect to see shamrocks, to hear "the lilt of Irish laughter" and a bit of blarney, perhaps to dance a jig or a reel. But why have we gathered in a *church* this morning—before the revelry begins?

The answer to that question lies shrouded in legend and ancient tale, in ballads sung and history recorded in shrines, statues, and stained-glass windows. The answer lies in the power and mystery of the saint we honor today as bishop and patron of Ireland: Patrick.

The facts of his life may be difficult to determine with accuracy, but the results of his ministry remain visible in the Irish people who have tenaciously held on to their faith through all the vicissitudes of the intervening centuries. We readily conclude that Patrick was a very effective evangelizer and teacher and that he loved Christ. And so, out of the mists of the past, Patrick comes to us as a model, for we, too, are called to deepen our faith, to apply it in our own circumstances, and to develop an intimate relationship with the Lord.

436

Patrick understood that the gospel can be proclaimed effectively only if the evangelizer first understands and loves the people to whom it is proclaimed. So he learned the language, culture, customs, and characteristics of the Irish to whom God had sent him. Great indeed must have been his love for them because they were the very ones who had enslaved him as a youth!

The faith of the Irish has been a noteworthy phenomenon throughout history because of Patrick's ability to unite faith and culture. Ireland has been called the "land of saints and scholars" because Patrick and his successors understood that the pursuit of truth through learning and the quest for God are not contradictory, but complementary, tasks.

Patrick also knew it was not enough simply to proclaim the gospel. People of faith need more than evangelization. Once the seed of the gospel has been planted in their hearts, it must be kept alive and nurtured through ongoing education of the faith and formation in Christian living. They must integrate the gospel's message into their daily lives in such a way that they discover its implications in ever new ways.

Patrick taught the people the implications of their faith. He taught them to respect the great dignity that was theirs as sons and daughters of God. He taught them that if they were truly to be the light of the world—as Jesus had called all his followers to be—they would have to overcome the barriers of race, culture, and language which separate people from one another.

Most of all, Patrick loved the Lord with all his heart and soul. That is why the faith took deep root in the hearts and minds of the Irish people. With Christ, in Christ, and for Christ, Patrick and his monks overcame every obstacle to the fulfillment of their mission. Patrick himself is said to have survived twelve attempts on his life. Undoubtedly the words of today's psalm response were often on his lips: "Though I walk in the valley of darkness, I fear no evil, for you are with me." His intimate relationship with Jesus assured the success of his efforts to sow the seed of the gospel and to make it come alive in all its beauty and richness—in the land to which he had returned.

We have gathered this morning in Old St. Patrick's Church, not simply to remember the past or to be overwhelmed by the pressures of the present, but to look toward the future. And that future will be infinitely brighter if all of us—whether we claim Irish descent or not—honor St. Patrick by imitating his example.

To follow the example of Patrick is to listen attentively to God's word and allow it to take deep root in our lives. It means learning more about the implications of our faith and how we are to apply it in the circumstances of the present moment. We truly imitate St. Patrick when we become a bright light to the world, when we carry our faith with us into the marketplace, the courtroom, the assemblies of government—wherever we work, wherever we go. This demands, on our part, honesty and integrity. It requires that we always place the common good above our own personal and sometimes selfish interests.

What we celebrate today, then, is not just a civic event. Neither do we honor merely a particular country or its sons and daughters. Rather, we commemorate the life of a saint—Patrick of Ireland—whose life, so filled with Christ's love, continues to be a model for us in our day. Our challenge is to follow in his footsteps; to take to heart, as he did, the words of Isaiah, so that in all we are and do and say, we may become the instruments which "bring glad tidings to the lowly . . . heal the brokenhearted . . . proclaim liberty to the captives and release to the prisoners . . . announce a year of favor from the Lord and . . . comfort all who mourn."

Homily

Prayer Service in Honor of Mary

Holy Name Cathedral, Chicago, Illinois

——April 4, 1986 ——————————————————

Recall for a moment the icons of the Eastern Church, the many musical settings for the *Ave Maria*, the *Pietà* by Michelangelo, the prayer-poems of St. Bernard of Clairvaux, the cathedral of Notre Dame in Paris, the hymns of St. Ephraem of Syria, the poetry of Gerard Manley Hopkins, the paintings of Giotto and Leonardo da Vinci. Sculpture, music, poetry, architecture, and painting—whatever the artistic medium, it has been utilized to represent and honor Mary, the mother of the Lord.

She has continued to inspire many different kinds of artistic endeavors. Could it be otherwise? She is, according to an ancient hymn in her honor, *Virgo pulcherrima! Mater melliflua! Dei Filia!*, "most beautiful Virgin! sweet Mother! Daughter of God!" Her holiness and her beauty provide an endless source of inspiration for writers, musicians, artists, sculptors, architects, and poets.

Mary, the mother of the Lord, is a person of intense complexity. She cannot be reduced to one dimension or to a single expression. All attempts to capture her and her spirit and impact—whatever form they take—will always remain partial and incomplete. She is woman, mother, sister, wife, prophetess, servant, leader, ordinary person, and creature endowed with extraordinary gifts. Her very complexity makes her a source of endless fascination and attention.

But complexity, fascination, and attention can be mere surface elements. They can lead one to meditation and deeper esteem or to distortion and exploitation. This evening I invite you to meditate with me on

439

the *deeper reality* of Mary and the reasons which generate our great devotion to her, our deep love for her.

When we contemplate Mary's life, what do we find—beneath the surface? Two aspects stand out among all others: her *fidelity* and her faith-filled *response* to God—both of which are models for us. Let us first consider Mary's *fidelity* to Jesus and to us.

She is faithful to *Jesus* because she is a woman whose life is open to the promptings of the Holy Spirit. She lives by unshakable faith, acts with loving generosity, and moves forward with great courage. Her fidelity to her Son, who is also her Savior, has none of the marks of a thoughtless fanaticism. Their intimate relationship is based on more than maternal affection. It stems from a basic trust: Mary holds fast to the promise of God who brings strength from weakness, glory from shame, and life from death.

Mary is faithful to *us* as well, to you and to me. Of course, she keeps and nurtures a living relationship with us, for we are the sisters and brothers of her Son. She is mother and sister and disciple with us. With sure instinct and complete confidence, Christians have always turned to Mary for help, protection, and support. They have trusted her and celebrated her fidelity to God's people. And, just as they have claimed her for themselves, they have sensed that she claims all God's people for herself.

Mary's fidelity is rooted in her close relationship with God and with us. Let us consider this fact more deeply as we try to understand the intimacy that creates such an enduring and faithful bond of love.

Mary shows us clearly that God has come close to us, has come among us, has been Emmanuel—"God-with-us." Our devotion to Mary ensures that we accept the full reality of Jesus Christ who is truly God and truly human. As long as we contemplate Mary, we can never forget that the Word of God became flesh, *true* flesh, someone "like us in all things but sin." As long as we contemplate Mary, Jesus can never be an abstraction for us, someone distant and removed.

Father Karl Rahner once said humorously, but accurately, that mothers do not give birth to abstractions. They give birth to real, live babies. So, as long as we keep Mary in focus, we will be delivered from the kind of abstract religion that ignores the great mystery of the incarnation and attempts to keep God at a distance from us, his people.

Mary is also a model of genuine and authentic *response* to God. As often and as long as we both contemplate and imitate Mary's response to God, our own response will be genuine and authentic. Let me explain what I mean.

Mary's response to what God did in her life and in the life of his people is not merely a matter of the head or a kind of routine or conventional nod. Her *fiat*—her "Yes" to God—is from her heart. It is a song filled with feeling. It acknowledges that exhausted human resources are not the end of our story. Rather, the Lord himself enters the lives of his people: he lifts them up, raises them up in their lowliness, and does great things for them.

When faith and gratitude converge as powerfully as they do in Mary, then the entirety of her life, her very bearing, becomes a song of grateful acknowledgment of what God has done:

> My being proclaims the greatness of the Lord, my spirit finds joy in God my savior, for he has looked upon his servant in her lowliness; all ages to come shall call me blessed. God who is mighty has done great things for me, holy is his name.

Mary's life and her response, then, are the same: the reverent acceptance of the great mystery of God at work within her. Its inevitable expression is praise to him.

The reverent acceptance of the mystery at work within *us* and *our* life of praise are the authentic responses we are to make to God. To contemplate Mary's "Yes" and to join her in this response assure us that we are being true to the great gift of new life in Jesus Christ which has been given us by the power of the Holy Spirit.

Mary's response to God was and continues to be one of praise. Knowing that there is nothing she can do to reciprocate his great gifts, she is simply grateful. All she can do is acknowledge with awe his greatness and generosity. Praise is also to be our response. We join our prayer of praise with hers in unceasing gratitude to God.

Mary's response to the Lord, however, does not end with praise. It is also embodied in her creative and courageous *decisions*. She reverently receives the word of the Lord. She makes active and conscious decisions to live by that word, to live creatively and courageously. For example, going against the cultural expectations of her time, she decides to bear Jesus, conceived by the power of the Holy Spirit. In doing so, she aligns herself in solidarity with the poor, the disenfranchised, the marginal people.

In effect, she decides to hope, to trust in God's word to her. Her courage and her creativity allow her to move forward without counting the cost, without a fear of personal loss, without accepting blindly the cultural values of her time.

As we join our response to hers, we, too, must respond with creativity and courage, not bound by the prevailing values of our culture but motivated by the coming of God's kingdom. We stand for the defense and enhancement of human life, for the poor, for justice, for peace, for reconciled relationships between women and men—in families, in our city, in our nation, among the nations of the world. Our imagination is unleashed, our courage strengthened, by joining Mary in her faithful, creative, and courageous response to the Lord.

My sisters and brothers, I have sketched a mere glimpse or reflection of Mary's true beauty. Her everlasting splendor is rooted in her fidelity to Jesus and to us. In her intimacy with the Lord and the human family, she offers us a marvelous witness to the humanity of Jesus and the accessibility of God. In her full response of praise and creative, courageous service, she shows *us* how to respond to the Lord.

The "Hail Mary," a prayer whose ancient roots are in the Gospels, sums up much of our devotion to Mary. In a few moments we will recite the rosary together, repeating this prayer many times. Before we do so, I wish to share with you a meditation on the "Hail Mary" drawn from a book sponsored by the National Shrine of the Immaculate Conception, a symbol of our nation's attachment and dedication to Mary.

I invite you to relax and follow this prayerful meditation. Close your eyes if you wish. Let us attend to this prayer that, for many of us, belongs to our earliest memories.

* * *

Hail Mary . . .

We are on a journey of faith. The journey takes us across level green plains or into deep valleys or, sometimes, through dry and empty deserts. Then we turn around or look ahead. You are there. We meet you. We greet you. You are an extraordinary person. In your presence we are reverent, perhaps with heads bowed. But we are also familiar with you. You are, after all, mother and sister and daughter and disciple with us.

full of grace . . .

An empty cup is filled up, brimming over. Mary, you are the poor one. You stand with hands upturned. God's grace, God's gift, has filled you. Our own emptiness, our aloneness, our neediness take a different shape when we look on you. The moments when we feel that we have little or nothing change into times of possibility. A path is cleared, a way is made for the Lord to journey within us, to fill us. Before you began to be, before we began to be, the richness of the Lord's mercy flowed into his dream for us.

the Lord is with you . . .

You wait and carry a child within you. You hold and feed and care for your child. You watch your son preach and heal and suffer and die and rise. He is the presence of God with us, Emmanuel. We do not make the journey alone. We look on you and we sense the presence of God within us, around us, among us, at the beginning of the journey, and at its conclusion.

blessed are you among women . . .

Mary, you live not by the great things you do but by who you are—hearing the word of God and treasuring it. You live the ordinary course of life in an extraordinary way. So, you are blessed, happy. You turn around our standards for greatness, happiness, and fulfillment. As the poor and lowly servant of the Lord, you are called blessed by all generations. We follow your movement into God, and we must change our plans for greatness and for happiness. Your one great good becomes our one great good—to be with him.

and blessed is the fruit of your womb, Jesus . . .

The Lord of life is so alive within you that you must give birth to him. You do not simply set him to rest in this world. You hold him up and out. You give the gift of the Blessed One as generously and as freely as he has been given to you. We walk with you. We speak the Word we have heard. We hold and share the Life that fills our hands.

Holy Mary, Mother of God . . .

Mary, you are holy. You are the mother of the Lord. Your holiness and our possibility for holiness is sketched in your eyes. They are eyes that wait and watch, eyes that wonder and observe and attend. They are eyes that weep and laugh. Your eyes speak to us of the holiness of God in human ways because they constantly look upon Jesus, who is the Holy One of God and our brother in human flesh.

pray for us sinners . . .

We freely ask you to pray for us. How can we not do so? You are with us and among us; you have walked with us and toward us. We are sinners, pilgrims on a journey who stumble and fall and struggle and imperfectly make our way. Your son has touched us and healed us and forgiven us. We can never forget or lose the memory of who we are—people in need of his love.

now . . .

Now is the time of our hoping and struggling. Today we hear his voice. We do not want to harden our hearts or dull his presence. Today is the time, and now is the prayer.

and at the hour of our death. Amen.

Mary, we can journey in our life only if we have the food of hope, only if we have some sense of our destination, only if we believe that we can follow your Son in his dying and, then, in his rising. Keep us alive and journeying in the memory that Jesus is Lord. He is the risen one who is our life and resurrection. Amen.

Ordination to the Permanent Diaconate

Holy Name Cathedral, Chicago, Illinois

—*April 26, 1986* —————————————————————

It all began around a table!

It all began when hungry mouths outnumbered helping hands. It all began when the early Church learned that the ministry of the word needs to be complemented by a ministry of deeds. It all began around a table, for it was in the everyday need and practical demand of the table that the diaconate was born.

This should not surprise us because the table has always been significant for Christians. Jesus often sat at table with his closest friends—enjoying dinner with them, teaching them the Good News of salvation. At table he called them to "live on" in his love. At table he gave them the mandate: "Love one another as I have loved you." At table he pointed out that it was not they who chose him, but he who chose them "to go forth and bear fruit."

We have gathered at the Lord's Table this afternoon to ordain thirty-four of our brothers to the diaconate. Never before in the Church's history has the diaconate been so complex and demanding as it is today. Complex undertakings need a simple dream, a clear focus.

Almost two thousand years have passed since that special gathering described in today's first reading. Since then the Table has grown—astoundingly, miraculously! Today it still has its own unique, critical, demanding needs. If the diaconate was born from the needs of the Table, should we not today return to the needs of *our* Table to capture the dream, to see clearly what we are to do? I will highlight three contemporary needs.

First, the "widows" are still crying. There are *many* around our Table whose basic needs are not being met. In each of our parishes there are people for whom life is a lonely, painful burden. We gather around the Lord's Table to listen to his word, to partake of his food and drink, to become more aware of our responsibility to help those in need. At the Table we find the nourishment and strength to reach out to them with helping, loving hands.

Assisting at the Table is an important function of a deacon, for the Eucharist is at the heart of our communities. Nonetheless, we must also move away from the Table each day to help others if our ministry is to be complete. The concrete needs of the community set the initial agenda for diaconal ministry. Today's deacons, too, must begin with the most vulnerable, the most needy in our midst.

Second, people are eager, hungry, to hear the gospel. Deacons are to proclaim the Good News using the particular gifts they have received from the Lord. Unfortunately, many in our communities have heard the gospel many times with their ears—to the point of boredom—but their hungry hearts remain tragically untouched. They have not yet heard the Christian story as their own story. They have not yet experienced the abiding hope, celebrated the wondrous victory, gotten a glimpse of the infinite, freeing possibilities of God's love.

My brothers, you are to proclaim the gospel in such a way that others can perceive its meaning for their lives. Your experience is different from that of priests, and, so, you bring a distinctive perspective to the proclamation of the gospel. You know personally how difficult it can be to keep love alive and growing in marriage. As parents you know the fears and dreams involved in raising children and seeing them through adolescence. You know firsthand the pressures and ethical compromises of the business world, the dehumanizing atmosphere of the workplace.

As you proclaim the word and help people hear the story as their own, use the particular gifts God has given you. Connect life to faith and vice versa. Proclaim the gospel from your heart, your strength, your experience.

Third, and most important of all, love as Jesus did and teach others to do the same. Jesus left a weak, faltering community of disciples to continue his mission and ministry in the world. He did not leave an intricate system of thought or a detailed book of instructions. He left a visible human community to represent him to the world.

In our day we are that community of disciples. Through us, through our love, God cares for his people. Jesus' love was eloquent—it spoke louder than words! By his own actions, he witnessed the truth of his words: "There is no greater love than this: to lay down one's life for one's friends." More important than any other function appropriate to a deacon, you must love—and teach us how to love—as Jesus did.

The first letter of Peter sums up your mission and the spirit in which you are to carry it out. Your love for others is to be constant. You are to put your gifts at the service of God's people. The message you deliver is God's, not your own. God will provide the strength you need to serve the Church. And, through all the turmoil, and despite the pace of ministry, you must remain calm so that you will be able to pray.

Know well your work. Give yourselves to the service of God's people. As the Lord gave his life for his people, lay down your lives that others may have life. Live on in Jesus' love. Strive so well in the Lord's service that I may never be held to blame for calling you to the diaconate, nor you for answering.

My brothers and sisters—deacons, wives, families, and friends—on behalf of the Church I thank you for your great generosity and depth of faith which has led you to this moment. Remember that it was not you who chose Jesus, but he who chose you. And, as you accept this office, know that the entire Christian people will gather round with their support. May God who has begun this good work within you bring it to completion.

As we gather around the Lord's Table, let us pray that we will remain close to one another and to the Lord. For all of us—and especially for deacons—all of life, all that we are and do, begins around the Table.

Homily

Religious Jubilarians' Celebration

Chicago, Illinois

——*December 6, 1986* ——————————————————————

What comes to your mind when you think of Chicago? Some think of it as the Windy City and claim that it belongs to the shifting moods and airs of feisty Lake Michigan. Some think of it as the City of Big Shoulders and suggest that it owes its allegiance and identity to the railroad lines, the gritty warehouses and factories that encircle the Loop, or the stockyards which used to anchor jobs on the South Side.

But these people do not know the city as we know it, for Chicago belongs, heart and soul, to its *churches!* One cannot walk for long in any direction and not have his or her path cross the shadow of a church. One cannot find a view of the city in which a church steeple does not rise, gracefully watchful, over the neighborhood tangle of chimneys, water towers, TV antennas, and ever-present billboards. One cannot spend a day in this city and not hear ringing church bells mark the noontime and passing hours.

Chicago's identity is intimately linked with its churches, the churches built by those who have gone before us, built with their immigrant sweat and toil, complex labors of simple love, magnificent testaments of faith that still speak silently but eloquently today. Chicago belongs to these churches, and, today, we celebrate the way these churches belong to you, our religious jubilarians.

I stand before you with profound awe and deep gratitude as I consider the countless hours and energies you sisters, brothers, and priests have lavished upon God's Church! Perhaps you didn't carry bricks, or mix the mortar, or hoist the wood that built the churches to which Chicago belongs. But make no mistake about it: you have built the Church—as fundamentally, as soundly, and as lovingly as human hearts and hands can manage. Yes, you have built the Church. Few can match, and no one can surpass your contribution, and the effect you have had upon this generation of God's Church.

It is beyond my capacity to reward you adequately for all you have selflessly offered. My tongue is too clumsy to tell of the wealth of your service. My prayer of thanks is too small to measure the endless expanse of your goodness. Any gift I could give would be hopelessly inadequate in comparison with the beauty of the lives you have given for the Lord and for the service of his people.

Nevertheless, on behalf of the hundreds of thousands of Catholics you have served, and on behalf of the Church you have built and love so dearly, I offer three simple *words* as gifts, as feeble attempts to sum up what you mean to us and to reflect all we would like, from the heart, to say to you.

The three words I give to you are *obedience, generosity,* and *gratitude.*

Let me hasten to explain what I mean by obedience lest you expect to hear echoes of your novice mistress or master! Father Henri Nouwen has often pointed out that the root meaning of the word "obedience" is "to listen attentively"—especially, at the deepest recesses of our hearts where God resides.

You heard God's call to religious life—for some of you many years ago, for others more recently—and you responded with your own *fiat.* To remain faithful to your religious vocation, however, you have had to remain obedient, listening attentively to God's voice, the kind of voice Isaiah refers to: "a voice from behind, sounding in your ears: 'This is the way; walk in it.'" At times the voice may have sounded a strong caution when you were tempted to turn to the right or to the left. At other times, it may have been a subtle whisper, reassuring you of God's deep affection for you.

Generosity. As God has called you to the religious life and to the service of his people, he has given you all the gifts you need to carry out your mission. The gifts you have received, you have generously shared with others.

Your gifts have been gentle humor and wisdom, long hours and patience, quiet humility, unshakable faith, compassion and kindness. You have shared your special gifts and the ordinary ones, too. You have diagramed sentences, preached homilies, brought healing to the sick, taught nuclear physics. But you also wiped noses, dried tears, challenged and comforted young people and old. As I have said so often, I cannot imagine what the church of Chicago would be like without you and your generous sharing of gifts.

Like the Lord Jesus, who was so full of compassion, you have shown great concern for the crowds whom you have found lying prostrate, like sheep without a shepherd. Like the Good Shepherd, you have been willing to put your life on the line for the flock entrusted to you.

And that brings us to the third word I have for you today: *Gratitude.* In the face of your continued graciousness, fidelity and generosity, gratitude is all we, as Church, can say to you. Gratitude is a word that cuts both ways. First and foremost, whether your jubilee celebration marks the passing of 25, 50, 60, 75, or even 80 years, I am sure you want to thank God who is the source of all your blessings and gifts. Today you celebrate in humble gratitude all the Lord has done for you in his tenderness and by his many acts of love. Your thanksgiving focuses on the myriad ways God has used you as his instruments through the years.

We also need to give thanks to *you,* God's willing instruments. Please, try not to hear merely *my* voice saying "thank you." Hear the thousands who have been touched and wonderfully changed by your faith, service, and love. "Thank you" from the children now grown, who are the backbone of the Church as it approaches the next millennium. "Thank you" from the wounded, lonely people whose broken hearts you so often mended. "Thank you" from the infirm, the aged and dying who, from God's throne, today sing your praises. Thank you for building up the church in Chicago!

My prayer for you is that "the Lord will always give you the bread you need and the water for which you thirst."

Homily

St. Mary of Providence School

Chicago, Illinois

—April 28, 1987 ————————————————

A very long time ago in a faraway land, there was a little lamb named Bink. Bink was the smallest lamb in all of the flock. And while most of the lambs had soft, beautiful wool, Bink's wool was rough and shaggy. Most of the lambs had sweet, gentle voices, but Bink's voice was squeaky and loud.

Bink was part of a very large flock. The owner of the flock hired shepherds to watch over it, to protect the lambs from wolves, to make sure that they always had plenty of food and water. But many of these hired shepherds were very cruel to Bink. They made fun of his wool and teased him about his voice. Sometimes they would forget to feed him, and three times they lost him in the wilderness. Bink was often very sad.

One day a new shepherd came to the flock. He seemed different than the others. He called each lamb by name and really seemed to care about them. When he saw Bink hiding behind a bush, he smiled and lifted Bink onto his shoulders. He brought Bink near the fire and gently combed his shaggy wool. He laughed kindly when Bink made his squeaky noises. The shepherd fed Bink and cared for him, and, for the first time in his life, Bink was happy.

This was a Good Shepherd, someone who cared about the flock—a shepherd who cared about all the sheep, even the smallest, the weakest, and the most vulnerable.

Jesus is a Good Shepherd. He cares for all of us—even the smallest, the weakest, and the most vulnerable. He doesn't care how we look or how we sound. He doesn't care if we are strong or weak. He loves us just as we are.

Pearl Buck once said, "The test . . . of any civilization is the measure of consideration and care which it gives to its weakest members." The same is true of the Church. The test of our faithfulness to the Good Shepherd is the consideration and care we give to our most vulnerable members.

St. Mary of Providence School has cared and cared well for those entrusted to it. The sisters, the lay staff, the parents of this community have made the love of the Good Shepherd a living reality here. In particular, I wish to thank Sr. Marcellina Erne for her fifty years of dedicated and loving service to God's children—and his Church.

Please accept my presence today as a sign of my esteem and affection for all of you.

And what about Bink? He is still very small, still very shaggy. He still has a squeaky voice. But he is also still happy because of the care of the Good Shepherd. Actually, we are all like Bink. We all need to be loved, and we all need the Good Shepherd to guide us. Let us listen to his voice.

WEORC Retreat

32nd Sunday in Ordinary Time
Techny, Illinois
—*November 8, 1987*

The story is told of a Chinese family that had a horse. And one day this horse, a mare, beloved by the family's only son, escaped and galloped off into the hills. The neighbors said, "What a curse!" but the aged father of the family said, "Maybe a blessing!"

A few days later the mare returned, and a stallion followed her. The neighbors said, "What a blessing!" but the old man queried, "Maybe a curse!"

The young boy who loved the mare now became attached to the stallion as well. He tried to ride it, but the stallion was too wild and threw the boy, breaking his leg. The neighbors said, "What a curse!" but the old man wondered, "Maybe a blessing!"

One day after the accident an invading army swept through the village and carried off every able-bodied man and boy. Only the injured son, unable to walk, was left behind. And no one dared to suggest to the father the nature of this blessing or curse.

My brothers and sisters, the title of your retreat is "American and Catholic: The Dream, the Reality." Having just had the benefit of a weekend of prayerful reflection on this topic, would one of you dare to suggest to us all the nature of this blessing or curse?

I do not mean to be flippant. Rather, I intend to frame today's elusive gospel parable within the context of these perplexing times. Today's Liturgy of the Word may go a long way towards pointing us into the enterprise of being "American and Catholic" in transformative and grace-filled ways.

Let me explain what I mean.

What *does* one do when the bridegroom is hours late, and you're in charge of the torches? What does one do when the unforeseen, the unexpected, the almost unthinkable happens? What do you do when life throws you a curve, and you were thinking fastball? Life has its surprises. After all, what self-respecting adult who cares about others is late for an important occasion?

But sometimes the groom doesn't arrive until midnight. Sometimes the stock market crashes. Sometimes the call to the priesthood or religious life and the charism of celibacy no longer seem as simultaneous and inevitable as once they did, and you find yourself a resigned priest or a former religious trying to fit into a Church in desperate need of ministers.

What does a believer do when the unforeseen and unexpected happens?

As I listen prayerfully to today's Scripture readings, this is what I hear: that the kingdom comes when people struggle to be faithful to wisdom in the midst of sometimes unforeseen circumstances. The kingdom appears whenever and wherever God's will is fulfilled, for God rules where his will is at work. And his will for us in situations of ambiguity and uncertainty is to be faithful to wisdom. When people struggle to be faithful to wisdom in the vagaries of life, the reign of God is made manifest.

The only difference between the five foolish bridesmaids and the five sensible ones seems to be that the five sensible ones knew, like Murphy the Irishman, that anything that *can* go wrong *will* go wrong. And, accordingly, they developed alternative plans. They were faithful to wisdom in the midst of a life where, all too often, things don't work out as originally planned. When people struggle to be faithful to wisdom in the vagaries of life, the reign of God appears.

What does this mean for us today? How can *we* be faithful to wisdom in these fast-paced, confusing, demanding times?

A beautiful line in today's reading from the book of Wisdom points the way: "He who watches for wisdom at dawn shall not be disappointed, for he shall find her sitting by his gate."

We must watch for wisdom, because it is closer than we know. We must believe in the accessibility of God's Wisdom for us, here and now. We can never give up, abandon the vigil, or assume that—for whatever reason—the issues we struggle with cannot somehow, someday be worked out. To do so would be a breach of faith. For nothing happens without God's knowledge; nothing happens without some purpose.

I am deeply touched by your organization, WEORC. As a group, you remain faithful to wisdom in the heart of the ambiguity of experience. You are people who continue to search for ways to serve the Lord in the church of Chicago in your present forms of life as resigned priests and former religious. I can only guess what the personal cost must be. I bless your sacrifice and struggle.

And this is the heart of what I want to say to you: let's not give up on one another, the Church, or the belief that—within this struggle, within this vigil for Wisdom—we shall find her sitting by our gate!

There are no easy answers. Church law, for reasons which are not always understood or appreciated, places restrictions on you and me which we must respect. As one who has taken an oath to uphold Church doctrine and discipline, I know you would not expect me to do otherwise. Yet, in the midst of this ambiguity, you might ask: Where is Wisdom?

I cannot say for certain, but I will promise that I will struggle with you to discern where the Spirit is leading us. As with so many other complex, sensitive issues, I do not know the answers. But I do know that, if we do not work together, if we do not keep watch together, our answers will be stillborn.

I firmly believe that God's Spirit is present in today's ambiguity and that we are called to a communal vigil, even though we may not be able to exercise together the ministry for which many of us were ordained. Because I know WEORC and what you stand for, I know that you have been and are committed to that belief as well. For some of us, the answers will come too slowly. Some of us will be worried about undue haste. But, as Paul told the Thessalonians, "let us not yield to grief, like those who have no hope."

When people struggle to be faithful to wisdom in the vagaries of life, the kingdom of God is made manifest. I have no facile solutions today, my sisters and brothers—only the deep belief and trust that our vigil in the night of this ambiguity will meet God's transforming Wisdom.

I promise to watch and struggle with you, and for that honor today I am deeply grateful.

I make my own Paul's blessing to the Thessalonians: "May the God of peace make you perfect in holiness. May he preserve you whole and entire, spirit, soul, and body, irreproachable at the coming of our Lord Jesus Christ. He who calls us is trustworthy, therefore he will do it."

Homily

National Conference of Catholic Bishops Annual Meeting

Washington, D.C.

—*November 11, 1987* ————————————————————

Perhaps you approach these annual meetings, as I do, with mixed feelings. I look forward to being with good friends, with true brothers, with whom I can freely share dreams and frustrations, joys and heartaches, knowing that they care about me as I do about them. Then, realizing the importance of individual items on the agenda, I experience some anxieties about the decisions to be made, wondering if we have all the pertinent facts and how we will handle especially sensitive issues. And from experience I know that, if I have arrived a bit tired, I will be bone-weary by the time I head back to Chicago!

My experience of the solidarity of our Episcopal Conference is nowhere more striking than when we gather around the Book and the Altar to listen to God's Word and to be nourished by his own Body and Blood. Our eucharistic assembly reflects the unity which we have already achieved with God's grace and has the capacity to bring healing and reconciliation where divisions may remain among us. As faithful followers of Jesus, we share a deep love for God and for the Church. That is the source of our strength, our inspiration, our perseverance, our ability to work together for the well-being of the Church in the United States and throughout the world.

This morning's parable of the silver pieces is fairly straightforward. Those who receive five and two thousand silver pieces respectively show their resourcefulness by doubling those accounts in their master's absence.

It's surely not difficult for a bishop to understand the owner's pleasure at the results when he returns home!

The parable, however, focuses on the third person who also knew that there would be a reckoning when the master returned. He was free to make his own decision about what to do with his master's funds. He expects to be thanked for his efforts, but it is not his master's gratitude that he receives. Instead, he ends up alone in the darkness outside, wailing and gnashing his teeth.

Where does he go wrong? Some commentators point out that hiding money or treasure in the ground was a common method of preserving it in first-century Palestine. Frankly, when I prepared to return home from the synod in Rome after the Wall Street meltdown, the thought crossed my mind that it might be better to *bury* our archdiocesan funds for a time!

The problem lies in his being overcautious, unenterprising, too careful, too fearful. He takes no risks. He hopes for a safe bargain. Although he knows beforehand that the owner of the silver pieces is demanding, the fearful man acts irresponsibly. And he does *not* live happily ever after.

The parable gives rise to certain questions. How many people have you met who truly acknowledged receiving the equivalent of the five thousand silver pieces? In my experience, a *few* do so readily and boldly, but the suspicion arises, at times, that some inflationary measure has been at work in their lofty self-esteem. On the other hand, how many people have you encountered who simply assumed that they had only received the equivalent of the one thousand silver pieces? Again, in my experience, *many* people do so. But, again, the suspicion arises that there has been a devaluation of currency or recessionary measures at work in their low self-esteem.

Today it is more fashionable for many to admit to the equivalent of the two thousand silver pieces—not too wealthy, not too poor, safely (it is assumed) in the middle of the road.

Through the twenty-one years that I have been a bishop, I have come to know most of you quite well. Frankly, I do not lose any sleep worrying whether the Catholic bishops of the United States are using their personal talents well. We make our modest allowances the old-fashioned way: we earn them! And although we know quite well the risks entailed in being faithful shepherds in the Church today, this does not deter us from carrying out our ministry with generosity and courage.

Nevertheless, the parable does pose a personal challenge to us. As pastors, we have a responsibility to the "owner"—to use all the resources he has given to his Church as wisely and effectively as possible. Each of us is called to be an effective steward. And today more than ever, that implies that we must acknowledge, help develop, and use well our greatest resource in the Church, humanly speaking—the people entrusted to our care.

As you know, our four elected delegates to the synod chose the theme of co-discipleship as the thread which gave an underlying coherence to their individual interventions. And, in effect, the synod reaffirmed the teaching of the Second Vatican Council which highlighted the fact that all members of the Church, in virtue of their baptism, share a responsibility for carrying out the Church's mission in the world.

As Church leaders, we are called to implement this teaching. As a matter of fact, the specific agenda for the plenary assembly this week gives us an opportunity to witness to our concern and care for certain of our co-disciples in the Church: priests and religious, theologians and health care workers, teens and their families, Hispanics.

Besides the specific issues about which we will make decisions this week, we have a broader responsibility to call the laity, the "sleeping giant," to their full and proper role in regard to the Church's mission. For some, this may mean convincing them that they have two or five thousand silver pieces, that they should not underestimate the contribution they can make. For others, it may mean gently persuading them that they should not overestimate the contribution they have set out to make. For many, it implies convincing them that, whatever silver pieces they have received, they should invest them wisely and generously—for the sake of the kingdom.

The first reading from the book of Proverbs, the description of the ideal wife, may have caused many celibate males to shudder this week as they were preparing homilies for this morning. One would hardly accuse the human author of the passage with being theoretical or romantic! However, the passage does indicate that material prosperity and a good standing in the community went hand in hand in ancient Israel, and a good wife was considered necessary for both. It paints the portrait of a wife's managerial responsibility and partnership with her husband.

Sharing responsibility for the Church's mission in the United States with our co-disciples undoubtedly involves risks. While we must be wise and prudent, we must also guard against the debilitating fear and misguided caution of the person who received the one thousand silver pieces. And in the process we may learn from the wisdom of ancient Israel that the Church's well-being will depend now more than ever before in human history upon our willingness to share responsibility with women for the sake of the kingdom.

My brothers and sisters, I pray that when the Lord comes, he will find the Church he has entrusted to us one or two or five steps closer to the full realization of that kingdom.

Homily

The Catholic Church Extension Society

Chicago, Illinois

——*May 7, 1988* ——————————————————————

In one of Robert Frost's best-known poems, the poet reminisces about a decision he made one day. He writes,

> I shall be telling this with a sigh
> Somewhere ages and ages hence:
> Two roads diverged in a wood, and I—
> I took the one less traveled by,
> And that has made all the difference.

For St. Paul, the divergence of "road in a wood" came quite unexpectedly, on the road to Damascus. He had intended to harass and persecute the minority Christian community there. But, after he encountered the risen Lord on this journey, Paul joined the young community and became a courageous co-disciple, an ardent apostle, a persistent preacher of the Good News.

With seemingly endless energy and enthusiasm—with great passion— Paul carried the light of the gospel to many regions of Asia Minor and Greece, and, eventually, to Rome itself. Once he had set his foot upon the Christian Way, he traveled far and wide with a single purpose. And that made all the difference in his own life and in the lives of the communities he founded and nurtured. As the Acts of the Apostles points out, "the congregations grew stronger and daily increased in numbers." The New Testament also bears witness to Paul's deep and abiding concern for the poorer Christian communities of his day and his fundraising efforts on their behalf.

Those were exciting, challenging times for the early Church, and God raised up men and women equal to the task—even throwing Saul off his horse and directing him to a road "less traveled by." Today, we acknowledge that the excitement and challenges have not diminished for the Church. And with gratitude we also affirm that, in our own day, God continues to send gifted men and women to carry on the Church's mission and ministry in particular places throughout the world.

For over eighty years, the Catholic Church Extension Society has helped support such missionaries and pastors in rural areas of the United States, in regions with few Catholics. The society was established to foster and expand the Catholic faith as well as to develop a missionary spirit in clergy and laity alike. Through the decades it has faithfully provided support for priests living in out-of-the-way places and helped pastors and their parishioners to build adequate structures for worship, and for educational and social life.

And so, we gather this afternoon in prayer and friendship. We thank God for the generous and dedicated support provided to many poorer Catholic communities throughout the United States by the Extension Society. In my own name, and in the name of all those who have benefited from your endeavors, I wish to thank all of you for your assistance, collaboration, and leadership in the Catholic Church Extension Society.

This occasion also gives us a splendid opportunity to recognize and honor a very special person, Father Joseph Valine. He has been described in many ways—as perhaps the nation's oldest full-time active pastor; as perhaps the youngest of heart among us this afternoon; as a pioneer in the use of automatic irrigation systems; as a town caterer; as the "doughnut" priest. While all of this is undoubtedly true, his doughnuts may tell us more about *him* than his fundraising concerns. Someone once said that

> 'Twixt the optimist and the pessimist
> the difference is droll:
> The optimist sees the doughnut,
> but the pessimist sees the hole!

From all that I know about him, I can assure you that Father Valine is not a pessimist! Neither is he a "homebody." He has well outdistanced St. Paul as a seasoned traveler. Father Valine estimates that he has logged two million miles in the service of the Church! I must admit that I was somewhat relieved at first when I learned that he has cut back on his weekly 600 miles of travel—until I read that he still logs 300 miles a week!

There have been several divergences of "roads in a wood" in Father Valine's life. His family moved to California from the Azores while he was a young boy. Later he entered the Dominican novitiate in Ohio and then studied in Kentucky, Illinois, and Switzerland before completing his theological studies back home in California. When he was ordained a priest, he first served in the dioceses of San Francisco, Los Angeles, and Portland before answering the call to minister in the Diocese of Salt Lake City.

In Utah, on a road less traveled by Catholics, he has faithfully served the Catholic communities there for forty-seven years. Through these years Utah Catholics and hundreds of thousands of tourists have come to know and love Father Valine. He has shared with them the Lord's goodness and forgiveness, his wisdom and nourishment.

Bishop William Weigand, the bishop of Salt Lake City, says that Father Valine has an "invincible zest for life" and a deep "love for the Lord." He is a good pastor and a zealous missionary. He is humbly grateful for the great gift of the priesthood. And, despite the fact that he has been a priest for fifty-nine years, he still "has lots more work to do in his service of the Lord."

The bishop has also said that something special commends the nomination of Father Valine for the Lumen Christi Award. We have already seen it here this afternoon: the twinkle in his eyes! Some of us have already heard it for ourselves: the merriment in his voice! In Bishop Weigand's own words, "Here is a man alight with the Lord. Here is a man to whom people in darkness are drawn for warmth."

Father Valine, my purpose this afternoon has not been to embarrass you with praise but to invite all of us to give glory to God who continues to raise up for his Church wonderful, gifted, dedicated men and women to carry on its mission and ministry.

You are, indeed, such a person, and the Extension Society is honored by your presence with us today.

The road *you* have taken is the one less traveled by, and that has made all the difference!

Homily

"Theology on Tap" Mass

21ˢᵗ Sunday in Ordinary Time
Holy Name Cathedral, Chicago, Illinois
—*August 21, 1988*

Tom had always prided himself on the fact that he had a *career*. He wasn't like his father, Mike. His father didn't have a career; he had a *job*.

Tom's father was a forklift driver at the Ford assembly plant. He punched in at 7:00 A.M. and punched out at 3:30 P.M., glad to leave the pressure and sweat of work behind. He punched in and out for thirty-five years, working that job—not out of love for the work, but out of love for his wife and family. Mike had a job, nothing more—it was something he did for a living, not something he *was* in life.

Tom, however, was different: He had a career. It was *who* he was in life. It demanded a dedication that went beyond a five-day, nine-to-five schedule. It required a determination to postpone other commitments until certain career goals had been accomplished. His career gave him identity and self-worth. His career meant everything to him—he loved its pace, its perks, and the path it made of his life.

But lately the path has seemed less full of surprises.

As Tom has grown in his profession, his work has become more predictable. It saps his energy and tires him more than it used to. The demands on his time, which used to be a discipline in which he delighted, now seem to be unreasonably intrusive. The sacrifices he has made for his career seem not always to be recognized or reciprocated. And as Tom approaches his mid-thirties, he is discovering that there might be more to life than the pursuit of his career.

461

Where do you go in such circumstances? Where do you go when you realize that your *career* has become just another *job?*

* * *

Here it was, almost Labor Day, and what Lisa thought was only another summer romance was turning into something far more scary. She hated to use the "L" word, but she simply had no choice. She was in *love,* love of the terminal kind, the sort of love that calls one's bluff. Her heart beat like a teenager's while, simultaneously, the sound of her biological clock ticked in her ears.

She was terrified at the thought of being married, of closing down her options, of working a lifetime at keeping the romance alive once love had become habitual. But Lisa was equally terrified of facing life without Jeff, her aloneness having been made more explicit by the grace they found in and with each other. So Lisa sat, caught midway between Bennigan's and the Bridal Shop, dreading the questions that autumn would bring.

Where do you go? Where do you go when love calls your bluff?

* * *

She sleeps not two blocks from where we now pray. Usually you can find her spending her nights leaning against the doors of Quigley North Seminary, at Rush and Pearson. She refuses any offer of help, shrinking like a turtle into the layers of her filthy clothes. At her feet are two Jewel shopping bags filled with all of her worldly possessions. Sometimes empty whiskey bottles stand like sentries before her. Her eyes dart like rabbits, watching the well-scrubbed, tanned, beautiful young people making their way down Rush Street. Sometimes they make jokes about her. It has been a long time since she has cared to notice.

She is one of the thousands who call the streets home. I have passed her, and people like her, too often. This afternoon our ears are full of the rhetoric of partisan politics, and our hearts are full of religious sensibility. But too soon and too often we will pass the street lady again. Although deep in our heart we may know better, we can become so accustomed to seeing people who are destitute, or disconnected from reality, that we take them for granted.

Where do you go? Where do you go when your contact with human suffering becomes commonplace, and you pass by without practicing the gospel you preach?

* * *

My brothers and sisters, today's gospel presents us with a significant challenge. Throwing the ball into our court, Jesus aims his question directly at us: "Do you want to leave me too?" Where do you go? Where do you go when significant things happen in life?

One of the most religious times of human life occurs during the young adult years. More things of significance, more momentous decisions, more deeply affective encounters seem to happen in our twenties and thirties than in other, more settled periods of our lives.

Where do you go when your career becomes just another job? Where do you go when love calls your bluff? Where do you go when contact with human suffering becomes commonplace, and you pass by without practicing the gospel you preach? These are all *religious* questions—even if they don't smell like incense or sound like church bells.

These experiences are contacts with the loving mystery of God. They are a divine summons to a more fully human, graced style of living. We are drawn into the endless love of God through the specific life experiences that hold our attention and call forth our best energies.

Divine revelation always demands a response. In the face of God's free self-disclosure, a decision from the viewer is required. Faith is not a spectator sport. To encounter the mystery of God in life demands a realignment of our hearts, either for or against the grace encountered. *What* we decide is up to us; *that* we decide is a necessity.

The heartbreak of today's gospel is the desertion of so many of Jesus' followers. When faced with the decision that divine revelation requires, they break off contact with Jesus, the source of life, choosing the oblivion of isolation over the risk of graced involvement. Only Peter, speaking for the Twelve, chooses to align his life with Jesus. He says, in effect, that to follow grace, although not easy, is the *only* life worth living. To turn one's back upon divine revelation would be to settle for a kind of living death.

What about you? Where are you going with the important questions of your life? What are those questions, and how is God calling you to a more fully human life through them? In your life struggles, where is the deepest grace? What realignment does it ask of you?

My sisters and brothers, don't run from grace. Don't avoid the hard questions. Don't rule out the summons of divine revelation and the risks it may ask of you. Everyone here this afternoon has walked into this cathedral with at least one major question in his or her life. Tell me where significance lies in your life, and I will show you where divine revelation summons you. Don't leave this church until you more clearly hear God's call.

As you listen to God, know that you don't have to walk alone. When one struggles to find God's grace in the significant experiences of life, one needs community. Stay involved with the community of faith.

"Theology on Tap" is a good example of the kind of Church involvement to which I am referring. There are over eight hundred of you here today! For the past five weeks, thousands of you have met in thirty parishes across the archdiocese. You have looked for the depth dimension in life, asked the hard questions, nurtured a religious sensibility, and tried to connect the faith of your youth with the experience of your adulthood. And you have done all this together! Don't give up on such a life-giving enterprise!

In discerning the movement of God in your life, continue to look to the Church community, its tradition, sacraments, Scriptures, and theology for help. Without you, the People of God suffer because you bring special grace to our community. Without faith or a life ennobled and transformed by grace, you suffer from undernourishment and a flattening out of your horizons.

Don't walk alone. And know that there is at least one balding, former young adult, named Joseph, who loves you, who will walk with you, and who will pray for you each wonderful step along the way.

Homily

Parish Visitation

31st Sunday in Ordinary Time
St. Gerard Majella Parish, Markham, Illinois
—*October 30, 1988* ——————————————

A wise and courageous prophet once journeyed to a distant city to convert its many inhabitants from years of apathy, indifference, and ignorance. As he spoke to the people of this distant city, he did so with great power and conviction, for the words were truly God's words. He spoke of truth, justice, and peace. He spoke of responsibility and passionate commitment; and, above all else, he spoke of sacrifice—the sacrifices we all must make if God's kingdom of peace is no longer to be an elusive dream, but a living reality for all people everywhere.

At first, the people of this distant city listened to his proclamations about truth, justice, and peace. But as the weeks passed, his challenge to them became more personal and demanding. Gradually they drifted away until there was not a single person to listen to him when he spoke. Still, he continued to speak and with even greater conviction—despite the fact that no one listened.

One day, after many weeks of preaching to the wind, the prophet was approached by a traveler who asked him, "Why do you go on preaching when no one is here? When no one listens? Can't you see how hopeless this situation is?"

The prophet then shook his head very slowly and responded solemnly: "In the beginning I had hoped to change the people. If now, all alone, I still shout for justice and preach of the wonder of love, it is only to prevent them from changing me."

In today's gospel Jesus speaks seven simple, challenging words from Jewish tradition—words so powerful that, if taken to heart, they can and will change the face of the earth. However, those words are so old, so familiar, so well worn that we may have forgotten their tremendous power and lost sight of their significant challenge: *"You shall love your neighbor as yourself."*

As Christians, we have heard these words a thousand times and more. Cynics may scoff at them as trite and naive. The worldly may look upon them as mere folly. The sophisticated may regard them as quaint. But for us who believe, who struggle, and who hope, they are worth listening to again and again: *You shall love your neighbor as yourself.* Let us listen to these words this morning. Let them touch our hearts. Let them fill our souls. Let them change our lives.

My brothers and sisters of St. Gerard Majella parish, I am grateful to have this opportunity to worship with you this morning. I am here to listen to God's word with you, to recall that our love for God is revealed in and through our love of neighbor—down the streets of Markham, across the metropolitan area, throughout the world. Do not be afraid to speak the words of love and compassion to others. Do not hesitate to preach the gospel of forgiveness and to share with others the beautiful dream and goal of unity and understanding.

If it seems to you as though no one is listening, know that *I* am listening. If no one seems to respond, know that *God* cares. If no one follows, know that you are leading by your example and your refusal to let others change what you know to be the truth. When you love God with all your heart, with all your soul, with all your mind, and with all your strength—and your neighbor as yourself—you are not far from the reign of God!

When Jesus calls us to love our neighbor, he is not giving us yet another command to obey, a rule to follow, an obligation to fulfill. He is offering us a *new way of life*. Life is to be lived not only for ourself and those like us, but also for those who may be different, those who are in need, those who may make us uneasy in their want.

Love of God and love of neighbor are inseparable twins. Where you find the one, you find the other. And where you don't find one, you won't find the other. A popular saying expresses this very poignantly:

> I sought my soul, but I could not see.
> I sought my God, but God eluded me.
> I sought my brother, and I found all three!

G. K. Chesterton once wrote that "we make our friends; we make our enemies; but God makes our next-door neighbors." Those neighbors, whatever language they speak, whatever the color of their skin, however they worship God—they were all made in God's image and likeness, and they are all created to be loved—especially by all who follow the Lord

Jesus. Father Sullivan has told me that you have just completed a three-day mission and that one of your themes was service to others. If you carry out that objective, you will not be far from the reign of God.

I wish to thank Father Sullivan and all of you for inviting me to be with you this morning. I am aware that you have come through some difficult times, especially with the closing of your parish school. I also know that you have developed a vibrant religious education program for elementary school children. Thank you for the many ways in which you remain active in this community of faith. I encourage you to continue to deepen your faith, to support your parish, and to give expression to the love that God has planted in your hearts.

Our love for others may not change the world overnight. But the world's indifference will not change our firm belief that love is the way, the truth, and the source of all life. Love does not come to an end. It lasts forever!

Parish Mass with the Ephphetha Ecumenical Choir

13th Sunday in Ordinary Time
Holy Name Cathedral, Chicago, Illinois
—*July 1, 1990* ——————————————————

Before my nephew, Joe Addison, moved to Chicago after graduating from college, he stayed with me whenever he came to town. Of course, this was quite convenient for him, and it was always an adventure for me. It changed my life a little whenever he visited Chicago. It certainly changed the atmosphere of my home. Sounds, conversations, and schedules change greatly when a teenager or young adult visits you. Over the years Joe came to know other young people in Chicago and brought them to my residence for a visit. Sometimes he would borrow my car, and I would have to get a ride with someone else!

Probably the most memorable of Joe's visits occurred when he was in college. I learned a lot about things that I'm normally not in contact with on a daily basis. Sharing breakfast and dinner with a college football player allowed me to tap into the searching, seemingly irrational, irregular, yet energetic and exciting life that he and so many young people live.

Offering my nephew hospitality involved some sacrifice and understanding, but also many unexpected rewards. Whenever we extend hospitality to someone, we give something of ourselves—for example, our time, our attention. But we also receive something in return—the gift of the persons we welcome, the gift of their uniqueness, their presence in our lives.

This morning, we welcome to this cathedral the Ephphetha Ecumenical Choir from Peoria. This choir, codirected by Mary Ann Fahey and Reese Nelson, gives the proceeds from its concerts to assist the poor. In

August they will be in Rome to sing at St. Peter's Basilica and give a concert at the Church of St. Ignatius. We are grateful for their spirited presence this morning; their talents and prayerfulness are obvious. And their gifts will echo in our thoughts and prayers throughout this day and in the days to come.

The Scriptures today call us to extend hospitality to others. In the book of Kings we heard of the woman of Shunem who welcomed Elisha with food and lodging. She recognized that he was a prophet, a man of God, and volunteered to provide for his needs. In return, Elisha rewarded the woman and her husband, who were childless, by promising them that within a year, God would bless them with a child.

In the gospel Jesus reminds us that, when we welcome someone into our lives or our home, we receive the gift of that person's presence. When we welcome a prophet, we receive his wisdom and vision, but also opposition and hostility a prophet often experiences when he teaches in God's name. When we welcome a holy person, we are gifted with that person's sense and love of God, but also the demands of holiness. When we welcome a disciple of the Lord, we receive the gift of the joy and the sacrifice of service. We receive the reward of a follower of Jesus: Those who welcome others truly welcome Jesus himself and God who sent him.

Hospitality, then, is an important virtue for the entire Church, as well as for the individual Christian.

For decades, the Catholic Church in metropolitan Chicago has extended welcome and hospitality to the many, diverse waves of immigrants who came here seeking a better life. The church continues to do so today, as immigrants come from all parts of the world, particularly Central and South America and Asia. While responding to the specific needs of each racial or ethnic group involves understanding and sacrifice, the church is greatly enriched by the diversity of its members. We must make every effort to continue to be a hospitable, welcoming community of faith.

Hospitality becomes highly personal as we, as individual Christians, welcome others into our lives, our homes. It is not only a matter of welcoming outright strangers; it also includes opening up our lives to those who should be familiar to us but have become strangers—estranged family members, for example, alienated friends. Sometimes people simply need a safe harbor in which to rest awhile on their difficult journey through life. It is not always easy, but, with effort and compassion, we can open up our lives to allow them to rest with us, to be nourished by wholesome and encouraging conversation, or simply letting them know we care. If they depart encouraged, with a renewed spirit, with a sense of hope they didn't have before—then we know that we have been truly hospitable.

St. Benedict, in his guidelines to religious communities, states that "all guests should be welcomed as Christ." That simple rule holds the profound truth that, when we extend ourselves in hospitality, we meet the Lord himself in our world and know God in our lives. As Jesus said, "Anyone who welcomes you welcomes me; and those who welcome me welcome the one who sent me." Moreover, if we welcome everyone as Christ—strangers, friends, guests, and family, especially those who are estranged and alienated from us—we will know the reward of God's presence through even the most unexpected people—even nephews!

Mass for the Colloquy
of Bishops and Scholars

Center for Development in Ministry
University of St. Mary of the Lake, Mundelein, Illinois
— *September 26, 1990* ————————————————

It is surely not the most important thing, and I should hope that it is not the most telling thing, but *one* thing perhaps, which distinguishes those of us in this room from many others, is our accumulated total of frequent-flier miles!

Our roles in the Church today—as bishops and theologians—often require us to travel. Our presence is required or desired at conferences and symposia, lectures and liturgies from Washington to Rome, from Jerusalem to Jakarta, from Melbourne to . . . Mundelein. If we had spent our time in other pursuits during these past few days, our combined experiences and shared wisdom could have resulted in a highly publishable travel guide; something to challenge "Michelin." The chapters might read, "How to Look Alert at a Papal Liturgy When Your Internal Clock Reads 4 A.M."; or, "How to Survive Seventeen Seminars in Six Languages in Four Days."

"Take nothing for the journey, neither walking staff nor traveling bag; no bread, no money. No one is to have two coats. Stay at whatever house you enter and proceed from there."

Thus did Jesus send his apostles forth to proclaim the reign of God and heal the afflicted. The image of the disciple as a traveler or explorer is one to which most of us can relate, even if our trips are seldom so unencumbered. And even when we exercise our ministries—as bishops and theologians, and even more simply, as believers and servants—even when we

471

exercise our ministries in those places we call "home," the image of traveler is an evocative one. For we minister within a Church which calls itself the "pilgrim" People of God. We are a dynamic community, not a fixed treasure or museum piece that is to be guarded until the end of time. We are a people on the move!

As Jesus' disciples, we, too, are sent forth with a great treasure, the Good News of the reign of God. We have humbly inherited this gospel from the pilgrims who have gone before us. Each of us has received it, personally, as a gift that has transformed our lives, as it did those of the Twelve long ago. And yet we cherish it *together*. For like all truly priceless gifts, it is given to us to be treasured, but never owned; it is meant for us, but is never really ours.

Impelled by this gift we share, we set out from village to village across this beautiful, suffering planet, sacraments of a sort of the One who sends us. We spread the Good News to all our brothers and sisters, friends and strangers alike. We bring the Lord's healing power to the afflicted, to the most vulnerable among us.

But we always keep one eye on the horizon. We watch for the day when our mission will come to its end, when every tear will be wiped away and every day will end in laughter. We look for that day when this banquet which we share will be fulfilled; when none of us will have to rush from the table to journey elsewhere. There will be no place else where we'll have to be, for on that day we'll already be home—with the risen Lord and all who have gone before us in faith.

My friends, may our earthly pilgrimage and travels—wherever they may take us—bring us back together one day in the Lord's own house.

32nd Sunday in Ordinary Time

Holy Name Cathedral, Chicago, Illinois

— November 11, 1990

When I was a little boy, growing up in Columbia, South Carolina, a summer day seemed to be without end. Once school had let out for vacation, my day was fairly unstructured—with the exception of mealtimes, and an Italian hardly needs a watch to know when it is mealtime! There was no need to mark time at all. There were no schedules to observe, no timetables to keep, no dates to make. Time could be gloriously wasted on frivolous play. I could simply do nothing, if I would so choose. Nothing seemed to matter, for the days then were without end. At least until Labor Day would come around.

How I long for even the slightest taste of those endless summer afternoons. There are so many deadlines I now have to make, so many time commitments I need to observe. Too rare are the moments when I am allowed the opportunity to just "kick back" and do nothing.

Recently, I had the opportunity to listen to the experiences of a man, who after thirty-some years, was "let go" by an employer for whom he had practically given his life's blood. Among the many struggles he had to face was the hardship of timelessness. When he was working, he moved at a frantic pace. He had too many schedules to keep, too many appointments to make. Like me, he would often long for a return to those days when there was absolutely nothing to do.

And then, in an unwelcomed way, those days came. The one who never had a moment's free time suddenly found that he had nothing but free time.

At first he attempted to keep up his standard pace in seeking out new employment. But he was unsuccessful. As the weeks of unemployment turned into months, there seemed little reason to observe time. There was nowhere to go and nothing to do. So much time without purpose deepened the man's depression, for he felt his life was now without purpose and meaning.

Eventually, he learned to create a structure for his day, to observe a schedule that enabled him to sense some purpose. Perhaps we do need some kind of deadline, some lines of demarcation, in order to appreciate the meaningfulness of our lives.

The liturgy in this month of November directs our attention to *the* end-times, *the* lines of demarcation, *the* deadlines. In accord with nature's move toward the death of winter, our worship celebrates All Saints and All Souls. The Scriptures we hear forthrightly proclaim the end of the age and the dawn of a New Heaven and a New Earth. Death becomes a theme for us to celebrate, from the perspective of our faith, of course.

In today's gospel, Jesus tells a parable which emphasizes the importance of a deadline. In the story, the bridesmaids have but a single purpose: to provide the groom a proper welcome. It is only the promise of his arrival that gives meaning to their waiting. Even though the deadline is unexpectedly extended by the groom's delay, it is the belief that he will come that gives the reason for the bridesmaids doing what they do: waiting with lamps burning.

The promise of the Lord's return in glory gives meaning to the Church's life. Because we believe in his words that the present age will pass and a new world will be born, we keep our lamps burning. We await his coming. We are ready.

The hoped-for deadline reminds us that the present time must be spent well. Like the clever bridesmaids, we are to be well prepared. We are not to forget our purpose. No matter how long the delay, we must be ready to give the Lord a proper welcome.

What is true for our life as a Church is also true for us as individuals. In the moment of our death, when time ends for us this side of eternity, the Lord comes to meet us. God willing, we will be ready.

Some would suggest that death robs life of its meaning. In life, we struggle and we toil. We engage in the many challenges we encounter in our human development. Because these struggles ultimately result in death, the process of life may seem absurd. Death's inevitability may make the tasks of life appear ridiculous.

But faith provides us with a different perspective on death, the ultimate deadline. Faith helps us recognize that, because life does come to its completion, what we do in the here and now is very important. Our waiting has a purpose. We await the One who meets us in death. We live our lives in a way which will give him a proper welcome. We bring the extra oil so that our waiting will not be in vain.

Faith reminds us that there's a wedding feast to attend *after* the groom is properly welcomed. Beyond death is God's mysterious future, a future which can only be described in a metaphor: it is like a wedding banquet!

As St. Paul reminds us, "We would have you clear about those who sleep in death, brothers and sisters, otherwise you might yield to grief like those who have no hope." We have hope. We believe God brings forth from death those who have trusted in the Bridegroom and await the future he has promised.

The Eucharist is a foretaste of God's heavenly banquet. At this table, we meet the Bridegroom who will come to us at the end of life and of time. May he strengthen us in our resolve to keep the life-lamps of our lives burning brightly!

Homily

Priesthood Ordination

Holy Name Cathedral, Chicago, Illinois
—*May 18, 1991*

My dear brothers and sisters in Christ: What a happy day this is for the church of Chicago! To the parents, families, friends, parish priests and seminary faculty: thank you for all you have done to make this day possible. If you will permit me, I'd like now to address in a very personal way, those who have presented themselves for ordination.

My dear brothers: You know how some people in positions of leadership and authority try at times to make their importance felt: fancy cars, the best tailor-made suits, high-power, high-profile lifestyles, the finest in material comfort. They climb the academic, corporate, or ecclesial ladders of success and assume the trappings which announce, "I've made it. . . . I'm successful. . . . I'm a leader. . . . I'm important!"

It cannot be that way with you, my brothers, who are about to be ordained.

As priests, you are certainly going to assume high-profile positions of leadership in the communities where you are assigned to serve. The Church needs you; it wants you to exercise wise and competent leadership.

But beware. Leadership and authority—even religious leadership and authority—can be a seductive, slippery slope. It is easy to lose perspective, to lose balance. It is easy to fall into the trap of self-centeredness.

I know that you have been blessed with many gifts for leadership. You are bright, articulate, skillful men. But keep your gifts in perspective. As St. Paul reminds us in today's second reading, your gifts, manifestations of the Spirit, have been given, not for your own self-aggrandizement, but for the common good, to build up the body of Christ.

I truly hope that, as priests, you will experience a profound sense of your giftedness and efficacy; I pray that you will be creative, vigorous preachers of the gospel; I pray that your people will be able to trust you and turn to you for direction, wisdom, and counsel.

But I also pray that you never begin to believe that any authority or power you may have is rooted in yourselves. To believe that is to open yourselves to an insidious, destructive clericalism which leads to a life of self-seeking entitlement, not to one of serving the common good of God's people. Ultimately, it leads to profound dissatisfaction, unhappiness, and isolation.

I have traveled this archdiocese extensively, and the most effective, satisfied priests I know are those who carry their authority gracefully, without trying to lord it over people. They realize from their own prayerful reflection, that, if they have any authority at all, it is the authority of love, Christ's love. They root themselves deeply in this love and seek to lead their people by serving them in the Spirit of the Lord.

I pray that this is the kind of leadership you will exercise throughout the course of your priestly ministry.

In times of rapid change and confusion, some people become frozen in fear, desperately searching for certitude, rigidly clinging to what is familiar and comfortable, closing themselves off from any possibility of an encounter with what might challenge or shake their carefully constructed worlds. You may know some people who live like that—insulated and isolated from the realities of life.

It cannot be like that with you.

As priests, you will be called to exercise the prophetic ministry described by Isaiah in the first reading. Anyone who hopes to exercise this ministry effectively must be willing to get close to people, the kind of people Isaiah describes: the lowly, the brokenhearted, the captive, the imprisoned, those who mourn.

People want you to be close to them so that you can touch their lives with Jesus' healing power. You need to know them intimately so that you can relate the gospel to their concrete life situation.

To be an effective priest also means that you must be willing to get your hands dirty. No matter how confusing, messy, or bewildering life may seem, it is there that you will encounter the Lord. You will not find him in fancy vestments or fixed formulas; you will not find him in complex structures or in bricks and mortar, as important as these may be at times for the well-being and good order of the faith community.

But you *will* encounter him in the lives of the people you serve. So listen closely to them as they articulate their needs and wants, their hungers and aspirations. If you listen attentively, you cannot help but hear the voice of him who calls you out of your fear and doubt and anoints you to proclaim, boldly and lovingly, the glad tidings he has revealed to us. Yes, know them, really *know* them, so that you can recognize in them Christ's voice, and help them to celebrate those moments when their lives are transformed by his life-giving word.

Do you know why some people—good, well-intentioned people—have a difficult time making a permanent commitment? They approach life and commitment with an attitude of "if this does not work out for me, I will try something else."

It cannot be that way with you.

My brothers, I am confident that you will find much joy and fulfillment in your priestly ministry. I certainly have. But I also know that there will be moments when things will not be so joyful or fulfilling. You can count on it.

There will be times when, perhaps due to the stress of ministry or the challenge of celibacy, or some other personal difficulty, you will ask yourself, "Why in the world did I ever become a priest?"

Let me assure you, those kinds of questions are normal, even healthy. I can assure you that I have had to face the questions and challenges many times during the nearly four decades I have been a priest and bishop. Talk to any married couple, and they will assure you that they sometimes ask themselves similar questions.

It is precisely during those difficult times that you will need to rely on your commitment to carry you through.

You will be able to do this because commitment is a two-way street; there is an element of mutuality in it. Not only do you make a commitment to give your life to the risen Lord by serving his people as a priest, but Christ affirms what you do, and makes a commitment to give his life to you through his body, the Church. Through his Church, in which both his word and sacrament are celebrated, he will offer you the sustenance and strength you need.

To put it another way: the Church lays claim on you in the commitment you make today. But you also lay claim on the Church in order to receive the support and nourishment you will need to exercise your ministry effectively.

When you entered this cathedral this morning, you noticed that it is crowded. It is filled with people who love you and support the commitment you are making. So you are not alone. Just as people can rightfully expect to turn to you for ministry, so you have a right to rely on your fellow disciples—both lay and ordained—to support you.

I pray that, through the course of your priesthood, you will allow the commitment, which you make today and will repeatedly reaffirm in the future, to see you through the difficult times, and lead you to experience, at ever-deeper levels, the purifying power of Jesus' love.

My dear brothers, I have been a priest for thirty-nine years, twenty-five of them as a bishop. I would like to repeat something I said at my anniversary celebration last month, when I spoke of the paramount importance of an intimate relationship with the Lord Jesus:

> If we are totally caught up with Jesus; if we are in love with him and convinced that he will ever be at our side to support us, we will never surrender to discouragement. The trials and disappointments of daily life will only confirm our faith and strengthen our resolve to proclaim the gospel to all people, whatever the cost to ourselves.

I believe that with all my heart, and I am convinced that if, as priests, together with me, you cling to that relationship with the Lord, you will offer the kind of faith-filled, courageous, committed leadership which the Church so needs today. You will be, as your class motto so beautifully states, true disciples, true servants.

Homily

Festa Italiana

20th Sunday in Ordinary Time
Grant Park, Chicago, Illinois
—*August 18, 1991* ————————————————

"Are you hungry?"

Traditionally, that question has played a key role in Italian homes. Sometimes it's spoken, but often it's merely implied. In any case, we know that the answer almost always is "Yes!" A few weeks ago, I visited my family and friends in northern Italy—in the Trentino region—and enjoyed their wonderful cuisine. Whatever part of Italy one may be from, there is a long and proud culinary tradition that prompts us to respond positively to the question, "Are you hungry?" What Italian family doesn't have special recipes handed on from generation to generation—linking us today with an important part of our rich cultural heritage?

But the important thing is not simply the unquestionable delights of Italian food itself. Meals do more than fill empty stomachs; they bind family members together in close relationships; they create an intimacy which is so vital, so important to our well-being. On special occasions, we include our broader family—grandparents, aunts and uncles, cousins and second cousins—depending on the size of our dinner table or backyard! Moreover, offering warm hospitality to friends—and strangers—is also an important part of Italian tradition. In short, eating tasty food together, enjoying good conversation, sharing experiences and memories—all these things build up a united, harmonious community.

If you look around you this afternoon, you'll see what I mean. You may know many people here, but there are undoubtedly very many with whom you're not familiar. It makes no difference. We're a *community* which is celebrating its common Italian heritage!

480

But there's an even more profound and marvelous dimension to our being together this afternoon. It may not be immediately obvious to each of us, but it is at the very heart of our celebration and, specifically, this Eucharist. Today, *God* asks us, "Are you hungry?"!

Let me caution you against answering the Lord's question too quickly. The answer may seem more evident than it truly is in the reality of our daily lives.

An old Italian saying points out that "the full stomach does not believe in hunger." There is much wisdom in this proverb. It reminds us that it is fairly easy today, when we are successful and enjoy a prosperity which our ancestors could only dream about, to become complacent, confident in our own abilities, no longer anxious about the future. It is easy to get so caught up with material things and our work that we no longer sense the deeper—indeed, the *deepest*—hungers of our heart.

But, sometimes—in quiet, reflective moments—we may ask ourselves questions like, "Is this all there is to being married and raising a family? Is this all there is to having a career? Is this all there is to *life?!*" While these may be unsettling questions, they are very important because they begin to bring us back into contact with the deeper hungers of our heart. And that is when we are able to respond—directly and honestly—to God's question, "Are you hungry—for something more?" with a profound "Yes!" "Yes, only you, God, can satisfy the deepest hunger of our hearts." It was Jesus who told us, as we heard in today's gospel, that only he could give us the kind of food that would satisfy our deepest hungers. "I myself," he said, "am the living bread come down from heaven. If anyone eats this bread, he shall live forever; the bread I will give is my flesh, for the life of the world. . . . Let me solemnly assure you, if you do not eat the flesh of the Son of Man and drink his blood, you have no life in you."

The reading from the book of Proverbs describes the marvelous banquet which Wisdom prepares for the wise—its choice meats, its splendid wine. This dinner finds fulfillment in the Sacred Meal in which the Lord becomes the living bread which he promised to the disciples nearly 2,000 years ago. In this Sacred Meal, in which we eat his Body and drink his Blood, under the appearance of bread and wine, Jesus promises to abide with us forever.

My dear friends, as we gather around this table as a family of faith, let us respond wholeheartedly to the Lord's question: "Are you hungry?" Yes, we are hungry; we are hungry for the Bread of Life! Let us give thanks to the Lord for giving us such a great gift. As St. Paul told the Ephesians, "Give thanks to God the Father always and for everything in the name of our Lord, Jesus Christ."

Homily

Association of Catholic Diocesan Archivists

18ᵗʰ Sunday in Ordinary Time
University of St. Mary of the Lake, Mundelein, Illinois
——*August 2, 1992* ——————————————————

We gather for worship on Sunday not only to thank God for the past week, but also to acknowledge that, no matter how hard we work, everything in the future is, ultimately, in *his* hands.

We also gather to listen to the word of God which both comforts and challenges us. I think you will agree with me that the readings for this eighteenth Sunday of the year present more *challenge* than comfort.

The first reading, from the book of Ecclesiastes, opens on a rather dismal note: "Vanity of vanities! All things are vanity!" The whole enterprise of human life and activity is only a "puff of wind," a single breath, nothing more. The author says this even though he had buried himself in his work. He apparently has been successful but cannot sleep at night. Why? Because he does not know how long he will live before death overtakes him. And, like the rest of us, he will leave his inheritance and all that he has accumulated in life to someone else—who may be wise or foolish. Was it all worth it, then? he asks himself—and us.

Throughout the centuries, Jews and Christians have often asked what this gloomy book is doing in the Bible! But can any of us deny that there are dark moments in our own lives, moments when we wonder whether what we are doing is really worthwhile? Moreover, we seek to discern God's will for us, but, at times, we may very much feel like the author of Ecclesiastes. He believed that everything was in God's hands and happened according to his plan. But at times he did not have a clear idea of what God's will was for him. We, too, are believers but, at times, are we not like the author of Ecclesiastes? Do we not sometimes feel a disquieting emptiness in our lives? Do we not experience God's absence more than his presence? Are there not times when we can only pray, in faith, "thy will be done" without having the slightest clue as to what the future holds for us?

Today's gospel builds on the first reading. Its context is a dispute two sons are having over their inheritance. We often hear about this kind of conflict—arguing over who gets grandmother's china, mother's silverware, father's fishing equipment, the family home, the savings accounts, etc. Even the closest family may find it easier to accept their grief upon the death of a loved one than to settle amicably the provisions of the will and the distribution of the inheritance.

Despite the fact that the young man in the gospel brashly interrupts Jesus' discussion with his disciples, it is not difficult to identify with his plight. There were provisions in the Law of Moses for dividing up an inheritance. Apparently, the young man did not think they were being followed. So he asked Jesus for his counsel and advice.

But Jesus refuses to referee the family dispute. Jesus was not really concerned about *who* would get *what* in this particular instance. Rather, Jesus' concern is the attitude we have toward our riches or possessions: the way we use them; whether we become so attached to our possessions that we give no time or attention to God and our neighbors, no time and attention to those things that really matter.

In many respects the rich man in the gospel parable is a good example of how the "work ethic," which we value so highly, pays off. He is a hard worker whom nature has blessed with abundant harvests. Who can argue with such success?

Jesus can and does! The successful farmer of the parable hoards his goods. They take the central place in his life, not God, nor the needs of others. He thinks only of himself; he plans only for himself. He even congratulates himself!

But his sudden death reveals the folly of his attitude, the folly of his approach and his actions. Despite his apparent success, he lived as a fool. And he dies as one. Jesus' message is quite clear: hard work, the accumulation of possessions, and even success do not, of themselves, make life worthwhile. Rather, it is only *wisdom* that can help a person find meaning in life. It is only wisdom that can show us how to live in accord with the word of God; it is only wisdom that enables us to live in God's presence and to be concerned about the needs of our brothers and sisters. All else is foolishness; all else, as we heard in the first reading, is vanity that quickly vanishes.

My brothers and sisters, I know you work hard on behalf of the Church. I share your dedication and encourage you to continue to develop diocesan archives which are the local church's institutional memory. You do much more than simply put order into stacks of correspondence and reports and innumerable files. The materials which are preserved in our archives tell the story of how God has been present and active within our respective communities of faith. By preserving the records of the present and past, and making those records available to others, you help witness to the larger community what God has done through his Church, through his people who are on their pilgrim way. Your work is indeed an important part of the Church's ministry.

I myself have had a personal interest in archives and a certain responsibility for them for the past thirty-eight years—in three dioceses: Charleston, Cincinnati, and Chicago. And I should also mention the five years I was general secretary of the Bishops' Conference and had ultimate responsibility for its archives.

When I was appointed chancellor of the Diocese of Charleston in 1954, I found all the records of the diocese in cardboard boxes, deteriorating in a dank basement vault, covered with mildew. The first summer I sent two seminarians to a local college to learn the basic elements about processing documents, and then each summer after that they worked on the archives. Before they were ordained, they trained two other seminarians so the work continued. In 1957 we built a special fire-resistant, humidity-controlled room for our records. I mention this simply to let you know of my own personal involvement, as a novice, in your work.

Please accept my presence here this morning as a sign of my respect and appreciation for what you do and my gratitude for all that you do for the Church. Some of you are only beginning this kind of work; others are veterans with considerable experience and expertise. The contribution of each of you is invaluable, and I thank you.

With the words of today's readings still ringing in our ears, I pray that all of us will hear the challenge of the word of God and strive, with his help, to be truly wise persons. In the final analysis this is all that counts. All else is foolishness and vanity.

Calvert House

28ᵗʰ Sunday in Ordinary Time
University of Chicago, Chicago, Illinois
———*October 11, 1992* ————————————————

A couple of years ago, some scientists and engineers in Scotland designed a special kind of mirror. You know that when you see yourself in a normal mirror, everything is reversed. Your right arm is on your left; your left ear is on the right. The technicians managed to create a system that showed people as they really are, as they looked to others, without being reversed.

When the scientists allowed people to try out the mirror, they found something odd. People preferred the regular kind of mirror. People did not, as the poet Robert Burns thought they would, prefer to see themselves as others saw them. There was something slightly unnerving about seeing oneself that way.

It may be true, as T. S. Eliot said, that we humans cannot stand too much reality. Yet we know that we need to face ourselves and our world directly and be willing to ask and answer tough questions. Otherwise, we live a kind of "half life," an inauthentic existence. The unexamined life is not worth living. If we fail to look honestly at ourselves, our world, and its problems, we will never grow beyond self-delusion and grand illusions.

This has never been more true than now, at the end of the twentieth century, when we are confronted with an "age of limits." No longer can we let ideologies of unchecked growth and development hold sway. We must honestly look at our lifestyles and begin to pursue more realistic models of development, if only for the selfish motive of mere human survival on this planet.

485

The search for answers to both age-old and new human quests takes up much of your time here at the University of Chicago. No matter what shape our quest takes, no matter what our field may be, we believers find that the starting point and the place we return to again and again is God's Word.

God's word is summed up in the gospel which Jesus Christ preached: "Repent and believe in the Good News." Jesus invites us to live an authentic human life by, first, honestly looking at ourselves, seeing ourselves as God sees us, and then accepting God's power to heal us. All our searching thus becomes informed and energized by our experiences of God's love and healing power. Our search for the truth is then not grounded on a false notion of objectivity, but on an honest assessment of how we contribute to our own problems and an acknowledgment that we cannot rely solely on our own power for solutions. Like the leper in the gospel story, we return to the One who offers us wholeness in order to give thanks.

We Catholics believe that the Catholic faith offers the best vantage point from which to see how God's word, which cannot be chained up, is at work in the world. Because of that, as Pope John XXIII and the Second Vatican Council said, we need to read the signs of the times. Because of our vocation as believers, as Catholics, we must be ready to live at the intersection of every human search, every human quest. Let me explain what I mean.

Whenever I visit this university, I am struck by its two dominant architectural styles. These two styles present a paradigm for the human quest as we have known it in the twentieth century.

On the one hand, the Gothic spires of Mandell Hall and the buildings surrounding the quadrangle raise our eyes to the transcendent and recall the origins of universities as great, medieval centers of learning which focused on God's word in Scripture as the point of departure for all human learning. The Gothic style reminds us that many of our answers must come "from above."

At the same time, the Regenstein Library, with its massive, horizontal blocks, like a pyramid whose upper part pointing to heaven has been sliced off, brings us back firmly to earth. Like the angels who appeared to the apostles after the Lord's ascension, the Regenstein's horizontal architecture asks us *why* we stand looking up to heaven. DNA roots us in, and connects us to, all other life. The molecules of the elements that constitute us, witness to the fact that we are of the earth and descended from star stuff. We are not angelic beings. We must live in communion with everyday, earthly realities.

At the end of the twentieth century, at a time when many claim a postmodernist perspective, we are more aware than ever that both the vertical and the horizontal emphases are necessary. There is not a confrontation between two cultures, but a rich dialectic emerging between religious and scientific faiths.

The Catholic faith has always invited its members to respond to God's word at the intersections, at the point of the cross between the transcendent and the immanent. Our faith proclaims that God's word cannot be controlled. God is at work in the world to heal and shape the future. That is a hopeful vision to offer to a world which, in modern times, has chosen to wallow in nihilism, in isolation and alienation.

As in the story of Naaman and Elisha, the Catholic faith offers a vision of God's power at work in the limited, earthly, human reality. We believe that the answer to our deepest human yearnings is available to us, if only we seek it.

However, the search begins by facing the truth. And the truth, quite simply, is that we need healing, we cannot heal ourselves, and the ultimate source of healing is the Lord Jesus, whose loving, healing power is available to us through the Church.

In your time at the university you will sometimes hear of—and you will certainly read about—critiques and reevaluations of the history of Christianity and, in particular, of the Catholic Church and its role in history. A timely example is the extremely negative views, put forward by some during this Columbian year, of Christianity's role in the history of the European settlement of the Americas.

Certainly, the Church is and has been made up of sinful men and women. The phrase, *semper reformanda* (always in need of reform), applies to the Church as much as any other institution. Honestly seeing ourselves as God sees us is the beginning of the gospel.

But I hope that you will also hear and read about the great women and men of the Catholic faith who have tried untiringly to work for justice and peace for all people in every age. Through them the Church affects human development in many untold, positive ways and has done so through the centuries. The positive effects of our faith can get lost in the ideologically motivated critiques of the Church and its place in history. In part, this is because too few of us return, like the healed man in the gospel, to praise God for the benefits of our faith in the modern world.

Like Calvert House itself, the Catholic faith offers you direction in a demanding life and a quiet place in which to sort out the important from the nonessential. Our faith offers a quiet place to discover a convergence of many perspectives along with other believers and, so, to discover the Lord who heals us from our isolation and sin.

In the calm, secure place that our faith provides for us, we are not afraid to see ourselves as we are: as sinners who continue to need and to find healing from the spiritual, cultural, and social wounds that harm our communion with one another and with God.

My prayer for you today is that you discover the great advantage, indeed the great gift, you have in your Catholic faith. Through your faith, may the Lord guide you in the way of all truth. Through this communion we are about to share, may we all obtain the healing which is only in Christ Jesus.

Homily

Diaconate Ordination

Mundelein Seminary, Mundelein, Illinois

—— December 11, 1993 ————————————————

My dear brothers and sisters in the Lord, at the heart of Christian faith is a drama. What has captivated Christian saints, scholars, poets, mystics, and artists over the centuries is the shocking and unexpected drama of the incarnation. In Christ Jesus, the God of the universe, the Creator of all things, has become a creature, has embraced the world in all of its limitation and imperfection. Indeed, on the cross, tasting the bitterness of despair and death, he even felt abandoned by his Father. In this great dramatic embrace, God shows that no one is beyond the reach of his love, that all have been invited to a share in the divine life. In this sense, God's bending low is "glad tidings to the lowly"; his acceptance of slavery, a proclamation of liberty to captives; his own heartbreak, salvation to the brokenhearted.

My brothers, in a few moments, I will ordain you for ministry and service as deacons in the Church of Jesus Christ. The servant of Jesus is not primarily a psychologist, social worker, or counselor. Rather, he is someone who has been drawn into the dynamism and energy of the incarnation, someone who is overwhelmed by the romance and drama of what has occurred in Christ, and who, therefore, wishes to participate in the process by which all people are invited to salvation. The deacon, the servant of Jesus, is the one who, like his master, goes out to the poor, the lowly, the rejected, those in the shadow of death. He carries to them the Father's infinite and unconditional love. And he does so, not "at a distance," but through identification: he becomes poor with the poor; he suffers with those who suffer; he enters into the hopelessness of the desperate in order to convince them that "nothing can ever come between us and the love of Jesus Christ." As deacons, and one day as priests, you will enter into the drama of the incarnation and thus help to light on the earth the fire of God's compassionate love.

During the ordination rite, you will promise to celebrate the Liturgy of the Hours "for the Church and for the whole world." You cannot be a servant in the spirit of Jesus unless you "pray constantly," unless you give yourself to a regular contemplation of the beauty that has appeared in the incarnation. In praying the Liturgy of the Hours, day in and day out, you will be drawn into intimacy with the Lord. You will find yourself more and more conformed to the image of Jesus. In prayer, you will take on the mind and heart of Christ Jesus. You will learn to imitate the gestures and movements of the Son of God, becoming an apprentice to the Incarnate Word.

My brothers, prayer is not optional for Jesus' minister. It is his lifeblood, his source of inspiration, his indispensable support. It is also, as St. Paul points out, his joy. Drawn into the awesome drama of the incarnation, how can one not rejoice? How can one not be enlivened? If, throughout your life, you want to be a minister who radiates the message of the gospel, never stop praying. Never cease to stare at the beauty and wonder of Christ. I can tell you, my brothers, it is intimacy with the Lord—an intimacy nourished each day by prayer—that has given me the strength I have needed this past month, and the peace I have experienced.

Today, you commit yourselves to service, prayer, and also celibacy. My brothers, this may be the most difficult and demanding promise that you will ever make. Why? Because the celibate life is inherently challenging. It is also so "politically incorrect," so countercultural. To many people in our society, celibacy appears strange, psychologically unhealthy, even bizarre.

However, like Christian service and prayer, celibacy must be understood against the background of the admittedly bizarre claim that God has become a human being. What God accomplished in Jesus is surprising, shocking, overwhelming. No one had ever imagined the range and intensity of the divine love that appeared in Jesus' dying and rising. No one could ever have dreamed that God would enter into our humanity and embrace us with such compassion and intimacy. God's love is disclosed as excessive, extravagant, surprising—and, yes, unreasonable.

Celibacy is an expression of that radical gift of self. Are there "reasons" for celibacy, arguments that can be used to "explain" it? Some have said that the celibate lifestyle frees one for more intensive ministry. It allows one to channel more of one's energies into prayer. Some suggest that the celibate is effectively "married" to the people he serves. These explanations are not entirely without merit. But they do not get to the heart of the matter, because they try to rationalize something which is deeper than reason. You are embracing celibacy because you want to make of yourself a gift to the One who has loved you so surprisingly, so overwhelmingly, so completely. Like the woman at Bethany, who unreasonably and excessively broke open the whole bottle of perfume at Jesus' feet, you also wish to break open your lives in gratitude, responding extravagantly to the Creator who is unreasonable love.

Brothers, in your service, your prayer, and your celibate commitment, you fulfill the role of John the Baptist. You become living witnesses to the Light. Everything you are and everything you do will be based upon, and will revolve around, the blazing light which is the incarnation. Your ministry will reflect Jesus' saving work. Your prayer will draw you near to the risen Lord. Your celibacy will speak of the overwhelming drama of God's action in Christ Jesus. You go as heralds to your respective dioceses and countries, testifying to Jesus in different languages, in different cultural contexts, in good times and bad, in season and out, despite opposition, with the joy and serenity that comes from living in the Light of Christ.

* * *

I offer a special word of gratitude to the parents, grandparents, relatives, and friends of these candidates. You are the ones who first introduced them to Jesus. In your words, your struggles, your patience, your joy, you spoke to them of the Incarnate God to whom, today, they commit themselves to serve. Through you, God has been mysteriously at work, guiding these men to this day. For you, for them, and for the Church which enlivens and nourishes us all, I give thanks and praise.

Priesthood Ordination

Holy Name Cathedral, Chicago, Illinois
—*May 21, 1994*

My dear brothers in the risen Lord,

This is a day of great joy for the church of metropolitan Chicago. For, in the presence of those who have nurtured and supported you over the years—your parents, brothers and sisters, relatives, friends, seminary faculty and staff, and priests of the archdiocese—I will ordain you priests. In you, the Lord will continue to fulfill his promise to be a Good Shepherd, one who knows his people and cares for them.

In my years as a priest and a bishop, especially during my years here in Chicago, I have learned that, while people may be very different on the surface, deep down we are all pretty much alike. Whether a person lives in an inner-city housing project, a bungalow on the South Side, or an affluent mansion on the North Shore, people often share the same needs, fears, hopes, dreams, flaws, and joys. Whether someone is the head of a great corporation or a janitor, whether someone is a famous surgeon or a homemaker, whether someone is a senior citizen in a nursing home or a teenager in high school, we all share the same basic human condition with its wonderful possibilities and its frustrating limitations.

So, beneath the surface, our deepest joys and concerns are very much alike. Whether we are rich or poor, African-American or Caucasian, young or old, English-speaking or Spanish-speaking, we all search for friendship, respect, and understanding. We rejoice when a new baby is born into our family. We want those whom we care about to know that someone truly loves them both in good times and bad. When we make a mess of life, we try to make a new beginning. We want to learn from our mistakes. We want to reach out and help one another. When we are sick, we hurt just the same as others. When we are afraid, we seek people who understand us.

My brothers, who are about to be ordained, why do I focus on all of this on your day of ordination to the priesthood? Because it is the unique privilege of the priest to be with so many people during the special moments and experiences of their lives. When a new baby is born, what happens? The family calls the priest to arrange a baptism. The priest can see this as merely another baptism—perhaps one of seven or eight he celebrates on a particular weekend. Or he can see it for the very special moment it is in the life of this family. Likewise, when youngsters come to the time for First Holy Communion, they and their families celebrate this milestone with the priest. On such an occasion the manner of the priest in celebrating the Eucharist and the words he shares in his homily can touch hearts and rekindle faith in people who may have been away from God for years, or, unfortunately, it can be only a routine, run-of-the-mill ritual.

The same is true of weddings, confessions, illnesses. All of these can be truly grace-filled encounters with the living God—or they can be stale, dull, routine, empty, listless ceremonies. People come to us at the pivotal moments of life. As Jesus says in the gospel, we want to give them nourishing bread rather than a cold stone. We want to give them an egg rather than a scorpion. For, at the very core of ordination is the profound reality that you, members of the Ordination Class of 1994, can really make a profound difference in the lives of many, many people. That is an essential point for you and all of us to remember.

We live in a world in which many people deeply appreciate the Church and the priesthood. But there are others who have difficulty understanding why a group of talented, intelligent, energetic people like yourselves would want to spend their lives as priests. It's not a highly remunerative occupation. It's not the kind of position which provides much opportunity to become a mover or shaker in our society. You sacrifice a wife and family of your own in order to serve the kingdom of God. It is not a ready avenue to fame or fortune. You know all of that. So why are you taking this step today?

Why? Because you have become increasingly aware of the deep hungers of the human spirit. You are aware of people who try to have it all, only to discover that possessions do not satisfy the profound yearnings of the human spirit. You realize that the priest is the unique person who is privileged to be invited by so many to enter into the key events of life as the Church's representative—indeed, as God's representative. You realize that you will be privileged to baptize babies and catechumens, celebrate weddings and First Communions, anoint the sick and comfort the dying, and lead the confused or brokenhearted to the experience of God's compassion, mercy, and forgiveness. You will gather the community to break the bread of the Eucharist and to ponder the mysterious meaning of God's holy word. You will be the shepherds of the flock, the heralds of the Good News, the mediators between God and his beloved people.

As you await the moment of ordination, you may very well be pondering the mystery of it all, as the prophet Jeremiah did so many centuries ago. Why me, Lord? I am so unworthy. I am too young. There are many others who are more capable. In reply, the Lord God says to each one of you, as he said to those of us who have preceded you in this marvelous and mysterious vocation, "Do not be afraid, for I am with you. I will give you the words to say." I will be your strength. I will not leave you alone in the desert.

A second thought that may enter your mind as you await the time of ordination may well be: what am I getting myself into? These are challenging times in the Catholic Church. We are experiencing a shortage of priests. Many parishes face difficult financial problems. Communities are polarized by all kinds of disputes or tensions. If it is any comfort, you will realize that the Church has never been a community without challenges. Jesus faced problems. Peter faced problems. Athanasius, Augustine, Dominic, Francis of Assisi, Gregory the Great—all faced problems. Mary Magdalene, Catherine of Siena, Teresa of Avila, Thérèse of Lisieux, Frances Xavier Cabrini—all faced problems.

But the words of St. Paul in today's second reading put those challenges into perspective. Paul says to me and to you and to all of us who have been called to the priesthood: "Lead a life worthy of the calling to which you have been summoned. Bear with one another. Make every effort to maintain the unity of the Spirit in the bond of peace."

And then Paul launches into his beautiful litany of unity. You and I are called to be spokesmen for unity in the Church wherever we are assigned—in the inner city or the outer city, in an ethnic parish or a suburban parish. Wherever and whenever and however we work as God's servants, we are to serve the unity of the community. For as Paul says, "There is one body, one Spirit, one hope, one Lord, one faith, one baptism, one God and Father of all."

And so, my hopeful and beloved brothers, my prayer for you this day is that you will find great joy in the priesthood and that you will be messengers of joy to the people of the archdiocese who so hunger and thirst for God. As Jesus said in John's Gospel, "As the father has loved us . . . so I love you. I have appointed you to go forth and bear much fruit, fruit that will last."

Homily

Church of St. Felicitas

25ᵗʰ Sunday in Ordinary Time
Chicago, Illinois
—*September 18, 1994* —————————————————————

It was Tanisha's first day of kindergarten, and, since she was the youngest of three children, it was also a major trauma for the family. Her father, an office manager, sneaked into her bedroom before leaving for work and sang into her ear, "School days, school days, dear old golden rule days." Although he looked at a groggy five-year-old, all he could see was the memory of his newborn baby daughter. He kissed her a prayer and left like a man carrying a secret treasure.

At breakfast, Natasha, the seventh grader, gave up some of her precious bathroom time to comb out and braid Tanisha's hair. She explained that she didn't want to be embarrassed by her "geeky" little sister, but the tenderness of her brush strokes told a different story. Derrick, the world-wise eighth grader, broke his vow of adolescent silence long enough to tell Tanisha to look both ways before crossing the street. He also whispered that she could use his Sony Walkman after school if she didn't say hello to him on the playground.

And Mom—she just sniffled a bit. She said it was an allergy, but everyone knew different. And later, when Mom hugged Tanisha at the door of the kindergarten room and told her that she was "the best!" Tanisha believed her. She had heard it all before.

"Then Jesus took a little child, stood him in their midst, and putting his arms around him said to them, 'Whoever welcomes a little child such as this for my sake welcomes me.'"

Jesus knew something about little children. He knew something about the wonderful ways children affect our hearts. Today, my dear brothers and sisters, during this seventy-fifth anniversary year of your parish, the Lord places that same child of the gospel in your midst that you might better know as a parish community the future to which you are called.

Think of the children in your life. How do they affect you? To what do little children in our midst call us? Please allow a celibate—someone who loves children as you do—to speculate.

The innocence of children challenges our cynicism. Their energy calls forth our wisdom. Their joy and wonder nudge us into awe in the face of life's mysteries. Their preciousness jolts us out of apathy. Their vulnerability and need evoke from us unconditional love and generosity. In short, children call forth our best selves. Children call us beyond self-concern into the enterprise of selflessness.

Jesus was a brilliant teacher. He used the example of a little child, and the spontaneous love which children elicit from our hearts, as a way of settling the argument among his disciples as to who was the most important. The most important in God's kingdom is the person who is the last and the servant of all. Children make servants of us all—in a good sense. It is not a question of spoiling children. Rather, loving parents don't put their own needs and wants before their children's. Children make us spontaneously and incredibly selfless lovers. And that is precisely Jesus' point. The most important in the kingdom of God is the person who loves and serves others in the way we naturally love children. Jesus is trying to expand the scope of our selfless love. He's saying that we are to be to the whole world what we are to our children.

Have you ever noticed the effect a newly born baby has on a room full of adults? Everyone wants to hold the baby! Everyone responds instantly to the baby's cries—for food or whatever. Everyone wants to make the baby laugh, feel more comfortable, stay at peace.

Jesus says: if you want to be most important in the kingdom, do that for one another. Defer your own needs and wants in light of the wonderful opportunity to care for another. Place each other's welfare before your own. Respond as generously and lovingly to one another as you would to the most precious and vulnerable child because, after all, isn't there a frightened and lonely child within each of us?

What does this gospel mean for you? My brothers and sisters, God calls you, as a parish, to be a living sign of the way members of a Christian community care for one another. It is an invitation to imitate Jesus who provides us with a model by caring for us all. He invites you to be a community of disciples whose only concern is to care for one another as deeply as you are able.

Let your loving concern extend beyond this community to include the entire city of Chicago, the entire archdiocese, the country, the world.

Factions are inappropriate in such a community. Collaboration among multiple ministries and services is, on the other hand, very fitting. Such a community is not arbitrarily divided by reason of age. Instead, it enables old and young to feel young and old enough to be at home. A community of Jesus' disciples is a place where those who do not belong to the Church can confidently come to enjoy hospitality and solidarity. In such a community everyone's gifts find opportunity for development and sharing, and all the spiritual and corporal works of mercy are carried out generously and effectively.

On this occasion, I thank all who have made this parish such a community over the years—the priests, the permanent deacons, the religious, and the laity. I wish to acknowledge the presence of Father Thomas Boyle, your pastor emeritus, and Father Howard Tuite, your former pastor. In a special way I pay tribute to Father John Boyle, your present pastor, and Sister Rosemary Brennan, your principal. Parishes don't just "happen." Neither do Catholic schools! It's the faith, dedication, and generosity of the people—the parents—and those who minister to them that give our parishes and schools their distinctive quality and personality. So, I thank you for all you have done to make St. Felicitas the vibrant community that it is.

My dear friends, thank you for inviting me to join you for this Sunday Eucharist during your seventy-fifth anniversary year. I am especially delighted that we have gathered for this first Family Mass of the new school year. My prayer for all of you is King Solomon's prayer for his people taken from the first reading:

> May the Lord God listen to your cries and prayers uttered before him.
> May his eyes be ever upon this community night and day. And may you
> be forever worthy of his name.

My prayers go with you as you seek to become the greatest in our midst by becoming the servant of all.

Homily

Celebration of 103 Korean Martyrs

Chicago, Illinois

── *September 25, 1994* ──────────────────────────

Annyong Haship Nikka? (Greetings/How are you?) *Yo-ro-boon ban-kap soup-ni-da!* (I am glad to see all of you!)

Anthony de Mello, in his book *One Minute Wisdom*, tells the following story:

> The Master said to his disciples: "Suffering can bring about growth and new life." The Master went on to explain: "Each day a bird would shelter in the withered branch of a dying tree that stood in the middle of a vast, deserted plain. One day a storm uprooted the tree, forcing the bird to fly a hundred miles in search of shelter till finally it came to a forest of fruit-laden trees."
>
> The Master concluded: "If the withered tree had survived, nothing would have induced the bird to give up its security and fly."

My dear brothers and sisters in Christ, how good it is for us to be here today as we celebrate and commemorate the life and the death of the 103 Korean Martyrs. These holy men and women were canonized by our Holy Father Pope John Paul II in 1984 during his pastoral visit to Korea. We honor those martyrs who took Jesus' words to heart and were willing to take up their Cross each day and follow in his steps. The holy martyrs risked and lost everything that the world deems important and in doing so were given a new and resurrected life in Christ.

We are all aware that in the history of the Catholic Church in Korea there are literally thousands of men and women who gave their lives for

498

the sake of the gospel. The 103 saints we remember and reverence today represent so many others whose names are known to God alone. The terrible suffering and the shedding of the martyrs' blood is directly responsible for the tremendous growth of the church in Korea. The suffering and the death of so many, done with a deep and abiding faith in the Lord, has brought new life and hope to the people of Korea and beyond.

We believe, as we just heard from the book of Wisdom, that "the souls of the just are in the hands of God and that no torment shall touch them." We believe that the martyrs of Korea "shall judge nations and rule over peoples and that the Lord shall be their King forever. We believe that God's grace and mercy are with his holy ones, and his care is with his elect." We are grateful to the Korean martyrs for their courageous example of faith.

The Catholic Church in Korea has a unique history in the larger history of the Catholic Church. Christianity came to Korea, not by foreign missionaries evangelizing the people, but rather by a Korean layman. The Korean Church was founded by Yi Sung-hun. Yi Sung-hun was baptized in Peking in 1784 by a Jesuit priest and given the name Peter and then returned to Korea to spread the Good News of Jesus. Yi Sung-hun and his early Christian community suffered greatly because of their faith, and in 1785 the persecutions and bloodshedding began.

Nonetheless, because of the heroic example of Yi Sung-hun and many other committed disciples, the Catholic Church in Korea survived and thrived. Those who had come to know the Lord would not allow themselves to be separated from him. As St. Paul says so eloquently in his letter to the Romans: "Who will separate us from the love of Christ? Trial, or distress, or persecution, or hunger, or nakedness, or danger, or the sword?" He goes on to say that he is "certain that nothing will be able to separate us from the love of God that comes to us in Christ Jesus, our Lord." This is certainly evident in the early history of the Korean Catholic community.

As a Church, we know that suffering, sacrifice, and pain, when endured in faith, produce life abundantly. I am grateful to you that the collection we will take up today will be given to the refugees of Rwanda. Our hope is that the tremendous suffering of these people will end soon and not be in vain. Again, our faith tells us that out of death, new life is possible. We pray that the Rwandans will indeed experience new life after their present trials are over.

Today the church of Korea is experiencing enormous growth. I am told that each year over 100,000 adults are brought into the Catholic faith community at the Easter Vigil. I am also told that there is a great interest in religious life and the priesthood with over 1,000 candidates entering the seminaries each year. The blood of the martyrs has indeed become a fertile soil in Korea.

The Catholic Korean community here in the Chicagoland area also continues to enjoy rapid expansion. There are four Korean communities which are comprised of over 1,200 families—over 5,000 people. These good numbers will continue to grow through your personal witness and evangelization within the Korean community and beyond.

The history, the traditions, the culture of the Korean Church have much to teach the larger Church. I am personally grateful for your support. Know that my presence here with you today is a sign of my love and respect for you.

Do you remember the story I told at the beginning of my homily? I am convinced that the little bird would still be sitting in the withered, dying tree . . . not knowing of the beautiful fruit-laden forest had it not experienced suffering, loss, and sacrifice. The same holds true for the Catholic Church in Korea and the Korean Catholic Church here in the Chicagoland area. All the Scripture readings today remind us over and over again that being a follower and friend of Jesus involves risks, suffering, misunderstandings, and yes, for some, even martyrdom.

And so my friends, we gather at the table of the Lord to share in this Eucharist, this sacred meal and sacrifice, to be nourished and strengthened by Christ. As we break bread and drink from the cup of salvation, we remember that his Body is broken, his Blood is poured out so that we might experience new life. We pray this day and always that we might be faithful followers of the Lord, willing to take up our Cross in the sure promise that Jesus is with us now and will be forever.

Homily

Mass Inaugurating the New Academic Year

Casa Santa Maria dell'Umilta, Rome, Italy

── *October 15, 1994* ────────────────────

> Anyone among you who aspires to greatness must serve the rest; who-
> ever wants to rank first among you must serve the needs of all. The Son
> of Man has not come to be served but to serve . . .

About twenty-three or twenty-four years ago, when I was general secretary of the Bishops' Conference, my mother visited me in Washington.
On the first evening, she had dinner at the staff house where I lived with
twenty priests. After cordially greeting Mother, they began to talk shop—
mentioning important people whom they had met during the day, as well
as significant meetings they had called or attended. Mother just listened.

Later, when we had returned to my private quarters, I asked Mother
what she thought about what she had experienced. "Oh, it was all very
nice," she said, "but, Joe, you and all those priests would be better off—and
the Church would be also—if you all went out and did a good day's work."

In the intervening years I have often thought about what my mother
said. And I was reminded of it again as I reflected on today's gospel in
preparation for this Eucharist. I have received many honors in the last
two decades. Humanly speaking, I cannot say that I have not derived
some satisfaction from them. And—to be quite candid—there have been
times when I was somewhat anxious because I thought that I would not
be recognized. But my mother's counsel has helped me to put things in
correct perspective.

For my mother, putting in a "good day's work" meant attending to the
spiritual and material needs of others—and doing so in a very concrete

501

way, a way that does not usually attract public attention. It meant teaching the young, counseling those in need of guidance and direction, visiting the sick, burying the dead and consoling their loved ones. It meant preparing couples for marriage, supporting families, especially those experiencing difficulties, providing for the needs of the poor and marginalized and speaking out on their behalf. It meant bringing people into greater intimacy with the Lord through prayer and the celebration of the sacraments, especially the Eucharist.

This, I am sure, is what Jesus had in mind when he rebuked James and John, who asked that they be permitted to sit on either side of him when he came into his glory. Our ministry, like that of Jesus, is one of service to the people committed to our care. Sometimes this service will be very visible and will elicit commendation and recognition by others. But at other times—and, indeed, this is usually the case—it will be quiet, hidden service, not generally known, at times even unappreciated by those whom we serve.

It is then that we need inner strength, patience, determination to persevere—and we receive it *not* so much from external honors and acclamations as from the knowledge that we are instruments in the hands of Jesus, chosen by him to continue his mission. It is then that his strength becomes our strength. As the letter to the Hebrews says, we can confidently approach his throne of grace to receive mercy and favor and to find help in time of need.

Sometimes it takes more than a casual remark—even if it comes from your own mother—to bring matters into clear focus. Sometimes it takes a traumatic event. Permit me to speak with you very personally. You recall, I am sure, that last fall I was publicly accused of abusing a young man some seventeen years ago. It immediately became a *cause célèbre;* a media frenzy ensued. Within a few hours—thanks especially to CNN—I was literally standing before the world, accused. At that moment, the honors did not help me; indeed, they fueled the frenzy. The only thing I had to rely on, in that moment of total humiliation, was my own integrity, my fidelity to my priestly commitments, my forty years of service which in both public and hidden ways had touched the lives of so many people, but *above all* my intimacy with the Lord who literally stood beside me to support and sustain me.

As I look back on that dark night, I become more and more convinced that the Lord permitted it to happen for a purpose: to make sure that, in whatever years I have left, I will never forget that what is important is not where I sit (or may want to sit) but whether I can drink the cup which Jesus has drunk and be immersed in the same bath of pain as he.

My dear brothers, you are beginning a new scholastic year. Some of you are here for the first time; others have been here for a while. But in either case, you are preparing yourselves for service to the Church. There will be times when you may be discouraged, times when you may wonder whether you should be here at all. But remember that you are here *not* to enhance your own personal status but to prepare yourself so that you can serve God's people more effectively when you return home. Remember that you are an instrument through which the Lord Jesus ministers to the people whom he has redeemed and whom he loves. So place your complete trust in him, and you will receive, in great abundance, his mercy and favor in time of need. And be assured of my own personal prayers and support.

Sixth Sunday in Ordinary Time

Holy Name Cathedral, Chicago, Illinois

—*February 12, 1995* ─────────────────────

Winston Churchill once said, "Never trust a man who has no enemies." What the great wartime Prime Minister knew was that the taking of a principled stand always entails opposition, and so, someone who inspires no healthy contempt probably has no character. Churchill faced the critique and the scheming of enemies throughout his political career, from his early days in the Parliament, through his service in the Cabinet during the First World War, through the dark years of his "exile" from power, and especially during the period of his dynamic leadership during the Second World War. For several decades, he was the most reviled political figure in Britain, yet it was to him that the English people turned during their time of greatest trial and difficulty. Even—I might say especially— Churchill's enemies knew that this was a man upon whom the nation could rely, a man of decisiveness and character.

Abraham Lincoln was, without a doubt, the most hated politician of his time. His election to the presidency caused half of the country to secede from the Union and enter into a terrible war. During the worst days of the Civil War, as the body counts grew and grew, he was routinely described in the press as a butcher and a barbarian. His country accent and coarse manners were constantly ridiculed by the representatives of polite society. Once he was even described as the "great ape." His own party rebelled against him and almost denied him nomination for a second term. And, most dramatically, threats on his life flooded daily into the White House during his tenure, and numerous attempts to assassinate him were made before John Wilkes Booth finally succeeded. What so excited this animosity, of course, was the strength and assuredness of Lincoln's stances. He was a man utterly convinced of the rectitude of two basic principles—union and liberty for the slaves. Armed with this singleness of purpose and strength of character, Lincoln saw this country through its most painful crisis and came to be generally regarded as our greatest president.

What the examples of Churchill and Lincoln teach us is that clarity of focus, a sense of identity, rootedness in the truth—all *necessarily* call forth opposition. Precisely those qualities that make a person great tend to make her or him, at the same time, disliked by many. This paradoxical truth is one of the most difficult to accept, for all of us want to be popular, well-liked, esteemed. We all, naturally enough, find great pleasure in the attention and approval of others, and thus we learn, from the time we are young, to adopt patterns of behavior and thought that help us to fit in, to be accepted. The problem, of course, is that this need to be liked can cause us to become chameleons, adapting ourselves to the environments in which we move, conforming ourselves to the attitudes that surround us. Or it can force us into a blandness of character, refusing to take any stand or to assume any self-definition. Too hungry to be highly thought of, we can lose our ideals, ourselves, our very souls.

All of this comes to mind in light of the last "warning" that Jesus offers in today's gospel. Significantly, in Luke's Gospel, there are both Beatitudes and "curses." Jesus says not only, "blest are you," but also "woe to you." The most powerful and painful of his four "curses" may be this one: "Woe to you when all speak well of you. Their fathers treated the false prophets in just this way." In other words, beware when you find yourself universally liked. Beware when you have no one who thinks poorly of you. Beware when everyone holds you in esteem. For, if this is the case, you have most likely lost yourself. If all we hear are approving voices, there is probably little substance behind the facade of our charm.

Of course, from the moment of his arrival on this earth, the Lord Jesus excited violent opposition: Herod, we read, and with him all of Jerusalem, trembled in apprehension at the news of the newborn king. And when he began his public ministry, Jesus was immediately opposed by scribes and Pharisees and, more dramatically, by the demons: "We know who you are, Jesus of Nazareth; have you come to destroy us?" Because he is the Word of God, which is more cutting than a two-edged sword, the Lord Jesus inspires fear and anger on the part of those who cling to their sin. Because he is the divine voice, he is an annoyance to those who have purposely stopped their ears.

My dear friends in the Lord, sometimes it concerns me that we Christians have grown too complacent. We are, perhaps, *too* much at home in a society that countenances the violence of abortion, that looks away from the killing in our city streets, that accepts a growing militarism, that explicitly or implicitly approves of racism, that turns a deaf ear to the cries of those who, in the midst of affluence, go without the basic necessities of life. Perhaps we desire too much to fit in. Maybe, out of a sense of politeness, we do not want to bring up disturbing or controversial matters, preferring the bland and harmless discourse of polite society.

But if we are to be followers of the Lord Jesus, and bearers of his dangerous memory, we must avoid the temptation of "popularity." We must speak the words and perform the actions of radical love, both in season and out, whether we are met with accolades or brickbats, whether such love inspires affection or hatred.

It is not the opinion of the crowd that matters in the end. No, it is the integrity and courage of our commitment to the gospel. So beware, my friends in the Lord, when all speak well of you. Others have treated the *false* prophets, the superficial, the cowardly in just this way. But if we want to rejoice and exult some day in heaven, like the *true* prophets, we will have to stand in solidarity with the poor, hunger for justice and peace, weep for the victims of violence in our streets and playgrounds, and profoundly disturb those who will neither listen to nor live in accord with God's word.

Special Occasions

a. Personal
b. Archdiocese of Chicago
c. Other

a. Personal

Mass on the Occasion of Being Named to the Sacred College of Cardinals

Holy Name Cathedral, Chicago, Illinois

─── *January 5, 1983* ─────────────────────────

I was eager to celebrate this Eucharist with you in thanksgiving for the many blessings God has showered on us all.

The honor given to me by our Holy Father, Pope John Paul II, is a tribute to the archdiocese—to all of you: the bishops, priests, deacons, religious, and laity who make up the family of this local church. There is surely a personal dimension to the Cardinalate, and I am deeply moved by the appointment. But in the final analysis it is the church of Chicago that is being honored. It is your dedication that makes the difference. You have shaped this local church through your faith and fidelity, giving it recognition throughout the country and, indeed, the world. May we always live up to the expectations others have of us. In particular, may we always support our Holy Father whose unique role in the Church is highlighted by this honor he has given us.

It is fitting that we celebrate today the feast of St. John Neumann. John Neumann was the bishop of Philadelphia in the last century. He was a simple, holy man, a good pastor who spent himself in the service of his people, bringing to them—both by word and example—the riches of the gospel.

John Neumann was not appreciated by all his contemporaries. There were those who wanted him removed from office. They thought he was too much out of step for the sophisticated society which existed in Philadelphia at the time. John Neumann probably agreed with them because he had no pretensions about himself personally. But he committed himself totally to the diocese. He was an outstanding pastor who was very sensitive to his people's needs. Ultimately, he was canonized. John Neumann is a model for all bishops. His simplicity, commitment, piety, and humanity are a wonderful example for all of us.

On this day, when my appointment to the Sacred College of Cardinals is announced, I am pleased to be reminded how a good bishop should conduct himself. It is not the external honors that count but what goes on inside one's heart; not so much what others think as what God thinks. It is good to be reminded that unless one's life is patterned after that of the Lord, all honors are hollow, superficial, because they fail to represent the deeper spiritual realities which make the difference with the Lord.

In the first reading, taken from his first letter, St. John the Apostle casts both God and us—and our mutual relationship—in the context of love. "God is love," he said, "and he who abides in love abides in God and God in him. . . . Love has no room for fear; rather, perfect love casts out all fear . . ."

Whatever other qualities may come into play, ultimately it is love that makes the difference. It is love that makes the Church a true community of believers, one filled with life and vitality. It is love that gives meaning to all the external structures and honors in the Church, giving them a dimension of the Transcendent.

I ask you, my brothers and sisters, to support me in the months and years ahead. Help me to become a good and holy shepherd like St. John Neumann. I, in turn, promise to support and help you. Together, may we become the body of Christ, loving one another so that God can dwell in us and bring us to perfection. Only in this way will the honor which has come today to the archdiocese and to me have meaning. Only in this way will it be an instrument which can help us respond more wholeheartedly and completely to the Lord's call.

Ceremony of Taking Possession of the Titular Church, Jesus the Divine Worker

Rome, Italy

── *February 4, 1983* ───────────────────

On Wednesday, Pope John Paul II added eighteen new members to the Sacred College of Cardinals. They represented the diversity and richness of the Church which is incarnated in every land. During these days following the consistory, each of the new cardinals will take possession of a particular church in the Diocese of Rome. It is my privilege today to take possession of this parish church named in honor of Jesus, under the title of the Divine Worker.

Undoubtedly the assignment of a titular church in Rome to a cardinal is a source of wonderment to many people. Is the significance of this celebration simply historical? Is it just the remnant of the days when the parish priests of Rome elected the Bishop of Rome who, in virtue of that office, is also pastor of the universal Church? Or does this assignment of particular Roman churches to each of the cardinals, who today are the electors of the popes and special advisors to them, have a deeper significance? Is the celebration in which we participate in this parish church which attends to the spiritual needs of some 46,000 people symbolic of a deeper reality that is present in the Church here and now? I believe that what we are doing this morning is very much related to the life and ministry of the Church today. Let me explain.

In the gospel which was just proclaimed we heard Jesus' priestly prayer which he prayed during his last discourse the night before he died. This prayer was for unity, a special kind of unity. Jesus prayed that the intimate bond which united him with his Father would also embrace his followers. "I do not pray for them alone," he said. "I pray also for those who will believe in me through their word, that they all may be one as you, Father are in me, and I in you; I pray that they may be one in us, that the world may believe that you sent me."

It is the Spirit of Jesus, the Paraclete whom he sent after he returned to his Father, who is the source of unity within the Church. It is the Spirit who unites us in faith—making us a true community which witnesses to the goodness of Jesus and his power in our lives and enables us to share his divine life of grace. The Church is a mystery; it is a spiritual reality which exists in the world and is influenced by the world. But it can never be fully understood; its mission cannot be truly appreciated unless we go beyond the human, visible structures of the Church so that we can see and experience the power of Jesus and his Holy Spirit at work.

And yet the visible structures are important. They are the instruments through which the Spirit continues the mission of Jesus. They provide the framework in which we humans can literally encounter the Lord and experience his saving grace. They are the signs of the inner dynamism which gives life and vitality to the community of believers.

One of these structures, established by Jesus himself, is the papacy. The Holy Father is Christ's Vicar, the visible head of the Church. He is the visible sign of the Church's unity. It is his duty, as Christ's Vicar, to exhort, encourage, confirm and—when necessary—correct the entire community of believers so they will always remain faithful to the Lord who alone is the Way, the Truth and the Life. It is the task of the Holy Father to help people witness to the Lord in their daily lives and to avoid any obstacle which might impede the saving action of the Holy Spirit.

The church which I serve in Chicago, under the leadership of the Holy Father, has nearly two and one-half million Catholics out of a population of over five million; some 2,500 priests and 5,000 religious. It is a large, dynamic community of faith, worship, and service. By making me a cardinal and giving me this titular church, the pope has made manifest the unity of pastoral ministry throughout the universal Church.

The cardinals, who serve as special advisors to the Holy Father, are a reminder of his unique and, indeed, indispensable ministry in the Church. By being assigned a church in the pope's own diocese, attention is focused on the fact that all ministry is ultimately pastoral; all ministry—no matter what form it takes—is aimed at bringing people closer to the Lord. Through the proclamation of the word and the celebration of the sacraments, which take place in this parish church and in every parish throughout the world, people are enabled to come into contact with Jesus; they are encouraged and motivated to turn away from sin so they can experience Jesus' mercy, love, and compassion in their lives.

The ceremony of taking possession of this church, then, is a forceful affirmation of the unity of the Church's ministry and its ministers. My identification with this parish church of Jesus the Divine Worker in Rome is a clear sign that the church of Rome and the church of Chicago are united in their service of the Lord and in the service of their people for the Lord's sake. My affiliation with this church in the Holy Father's diocese is visible testimony of my personal union and solidarity with him. There is, as St. Paul told us, only one Lord, one faith, one baptism. In the final analysis, the well-being of the universal Church is dependent on the well-being of each of its parts; it is directly related to the dynamism and health of each of the local churches.

I take this occasion to reaffirm my own personal commitment to the Church and to my ministry as a bishop and priest within the Church. I reaffirm also my loyalty to the Holy Father whom I will now serve in a special way—as symbolized by my affiliation with this church in his diocese. I will leave Rome determined to be the best pastor possible in Chicago, convinced that my worth to the Holy Father and the universal Church is in direct proportion to my effectiveness as a residential bishop.

* * *

And now may I add a special word, a personal word, to all of you who have joined me on what, in effect, has been a kind of pilgrimage. To you, the members of my family, I extend my deepest gratitude for being here. Your love and support over the years have meant a great deal to me. Having all our family together, from the United States and Italy, has been a great joy for me and, I am sure, for you.

I wish also to thank my brothers in the College of Cardinals, my brother bishops and priests. Your generous gift of time to celebrate the events of these days with me is but an added sign of the closeness that we have for one another. As I have relied on you in the past, so I will rely on you in the future. Your prayers, your presence, your friendship has made this challenging week a time of real joy.

To the priests and parishioners of Christ the Divine Worker, I extend a special word of greeting. In the mystery of Divine Providence, our lives have been joined. I look forward to celebrating the Eucharist on a Sunday in the fall when I return for the synod of bishops. I want to get to know you better. I ask you to keep me in your prayers as I return to Chicago. Be assured that I will give you a special remembrance at Mass each day.

Finally, I would like to express a special word of thanks to you, my friends of the media. The decision not to encourage a large number of people to accompany me on this pilgrimage of faith was a difficult one. I would like to have had all the good people of Chicago, Cincinnati, Atlanta, Charleston, and Columbia share the joy that has been ours during the past few days. But through the wonders of the media, many have indeed been able to take part in the festivities related to the consistory. I thank you for your understanding, your sensitivity, and your kindness to me and my family. I will pray for you and your families. May the good work you have done be a source of joy and accomplishment for you as well.

There are some people missing from this pilgrimage. They are the poor of Chicago, indeed, the poor of the world. Although they are not physically present, they are present in my heart. I take this occasion to thank all who have contributed to the special charity fund I established at the time of my appointment. I have already given the Holy Father half of what had been received when I left Chicago. When I return to Chicago, I will share the remainder with those in need. How wonderful it is when those who have are willing to share with those in need, regardless of sex or race, nationality or creed. This is truly a sign of our unity as a human family. This is, in a very real sense, the continuation of Christ's ministry to which we are all committed as his followers. It is this kind of concern and sensitivity that gives substance and meaning to the honors which have been given this week.

Homily

Mass Commemorating the 20th Anniversary of Episcopal Ordination

Fifth Sunday of Easter
Holy Name Cathedral, Chicago, Illinois
—*April 26, 1986* ————————————————

The first reading of this evening's Mass told us about the evangelizing efforts of Paul and Barnabas. They went from town to town preaching the Good News, encouraging the new Christian communities to keep the faith, and providing counsel and direction for their growth and development.

Today, nearly twenty centuries later, the work of evangelizing and pastoring continues. Times have changed; many of today's challenges and problems are new. But, in the final analysis, the Church's mission today is the same as it was in the days of Paul and Barnabas. Twenty centuries ago, it was Derbe and Lystra, Iconium and Antioch. Today—for me personally, at least—it has been Columbia and Charleston, Atlanta, Washington, Cincinnati, and now Chicago.

Twenty years ago today I was consecrated a bishop in Charleston. And on that very same day—fourteen years earlier—I was ordained a priest in my home parish in Columbia.

Please don't be alarmed! I don't intend to review all that has happened in the years since my ordination and consecration. But there are a few changes—other than my loss of hair and diminished eyesight—that I would like to share with you.

When I was consecrated twenty years ago, I'm afraid I thought I was God's gift to the Church. It was probably even worse thirty-four years ago when I was ordained a priest. Like most young people, I thought I had all the answers. All I needed was the opportunity to show people how

517

things should be done. My dear mother, who is here in the cathedral with me this evening, sensed the problem. She wisely told me just before the consecration ceremony began: "Joe, make sure you walk straight, but don't look too pleased."

I understand much better now what she meant, because in the intervening years I have matured. I now realize—in a way I didn't before—that the human condition is very complex and at times paradoxical. While there is surely a wonderful clarity about our Catholic faith, just how that faith is to be lived out each day in our highly secularized, consumer-oriented society is not always so clear. So I have learned to be a little more realistic, a little more humble in terms of my ability to set things right, to provide answers to the challenges and problems of daily life.

In the final analysis, it is not so much our human efforts that are responsible for the good things in life as it is God's grace. So we should not pretend that everything depends on us. Rather, we should see ourselves as instruments in the Lord's hands. I know that my best planned efforts often produce little or nothing while, at other times, in spite of my blundering, things turn out well. I'm sure that you have experienced this also.

We simply have to place our faith and trust in the Lord. And why shouldn't we? As we heard in the second reading, taken from the book of Revelation, God dwells with us; we are his people and he will be with us always. If we are faithful to him, "He shall wipe every tear from our eyes, and there shall be no more death or mourning, crying out or pain . . ."

There is a final lesson I have learned, though admittedly not perfectly. The only way we can become an authentic community of faith, one totally committed to the Lord, is to follow the new commandment Jesus has given us: "Love one another. Such as my love has been for you, so must your love be for each other. This is how all will know you for my disciples: your love for one another."

Such love can be very demanding. It requires patience, compassion, a willingness to forgive, a willingness to give and to sacrifice—even when what we offer is rejected or not appreciated. It also requires a certain toughness at times, a willingness to be honest, to correct when it might be easier to look the other way. But love is never vindictive, mean-spirited. It never loses heart or abandons anyone. Such love, in practice, is not always understood or appreciated. It is criticized, at times taken for weakness. But in the end, only love prevails. Only love brings about lasting results, because it is only through human love that God's love can make all things new again.

This evening, as I reflect on the years I have been in the Lord's service, I am deeply grateful for the love he has showered on me through the many people who have been so much a part of my life. In a very special way, I thank you and all the people of the archdiocese who received me with such openness and warmth nearly four years ago. You have shown me in so many wonderful ways that you do love and support me. You took me at my word when I first presented myself as your brother, Joseph. I promise that I will continue to do all I can to be a good pastor for you.

As I thank you for all you have done for me, I invite you to continue the journey with me, as we prepare for the third millennium of Christianity. May I share with you my vision of the church of Chicago, which I love so much and to which I have committed every fiber of my being? In that vision I see a community of deep, vibrant faith over which the risen Lord truly presides; a community which continues, in our contemporary context, the life and ministry of the members of the first Christian community who were ministered to by Paul and Barnabas and the other apostles.

It is a community in which all members, in virtue of their baptism, witness to Jesus' saving deeds before the entire world and work for the emergence of the kingdom he proclaimed. It is a community whose members—laity, religious, priests, deacons, and bishops—understand and accept their uniquely different but complementary and necessary responsibilities and roles, working together for the good of all.

It is a community whose faith in Jesus is far more compelling than any human consideration; one which honors truth more than idle speculation and bias; a community in which respect for persons rules out pettiness, unfairness, and mean-spiritedness—promoting instead dialogue, reconciliation, and unity. It is a community in which Jesus' love and mercy, his justice, his compassion and healing power are tangibly evident each day.

Won't you join me in shaping that kind of community for the church of Chicago? Together, with God's grace, let us make the vision come true. That is the best gift you could give me on my anniversary!

God bless you always.

Homily

Mass Commemorating the 25ᵗʰ Anniversary of Episcopal Ordination

Holy Name Cathedral, Chicago, Illinois
—April 28, 1991 ─────────────────────────

Some time ago, a resident at the home where my mother lives entered Mother's room and asked her *what* I was. What prompted the question was many photographs of myself dressed in various colorful robes and vestments. Given her poor memory, Mother answered that she was not sure but she thought I was a priest. The lady insisted that, given the funny clothes I was wearing, I must be more than a priest. She kept pressing Mother, and finally she responded, "I really don't know, but I think he is a patriarch."

Well, I'm not a patriarch, but twenty-five years ago this past Friday, I was ordained a bishop in the Cathedral of St. John the Baptist in the historic See of Charleston, South Carolina. The Second Vatican Council had just completed its work four months before, and there was much excitement about the changes that were already taking place, especially in the liturgy, and the direction that a renewed and revitalized Church might take in a fast-changing world.

A week after my ordination, I went to Atlanta as auxiliary to Archbishop Hallinan, who had been my bishop several years earlier in Charleston and now needed help because of illness. Atlanta was a thriving Southern metropolis where the church was small but respected and growing. My two years there were happy ones because Archbishop Hallinan was both a close friend and an excellent mentor, and, together, we began the work of renewal envisioned by the council. During those two years, I was also pastor of Christ the King Cathedral parish—my first and only experience as a pastor. To be honest, I liked parish work more than diocesan administration, and so spent more time in the parish. Several times the archbishop reminded me that he didn't ask for an auxiliary bishop because he needed a pastor!

Shortly before the archbishop died in 1968, I learned that I was to be the general secretary of the National Conference of Catholic Bishops and the United States Catholic Conference. Actually, I resisted the appointment as long as I could because I preferred to stay in diocesan ministry. But the persistence of Archbishop (later Cardinal) Dearden, who was then president of the Episcopal Conference, prevailed. So, I went to Washington shortly after Archbishop Hallinan's death. And what an experience that was! I came into contact in a very direct way with the larger Church, both in this country and abroad.

The single most influential factor in my life during that period, however, was Cardinal Dearden himself, who, like Archbishop Hallinan, was a forward-looking, committed churchman. Just as I had learned so much from Archbishop Hallinan, so now in Washington I learned a great deal from Cardinal Dearden. He taught me to take the long view of things, to trust the Lord and the basic goodness of people, to be patient, and not to be discouraged because of human shortcomings and failures—whether my own or those of others.

In Washington, I was very much involved in the reorganization of the conference and the implementation of many new initiatives such as the Campaign for Human Development and the National Advisory Council. No doubt my five years there set the stage for many things which would happen to me later. At the time, however, I was eager to return to diocesan ministry.

I remember vividly when the apostolic delegate, then Archbishop Luigi Raimondi, told me that Pope Paul VI planned to send me to Cincinnati. The archbishop asked me to go to his chapel and pray about it before accepting. "No, Archbishop," I replied, "I accept *now*. Then I'll go to the chapel and say a prayer of thanksgiving!"

What wonderful years I spent in Cincinnati! I was like a pastor with his first parish. Cincinnati was a well-organized archdiocese. Under the leadership of Archbishop Karl Alter, who was still alive, and his successor, Archbishop Paul Leibold, who died suddenly after less than three years in office, great strides had already been made in implementing the teaching of Vatican II. The priests, religious, and laity were very receptive and supportive. During those years, too, I was elected president of the Episcopal Conference and delegate to several world synods of bishops.

Then in early July 1982, I was called to Rome and personally told by Pope John Paul II that I was to succeed Cardinal Cody, who had died on April 25, as archbishop of Chicago. I will never forget the night I first met all the priests here in the cathedral. My knees were literally knocking as I carried a heavy paschal candle down the middle aisle of the darkened church. But when the lights went on, what a tremendous reception they gave me! "As our lives and ministries are mingled together through the breaking of the Bread and the blessing of the Cup," I told them, "I hope that long before my name falls from the Eucharistic Prayer in the silence of death you will know me well. . . . You will know me as a friend, fellow priest, and bishop. You will know also that I love you. For I am Joseph, your brother!"

And the next day, at the formal installation, I spoke to the assembled guests and representatives of the parishes. "I have come to Chicago with only one desire," I said, "to do all in my power to proclaim the Lord Jesus Christ and his Gospel in word and deed."

Those brief, simple words—first spoken when I was ordained a bishop, repeated when I entered Cincinnati nearly nineteen years ago, and reaffirmed most recently in this cathedral on the day of my installation—sum up the driving force of my life and ministry as a bishop, as one who has been charged by the Good Shepherd to lead, encourage, nourish, and protect the flock committed to my pastoral care. That was the task of the original Twelve. In today's first reading we were told how Paul, recently converted and sent on mission by Jesus himself, was introduced to the other apostles. Because of their evangelizing efforts, the Church throughout all Judea, Samaria, and Galilee was built up and made steady progress, enjoying all the while the "increased consolation of the Holy Spirit."

Today, nearly 2,000 years later, the task remains the same: to proclaim the gospel to every creature. To carry out such a task, as the Second Vatican Council told us, the Church must constantly scrutinize "the signs of the times," interpret them in the light of the gospel, and show how the gospel speaks to the hopes and aspirations, the anxieties and concerns of each generation. The genius of the council was that it addressed some of the most important issues of our time, setting the course for the Catholic community as we approach the third millennium of Christianity. Significantly, my episcopate began just four months after the close of the council, and I have spent the past quarter century implementing its teaching and insights.

Today, some feel that the council's teaching is depleted, that both the Church and society have moved *beyond* it. They are ready for Vatican III. Others seem to be committed to a "restoration" of things to what they were *before* the council; they would turn the clock back. Still others—perhaps the majority—really do not know or fully understand the council's teaching and often fail to see its relevance in their lives.

I am convinced that we do not fully understand all the implications of the council's teaching, and that is why we have not yet adequately implemented it. While much has changed in the past quarter century, it takes more than a single generation to assimilate fully the teaching of an ecumenical council, especially one whose purpose was primarily pastoral and whose scope embraced so many important topics and concerns.

Today, as I mark the twenty-fifth year of my episcopate, I recommit myself to implementing the teaching of Vatican II and providing the pastoral leadership needed to energize this local church so that it will realize fully its God-given mission of proclaiming the gospel to all people, showing—through word and deed—how the gospel speaks to our deepest yearnings and questions about the present life and the life to come.

Today's gospel helps us understand how we must go about our task. We carry out our mission in the world—with all its hopes and aspirations as well as its ambiguities, frustrations, and failures. But the Church's ultimate goal is spiritual. Nothing we do is of real value unless it brings about a change of mind and heart, a genuine conversion which enables us to enter into a closer union with the Lord. Jesus expressed this so beautifully in the gospel: "I am the vine, you are the branches." What relationship could be more intimate, more life-giving? And he goes on to tell what the Father, the vinegrower, will do to make sure that this union of vine and branches is vibrant and fruitful. "He prunes away every branch," so that the plant will not be hindered by lifeless and decaying branches. "But the fruitful ones he trims clean to increase their yield." Then to make his point more emphatic, he adds: "A man who does not live in me is like a withered, rejected branch, picked up to be thrown in the fire and burnt."

It is that intimate relationship with the Lord Jesus that gives us vision and strength. If we are totally caught up with Jesus; if we are in love with him and convinced that he will ever be at our side to support us, we will never surrender to discouragement. The trials and disappointments of daily life will only confirm our faith and strengthen our resolve to proclaim the gospel to all people, whatever the cost to ourselves.

As archbishop of Chicago, I have many fond memories of the nearly nine years I have served this local church. For me, one of the most significant events was the Mass in Grant Park—in August 1982, the first Sunday after my installation—with nearly one hundred thousand people from all the parishes of the archdiocese. I chose as the theme for the homily that day the fact that, as Church, we are a family. "To be a member of a family," I said, "is a beautiful human experience. But to us who are the family of the Church, it is that and *more*." In my recent pastoral letter, *The Family Gathered Here Before You*, written after nearly seven years of serving the people of Cook and Lake counties, I shared my vision of this wonderful family of faith: its history which helps us understand its present vigor and dynamism, its richness and diversity, its accomplishments and potential. And, as its bishop, I also shared some of my own hopes for the future, which I reaffirm today:

—May we always be faithful to our Catholic heritage which, in union with our Holy Father, Pope John Paul, we share with all our brothers and sisters in faith throughout the world.

—May we be an evangelizing Church, continually renewing ourselves and reaching out to others, especially the unchurched and the alienated.

—May we be a prayerful people so that we may enter into a close relationship with the Lord—the kind described in today's gospel.

—May we be a source of unity and reconciliation, helping to bring people together, not fearful of the cost, not impatient with slow progress, not discouraged by prophets of doom, not intimidated by those who foster division.

—May we speak clearly and persuasively about the many life issues which, rooted in the God-given dignity of every person, are central to the well-being of the human family, from the moment of conception to natural death.

—May we recognize, encourage, and support all ministries, in particular vocations to the priesthood and religious life.

—May we develop and assimilate a deeper understanding of stewardship, a commitment to the Church's life and mission which calls all of us to assume responsibility for its welfare by giving our time, our talents, and our treasures.

* * *

As I look at you who are gathered with me in the celebration of this Eucharist, I am deeply moved. I see faces—young, old, middle-aged, black, white, yellow, red, and brown—which reflect histories of struggle and pain mixed with joy and hope. As I look at you, I see our forebears in faith who came from Africa, Asia, Europe, and Latin America to make this archdiocese the wonderfully rich and diverse community it is.

Yes, as I look at you who represent the nearly four hundred parishes of the archdiocese, I am deeply touched. For I love you very much, and, united with Jesus, the Good Shepherd, I am ready to lay down my life for you.

It is in you, gathered with me in prayer, that I experience the Church at its deepest level. For me, the Church is not an abstraction. It is a people who have a rich heritage, a people who are able to see beyond the present struggles to the future with its hopes and promises. It is a community and a way of life which depend totally on God's grace and our free human response.

Yes, it is in you, the people of the archdiocese, that I see a future prom-ise taking hold. In deep and mysterious ways, God's reign breaks in upon us—a kingdom of truth, justice, mercy, and peace. Our present experi-ence as Church is admittedly provisional, temporary. But in the heavenly kingdom, when we stand together before God's throne and share in his glory as human members of the divine family, it will be forever!

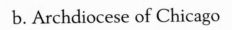
b. Archdiocese of Chicago

Liturgy for Sending Missionaries to the Diocese of Chilapa, Mexico

Chicago, Illinois

─── *June 30, 1989* ──────────────────────────────

The gospel narrative of the sending of the Twelve on mission leaves many details to our imagination. We hear the few things Jesus told the disciples: *what* they should say and do, and *how* they should rely upon the Spirit of the Father to shape their message. But we learn nothing of what was in the disciples' minds and hearts on this occasion. What were their thoughts and feelings?

Was Peter eager to march off boldly—perhaps feeling ready to walk on water, if necessary? Did Thomas have doubts about what, if anything, would come from the mission? Did James wonder how his mother would get along without him while he was on the journey? Was John already confident of his eloquence in proclaiming the Good News of God's kingdom? Did Levi look back with nostalgia upon the more stable responsibilities of a tax collector? Was Judas quietly calculating the mission's potential revenues and expenses?

Undoubtedly, because they were human, the disciples had mixed feelings about being sent on mission. On the one hand, they were surely pleased that Jesus considered them ready to undertake such a responsibility in his name. On the other, they probably also felt that they were not yet ready for such an important task. Facing the coming adventure with a mixture of anticipation and apprehension, they may well have wondered how it would all turn out.

As I said, the gospel is silent about such specific, personal details. What *is* significant, however, and worth emphasizing, is that Jesus *sent* them on mission, and they *went*. It's as simple—and profound—as that.

Matthew's Gospel does not record what happened while they were on mission or what the disciples learned from the experience. But the gospels of Mark and Luke report that, when the disciples returned, Jesus invited them to join him in an out-of-the-way place to rest. The crowds, however, found him even there, and there was no time for a debriefing of the disciples' missionary experience.

Perhaps this experience gave them only a brief foretaste of what they would learn later—after Jesus' resurrection and ascension—when they began to carry out his command to proclaim the gospel to the entire world. Like all missionaries since then, they learned that being a missionary means *letting go*—of one's family and friends, of one's first language and native land, of one's culture and food and clothes and ways of thinking. Being a missionary means *letting go* of *everything* in order to allow God's Spirit to work through him or her for the sake of the kingdom. It means *letting go* so that the people, to whom the missionary is sent, can also teach him or her about God and his kingdom.

Paul, Jeri, Ted, Carol Ann, and Gary—conflicting thoughts and feelings are undoubtedly racing through your minds and hearts this evening as we prepare to send you on mission to Chilapa. I'm sure your families and friends have similar mixed reactions. We are eager to send you to Mexico—we have been working on this project for many months—but we also want to keep you with us!

What is *most* important in our celebration this evening, however, is that the church in Chicago *is* sending you on mission in Jesus' name, and that you *are going!* As important as personal thoughts and feelings are, what we are celebrating this evening transcends purely personal matters and touches the very heart of the Church's mission in the world.

In the past few years, since the Partnership in Mission was announced, many have commented on it, expressing different views.

Some have said, "A mission!? You must be crazy! Leave that work to religious communities who were founded for that very purpose and know what they're doing!"

Others were also pragmatic in expressing their concern: "How can we send away two priests and three pastoral associates at a time when our own local church is beginning to feel the pinch of a shortage of priests? We need to hang on to our personnel, not allow them to work outside the diocese!"

Still others mused, "We have enough issues and problems confronting us in the archdiocese without taking on another one! We can't be responsible for the whole world!"

These are legitimate concerns; indeed, they have crossed my mind. However, it has been the Church's conviction, from its earliest days, and it is my firm belief as well, that we cannot allow local concerns, important and demanding as they are, to prevent us from reaching out in solidarity, generosity, and mission to other peoples and cultures.

This missionary impulse flows from the very nature of the Church. To be Christ's Church is to be people *in mission*. The universal Church—and each local church—continues Jesus' own mission and fulfills his mandate to proclaim the gospel to everyone.

That is why, like those who have gone before us in faith, we must move beyond our own familiar comfort zone in order to embrace a wider and deeper understanding of what it means to be God's people. And as the Church's experience has shown through the ages, we build up the kingdom by reaching out and giving our very lives in service of God's people. As an archdiocese, we have indeed been blessed by our missionary outreach. At present, 280 priests, religious, and lay missionaries from this local church serve in lands and cultures other than their own.

In regard to our partnership in ministry with Chilapa, we are not simply releasing personnel to work in another diocese. Rather, we are entering into a new *relationship* with the people of the Diocese of Chilapa. As a sign of this new relationship, we are sending five of our brothers and sisters to live and work in Chilapa, and the people of that diocese are sending one of their brothers, Father Rodolfo Gutiérrez, to live and work among us here in Chicago.

So, it is not a one-sided relationship. It is a *mutual exchange* of gifts which will expand our experience and understanding of what it means to be God's people and enable us to carry out more fully the Church's mission. This evening, then, we are both *sending* missionaries to Chilapa and preparing to *receive* a brother from Chilapa who will minister among us.

Paul, Jeri, Ted, Carol Ann, and Gary, you are our gifts to our brothers and sisters, the people of Chilapa. You have been faithful, dynamic, and successful in your ministry here in the archdiocese. You have won the esteem of your colleagues and the affection and love of those among whom you have ministered. Through your words and actions, you have proclaimed the gospel in ways that have truly been fruitful.

You have helped others come to a deeper understanding of the risen Lord's presence and power in their lives. You have also allowed others to preach the gospel to *you*, and you have been transformed by that experience. Your minds and hearts have been expanded to allow you to embrace a wider, deeper, and fuller image of the Lord Jesus.

In a few moments each of you will be given a Spanish-language Bible to symbolize your ministry in Chilapa. My prayer is that you will hold God's word close to your hearts and allow it to penetrate your whole being. This will enable you to fall in love with your new people, and they, in turn, will take you into their homes and hearts, and your lives will be transformed once again. And, through you, the church of Chicago will also be affected and changed for the better.

We are all very grateful for your willingness to be sent on mission. What you are beginning is exciting. I am confident that our partnership in mission with the people of Chilapa will be successful, in part, because of the faith and enthusiasm you bring to this enterprise.

Our prayers, our support, and our love go with you as you begin your new ministry. We send you forth in faith and joy, relying upon God's gifts and the Holy Spirit who will always be at your side.

Homily

Columbus Day Mass, Fifth Centenary

Holy Name Cathedral, Chicago, Illinois

——*October 12, 1992* ————————————————————

Inspired by God's Spirit, the prophet Isaiah had a vision of what would happen "in days to come": the word of God will go out from Jerusalem and teach all nations how to walk in his paths. And when they hear the word of God, they will "beat their swords into plowshares" and "one nation shall not raise the sword against another."

In a sense, Jesus echoes Isaiah's words in today's gospel. When he met with his disciples, moments before he "was taken up to heaven," he gave them a challenging message to proclaim to all the world: they were to preach a crucified Messiah and to offer repentance and forgiveness of sins to all people. But neither the fundamental message nor the offer of universal salvation matched their natural inclinations. They did not find it easy to talk about the Cross. Moreover, they were reluctant to leave Jerusalem, let alone the regions of Judea, Samaria, and Galilee. They were more comfortable with their fellow Jews than with Gentiles. Jesus' disciples would first need to receive the gift of God's Spirit who would empower them for their mission to the world.

This has been the history of the Church's mission throughout the centuries. With the help of the Holy Spirit, and despite the inherent difficulties in the task, Christians continued to proclaim the Lord Jesus and his gospel wherever they went.

Twenty centuries later, the Church still struggles with the challenging task of preaching faithfully a crucified Christ and accepting equally all people. Today, we, too, must rely on the same Holy Spirit to guide our work of evangelization and our effort to achieve unity and harmony among all people.

St. Paul points out that, through the shedding of his blood, Jesus reconciled the human family with God and made it possible for "those who are far off" and "those who are near" to be reconciled with one another. Whenever the gospel is proclaimed faithfully and effectively, strangers become fellow citizens, enemies become friends. The fruit of evangelization is peace and harmony—the peace and harmony for which we all yearn.

Today, we observe the 500th anniversary of Christopher Columbus's first arrival in the Americas. The motivations for his voyage were fascinatingly complex. The inquisitive nature of the human spirit, the expansion of trade routes, a search for new wealth, and national pride—these were some of the reasons for his epic journey into the unknown.

Another integral purpose which Columbus envisioned for his voyage was to help evangelize those who had not heard of Jesus. Much evangelization has taken place in the intervening years. Still, today—five hundred years after his voyage—Pope John Paul II has called for a "new evangelization"—new in its zeal, its methods, and its expression.

Some have questioned the celebration of the quincentenary, referring to it as an ambiguous, controversial moment in the history of the Americas. In a pastoral letter published in November 1990 for the observance of the fifth centenary of evangelization in the Americas, the U.S. Catholic bishops called for 1992 to be a time of "looking back at where we have been and looking ahead to where we should be as a people and a nation." In a more recent statement, the bishops asked that the fifth centenary become an occasion for *remembrance, reconciliation*, and *recommitment*, through continuing conversion to Jesus Christ and his values, rather than merely the celebration of a past event.

What are we to *remember?* In an apostolic letter on the evangelization of the New World, Pope John Paul II reminds us that the evangelizing process five hundred years ago was uneven, both in space and time. Peoples were baptized without adequate religious instruction. Instead of discerning what was good in native spiritualities and harmonizing it with Christianity, they were often outlawed in a way that destroyed the culture, the customs, and the way of life of the indigenous peoples. Unfortunately, many of those who were associated with the colonization of the land failed to see in the natives the workings of the same God they professed.

Our remembrance of the violent exploitation and, even, the brutalization of the land and its inhabitants fills us with a deep sense of indignation and sorrow. Father Gustavo Gutiérrez, a theologian of great historical insight, who speaks for the poor of Latin America, urges us to look at the past with hope, not nostalgia. We do not need a "fixation on the painful and traumatic events of the past," he tells us, "but rather, a concern about contemporary poverty." Only a people which has retained its memory and looks at the implications and lessons of the past for the present and future can change its situation and build a better world.

As the U.S. bishops pointed out, "the effort to portray the history of the encounter as a totally negative experience in which only violence and exploitation of the native peoples were present is not an accurate interpretation of the past. From the earliest days there were (Catholic) missionaries who exercised a humanizing presence in the midst of colonization." Pope John Paul II echoed this sentiment in his letter to Latin American men and women religious, when he said, "The first sowing of the word of life" in the Americas occurred "amid darkness and light—but more light than darkness, if we consider the lasting results of faith and Christian life on the continent."

Indeed, the first people with whom we are to seek *reconciliation* must be the missionaries who, five hundred years ago, came—in good faith—to bring the gospel to a new land. While we cannot ignore the limitations of their process of evangelization, we also cannot apply contemporary criteria to methods of catechesis followed five centuries ago. Reconciliation, at this level, helps us to recognize the fidelity of these early missionaries to the gospel and their unlimited Christian love. Many sought to live with the native peoples and to promote a native church. Their efforts brought to the New World the gift of Christian faith with its powers of humanization and salvation, dignity and fraternity, justice, and love. The Good News was proclaimed to a people who had never heard of Jesus Christ or his gospel.

There is also great concern in the Church today for reconciliation with the peoples whose ancestors were here long before the first Europeans came to these shores five hundred years ago. For us, these peoples are the Native Americans and, later, the Africans brought here as slaves.

The challenge of reconciliation in Jesus Christ requires greater awareness and understanding of the need to bring the saving word of the gospel to every people and culture, but to do so in ways that challenge and purify all cultures, enhancing the best in them, and respecting the diversity and uniqueness of each.

The challenge is also to learn from our failures and our success in this encounter, for authentic evangelization begins with a respect and recognition of our rich cultural diversity in the Americas. When people welcome one another with respect, peace flourishes. But this is accomplished only after patient listening, mutual sharing, and trust. In this context, the gospel can be joyfully and energetically proclaimed.

Five centuries after the arrival of the Good News, there is still a great need for the healing, saving, transforming power of Jesus. Let this anniversary mark a new moment in our history. Let us *recommit* ourselves to the Church's important and unending voyage bringing the gospel to all peoples as the message of salvation and humanization, dignity, justice, love, and eternal life. Let us Catholics hear anew the word of God so that it can take deep root in our lives and make us credible witnesses to the gospel. Let us also pray fervently for the fruits of evangelization, which are mutual respect, harmony, and peace among all people.

May this Mass, which we celebrate today to commemorate the 500th anniversary of Columbus's voyage, be an act of *gratitude* for all that has been accomplished, an act of *repentance* for our human failings, and a fervent *petition* for the strength and grace needed to live up to our commitment, as followers of Jesus, to proclaim the gospel in our time.

Homily

Feast of Christ the King
Mass for the Opening of the Archdiocesan Sesquicentennial Year

Holy Name Cathedral, Chicago, Illinois

—November 21, 1993 ————————————————————

Eleven years ago, when I was installed as archbishop of Chicago, I said from this very pulpit:

> Jesus tells us that the good shepherd is one who lays down his life for his people. Some live this calling literally, shedding their blood as martyrs. Others live it in the unstinting giving of their time, their energy, their very selves to those they have been called to serve. Whatever the future holds for me, I pledge this day to live as a good shepherd who willingly lays down his life for you.

Today, as we begin the 150th anniversary of our diocese, I return to you to reaffirm my pledge. In the light of what has occurred during the past week, I know much better the pain and suffering that a good shepherd must endure to care for his flock.

But I am only a *human* shepherd, and, like you, I need the care and the love of the *divine* Shepherd. In faith, you and I know that the divine Shepherd is always with us. So, we need not fear, not even in the worst situations. For, Jesus, who is the Good Shepherd of us all, takes loving care of his flock.

We, too, must love and care for *one another*, especially our brothers and sisters in need. In today's gospel, Jesus explains to his disciples that, at the

537

Last Judgment, the decisive question for each member of his flock will be: did you love the poor by concrete works of mercy? Did you express your love in practical ways each day? These are Jesus' final words to his disciples before his passion and death. On the cross, the Good Shepherd fully identifies himself with his brothers and sisters and gives his life for them.

My dear brothers and sisters, this morning we stand at the threshold of a new era. Behind us lie 150 years of ministry and service in the Archdiocese of Chicago. Before us lies the future of our Church. Today, and throughout the coming year, we will pause from time to time to reflect on, celebrate, and learn from our past. We will also look forward and plan for our future. We will do this with confidence in the abiding presence of the Good Shepherd among us. So, this is a special time of gratitude and joy, a time for faith and courage.

When the Diocese of Chicago was established 150 years ago, on November 28, 1843, it embraced the entire state of Illinois. Several thousand Catholics were scattered in small settlements throughout the state. They were immigrants, farmers, laborers. For the most part, they were poor, and their lives were very difficult. They had to struggle to build churches, and there were very few priests. Nowhere was the situation more desperate than right here in Chicago, where there was only one church in 1843.

Yet, within a few years Catholic institutions dotted the landscape, powerful symbols of the progress and promise of Catholicism in Chicago. How did this come about? The several hundred Catholics who had set down roots here in Chicago faced enormous obstacles. But they had *faith:* faith in themselves, faith in this community, faith in the Catholic Church, and, most importantly, faith in the Lord Jesus. No matter what challenges they faced, and there have been many, the people of this local church—and this wonderful cathedral parish—have always risen to their call.

Let me illustrate what I mean. All the buildings of Holy Name parish were destroyed by the Great Chicago Fire of 1871. But four years later, 118 years ago to the day, this great cathedral was dedicated. Then, as now, the people of the church rose to their call and built anew. In fact, not long after the 1871 fire, when the diocese was designated an archdiocese, a fitting symbol was chosen for its new coat of arms: a rising phoenix—the legendary bird that rose from its own ashes—to represent the faith of the Catholics of Chicago "rising from the ashes" of the great fire.

Each new generation of Catholics contributed its special talents and gifts, and new people—whatever their origins, whether from across the country or from across the seas—set down roots in Cook and Lake counties. Despite the diversity of their backgrounds, their faith united them—faith expressed in the establishment of Catholic parishes, schools, hospitals, colleges and universities, and charitable agencies which serve those in need. During the past century and a half, our schools alone have educated millions of students, many of whom have made significant contributions to the Church and our civic community.

One such person was the late Bishop Michael Dempsey, who grew up here in Chicago. As a young man, Michael Dempsey acquired the spirit of generosity and compassion that has been characteristic of this local church. In 1970, he, more than anyone else, was instrumental in the establishment of the Campaign for Human Development. I had the honor of working very closely with him in those early years. Today, thanks to his vision and courage, the archdiocese leads all other dioceses in collecting funds for the Campaign for Human Development. The campaign, as you know, supports landmark programs that promote human dignity by putting people to work, helping people start businesses, building houses, fighting crime, and developing leaders who will help shape a better future.

It is tragic, but true, that there are many in our midst today who are not much better off than our pioneer Catholic forebears. I believe that it is God's providence—not mere coincidence—that combines today our sesquicentennial's call to action with CHD's call to reach out to help our brothers and sisters in need. Your gift to the Campaign for Human Development will help bring the kingdom of God closer to reality for the poor. Recall Jesus' words: "As often as you did it for one of my least brothers, you did it for me."

* * *

We should savor this historic occasion of our sesquicentennial and take pride and strength from the accomplishments of those who laid and built upon the foundations of faith. We will need that strength for tomorrow. And what will tomorrow bring?

A great deal depends on *us*. We can either ignore the problems confronting our Church and society—we all know what they are. Or we can provide the *leadership, creativity*, and *vision* needed to make a difference—the difference that will give greater meaning to our lives and provide a brighter future for our children.

The Great Chicago Fire of 1871 caused considerable damage to property. Today, a similar conflagration is burning out human hearts and searing ugly memories in our children. Struggling families, broken families, escalating and senseless violence, and numbing poverty stalk the Chicago metropolitan area, wreaking havoc everywhere.

During this sesquicentennial year, let us focus our attention and compassion on the members of our church and community who are homeless, who are jobless, those who are newly arrived immigrants, those who are trying hard simply to survive. Let us reach out to families struggling to improve their lives and their neighborhoods in a hostile, violent society that offers little hope. Let us recommit ourselves to helping the children of our metropolitan area, so many of whom know poverty, and fear the dangers that surround them. We must help people to rise anew from the ashes of their lives. I pray that you and I will not allow whatever success or comfort we have achieved to blind us to this God-given mission.

The theme for our sesquicentennial celebration is "Rooted in Faith, Rising to Our Call." Today, I call upon all Catholics to *rise to our call.* Let us take action. Let us take control of our future. Let us build upon our proud Catholic heritage and face the future with hope and courage. Let us dispel all fear and gloom from our hearts. I am Joseph, your brother, and I will walk with you. Will you make this journey of faith and compassion with me? We will not walk through the dark valley alone. The Good Shepherd, Christ the King, is with us. So, let us walk into the future with quiet confidence.

At noon today, all the bells in every Catholic church in Cook and Lake counties will ring in this glorious moment in our story. Listen to those bells! They are calling everyone to meet the challenges before us. I know that we can successfully do this because we are a people of faith with enormous energy and endless creativity. Those bells are truly the sound of courage calling us to commit ourselves, whatever the cost, as never before, to our children and families, our communities, our future, our faith!

Homily

Liturgy by the Lake
150th Anniversary of the Diocese of Chicago

19th Sunday in Ordinary Time
Chicago, Illinois
—— *August 7, 1994* ——————————————————

WELCOME! *Bienvenidos, Mabuhay, Witámy, Chao mung, Benvenuti!* How good it is for us to be here!

LOOK! Look Around! Take Notice! *Mira! Tignán Natin! Patrz! Nhin! Guarda!* See the People of God, the church in metropolitan Chicago! How good it is for us to be here!

Look and see! We are a very large and diverse people; we are a wonderful reflection of God's miraculous, creative power! We are African-American and German, Haitian and Italian. We are Irish, Slavic, and Hispanic. We are Asian and Caucasian. We are the People of God; the church in Cook and Lake counties; and how good it is for us to be here!

Look and see! We are old and we are young, energetic and tired. We are healthy and not so healthy. We are rich and we are poor; we are saints and we are sinners. We are a people of faith; the People of God, the church in Chicago; and how good it is for us to be here!

You are the great treasure of our Church—all of you! As I look out today, I see the tapestry of God in his people. We are woven together by our common faith and baptism in the Lord Jesus. We are a reflection of the risen Lord!

In today's gospel we hear that the people came out in great numbers to be with Jesus. Why did the crowds come to Jesus? Out of curiosity? Because their friends and neighbors were going? Because parents insisted that their children accompany them?

541

Perhaps, but there was also something *deeper* that attracted the crowds to Jesus.

Closer to home, when the immigrants came to metropolitan Chicago during the past 150 years, why did they establish—almost immediately—Catholic parishes and schools? Because they wanted to preserve their religious heritage? Because they wanted to belong to a community in their new environment?

Surely, but there was also something *deeper* that motivated them to make enormous sacrifices to establish and support their parishes and other vital Catholic institutions.

My dear brothers and sisters, why have *we* come to Grant Park this afternoon? Out of curiosity? Because our friends and neighbors were coming? Because we had to? Because we are lonely and like crowds?

Is there something *deeper* that brings us together?

Our setting for this Eucharist may provide a clue. Look toward the west. Enjoy the beautiful Chicago skyline. Yes, there is much poverty and suffering beyond that skyline. But the magnificent architecture before us reminds us that human creativity and determination can overcome enormous obstacles and create something good, beautiful, and beneficial for the human family.

Now look toward the east. Gaze at the blue waters of Lake Michigan. The lake stretches our vision toward the distant horizon and adds perspective to our lives. The lake is a *gift*. We did *not* create it. It reminds us that, ultimately, all we have and all we are is a gift from God.

And so, this afternoon, we gather on the frontier, as it were, between the *city* built by human labor and the *realm of God*. Now, let us return to our question: why are we here?

The crowds who came to Jesus may have had many different reasons for doing so. But Jesus looked at each of them and saw the truth: they came to him in order to *satisfy the deepest hungers* of their hearts.

There are many hungers of the human heart—the hunger for understanding, for meaning, for belonging, for acceptance, for dignity, for safety, for security, for love, for justice and peace. And whether we recognize it or not—like those who flocked to Jesus and those who established parishes, schools, and other Catholic institutions in metropolitan Chicago—we are hungry for God, starved for his word, unsatisfied by all that the world has to offer us.

My dear friends, today's readings remind us that, ultimately, our deepest hungers—the hungers of the heart—can only be satisfied by God. The readings also proclaim that God is more than willing to do just that: feed us, nourish us, and give us strength for our journey. God sends his own bread from heaven to give new life to the world. This is Good News, indeed! It is at the heart of our faith! Let us share it with our neighbors!

Why, then, have we come to Grant Park this afternoon? We have come to celebrate the 150th anniversary of our archdiocese, the community of faith here in Cook and Lake counties to which all of us belong, a community of which we are all so proud. The dominant sentiment in our hearts, of course, is gratitude. We thank God who has showered so many blessings and gifts upon us—gifts that have satisfied the hungers of our hearts. Our celebration in this historic park is a public acknowledgment that we are truly "rooted in faith" and that we are grateful for the witness and the sacrifices of those who have gone before us. They have shown us what fidelity to the gospel, creativity in ministry, and selfless love can accomplish. And today we pay tribute to them.

We also celebrate a very special gift, one that has been shared daily for the past 150 years in the churches and chapels of this archdiocese, one that has shaped our life as a community of faith. We celebrate the Eucharist, the Lord's precious gift of himself, the Bread of Life that provides wisdom and nourishment for our earthly journey.

Today, we gather as *one* church, a church made up of many local communities of faith; a church united in its faith in the Lord Jesus; a church enriched by many nationalities, races and cultures; a church whose witness and ministry were never needed more than now.

Today, the call is the same as it was two millennia ago when Jesus first commissioned the disciples: "Go—and make disciples of all the nations," he said. "Teach them to carry out everything I have commanded you." You and I stand at a new frontier of faith; we stand between the past, to which we are so indebted, and the future, whose challenges are still not totally known to us.

So together, let us recommit ourselves to the Lord and his Church; let us "rise (anew) to our call"—a call that beckons us to build upon our proud Catholic heritage, and to face the future with courage and determination. Assured that the Lord will be with us "always, until the end of the world" and nourished by the Bread of Life he has shared with us, there is no reason to fear, no cause for gloom, no matter what the challenges might be. With his help and our own efforts, carried out with perseverance and fidelity, we *can* make a difference! As brothers and sisters *united* in Christ's love and *driven* by that love which knows no limits, no barriers, we *can* change the face of the earth.

Today, I challenge you to rise to that call! As your bishop and brother, I will walk with you, so that together we can move into the future, so that together we can prepare ourselves and the world for the third millennium of the Lord's reign.

May the grace of our Lord Jesus Christ and the love of God and the fellowship of the Holy Spirit be with you all, now and forever. Amen.

Mass for the Closing of the Archdiocesan Sesquicentennial Year

Feast of Christ the King
Holy Name Cathedral, Chicago, Illinois
——*November 20, 1994* ——————————————

My dear brothers and sisters, we began our observance of the sesqui-centennial anniversary of the Archdiocese of Chicago exactly one year ago, on this feast of Christ the King. We ushered in the yearlong celebration with the ringing of church bells at noon that day throughout our local church. The wonderful sound of the bells was heard throughout Chicago-land, a powerful reminder of our unity. But the individual tones of the parish bells also echoed the rich racial, ethnic, and cultural diversity of our parish communities. Throughout our sesquicentennial celebration, we have celebrated our unity in faith amidst our great diversity.

This afternoon, we gather in this cathedral church as representatives from every facet of Catholic life in Cook and Lake counties. We represent parishes, elementary and secondary schools, colleges and universities, social service organizations, hospitals, religious communities, archdiocesan agencies, and many, many more entities.

Today's scriptural readings help shape our celebration. They offer a sharp contrast between Daniel's comforting vision during the night and the stark reality of Jesus standing before Pilate in broad daylight.

We listen in awe and wonder to Daniel's vision of "one like the son of man coming on the clouds of heaven" to receive an everlasting dominion over the entire earth. It is the vision of a human being who is given power by God to gather people of every nation and language in a kingdom of justice and peace. Daniel's vision pierces the darkness of human disunity and conflict, and gives us new hope for the future, a hope based on God's all-powerful word. This vision continues to comfort God's people in every age, especially when their hearts are full of anxiety and the future is uncertain.

Dare we dream such a dream? Dare we dispel the nightmare of beastly ignorance and violence? Dare we dream of harmony, unity, and collaboration? The history of our local church reminds us that, because they were rooted in faith, those who have gone before us have always risen to God's call, especially in times of difficulty or crisis. Are we willing to rise to our call today? That is the question each of us must answer.

The gospel reminds us that God reigns even in the midst of hostility. Jesus stands like a beacon in the darkness caused by Pilate's ignorance, cowardice, and dishonesty. The Lord's light reveals the truth of the situation: it is Pilate, not Jesus, who is on trial. Confronted with the one who is the Way and the Truth and the Life, Pilate prefers the darkness of being a dupe for the violence of the crowd. Faced with the opportunity to accept the Lord, Pilate turns away, a prisoner of his own past and of fear.

Jesus affirms that proclaiming the *truth*—indeed, being the truth—is at the heart of his kingship. He reveals the truth about God's enduring love in his person, his teaching, his actions. Jesus tells the Roman procurator that those who are committed to the truth hear his voice—the voice of the Good Shepherd who willingly lays down his life for his flock.

Pilate had the power under Roman law to condemn Jesus to death, but his decree was overturned by Jesus' glorious resurrection from the dead. The truth of Jesus' victory over the powers of darkness and death itself is highlighted in our second reading. Its song of praise is directed to the risen Lord who has freed his beloved community from its sins by shedding his own lifeblood for the salvation of the world. Having conquered death and given new meaning to human suffering, he now wants to reign in our hearts.

To make Jesus the Lord of our lives, we must live the truth; we must reveal God's love to the world by our words and actions. All who hear the voice of the Good Shepherd share in his ministry as prophet, priest, and king. My dear brothers and sisters in the faith, you and I are called to carry on Jesus' mission as a *prophetic, priestly,* and *royal* community.

As a *prophetic* community, we proclaim Jesus and his gospel to a world that desperately needs to hear the Good News. Violence plagues our streets and our playgrounds. Poverty robs the poor of the necessities of life. The homeless can be found right outside this cathedral. Families struggle to make ends meet and, often, simply to stay together. People are thirsting for a sense of direction in their lives. To the downcast, the dispirited, the hopeless, we are to proclaim the truth of the gospel—about

God's love for each of us, about the precious gift of every human life that must be protected and nurtured from conception until natural death, about the mandate to work for justice and peace.

That is why we have given such an important emphasis to evangelization and education in *Decisions*. Our archdiocesan plan for the next five years is not a theoretical or bureaucratic pipe dream. It is based on consultation with over 8,000 members of our local church. Its prophetic quality will help us chart our course, as a community of faith, with vision, creativity, and determination. Evangelization is at the very heart of our mission. And Catholic schools, together with other forms of Catholic education, are essential to our evangelizing efforts.

As a *priestly* community, we carry on Jesus' mission of bringing to the world God's healing power, the reconciliation of the world with God in Jesus, the eternal High Priest. Liturgy is central to all we do, and our daily lives must reflect this by our actions. Instead of sacrificing on the altars of materialism, consumerism, and an exaggerated individualism, we are called to sacrifice our lives on the true altar of God, like Jesus. We must be willing to give our all for struggling families, widows and widowers, orphans and abused children, the poor, victims of violence and spousal abuse—indeed, everyone who needs healing, reconciliation, and new life with God.

As a *royal* community, the Church witnesses to the fact that the reign of God is already present in the world. Despite all appearances to the contrary, God's kingdom *has* taken root. There are unmistakable signs of its existence throughout our local church. It is found wherever believers, in imitation of the Good Shepherd, love their brothers and sisters, without counting the cost. As a royal community, we will need effective ministerial leaders—priests, deacons, and the lay faithful. To ensure that we have such leaders is a vital dimension of our pastoral plan for the immediate future.

* * *

During this sesquicentennial year, we have recalled the wonderful accomplishments of those who have gone before us. We have also acquired greater appreciation for all that the Catholic Church presently does for people in Cook and Lake counties. Now is the time to face the future with renewed faith, courage, enthusiasm, and hope.

What is the truth about the future of the Archdiocese of Chicago? It is a very complex reality, and, yes, we face many challenges. But people are also rediscovering the Church. There is much untapped talent in our parishes. People, especially young people, want to be more involved in the Church's life and ministry. This leads me to believe that two themes are key to our future.

First, during our sesquicentennial year many people have come to realize that the Church is larger than the individual parishes, and that collaboration is more appropriate than competition. All parishes must work together for the good of the whole Church. A creative, new approach to collaboration will break down barriers and resistance to change. Moreover, in order to be an effective minister today—whether ordained or lay—one must be able to work collaboratively with others and to respect their ministries.

There is another vital dimension to our future. In the past 150 years, our local church experienced phenomenal *growth*. While some areas of the archdiocese continue to grow, the challenge of the future is not so much the demands of physical growth as the need to *deepen* our commitment to the Lord Jesus and his gospel, to deepen the roots of our faith. We must give people the hope needed to help drive away the cynicism of our time. We must love one another in concrete ways that will make a difference in their lives and ours. In short, the challenge will be to reach minds and hearts.

My dear brothers and sisters, we live in tension between the comforting vision of Daniel that God is with his people and the sobering reality of how much it will cost us to make Jesus the Lord of our lives, and to work together to build up his kingdom of justice, peace, harmony, and love in metropolitan Chicago.

As we forge ahead in the years to come, may we seek the intercession of the Blessed Virgin Mary. I take this occasion to dedicate our archdiocese to the Mother of Jesus and our own spiritual mother, our patroness, under the title of the Immaculate Conception.

Together with Mary, may the spirit and enthusiasm of our sesquicentennial celebration carry us confidently into the future and our next 150 years. ROOTED IN FAITH, MAY WE CONTINUE TO RISE TO OUR CALL!

c. Other

Homily

50th Anniversary of the Cathedral of Christ the King

Cathedral of Christ the King, Atlanta, Georgia

—May 4, 1987 ─────────────────────────

If these cathedral walls could speak today, what stories they would share with us about the events they have witnessed throughout these past fifty years! They would speak of glorious celebrations when this building was packed with people, when festive music filled this space with wonderful sounds of joy. These walls would also speak of familial events—baptisms, First Communions, confirmations, weddings, funerals—milestones marking the recurrent cycle of our lives.

They would also speak to us of dim, quiet days when the pews were empty and silent save for one or two isolated individuals who came to this special place to find solace, comfort, peace in the presence of God. Some of the most poignant stories would recount the quiet sobs of someone whose life was shattered, the bowed head of a person struggling to make sense out of life's twisting and turning, the desperate doubts and struggles of a man or woman or child searching for God who writes straight with crooked lines.

As I speak, many of you may be pondering a special event in your own life which took place in this unique place, the Cathedral of Christ the King, the mother church of this great metropolitan area.

I myself remember the two short, happy years I spent here as pastor—from 1966 to 1968: the only time in my thirty-five years of priesthood that I have ever been pastor of a parish. I remember the day—twenty-one years ago this week—when you received me, a young, newly consecrated bishop, as pastor and auxiliary bishop. I remember the day—two years

551

later—when together we bid a sad farewell to Archbishop Paul Hallinan, the first archbishop of Atlanta. And I remember the day—three and a half months later on the eve of my departure for Washington—when we joyfully received Archbishop Thomas Donnellan whom I salute today.

Fifty years! So much has happened in our world since that day in 1937 when this cathedral was consecrated. Those were the days when the Great Depression stalked the land, when people wondered if there ever would be a job for them, sufficient food for their families, hope for the future.

Then came that terrible day of Pearl Harbor when war entered our lives and disrupted our family life. Countless people came here to pray for husbands, sons, fathers who were fighting, suffering, dying thousands of miles away. And when the war ended, we gathered here to celebrate the victory, to mourn the heroic dead, to pray that we might learn the lessons which would preserve peace in the future.

So much has happened since then. We struggled to understand the meaning of events which unfolded so rapidly, challenging our faith, changing our lives. We gathered here to ask the Lord to enlighten our minds and soften our hearts. As we had faced the challenges of poverty and war, now we faced the new challenges of prosperity and social change.

In these past fifty years, historians estimate that more change has affected the human family than occurred in the previous fifty centuries. The atomic bomb. Civil rights and the quest for equality. Instant worldwide communication. Communism. The Vietnam War, Watergate, Iranian hostage-taking. Space exploration. Divorce, alienation, and the immense pressures on family relationships. Tremendous internal and external migrations of newcomers from overseas and from other areas of the United States.

We have lived in challenging times, indeed. This cathedral has been part of all this. It is a place where we come not so much for answers, as to raise up and clarify our questions in the light of the gospel of the Lord Jesus, in the presence of a community of faith, and in the strength of the Holy Spirit who has pledged never to leave us orphans.

In reflecting on the meaning of this beautiful building and its fifty-year history, I'd like to share a delightful story. A woman who teaches religion to very young children, preschoolers five years old or younger, once said that adults sometimes forget how literal-minded children are. She said, "We feel that we are simplifying things for youngsters if we tell them that the Church is God's house. But do you know what that means to a child? He thinks of his own house and is puzzled. He spends all his time in church trying to figure out where God's bed is. Where is God's kitchen? Where is God's television set? Rather, we should say that the church is a special place where God gathers his family together so that he can be very close to them."

I mention that little story on this solemn occasion because it helps us get to the heart of the matter. This cathedral is, indeed, a very special place where, for the past fifty years, in good times or in bad, in wartime or in peace, on feast days or ordinary days, God gathers his family together so that he can be very close to them.

Today's Scripture readings expand upon that childlike description. King Solomon asks the ultimate question, "Can it be that God dwells among us on earth? If the heavens and earth cannot contain you, O God, how much less this temple which I have built."

We will never fully understand the true significance of this place and this day until Solomon's awe-filled question becomes our own. Theologians speak of the necessity of firmly grasping the twofold qualities of God, namely *transcendence* and *immanence*.

Transcendence: God is the totally other. Eye has not seen; ear has not heard. The human imagination cannot begin to capture the glory, the majesty, the immensity of God. A few weeks ago the scientific world was astonished by the discovery of the explosive birth of a new supernova. It is 100,000 light-years away. The light from that explosion began its journey to earth one thousand centuries ago. Facts such as that boggle our minds. They confront us with the vastness of space and the marvelous immensity of God the Creator. And Solomon's question takes on new force and meaning.

Humbled, we ask, "Can it be that God dwells among us on earth?!"

But God's transcendence must be linked with the equally magnificent reality of God's *immanence*. St. Paul's question must be placed alongside that of King Solomon. He says, "You are God's building. Are you not aware that you are the temple of God and that the Spirit of God dwells within you?"

Are you not aware? We gather today to celebrate the astonishing reality that the God of supernovas and galaxies, the God of majesty and immensity bends down to meet his people in a place like this cathedral. But we also attempt to expand our minds, our spirits, our lives around the even more remarkable reality that God dwells within us as individuals and among us as a community. As beautiful as stones and stained glass, wood and metal, weavings and artistry are, even more beautiful are the living temples of flesh and blood, sinew and spirit, memory and imagination.

These are such profound realities that they are almost too much for us to bear. This Good News is so extraordinary that it exceeds our capacity to hold it. Our hearts are too small. Our minds are too limited. We pray for the gift of magnanimity—greatness of spirit—so that we might grow and expand to the degree that all of this might sink in. On rare occasions when we are at the height of our powers, when we leap beyond our capacity to understand; at such peak moments we can begin to glimpse what Solomon and St. Paul and all the other great men and women, saints and mystics and poets, have tried to tell us about the reality of God in our world and in our lives.

Perhaps we can deal more comfortably with the words of Jesus at the Last Supper as they are recounted in John's Gospel, for they make the same point in more familiar terms.

Jesus says: "As the Father has loved me, so I have loved you. Live on in my love."

We answer: "How hard it is sometimes for us to accept the fact that we are loved, that we are loveable, that we can love another."

"Live on in my love," *Jesus says.* "All this I tell you that my joy may be yours and your joy may be complete. I call you friends."

We answer: "Lord, we want to be joyful persons. But some days we feel so burdened, so unworthy, so confused. Sometimes life seems so meaningless. Other people seem to be hostile, untrustworthy. Sometimes we're not sure you are there, or that you care."

"I call you friends," *Jesus says.* "It was not you who chose me, but I who chose you to go forth and bear fruit."

We answer: "Yes, Lord, once in a while we begin to realize that you are present, gently calling us, prodding us to grow, to become more than we think we can be. Your amazing love astonishes us. We don't know why, but we are beginning to believe that you have indeed chosen us to be small but significant instruments for your work in this world."

My brothers and sisters, as we celebrate the fiftieth anniversary of this cathedral, let us hold in our hearts those simple but profound messages of Jesus:

"Live on in my love."
"I call you friends."
"Go forth and bear fruit."

Homily

Funeral Mass for John Cardinal Dearden

Cathedral of the Blessed Sacrament, Detroit, Michigan
—August 5, 1988 ————————————————————

He came to Nazareth, where he had been brought up, and went into the synagogue on the Sabbath day as he usually did. He stood up to read, and they handed him the scroll of the prophet Isaiah. Unrolling the scroll he found the place where it is written:

"The spirit of the Lord has been given to me,
for he has anointed me,
He has sent me to bring the good news to the poor,
to proclaim liberty to captives
and to the blind new sight,
to set the downtrodden free,
to proclaim the Lord's year of favor" (Luke 4:16-19).

God's people have never been without their prophets—holy and wise leaders who are sent to bear a personal testimony to the reality of God. Their prophetic voices never speak and are never heard in a vacuum, for they are always very much a part of the historical moment in which they live. They share the same needs and the same hopes and aspirations as the people among whom they live and work. It is precisely to them that the prophets speak, bringing them the good news of all that God has done for them, giving them the hope needed to transform their human misery into joy.

Today we gather to honor the memory of one whose voice in the contemporary Church was truly prophetic. We have come to express our

555

gratitude to God for a man who understood and accepted the challenges of the present because his vision was deep and broad enough to encompass both the past and the future: Cardinal John Dearden, archbishop-emeritus of Detroit.

It is not necessary for me to give you the cardinal's biographical data. You have read this in the many stories which have appeared since his death. Besides, what is really important is the man himself. I want, therefore, to speak to you today about a fully human person who loved people and life. I want to trace, briefly and simply, the image of a dedicated, faith-filled man whose every moment was spent, both in word and example, convincing people that God really loves and cares for them and that, because of this, the world is not such a bad place after all.

First, the cardinal was a man of deep *faith*. Both in life and in death, he walked, as St. Paul told the Corinthians, "by faith, not sight." It was this faith that gave him the inner peace and tranquillity which he always seemed to possess—no matter what challenge or crisis he faced. As late as last Friday, he told a priest of the archdiocese not to be fearful about an important responsibility he had been given. "The larger the task," he said, "the more the Holy Spirit will be given to you." It was this faith that shaped the cardinal's life and ministry.

The cardinal also had a great *confidence* in people. He was certainly not naive; he knew that people would fail, that they would not always live up to the expectations others had of them. But he also believed that there was a basic goodness in people and, if encouraged and given a chance, they would rise to the occasion. I know, for example, that he placed much more confidence in me than I deserved. When I served as his general secretary at the National Conference of Bishops in Washington, he just took it for granted that I would be able to accomplish what he expected. That gave me a motivation which enabled me to do far more than I would have accomplished on my own. But it was also somewhat frightening.

It was this combination of faith in God and confidence in people that gave the cardinal an extraordinary serenity, even when things were not going well. He did not panic because he believed that, in the end, problematic situations would correct themselves, that the grace of God and the good will and good sense of people would ultimately prevail.

Another quality of the cardinal was *courage*. He seldom faltered when he was convinced of the correctness of a particular decision or course of action. He was a secure, humble man who never held back because he was afraid of the personal repercussions his stand might have. Indeed, sometimes he changed his position, but not because of weakness or a lack of resolve. Rather, it was because he listened to people and was not reluctant to make a change when the circumstances warranted it. In taking difficult positions, however, he was always respectful of people. His position was always rooted in sound argumentation, not *ad hominem* arguments. He tried never to embarrass the person with whom he disagreed. If he felt that he had done so, he was quick to apologize.

Finally, there was an extraordinary *human quality* which the cardinal possessed. I did not know him when he was called "Iron John." Whatever there was that gave rise to that title, it was—I am convinced—simply a mask for the warmth that lay underneath. He was always a gentleman and had respect and affection for a wide range of people. He could relate equally well to poor and rich, young and old alike. He also had a good sense of humor and was always ready to help people see the lighter, more joyful side of life.

There was one group for whom he had a special affection, although not all of them may have realized it at the time. I am referring to his priests. He told me many times that he was blessed in both dioceses by good priests. He trusted and supported them. If any experienced difficulty, he was always kind and understanding. As president of the Episcopal Conference (which I will talk about in a few moments), one of his special interests was the priesthood study. So important did he consider this project that he asked Cardinal Krol, the vice president, to chair the committee responsible for the study. Before leaving office as president, he also saw to it that the Committee for Priestly Life and Ministry was properly staffed. The priesthood was very important to him. He saw the charity and unity which join together a bishop and his priests as essential to the life and well-being of the diocese.

As I have reflected on the cardinal's life and ministry, one word stands out above all others. And that word is *Church*. He was truly a "churchman"—a man of and for the Church.

First of all, he had a great *love* for the Church. That love manifested itself in so many ways—his affection for and loyalty to the Holy Father; his esteem for his brother bishops; his devotion to his priests and people. He saw the Church as a family, and he was ever concerned about the spiritual and material well-being of every member of that family, no matter what his or her status might be. This esteem and affection created a climate of warmth and acceptance, even on the part of those who felt alienated from the Church.

Love, as we know, begets *wisdom*. And Cardinal Dearden had a great wisdom regarding the Church. He understood the Church as few people do. He was steeped in its theology, tradition, and history. He understood and tenaciously defended those elements which are part of the Church's God-given heritage. He also understood that the Church is a dynamic, living reality, always subject to growth and renewal. He fully agreed with Pope John XXIII that "the substance of the ancient doctrine of the deposit of faith is one thing, and the way in which it is presented is another," and that the Church "must ever look to the present, to the new conditions and new forms of life introduced into the modern world which have opened new avenues to the Catholic apostolate" (Pope John XXIII, Opening Address, Second Vatican Council).

For this reason, the Second Vatican Council, in the cardinal's judgment, was a great grace for the Church as it approached the remaining decades of the second millennium. He took an active part in the preparatory sessions, as a member of the commission that prepared the draft of the Pastoral Constitution on the Church in the Modern World. In particular, he chaired the subcommission which wrote the chapter on marriage and family. He told me that after the completion of the chapter, which has made such a substantial contribution to the Church's theology of marriage, Pope Paul VI called and asked that he brief him on its content. The cardinal reviewed it with him, line by line. Subsequently, the Holy Father sent the cardinal a personal note thanking him for the leadership he had given. Cardinal Dearden often spoke about the rich exchanges that marked the commission's meetings. Together with others, I encouraged him to make a record of this living history, but to my knowledge he did not.

The cardinal returned from the council ready and eager to implement its teaching. And this he began to do in the archdiocese. I might add that the growth and renewal to which the council called the entire Church also had a profound effect on the cardinal personally. He underwent a significant change as a result of his participation in the council.

Toward the end of the first year after the conclusion of the council, the cardinal was called to exercise leadership at the national level. In November of 1966 he was elected president of the Episcopal Conference. Together with Cardinal Krol, the new vice president, and the other officers, he was given the challenge of reorganizing the conference so.that it could play the role in the Church's life which was envisioned by the council. The implementation of the conciliar documents called for the conference to make decisions and determinations in many areas, such as liturgy and ecumenism. In a very real sense, Cardinal Dearden was the father of our Episcopal Conference as we know it. We owe him a great debt of gratitude for all he did in this regard.

In recent years, especially since his retirement, I often spoke with him about the council and its aftermath, especially in this country. Usually these conversations took place while we were together on vacation in Harbor Springs, Michigan. While he was saddened by some of the tensions and divisions which have subsequently developed, he was always optimistic because he was convinced that the council was the work of the Holy Spirit. He was equally convinced that the council's vision of the Church was not yet fully realized, that it would take several more generations to appreciate and assimilate fully the depth of that vision.

Cardinal Dearden's death is a great loss to all of us. I wish to extend my sympathy to Cardinal Szoka and to all the bishops, priests, religious, and laity of the Archdiocese of Detroit. My condolences go as well to the members of his family, especially his brothers. My sympathy also goes to the many friends who have known and worked with the cardinal in Cleveland, Pittsburgh, and Detroit, and to his classmates, especially Father Steve Towle to whom he was so close and who was with him when he died.

I cannot express adequately my own personal feelings on this occasion. For the past twenty years our relationship has been a very close one. He was both a brother and a father to me. We shared our ideas and our hopes as we worked together for the Church. He was my teacher and counselor. Above all, we were friends, and I will miss him very much.

But we must not dwell too long on the past. What is important is the *present* and *future*. Cardinal Dearden has left us a legacy which we must not forget. He saw more clearly than many of us the real challenges of our times. He understood that renewal is more than a matter of external, superficial changes; that it is basically a change of mind and heart which is much more difficult to achieve. He was realistic enough to know that we must have order, that without structure our human condition would become chaotic. In faith he accepted and took seriously his role as bishop and shepherd. But he also believed that structure was always intended to help people, to bring out the best in them and never to stifle them. By putting this conviction into practice in his own life, he opened the door of hope for many who otherwise would have been disillusioned or frustrated.

I cannot conclude without reference to another great churchman, Archbishop Paul Hallinan, whom I served as auxiliary bishop in Atlanta. Cardinal Dearden and Archbishop Hallinan were close friends, and my life, as priest and bishop, has been closely intertwined with theirs. I had the privilege of preaching the homily for the archbishop's funeral. What I said about Archbishop Hallinan twenty years ago applies equally to Cardinal Dearden today:

> There may be some who say that he was ahead of his time. Perhaps he was. But I think his genius was that he saw that time was running out. He had the courage to take a bold step—that necessary, decisive step needed to bring the Church into the mainstream of contemporary life. It is for this reason that he was a prophetic figure. It is for this reason that his influence will long be felt.

Farewell, Cardinal Dearden, farewell! May God grant you the eternal rest you so richly deserve.

Homily

Celebration of the Millennium of Christianity in the Ukraine

National Shrine of the Immaculate Conception, Washington, D.C.

—*November 13, 1988*

Slava Isusu Chrystu!

My dear sisters and brothers in the Lord Jesus,

With great joy and gratitude to God we gather in harmony and unity as God's family to celebrate one thousand years of Christianity in the Ukraine. And how fitting it is that the gospel for today's Divine Liturgy is about the commissioning of the apostles. In this passage from St. Matthew, which follows the account of the resurrection, the risen Lord tells his disciples "to go therefore and make disciples of all nations." In effect, the Lord said to his disciples that they should be willing to leave behind the comfort of the culture and religion of their ancestors to set out on a new pilgrimage—one which was to bring the Good News of the kingdom of God to all peoples.

It was this evangelistic spirit that brought the gospel of Jesus Christ to the great cultural centers of the Roman Empire and from there to its distant borders. Although those of us from the West have all too easily identified that empire with the city of Rome, history tells us that for centuries the real political and economic center of the Roman Empire was Constantinople. It was in Constantinople and the other great religious and cultural centers of Byzantium, the eastern part of the empire, that Christianity flourished and developed its own unique theological traditions, deep spiritual yearnings, and distinct ecclesial discipline.

And it was this Eastern experience of Christianity that was to be carried, as the Lord had said it should, simultaneously with developing political and commercial links, to the emerging state of Kiev. Following the example of his grandmother, Princess Olga, Prince Volodymyr the Great responded to the proclamation of the death and resurrection of the Lord. He converted, along with a great crowd of his subjects, and was baptized on the bank of the river Dniepro on August 14, 988—one thousand years ago.

And what a conversion it was. An entire people came to be followers of the Lord with a dedication and a tenacity that were to survive a complex history of trial and triumph. And throughout these thousand years, the spirit of sharing the Good News that Jesus had given to his disciples has remained a hallmark of the community of faith that was born at the river Dniepro. Part of the giftedness of that spiritual heritage is that its roots were to be found in the tradition of Byzantium. United with the ascetical traditions and liturgical practices used in Palestine, Antioch and Cappadocia in the earliest days of Christianity, the ecclesial experience born at Kiev was to mature and develop its own unique identity.

Unfortunately, this religious and cultural diversity which was a distinctive feature of Christianity for over a thousand years eventually came to be a source of division that was to affect profoundly the ecclesial tradition born in the Ukraine.

But this brings us to the first reading in today's Divine Liturgy. In baptism we are all united with the one Lord, with a likeness to his death so that we might also share in his resurrection. In the end there is but one Lord, one faith, one baptism.

It was this profound Christ-centered instinct for unity of faith that was to be a distinguishing characteristic of Christianity in the Ukraine. Although Eastern and Western Christianity were tragically to split in the eleventh century, many people, together with the Metropolitan of Kiev, wanted to remain in communion with the church of Rome. This was not an easy goal to achieve. The spiritual traditions and ecclesial disciplines of the East were, and I might say still are, deeply treasured by Ukrainian Christians. But so, too, was the conviction that the Church of Christ was to be a communion of churches united with the Apostolic See of Rome. This dream of ecclesial unity was to be realized in the union of Brest-Litovsk in 1596.

The call to evangelize and a sense of ecclesial unity—these are two aspects of the Ukrainian spiritual tradition which we celebrate today. Unfortunately, the story of that tradition is also one of two countervailing forces: an attempt to restrict the life of Ukrainian Catholic Christianity as well as a lack of appreciation for the giftedness of its distinctive ecclesial and spiritual heritage.

The first force is more recent. How can we forget the sufferings of the "unknown Holocaust," the artificially engineered famine which took the lives of some six to seven million Ukrainians during Stalin's reign of terror? Nor can we pass over the tremendous loss of life in the Ukraine during the Nazi occupation and the Second World War. And finally, it is difficult to appreciate the violence that was done to the life of faith in the Ukraine during the infamous "Council of Lviv," when the Ukrainian Catholic Church was outlawed and its members forcibly joined with the Russian Orthodox Church.

The second force—a lack of appreciation for the distinctive Ukrainian heritage—is older and deeply troubling for us as sisters and brothers in the Lord. We must admit, with honesty and sadness, that Latin and Ukrainian Catholics have not always lived as brothers and sisters of faith. In a particular way here in the United States, Ukrainian Catholics were little understood by Latin-Rite Catholics and were treated, at times, with outright hostility. Although some Latin-Rite pastors accepted them into membership in their parishes, there was little effort to meet the unique religious and cultural needs of Ukrainian Catholics.

And finally, when the Ukrainians were sent their own priest, he was rejected by Latin-Rite bishops and pastors because, as permitted by the Eastern tradition, he was married.

Fortunately, today we are able to celebrate the great progress that has been made in the development of mutual respect between Ukrainian and Latin-Rite Catholics. Faithful to the teaching of the Second Vatican Council, we all recognize the legitimate and honored place of the ecclesial traditions of the East within the universal communion of faith. Although in times past we Latin-Rite Catholics may have passed by Ukrainian Catholics along our journey, today we acknowledge, with affection and respect, that we are all united, as sisters and brothers, in the one Church of the Lord. We ask your forgiveness for the times when we, your Latin-Rite neighbors, may have misunderstood you or failed to appreciate your valuable contribution to the Catholic heritage. While we cannot undo the mistakes of the past, we *can* work together closely, as we have for many years now, to ensure that they are not repeated and that we might manifest more clearly the unity of the Church in the diversity of its venerable rites, a unity that has been so essential to Ukrainian Catholicism.

Unfortunately, the same progress has not been made within the church in the Ukraine. The same forces that sought to repress the vitality of that church remain at work today. Despite the beginnings of *glasnost* and certain ecumenical gestures, it seems likely that, for now, the church in the Ukraine—whether in the catacombs or in the bright light of sunshine—will continue to walk the Way of the Cross.

This, then, is the context in which we come to celebrate the end of the first millennium of Christianity in the Ukraine and the beginning of the second. As one communion of faith, diverse in traditions and spirituality, we celebrate the spirit of proclamation that brought the faith to Kiev a thousand years ago and that keeps it alive today: in the Ukraine and in its diaspora. And, as sisters and brothers in the Lord, we Latin-Rite Catholics stand in solidarity with our Ukrainian sisters and brothers throughout the world. Together, our hope and prayer is that the Catholics of the Ukraine will soon be free to practice their religion.

As we celebrate this heritage and offer this prayer for freedom, we do so aware of the special gift which is yours, my dear Ukrainian brothers and sisters: the intercession of the Mother of Jesus. You honor her in the icon of the loving Oranta in St. Sophia Cathedral in Kiev. Today, the Virgin Mary holds each of you in her arms, for each of you is an icon of her divine Son. She is *your* mother also, the Protectress of all your people.

May the Virgin of Kiev guard and protect you, your families and your loved ones. May love and wisdom of God lead you safely into the second millennium of Christianity among Ukrainians.

Slava Isusu Chrystu!

Homily

Diamond (75th) Jubilee of the Theological College

Feast of St. Thérèse of Lisieux
The Catholic University of America, Washington, D.C.
— *October 1, 1992* ——————————————————

When individuals begin a journey into the unknown, one of two initial emotions usually predominates. Some begin with great enthusiasm; others, with considerable reluctance. As the journey continues, enthusiasm may give way to reluctance, and reluctance, in turn, to enthusiasm. But there is no hard and fast rule. It depends on the individual's attitude, the circumstances, and his or her faith in God.

St. Theresa of the Child Jesus, whose feast we celebrate today, was very enthusiastic when she heard God's call. Although she was only fourteen years old, she immediately began the journey toward the Carmelite convent in Lisieux. When the Carmelite superiors and the bishop of Bayeux refused to allow her to enter at that tender age, she did not give up. Later that same year, during a pilgrimage to Rome for the priestly jubilee of Pope Leo XIII, she boldly broke the tradition of respectful silence during an audience with the Holy Father. She asked him to allow her, in honor of his anniversary, to enter the Carmel of Lisieux the next year, when she would be fifteen. She made a favorable impression on the kindly Pope, but he wisely told her that he would not countermand the decision of the Carmelite superiors. She was undeterred at not having received a positive decision at the highest level of the Church. A short time later, she successfully persuaded her bishop to allow her to enter the monastery soon after her fifteenth birthday.

The Little Flower, as she is fondly called, is especially remembered for her "Little Way," her humility, and her profound spiritual wisdom. But

564

she also had great courage, strength, and even boldness when she became convinced that God wanted her to serve the Church—and, in a special way, to pray for priests—as a Carmelite. St. Theresa was in a hurry. Although she did not know it at the time, she had only nine more years to live. She entered into an intimacy with God seldom matched by others in such a short time—less than a decade! Her enthusiasm for life in the service of God and the Church never waned, despite the great suffering which she experienced before her death.

Her eagerness to enter God's service stands in sharp contrast to Jeremiah's reluctance: "Ah, Lord God, I am too young! I do not know how to speak." His hesitation, which resurfaced from time to time during his prophetic mission, was due not only to his youth but also to the hardship of his prophetic ministry. Being God's spokesman is often difficult. It is not easy to proclaim God's challenging word to those who do not want to hear it, or those who are apathetic or hostile toward it. So, Jeremiah's reluctance is understandable even though we may find St. Theresa's enthusiasm more attractive.

As we listen to the stories of St. Theresa and Jeremiah, we quite naturally react differently. Some of you—especially the students at Theological College—are young like Theresa and Jeremiah. You can identify with their responses to God's call. Others, myself included, have only the memories of our youth—some of them rather distant memories! We tend to focus our attention more on *God's* words and actions than on Jeremiah's response.

There are some who think that the first words in the book of Jeremiah, including those we just heard, were written relatively late in the prophet's life, perhaps toward the end of his ministry. That is, it was only *then* that he could articulate so clearly the significance of God's call and his own response. Regardless of when Jeremiah wrote these words, I can personally attest that, the longer I am a priest and a bishop, the clearer my vocation has become. It is a lifelong challenge to surrender every dimension of our lives to God, holding nothing back from his loving care and the service of his people. Indeed, there are many twists and turns in our lives. But in retrospect and in faith, we often see how God was present each moment, guiding and leading us. That has certainly been my experience, as it was Jeremiah's.

When Jeremiah looked back over his life, he was able to trace God's call to the first moments of his existence. God helped to shape him in his mother's womb, like a potter who shapes clay into a beautiful vessel. God knew him at the very beginning of his life and drew him into an intimate relationship. He set him aside for a special mission. Thus, Jeremiah did not stand alone before his enemies. God's divine power always strengthened and sustained him.

In our priestly ministry, many of us have faced obstacles, opposition, and outright hostility. But the risen Lord has strengthened and sustained us in both good and difficult times. His Holy Spirit has guided and comforted us. At the same time, as his disciples, we have been called by Jesus to walk with him—on a journey that always leads to Jerusalem, a journey that always leads to suffering.

At a turning point in St. Luke's Gospel, the evangelist tells us that, one day, Jesus "made up his mind and set out on his way to Jerusalem" (9:51). We are not told whether Jesus was enthusiastic or reluctant. It was enough for him that it was his Father's will that he go. The journey, of course, was not into the unknown, for Jesus knew what awaited him in Jerusalem. But his disciples did not because they had not listened to what he had told them about *why* they were going to Jerusalem. So, they were enthusiastic. And their enthusiasm was greatly bolstered by the *Hosannas* which greeted his entrance into the Holy City. But this gave way later in the week—not to reluctance so much as betrayal, denial, and flight.

In the gospel reading just proclaimed, Jesus, on the night before he dies, offers himself to his disciples in the form of bread and wine. His self-offering institutes the New Covenant, sealed with his own Blood. He gives this wonderful gift—the Eucharist—to the community of faith and invites them to celebrate it often in his memory. And he challenges them to be willing to lay down their lives for others, as he would do the next day. But the initial response of the Twelve is not very edifying. An argument about which of them would betray the Master deteriorates into a dispute about which of them is the greatest. Jesus points out, as he had done so many times earlier, that in his kingdom those who lead are to serve the rest, not lord it over them. Elsewhere he makes this point by washing their feet, giving them an example to imitate.

* * *

God always takes the initiative and calls men and women to the service of his Church. Everyone he calls is human—that is to say, limited, inadequate, inexperienced. But that should not deter us because we know that God also provides everything we need for our journey. When we walk with Jesus as his disciples—and continue his mission and ministry through the Church—we cannot avoid going to Jerusalem. We may be reluctant to embrace the Cross, but embrace it we must. We cannot turn back or find an easier route. So, let us pray for the grace given to St. Theresa who could find joy, strength, and enthusiasm even at times of great suffering.

Most important of all, at the very heart of priestly service and the Christian life is the Eucharist, the source of strength, wisdom, and perseverance. It is at the Lord's table that we encounter him most intensely—

in word and sacrament, in priest and congregation. It is also from the risen Lord present in the Eucharist that we learn how to serve one another and to be willing to lay down our lives for the sake of the gospel.

My dear friends in the Lord Jesus, the themes of today's Scripture readings reflect the significance of the diamond jubilee of Theological College. For seventy-five years, this school has prepared candidates for the priesthood for dioceses throughout the country. The dedicated faculty and formation staff have been God's instruments, forming priests who would minister in the Church in imitation of the Good Shepherd— with love, dedication, compassion, and great care.

We have gathered in *gratitude* to thank God for the many wonderful people who have worked diligently at Theological College to prepare successive generations of good priests. In a special way, I wish to commend and thank the Sulpician Fathers who have sponsored and staffed Theological College since its founding. Those of us who prepared for the priesthood here are especially grateful to everyone who walked with us during our seminary years.

We also gather with great *hope* for the future. Faithful to the gospel and to the Church's teaching, Theological College will continue to prepare future priests for the Church in this country.

I now wish to speak a special word to you who are currently studying for the priesthood. This year I celebrated the fortieth anniversary of my priestly ordination. If I had to do it all over again, would I choose priesthood? Absolutely—and without reluctance or reservation. I wish I could sit down with each of you and share the many reasons why. Since I cannot, I will simply say that the priesthood for me has been a tremendous source of satisfaction and joy. It has given me opportunities to love the Lord and serve his people that I never thought possible. My prayer for you this evening is that you will persevere in the vocation God has given you so that you, too, will experience the challenge, joy, and satisfaction of priestly life and ministry.

* * *

I invite all of you to join me in prayer for those who will come after us—that the stories of St. Theresa and the prophet Jeremiah, among others, will continue to inspire them and give them confidence for their journey of faith. And as God continues to call men and women to priesthood and religious life, may he give them the *faith* to hear his call, the *confidence* to respond, and the *generosity* to serve.

25th **Anniversary Mass**

National Federation of Priests Councils
— *May 4, 1993* ————————————————————

It is an honor for me to celebrate with you today the twenty-fifth anniversary of the founding of the National Federation of Priests Councils. It is fitting that we gather here in Chicago, the Windy City, the City of Big Shoulders, because NFPC originated here. So I welcome you back home. I congratulate you for your accomplishments during this past quarter-century, and I thank you for your faithful service to God's pilgrim people.

This is indeed a very special day. However, if you are like me, I'm sure you have a mixture of good days and bad. Our lives as priests are often like a roller coaster of ups and downs. Some of you may know that I started college in South Carolina with the intention of becoming a physician. When I have had an especially bad day, I sometimes fantasize about what my life would be like today had I pursued that goal instead of priesthood. Of course, in my fantasy, I would have been the type of doctor who is not only extremely competent but also warm and compassionate. And my patients would be devoted and loyal. But then I think of some friends of mine who are physicians and their headaches with malpractice insurance, mountains of paperwork, and the like.

Then I think I'd have a lovely wife to come home to and a bunch of wonderful children who idolized me. However, I pause in the realization that some of my friends have had very difficult marriages. In some cases their wives have been plagued by serious illness. In other cases, there have been divorces involving much anger, hurt, and bitterness. And the relationship with their children has run the gamut from very loving, close friendships to situations where they aren't even on speaking terms. As priests, we have dealt with many situations such as these.

And so, on my bad days when I tend to feel sorry for myself, my attempt to escape into fantasyland runs headlong into reality. And reality reminds us that everyone has bad days, whether he or she is married or single, ordained or not. We are all in the same boat. That awareness helps me to put my problems into perspective. I say this not to minimize the difficulties which we face. The challenging and profoundly disturbing cases of misconduct by clergy and by other Church employees. The necessity of closing or consolidating parishes and schools which have been in existence for many years. The persistent shortage of priests. The polarization in so many of our parishes between people who feel we move too slowly or too fast for them. The heartbreaking reality of violence, poverty, racism, exploitation in our society and in our world. These problems can weigh us down, stifle our spirits, drain our energy, test our faith, and break our hearts. At such times we may well ask ourselves, "Why did I ever become a priest? If I had to do it over again, would I say yes to God's invitation?" When we were ordained, we made a commitment. Each day, be it a joyous day, an ordinary day, or a disastrous day, we are challenged to say *yes*, again and again and again.

But to what are we giving this affirmation? In some ways both the Church and the priesthood have changed dramatically in the forty-one years since I was ordained. One veteran priest said, "I sometimes feel that I signed up to play football, and I became a pretty good player at my position. But at halftime the coach said, 'Guess what fellows, we're going to play baseball from now on.' So I adjusted as well as I could, but it's not always easy." Yes, things have changed, and we have had to adjust. But we are not alone. Lawyers, physicians, teachers, police officers, and many others in our society could make the same observation about their professions. Change is a fact of life in our modern world and in our Church.

Amidst all of this change, what is it about the priesthood that remains constant? What is the fixed star by which we navigate? What is it that causes us to say *yes*, again and again?

The title of the talk by Father Gerald Fogarty which you heard this morning provides a clue: "From Cultic Authority to Charismatic Bridge-Builder." Whether we are bishops or priests, pastors or associates, hospital chaplains, teachers, diocesan officials or whatever, the fundamental image of the Church we serve has switched from a pyramid to a circle. While prophecy is part of our mission, and we are charged to proclaim the gospel message in season and out of season, no longer are we the cultic authorities who stand in isolated splendor atop the pyramid. Rather, we are the bridge-builders who strive to coordinate, integrate, and animate our brothers and sisters who live together in the circle of God's love. As the psalm response in today's Mass says, "And of Zion they shall say 'One and all were born in her' and all shall sing 'My home is within you.'"

We are challenged by our vocation to be a true *pontifex*—a builder of bridges between the young and the old, between males and females, between the affluent and the poor, between black and white, between Hispanic-Americans and European-Americans, between conservatives and liberals. That is the duty of a Good Shepherd. As Jesus said in this evening's gospel, his sheep follow him because they hear his voice and know that he will care for them and shelter them, despite their differences.

Such bridge-building, such building of community, sounds very noble when you consider the litany of interest groups within the Church today. But we all know how frustrating it can be in actuality when you enter a meeting with some people whose demands, needs, and expectations are exactly the opposite of the previous group which sat in exactly those same chairs and around exactly the same table.

I think that we can look to Barnabas, who figures prominently in today's first reading, as an example of the charismatic bridge-builder whom we are called to be.

However, as an aside, I must confess that I am personally much more comfortable with the notion of "bridge-builder" in Fr. Fogarty's title than I am with the idea of "*charismatic* bridge-builder." As some of you know, I meet often with the priests of our archdiocese. Often I talk to them, but more often I listen to what is on their minds. I'm happy to report that they are very open and honest with me . . . indeed, sometimes their honesty is unsettling! But we have a good, straightforward relationship. In their honesty some of them have said to me, "You are a fine man. We are fortunate that you are our bishop. But couldn't you put a little bit more zing into your homilies? You're not very charismatic, you know." So, as I say, I'm more at ease with the notion of bridge-builder. I think I do that well. But not all of us are charismatic, no matter how hard we try.

At any rate, I'm not sure if Barnabas was charismatic either. Paul certainly was. Stephen was also. But Barnabas seemed to be the kind of person who worked behind the scenes to calm troubled waters, to heal wounded egos, to patch up disputes and arguments. And so he deals with the Greeks who complain that their widows are being neglected. He is sent by the church in Jerusalem, and on his arrival, we are told, he rejoiced with them and he encouraged them. Next he went to Tarsus to look for Saul and he brought him back to Antioch. In these few sentences what a wonderful portrait is drawn by the New Testament of this man Barnabas—diligent, intelligent, fair-minded, compassionate, patient, knowing when to speak and when to listen, knowing when to be firm and when to be flexible, always seeking what is best for his community, searching for hints of the Spirit of Jesus in the challenges and opportunities which faced him. What a wonderful evaluation of his activity is contained in that one sentence of Acts: "He himself was a good man filled with the Holy Spirit and faith!"

Isn't that what we strive to be? Isn't that what the National Federation of Priests Councils has stood for throughout these twenty-five years? And so we stand at the crossroads, at the intersection of the accomplishments of the past and the dreams of the future. As one of your statements puts it, "We are walking in the spirit of Vatican II, ministering in the faith of today and collaborating for the Church of tomorrow."

In my own name and on behalf of my brother bishops, I want to thank you for your dedication, your hard work, your creativity, your enthusiasm on the best days, and your perseverance on the difficult days. In particular, I want to congratulate the past presidents of the NFPC whose leadership has guided you. Many of them are with us today.

May the Holy Spirit who guided Barnabas, Peter, Paul, and Stephen also guide us as we continue to serve as bridge-builders between God and the people he has chosen to be his very own.

God bless you all!

"Promoting the Common Good through the Practice of Virtues"

John Carroll Society

Cathedral of St. Matthew the Apostle, Washington, D.C.

── *October 3, 1993* ─────────────────────

My dear brothers and sisters in the Lord:

I am grateful to Cardinal Hickey for the invitation to be the homilist for this year's Red Mass, sponsored by the John Carroll Society. This Mass on the Sunday prior to the first Monday in October, which traditionally marks the opening of the Supreme Court's new term, is an appropriate occasion for us to gather in prayer. We ask God's guidance and wisdom for the president, the Congress, the judiciary, the diplomatic corps, and for all who serve our nation.

The scriptural readings we have just heard give us the image of a vineyard. As described by the prophet Isaiah, this vineyard was very valuable property which symbolized the wealth of the land. The parable suggests that this wealth had not produced a just society. The threat that the vineyard would be turned into a ruin was fulfilled quite literally after the Assyrian invasions during the eighth century B.C.

Isaiah used the song of the vineyard to establish why judgment was appropriate for God's people, and to show that their behavior was tantamount to a total failure to live up to the demands of their privileged position. The song, therefore, is a sophisticated form of legal indictment of those who had broken the covenant of justice and love.

The Gospel of St. Matthew continues Isaiah's image of the vineyard. The interpretation of this gospel parable is made clear to us by its connection to Isaiah's song of the vineyard: God is the owner of the vineyard; the vineyard is the community; the vinedressers are the religious and political leaders who have been entrusted with the care of the community; the servants who were sent to the vineyard were the prophets, but they all met the same bad fate. The son is Jesus Christ. The owner expects that at least his son (Jesus) will be received with respect. In fact, he receives even worse treatment, to the point of being killed. His murder is the rejection of the gospel message by the people of the community and their leaders.

The threat that the vineyard would be taken away and given over to others, who live in accord with justice, is a cogent reminder for us who exercise leadership positions in our religious and political communities. If we do not act as responsible stewards and servants of the communities in our care, our leadership will be taken away and given to those who *will* act responsibly and in accord with the demands of justice. (Those of you who face the prospect of a reelection campaign know all too well the reality of that challenge!)

As we look out across the nation, the vineyard in our care, we see a valuable community of people with a wealth of talents and resources. But it is threatened with destruction and ruin by the forces of violence and narrow self-interest. Perhaps now as never before, people in many of the communities of our nation live in fear of crime. Perhaps now as never before, human life cries out for dignity and respect at every stage and in all circumstances. Perhaps now as never before, our failings as individual citizens threaten the common good of the vineyard in our care, the vineyard of our nation.

May I suggest a way to address this threat, a way which will entail no new government programs, no new laws, and best of all, no new expenditures of funds! That is because the means I suggest are not political, legal, or material, but *spiritual*. My suggestion is that, as a nation, we embark on a concerted effort to promote the common good through the practice of virtues. Although not requiring any new government programs, new laws, or new expenditures of funds, the promotion of the common good in this way *does* call for a change of focus, a change of emphasis, a change of direction, a change of attitudes, and a change of heart.

When considering the common good, it is far too easy to fall into the trap of seeing the common good as somehow opposed to individual rights and freedoms. This is a false dichotomy since individual concerns are inherently contained in consideration of the common good. The common good is not concerned with the good of the community in a way that sets itself in opposition to the rights and freedoms of individual persons. In fact, the common good of the community is harmed when individual rights and freedoms are not respected. On the other hand, the individual is harmed when narrow self-interests and the pursuit of purely private gain are pursued without reference to the needs and interests of the community as a whole.

As described by the Second Vatican Council in the Pastoral Constitution on the Church in the Modern World, "The common good . . . is the sum total of all conditions which allow people, either as groups or as individuals, to reach their fulfillment more fully and more easily."[1] Thus, there is a dynamic relationship between the individual and the rest of society in promoting the common good. This relationship is reflected in the law of the Church, which says that "in exercising their rights, individuals and social groups are bound by the moral law to have regard for the rights of others, their own duties to others and the common good."[2]

While the United States Constitution has no similar provision, the common good *does* have a special place in our nation's understanding of its laws and system of justice. The Constitutional Convention of 1787 voted unanimously against adding a Bill of Rights to the Constitution, considering it unnecessary. It was not that the delegates were against such rights; they simply considered the matter already covered inherently in the Constitution and its parameters for governance of nation.[3] As Alexander Hamilton said, an enumeration of rights "would sound much better in a treatise on ethics than in a constitution of government."[4]

As we all know, proponents for a specific listing of protected rights, led by Thomas Jefferson, prevailed within two years of the Constitution's ratification and amended the document to include the first ten amendments as the Bill of Rights. This listing has made us keenly aware of the individual rights which we enjoy in this country. May I suggest that, even though not mentioned specifically in the Constitution, the common good is a fundamental principle which serves as a basic pillar of our nation's understanding of its laws and system of justice.

Just as respect for individual rights is inherent in promoting the common good, may I further suggest that, when individuals conduct their lives in accord with the virtues, the common good is promoted. Perhaps this is

---

[1] Vatican Council II, Pastoral Constitution on the Church in the Modern World, *Gaudium et spes*, no. 26.

[2] Vatican Council II, Declaration on Religious Liberty, *Dignitatis humanae*, no. 7; see also canon 223.

[3] Catherine Drinker Bowen, *Miracle at Philadelphia: The Story of the Constitutional Convention—May to September 1787* (Boston: Little, Brown & Co., 1966) 245–47.

[4] *Federalist Papers*, no. 84.

more easily seen by considering the opposite. When individuals fail to live their lives virtuously, that is, when their conduct is marked by a life of sin and vice, then society as a whole, and thus the common good, is harmed.

Although it is impossible to provide a list of virtues upon which everyone would agree, the ethics of virtue has certain common features which primarily involve a focus on individual character: Actions are important because they show a person's values and commitments. It is a person's good character that produces practical moral decisions "based on beliefs, experience, and sensitivity, more than on (instead of) rules and principles."[5]

The new *Catechism of the Catholic Church*, reflecting our Catholic tradition, defines virtue as "a habitual and firm disposition to do good. It permits a person not only to do good deeds, but also to give the best of himself or herself."[6] We distinguish virtues as being *human* and *theological*.

Human virtues are attitudes, dispositions, and understandings by which we regulate our actions, control our passions, and guide our conduct in accord with reason and faith.[7] Four virtues are called *cardinal*, not because they apply only to cardinals (!), but because, coming from the Latin word, *cardo*, which means "hinge," all other virtues hinge on these: prudence, justice, fortitude, and temperance.

Prudence is the virtue which disposes practical reason to discern in every circumstance our true well-being and to choose the correct means to achieve it. St. Thomas Aquinas, following Aristotle, described prudence as the "right rule of action."[8] It is prudence which directly guides the judgments of conscience.[9]

Justice is the moral virtue which consists in the constant and firm willingness to give to God and neighbor that which is due. Justice disposes one to respect the rights of all and to establish in human relations that harmony which promotes the common good and fairness respecting all persons.[10]

Fortitude is the moral virtue which secures strength and constancy in the search for well-being when faced with difficulties. The virtue of fortitude is able to conquer fear, even fear of death, so that a person is willing to sacrifice his or her own life in order to defend a just cause.[11]

---

[5] William C. Spohn, s.j., "The Return of Virtue Ethics," *Theological Studies* 53 (March 1992) 61.

[6] *Catéchisme de l'Eglise Catholique,* unofficial translation (Paris: Mame-Libraire Editrice Vaticane, 1992), p. 381, art. 7, par. 1803.

[7] Ibid., par. 1804.

[8] *ST* II–II q. 47, a. 2.

[9] *Catéchisme,* par. 1806.

[10] Ibid., par. 1807.

[11] Ibid., par. 1808.

Temperance is the virtue which moderates the attraction of pleasures and provides a balance in the use of created things. Through temperance, persons are able to exercise control over the instincts and appetites of the senses and maintain their desires within appropriate limits.[12]

The human virtues are rooted in the theological virtues of faith, hope, and love. They are called theological virtues because their reference point is God himself, leading human beings to a participation in God's divine nature.[13]

Faith is the theological virtue by which we believe in God and all that he has said and revealed, and which the Church proposes, because God is the essence of Truth.[14]

Hope is the theological virtue by which we aspire to the kingdom of heaven and to the happiness of eternal life, placing our confidence in the promises of Christ and in the assistance of the grace of the Holy Spirit rather than in our own powers and abilities.[15]

Charity or *love* is the theological virtue by which we love God above all else and our neighbor as ourselves.[16] Loving one another, the disciples imitated the love of Jesus.[17] For this reason, Jesus said: "As the Father has loved me, so I have loved you; live on in my love" (John 15:12).

Charity is greater than all the other virtues.[18] The exercise of all the virtues is animated and inspired by charity.[19] As St. Paul wrote, "There are in the end three things that last: faith, hope, and love, and the greatest of these is love" (1 Cor 13:13).

Although I am speaking to you as a pastor in the context of a Catholic celebration of the Mass, my message of promoting the common good through the practice of virtues is by no means limited only to Catholics. Indeed, we have the example of none other than St. Paul, who relied on the ethical teaching of the Stoics and not on any uniquely Christian doctrine when he wrote the words we heard in today's second reading from his letter to the Philippians: "Your thoughts should be wholly directed to all that is true, all that deserves respect, all that is honest, pure, admirable, decent, virtuous, or worthy of praise. Live according to what you have learned and accepted, what you have heard me say and seen me do. Then will the peace of God be with you" (Phil 4:8-9).

[12] Ibid., par. 1809.
[13] Ibid., par. 1812.
[14] Ibid., par. 1814.
[15] Ibid., par. 1817.
[16] Ibid., par. 1822.
[17] Ibid., par. 1823.
[18] Ibid., par. 1826.
[19] Ibid., par. 1827.

Just as St. Paul did not assert that there was anything distinctively Christian about this exhortation, neither do I contend that my call for promoting the common good through the practice of virtues is uniquely Catholic or even Christian. Nor is there really anything novel about the concepts of the common good and the virtues. Moreover, we should not necessarily expect this message to have great popular appeal. As Mark Twain said, "Virtue has never been as respectable as money."[20] Nevertheless, I believe that this message has great timeliness and necessity for us at this time in our history.

This timeliness and necessity was recognized recently by three organizations representing some 100 million American Christians and Jews. A joint statement issued a few months ago by the United States Catholic Conference, the National Council of Churches, and the Synagogue Council of America said:

> The common good is an old idea with a new urgency. It is an imperative to put the welfare of the whole ahead of our own narrow interests. It is an imperative which we fervently hope will guide our people and leaders at this new moment. It is an imperative for a national embrace of responsibility and sacrifice, of compassion and caring as building blocks for meaningful lives and for a healthy society. We believe we can and must do better.[21]

I, too, believe that we can and must do better, and I echo the call of our nation's religious leaders that our "faith communities must continue to strengthen our ongoing efforts to engage our constituencies in study, dialogue and action in pursuit of the common good. Let then the leaders of our nation pursue this call and pursue its direction with urgency and creativity."[22]

[20] Quoted in Charles E. Bouchard, O.P., "Make Virtue Your Habit," *The Catholic Digest* (March 1993) 110.

[21] "The Common Good: Old Idea, New Urgency," *Origins* 23 (June 24, 1993) 83.

[22] Ibid., 85.

The Challenges of the Last Years

Priests of the Archdiocese of Chicago

Niles College Seminary, Niles, Illinois

—*November 19, 1993* ————————————————————

My Dear Brothers in Christ,

For a few moments, I thought you wouldn't give me a chance to speak to you. Needless to say, my heart is full to the brim and overflowing with gratitude—gratitude for the tremendous support that I've gotten during the last week. But in a very special way, gratitude for the support and the love that you have shown to me, you, the priests of this archdiocese, whom I love and respect so much.

I know that many of you have written letters to me. Some have called. There have been so many letters that I have not had a chance to go through them all. But in due time, I will. I am very happy to have this opportunity to pray with you this afternoon. What better thing is there to pray for than healing—in our Church, first of all—but also in this world in which we live. And I must tell you that I am deeply moved by the tremendous turnout of priests this afternoon.

For a few minutes, I would like to reflect with you on three points. The first is very personal: I want to share with you my personal reaction to what has happened. And then, I want to speak for a few moments about our response as priests to sexual abuse, especially the sexual abuse of minors: our response both to the victims and to the priests who are involved. And third, I would like to talk for just a few moments about our future together in this wonderful local church.

First, the personal dimension. I was very humiliated. It was total humiliation. Last Friday morning, as I always do, early in the morning I was

581

praying my rosary, and on Fridays we use the sorrowful mysteries. The first mystery, as you so well know, is the Agony in the Garden. And as I prayed that decade of the rosary, I said to the Lord, "In all my sixty-five years, this is really the first time that I have really understood the pain and the agony you felt that night." And then I said, "Why did you let it happen?" I have never felt more alone.

Last Friday afternoon, just a week ago, at 1 P.M., I had to stand before the world, and I did feel very much alone. Up to that point I had felt supported, but when I went into the conference room on the first floor of the Pastoral Center—and saw some sixty or seventy media representatives—I did feel very much alone. And the only thing I had going for me at that moment was my own forty-two years of ordained ministry, my name, my reputation. But there was an inner strength. And I am convinced that that inner strength was the strength that the Lord had given me.

For me, it was a moment of grace. A moment of pain, but also a moment of grace, because after that I began receiving the kind of support, the expressions of love, that I did not think were possible. But it was also a moment of grace because, for me personally, it was a time of spiritual growth. I have talked to many of you about my own spiritual journey, but I can assure you that I am entering into a new phase of that journey because of all that has happened during the past week.

I would like to speak to you also about my personal feelings toward Steven Cook. I said in that interview that I do not remember the man. He was enrolled in what was called, at that time, the Gregorian program for high school students, and then after that, for some time—I don't remember how long—he was a student in our college seminary. I am sure I must have met him because I visited the seminary frequently, as I visit the seminaries here in the archdiocese, but I don't remember him.

When this first occurred, my feeling was that of disbelief, bewilderment, "This cannot be." And then it turned to anger, real deep-seated anger: "Why has this person done this to me?" And then, it turned to compassion and sorrow. And that's where I am now. I only know Steven Cook by what I have read about him in the papers, what I've seen on television, and he has had a very troubled history. I also understand that he has AIDS, a devastating illness, a terminal illness. And so my heart goes out to him. And I have a great desire to meet him personally. I want to pray with him, and I want to comfort him. And I will write to him and ask if he will see me. I will go to him. I feel that need.

The second point is our response to sexual abuse, our response to the victims of sexual abuse. And our response to the priests who, regrettably, sometimes are involved in this.

First, the victims. My brothers, we must not let our distress over this false accusation or any other false accusation lessen our concern for true victims. I have said to the media several times during the last week: yes, I want to protect my name, I want to protect the image of the archdiocese. But I do not want to do it in any way that would scare off true victims. They must come forward to us to receive our pastoral care. And we must make sure that no child, no minor will ever be at risk in this archdiocese. And it's for that reason that I established the commission two years ago; it's for that reason that we have put into place our new policy and independent review board. We have a full-time Fitness Review Administrator and a full-time Victim Assistance Minister. I know that many of you were concerned about this—you were afraid that the new policy would be used against you. But I knew that it was needed. And I am happy to say that this new policy is working, and it is working well.

What about our response to priests who have engaged in sexual misconduct, who have abused a young person? We must also be very concerned about them. We must help them; we must help them both understand and accept the seriousness of such abuse and its consequences. As they try to rebuild their lives, we must walk with them when they are in therapy, whether it's psychological or spiritual. We must walk with them. And if later they are able to return to some kind of restricted ministry, we must continue to walk with them, so they will not feel alienated from us, so that they will not feel abandoned. We must love them, and we must care for them even when strong measures have to be taken. We have all heard of tough love, but tough love frequently is true love.

And what about the priests who are falsely accused? We must be very concerned about them too, because false accusations have a chilling effect. Some of you in this chapel know that, and certainly, I know that. Most of these cases of false accusations are not publicly known. But whether they are publicly known or not, if any one of us knows of someone who has been falsely accused, we must reach out to that person, just as you have done for me during the past week, and just as you are doing for me today.

And the third point is that I firmly believe, from the bottom of my heart, that this is a moment of grace for all of us, for the presbyterate of the church in Chicago. You will recall that a little over eleven years ago, on the twenty-fourth of August in 1982, we met for the first time in Holy Name Cathedral. Remember the thunderstorm that took place that evening? A great evening. And on that evening, I pledged to you my love; I committed myself totally to you as my priests. I would like to read you the last paragraph of the talk that I gave on that occasion.

> As our lives and ministries are mingled together through the breaking of the Bread and the blessing of the Cup, I hope that long before my name falls from the Eucharistic Prayer and the silence of death, you will know well who I am. You will know because we will work and play together, fast and pray together, mourn and rejoice together, despair and hope

together, dispute and be reconciled together. You will know me as a friend, a fellow priest, and bishop. You will also know that I love you, for I am Joseph, your brother.

That was a promise eleven years ago. I hope, in some way, you feel that both of us have kept that promise. I want you to know that I'm very proud of the priests of this archdiocese. Too often when we come together it's to discuss a problem or to respond to some kind of crisis. But when I am outside the diocese, I speak so highly of you. I tell my brother bishops that you are the best presbyterate in the country. I brag about you—they get tired of hearing me talk about you.

But there is one little disappointment I want to share with you. I have shared it with you before, but I want to share it with you this afternoon. Outside of the great moments of crisis—such as this—or moments of great jubilation—such as our convocation last year—we simply do not affirm and support one another as much as we should. Somehow, if a rumor comes along, we are too prone to pass it on instead of giving our brother or brothers the benefit of the doubt. When we hear someone is in trouble, we know that we should go and support him, but we delay doing it, and then we forget about it, and then we feel very badly later when we realize that we did not extend a hand to our brother-in-need. And we let petty jealousies and petty hurts come between us so that they become obstacles to our lives, to our ministry. In a word, we have not been brothers to each other as much as we should.

But enough of the negatives. I started out by saying that you are the best presbyterate in this country, and now I would like to add that this is a wonderful moment of grace for all of us.

It's a time to acknowledge, openly, our weakness, our dependence on one another—let's not be ashamed to do that. But it's also a time to acknowledge the many wonderful gifts God has given us, our potential as human beings and as ordained ministers. Now is the time to bring our rich diversity into much clearer focus, with a common vision of what we are about as priests in this local church. Now is the time to pledge to each other mutual support as we go about the work which the Lord has entrusted to us. Can you imagine what we could accomplish in this archdiocese if we loved each other that way, if we lived together that way, if we worked together that way?

My brothers, again, thank you. I love you, and you will always be close to my heart.

Prayer Service with the Presbyterate

Holy Name Cathedral, Chicago, Illinois
—September 25, 1995

In *August 1982*, we came together in the cathedral to pray and to get to know each other. Then in *November 1993*, after I was falsely accused, you invited me to gather with you at Niles College Chapel so that you could pray for and with me. Now in *September 1995*, we gather again at the cathedral to pray *for* and *with* each other, and to support each other, both personally and ministerially.

It is good for us to be here! I thank you for accepting the invitation. And I thank Jim Kaczorowski and the other members of the Executive Committee of the Presbyteral Council for their part in planning this prayer service.

I intend to speak very personally with you this evening in the hope that my insights and experiences will be of some help to you. I chose the passage from St. Paul's letter to the Corinthians for this evening's reading because I have gotten much comfort from it in the past several months.

> We have this treasure in clay jars, so that it may be made clear that this extraordinary power belongs to God and does not come from us. We are afflicted in every way, but not crushed; perplexed, but not driven to despair; persecuted, but not forsaken; struck down, but not destroyed; always carrying in the body the death of Jesus, so that the life of Jesus may also be made visible in our bodies. For while we live, we are always being given up to death for Jesus' sake, so that the life of Jesus may be made visible in our mortal flesh. So death is at work in us, but life in you.

Several years ago, in a conversation I had with several priest friends, I was asked what were my two greatest fears. Without much reflection I told them that I had always had two fears: one was being falsely accused of anything serious; the other was being afflicted with an aggressive type of cancer. Within two years, both occurred!

The first has had a happy ending. Steven Cook and I were reconciled. More importantly, he was reconciled with the Church. During this past summer he wrote and called me several times to assure me of his prayers. Last week he died peacefully—no longer an angry, alienated man. He died with his family and friends around him, praying with them. He prayed for me. Last evening I had a long talk with his mother, who told me about the last hours of Steven's life. She told me that, after he had received the sacraments, he winked at her and smiled, saying, "This is my gift to you." At this very moment, his funeral Mass is being celebrated in Cincinnati. I consider it a great blessing that I could be instrumental in his reconciliation with God and the Church. May he rest in peace.

The second *fear* was realized, as you know, this past June. I was feeling great, had many good things planned for the summer, including a vacation. For the first time in my life I was confronted with not only the possibility but also the probability of a premature death.

Somehow, with God's grace and the prayers and support of many people, including yourselves, I was able to move beyond the fear; I was able to put aside the non-important, nonessential things that so often hold us hostage. I was able to see things from a new perspective. Suddenly, the difference between the important things and the non-important came more sharply into focus.

The important things are those that truly help people, both personally and communally; the things that unite them and enable them to realize the full potential of their God-given gifts; the things that promote the common good; the things that promote justice rather than injustice and discrimination. It is better to focus our time on these matters than on petty squabbles that divide and alienate, on posturing that is self-serving and inauthentic, on bureaucratic red tape that does not contribute very much to the individual or common good.

Someone who helped me greatly during this period was Henri Nouwen, who visited me in July. We talked very candidly about life and death issues, and he gave me one of his latest books, entitled *Our Greatest Gift— A Meditation on Dying and Caring*. He said that death incites fear when it is perceived as an enemy. If we consider death an enemy, we avoid talking about it. If we do think about it, it causes us to be depressed, even angry. Rather, we should see death as a *friend*, as a very normal phenomenon, as a gateway to eternal life. When we see death in this way, our fear subsides; we are enabled to prepare ourselves so that we can die peacefully, united with the Lord who will accompany us home.

As St. Paul told the Corinthians,

> Even though our outer nature is wasting away, our inner nature is being renewed day by day. For this slight momentary affliction is preparing us for an eternal weight of glory beyond all measure, because we look not at what can be seen but at what cannot be seen; for what can be seen is temporary, but what cannot be seen is eternal.

As a result of my cancer surgery and the subsequent therapy, I have become the "unofficial chaplain" for all the cancer patients in Cook and Lake counties. Each day I receive requests to call or write notes to people suffering from cancer. I have invited a number of them to come to the residence for Mass. One family brought their mother on a stretcher. Let me tell you three stories.

The first story is about *Amanda*, a five-year-old Protestant girl who has leukemia. She was at the Loyola Hospital the same time as I. Having seen the doctors' report on me for several days on TV, she told her mother: "I've got to see that 'pope-man.' I'm not a Catholic, but we both have cancer. I've got to see him!" I couldn't visit her then, but I sent her some flowers and a teddy bear someone had given me. Subsequently, I saw her a number of times at the Loyola Cancer Center where we were both receiving chemotherapy. Each day she would give me a picture she had painted for me.

The second story is about *Lottie*, a lovely woman in her seventies who had had cancer for some years and was undergoing radiation. During the more than a month that I saw her on an almost daily basis, we became friends. Later, her daughter told me that she began to decline very rapidly. On Labor Day I went to her daughter's home in Western Springs, where she was staying, to anoint her. Her daughter told me that for some time she had seemed to be quite agitated; she was not reconciled to dying. She further told me that she thought the reason was that her father kept telling Lottie that she could not die; she could not leave him. I had a good talk with Lottie's husband. I suggested that he put Lottie in the hands of the Lord.

After I left, Lottie's daughter told me that she heard her father whisper to her mother: "You may go now, Lottie. I don't want you to suffer anymore. The Lord will come to get you." Several days later, Lottie died peacefully. And her husband was at peace also.

The third story is about *Kathleen*, a beautiful thirteen-year-old girl who has cancer. I was supposed to meet her and her family when I visited St. Mary's Church in Riverside, but the night before she had to return to Children's Memorial Hospital because she began to have a fever. I promised her parents I would visit her at the hospital, and I did that Sunday afternoon. Her parents told me before the visit that Kathleen had said to them: "I go to church every Sunday, but many of my classmates do not. Why do I have cancer, and they do not?" While I did not tell Kathleen I knew she had said this, I kept her question in mind as we talked. We had a wonderful visit.

During the past three months I have received between 10,000 and 12,000 letters and cards. Many of these letters were from you. I thank you. Besides assuring me of their prayers and support, many of the lay people who wrote spoke candidly of their expectations of us as priests. It became evident in what they wrote that they do not expect us to be men who have a lot of political savvy. They do not want managers (though if we do not manage well, they will be the first to criticize); they do not expect us to be "fixers" or have the solution for every problem. No, they want *holy men*. They want us to be *signs* of *God's presence* and *symbols of hope*.

We fulfill this expectation by very simple things—being present to people in their moments of joy and sorrow, saying a kind word to them, giving them a sympathetic ear, assuring them that God loves them and will never abandon them—no matter what happens.

And now, I will conclude by sharing with you my hopes for the future. In my pastoral letter on the Church ("The Family Gathered Here Before You") I articulated fourteen specific hopes I had for the future of our local church. Don't worry: I will not repeat them all now! I concluded by saying that "my deepest experience of the Church (is) people gathered together with a rich heritage of the past, with present struggles and celebration, with a future hope." "The Church," I said, "is a community and a way of life which depends totally on God's grace and our free human response."

Then several years later, I shared with you the *Decisions* document in which I spelled out my vision and my hopes in two specific areas, Evangelization and Education, and Ministerial Leadership.

This evening I wish to conclude *not* by focusing on that vision and those hopes, but by telling you how I hope I can be of help to you—personally and ministerially—as together we walk into the future.

At the administrative level, I will continue to do all I can to support and facilitate your ministry and outreach. I pledge that to you this evening.

But in the final analysis, my best contribution or gift is to help you grow in the Lord who alone can bring your efforts to fruition. My best gift to you is *myself*. Beneath the titles of archbishop or cardinal is a man—Joseph Bernardin—who is weak and sinful like you, in need of affirmation and support, at times full of doubts and anxieties, very sensitive, easily hurt and frustrated.

But this Joseph is a man of great faith, one who is in love with the Lord, one who struggles each day—sometimes with little obvious success—to decrease so the Lord can increase in him, a man whose life is full of crooked lines but who is willing to let the Lord write straight with them.

My brothers, know that this man, Joseph, has a great affection for you. Know that when you fail, he understands. Know that when you do crazy things that bring grief to others (as he himself does so frequently), he forgives you. Know that as you try to cope with the realities of life—both personally and ministerially—he is at your side, ready to help in every way he can. Know that when you succeed, he smiles and shares your joy and satisfaction. Know that when you are sad, hurt, demoralized, he cries with you. Know that this man, Joseph, loves you; that he is proud of you; and that for the sake of the Lord, he is ready and willing to give his life for you!

Homily

"Theology on Tap" Mass

19th Sunday in Ordinary Time
Holy Name Cathedral, Chicago, Illinois
—————*August 11, 1996* ————————————————————

It will happen to you. As a matter of fact, it might have happened to you already. At my age, it has happened many times. It might be something *minor* that triggers it, like making a mistake at work that we blow completely out of proportion. But it can also be a *major* setback. For example, someone tells you that your mother has just died: "She put up a good fight, and we did everything we could. We're so sorry." Or a doctor tells us: "The tests results are in, and they indicate that you have a cancer that must be treated." Last year that is precisely the news I personally received. At first, I was so dumbfounded, I couldn't say anything. Then, when I got my bearings, I asked: "Why me? After all, Lord," I added, "wasn't the humiliation of the false allegation of sexual abuse brought against me enough?"

The immediate human reaction to almost any and every painful situation is to be saved from it. Inside us, in the deepest recesses of our mind and heart, we cry out to be lifted beyond the present situation to a better place in life. Sometimes what we hear ourselves saying deep within us comes racing out as the most simple, yet powerful, prayer we can utter, "O my God, save me! Help me! Spare me!" That is why the cry of Peter in today's gospel is so easy for us to identify with. "Beginning to sink, he cried out, 'Lord, save me!'"

But we must be very careful for what we are asking. Are we asking to be *spared* by God? Or are we asking to be *saved* by God? There is a very big difference. We will not be spared or saved from dying. We will all die

590

someday. Sometimes we will suffer. That, too, will not pass us by. Broken hearts, diseases, and tragedies are a part of life. The news media and our personal experience confirm that for us every day.

What are we crying out for when we echo St. Peter, "Lord, save me!"? Perhaps, we will find an insight from our first reading, from the first book of Kings. Elijah went out of the cave to look for the Lord God to pass by. But the prophet did not experience God in the great wind, the earthquake, or the fire—as Moses had centuries before. Those were the expected places and experiences to encounter God. Everybody thought so. But Elijah had to look for God in some other experience. Elijah discovered God's presence in the totally unexpected, in a tiny whispering sound as the Lord God was passing by.

We are no different. We may well have assumed that we will encounter God in certain situations only—usually good, happy, positive experiences. And the painful things of life, many people assume, are God's punishments. Have you ever heard someone say, after reading about a natural disaster, "I wonder why God is punishing those people?" Yet, the amazing thing about our religious tradition is that the Lord God is with us when we least expect the divine presence.

My dear brothers and sisters, we firmly believe that the Lord Jesus is with us in every moment of life. All of life is charged with God's presence—good times and bad, sickness and health, day and night, summer and winter, whether we are alone or with others. It makes no difference when or where.

So, why do we cry out to be saved? Because we do not want to be alone. Because we want to experience God's faithful love, especially when we feel unloved. We want to become more aware of the ever-present God, especially when we are lonely. And when we are convinced that nobody can possibly understand what we are going through, we need reassurance that very close to us, indeed within us, is the divine presence. If we listen carefully in the deepest recesses of our being, we will hear Jesus say to us what he said to the apostles in the boat: "Take heart, it is I; do not be afraid."

We will not be spared the painful moments of life. But it is in those moments that the salvation, the love, the gentle and healing presence of the Lord is with us. We are not alone. We live in God, and God lives in us. That is the wisdom we heard in St. Paul's letter to the Romans: "[T]here is great grief and constant pain in my heart." Yet, there is more there, too. There is the presence and witness of the Holy Spirit as well.

So, when life hits you hard, and we all know that life will, keep the eyes of your faith wide open so that you may see God's presence when you think you are very much alone. At the same time, keep in mind that being *saved* is not the same as being *spared*. There is a good chance that Peter wanted both, and his immediate concern was being spared from drowning. Yet, in the Lord Jesus we are not spared the injustices and pains of life. But we know there is more. He is the one who offers us salvation.

"Save me, O Lord" is our prayer and our belief. To be saved means that we accept God's love into our lives. And no matter what transpires, we will not lose God's love. God will *not* abandon us. But in order to experience the Lord's salvation, we must know always who we are. In times of fear and in moments of joy, whether we are afraid or extremely confident, we are God's sons and daughters. We have no greater title, and God will relate to us as nothing less.

Nevertheless, if we are so loved and cared for by the Lord Jesus, it is not enough for us merely to recognize that fact. Because we are Jesus' followers, his disciples, we need to be bearers of that love, care, and salvation to all we meet. This means that when people are hurting, suffering, and living in fear, we will be there for them. We will bring God's saving love and care to them. We will walk with them in good times and in bad, in sickness and in health, when life is fair and when life is terribly cruel. Day or night, summer or winter, may the Lord Jesus count on us to care for others as he did for us.

My friends, let us pray that the actions of our lives will give meaning to Jesus' words, "Take heart, it is I; do not be afraid!"

Communal Anointing of the Sick

Church of St. John de Brébeuf, Niles, Illinois

—August 24, 1996 ————————————————————

My dear brothers and sisters in the risen Lord: It is good, indeed, for us to come together this afternoon to celebrate this communal anointing of the sick. I have wanted to celebrate this sacrament with you for a long time, and I thank God for bringing all of us here today. God has brought us together for a very special purpose. And the Scripture readings that we just heard help explain what this purpose is.

The reading from the book of Wisdom reminds us gently but firmly that *our own* plans for our lives are not always *God's* plans for us. Moreover, his plans are often shrouded in mystery. We make elaborate plans for ourselves, but often they wane or disappear altogether as we get older or face a serious sickness. I know this in a very personal way. In early June 1995, I was very busily and happily engaged in my pastoral ministry. My calendar was filled well into 1996 and, in some instances, to the end of this century. Then I learned one day that I had pancreatic cancer; I underwent radical surgery only three days later. All of this took me totally by surprise because I had had no symptoms of such an aggressive malignancy. Suddenly, for the first time in my life I had to face directly the prospect of a premature death. In one brief moment, all my plans for the future had to be put on hold; *everything* in my life had to be reevaluated from a new perspective. I know that many of you have had a similar experience, and you know how vulnerable it makes one feel!

After coping with the initial shock of such a discovery, it is quite natural to ask, "Why me, God? What have I done to deserve this?" That question crossed *my* mind, I assure you. As you know, the previous year I had suffered the humiliation of a false accusation of sexual misconduct. So, when I discovered that I had cancer, I wondered why God had also allowed this to happen to me.

The question, "Why me?" has been asked by countless people through the ages. We often tend to assume, for some reason, that, when hardship or tragedies occur, God has punished or abandoned us. But in his letter to the Romans, St. Paul lays that assumption to rest once and for all. As we heard, the apostle states with great confidence that no creature—absolutely no one—can separate us from God's all-powerful love that comes to us through his Son, Jesus. No adversity can prevent our access to God's love. God has *not* rejected or abandoned us. His love for us is absolute, not conditional. And, if we have God's love, we have all we need. We lack nothing.

But, at times, it is difficult for us to believe this. When we are ill or no longer able to function as we used to, it is not only the physical pain or incapacity that affects us. Our mind and our heart, our imagination and our will, are also affected. In 1987, on a pastoral visit to New Zealand, Pope John Paul II celebrated a communal anointing of the sick as we are doing this afternoon. He told the people, "when pain dulls the mind and weighs down body and soul, God can seem far away; life can become a heavy burden. We are tempted not to believe the Good News." We "may even be led to the verge of despair." But as the Holy Father pointed out, "the anointing of the sick responds to these precise needs, for it is a sacrament of faith, a sacrament for the whole person, body and soul."

The anointing of the sick reminds us of God's plan for our salvation: how God allowed his own beloved Son to suffer, die, and rise again so that we might be saved, so that we might be forever convinced of his enduring, unconditional love for each of us! The death and resurrection of Jesus—the paschal mystery—is the triumph of life over death and suffering. This sacrament sweeps us up into that victory—that triumph—by drawing us into the healing, loving embrace of God.

In the gospel passage we just heard, Jesus invites us to come to him, to learn from him as his disciples. Let us listen again to his beautiful, consoling words:

> Come to me, all you who are weary and find life burdensome, and I will refresh you. Take my yoke upon your shoulders and learn from me, for I am gentle and humble of heart. Your souls will find rest, for my yoke is easy and my burden light.

What beautiful, comforting words. For a few moments, let us reflect on them. Let us draw out their full meaning and significance for our lives.

As we know, Jesus practiced what he preached. He was gentle toward the people he served—especially those who came to him for healing. And he was humbly obedient to his heavenly Father's will. The "rest" Jesus offers us comes from adopting and living each day his attitude toward illness and human suffering, his ministry of loving care for others, his submission to his Father's will—in whatever circumstances we find ourselves.

But what makes Jesus' yoke "easy?" A good yoke, which is usually seen around the neck and shoulders of cattle, is carefully shaped to reduce chafing to a minimum. Jesus promises that his yoke will be kind and gentle to our shoulders, enabling us to carry our load more easily. That is what he means when he says his burden is "light." Actually, it might be quite heavy, but we will be able to carry it. Why? Because Jesus himself will help us. It is as though he tells us, "Walk alongside me; learn to carry the burden by observing how I do it. If you let me help you, the heavy labor will seem lighter."

My brothers and sisters, when I learned that I had cancer, I prayed as I had never prayed before that I would have the courage and grace to face whatever lay ahead. That has been part of my daily prayer ever since. And God has answered my prayer. I have been blessed with an inner peace that I have never experienced before. This does not mean that I am spared the anxiety and fear that serious traumas cause. I have made no effort to hide or deny my fear, my anxieties, and, at times, my tears. But the important thing is to find ways to move beyond these normal human emotions and, in faith, to live life in God's presence as fully as possible each day.

Sometimes we tend to look outside ourselves to find Jesus. But he is actually inside ourselves in the same way that a vine is present in all its branches. So all we need to do is open our minds and hearts to him so that his love and healing power may fill every part of our mind, heart, and will; indeed our very being; so that we can truly say with St. Paul: "Now I live, not I, but Christ lives in me."

In a few moments, we will lay hands upon the heads of those of you who are sick or elderly. We will also anoint your forehead and your hands with consecrated oil. I, too, will be anointed because, like you, I need strength and healing. These gestures and their accompanying words will assure us that God is with us always—especially in our times of trial and suffering. They will assure us that the risen Lord and the whole Church will walk with us, helping us to carry our burdens. In a special way Mary will accompany us—in the same way she followed her son, Jesus, showering upon him and consoling him with her tenderness, compassion, and love in the midst of his suffering and death.

My dear friends, may the peace that God alone can give—the deep peace of mind and heart and soul and spirit—be with us today and all the days of our life!

Communal Anointing of the Sick

Church of St. Barbara, Brookfield, Illinois

—*August 31, 1996* ————————————————————

1. It is good for us to be here.

- We are all facing illness or the infirmity that comes with advanced years.

- So, it is good that we have come together to acknowledge our *physical* vulnerability, but also the *strength and grace* we have because of our faith in the Lord Jesus.

- Through this anointing we will have an opportunity again to place ourselves in the hands of the Lord, asking him to give us peace of mind, as well as physical healing if that is his will.

2. I would like to share with you a little of my own personal journey. I do so just to let you know that I am going through the same thing that many of you have experienced. Perhaps in that way we can be united even more closely as we live our lives in fidelity to the Lord's will.

- June 1995—diagnosed as having pancreatic cancer. First reaction: surprise, anxiety, fear. Lord, why me? (especially since I had been through the trauma of a false accusation of sexual abuse). But then, I turned to the Lord and asked for courage, strength, and healing.

- Surgery was *successful*. For fifteen months I was cancer free. Trouble with my back, but that was minor in comparison with the cancer.

- Then on Wednesday, August 28, I was told the cancer had returned. Terminal. Year or less to live.

- Needless to say, I was surprised at the *quick* return. In one moment everything changed. But I am tranquil. Even though I know that, humanly speaking, I will have to deal with difficult moments, I am at peace. There have been tears—and there will be more. But they are tears of gratitude and joy. *Why* am I at peace?

3. When we are faced with serious illness (or any serious difficulty), we should do several things—and these are the things that have given me peace of mind personally.

- Put ourselves *completely* in the hands of the Lord. "Come to me all you who are weary and find life burdensome, and I will refresh you." We must believe that the Lord loves us, embraces us, never abandons us (especially in our most difficult moments). This is what gives us hope in the midst of life's suffering and chaos.

- We must try to see death as a friend, not an enemy.

- What follows from that is that we must be willing at a given point to let go, to let Jesus come to get us, not resist. If we resist, we will be anxious, fearful, etc. Let me give the story of one of my cancer friends. Her name was Lottie . . .

4. *And now let us be anointed.* I will be anointed first so that then, together with the other bishops and priests, I can anoint you. May this anointing be both a *sign* of our faith in the Lord and the *instrument* he uses to give us the strength and grace we need.

St. Joseph College Seminary

Chicago, Illinois

——September 5, 1996 ——————————————————————

This is an occasion of new beginnings. Some of you are entering the seminary for the first time. All of you are beginning a new school year here at St. Joseph Seminary. We are also inaugurating a new era in the life of this community by installing Father Jim Presta as your rector. And my dear brothers and sisters, as you know, I have begun a new era in my own life as I prepare to meet the Lord.

There are often conflicting emotions at the beginning of a new endeavor, and today's Scripture readings address some of these: fear and hesitation, eagerness and enthusiasm, honor and shame.

Jeremiah's response to his initial call to be God's spokesperson is both fear and hesitation. Yes, he was quite young—younger than Father Jim Presta and I or any of you. Jeremiah was probably a teenager when God called him to be a prophet. While Jeremiah's youth and inexperience may seem obvious causes for his hesitation, a deeper level of his fear may have surfaced from his familiarity with the traditions of Israel: knowing, for example, how lonely a prophet's life could be or how often people laughed at prophets, ignored their message, and even rejected them and their God-given message.

But God has the perfect antidote to Jeremiah's fear and hesitation. "I will be with you," God says quite simply, and that makes all the difference in the world—to Jeremiah and to each of us! Living in God's presence, we need not fear or hesitate to respond to his call, no matter what he asks of us—even our very life! My friends, I can attest to this from my own personal experience. I have never felt God's presence more keenly than in the past days, weeks, and months. He has given me a wonderful gift—the gift of peace, tranquillity, and total confidence in his love for me.

Sometimes, when we are called by the Lord, instead of fear and hesitation, we launch new endeavors with great eagerness and enthusiasm, like the three disciples in today's gospel. For example, called to discipleship by Jesus, Peter, James, and John immediately leave behind their nets, boats, and families in order to walk with the Lord. In effect, Jesus throws his net over the three fishermen, and they were caught. Then he promises to make them fishers of others.

We should not be misled by their enthusiastic response, however. Remember that Peter, after identifying Jesus as Messiah and Son of God at Caesarea Philippi, will chide the Lord for predicting that he would suffer, die, and rise again in Jerusalem at the end of their earthly journey with him. James and John are well known in the Gospels for their personal ambition. All three will fall asleep in the Garden of Gethsemane, leaving Jesus to pray alone in his agony. And shortly thereafter Peter will deny that he ever knew Jesus.

My friends, it is quite apparent that Jesus does not choose disciples on their own merits. It's not that Peter was the least impulsive or most trustworthy person on the lakeshore that morning, or that James and John were the most humble or altruistic brothers available. Indeed, they were just the opposite! Nevertheless, Jesus takes the initiative and calls them to discipleship—as he has continued to do through the ages.

And to the extent that the disciples walk with him, listen very attentively to what he says, and, most importantly, learn to model their lives on Jesus' life, to that extent they will become effective fishers of others. They then will be able to proclaim credibly God's reign of justice and compassion, to reach out compassionately to the sick and suffering, to love others generously as Jesus loved them.

Father Presta and I, together with all of you, are aware that none of us is today a perfect disciple of the risen Lord. But if we allow him to do so, Jesus will form and mold us as a potter molds clay—until we become useful vessels of God's word and love to be shared with others. God simply is not finished creating any of us yet.

And that brings us to St. Paul's advice to the Romans, in our second reading. His message hinges on the ancient notions of honor and shame. Today, honor is often popularly given where it is little deserved, and a sense of shame is tossed aside in the interests of an exaggerated individualism that knows no limits, no boundaries, of behavior. It cannot be that way with Jesus' disciples. Honor and shame set limits or boundaries to our behavior. In effect, Paul says simply: Do what is honorable; avoid what is shameful. For example, acknowledge, develop, and use wisely your God-given gifts—

for the sake of the community, not your own self-aggrandizement. And acknowledge one another's gifts; help others to develop their God-given talents further and to use them well to build up the reign of God. Do what is honorable. The reputation of St. Joseph Seminary depends on the honor of all of you—rector, faculty and staff, students.

My dear friends, knowing that God is truly with us and being willing to walk with the Lord Jesus and one another, may we have hope and, indeed, confidence for the year that lies ahead of each of us. As St. Paul counsels, let us be patient under trials and remain in close contact with God through prayer. Above all, let us love one another as brothers and sisters in the faith, co-disciples of the risen Lord.

Mass of the Holy Spirit

Mundelein Seminary, Mundelein, Illinois

——September 13, 1996 ————————————————

Sometime in the past two weeks, each of you arrived here, some of you returning after an absence of months, some of you arriving, if not for the first time, at least for the first time as one who now calls this place "home." I trust that as you pulled onto the grounds, and in the days since, you have been struck, or struck again, by the sheer beauty and grace of this privileged place.

Some of you may know that, ever since I arrived in Chicago, Mundelein has occupied a fond place in my heart. Although I have often used it as a sort of "retreat," and have made countless visits, both official and unofficial, I never tire of its quiet splendor.

But of course, the beauty of these grounds and the sweeping elegance of this campus are not the only, or even the primary highlight of their heritage. This year, as you know, we will commence the celebration of the Diamond Jubilee of St. Mary of the Lake. And as we will no doubt become more deeply aware, the singular boast of this jubilee observance will be the hundreds of men, sent forth from these thousand acres, to serve—how many millions of God's people in Chicagoland and beyond?

My younger brothers, by your presence here, each of you now stakes a claim to this honored tradition. You join a noble procession of men, called from the Church, shaped in its tradition, formed in its ideals, and sent again into its vineyards. I pray that, in the brief time you have here, you may come to share my pride in having been blessed to be a part of this place called "Mundelein."

One of the blessings of a jubilee year, such as the one upon which we shall soon embark, is the opportunity it affords us to retrieve and reclaim the treasures we have inherited. What are the treasures, the legacy, the "birthright," if you will, to which you are now heirs?

You have just come from an address during which Father Joncas spoke of the liturgical heritage of the Church, a legacy in which St. Mary of the Lake had no small part. In your courses in liturgy you will no doubt learn that in its earlier phases, the liturgical movement of this century was largely the fruit of monastic labors. Although its aims were primarily pastoral, the liturgical movement sprang first from monasteries in Europe and the United States.

It was to a great extent here, at St. Mary of the Lake, that the pastoral implications of liturgical renewal were foretold and conceived. Today, it is sometimes forgotten that, in those early years, the liturgical movement was not embraced as an end in itself, but as a means to the Church's renewal. The purpose was not simply to "dress up" the liturgy, to give it a "facelift" after centuries of disregard; rather, it was to retrieve the liturgy's power to transform the Christian life. The link between liturgy and active Christian engagement in society and the world was one of the singular contributions to American Church life in this century.

A number of years ago, in one of my pastoral letters, I meditated on this link in these words:

> At this table we put aside every worldly separation based on culture, class, or other differences. Baptized, we no longer admit to distinctions based on age or sex or race or wealth. This communion is why all prejudice, all racism, all sexism, all deference to wealth and power must be banished from our parishes, our homes, and our lives. This communion is why we will not call enemies those who are human beings like ourselves. This communion is why we will not commit the world's resources to an escalating arm's race while the poor die. We cannot. Not when we have feasted here on the "body broken" and "blood poured out" for the life of the world.

The words are mine, but they could have been spoken here in this chapel sixty years ago. Each of us is now heir to this deep conviction, and we are all better—more authentic and faithful disciples—for it.

This conviction gave rise, in the 1940s and 1950s, to a host of efforts—bundled together under the umbrella of "Catholic Social Action"—a host of efforts to apply the gospel to the everyday lives of Catholic men and women. If today some of those efforts are forgotten, the core conviction that fueled them has become an axiom of Catholic life and teaching.

But liturgical renewal, like renewal of the Church itself, is a perennial labor. And in our own time, no less than in that of our forebears, the Church of Jesus Christ is stirring, foretelling anew its rebirth.

Today I charge you, my friends, with the nurture and care of this Church still unborn. You shall be its nurses; you shall be its guardians; you shall be its teachers; you shall be its priests. This newborn Church will, no doubt, bear the unmistakable likeness of the Church today. But surely it will bear features, too, of the new millennium that will bring it to birth.

How shall you prepare for it? The skills and resources to be demanded of you are more thorough and more broad than ever before. While philosophy and theology must still be the foundation of your preparations, in addition, you must develop and master a broad range of pastoral skills, from counseling to management, from second languages to computer programs. I urge you to use these years of preparation well, not only for the good of the Church, but for your own future success and happiness as well.

But just as knowledge and skills alone do not make a good parent, neither will your knowledge and skills alone make you a good priest. You will also have to develop the gift of love, and the capacity for love, that is the mark of great parents, the mark of great priests. Your love for the Church, your love for your people, will reveal itself in the conviction and compassion with which you apply your knowledge, and in the conviction and compassion with which you exercise your skills. Where, we might ask, will you acquire this love; from whom will you obtain this conviction and compassion?

Has the answer ever been any different? The paradoxical wisdom, revealed to us in Jesus Christ, is that the one who seeks to save his life will lose it, while the one who loses his life for the sake of the Lord will find it. In order for your learning, your skills, your prayer, your very priesthood to bear any fruit, they must be expressed in the words, the gestures, the habits of the Cross. Otherwise, you may gain the world's esteem and flattery, but it will be at the risk of your very self.

My brothers, in your years here at the seminary, and with however many years the Lord blesses you with priesthood, you will have no greater duty than to lose your life, again and again, to the love of Jesus Christ. No greater duty!

And do not be deluded; this love is no romantic notion intended to comfort the fainthearted. This love of Jesus Christ can be recognized. It has symptoms. It leaves evidence.

- It looks like the faithful man, sitting at the edge of the dying man's bed, whispering the last prayers of his journey.

- It looks like the patient man, standing between the warring couple, searching for what has been lost.

- It looks like the just man, forsaking the privilege of his status, dishing out soup and bread for the hungry and the homeless.

- It looks like the helpless man, his mouth empty and his mind gone blank, listening to the heartbreak of a grieving mother.

- It looks like the unworthy man, standing at the altar in the place of Christ, interceding for his people in words not his own.

- It looks like the sinful man, tracing the cross out of thin air, absolving another for sins all-too-familiar.

My brothers, let the love of Christ possess you! Let the love of Christ transform you! Let the love of Christ impel you! For, it is the love of Christ, made flesh in the hundreds of men ordained from this place, that is the true heritage of Mundelein Seminary. It is not programs or movements; it is not skills or strategies; it is not knowledge or learning or aptitude. The heritage of Mundelein Seminary is disciples: men who wished to follow the risen Lord—who denied themselves, took up their cross, and followed in his steps. The heritage of this holy place is men like yourselves who took the chance that, in losing their lives, they might save them.

And you are their heirs. It gives me great comfort to look out at you, trusting that a Church yet unborn will be in good hands. And what is the source of this confidence of mine? It is no more or less than this: it is this love of Jesus Christ that we share.

My dear brothers and sisters, allow me to echo the words of the apostle:

> May the God of our Lord Jesus Christ, the Father of glory, grant you a spirit of wisdom and insight to know him clearly, may he enlighten your innermost vision that you may know the great hope to which he has called you, the wealth of his glorious heritage . . . and the immeasurable scope of his power in us who believe.

Homily

Prayer Service with Priests

Holy Name Cathedral, Chicago, Illinois

—*October 7, 1996* ————————————————————

As you all know, two weeks ago Ken Velo and I were in Rome. After we had completed our meetings, we decided to go to Assisi. During our visit to Assisi we offered Mass for all the priests of the archdiocese. All of you were very much in my mind and heart during that time.

I take this occasion to thank you for coming together this afternoon to pray with and for me. In a special way, I thank the Presbyteral Council and the Association of Chicago Priests for arranging this prayer service. It is good for us to be here!

When I first learned that we would be gathering this afternoon, I asked that we broaden our intention to include all sick persons. In a particular way, let us remember our Holy Father who undergoes surgery tomorrow. May it be successful. Let us also remember all the members of our families and parishes as well as our friends who are ill.

Today, the focus of our prayer service is on the Cross—which is a symbol of suffering and death as well as victory. The Cross, in so many ways, is reflective of life—both its agonies and its ecstasies. For the person of faith, despite all the suffering, it is ultimately both the symbol and cause of victory. In recent months the Cross, my brothers, has never been more difficult or sweeter to me.

My spiritual journey goes back for many years. But it did not really begin to take shape until I learned, with my heart as well as my mind, who Jesus is and what he expects of me. The answers to these two questions came over a period of time through study of the Scriptures, prayer, exchanges with my fellow priests, and my ministerial experiences—but especially through prayer and the Scriptures. It is both the discovery and the internalization of the answers to those two questions that have given me the strength to carry the cross that Jesus has given me the privilege to share with him.

The first question is: *Who is Jesus for me?* I can assure you that I do not have an abstract notion of who Jesus is. For me, he is

- a man who was in *touch with his humanity, his manhood,* though he is God's son. He was a man who experienced the same human longings and passions as we, though he never sinned. Down-to-earth, he was sensitive to human feelings. He was compassionate and not reluctant to show emotions of joy, sorrow—and once, anger.

- *a teacher.* He was not sophisticated. He often preached in parables, using images and realities with which people were familiar. He never hedged, never avoided the "hard sayings," but took people where they were. He was not upset if at first they did not understand him or even walked away.

- *a person of integrity.* There were no contradictions in his message, his life, or his ministry.

- *a lover.* He constantly talked about love. When asked which is the greatest commandment, he answered: "You shall love the Lord, your God, with all your heart, with all your soul, and with all your mind. This is the greatest and the first commandment. The second is like it: You shall love your neighbor as yourself. The whole law and the prophets depend on these two commandments" (Matt 22:37-40). He invited people to share his love and be intimate with him. This love would also connect people with his Father.

- *a patient man.* He was not given to panic. He was stable. The one exception was his anger at the money changers in the Temple. He was patient even with those who maligned him, knowing that in the end his truth would prevail. He was able to convince others by the sheer power of his personality and message.

- *a man who understood that suffering and death* were the key to ultimate success—his resurrection. We can expect no less.

The second question is: *What does this Jesus expect of me?* I would like to talk about this in the first person plural. What does he expect of *us*? He expects

- *that we focus on essentials,* not accidentals or peripherals. By essentials, I mean such things as

- ► acquiring authentic spiritual growth
- ► understanding the demands and implications of love and justice
- ► working for unity, not disunity
- ► making evangelization our priority
- ► giving personal witness
- ► striving for clarity and simplicity of teaching

- *that we speak the truth with love.* We should never hesitate to present the truth, never compromise, but also be humble and gentle in presenting it, taking people where they are.

- *that we minister in a special way to our brother priests.*

  - ► We must convince them that we do minister *in persona Christi.*
  - ► Therefore, our lives must be filled with love—not with bickering, rumors, jealousies, or inappropriate behavior.
  - ► They must be in touch with themselves and the Lord in prayer.
  - ► We must support our fellow priests. The best way is by example and loving outreach, though sometimes also "tough love."

- He expects us to live a *simple lifestyle.* How do we accomplish this in the midst of plenty?

- He expects us to live a *pure, chaste life.* The promise of celibacy means that, while I may (and should) have many intimate friendships, none can take the place of Jesus.

- He expects us to *nourish our relationship,* our friendship with him *through prayer,* both public and private. This means that we must devote quality time to prayer. I have told you my own story many times.

To accomplish the above (and more) requires that:

- we *love* the Lord more than anyone or anything else.

- we have a deep and abiding *faith* in him.

- and, with faith as a foundation, that we *trust* him, really trust him, as he accompanies us on our journey.

- and finally that we "let ourselves go," that is, that we put ourselves totally in the hands of the Lord—which can only be done if there is a lot of *love, faith, and trust.*

My brothers, I am in the midst of this "letting go." It is like the Cross: sometimes it is sweet and easy; sometimes it is very difficult.

My faith is unwavering. It shapes my mind and will and keeps me on the right track. But human emotions can be quite fickle, as all of you so well know. But there is no reason to hide those emotions. In no way is there a contradiction between them and our faith and trust.

* * *

Many people (mostly journalists) have asked me what unfinished business I wish to complete before I pass on to the glory that Paul spoke about in his letter to the Romans. My standard answer is *nothing;* that is, I intend simply to continue doing as best I can the things I have done for the last fourteen years.

But this afternoon I do wish to share something with you, my brother priests, something that has been on my mind for several years. I am talking with some of our very best priests about how we might attend more effectively to the spiritual needs of our priests. Together, we have done a great deal in this regard. I need not give you a litany of what has been accomplished during the past fourteen years. But there is still a missing link, and before I leave, I want to find it. If I do, that will be my final legacy to you.

* * *

Fourteen years ago when I was first introduced to you the evening before the formal installation, I said:

> As our lives and ministries are mingled together through the breaking of the Bread and the blessing of the Cup, I hope that long before my name falls from the Eucharistic Prayer in the silence of death you will know well who I am. You will know because we will work and play together, fast and pray together, mourn and rejoice together, despair and hope together, dispute and be reconciled together. You will know me as a friend, fellow priest, and bishop. You will know also that I love you. For I am Joseph, your brother!

That moment of silence will soon be here. I pray that my initial hope has been realized. May God bless you all!

Homily

Church of the Queen of Angels

Feast of SS Simon and Jude
Chicago, Illinois
— *October 28, 1996* —————————————————————

My dear brothers and sisters in the Lord, I am happy to be with you as we thank God for all the blessings he has given to Queen of Angels parish. I am sorry that I am unable to join you for the reception in the Guild Hall following this Eucharist as I had originally intended, but I will be with you in spirit. I trust that your gathering will be a continuation of our celebration here at the Lord's table and a celebration of your parish's unity and strength. I have been told that, when you enter the Guild Hall, you will be met by an ice sculpture of an angel. Let me assure you, the angel is not in any way meant to remind you of Father O'Brien!

We celebrate this Eucharist on the feast of two apostles: Saints Simon and Jude. Simon was a member of the Zealot party, a group of people known for their zeal on behalf of the Jewish law. Jude may have been a cousin of the Lord. After Jesus' ascension, tradition says that Simon and Jude preached in Egypt and Persia where each suffered a martyr's death. St. Jude is often called the "Patron of Hopeless Cases."

What do these two men have in common? What do they mean to us and to Queen of Angels parish? Both men found that their lives were totally changed when they met the Lord. Jesus and his gospel became everything for them. They were so convinced that Jesus' name and message should be heard by all nations that they left their familiar surroundings and went to distant lands as the first preachers of his gospel. Their

609

ministry welcomed new believers into the growing Christian family. Their strength helped them face a martyr's death. That same combination of ministry and strength that has marked the history of Queen of Angels parish since it was founded in 1909 and, I pray, will characterize your future as well.

In our first reading, St. Paul wrote what could easily have been motivating words for Simon and Jude, "You are strangers and aliens no longer. No, you are fellow citizens of the saints and members of the household of God." Queen of Angels parish, like so many other parishes and communities in our archdiocese, faces a very difficult task: how to sustain the life of long-established parishioners while also welcoming newcomers. This ministry of welcoming is even more challenging when the newcomer and the longer-established parishioners speak different languages.

This evening, I ask all of you to look into one another's *hearts* rather than listen to one another's languages. You will find that the human heart and longing for faith is very much the same within all people. The search I propose to you is one where *all* people of *all* ages and *all* backgrounds look into each other's hearts, minds, and lives with reverence, trust, and love. St. Paul gives us the reason for our search when he writes that we *all* "are members of the household of God." So, I urge you to find the common ground that unites you. That common ground is Jesus in whom all are "fitted together."

This unity in faith motivated the apostolic work of Simon and Jude. I ask that Queen of Angels parish be the new Simons and Judes in Ravenswood. May the tower on the top of this church—visible for blocks around—guide people to this temple where all find "a dwelling place for God in the Spirit."

St. Paul says that "you form a building." He is speaking here of a spiritual building. *You* are a building in the Holy Spirit. Among other things, you have recently completed the Tomorrow's Parish Planning Process, outlined goals for your school board, expanded your religious education programs, begun high school and young adults groups, adopted new policies for athletics, and are forming your renewed Parish Pastoral Council. I am also well aware that you are undertaking an ambitious and necessary renovation project on all of your parish buildings, literally from the boilers to the roof! I know, as you do, that it will be costly. It will involve sacrifice and work on everyone's part.

Please don't get discouraged! At times, when you see all that has to be done, you might "groan inwardly" as is written in our second reading. Please remember this. The word of God, the sacraments, teaching the young, protecting all of human life, and caring for the poor are the first responsibilities of all believers. However, the attention you give to your buildings—especially this beautiful church—is a visible sign of your faith and your desire to have fitting places where your liturgy, ministries, education, and social gatherings can flourish. I assure you that the archdiocese will continue to work with you in a mutual partnership.

What is the cord that draws together all that you and I must do? Prayer! In today's gospel Jesus—though he is Son of God—goes off to pray to his Father before he chooses his first disciples. In fact, before Jesus made any important decision or began any journey, he prayed. Prayer always comes first.

Be people of prayer! In a special way I say this to the young people at this Mass who are preparing for confirmation. It is so good that you are here. Talk to God. That's what prayer is: talking to God. And it takes a lot of talking—and listening! Prayer is also opening myself to God's ways and words every day. Prayer is asking God, "How do you want me to live this day?" Prayer is praising God for all the good that is around us. Prayer is seeking God's wisdom when we are unsure. Prayer is searching for God while also realizing that God is already within us.

This, then, is the last request I make of you—as your bishop, your friend, and a fellow believer in the Lord: pray and pray often. When people look at your buildings, let them say, "They are beautiful." When people see your ministries and your activities, let them say, "They are a parish guided by the Holy Spirit." But when people pray with Queen of Angels parish, let them say, "We have seen the Lord!"

My dear brothers and sisters, at this Eucharist, I lift all of us up to the Lord whose glory and goodness is beyond all comparison. I put before you the example of the apostles Simon and Jude for you to imitate so that you truly will be the household of the saints. And I place us all under the protection of Mary, the Queen of Angels, that she might reunite us before Jesus, her Son, in heaven. May God bless you all.

Index